MUTUAL FUNDS

"This marvelous compendium of mutual fund information is an answer to the prayers of investors who want to dig beneath the superficial to reach the fundamental. Dr. Haslem's book is more than a textbook. It is perhaps the first substantive attempt to evaluate mutual funds from an academic and historic perspective. I commend it highly to the serious investor."

John C. Bogle, Founder and Former CEO, The Vanguard Group

"Like a master anthologist, Professor Haslem has collected the best ideas of the past twenty years on how to select and evaluate mutual funds, and he's assembled them into a cohesive, highly readable work. If you're seeking order out of the chaos of competing lists of '10 Funds to Buy Now,' then this is the book for you."

Don Phillips, Managing Director, Morningstar, Inc.

"This book is the most comprehensive, detailed textbook treatment of mutual funds available. It contains a complete, thoroughly researched and documented discussion of the important issues involved with funds."

Charles Jones, North Carolina State University

"This masterfully written book is a 'must read' for those who want to make informed decisions about mutual funds. Jack Haslem's definitive treatment of the subject sets a new standard for excellence. His clarity of style and solidity of research result is fascinating reading!

H. Kent Baker, American University

"Haslem's realistic, thoroughly researched perspective on mutual funds is must reading for both investors and fund managers. This is one of those solid books that results from a strong academic background in investments and a balanced view of the financial markets."

Bob Edmister, University of Mississippi

"Professor John Haslem has written a very thorough and detailed book on mutual funds. This book will be very useful as a text for a course on mutual funds, a supplementary text for a standard investment course, and a must reading for anyone aspiring to be a certified financial planner."

Robert Krainer, University of Wisconsin

This book is dedicated to the World War II generation and two family heroes: Lieutenant Colonel Andrew J. Nehf, Commander, 250th Combat Engineering Battalion, and Major John R. Haslem, MD, FACS, Surgeon and Neurosurgeon, 32nd General Hospital. Colonel Nehf served in Europe and built bridges crossing into Germany, and was awarded two Bronze Stars. Dr. Haslem served three years in the European and Pacific theaters, including Normandy and the Battle of the Bulge, and was awarded four Bronze Stars.

MUTUAL FUNDS

Risk and Performance Analysis for Decision Making

John A. Haslem
Robert H. Smith School of Business
University of Maryland

350 Main Street, Malden, MA 02148-5018, USA
108 Cowley Road, Oxford OX4 1JF, UK
550 Swanston Street, Carlton South, Melbourne, Victoria 3053, Australia
Kurfürstendamm 57, 10707 Berlin, Germany

First published 2003 by Blackwell Publishing Ltd

Library of Congress Cataloging-in-Publication Data

Haslem, John A.
    Mutual funds : risk and performance analysis for decision making / John A. Haslem.
        p. cm.
    Includes bibliographical references and index.
    ISBN 0–631–21561–1 (alk. paper)
    1. Mutual funds.   2. Portfolio management.   3. Investments.   I. Title.
HG4530 .H387 2003
332.63′27—dc21

                                                                    2002026257

A catalogue record for this title is available from the British Library.

Set in 10/12.5pt Ehrhardt
by Graphicraft Ltd, Hong Kong

For further information on
Blackwell Publishing, visit our website:
http://www.blackwellpublishing.com

CONTENTS

FIGURES

PREFACE

This book is the culmination of some ten years' teaching analysis of mutual funds to undergraduates and MBAs. And what great student teams they were. At the time the course was created, it was the first security analysis course dedicated to mutual funds. These several thousand students have provided research reports that improved our knowledge and approaches to this topic. For example, students taught me identification of investor risk preferences does not have to be an ordeal, but can be very simple. Or, as "Pop" Hansen used to say in his Harvard Control classes: "Use your squash" and "Keep it simple." We do that here while providing a comprehensive treatment of mutual funds.

The book is the result of this learning about mutual funds and its accompanying investing. Discussions of the analysis of mutual funds are followed by checklists to ease the analysis and selection of specific mutual funds and fund portfolios. The book is thus designed for serious investors who focus on the textual material to learn about the analysis of mutual funds, but also for those who want to improve their decisions by focusing more so on the checklists.

As a brief introduction, the chapters are generally self-contained, which facilitates reader attention to particular fund topics. Let's look at the chapters. Chapter 1 tells us what mutual funds are and how they fit into investment company and regulatory schemes. Chapters 2 and 3 tell us about the advantages generally ascribed to mutual funds, and how to evaluate them for particular funds and investors. The concept of diversification risk and how its elements may constrain attainable diversification is also introduced.

Chapters 4 and 5 do the opposite of chapters 2 and 3. They tell us about the general disadvantages of mutual funds, and how to evaluate them for particular funds and investors.

Chapter 6 tells us about the value and performance of long-term equity investing and the shortcomings of market timing. It also describes contributions of modern and behavioral finance to fund analysis. And the chapter provides the process for determining the basic stock/bond allocation of investor fund portfolios, as a guide to further portfolio allocations.

Chapter 7 tells us how to evaluate and assess fund diversification risk and how the elements may be measured and assessed overall. It also discusses equity style allocation, style analysis, Morningstar on investment style and measures, mutual fund risk, and value versus growth investment style.

Chapter 8 tells us how to measure fund returns, risks, and risk/return performance measures and how to assess them overall. The chapter also tells how to bring together the buy/sell criteria and how to make fund buy/sell decisions.

Chapters 9 and 10 tell us how to assess and determine mutual fund portfolio allocations beyond stock/bond allocations. These additional allocations include international and domestic value/growth and cap. size investment styles, along with international and domestic bond allocations. The process and criteria for assessing and selecting specific index fund portfolios are provided (chapter 9), as well as those for selecting actively managed funds to supplement core holdings of index funds (chapter 10).

Portfolio allocation and mutual fund selection decisions are made in the context of research findings concerning the determinants of improved fund portfolio strategies and performance. Professor Russ Wermers culminates these findings with an authoritative essay on factors that differentiate fund performance. This is done to answer the question: Should investors use index funds or actively managed funds?

Chapter 11 reviews current problems with mutual funds and how these will increasingly affect the future of the funds industry. The focus of the chapter is the major threat to the industry – exchange-traded fund shares. As funds become less personalized and trade more as index fund commodities, the threat of exchange-traded fund shares will become even greater. These fund hybrids have numerous advantages.

Finally, chapter 12 provides an optional treatment with checklists of how to use specific indicators of future economic and market outlooks to time implementation of fund buy/sell decisions or just to get the context of the market.

A comment is needed concerning the book's organization, content, and chapter sequence. This book has two concurrent purposes. The first is to inform readers concerning the nature of mutual funds. The second is to do this while providing a step-by-step approach to the analysis and selection of equity mutual funds. The decision checklists and required information begin in chapter 2, and by the time the checklist results are completed and summarized in chapter 8 the information in the previous chapters is assumed. The first eight chapters thus carry the burden of providing adequate background for the analysis of a sample fund. The last four chapters include checklists for selection among index funds and actively managed funds, determining advantages/disadvantages of exchange-traded funds, and analysis of the economic and market outlooks. Thus there is a method behind these in-depth chapters.

ACKNOWLEDGMENTS

We live in a world of technology, which reminds us of the importance of maintaining our personal "computing machinery" under warranty for the long haul. In this regard, thanks are due to several Johns Hopkins professors: Donlin M. Long, MD, PhD; Michael J. Holliday, MD; Alan W. Partin, MD, PhD; Glenn J. Treisman, MD, PhD; and principal care provider John A. Flynn, MD, MBA (yes!). John Flynn followed his father into medicine and I did not, but we both made the right decisions. John Flynn and Glenn Treisman are very special people, as are the others.

My family is, of course, my mainstay and best critic (in nice ways) of this book. It goes without saying that I did all that I was told to do. First, I thank my wife, Jane Haslem, my soul mate since high school. She is also variously known as Mom, Grandma Jane, artline.com and Haslem Fine Arts. Next, thanks go to three great sons and their families. In Galesburg, IL, there are John A. Haslem, Jr., PhD, Lorie Schroeder Haslem, PhD, and their Shakespeareans, Katharine Ruth, Abigail Jane and Sophia Louise. In Santa Barbara, CA, there are James R. Haslem, JD, Catherine Oppen Haslem, and their movie stars that read, John Robert and Charles Andrew. And, in Redwood City, CA, there are Jeffrey A. Haslem, MBA, and Deborah Horn Haslem, MBA, "product managers" for Andrew Stephen and Sarah Elizabeth. What a group!

Back to the book. I wish to thank several other persons who made it possible. They include top academics, friends, and ace editors, Robert O. Edmister, PhD, University of Mississippi, H. Kent Baker, DBA, American University, and Charles P. Jones, PhD, North Carolina State University. Other reviewers who provided assistance include Robert W. McLeod, PhD, University of Alabama; Karin Bonding, PhD, University of Virginia; James Yoder, PhD, University of West Georgia; and Malek Lashgari, PhD, University of Hartford. As noted, colleague Russ Wermers, PhD, University of Maryland, authored an essay updating research on fund performance. Jennifer S. Leete, JD, and Francis E. Dalton, MBA, both of the SEC, provided guidance on regulatory issues. Lisa Rawlings, MBA, doctoral student at the University of Maryland, expertly created the tables. Al Bruckner, former Executive Editor, initiated this long-running show, and Colleen Capodilupo and Elizabeth Wald, patient editors, guided it to production. The manuscript was expertly steered through the production process by Valery Rose.

J. A. H.
Washington, DC

CHAPTER ONE

UNDERSTANDING MUTUAL FUNDS

> [M]utual funds embody the American Ideal . . . whereby the individual is treated to the privileges of the elite.
>
> (*Don Phillips, in* **Morningstar Mutual Funds,** *April 3, 1992*)
>
> [T]he Investment Company Act of 1940 [is] one of the world's most perfect legal documents.
> (*Jason Zweig, Money, in* **Morningstar Mutual Funds,** *August 18, 1995*)
>
> The art of investing in mutual funds . . . rests on simplicity and common sense.
> (*John C. Bogle, Vanguard Group, in* **Common Sense on Mutual Funds:**
> **New Imperatives for the Intelligent Investor,** *1999*)

When the financial history of the twentieth century is ultimately written, one chapter will be dedicated to mutual funds. This industry has been and continues to be one of the extraordinary growth stories in the history of US financial markets. The Investment Company Institute (ICI) (1997c), the industry trade association, reported industry assets were $35.8 billion in 1974, and by 1996 they had escalated to $3.5 trillion – an annual growth rate of nearly 24 percent! And, by the end of the century, ICI (2000c) reported mutual funds assets were off the chart at over $6.8 trillion – almost doubling assets in three years! Over 8,000 named mutual funds are offered by over 400 different sponsors. Mutual funds are not only the most rapidly growing financial institutions, they are second in size only to commercial banks, and closing rapidly. In fact, mutual fund assets are equal to some 70 percent of the country's annual gross domestic product.

Several major forces explain most of this industry growth. But the first and essential force has been the demonstrated effectiveness of mutual funds as vehicles for providing individual investors with market rates of return, along with investment alternatives and services traditionally available only to institutional and other large investors. This is seen in the immense wealth generated by the historically unsurpassed duration and performance of equity securities since 1982. This performance has contributed enormously to the total of assets managed by mutual funds.

Mutual funds have thus effectively brought Wall Street to Main Street by providing single packages of securities that provide portfolio diversification, professional portfolio management, shareholder services, and a variety of investment objectives, among others. But mutual funds have also attracted huge investments from institutional investors, business organizations, and nonprofit organizations.

This first chapter has several goals. The first goal is to describe the role of mutual funds as financial institutions in the financial services industry that engage in financial intermediation. Investors utilize mutual funds to acquire financial market assets. This intermediation process helps channel savings to productive uses.

The second goal is to describe mutual funds and related investment vehicles within their regulatory and historical contexts. Mutual funds are a type of investment company primarily regulated under the Investment Company Act of 1940. The two major types of investment companies are unit investment trusts (UITs) and management investment companies. Management investment companies are further subclassified as open-end funds or closed-end funds. Open-end funds are called mutual funds. The 1940 Act mandates a critical role for mutual fund independent directors as shareholder watchdogs.

The third goal is to describe mutual funds as entities with regulatory and director oversight and external service providers, including investment advisors. Mutual funds are shell entities with portfolios and management functions performed by external service providers: (1) investment advisors, (2) administrators, (3) custodians, (4) transfer agents, (5) principal underwriters, and (6) auditors and legal counsel. Mutual funds are sponsored, staffed, and managed by management companies that in their roles as investment advisors manage fund portfolios for asset-based fees.

MUTUAL FUNDS AS FINANCIAL INTERMEDIARIES

Mutual funds are part of what is known as the *financial services industry*. This industry includes two basic types of *financial institutions*: depository and non-depository. Depository institutions include commercial banks, savings and loans, mutual savings banks, and credit unions. Non-depository institutions include mutual funds, as well as insurance companies, pension funds, finance companies, investment banks, and venture capital firms. Financial institutions are also called *financial intermediaries* because they channel surplus cash assets from economic units to economic units with deficit savings and productive needs for cash. This *intermediation* process thus channels savings to productive uses.

Financial intermediaries have evolved by providing customers with financial assets more efficiently and conveniently than they can obtain them directly in financial markets. For example, a common approach to intermediation has savers acquiring financial assets by opening bank savings accounts. The savers receive assets (savings accounts) and banks simultaneously acquire deposit liabilities. Banks then use these funds to create assets by loaning funds to firms, such as for seasonal inventory buildup. In these cases, intermediation channels savings in the form of saver assets and creates deposit liabilities used to acquire financial assets.

There are several versions of the intermediation process. First, there is classic intermediation, which has savers acquire financial assets directly from financial institutions. For example, a Redwood City, CA, executive buys a CD from his local bank. A second version has savers utilizing intermediaries to acquire assets in financial markets. This is the form of intermediation provided by mutual funds, among others. Purchases of mutual fund shares represent proportional ownership of portfolios acquired by these same mutual funds. Third is an alternative to intermediation in the direct acquisition of financial assets in financial markets. For example, a Santa Barbara, CA, lawyer buys shares direct from a closely held technology company.

Purchase of mutual fund shares is thus an alternative to direct purchase of securities from issuers. It is a simple alternative to implement. Opening an account involves completing a mutual fund account application and mailing it along with a purchase check, or calling a broker or financial advisor to open an account. Many funds provide applications on their Web sites. Mutual funds pool these checks to buy portfolio securities managed for shareholders. This book provides a guide to the selection of the right funds, one fund at a time.

INVESTMENT COMPANIES AND UNIT INVESTMENT TRUSTS

Regulatory framework and classification

The term *mutual fund* is well known, as is its shorter version, *fund*. Mutual funds are a type of investment company primarily regulated under the Investment Company Act of 1940 (the 1940 Act), which assigns primary regulatory oversight to the Securities and Exchange Commission (SEC). The 1940 Act and laws governing investment advisors to mutual funds are summarized in table 1. The Act defines an investment company as primarily engaged in the business of investing, reinvesting, owning, holding, or trading in securities, with at least 40 percent of assets so invested, exclusive of subsidiaries and US Treasury securities. Chapter 4 notes concerns associated with SEC oversight.

The 1940 Act includes two major types of *investment companies: unit investment trusts* and *management* ("*managed*") *investment companies*. A third type, "face amount certificates," is of minor importance and not discussed. Unit investment trusts (discussed in detail below) are investment companies with generally fixed portfolios (not actively managed) and finite lives. Management investment companies are further subclassified as *open-end funds* (*open-end management companies*) or *closed-end funds* (*closed-end management companies*). Open-end and closed-end funds are further classified as *diversified* or *non-diversified* (legally defined below).

The legal notion of diversification as a good thing is validated by finance theory, which shows the portfolio risk reduction properties of effective diversification. Management investment companies are organized and managed by investment advisors, usually with assistance of other service providers. The portfolios are managed to meet stated investment objectives and are either passively managed or actively managed portfolios (discussed below).

Each type of management investment company has unique characteristics, as well. In summary, open-end funds are called mutual funds, but the latter term is not defined in the 1940 Act. However, when people say mutual funds or funds, this is interpreted to mean open-end management investment companies, diversified or non-diversified, which offer continuously redeemable securities. Mutual funds shares are both sold and redeemed continuously at portfolio *net asset value* (NAV) per share – total assets less liabilities, divided by number of shares outstanding at close of trading.

On the other hand, closed-end funds have initial, and perhaps intermittent, share offerings, just as regular companies do. The shares are not redeemable and are traded like companies' shares at prices determined by supply and demand. Their lives are perpetual.

Management investment companies are legal entities, usually corporations, but they may be organized as business trusts or partnerships. They pool investor dollars with the same investment objectives and create, organize, and manage securities portfolios. These pooled dollars are obtained from the public sale of shares through which investors receive proportional ownership in portfolios, typically diversified, that are actively or passively managed by investment professionals.

Investment management companies

In addition to management investment companies, including mutual funds, there are *investment management companies*, also known as management companies, investment advisors, investment managers, fund managers, fund advisory firms, and fund advisors. These companies are easily confused with the legal term "management investment companies" discussed above – note the word reversal. Management companies sponsor (create), organize, staff, and directly/indirectly manage mutual funds. Most important, they are responsible for managing fund portfolios for fund shareholders on a fee basis. In a few words, mutual funds are shell entities with real portfolios that contract with management companies to provide investment advisory and usually other services. Technically, mutual fund entities hire management companies as investment advisors to provide professional portfolio management and usually other services.

THE 1940 ACT AND REGULATION OF INVESTMENT COMPANIES

The 1940 Act is generally considered model federal legislation and is summarized in table 1. The 1940 Act was enacted at the end of the Great Depression that followed the 1929 stock market crash. Congress determined that the disclosure and anti-fraud provisions of the landmark 1933 and 1934 securities laws (discussed below) were inadequate to protect investment company investors. The 1940 Act's mandate is wide and includes investment companies but also investment advisors, distributors of fund shares, directors, officers, and fund employees.

The 1940 Act requires investment companies to register with and report to the SEC, which has regulatory oversight. The Act's major objectives are to (1) ensure investors receive adequate and accurate information, (2) protect fund assets, (3) prevent abusive fund self-dealing, (4) prevent issuance of shares with unfair or discriminatory provisions, and (5) ensure securities bought and sold are fairly priced.

Investment company activities

Ratner (1998) summarized 1940 Act provisions concerning regulation of investment company activities. First, investment companies must register with the SEC by filing notifications that include investment policies and other required information. Registered investment companies must file annual reports with the SEC. Second, to protect investment company assets, all securities must be held secure with bank custodians, stock exchange member firms or under procedures established by the SEC. All persons with access to the securities must be bonded.

Third, there are capital structure limitations. Investment companies may not issue senior securities (debt or preferred stock) other than notes payable – banks. Closed-end funds may not issue more than one class of debt securities or preferred stock and are restricted in amount. Registered management companies may not issue rights or warrants to purchase securities. And investment companies may not issue securities unless their net worth is at least $100,000.

Fourth, investment companies may not pay dividends from sources other than accumulated undistributed net income, or net income for the current or preceding years, unless accompanied with written disclosure of sources of payments. The Internal Revenue Service (IRS) requires that investment companies must distribute shareholder dividends equal to at least 90 percent of taxable ordinary income, to avoid taxation.

Fifth, the investment activities of investment companies are regulated along several dimensions. Investment companies may not purchase securities on margin, sell securities short, or participate in joint trading accounts. Underwriting commitments totaling more than 25 percent of total assets are prohibited.

There are also numerous activities that require approval of a majority of shares voting: (1) borrowing money, (2) issuing senior securities (prohibited for mutual funds), (3) underwriting securities, (4) engaging in real estate or commodities transactions, (5) making loans, (6) changing investment policy concerning concentration or diversification of assets, (7) changing investment company subclassification, and (8) ceasing to be an investment company.

Investment companies are not limited to "legal lists" in making investments and are not subject to "prudent man" rules. Managers may not be held liable for losses from bad investments or even those deemed imprudent by conservative investors. Managers are subject to SEC sanction for failure to provide the kind of investment management and supervision stated in advertisements or statements of policy. In such cases, courts have held directors civilly liable under state laws for losses due to mismanagement.

Sixth, investments in other investment companies are limited. No investment company may own more than 3 percent of stock in other investment companies, invest more than 5 percent of assets in any one investment company, or invest more than 10 percent of assets in other investment companies generally.

Company management and control

Ratner (1998) next summarized 1940 Act provisions concerning investment company management and control. First, regulations include investment company shareholders, directors, and officers. Shares issued must have equal voting rights and voting trusts are prohibited. Solicitation of proxies is subject to approximately the same rules applying to listed companies generally. In addition to voting rights under state law, shareholders are entitled to vote on several important changes: (1) investment policy or status, (2) approval or assignment of investment advisory contracts, (4) filling more than specified minimum numbers of director vacancies, (5) sale of stock in closed-end funds at prices below net asset value, and (6) appointment of independent public accountants.

There are also provisions designed to ensure integrity of investment company directors and officers, as well as independence of directors. No persons convicted within ten years of securities-related felonies or enjoined from securities-related activities may serve as directors or officers or in other specified capacities. Directors or officers may not be indemnified against liabilities arising from willful misfeasance, bad faith, gross negligence, or reckless disregard of duty.

To assure director independence, no more than 60 percent of board members may be "interested persons" of investment companies. However, "no load" (no up-front sales charges) funds managed by registered investment advisors are required to have only one "non-interested" director. Interested persons include broker-dealers, persons who served as legal counsel within the past two years, immediate family members of affiliated persons, and any persons determined by the SEC to have "a material business or professional relationship" with investment companies or principal executive officers within the past two years.

Second, management compensation is regulated. Acting under board of director supervision, investment company officers normally contract with separate entities called investment advisors to provide all management and advisory services for fees. Investment advisors may be partnerships or private/public corporations. Investment advisors normally create one or more mutual funds as corporate shells to provide vehicles for pooling investor monies. Investment advisors must serve under written contracts approved initially by vote of shareholders and subsequently approved annually by directors. Investment advisory contracts typically call for compensation based as percentages of net portfolio assets.

The SEC has criticized advisory fees as bearing no relation to value of services provided and grossly higher than fees charged by pension fund managers and others for portfolios of comparable size and investment objectives. Shareholder suits on behalf of a number of mutual funds have alleged "waste" of corporate assets and "breach of fiduciary duty" under state and federal laws. In fully litigated cases, courts have found advisory fees high, but not so much as to be considered waste. Some cases have been settled with reduction of advisory fees as portfolios reached specified sizes, and other adjustments.

A 1970 amendment to the 1940 Act provides that investment advisors are deemed to have a "fiduciary duty" with respect to reasonableness of fees. Fiduciary duty is interpreted to prevent investment advisors from increasing fees, even with shareholder approval, if increases provide no benefit. This duty may be enforced in court, by the SEC, and by shareholder suits, without prior demand of directors. In addition, the provision provides that any amendment in renewal of investment advisory contracts must be approved by majority of *disinterested* (*independent*) *directors*, who are "under duty" to request information reasonably necessary to evaluate contracts.

Third, to prevent "trafficking" in investment advisory contracts, transfer of management is regulated. To prevent investment advisors from assigning advisory contracts to other entities, all contracts automatically terminate upon assignment. Assignment includes transfers of controlling interest in investment advisory firms, which also require shareholder approval. The court has held payments of fees to former advisors in connection with changes in advisors to be breach of implied advisor fiduciary duty. A 1975 addition to the 1940 Act provides that sale proceeds of investment advisory firms are protected if for periods of three years at least 75 percent of affected investment company directors are disinterested, and as long as no unfair compensation burdens are placed on investment companies resulting from sales.

Transactions with affiliates

Ratner (1998) next summarized 1940 Act provisions for investment company transactions with affiliates. Such transactions are obvious potential sources of conflicts of interest. The primary concern is to prevent investment companies from buying/selling securities at prices that favor affiliates. Affiliated persons, promoters, or principal underwriters of investment companies may not buy or sell investment company property without specific SEC approval. Approval requires transactions to be fair and reasonable without "overreaching" by any parties, consistent with investment company investment policies, and within the general purposes of the 1940 Act.

First, investment company joint transactions are regulated. Investment companies are prohibited from "joint participation" with affiliates in which arrangements are less than advantageous. These transactions require prior SEC approval. Patterns in which investment company officers or directors repeatedly make the same investments as investment companies are considered joint participations.

The definition of "affiliated person" includes not only those who control investment companies or own more than 5 percent of their shares, but also any entities in which investment companies owns more that 5 percent of shares. Any understandings between investment companies and "portfolio affiliates," such as stock acquisitions in connection with takeover bids, constitute joint arrangements.

Second, investment company brokerage transactions are regulated. Affiliated persons are barred from receiving any compensation for acting as agent or broker in investment company transactions, except where commission are "usual and customary." This latter exception permits brokerage firms that are investment advisors to also act as investment company brokers. The SEC has standards for satisfying this requirement. The larger problem had been routing of commission to brokerage firms that provide other services to investment companies and their advisors. These so called "give ups" were traditional prior to prohibition of fixed commission rates. Investment companies would direct trades to brokerage firms skilled in trade execution with instructions to give up part of the commission to other brokerage firms that provided services.

Following prohibition of fixed commission rates in 1975, new legislation provided investment advisors have not breached fiduciary duty by causing investment companies to pay higher than competitive commission. But only if the commission is "reasonable" in relation to the value of brokerage and research services provided to all accounts under management. The purpose was to allow investment advisors to use the commission they pay to acquire research as well as trade execution services. These *soft dollar payments* are discussed in a later chapter. The SEC ruled such payments could *not* be made for readily available products and services. Ten years later, this rule was terminated as too difficult to apply or unduly restrictive. The SEC decided soft dollar payments are permissible as long as services/products provided are lawful and appropriate to portfolio manager performance.

Sale of fund shares

And, finally, Ratner (1998) summarized 1940 Act provisions concerning investment company sale of fund shares. Closed-end funds are like regular corporations and issue fixed numbers of shares at one time or more. Open-end funds make continuous offerings (sales) and redemption (sale) of shares at prices equal to fund net asset value. Open-end funds include both *load funds* and *no-load funds*. Traditional load funds imposed upfront sales fees to compensate brokers and financial advisors for selling shares received through captive distributors. Traditional no-load funds did not impose sales fees, but sold shares direct to shareholders through distributors. Principal underwriters of fund shares operate under written contracts renewed at least annually by shareholders or directors. The various sales fee arrangements are updated and discussed in chapter 3.

First, the disclosure requirements of the 1933 Act were modified under the 1940 Act as they apply to investment company registration statements. Further, any sales literature that supplements the required *prospectus* must be filed with the SEC. The required content of the prospectus is in table 2. Also, because mutual funds make continuous offerings of shares, dates of amendments to registration statements are considered the effective dates of registration statements and original dates of fund public offerings.

In 1979, the SEC took steps under the Securities Act of 1933 (the 1933 Act) and the 1940 Act to reduce restrictions on what mutual funds may say in advertisements. Those that include only information that *could* be included in the prospectus satisfy "prospectus delivery [to shareholder] requirements." Also, requirements governing what makes investment company sales literature "false or misleading" were reduced. The SEC was also authorized to permit investment companies to use a prospectus that includes information not in the prospectus filed with the registration statement. In 1988, the SEC required mutual funds to provide a standardized "fee table" in the prospectus.

The 1933 Act is the original "truth in securities" legislation for sales of new securities, including mutual fund shares. Mutual funds are required to register their continuous public offering of shares, and are prohibited from fraudulent and misleading advertising. Investors must be provided with a prospectus of "material facts," including investment objective and policies, investment strategies, performance, expenses, and fees.

Upon request, investors must also be provided *statements of additional information* (SAI). The prescribed content of the SAI is in table 2. This much more detailed document has been required since 1983 for the purpose of reducing information overload in the prospectus. In 1998, additional information was moved to the SAI, including disclosure of shareholder voting rights.

Funds must also distribute *annual* and *semi-annual reports* of financial condition and performance, including portfolios. These documents are oriented towards fund performance, current and historical.

Second, the 1940 Act imposed controls on prices at which investment companies may sell shares. The purpose is to prevent dilution of shareholder share values or unfair discrimination between shareholders. Closed-end funds may not issue shares at prices below net asset value without consent of a majority of shareholders. This control effectively prevents new offerings because closed-end funds normally trade at a *discount* to net asset value.

For open-end funds, the National Association of Securities Dealers (NASD) is authorized to adopt rules that prescribe prices at which security dealers may buy mutual funds shares and resell them to the public. The NASD is the industry's legally defined self-regulatory authority. It also performs on-site examinations and investigates investor complaints. It administers and interprets the SEC's legal framework for fund advertising and sale literature. And it regulates the required certification of broker/dealers as "registered representatives" and enforces rules of conduct.

Mutual fund shares may be sold only at current offering prices described in prospectuses, including any sales *loads*. In 1966, fixed brokerage commission on sales of stock was prohibited to ensure competition. However, the 1940 Act was amended to prevent abolition of fixed mutual fund sales fees. The NASD was given responsibility to ensure maximum loads are not "grossly excessive." excessive, but provide reasonable compensation for sales agents and underwriters. The maximum sales load is 8.50 percent.

The 1940 Act prohibits mutual funds from distributing their own shares, except in compliance with SEC rules. Prior to 1980, mutual funds were effectively prohibited from paying distribution costs from fund assets. Sales expenses were paid from sales loads received by distributors or, in the case of no-load funds, by the management companies.

This prohibition was removed in 1980 when the SEC adopted rule 12b-1 (12b-1 fees), which is discussed and assessed in chapters 2 and 3. If approved by shareholders and directors, mutual funds may act as distributors of their own shares and pay all or part of the costs from fund assets. The SEC has moved against some mutual funds for charging fund assets for costs unrelated to sales, and for charging 12b-1 fees and advertising as no-load funds. The definition of "no load" was later changed so funds with small 12b-1 fees can advertise as no-load funds (discussed in chapter 3).

The sanctions that may be applied to mutual funds for violations of securities laws and regulations are also discussed in Ratner (1998).

Other regulatory acts

Investment advisors, including those for mutual funds, must register under the Investment Advisors Act of 1940. This Act, summarized in table 1, imposes general fiduciary responsibilities and antifraud provisions. It also imposes record-keeping requirements and provides for reports and disclosure to shareholders and the SEC.

The SEC was created by the Securities Exchange Act of 1934 (the 1934 Act), which also extended the 1933 Act to outstanding securities. This Act regulates broker-dealers, including distributors of mutual fund shares. They must meet financial responsibility requirements, maintain financial and customer records, provide custodial accounts for customer securities, and file annual reports with the SEC.

The National Securities Market Act of 1996 (the 1996 Act) extended the 1940 Act and provides for more efficient management of investment companies with more effective, but less burdensome, regulation. The federal government is given sole authority to regulate investment company disclosure and advertising. States may still require investment companies to register and submit their SEC documents, and they do retain jurisdiction for fraud, deceit and unlawful broker-dealer conduct. They also maintain jurisdiction under laws regulating registered corporations generally.

Diversification requirements

As noted above, the 1940 Act also classified investment companies as diversified or nondiversified. This is a different brand of diversification than assumed when discussing portfolio diversification (chapter 2). Legal diversification requires that, as to 75 percent of assets, diversified investment companies may *not* (1) acquire more than 10 percent of voting shares of any single security issuer, or (2) invest more than 5 percent of fund total assets in any one security issuer. No limits exist on the remaining 25 percent of fund assets, but, in practice, funds rarely invest more than 10 percent of assets in a single security.

Subchapter M of the Internal Revenue Code also imposes diversification requirements on investment companies. However, these requirements are less restrictive than those required under the 1940 Act. They state that no single security may exceed 25 percent of assets, and, as to 50 percent of total assets, no one security may exceed 5 percent of assets. Cash, cash items, US Treasury securities, and securities of other regulated investment companies are excluded.

Distribution requirements

Investment company distributions are further regulated under subchapter M of the Internal Revenue Code. This Act also requires registration under the 1940 Act. Importantly, investment companies must meet exacting income distribution requirements to qualify as *regulated investment companies* and receive *pass-through tax treatment* (*tax conduits*). This is crucial because eligible investment companies are exempt from federal income and excise taxes. This exemption requires investment companies to receive at least 90 percent of gross income from security holdings, and they must distribute annually at least 90 percent of ordinary income and realized long-term capital gains to shareholders. Exemption from excise taxes requires them to distribute annually at least 98 percent of annual ordinary income and realized net long-term capital gains (the latter for the year ending October 31), as well as any previous year income not distributed.

Mutual fund dividend and interest income, less management fees and other operating expenses, plus net realized short-term capital gains, is paid to shareholders as *dividend* (*income*) *distributions*. These distributions are reported for tax purposes as ordinary dividends. Mutual funds pay realized long-term capital gains to shareholders as *capital gains distributions*. These distributions are reported for tax purposes as long-term capital gains. Although qualifying investment companies receive pass-through tax treatment, distributions are taxable income to shareholders, whether reinvested in additional shares or paid by check. Capital gain distributions are taxed preferentially as long-term gains. But the key is no federal income taxation of mutual fund income.

State regulation of directors

States impose two types of responsibilities and specific duties on directors in general. The first is a "duty of care," which requires diligence, care, and skill that persons of "ordinary prudence" exercise in serving corporate interests. Directors must obtain adequate information and exercise "business judgment" in decision making. The second is "loyalty," which requires "good faith" dealings favoring corporate interests in resolving conflicts of interest. Specific corporate director duties include selection of principal officers, declaration of dividends, setting shareholder meetings, and determining shareholder dates of record for dividends.

INVESTMENT COMPANIES AND UNIT INVESTMENT TRUSTS: CHARACTERISTICS

Open-end investment companies (mutual funds)

Historically, mutual funds have been what are called *actively managed funds*. They seek to earn superior returns by actively managing their portfolios. But, increasingly, funds are becoming what are called *index (passively managed) funds*. Index funds manage their portfolios to mimic performance of particular benchmark market indices, such as the S&P 500 Index. In any case, the defining characteristic of mutual funds as open-end funds is continuous offering of new shares to investors and, under normal market conditions, continuous readiness to redeem (buy back) outstanding shares upon request. Numbers of outstanding shares fluctuate as they are bought and redeemed. If fund share purchases exceed redemptions and *exchanges*, the result is *net cash inflows* and more dollars to invest. Conversely, if redemptions and exchanges exceed purchases, the result is *net cash outflows* and fewer dollars invested. Net cash outflows are covered from *cash assets (reserves)*, sales of securities, and/or pre-established bank lines of credit.

Mutual fund shares are priced daily at net asset value, which, as noted, is computed by taking total market value of the portfolio, less fund liabilities, and dividing the remainder by number of outstanding shares. Shares are sold at net asset value (plus any sales charges) and redeemed at net asset value (less any fees). Fund shares are sold to investors in two basic ways: direct to investors or indirectly through sales agents, such as financial planners.

Closed-end investment companies

As noted above, closed-end funds are similar to regular corporations – their shares outstanding are fixed following public offerings. Thus they stand ready neither to sell nor to redeem shares on an ongoing basis. As a result, closed-end funds are not concerned with potential investor redemptions, which allows them to buy less liquid securities. Share prices vary and are determined by market supply and demand. Their portfolios are actively managed, typically diversified, and managed in accordance with fund objectives and policies. Any ordinary income and realized long-term capital gains are distributed to shareholders. Closed-end funds normally have perpetual lives.

In 1999, ICI (1999c) reported 476 closed-end funds with total assets of $151.6 billion. Domestic closed-end funds represent 77 percent of total closed-end fund assets. These funds include equity funds, specialty stock funds (*sector funds*), US Treasury bond funds, and municipal bond funds. Foreign closed-end funds include equity funds, government bond funds, and corporate bond funds, some of which are defined by country or region.

Initial public offerings of closed-end funds generally sell at a premium to net asset value of approximately 10 percent, which reflects investment banking fees. Subsequently, outstanding shares trade in secondary markets, including exchanges and over the counter, in exactly the same way as common stock. Prices reflect supply and demand, and investors pay transaction costs in both initial public offerings and secondary market transactions executed through broker-dealers.

In the secondary market, closed-end fund shares tend to trade at discount to net asset value of about 10 percent. Occasionally, they may trade at premium to net asset value. Thus unlike mutual fund shares, closed-end fund shares do not normally trade at net asset value. Shares selling at discount may provide above-average returns if discounts narrow or disappear. Jones (1998) and Malkiel (1995) provided a brief discussion and analysis, respectively, of closed-end fund discounts/premiums.

Because closed-end funds normally do not sell at net asset value, Zweig (1996) offered the following guidelines: (1) do not buy bad funds at discount to net asset value, (2) do not buy funds at initial public offerings to avoid underwriting fees – wait for prices to settle, (3) never pay premiums to net asset value and buy only at discount, (4) reinvest dividends to buy additional shares selling at discount, (5) invest long-term to minimize commission, and (6) buy funds with low expense ratios. Rekenthaler (1994a) also recommended buying closed-end funds at discount, but added that this does not make them preferable to mutual funds. Also, with the subsequent introduction of *exchange-traded funds* (ETFs), closed-end single *country funds* do not have exclusive offerings in these markets.

Unit investment trusts

Unit investment trusts differ from open-end and closed-end funds in three major ways. First, UITs are organized by sponsors under trust indentures with trustees that represent investors, rather than directors and shareholders. Portfolio assets are placed with trustees, normally banks or trust companies, for safe keeping and administration. Second, portfolios are fixed at inception, but they are monitored and may be changed if issues of creditworthiness arise. The portfolios are preselected to meet investment objectives, not actively managed, and require few service providers. Third, unlike mutual funds, they do not have perpetual lives but instead terminate at predetermined dates, which vary widely with the nature of the securities held.

Unit investment trusts (*fixed trusts*) are organized by single or "syndicates" of broker-dealers that purchase the portfolios and sell the trusts. Trusts distribute dividend and interest income plus any cash proceeds from maturing bonds, bonds redeemed by issuers, and disposition of bonds with deteriorating creditworthiness. Investors are charged modest annual fees, reflecting unmanaged portfolios, to cover trust and administrative expenses.

There are approximately twelve broker-dealers that sponsor UITs. As noted in ICI (1997b), there are 12,386 trusts with assets of $78 billion. Broker-dealers initially sell the redeemable *trust certificates* (*units*) at net asset value plus sales fees of some 3–4 percent. Fees may be delayed to allow purchasers to first earn some income. Normally, units trade at offering prices for about one month following initial offerings. Performance information is usually provided to investors monthly.

After initial sale, units normally trade in secondary markets, where they are priced by supply and demand. Typically, investors may sell units to the broker-dealers who organized the trusts or other dealers that make markets in the units. These broker-dealers resell the units at ask prices that approximate net asset value plus fees at initial offering. The markets are usually relatively illiquid, with large trading costs. Thus there are significant investor transaction costs at initial offerings and secondary market trades.

In the absence of secondary markets, investors may redeem units (limitations may apply) with the trustees prior to termination, which may range from six months for trusts holding money market securities to twenty or more years for bond trusts. Trustees may sell securities as needed to meet unit redemptions. Trust assets are liquidated at termination, with investors receiving return of bond principal and equity capital.

Historically, unit trusts predominantly held fixed-income securities, especially tax-exempt bonds. Times have changed and equities now represent over 50 percent of unit trust assets. These equity trusts hold stocks and generally have shorter lives than bond trusts, such as five years. The trusts are designed for particular: (1) investment strategies, (2) indexed portfolios, including broad and narrowly defined market indices, (3) demographic markets, such as retirees, and (4) types of investors, such as individual investors.

Fixed-income trusts were traditionally primarily designed for high tax bracket investors desiring tax-exempt securities. Other widely used trusts also invest in money market instruments, corporate bonds, international bonds, mortgage-backed securities, and US Treasury obligations.

INVESTMENT COMPANIES: A HISTORICAL NOTE

Investment companies have a longer history than suggested by their great visibility and growth since the 1980s. They originated in London in 1868 with the first of what are now called closed-end funds. By the 1880s, closed-end funds were operating in the United State, where they became the dominant class of investment company. But this ended with poor performance after the 1929 market crash and subsequent depression. These events obviously greatly reduced public confidence and ability to invest, as well as securities and financial institutions generally. Worse, however, numerous closed-end funds were excessively leveraged and often engaged in speculative and fraudulent practices. As a result, closed-end funds were largely discredited and, to this day, they have never regained their once dominant position. There are now about 500 closed-end funds, many of which focus on single country markets, such as the Germany Fund.

Mutual funds are now the dominant class of investment company. The highlights of this growth are outlined and discussed in Zweig (1999a, b). The year 1924 marked organization of the first modern mutual fund, the Massachusetts Investment Trust (MIT). The second fund, State Street Investment Trust, followed just four months later. In 1925, MIT organized Investment Trust Fund A on the then wild premise that common stocks outperform bonds and cash over the long term. In 1928, First Investment Counsel Trust, now Scudder Income Fund, was organized as the first no-load fund. And, in 1932, MIT employed the first industry research director, who initiated the industry practice of preparing stock research reports. MIT continues to be located in Boston, MA, a city with a long tradition of trust management.

As the first mutual fund MIT was the model for what was to become the mutual fund industry. First, from its beginning in 1924, MIT's portfolio was 100 percent common stock. This was at a time when bonds were considered the only prudent investment. Stocks were speculative! Second, MIT used only conservative investment principles, none of the speculative antics of numerous closed-end funds. And, third, MIT's portfolio was publicly disclosed, which was a real shock to Wall Street. Disclosure was the exception to accepted practice at that time. In this regard, MIT's first portfolio is reprinted in table 3. Other than the predominance of railroad, railroad-related and utility shares, industrial holdings include a fair number of household names that today look like anything but speculative common stocks: Standard Oil, Texaco, United Fruit, US Steel, General Motors, General Electric and Eastman Kodak. Fourth, and most important, MIT introduced the mutual fund's defining attribute – the continuous offering and redemption of shares at net asset value.

As, if this were not enough, MIT also contributed importantly to writing mutual fund legislation and to subsequent industry growth. MIT officials actually assisted in drafting the 1940 Act, which was patterned after MIT's own bylaws. Further, MIT worked hard to win congressional approval of mutual fund pass-through tax treatment for mutual funds. This tax conduit for qualifying funds greatly enhanced investor interest in mutual funds. Without this tax break, it is unlikely the fund industry would have anything approaching its current amount of assets under management.

Nonetheless, the 1929 market crash and subsequent depression had tremendously adverse effects on the mutual fund industry. The crash and depression, along with wide use of speculative investment practices, led to the landmark 1933 and 1934 Acts, which were designed to protect investors and regulate securities markets. The 1940 Act extended this legislation and subjected mutual funds to very extensive regulation. This has also been very important to investor confidence and eventual success of the mutual fund industry.

When, years later, *Time* ("The Prudent Man," 1959) featured the then still very modest-sized mutual fund industry, it was MIT's chief investment officer who was the cover story. This success story continues today in Boston. The MIT is now the MFS Massachusetts Investors A fund, and the investment advisor is Massachusetts Financial Services, a subsidiary of Sun Life Assurance of Canada.

In subsequent years, mutual funds continued to experience both good times and bad. Funds were not especially popular during the 1950s, but they became quite the thing during the short-lived growth stock mania of the 1960s. A few *portfolio managers*, such as Gerry Tsai, even acquired celebrity status. His fifteen minutes of fame lasted about as long as his fund's superior performance did, which was not very long at all. Numerous other star portfolio managers also came and went, and the star icon soon generally disappeared until reborn again in the 1980s. These early *star* (*portfolio*) *managers* (*stars*) had quite consistent patterns – short-lived hot streaks followed by often disastrous flame-outs.

However, introduction of *money market funds* in 1971 did much to spur investment in mutual funds. These funds invest in short-term securities, such as Treasury bills, bank certificates of deposit and commercial paper. Money market funds are competitive alternatives to bank interest-paying deposits. They are normally managed to maintain a $1 net asset value. The first money market fund, the Reserve Fund, opened when inflation was over 10 percent. The fund offered individual investors something they were not accustomed to – money market rates of interest on small accounts, which were over 20 percent when inflation was at its highest. Mutual funds also offered an increasingly diverse menu of shareholder services. In 1974, Fidelity Daily Income Trust became first to offer the most important service – check writing on fund accounts.

Developments following the severe bear market of 1973–4 also encouraged investor interest in mutual funds. Investors were provided with increasing numbers of mutual funds and expanding variety of investment objectives to meet their needs. This spectrum increased some threefold from the mid-1970s to the present. Increased choice was seen in expanded offerings of bond funds, such as tax-exempt municipal bonds, as well as international funds that facilitated increased global investing. And, in what has become a huge success, 1976 marked the shaky introduction of the first retail index mutual fund, the First Index Investment Trust. This fund is now the Vanguard 500 Index Fund, by far the largest retail index mutual fund, with assets over $70 billion (one fund!). For a while, when its assets exceeded $100 billion, the fund was the largest mutual fund.

Innovations in retirement and savings vehicles have also increased demand for mutual funds. These innovations included 401(k), 403(b) and 457 salary reduction pension plans, Keogh plans and SEP IRA self-employed retirement plans, SIMPLE 401(k) small company pension plans, SIMPLE IRA and ROTH IRA individual retirement plans, and EDUCATION IRAs. These various savings vehicles provided new investment incentives for American workers and savers.

Moreover, much growth in mutual fund assets has been caused by major shifts in company pension plans from defined benefit to self-directed 401(k) defined contribution plans. This shift has "required" individuals to become more involved in retirement planning, and it has also increased awareness that bank Certificates of deposit are not the route to long-term retirement security.

Retirement assets represent an increasing share of mutual funds assets, and mutual funds represent an increasing share of retirement assets. ICI (2000e) reported mutual fund retirement assets as proportions of total mutual fund assets increased from 19 percent in 1990 to 35 percent in 1999. And, mutual fund proportions of total US retirement assets increased from 5 percent in 1990 to 19 percent in 1999. Even more impressive, mutual fund proportions of total 401(k) assets increased from 9 percent in 1990 to 45 percent in 1999.

Further, much growth in mutual fund assets is due to increased proportions of households that invest in funds. ICI (2000f) reported the percentage of households investing in mutual funds increased from 5.7 percent in 1980 to 49 percent in 2000. The percentage reached 72 percent for households with incomes of at least $50,000. ICI (2000c) found this growth very much reflected in increasing numbers of mutual funds – from 857 in 1982 to 7,791 in 1999.

Much of the growth in mutual fund assets since 1982 may be seen in the turnaround and increase in net cash inflows to funds. By 1981, mutual funds had endured ten consecutive years of net cash *out*flows, but since then net cash flows have been positive in each and every year, except 1988. The 1988 outflow was a major mistake that followed the October 1987 market collapse. Reid and Millar (2000) reported that, in 1989, $73 billion in net new cash was invested in mutual funds, but by 1999 it was $364 billion! Reid (2000) provided a review of fund industry developments during the 1990s.

But the largest incentive to mutual fund investing has been the unprecedented size and duration of stock market returns since 1982, early in the Reagan administration. The origins of this performance may be traced to the large reductions in income tax rates. While several downdrafts have lowered returns from time to time in subsequent years, the only years with negative returns have been 1990, a very small loss, and 2000. For example, annualized returns on the S&P 500 Index from August 1982 to 1996 exceeded 17 percent, compared to its historical 9–11 percent.

This unprecedented bull market is seen in table 4, which reproduces the extraordinary performance of the top fifty stock funds. The top-ranked fund had annualized returns of an amazing 23.8 percent, and the lowest of the ranked funds earned 18.6 percent. Thus it is no surprise that individuals and others invested heavily in mutual funds, especially equity funds, and these cash inflows mostly continue.

MUTUAL FUNDS AS ORGANIZATIONS

Mutual funds organized as corporations are like other corporations with shareholder-elected directors. Funds organized as business trusts are governed by shareholder-elected trustees. Use of the business trust organization is normally motivated by more favorable tax treatment. For example, the Vanguard group of funds reorganized as Pennsylvania business trusts owing to higher taxes they would have had to pay by remaining registered Maryland corporations.

As noted above, mutual funds may issue only common stock, with shareholders having "mutuality of interest" in fund assets and income. But, with rare exceptions, funds have been permitted to issue senior securities, including preferred stock. Funds may also borrow from banks to meet cash withdrawals from share redemptions. But, more recently, funds prefer to use less costly interfund loans under the same management. These "in the family" loans require SEC authorization, which limits loan size, terms and interest rates.

The most important change in mutual fund capital structure has been the issuance of *multiple share classes* (discussed later). Each class has a different menu of sales charges and fees (including none) attached to the same or equivalent portfolios. Multiple share classes enable funds to appeal to diverse types of investors through increased share distribution channels.

Service providers

Mutual funds differ from typical corporations in a very significant way – they are *not* managed internally. Mutual funds are basically shell entities holding securities, for which administrative, investment, and legally required functions are provided by external *service providers* (subcontractors). Investment management companies sponsor, organize, and arrange for provision of services required by funds. They act as fund investment advisors and provide the essential research and portfolio management services consistent with fund investment objectives, policies, and limitations. Summaries of fund service providers are in ICI (1996b) and Kunert (1993).

The specifics of services provided by mutual fund service providers vary, but a general description follows:

1 *Investment advisor:* provides research and portfolio management services consistent with fund investment objectives, policies, and limitations as stated in the prospectus; functions include formulation and implementation of investment style and strategies, security analysis, market and economic analysis, portfolio allocation, security buy/sell decisions, and performance evaluation.

2 *Administrator:* provides management and regulatory oversight; reviews and reports performance of other administrative service providers and ensures fund regulatory compliance; may
pay office, equipment, and personnel expenses; may provide general accounting services
and prepare/file SEC, tax, shareholder, and other reports.
3 *Custodian:* holds portfolio cash and securities in safe keeping; settles portfolio transactions
– receives cash and securities and makes authorized cash payments and security deliveries;
collects portfolio interest and dividends; pays authorized expenses, shareholder redemptions,
and disbursements; and maintains related records.
4 *Transfer agent:* fulfills shareholder transaction requests and receives and authorizes disbursement of monies from shareholder transactions; maintains and provides shareholder
account and transaction records; provides a wide range of shareholder services; provides
shareholder communications, including account and transaction statements, annual and
semi-annual reports, prospectus, proxy statements, and informational material; often serves
as disbursing agent for shareholder distributions.
5 *Distributor (principal underwriter):* as broker-dealer provides direct and/or indirect distribution
of shares to investors; distributes fund publications; and provides fund marketing and
advertising.

Auditors and legal counsel provide compliance services. Auditors determine whether fund
financial reports and records are in compliance and report to directors. Counsel ensures fund
regulatory compliance and advises disinterested directors concerning contracts with investment
advisors and other providers. Fund legal counsel is normally separate from that to investment
advisors. Figure 1.1 summarizes these relationships along with overviews of service providers.

Non-advisory service functions may be contracted directly by mutual funds and/or by fund
investment advisors, which in turn provide them directly and/or indirectly through one
or more affiliates and/or non-affiliates. Non-advisory contractual service relationships vary
considerably among funds. At one extreme, funds contract independently with each service
provider, which may directly and/or indirectly provide the particular service. Most funds
contract with investment advisors to provide inclusive "service packages," especially in the
case of money market funds. In any case, investment advisors normally provide administrator
services, as well. These various contracts, including transfer agents, require board approval,
including a majority of disinterested directors when providers are affiliates of advisors.

As noted above, the 1940 Act requires mutual funds to contract with custodians to ensure
safe keeping of cash and securities. These "shareholder trustees" hold fund assets to protect
them from fraud and negligence. Custody includes use of central securities depositories and
the US Treasury's book entry system to minimize the physical movement of traded securities.
Banks and trust companies normally act as custodians, but stock exchange member firms and
others may serve, if approved. However, custodians must be otherwise independent. Custodial
fees are normally based on fund asset size and volume of securities transactions. They also
reflect the complexity and scope of services provided. Custodial contracts require the approval
of fund directors, including a majority of disinterested directors, as well as shareholders of a
majority of shares voting. Normally, less than 10 percent of outstanding shares are voted.

Custodians may also be contracted to provide other services. For example, the Dodge &
Cox Fund contracts with Firststar Trust Company as custodian, transfer agent, and dividend
disbursing agent. On the other hand, Fidelity Low-priced Stock Fund has only a custodial

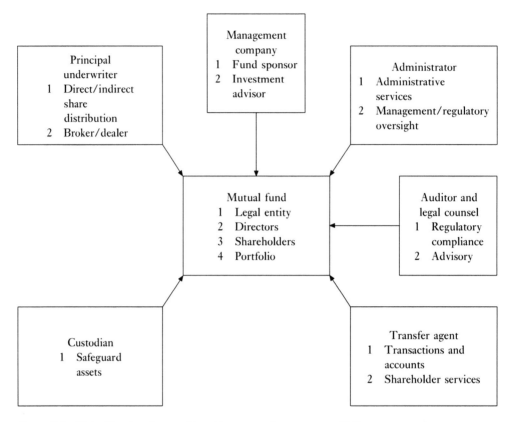

Figure 1.1 Mutual fund service providers. Management company: portfolio management. Administrator: administration and management/regulatory oversight. Auditor: accounting compliance. Legal counsel: legal compliance. Transfer agent: transactions, accounts, and services. Custodian: safeguard assets. Principal underwriter: distribute shares.

contract with Brown Brothers Harriman. Transfer agency, dividend disbursement, shareholder, and accounting services are provided by Fidelity Services Company, an affiliated company.

Mutual funds may not act as distributors (principal underwriters) of their shares, except in compliance with SEC rules. Prior to 1980, the distribution costs of shares sold without sales charges were borne by management companies. Mutual fund assets could not be used for this purpose. Distribution costs of shares with sales charges were paid from these fees.

The payment of distribution costs of mutual fund shares changed dramatically in 1980. As noted, rule 12b-1 allows funds to charge share distribution costs against fund assets. These fees are primarily used to pay sales commission, but also for other distribution expenses, such as advertising, marketing materials, and payments to sales agents and others for "continuing shareholder services." Use of 12b-1 fees must be pursuant to plans approved annually by fund directors, including a majority of disinterested directors. Directors must also determine that imposition of 12b-1 fees will "reasonably benefit" funds and shareholders. For example, Vanguard Windsor II imposes no 12b-1 fees, while the Robertson Stephens Contrarian fund charges a 0.75 percent annual fee. Distributors are generally broker-dealer affiliates of investment advisors. In these cases, disinterested directors must comprise a majority of board members.

The SEC regulates principal underwriters in their role as *registered broker-dealers*, and, under its legal framework, the NASD regulates mutual funds' advertising and sales practices. Fund shares are sold using either one or two distribution channels. *Direct-market funds* use direct sales methods such as newspaper and mail advertising to offer shares to investors. Sales force (*indirect-market*) *funds* solicit and distribute shares through full-service brokers, discount brokers, online discount brokers, *mutual fund supermarkets* (fund supermarkets), insurance agents, banks, and financial planners and advisors. Direct market fund shares are usually, but not exclusively, sold at net asset value without sales charges (loads). On the other hand, sales force fund shares are sold at net asset value plus loads, which are primarily used to compensate commission sales agents, such as brokers. For example, Fidelity Investments employs both direct and indirect sales methods, and some of their direct sale funds have sales charges.

Transfer agents must register with the SEC to provide mutual fund services. Contracts with transfer agents are negotiated and approved by fund boards, including a majority of disinterested directors. Approval is required because transfer costs are fund expenses. Average account size is the most important determinant of transfer agent fees. Other arrangements include asset-based fees and transaction-based fees. Out-of-pocket expenses may be reimbursed separately. Large management companies usually provide these services through affiliates to ensure quality and reduce expenses. Managers of small funds usually find it more economical to rely on external providers.

Investment advisors

Mutual fund investment advisors provide portfolio management services, and they normally also provide administrator services. In the latter case, advisors and administrators are often the same entities. If not the same, administrators may be affiliates of advisors or independent entities. Smaller fund operations usually contract with independent administrators.

In addition to contractual roles as mutual fund investment advisors, investment management companies normally also advise/manage other types of portfolios as well. This is normally the case because advisors normally began by managing money for private clients, such as large individual accounts, partnership accounts, trusts, pension plans, and foundations. For example, Harris Associates advised this range of private clients prior to sponsoring mutual funds.

Some management companies are stand-alone entities, such as Barr Rosenberg's Rosenberg Institutional Equity Management. Others are components or affiliates of brokerage firms, such as Legg Mason Fund Advisor, or insurance companies, such as Nationwide Advisory Services, or banking institutions, such as Wachovia Asset Management.

In the simplest case, management companies advise a single mutual fund entity. For example, Westchester Capital Management advises one open-end investment company, the Merger Fund. But as the market for mutual funds has expanded, management companies have generally added, incrementally, to the number of funds they advise. This has been done in different ways. In one, a single open-end investment company operates a series of distinct portfolios managed as separate mutual funds, For example, Fidelity Growth and Income Portfolio is a diversified portfolio of Fidelity Securities Fund, an open-end investment company organized as a Massachusetts business trust.

In other cases, multiple open-end investment companies are organized, each with a diversified series of distinct portfolios. Until recent changes, the Vanguard Index Trust was one of over thirty investment companies totaling more than ninety-five distinct portfolios. Sets of mutual funds and/or series of funds under the management of one investment advisor are called (*mutual*) *fund families* or (*mutual*) *fund complexes*. For example, Harris Associates advises the Oakmark Family of Funds and its six funds. One the other extreme, giant Fidelity Investments is the largest fund family, with over 150 funds/portfolios.

As mentioned, mutual funds are typically corporations (or business trusts) with boards of directors (or trustees) elected by shareholders. As such, they are technically shareholder-owned. But they are not shareholder-controlled through elected directors. Actual control of mutual funds normally lies with investment advisors – the management companies that sponsored them, obtained regulatory approval, organized them, nominated directors and staffed principal officers, among other functions.

Nonetheless, mutual fund shareholders must approve (affirm, actually) certain board decisions, including changes in investment objectives, policies, investment advisory contracts, and fee schedules, selection of directors to fill a specified number of vacancies, appointment of independent public accountants, and "fundamental" limitations on portfolio securities.

The 1940 Act requires mutual fund investment advisory contracts be approved by a majority of disinterested directors and owners of a majority of shares voting. This process initiates with appointing principal fund officers, who normally also serve on boards of directors – the same boards that officially named them officers. Further, principal fund officers/directors normally hold similar positions in the sponsoring management companies acting as fund investment advisors.

Investment advisory contracts should include advisor responsibilities and fees, expenses paid by the parties, any other service functions to be provided and fees, and portfolio investment objectives, policies, strategies, and limitations. Contracts could well include specific investment services, such as economic and market forecasts, portfolio manager and analyst services, and methods of security analysis, portfolio allocation, investment style, trade execution, and performance evaluation, among others.

Further, if investment advisors also provide some or all non-investment services, these and their fees should be specified. As noted above, non-investment services could include administration, managerial oversight, asset safe keeping, customer service, shareholder records and share distribution. These service suppliers and their responsibilities should also be specified, including those provided directly and/or indirectly through affiliated and/or unaffiliated firms.

It is not by some Evil Empire conspiracy that management companies control mutual funds in their roles as investment advisors, but because a business purpose is served. The motivation to sponsor, organize, and manage funds is for the purpose of attracting, pooling, and investing shareholder dollars for asset-based fees. One implication of this control has been that fund boards routinely renew investment advisory contracts. Exceptions occur more frequently if advisors subcontract one or more *subadvisors* to manage some portion or all of fund portfolios. Manager tenure in these cases is determined more by investment performance than by control.

The "lock" investment advisors have on mutual funds is not necessarily bad for share-holders. Shareholders usually focus on performance, not control issues. The best shareholder remedy when funds underperform is to cash-out and move to more user-friendly funds or fund families. Exceptions could occur if for some reason large individual or institutional share-holders found it advantageous to leverage their positions seeking improved fund performance and/or portfolio management.

Boards of directors

As suggested above, mutual funds have two general types of board directors: *interested* (*inside*) *directors* and disinterested (independent) directors. Interested directors are those affiliated with fund investment advisory firms and the funds themselves. The 1940 Act mandates critical roles for independent directors as shareholder watchdogs. These outside directors carry primary responsibility for ensuring the primacy of shareholder interests in mutual fund management. Their single most important function is approval of contracts between funds and investment advisors. Independent directors may not be affiliated with investment advisors and must satisfy various tests of independence. The other board members, the inside directors, normally have dual affiliations as fund officers/directors and investment advisory officers/principals.

To foster board independence, no more than 60 percent of directors may be interested and, conversely, at least 40 percent must be disinterested. Interested persons include: (1) affili-ated persons, or immediate families, with direct control relationships with mutual funds or investment advisors; (2) fund investment advisors, principal underwriters, broker-dealers or affiliates, and legal counsel within the last two years; and (3) persons determined to have "material business relationships" with funds. Moreover, specified persons are prohibited from serving as mutual fund directors. These include persons convicted of specified felonies or misdemeanors, and those enjoined from acting as broker-dealers, investment advisors, or participating in specified investment and financial activities.

Independent directors generally comprise nominating committees for new mutual fund directors, but they are required to do so if 12b-1 fees have been adopted. Independent dir-ectors are provided legal counsel and consultants for assistance in negotiating and approving service provider contracts, of which investment advisor contracts are most important. They must also approve transfer agent, custodian, and principal underwriter contracts. They may vote to remove investment advisors, but this is done only infrequently and requires shareholder approval, which is given even less frequently. Director responsibilities are summarized in ICI (1995), and their responsibilities under federal law are summarized in table 5.

To summarize, mutual fund directors are responsible for: (1) evaluation of portfolio per-formance; (2) renewal of investment advisory and subadvisory contracts; (3) pricing of fund shares; (4) securities valuation and maintenance of required portfolio liquidity; (5) regulatory compliance oversight; (6) oversight of compliance with investment objectives, policies, and restrictions; (7) rules governing transactions with investment advisor affiliates, and (8) approval of contracts with other service providers.

Moreover, investment advisory contracts are "fundamental" to mutual fund operations and must: (1) be approved initially by owners of a majority of shares voting; (2) specify advisor compensation schedules; (3) terminate, with notice, if ordered by the board or owners of a majority of shares voting; and (4) terminate if assigned to other parties. As stated, renewal of advisory contracts and approval of non-advisory service contracts require majority vote of independent directors, who have fiduciary responsibility for their terms and costs. Both independent directors and owners of a majority of shares voting must approve adoption of 12b-1 fees.

Mutual fund organization: an example

The varying aspects of mutual fund organizational and service provider relationships make an example useful. Tweedy Browne Fund (the corporation) serves well for this purpose. Tweedy Browne's prospectus (1998) clearly presented its relationships with service providers.

The corporation is a registered open-end investment company incorporated in the state of Maryland that offers a series of two diversified portfolios: Global Value Fund and American Value Fund. Each fund is a regulated investment company under subchapter M of the Internal Revenue Code, and are therefore exempt from federal income/excise taxes.

The corporation's directors supervise the funds, and shareholders have one vote for each share owned. No annual shareholder meetings are required or held, but special meetings may be called to elect/remove directors and to change fundamental investment policies.

The corporation contracts with Tweedy Browne, a registered investment advisor, to provide each fund's advisory services. Each fund's daily business and investment affairs are managed subject to board policies, legal requirements, and its investment objective, policies, and restrictions. Tweedy Browne's general partners manage each fund's portfolio and make the investment decisions. Their investment approach, decisions, and performance are discussed thoroughly in each fund's annual report to shareholders. Tweedy Browne receives an annual advisory fee of 1.25 percent of each fund's daily net assets.

Each fund is also responsible for directly paying the following other expenses: (1) legal, accounting and auditing fees; (2) custodian, transfer agent and dividend disbursing agent fees; (3) independent director fees and expenses; (4) fidelity bond and liability insurance premiums; (5) interest expenses, brokerage fees, and other trading costs; (6) taxes; (7) shareholder printing and servicing expenses; (8) litigation expenses; and (9) extraordinary or non-recurring expenses, etc.

First Data Shareholder Services Group is each fund's administrator. It provides management services for an annual fee of 0.09 percent of average daily net assets, subject to specified minimums and limitations. It also acts as each fund's agent for transfer, shareholder servicing, and dividend disbursement.

Boston Safe Deposit & Trust Company is custodian of each fund's cash and securities. Tweedy Browne, in its role as registered broker-dealer, acts as each fund's principal underwriter for share distribution.

CHAPTER TWO

MUTUAL FUND SERVICE ADVANTAGES

Mutual Funds . . . the Greatest Investment Ever Invented.
(*John C. Bogle, Vanguard Group, in* **Mutual Funds,** *April 1998*)

Mutual funds were designed to provide the do-it-yourself investor with professional investment expertise at relatively low cost. . . .
(*Kylelane Purcell, in* **Morningstar 5 Star Investor,** *January 1994*)

Fund managers are just like baseball players . . . You can measure the performance of both. That means fund managers can be franchise players, too.
(*Ken Phillips, Money Management Partners, in* **Wall Street Journal,** *September 7, 1999*)

The goals of chapters 2 and 3 are twofold. The first goal is to identify and discuss the service advantages provided by mutual funds generally. The second goal is to provide guidelines that facilitate determination of whether particular mutual fund services are actual advantages to particular investors. Mutual funds generally provide several major service advantages: (1) diversification, (2) investment objectives, (3) shareholder liquidity, (4) shareholder transaction costs, (5) shareholder services, and (6) professional management (chapter 3).

The key issue is not whether mutual funds offer general service advantages – they do – but whether particular funds offer them as specific service advantages in meeting the needs of particular investors. That is, do the specific service advantages of particular funds translate to specific service advantages for particular investors?

The extraordinary growth in the number and size of mutual funds is strong evidence they provide service advantages to investors. These services taken together motivate investors to pay the expenses and costs associated with ownership of fund shares. These expenses and costs along with other fund service disadvantages are discussed in chapters 4 and 5.

Diversification is a powerful tool for reducing portfolio unsystematic (other than market) risk and is a most important service advantage of mutual funds generally. However, there are funds that provide diversification only within narrow industry sectors. Domestic, but more so global, diversification allows investors to minimize portfolio risk for given levels of expected returns.

Constrained diversification refers to factors that limit portfolios from achieving attainable degrees of global diversification and risk. These constraints include fund investment objectives (primary), methods of security analysis and portfolio management, investment style, cash assets, geographic concentration, asset allocation, market liquidity, returns distribution, industry sector concentration, security concentration, and quality concentration.

Mutual funds generally provide a wide range of investment objectives to meet varying needs of investors. This is an important service advantage. The industry trade association classifies funds into twenty-one categories, some of which are more narrowly defined than others. Investors need to be alert to actual versus stated investment objectives and signals of change in investment objectives. In general, fund risk is consistent with that implied by investment objectives.

Shareholder liquidity is an important service advantage provided by mutual funds in meeting shareholder redemptions (sales of shares). There are several methods for requesting share redemptions, such as by mail, telephone, and special checks. The time necessary to receive payments varies from instant to several days. However, constraints on redemption may be imposed under specified conditions.

Shareholder transaction costs are a general service advantage of mutual funds. Transaction costs are what the term suggests – shareholder costs that relate to transactions with funds. Transaction costs may apply at the time of purchase, at the time of redemption, while shares are held, and combinations of the above. Or no transaction costs may be imposed.

Transaction costs range from front-end loads (sales charges), back-end loads, continuing loads, and combinations of loads to no loads. Use of multiple share classes with different load/ fee structures for different markets, but generally appended to existing portfolios, has complicated assessment as more funds employ them. A majority of funds impose transaction costs, but there are still numerous funds that do not. However, if trends continue, it will be necessary to categorize transaction costs as a general service disadvantage.

Shareholder services are a general advantage of mutual funds. They are wide-ranging in quantity, quality, and by fund family, and are generally favored over other financial service providers. Investors have several types of perceived needs best met by a variety of fund distribution channels. Investors prefer direct market fund services to most types of sales force services.

Professional management (chapter 3) is another most important service advantage of mutual funds generally. Factors affecting the quality of portfolio management include family background in investments, education, previous investment experience, portfolio manager tenure, personal investment in the fund, fund communication, portfolio management advisors versus subadvisors, and use of star and multiple portfolio managers.

The second goal is to provide guidelines that facilitate determination of whether particular mutual fund services are actual advantages to particular investors. This determination of fund performance across these and various other dimensions is a theme in this chapter and throughout the book. Specific guidelines are illustrated for each service advantage using Vanguard Windsor II.

DIVERSIFICATION

Concept and portfolio risk

Diversification represents the most important mutual fund service advantage derived from investment theory. The notion of diversification is well known from the adage "Don't put all of your eggs in one basket." More precisely, diversification is the process of adding securities to a portfolio for the purpose of reducing its unique security risk and, thereby, reducing its total risk. Diversification reduces investor risk below the risk of a single security by combining in a portfolio those securities whose changes in returns offset one another. The basic idea is to combine securities that average out each other's risk because their changes in returns are not strongly positively correlated. The result can be a level of portfolio risk that is less than the weighted average risk of the individual securities. To get the lowest portfolio risk, the correct mix of "eggs in the basket" is required. The reduction in portfolio risk from diversification is called the *diversification effect*. Optimally, the diversification effect reflects the elimination of all but market risk.

Diversification is one of the most important service advantages of mutual funds generally. This service advantage allows investors with normally limited resources to benefit from the diversification effect to a degree not possible by purchasing individual stocks. Mutual funds provide this advantage because each share represents proportionate ownership in the portfolio. For example, investors who desire diversification represented by the S&P 500 Index can do so simply. For example, for $3,000 investors can purchase shares in the Vanguard 500 Index Fund, which mimics the diversification and performance of the S&P 500 Index, less modest expenses. The S&P 500 Index is one of two most widely used *benchmark indices*, and is the one used here. Ownership of one share in the fund provides the diversification effect of holding all stocks comprising the index.

As suggested, diversification and its effect on reducing portfolio risk can be extremely powerful. Application of this concept is similar to how fire insurance companies limit overall risk by selling large numbers of policies with unrelated risks. The wonderful thing about diversification is that, properly done, it can reduce portfolio risk (volatility) without sacrificing return. And it can be done with a reasonable number of properly selected securities. This may be seen in the simple case where randomly selected stocks are used to construct portfolios, which is analogous to selecting stocks by throwing darts at newspaper stock listings.

Domestic diversification

The question of how many mutual funds are needed for diversified portfolios should be a concern to investors. Many investors probably think portfolios with large numbers of securities are well diversified by definition. O'Neal (1997) used simulation to test this assumption. Diversification across funds reduces risk to future terminal wealth over specified time periods. Risk decreases significantly as the number of funds held increases, but at some point the marginal risk reduction from adding one more fund decreases. The reduced risk to terminal wealth for all holding periods applies both to mutual funds focusing on growth and those emphasizing growth and income, but more so for the former. Portfolios of six growth funds reduce variability of returns to just 31–41 percent *of* that expected for single-fund portfolios. And portfolios of six growth and income funds reduce variability to 47–52 percent *of* that expected for single-fund portfolios. Thus more aggressive investors receive more diversification benefits. However, the risk reduction benefits do not differ significantly for the same time intervals across time. This suggests persistence in the benefits of fund diversification for given time intervals.

Sanders (1997b) also examined the number of mutual funds needed for effective diversification. In general, as the number of domestic equity funds held increases, short-term volatility declines and the range of long-term results narrows. On average, short-term volatility declines significantly for the first four funds, declines more with the next four or five funds, and then levels off. The larger the number of funds, the lower the probability of achieving maximum terminal wealth. But holding more funds increases the probability of achieving minimum acceptable terminal wealth. Portfolios of small cap. value funds benefit most from holding more funds because they have a wider range of performance, especially relative to large cap. funds.

Evans and Archer (1968) examined portfolio diversification using a random selection of stocks with equal portfolio proportions. A sample of 470 large stocks generated sixty simulated runs of forty randomly selected portfolios, each containing from one to forty stocks. Portfolio risk declined rapidly as the number of different stocks (not mutual funds) increased. The often cited conclusion is that the economic benefits of diversification are virtually exhausted when portfolios include ten or so stocks.

Statman (1987) tested the Evans and Archer conclusion with different results. Diversification should be increased until its marginal benefits equal its marginal trading costs. Holdings of ten stocks are inadequate to provide well diversified portfolios. A 500-stock portfolio was used as an attainable, fairly diversified portfolio. The findings were that well diversified portfolios of randomly selected stocks must include, at the very least, thirty stocks for borrowing investors and forty stocks for lending (*risk-free rate*) investors. This number of stocks could be out of the reach of many individual investors, which is consistent with observation.

The finding that thirty to forty stocks provide well diversified portfolios appears reasonable, based on Elton and Gruber's (1977) analysis of the relationship between portfolio size and variance of portfolio returns. While the first ten stocks are most important to portfolio risk reduction, the first twenty stocks reduce portfolio risk by 56 percent. Increasing portfolio size to thirty stocks reduces risk by only an additional two percentage points.

But how many securities would be required to eliminate the vast proportion of market risk? Beck et al. (1996) reviewed the findings of nine studies and concluded that well diversified portfolios require from eight to sixty stocks. The wide range of these results is due to the sensitivity of portfolio size to the methodology used. For example, based on 200 replications of sample portfolios, a portfolio of approximately forty-eight stocks is necessary to eliminate 98 percent of market risk.

Global diversification

Global diversification extends the boundaries of domestic diversification. Solnik (1974) found that portfolios of both international and domestic stocks reduce average portfolio risk by some

30 percent more than domestic portfolios alone. Although real world portfolios are not constructed randomly, nonetheless, these results illustrate the power of diversification.

As further discussed in Solnik (2000), domestic portfolios with more than forty to fifty stocks provide little additional risk reduction. Adding international stocks to purely domestic portfolios reduces risk much more rapidly than adding domestic stocks. Portfolios with only forty stocks equally spread among major domestic and international markets reduce the risk of domestic portfolios by more than 50 percent. The same results apply to actual and simulated portfolios over various time periods, including the era of volatile exchange rates. Solnik concluded: "In all cases, international diversification provided a better and quicker reduction in risk, even for a portfolio with a limited number of securities."

However, Paluch's (1995) evidence finds that identifying distinct mutual fund investment objectives is becoming more difficult. These higher return correlations may be due to the growing similarity of domestic and international stock markets and/or by individual fund portfolio holdings becoming more diffused. If so, diversification among investment objectives may not provide expected diversification benefits. This is seen in higher return correlations between bond portfolios of different quality, between domestic growth and Pacific stock funds, between asset allocation and international stock funds, and between specialty precious metals and growth funds. Nonetheless, adding precious metals funds provides the best bet for diversifying portfolio risk. However, Solnik (2000) disagrees. While the correlation of returns varies between these markets over time, there is still ample room for successful risk diversification. European markets are more correlated with domestic markets than Asian markets, and emerging markets are least correlated with the rest of the world.

Solnik et al. (1996) analyzed the correlations of international and domestic stocks and bonds and reported they fluctuate widely over time. Volatility is contagious across global markets in times of crisis, and international correlation of returns increases when volatility is high, which is not good news for global investors. But correlation of returns of individual international stock markets with domestic markets increased only slightly over the last thirty-seven years, and none in the last ten years.

Moreover, the correlation of returns of international *bond* markets has not increased over the last ten years. Moreover, bond and stock markets are not synchronized, which is good news. Overall, the benefits of international risk reduction are still present. A passive global diversification strategy of 80/20 domestic/international stock appears reasonable, especially if large weights to single countries are avoided and emerging markets are included.

PORTFOLIO THEORY AND RISK: A NOTE

Markowitz model

Markowitz (1952, 1961) developed the core model for measuring diversification effects on portfolio risk. The discussion here is limited to providing the rationale underlying the risk reduction benefits of diversification on portfolios of risky assets. Sharpe et al. (1999) provide comprehensive coverage of and references to portfolio theory.

Subsequent to its development, the Markowitz model became the cornerstone of modern portfolio theory. The model was the first to apply the concept of portfolio diversification in a precise, measurable way. The model demonstrates precisely, given expected returns, risks and co-movements of individual risky assets, how diversification reduces portfolio risk. The model applies a statistical risk measure to derive specific risk/return parameters of portfolios with varying asset mixes. Markowitz thus converted traditional subjective notions of diversification ("eggs in the basket") to quantitatively measurable concepts.

The Markowitz model generates, for a given set of risky assets, the mix that produces the least risky portfolio for a given return. This *efficient portfolio* has the least risk of all portfolios with the same expected returns. The set of all efficient portfolios comprises the *efficient frontier*. The frontier enables investors to select portfolios with the highest expected returns that match their risk tolerance. Ideally, all global financial, tangible, and human capital assets should be included in computing the efficient frontier. These assets should be included in their proportions of total global market value. In this context, portfolio risk reduction would be unconstrained by data problems and, therefore, optimal. But, in practice, optimal allocations are not possible.

Risk

Risk is usually associated with the likelihood that an asset's expected rate of return will not be realized. This likelihood reflects the uncertainty of future outcomes. The greater the uncertainty, the greater the expected variability (dispersion) between expected and realized returns. The *standard deviation of mean returns* is the standard risk measure. This absolute measure of expected (actual) mean returns uses the likelihood of each possible outcome to determine variability around expected (actual) returns.

Portfolio risk that can be diversified away is called *unsystematic (diversifiable) risk*. It includes the unique risks of specific firms and industries, such as unexpected strikes, product failures, etc. Optimally, diversification reduces unsystematic risk to zero. In practice, it allows minimization of unsystematic risk for given levels of expected returns. *Systematic (non-diversifiable) risk* is called *market risk* because it cannot be diversified away. Market risk includes unanticipated events and factors that impact securities generally and, therefore, cannot be avoided. Examples are market collapses (October 1987) and political assassinations, as well as monetary and economic factors such as increased interest rates, inflation, slower economic growth, and smaller corporate profits. Purcell (1994b) discussed these risks as they apply to mutual funds.

Several studies have investigated the importance of market risk in explaining stock returns. For example, King's (1966) classic study determined that market factors explain 52 percent of the variability in stock prices, while firm factors explain 38 percent and industry factors only 10 percent. Thus systematic risk is the largest, but not the only, major source of risk. Later studies by Meyers (1973) and Blume (1971) reported systematic risk is less important, but still representing 30–5 percent of total risk. In any case, unsystematic risk is large enough for mutual funds to provide significant portfolio risk reduction through diversification.

The 1940 Act also recognized the importance of diversification in regulatory matters. As noted in the previous chapter, the 1940 Act imposes standards for mutual funds to qualify as diversified investment companies. And, again, subchapter M of the Internal Revenue Code imposes diversification and distribution standards for funds to qualify as regulated investment companies.

CONSTRAINED ATTAINABLE GLOBAL DIVERSIFICATION

The impracticability of identifying and attaining theoretical global diversification led to the applied concept of *attainable global diversification*. This concept refers to the degree of diversification that mutual fund portfolios can attain globally. For example, domestic fund portfolios do not have the attainable degree of global diversification because of limited geographic coverage.

Next, the concept of *constrained attainable diversification* refers to the actual degree by which portfolio attributes preclude attainable global diversification. This finding is made specific here and later by analyzing particular fund attributes to identify those that constrain attainable degrees of global diversification. A fund that focuses on one industry sector provides a good example of constrained diversification. Of course, the constraint can be reduced by combining such funds into diversified portfolios. The broader the fund's diversification the fewer funds that are needed to achieve diversified portfolios.

Moreover, identified constraints also increase or decrease the relative degree of *diversification risk*. This concept is specifically applied later where specific fund attributes and their risk implications are identified. The constraints apply in various attributes of fund portfolio management and can result in either higher or lower diversification risk, depending on the measure (discussed below).

Fund investment objectives are the largest potential constraints on attainable global diversification. Without global objectives, mutual funds obviously cannot achieve attainable global diversification. Diversification constraints by investment objectives also affect fund peer group and benchmark index risk/return profiles.

Fundamental/technical method of security analysis is another important potential constraint on attainable global diversification. Use of either *fundamental analysis* or *technical analysis* constrains attainable diversification by method of security analysis. Use of both provides more methodological diversification than use of either one. These constraints also affect profiles of relevant fund peer groups and benchmark indices. However, this is not to say that use of either method can generate superior returns, but rather both are applied widely in practice and utilize different analytical frameworks.

Most portfolio managers use fundamental analysis to estimate the underlying worth (*intrinsic value*) of securities relative to market prices. A different fundamental analysis is used here. The analysis is applied to particular mutual funds and includes both objective and subjective criteria, such as portfolio manager background, *investment style* and diversification risk, risk, return, risk/return measures and performance attributes.

To see how investment style constrains attainable global diversification, assume a mutual fund with a growth investment objective that uses fundamental analysis to select a large portfolio of small domestic stocks with high growth expectations. This portfolio's diversification is constrained by its singular use of several variables: growth investment objective, fundamental analysis, active portfolio management, growth style, small company style, domestic securities, and common stock, among others. Thus the portfolio's attainable degree of diversification is constrained in all regards except by its large number of securities holdings.

Other analysts use technical analysis to forecast the price behavior of individual securities and/or the overall market. The analysis is typically based on identifying recurring patterns in historical price and volume data of individual securities and/or the overall market. Some portfolio managers use both fundamental analysis and technical analysis, in which cases technical analysis is often used to confirm fundamental analysis findings and to assist in timing implementation of buy/sell decisions.

Both fundamental analysis and technical analysis are used here, but the latter is applied only in the context of likely short-term movements in the overall market and economic outlook. Technical analysis is not applied to individual mutual funds. More precisely, particular market and economic indicators are often used to assess the short-term economic and market outlook for purposes of timing implementation of mutual fund buy/sell decisions.

Active/passive portfolio management provides another important potential constraint on attainable global diversification. Use of either active or passive portfolio management constrains attainable diversification by method of portfolio management. Use of both methods provides more methodological diversification than use of either one. These constraints also affect the profiles of relevant fund peer groups and benchmark indices. However, this is not to say that either method can generate superior returns, but rather both are applied widely in practice and utilize different analytical frameworks.

Actively managed mutual funds normally seek superior performance from stock selection while passively managed portfolios seek to match market returns – that is, passively managed portfolios are designed to benchmark particular indices, such as the S&P 500 Index. Active management normally implies fundamental analysis, but it also may include or refer only to technical analysis applied to particular securities, but as noted above, this is not the version of technical analysis used here.

Investment style is also an important potential constraint on attainable global diversification. The first dimension of this potential constraint is value/growth investment style, which indicates whether funds focus on value, growth, or a blend of both approaches to security selection. Use of the *value style* (or simply, value) seeks to identify and purchase stocks undervalued relative to their intrinsic value. Use of the *growth style* (or simply, growth) seeks to identify and purchase stocks with rapid earnings growth, and use of the *blend style* (or simply, blend) incorporates both value and growth investment styles.

The second dimension of this potential constraint is cap. size investment style, which indicates whether mutual funds focus on stocks with large or small market capitalization. Funds tend to focus on stocks with *large-cap. style* (*large cap.*), *mid-cap. style* (*mid cap.*), or *small-cap. style* (*small cap.*). Cap. size is measured by the *median market capitalization* of stocks in the portfolio.

Table 6 provides a conceptual checklist with examples of potential constraints on attainable global diversification and resulting degrees of diversification. In addition to the five constraints discussed above, the remaining potential constraints include cash asset allocation, geographic concentration, asset allocation, market liquidity, returns distribution, industry sector concentration, security concentration, and quality concentration.

The table 6 diversification constraints are modified later to make them useful in analyzing a particular mutual fund's degree of diversification and risk as measured relative to its peer group and benchmark index. The constraints are therefore not assessed relative to attainable global diversification, but rather to a fund's peer group and benchmark index. The implication is that some global diversification constraints are given rather than analyzed. The question is whether a particular fund's actual overall multidimensional degree of diversification and risk translates to an actual relative advantage in meeting the needs of particular investors in large-cap. value funds. In any case, each constraint's degree of diversification and risk is used to provide a rich comparative analysis of a particular fund, given its peer group and overall benchmark index.

As noted later, the constraints on degree of portfolio diversification also result in either an increased or a decreased degree of diversification risk. Again, the constraints are therefore not assessed relative to attainable global diversification, but rather to a fund's peer group and benchmark index. The implication is that some global diversification constraints are given. A partial analysis of this is seen in a fund that holds only AAA quality bonds. Assume the fund's highest quality portfolio is more constrained than that of either its peer group or its benchmark index. While its portfolio is more constrained, the fund's concentration in high quality bonds provides smaller relative diversification risk. That is, the portfolio's quality is far more constrained, but of higher quality than a more representative AAA quality portfolio. However, other examples may find more diversification risk in portfolios more constrained than its peer group or benchmark index, such as a portfolio of very aggressive growth stocks.

INVESTMENT OBJECTIVES

Mutual funds offer investors a wide range of choices as defined by fund investment objectives. These choices are consistent with meeting the diverse investment needs and risk preferences of investors, but not those seeking tangible assets. Funds are likely to provide particular investment objectives that meet the needs of particular investors. These needs might include single mutual funds or portfolios of funds. For example, funds with aggressive growth objectives might appeal to high-risk investors or to conservative investors as components of well diversified portfolios.

As discussed previously, mutual funds must provide shareholders with a prospectus that includes statements of investment objectives and policies, portfolio restrictions, and investment risks. It also has information concerning shareholder transaction costs, fund operating expenses and fees, and a ten-year summary of financial highlights. Statements of investment objectives and policies should be concise, but precise and clear enough to convey what the fund is trying to accomplish and how the portfolio manager proposes to do it.

For example, the Vanguard US Growth prospectus (1997) stated: "The Portfolio seeks to provide long-term capital growth by investing in equities of high quality, seasoned US corporations with records of exceptional growth. The portfolio contains companies with strong positions in their markets, reasonable financial strength, and low sensitivity to changing economic conditions." This concise and precise statement (printed in bold topic headings) provides the type of information investors need in selecting funds that match their investment objectives. The Vanguard prospectus also includes "plain talk" commentaries briefly discussing shareholder transaction costs, fund expenses, financial highlights, investment style, trading costs, the market capitalization of stocks held, portfolio diversification, portfolio turnover, derivatives, past performance, shareholder distributions, timing purchases for taxes, Vanguard's corporate structure, and portfolio managers. "Warning flags" mark notes about market risk, investment objective risk, and risks of derivative securities.

Categories of investment objectives

Table 7 presents a classification of mutual funds into twenty-one categories based on their basic investment objectives. The Investment Company Institute (ICI) (1997a), developed this scheme to help funds define themselves within a common framework of investment objectives. A fund's stated investment objective should readily correlate with one of the twenty-one categories. For example, "growth funds seek capital growth; dividend income is not a significant factor. They invest in the common stock of well-established companies." The Vanguard US Growth prospectus (1997) directly correlates with the ICI definition – the fund's objective is growth, and not in name only. The categories are further classified as stock funds, bond and income funds, or money market funds. Other classification schemes are also used.

Proper classification of mutual funds may be more complex and less obvious than usually thought because some investment objectives are not narrowly defined and are, therefore, more subject to interpretation by investors, advisory firms, and portfolio managers. The more ambiguous and broad the definitions are, the more flexibility portfolio managers have to deviate from investor expectations based on stated objectives. Investors should determine whether stated fund objectives are the actual ones perceived, but also from fund names and marketing and advertising messages. For example, "growth funds provides a lot of wiggle room for funds to game the objective and rank high for performance."

Rekenthaler (1994a) examined Morningstar's mutual fund objectives to determine which require most attention in selecting funds. As expected, some objectives are much more internally consistent than others. Thus more narrowly defined objectives should be less subject to incorrect classification. Among equity categories, the most internally consistent funds are specialty funds: utilities, precious metals, and health. The least internally consistent are the more broadly defined and aggressive investment objectives: small company, aggressive growth, and growth. Overall, equity fund objectives are more diffuse than fixed-income objectives. This is not surprising, but bond funds have to be assessed for use of derivative securities with less than obvious risks.

Interestingly, there are no major differences in the internal consistency of investment objectives of domestic and international equity funds. In order of their internal consistency, the stock fund investment objectives are: (1) Health, Precious Metals, and Utilities; (2) Growth-Income and Equity-Income Foreign; (3) World and Europe; (4) Aggressive Growth; (5) Growth and Small Company; (6) Pacific; and (7) Specialty Unaligned. The first category is much more internally homogeneous than the seventh objective.

On the fixed-income side of mutual funds, the investment objective with the most internal consistency is clearly municipal bonds. This finding argues, counter to most analysts, that the performance of one state's bonds can be compared with those of other states'. Next, the categories requiring most individual analysis are convertible bonds and international bonds. These investment objectives are quite diffuse. In order of their internal consistency, bond fund investment objectives rank as follows: (1) Municipal – NY and Municipal – CA, (2) Government – General and Municipal – National, (3) High – yield and Government Mortgage, (4) Corporate – General and Corporate – High Quality, (5) Convertible, (6) World Bond and Government – Treasury, and (7) Short-term World Income. Again, the first category is much more internally homogeneous than the seventh category.

As discussed later, Morningstar, the mutual fund research company, developed an alternative to the use of stated investment objectives based on the prospectus. The reason for this, as described by Rekenthaler (1992b), may be summed up as follows: "In some cases, a fund's name will imply one objective, its prospectus another, and its investment practices a third. Finally, that company's marketing department might wish that the fund be treated in a fourth category." So began Morningstar's search for improved fund classification for purposes of fairly and accurately reporting performance and performance attributes. This effort has made an important contribution to proper classification of funds.

Socially responsible funds

Socially responsible mutual funds lie outside the usual and traditional domain of fund investment objectives. These self-designated socially responsible funds do not invest in stocks of companies that fall within their definitions of sin, such as tobacco and alcohol. They believe it is possible to do well as investors while also doing good. Investors should make sure that doing well includes competitive risk/return performance and low expenses. This has not always been the case with these funds.

Interested investors should also make sure the fund definition of doing good matches their own. This sounds easy to do, but the definition of sin can take many forms, including environmental concerns, societal issues, personal preferences, religious preferences, fair labor practices, product safety, defense contractors and human rights issues.

To the extent "socially irresponsible" companies are concentrated in relatively few industries, funds could be excluded from investing in major sectors. For example, many companies in the cyclical industry sector, such as energy-inefficient auto manufacturers, are likely to be excluded from socially responsible portfolios. The problem is that most major corporations are diversified outside traditional core businesses, or at least operate as multinational corporations. As a result, firms that sin in one product line may produce the equivalent of goodness (such as Jell-O) in other lines.

Opponents of socially responsible investing, and the majority view, argue that the proper role of mutual funds is to provide investors with best possible risk/return profiles within their investment objectives, not to define morality for them. There is also the issue of whether socially responsible funds should vote proxies as investors or social activists.

The problem of defining company sin was examined by Damato (2000b). Three socially responsible funds were examined for their consistency in screening six major corporations. In no single case did all three funds agree. Damato concluded: "[T]he variations in stocks passing muster highlight the tricky task of deciding which stocks are indeed socially correct."

Signals of change

There are both obvious and less obvious qualitative signals of *potential* changes in *actual* mutual fund investment objectives, policies, limitations and style of portfolio management, among others. The potential implications of these signals deserve close attention because they are often not in the interests of shareholders. The media usually cover signals involving major funds and fund families, but coverage is less for smaller, less known funds.

The likelihood investment advisors make visible shareholder disclosure depends on fund perceptions of the implications of change for redemption of fund assets. But, in most cases, especially those involving changes in portfolio managers, only minimum required disclosure is made. Before considering signals of change, it should be noted that the implications are not necessarily bad for shareholders, but adequate disclosure is needed in either case.

Changes in portfolio managers may be obvious or less obvious signals of change. Mutual funds with less than stellar performance tend to hype new portfolio managers, but not those losing valued portfolio managers. This is unfortunate because these changes often have different implications for shareholders. To solve the problem of inadequate information, especially involving smaller fund families, Weitz (1999) created Fund Alarm to provide readily available information on portfolio manager turnover.

Gallo and Lockwood (1999) examined sixty-nine mutual funds that changed managers from 1983 to 1991. For poorly performing funds, performance improved with new portfolio managers. This is seen in better risk-adjusted returns and lower total risk. But increased systematic risk suggests changes in investment style that require monitoring. A positive implication of portfolio manager changes or fund liquidation (discussed below) is that investors may take any losses involved as offsets to future realized capital gains.

Cooley (2000) analyzed mutual fund performance following portfolio manager changes. Subsequent performance differs, depending on how well the funds are doing when the changes occur. The general rule is that if portfolio manager changes occur at strongly performing funds, investors should normally continue holding the shares. This is especially so if fund investment advisors have a reputation for well performing funds. However, if changes occur at poorly performing funds, this performance is likely to continue, especially if funds have been consistently poor performers.

Portfolio manager retirements with planned succession are least likely to have implications for subsequent mutual fund investment style and performance. Planned succession (discussed above) includes installation of trained protégés, installation of former portfolio manager team members, and family members with successful portfolio manager experience and the desire to succeed. Of course, no planning is foolproof.

When portfolio managers are terminated, the implications are very uncertain until new managers have proven themselves. Experienced replacements with good performance records reduce uncertainty. Abrupt resignations have the most uncertain implications for actual changes in investment objectives, investment style, and performance. Do resignations reflect problems within investment management companies? Probably not, if former portfolio managers go on to improved opportunities. And will new portfolio managers prove effective and apply the same investment styles? Changes in portfolio managers always cause at least subtle changes, even if not desired, because no two persons can manage in exactly the same way.

Changes in mutual fund stated investment objectives are obvious signals of change. They are normally made because of poor performance and the desire to more closely match fund objectives to in-house or subadvisor investment expertise. Changes in stated objectives could be made to reflect accurately what actual investment objectives are, rather than actual changes in objectives. Changes in fund names are other obvious signals. They may be changed to be more consistent with actual or changed investment objectives, or to free investment advisors from names known for poor performance.

Mutual fund names indicating particular investment objectives are only required to invest 65 percent of assets accordingly. This provides leeway for bond funds to hold 65 percent in US Treasury bonds, but also the remainder in risky securities in efforts to enhance returns. This broad limitation provides more than ample opportunity to mislead investors about fund risk/ return profiles. The limitation should be raised significantly, because funds, perhaps more so bond funds, have held securities not anticipated by shareholders, such as illiquid, risky derivatives.

Sales of fund assets to other investment management companies and mergers (rollovers) of assets into other family funds are obvious signals of change. Sales and mergers of mutual fund assets cause inevitable change even if assets are rolled over into funds with the same investment objectives. No two investment advisors share the same culture, and no two portfolio managers work exactly the same.

Mergers are the usual, preferred route because they keep assets under management. Mergers occur when fund marketing and/or fund performance has not attracted or maintained critical asset sizes needed for profitable management. Mergers also have no potential capital gains tax implications for shareholders.

Zweig (1998a) reported 257 mergers in the first seven months of 1998, up from 131 in the same period the prior year. Mergers are generally motivated to benefit fund managers more than shareholders. Goetzman and Peles (1997) determined that fund mergers are driven more by poor fund performance than net redemptions. Fund shareholders do not automatically punish poor fund performance with large redemptions. This may be partly due to investor hope or lethargy, but perhaps also to fund advertising reassuring shareholders. And, most important, mergers normally bury poor performance histories when assets are merged into better performing or new funds.

The SEC has facilitated the large number of mutual fund mergers by lack of strict guidelines. Funds are supposed to compare the attributes of surviving or new funds to determine which predecessor funds, if any, the surviving or new funds most resemble and use those performance histories. But, as noted by Dziubinski (1998), these guidelines leave plenty of wiggle room for funds to pick fund histories that look to perform the best.

However, on occasion the SEC objects to blatant examples of burying bad performance histories. Dziubinski (1999b) reported a case where a fund manager wanted to "bury" the history of a poor-performing fund in a new post-merger fund. The new fund, of course, had no performance history. In this case, the SEC ruled the old (bad) fund's history had to be attached to the new fund. The merger was cancelled. Investors can normally avoid such issues by investing only with fund families known for successful funds.

Fund liquidations and distribution of assets to shareholders are obvious end of game signals. Dziubinski (1997) observed over 400 liquidated or merged funds since 1996, and estimated about 5 percent of funds are closed each year. Liquidations occur when fund marketing and/or fund performance has not attracted or maintained critical asset sizes needed for profitable management. Liquidations, rather than mergers, can reflect concern for shareholders in cases where fund families do not have other funds with the same investment objectives. The down side for shareholders in liquidations is potential capital gains taxes.

Shareholders are advised to sell or exchange mutual fund shares as soon as liquidations are announced. There is no reason to share in the potential costs. As noted, investment managers usually prefer rollovers to liquidations to keep assets under management, with no refunds to shareholders, and new leases on life for funds.

Changes in the fine print of mutual fund stated investment objectives, policies, strategies, and limitations are less obvious signals. These changes reflect actions by investment advisors designed to free up portfolio managers to improve fund performance or efforts to rein them in to improve risk profiles. Shareholders should investigate reasons for the changes, but good past performance will not be one. In either case, changes will have risk/return implications for shareholders.

Finally, mergers or acquisitions of investment advisory firms themselves are obvious signals of change to come. These events are usually soft-pedaled to avoid shareholder redemptions. In any case, they cause at least subtle changes in actual investment objectives, investment style, and performance, even if not intended, because they involve changes in general management and organizational culture. And they may cause unintended changes in portfolio managers who prefer to leave rather than accept new management. Shareholders should investigate the implications of changes for their investment needs. This is not always easy because shareholders may not be aware until they receive proxy statements.

There are some potential good implications for mutual fund shareholders from sales of investment advisory firms. For example, they may include: (1) broader range of fund investment objectives, (2) more skilled portfolio managers, perhaps including access to star institutional portfolio managers, (3) wider range of investment expertise, such as international portfolio managers, and (4) reduced expense ratios due to larger fund asset sizes.

Barbee (1997a) noted that mergers/acquisitions of investment advisory firms are rapidly reducing the number of independent money managers. This reduction is seen in the number of acquisitions by insurance companies and banks. Mergers and acquisitions primarily serve the interests of fund advisory firms, not shareholders. Mergers and acquisitions occur for three major reasons, each with potential to negatively impact fund shareholders. The first reason is to offer wider choices to institutional and individual investors preferring one-stop shopping. They also improve chances shareholder asset withdrawals will be exchanged into funds in the same family. Similarly, shareholders can exchange assets into funds in the same family without paying sales charges. Thus mergers/acquisitions provide investment with improved opportunities to maintain and increase assets. But the potential in these actions for undesirable management changes and culture clashes may lead to loss of portfolio managers and shareholder assets.

The second major reason for mergers/acquisitions of investment advisory firms is that insurance companies and banks want to broaden services and share in the generous cash flows and profits investment advisors generate. Banks remember only so well how customers cashed in CDs and bought mutual funds in the late 1980s, and they want those dollars back. The major reason investment advisory cash flows are so large is that mutual fund management fees and expenses bear little resemblance to actual costs, especially considering fund economies of scale. Nonetheless, fund performance and services can suffer if new owners take cash flows out without making investments in technology and support for portfolio managers and analysts. This, of course, harms the new owners, but also the investment advisors and fund shareholders.

The third reason for mutual fund mergers/acquisitions is marriages of convenience by so-called *boutique funds*, which are specialized small niche funds. These actions are motivated to consolidate management and reduce expenses through greater scale economies, but not at the expense of maintaining and promoting each fund's unique identity. It should not be assumed shareholders will benefit from these savings: increased advertising expenses are more likely. These arrangements provide opportunity for sharing expertise, but also for significant clashes of culture and undesirable administrative changes. These umbrella organizations increase investor choices and increase the likelihood any shareholder redemptions will be exchanged into other family funds.

Purcell (1994c) noted several other motivations and implications behind investment advisor mergers/acquisitions. Motivations include the desire to bring together fund families with different strengths and weaknesses. For example, one family has good funds but poor distribution, and vice versa for the other fund. Other mergers might be motivated to increase the number of investment objectives offered. For example, one family has excellent domestic funds and the other has excellent international funds. Some acquisitions are motivated by desire to broaden product lines for additional profits. For example, a fund family wants entry into the huge market provided by company pension plans. Additional caveats for fund shareholders in mergers/acquisitions include sales loads, increased fund expenses, poor shareholder services, and loss of portfolio managers with particular investment style strengths.

Fund risk and stated investment objectives

Most *actual* mutual fund risks have been found consistent with those *implied* by their stated investment objectives. McDonald (1974) classified 123 funds by stated investment objectives and analyzed total risk over ten years. Actual total risk is generally consistent with that implied by investment objectives. Funds with higher risk investment objectives also evidence higher total risk. However, range of risk within investment objectives overlaps somewhat, which indicates risk boundaries are not discrete. Some funds with lower implied risk investment objectives have more actual risk than others with higher implied risk investment objectives, and vice versa. Thus investment objectives provide only a general measure of actual relative risks. Investors should not rely solely on fund stated investment objectives to judge actual relative risks.

Paluch (1997) extended the issue of performance consistency to fund families. Statistical analysis identified the most predictable fund families–those most adhering to strict investment style parameters. These families (and their grades) are (1) Putnam (A+), (2) Vanguard (A), (3) Van Kampen American Capital (A), (4) American Funds (A–), and (5) IDS (A–). The least consistent families are (1) Merrill Lynch (D–), (2) Franklin Templeton (D), (3) Dreyfus (D), (4) Janus (D+), and (5) Fidelity (D+). The price of performance consistency is less portfolio manager flexibility (and returns).

As discussed in DiTeresa (1999b), top-rated (A+) Putnam funds are well known for consistency of above-average performance. Team management and style-specific investing are applied to fund offerings along the risk/return spectrum. Clear guidelines concerning company size, price, and growth attributes maintain style purity. As discussed in DiTeresa and Granzin (1999), low-rated (D+) Janus focuses on companies with rapid, but sustainable, growth along the growth style spectrum. This leads to overweighting sectors with high growth and risk, such as technology. These brief descriptions make it easy to understand why the performance consistency of Putnam and Janus differs.

A related issue is whether mutual funds maintain actual relative risk over time, especially as market conditions change. Legally, funds are required to follow stated investment objectives until changes are approved and disclosed. Research has quite consistently shown that funds tend to maintain the risks of their *actual* investment objectives over time. That is, the best indicator of future fund relative risk is current risk. This is a valuable finding for investors.

Sharpe (1966) analyzed thirty-four mutual funds for the period 1954–63 and found that fund managers generally keep portfolio risk within the limits provided by their investment objectives. Risk was also reasonably consistent between each half of the study period. Next, Jensen (1968) analyzed 115 funds for the years 1945–64. Fund systematic risk appears to be independent of investor investment horizons. That is, systematic risk is approximately stationary over all investment horizons. This is also an important finding.

Further, Mains (1977) analyzed seventy mutual funds for the years 1955–64 and found a clear relationship between previous and current fund systematic risk, which reflects reasonable consistency over time. And, finally, Shawky (1982) analyzed the monthly performance of 255 funds for the period 1973–7. Again, fund systematic risk appears stationary over time. Good news!

MUTUAL FUND SHAREHOLDER LIQUIDITY

Mutual fund *shareholder liquidity* refers to the length of time it takes for shareholders to access fund shares as spendable bank account balances. This process is generally free to particular shareholders unless they require other than routine methods of payment, such as wire redemptions. The issue is not whether mutual funds generally offer effective shareholder liquidity services, they do, but whether particular funds offer these services as advantages in meeting the needs of particular investors. That is, do actual shareholder liquidity services of particular funds translate to actual service advantages for particular investors? The more quickly shareholders can access fund account balances, the more liquidity shareholders have.

It is probably safe to assume investors prefer less time (high liquidity) to more time (low liquidity) to get access to mutual fund balances. This preference could reflect shareholder precaution rather than actual current needs. It is generally true that actual shareholder liquidity services of particular funds translate to actual service advantages for particular investors.

Methods of obtaining liquidity

How long does it take for mutual funds to receive and process shareholder redemption requests, and how long does it take for redemptions to reach investors? The answers depend on the methods used to request redemptions, the time taken to process requests, and the methods selected to receive redemption payments.

For the purposes of this discussion, direct market rather than indirect market funds are assumed. Direct market funds transact directly with investors. In the case of indirect market funds, the brokers, discount brokers, insurance agents, banks, or financial planners who service investors normally transmit redemption requests. This may reduce the time for funds to receive requests, but the best method (discussed below) for obtaining liquidity remains unchanged in either case.

Mutual funds generally mail share redemption checks within two business days of receiving requests. The 1940 Act requires funds to honor redemptions on the trading day received, which determines the net asset value used to value shares for redemption. Requests received after market close are valued at the end of the next business day.

The shortest time for mutual fund shareholders to be able to access fund account balances is basically zero. This involves check redemptions, whereby shareholders make payments using pre-authorized fund checks drawn on their fund accounts and cleared through fund banks that honor the checks and are reimbursed by redemptions from shareholder fund accounts. But this assumes check payment options were established and checkbooks received prior to time of need, such as when fund account applications are completed. Not all funds offer the service.

Money market mutual funds generally offer check redemption services, but fund checks (drafts) usually require payments of $500 or more. In all other ways, these fund checks are used just like bank checks. The checks clear through fund banks that honor the checks and are reimbursed by redemptions from shareholder fund accounts. If investors deposit fund checks into checking accounts and write bank checks, the payment process is delayed. Fund checks must first clear for bank payment before they can be charged against shareholder bank accounts. This could take five business days. Use of fund account checks thus provides shareholders with the highest degree of liquidity.

Many investors write fund checks on taxable money market fund accounts to avoid taxable events on redemptions. Money market holdings have short maturities and small sensitivity to interest rate changes. Money market funds manage their portfolios so as to not "break the buck" ($1 net asset value), which effectively eliminates taxable gains or losses on share redemptions. Use of money market fund checks to make direct payments provides instant liquidity and no taxable events.

The longest time to access shareholder mutual fund accounts could be fifteen or more business days. This time period assumes: (1) shareholders prepare and mail written redemption requests to funds; (2) funds receive and process redemption requests; (3) funds mail redemption checks to shareholders; (4) shareholders deposit redemption checks and banks clear them to generate good funds in shareholder bank accounts; and (5) shareholders make payments from bank checking accounts. The time needed for steps 1 and 3 depends largely on the US Postal Service or express mail carriers, but also on fund processing time in step 2. Funds do not routinely send redemptions by express mail, but arrangements may usually be made in emergency situations. The clearing process for good funds in step 4 can take five business days.

Moreover, redemption requests of particular types of fund accounts, especially IRA and other custodial-type accounts, require written notification, which normally involve steps 1–5 above. No telephone redemptions or check redemptions are permitted. Funds that seek long-term shareholders often discourage redemptions by requiring written requests. For example, Vanguard requires written redemption requests for its index funds.

The time it takes for the shareholder written redemption process can be significantly reduced or practically eliminated if investors pre-select other redemption options normally available. These options, like check redemptions, are most efficiently selected when originally completing account applications. The *telephone redemption* option eliminates step 1 in the written redemption process. But steps 2–5 remain the same. The *online redemption option* using fund Web sites eliminates step 1 in the mail redemption process and may reduce fund processing time in step 2. But steps 3–5 in processing written redemption requests remain the same.

Better yet are telephone redemption requests coupled with previously pre-authorized options for *electronic redemptions*. Occasional electronic redemptions may be entered by telephone. These redemptions eliminate steps 1, 3, and 4, and reduce step 2, in written redemption requests. They are replaced with the time it takes for electronic redemptions to be good funds in investor bank accounts. And, even better yet, are previously pre-authorized options for electronic redemptions on fixed dates, such as the first of the month. These redemptions eliminate telephone calls plus steps 1, 3 and 4, and reduce step 2, in written redemption requests. These steps are replaced with the time required for bank accounts to receive electronic redemptions. Federal Reserve wire transfers normally deposit good funds in investor bank accounts the next business day. Automated bank clearinghouse electronic transfers normally deposit good funds in two business days.

Liquidity constraints

The SEC has authority to suspend mutual fund redemptions during market crises, but any such suspensions are expected to be short-term. Funds may also delay paying large redemptions for up to seven business days, if paying will disrupt fund operations or portfolio performance. Funds also reserve the right to delay or terminate redemption privileges at any time, including if the New York Stock Exchange closes or the SEC has determined emergency conditions exist. Funds may also make redemptions in kind, rather than cash, under specified conditions. But, more likely, funds will draw upon their established bank lines of credit. However, in the event of financial crisis, these lines may not be available without Federal Reserve guarantee of bank liquidity.

Cullen (1998a) reported that the mutual fund industry's vaunted easy access to investor accounts may not hold in times of turbulent markets. Funds may take a number of measures to minimize the impact on portfolio management and returns, which actually work to the benefit of long-term investors. These steps include (1) *fair-value pricing* (discussed later), rather than market prices by funds investing internationally, (2) increasing length of time to process redemptions and exchanges, (3) not allowing same-day changes in buy/sell orders, (4) requiring signature verification on large redemptions, and (5) paying redemptions in securities rather than cash. The latter has never been implemented, but is permitted by the 1940 Act in event of market panics.

Mutual funds may normally also reserve the right to limit the number of shareholder redemptions over time, such as four redemptions a year. This is done to discourage investors who use market timing strategies and others with short investment horizons. These transactions normally have fees (discussed below) to discourage frequent, costly, and disruptive redemptions.

Shareholder redemptions access mutual fund liquidity without the trading costs associated with sale of stocks to raise needed cash. These costs are borne by the remaining shareholders unless funds charge redemption fees adequate to compensate for such costs. These issues are discussed below and later.

SHAREHOLDER TRANSACTION COSTS

Shareholder transaction costs are imposed by most, but not all, mutual funds. It is very important to note that these are *not* expenses paid by shareholders for fund administration and portfolio management, nor are they the costs of trading fund portfolios. These costs are what the term suggests – shareholder costs that relate to their fund transactions. Transaction costs may apply at the time of purchase, the time of redemption, while shares are held, and combinations of the above. Or no transaction costs may be imposed.

The issue is not whether mutual funds generally impose shareholder transaction costs, many do, but whether particular funds do not employ them in meeting needs of particular shareholders. That is, do the actual transaction costs, if any, of particular funds translate to actual service advantages for particular investors? A majority of funds impose transaction costs, but there are still enough that do not for shareholder transactions costs to remain as general service advantages. However, if trends continue, it will be necessary to categorize transaction costs as a general service disadvantage, not an advantage.

Shareholder transaction costs include any charges imposed by mutual funds for distributing, advertising, and marketing shares. The particular types of costs vary by fund share distribution channels. As noted previously, predominantly direct market funds normally distribute shares directly to investors with no middlemen. Sales force funds (indirect market funds) distribute fund shares through middlemen, such as brokers, financial planners and banks. Increasingly, funds are using both types of distribution. Most direct market funds impose shareholder transaction charges and all sales force funds do to compensate sales agents.

Sales force fund sales agents are paid commission at the time of sale (up front), over time, and perhaps for "continuing client servicing." Sales agents include full-service brokers, discount brokers, insurance agents, banks, and financial planners. However, not all financial planners are paid commission. Other planners receive asset-based fees, say, 1 percent, while others charge hourly fees.

It is probably safe to assume, all else being equal, that mutual fund investors prefer zero transaction costs. However, the fact that many funds are able to impose these costs suggests most investors weigh other factors more heavily in fund selection. Nonetheless, a particular fund's actual zero or minimal shareholder transaction costs would normally translate, on its own merits, to an actual advantage in meeting investor needs and preferences.

Types of transaction costs

There are several types of mutual fund shareholder transaction costs that may be imposed: (1) *front-end loads* (sales loads or, simply, loads) paid at purchase, perhaps on reinvested dividends (loads on reinvested dividends), and purchase transaction fees paid into portfolios; (2) *back-end loads* (deferred loads) paid at redemption (sale) that include redemption fees, *contingent-deferred sales charges*, sales (redemption) transaction fees paid into portfolios, and exchange fees; (3) *annual fees/expenses* that include *rule 12b-1 fees* (annual distribution expenses) and account maintenance fees; and (4) *miscellaneous fees*.

Pure no-load funds literally have *no* shareholder transaction costs. This is an important distinction because the SEC allows funds with 12b-1 fees (discussed below) not exceeding 0.25 percent to advertise as no-load funds (really!). The rationalization for this may be that 12b-1 fees are technically expenses, not loads. In any case, this is misleading shareholder communication and should be prohibited.

Front-end loads were traditionally imposed on all mutual fund share purchases. The legal maximum is now 8.5 percent, but actual loads are now usually less, but still too high. For example, Livingston and O'Neal (1998) reported that 12 percent of equity fund front-end loads are 3.95 percent or less, 47 percent are between 4.0 percent and 4.95 percent, 38 percent are between 5.0 percent and 5.95 percent, and 3.0 percent are over 5.95 percent. Thus 88 percent of front-end loads are at least 4.0 percent. These smaller loads reflect increased competition, but, more important, front-end loads have increasingly been partly or completely replaced by annual 12b-1 fees. For example, the Westwood Equity Service fund has a 4 percent front-end load plus a 0.50 percent annual 12b-1 fee.

Sales force funds use sales loads and 12b-1 fees to pay sales commission and other distribution expenses, respectively. When used by direct-market funds, they may reflect investor demand and willingness to pay premiums for particular funds or to discourage short-term investors and market timers. For example, Fidelity Investments imposes low loads of 3 percent on sector funds and some general equity funds.

Most mutual funds that employ front-end loads offer reductions and perhaps temporary or ongoing fee waivers under specified conditions. The reductions apply to specified minimum purchase amounts (*breakpoint discounts* or *break points*) required for increasingly large discounts. That is, front-end loads are further reduced at increasingly higher thresholds of minimum required purchases. For example, Fidelity Low-priced Stock Fund's load is reduced from 3 percent to 2 percent for minimum purchases of $250,000, and to 0 percent for minimum purchases of $1 million. Funds normally also offer other options for investors to qualify for threshold purchases (discussed below). Load waivers are usually also granted for specific types of large accounts, such as employee accounts under company benefit or pension plans.

Loads on reinvested dividends are technically "dividend reinvestments at offering prices." This grand phrase means dividend reinvestment prices include sales charges, which are generally the same as on initial share purchases. Fortunately, these loads are infrequently used today. After all, no additional sales effort is required, just minor processing. Some investors may not be aware of them, even when they receive transaction confirmations. Use of this load probably lacks economic justification and shareholder awareness, even with limited boilerplate disclosure.

More recently, some mutual funds impose *purchase transaction fees*. These are supposed to be good fees, if there are such things. These loads are normally smaller than traditional front-end loads, ranging from 0.5 percent to 2 percent. But there is an important difference in these purchase side fees. They are not paid to fund managers for distribution of fund shares, but rather added to portfolio assets. Their purpose is to offset trading costs new investors have traditionally imposed on current fund shareholders. These fees are most often applied to fund portfolios containing less liquid small company and international stocks, which often have large trading costs. Moreover, as noted, the fees protect long-term shareholders from the additional trading costs imposed by the actions of short-term investors. For example, Vanguard's five small capitalization stock index funds impose purchase transaction fees ranging from 0.25 percent to 1 percent.

Back-end loads on share redemptions include any redemption fees and contingent-deferred sales charges, plus any modest exchange fees for wiring redemption proceeds. They are designed to discourage short-term redemptions, especially before continuing service commission has been fully paid or up-front loads have been recouped. *Redemption fees* have normally been 1 percent of assets redeemed. More recently they have been reduced and imposed for short periods of time, say, three to six months, to discourage short-term traders. For example, Fidelity sector funds impose $7.50 maximum fees on shares held less than thirty days, and its Low-priced Stock Fund has a 1.5 percent fee on shares held less than ninety days.

Rocco (1998a, b) examined specialty funds to determine the effectiveness of redemption fees. The fees are ineffective in limiting redemptions during market downturns because they are too small and apply only to limited periods of time. They thus offer little protection for long-term investors seeking funds with minimum trading costs and capital gains distributions due to shareholder redemptions. The fees normally ranged from 0.5 percent to 1 percent and applied for three to six months. DeBlasi (1999) reported that 311 funds now use redemption fees, up 50 percent since 1997, and one-third of the fees apply for one year or more. A few funds now charge 2–3 percent redemption fees on shares sold within less than three years. These larger fees should be more effective in discouraging investors that chase hot performance or time the market.

Fortunately, there are precautions for investors to take in avoiding mutual funds subject to large redemptions in market downturns. Investors should focus on funds that: (1) invest in liquid markets, to minimize transaction costs; (2) have small portfolio turnover and capital gains distributions, resulting from small redemptions in previous downturns; (3) fully outline their portfolio risks and pursue strategies that attract long-term investors; and (4) identify short-term investors and refuse to accept their purchases.

Sales (*redemption*) *transaction fees are* alternatives to redemption fees, but with a major difference. As is the case of purchase transaction fees, sales transaction fees benefit fund portfolios, not fund investment advisors. They are not paid to fund managers for distribution of fund shares, but rather added to portfolio assets. As noted by Zweig (1996a), long-term investors should like these fees. Their purpose is to offset the trading costs investor redemptions have traditionally imposed on current shareholders. These fees are most often applied to fund portfolios containing less liquid small company and international stocks, which often have large trading costs. Moreover, as noted, the fees protect long-term shareholders from the additional trading costs imposed by actions of short-term investors.

Sales transaction fees are paid into fund portfolios to offset the higher trading costs of less liquid small company and international stocks, and help reduce capital gains distributions to current shareholders imposed by the actions of short-term investors. For example, Vanguard's Emerging Markets index fund has a 2 percent purchase transaction fee, a 1 percent redemption transaction fee, and a $10 account maintenance fee (discussed below). Both sales and purchase transaction fees work to the advantage of long-term shareholders by reducing costs imposed by actions of short-term market timers. But sales transaction fees are not as commonly used as purchase transaction fees.

Boitano (1999) later reported even tougher action by Vanguard in its fight against "hot money" chasing fund performance. Vanguard Health Care Fund was closed to new investors when evidence of hot money underlay large net cash inflows. Moreover, imposition of the fund's redemption fee was extended from one to five years. The former move is really what best serves long-term investors and the funds that invest long-term. But most funds are never closed.

Contingent-deferred sales charges are redemption fees designed to discourage shareholder redemptions before up-front sales loads have been recouped or continuing service commission fully paid. They are typically 5–6 percent and decline by one percentage point per year down to zero. They normally apply to initial purchases, but some are applied to the smaller of purchases or sales. In particular, these sales charges ensure that sales and any continuing service commission will be paid if shareholder redemptions occur before they are paid from smaller annual 12b-1 fees (discussed below). They are also designed to discourage short-term investors, which is particularly sensible for funds employing long-term strategies with low trading activity.

Exchange fees are charges for exchanging shares in one family mutual fund to another. These fees may also serve to discourage short-term traders, but the fact they tend to be modest dollar amounts makes this doubtful. To some, they appear nitpicking efforts to charge yet another fee. For example, Fidelity charges $7.50 exchange fees on stock index and sector funds. Exchange fees are imposed less widely today, especially compared with other loads and fees, which may or may not be good tradeoffs for investors in given situations. *Wire-redemption fees* are charges for wiring funds to investor bank accounts.

Annual shareholder fees include *12b-1 fees* and account maintenance fees. Since 1980, SEC rule 12b-1 allows mutual funds, as specified, to pay distribution expenses from fund assets. Rule 12b-1 fees are technically expenses paid for compensation of broker-dealers and related expenses, administrative services, and advertising and sales promotion. However, from the shareholder perspective, 12b-1 fees are continuing annual loads. The fees are often used in conjunction with contingent-deferred sales charges to fully or partly reduce front-end loads. Annual 12b-1 fees are especially disadvantageous to long-term investors, who would be better served by front-end loads. Further, long-term investors may previously have also paid front-end loads prior to fund adoption of annual 12b-1 fees.

Livingston and O'Neal (1998) computed that 37 percent of 12b-1 fees are 0.25 percent or less, 17 percent are 0.26–0.50 percent, 9 percent are 0.51–0.75 percent, and 37 percent are 0.76–1.0 percent. Asset-based 12b-1 fees may not exceed 0.75 percent annually, but "service fees" of no more than 0.25 percent may be added to pay for continuing shareholder service. Thus actual maximum 12b-1 fees are 1 percent per year. Rekenthaler (1992a) stated use of fund assets for 12b-1 fees jeopardizes the industry's fiduciary integrity. Instead of offering investors another choice of fee structures, what 12b-1 fees do is bring "marketing considerations into the realm of actual fund management."

SEC approval of 12b-1 fees was based on the industry fairy tale that the fees would enable no-load mutual funds to advertise and therefore compete more effectively with sales force load funds. The resulting increased sales were supposed to increase assets under management, thereby providing *economies of scale* and lower per share expenses for shareholders.

Load mutual funds then joined in the hunt for larger revenue with the argument that 12b-1 fees would allow them to compete more effectively with no-load funds by generating larger funds with economies of scale and reduced expenses for shareholders. This growth would come from replacing or reducing front-end loads and making load funds look more like no-load funds. This issue is discussed further later.

Lucas (1992a) and Phillips (1993a) concluded that load mutual funds make the wrong argument in competing with no-load funds. Rather than argue for 12b-1 fees, they should have made the case with investors that load funds are properly for those who need financial advice. However, Rekenthaler (1993b) disagreed, saying that paying sales loads does not guarantee good advice or provide buffers to impetuous investor trading. As it is, financial advisors are left to explain to clients the differences between various load/12b-1 fee packages (see "Multiple share classes" below). Moreover, the ethics of the recommendation is made more difficult because the fee structure that is best for sales agents is worst for shareholders.

Kelley (1995) also made an interesting point about level annual 12b-1 fees. For load funds, the former large front-end loads sent shareholders this message: Pay up front once, stay invested, and don't pay another load. Funds with level annual 12b-1 fees now send shareholders quite a different message: Pay fees every year, make sure this is the right fund, and do so before the next annual payment. Now, which message is most likely to favor long-term shareholders?

The NASD allows mutual funds to make one of the most misleading uses of 12b-1 fees. As noted above, mutual funds with 12b-1 fees not exceeding 0.25 percent per year are permitted to advertise as no-load funds. As reviewed in Charlson (1993), NASD's sales load limits are based on whether funds impose asset based 12b-1 fees and servicing fees. If they do, combined 12b-1 fees, servicing fees, front-end loads, and back-end loads may not exceed 6.25 percent. If funds impose 12b-1 fees but not servicing fees, total fees/loads may not exceed 7.25 percent.

Account maintenance fees, if any, represent periodic fees imposed on mutual fund account balances under specified amounts. The rationale is that small accounts cost proportionately more to manage than large accounts. The fees are normally modest dollar amounts charged annually or quarterly. For example, Vanguard charges $2.50 quarterly on index funds and up to $10.00 per year for account balances less than $10,000. But, these fees appear a bit much in the scheme of management company profits. Funds could automatically redeem accounts below minimum amounts, if this is a serious problem.

Miscellaneous fees, if any, include several types of annoying little fees that add up big for fund managers. These less-than-routine fees apply to particular types of shareholder transactions or investment plans, such as account closeout fees, systematic withdrawal plan fees, automatic investment plan fees, and retirement account fees.

As noted by Sinha (1993), the only real rationale for miscellaneous fees, but also for exchange fees and account maintenance fees, is if they pay fund expenses not related to activities of other shareholders. This justification is valid only when the fees remain in fund portfolios and not paid to fund advisors. Investors should give careful attention to discovering which party benefits, fund advisors or current shareholders. The findings of this inquiry say something about fund advisors that is more than the sum of these small fees – are investors considered shareholders or customers?

Common loads and fees

Livingston and O'Neal (1998) identified the most common types of loads and fees and quanti-fied their relative costs for various holding periods. Approximately two-thirds (and growing) of domestic equity funds impose loads/fees, but happily one-third do not. Of funds that impose loads/fees, some 23 percent use front-end and annual loads, 22 percent use back-end loads and annual fees, 11 percent use only annual fees, and 7 percent use only front-end loads. The trend is definitely away from front-end loads. As reported by Dziubinski (2000), load funds held 67 percent of fund assets in 1989, but only 50 percent by 1999.

Livingston and O'Neal (1998) characterized typical mutual fund distribution arrangements. First, most mutual funds that charge front-end loads also impose annual 12b-1 fees. Maximum front-end loads vary from 1.0 percent to 8.50 percent. As noted, loads may be waived or reduced for very large purchases. Most front-end loads range from 4.0 percent to 6.0 percent. Second, back-end loads are usually combined with annual 12b-1 fees. Typically, back-end loads decrease as holding periods increase. Loads that decline to zero beyond specified holding periods are called contingent-deferred sales charges. Third, some funds charge only annual 12b-1 fees, but typically they are combined with front-end load or back-end loads. As noted above, maximum 12b-1 fees of 1.0 percent may be charged against fund assets.

The most common types of transaction costs are (1) front-end loads and annual fees, (2) back-end loads (that decline by 1 percent per year), and annual fees with conversion (from 1 percent to 0.25 percent after eight years), (3) front-end loads only, and (4) annual fees only (usually 0.25 percent). Except for type 3 loads, the present value cost of each increases as a percentage of initial investment as the holding period increases. The cost dispersion of types 1 and 4 costs across funds is high and increases with the length of the holding period.

Choice of load/fee structure is especially important for long-term investors. Annual fees only have the lowest present value cost at the fiftieth percentile for all holding periods through nineteen years. Front-end loads have the lowest cost for just the single twenty-year holding period. However, these load/fee cost rankings change at the tenth and nineteenth cost percentiles.

Table 8 provides examples of mutual fund loads and fees. The tables provide comparisons of loads/fees both within and among selected fund families. In particular, note that Vanguard Windsor II has no loads/fees (table 8a). Vanguard Windsor II serves as the text mutual fund sample for assessing whether a particular fund should be purchased or sold, relative to its peer group and benchmark index. Windsor II's lack of loads/fees (also table 40a) is excellent compared with its peer group's average front-end load of 1.30 percent and deferred load of 0.96 percent (table 42a). Comparison with the benchmark index is not valid because the S&P 500 Index is not an actual fund. The Vanguard 500 Index Fund is often used as a surrogate for the benchmark index in other uses, owing to its readily available data. Windsor II's excellent performance is summarized in table 27.

Wrap fees are not mutual fund fees, but brokerage-firm fees charged fund investors for private money managers. The arrangement folds investor fund holdings into one *wrap account* for management. These fees add 2 percent or more to the already imposed fees and expenses of each fund, and certainly guarantee the portfolios will underperform index benchmarks.

Wrap accounts are inconsistent with the basic advantages of mutual fund investing, which include professional management and public disclosure of returns. Wrap accounts may or may not provide improved portfolio performance, but the point is, why should investors pay twice for it? And, where is the disclosure of performance data that allows investors to compare performance with other wrap account managers?

Multiple share classes: costs

In 1995, the SEC adopted rule 18f-3 that allows mutual funds to offer mutual funds with the same underlying assets, but with multiple share classes. Previously, many funds received permission to do this under SEC exemptive orders. These share class arrangements are very similar across funds, but the acronyms vary. Multiple share class funds provide distributors with load/fee options designed to attract both short-term and long-term investors, while at the same time providing different schemes to compensate brokers.

O'Neal (1999) observed that 82 percent of retail growth funds are part of multiple share class arrangements. These shares are generally designated as Classes A, B, and C. Class A shares typically have 5.75 percent front-end loads plus 0.25 annual 12b-1 fees. Distributors pay brokers 5 percent initial sales commission plus annual 0.25 percent 12b-1 fees (trailing) as long as investors hold the shares.

Class B shares typically have 5 percent contingent-deferred sales charges that decline by one percentage point a year to zero over six years, plus 1 percent annual 12b-1 fees. Class B shares usually convert to Class A shares after some seven or eight years. At redemption, deferred sales charges are usually applied to the lesser of investor current or original investments. Distributors pay brokers 4 percent initial sales commission in the absence of front-end loads, plus 0.25 percent trailing 12b-1 fees. Fund distributors are repaid from annual 12b-1 fees of 1 percent, but the broker receives only 0.25 percent of this amount.

Level-load funds are the newest type of share class. These Class C shares normally do not impose front-end loads, but usually impose a 1 percent redemption fee during the first year. This fee is equal to the annual 12b-1 fee, thus level load. The shares are not convertible to other classes. Although Class C (and B) shares do not charge front-end loads, distributors do pay broker sales commission. But the commission is usually smaller than paid by Classes A and B shares.

Class C shares also impose annual 12b-1 fees that are generally similar to those imposed by Class B shares. However, distribution payments to brokers of Class C shares are larger than for Class B shares. Thus, even if 12b-1 fees are equal for both Class B and C shares, the splits between distributors and brokers differ. Table 9 provides examples of multiple share class loads/fees, including differences within fund families.

Multiple share classes and investors

Prior to O'Neal (1999), Livingston and O'Neal (1998) analyzed the same three types of retail multiple share classes to determine which classes best serve investors. Class B shares have the lowest present value costs for holding periods of six years or less. Class B and C shares each have the lowest present value cost for only the seven-year holding period. But for years 8–20, Class A shares have the lowest present value cost. Long-term investors are best served by paying loads up front and minimizing annual 12b-1 fees.

As noted, the multiple share classes followed SEC approval of 12b-1 fees. The use of multiple share classes was justified on the grounds they would enable the industry to meet the needs of specific distribution channels and markets. As discussed above, share classes are offered for retail markets, but they are also designed for large and institutional investors, as well. Institutional investors include limited-distribution plans, such as state supplemental retirement plans, state teacher retirement plans and corporate pension plans. For example, Vanguard offers its 500 Index Fund to individual investors and its clone portfolio, the Institutional Index, to institutional investors.

Mutual funds with multiple share classes initially began as separate clone funds, each with its own load/fee structure. Measured performance of each share class reflects its load/fee structure and its impact on fund expenses and net asset value. Later, so-called *hub-and-spoke funds* were created, also offering multiple shares (spokes) appended to new or, more often, existing single portfolios (hub). Each spoke has its own load/fee structure and, for the reasons noted above, is sold as a separate portfolio (fund). However, individual investors do not pay the lowest loads/fees.

Spoke funds do not present problems for portfolio managers because they see one portfolio regardless of share classes appended. But spoke funds add another element of investor uncertainty in the sense that actions of a given share class, such as large redemptions, can negatively impact returns of the other share classes. Phillips (1992) has characterized hub-and-spoke funds as providing "a sharing of interest without a sharing of information." Shareholders of one spoke account have "little idea about other spokes' existence, the stability and size of their asset bases, or the nature and characteristics of their owners."

Kelley (1994) analyzed the multiple share class phenomenon and reported it accelerating, with over 50 percent representing spinoffs of existing funds. A total of thirty-five separate share classes were identified, which lack consistent designations among fund families for the same load/fee structures. Multi-share funds average 2.5 share classes, and some are unique to particular fund families. In addition to retail share classes, there are classes for brokerage firms, discount brokerage firms, institutional investors, retail banks, bank trust departments, and qualified pension and benefit plans, among others. Funds have even been organized for single clients, such as corporate and city pension funds. Use of multiple share classes represent more shareholder confusion, rather than simplicity to assist shareholders.

The ICI attempted to simplify share class designations by defining the letters for particular load/fee structures. The guidelines remove much of the confusion in comparing load/fee structures among funds, but many fund families have not adopted them. As noted above, the consensus designations for retail accounts are Classes A, B, and C.

Not only do multiple share classes complicate the investor decision process, but the entire structure rests on 12b-1 fees, which Phillips (1992) concluded makes sense only if one accepts the logic "that 12b-1 fees must be retained." These charges "have utterly failed their stated mission of lowering shareholders' total costs." Also, multiple share classes provide sales agents with potential conflicts of interest in serving clients. Choice of load/fee structure impacts sales commission *and* investor net returns, which may not serve each equally well.

O'Neal (1999) examined this issue. In most circumstances and for most share class load/fee structures, brokers have monetary incentives to sell the share class that is least advantageous for investors. Brokers have incentives to guide long-term investors to low sales load, high annual 12b-1 fee funds and short-term investors to high sales load, low annual fee share class funds. Investors should be informed of the potential conflict of interest in buying funds through sales agents. There have been numerous cases where brokers have taken advantage of investors. The SEC should recognize this potential conflict of interest and consider alternative methods of paying brokers. The ideal solution would be to compensate brokers equally for all share classes sold.

Quantity discounts

As noted, mutual fund offerings of multiple share classes make it important for larger investors to understand the transaction break points required for increasingly larger front-end load discounts on Class A shares. Breakpoint rules are reported to the SEC and stated in the prospectus and statement of additional information. Funds and broker/dealers are responsible for enforcement.

The rules are designed to prevent unethical sales agents from using "breakpoint sales" to keep investors from obtaining breakpoint discounts available to them with Class A shares. They usually do this by steering investors to Class B shares, not Class A shares. For example, brokers receive higher commission by selling Class B shares than selling Class A shares that also qualify for breakpoint load discounts. This practice generates larger sales commission, but also lower returns for investors. To the credit of some mutual fund families, they do not accept large Class B purchases that qualify for breakpoint loads in Class A shares.

Mutual funds usually provide investors with several options to qualify for breakpoint discounts. Most fund families offer *combined purchase privileges* that base Class A share loads on total shareholder investment in its funds. This privilege may also extend to family members who pool purchases to qualify for breakpoints. Some fund families offer *rights of accumulation* (*cumulative quantity discounts*) that provide reduced loads on new purchases bringing total shareholder investment to break points. Most fund families allow investors defined periods of time to reach break points. To do this, investors sign *letters of intent* (*statements of intention*) that give them, say, twelve months to reach specified break points. These discounts apply to initial and subsequent purchases as long as investors satisfy the agreements.

Break points for Class A shares with front-end loads usually begin at $50,000, and again at $100,000. There are typically no loads on minimum purchases of $1 million. Again, Class B shares do not have break points and some funds do not sell them in amounts of $250,000–$500,000 because these purchases qualify for Class A share break points. As noted, funds often automatically convert Class B shares to Class A shares after some seven or eight years to reduce shareholder transaction costs.

Measuring the performance of pre-existing mutual funds with multiple share classes presents a real case of revisionist history to investors. Funds use the SEC's "standardized historical performance data" approach to compute the historical share class performance of share classes that have no history. Fund historical performance figures are restated, as deemed appropriate, to reflect any front-end and deferred loads that currently apply to redemptions within eighteen months. However, 12b-1 fees are reflected only from date of adoption. The results of this process are historical performance figures that never actually occurred for multiple share classes that never previously existed. This revisionist history should at least be disclosed with emphasis to ensure investors clearly understand the implications for historical accuracy and returns. ·

Fund attributes and transaction costs

Kihn (1996) identified the determinants of shareholder transaction costs from a 1992–3 sample of 2,500 mutual funds. The critical determinants are fund services and other marketing expenses, but not financial performance. Apparently, most investors are more concerned with service than financial performance!

The types of shareholder transaction costs vary with mutual fund attributes. Large front-end loads are associated with funds with (1) municipal bond portfolios, (2) small initial purchase requirements, (3) high expected returns, (4) high past returns, (5) at least a minimum of specified services, and (6) relatively long histories. Small front-end loads are related to (1) funds with deferred loads and (2) funds with 12b-1 fees. Large 12b-1 fees are associated with funds with: (1) deferred loads, (2) high management fees, (3) small initial purchase requirements, (4) high expected returns, (5) low risk, (6) a minimum of specified services, and (7) relatively short histories.

Sales force mutual fund investors are therefore faced with load/fee tradeoffs in selecting funds with desired attributes. That is, 12b-1 fees and deferred loads are at least partial substitutes for front-end loads. Front-end loads are positively associated with fund performance, but 12b-1 fees are positively associated with management fees, and front-end loads and 12b-1 fees are positively associated with a minimum of specified shareholder services.

Mutual fund shareholder transaction costs are not trivial. Investors should give them serious attention in the context of their investment horizons. Table 10 illustrates a calculator for determining and assessing transaction costs for various horizons. Transaction costs reduce shareholder returns from fund investing, and, to the extent assistance is not needed, it is not necessary to pay loads or annual fees. If advice is needed, the tradeoff of load/fee structure remains an important issue. The loads/fees associated with advice are especially burdensome when they do not generate additional returns sufficient to cover their costs. On average, it would seem that funds with minimal to no loads/fees are more likely to generate additional returns to shareholders. This issue of performance and loads/fees is important and is considered again later.

SHAREHOLDER SERVICES

Mutual funds offer a wide and increasing range of shareholder services. Investor perceptions of these services play an important role in their choice of funds. As stated previously, fund industry growth provides overwhelming evidence that funds, in general, offer distinct service advantages. However, the issue is not whether mutual funds offer effective and useful shareholder services – they do for the most part – but whether particular funds offer specific services as advantages in meeting the needs of particular investors. That is, do the actual shareholder services of particular funds translate to actual service advantages for particular investors?

There is ample evidence that mutual fund shareholders support this general finding. As discussed below, fund shareholders appear to have clear perceptions of: (1) personal needs and requirements in purchasing funds; (2) fund services compared with other financial service providers; (3) improvements needed in fund services to better serve their needs; (4) services of direct market and sales force funds, respectively; and (5) services of direct market and sales force fund distribution channels.

Shareholder investment needs

The ICI (1994a) analyzed the perceived needs and requirements of mutual fund shareholders. A shareholder sample of nearly 1,500 persons participated and about 50 percent completed the study. Factor analysis identified five shareholder clusters, each with similar needs and requirements in purchasing mutual funds. The shareholder clusters are characterized as (1) "confidence guidance oriented," (2) "advisor-dependent," (3) "fee-sensitive independent," (4) "cautious," and (5) "uninvolved."

Confidence guidance mutual fund shareholders are self-reliant investors who make their own decisions, but do value advice and are willing to pay for it. Advisor-dependent shareholders are not self-reliant and depend on financial advisors. Fee-sensitive independent shareholders make their own decisions with little guidance, and wish to avoid high sales fees and commission. Cautious shareholders are quite self-reliant investors, but they need financial guidance and are somewhat sensitive to sales fees and commission. And, last, uninvolved shareholders not only lack self-reliance in investing, but they do not express much need for financial guidance. These are especially vulnerable investors. These findings also suggest shareholders are generally best served by a variety of mutual fund distribution channels.

Mutual funds as service providers

A strong minority of shareholders perceive mutual funds provide the best overall service relative to other financial service providers. The ICI (1994b) computed that the following rounded-up percentages of shareholders favor each service provider:

Mutual funds	40
Banks	27
Brokerage firms	21
Credit card companies	7
Insurance companies	6
	100

Thus shareholders clearly perceive mutual funds as best relative to other service providers. This is also seen in that mutual funds are perceived best in providing seven of fourteen specific service and investment needs:

1 Understanding customer needs.
2 Providing high returns.
3 Providing retirement investments.

4   Providing innovative products and services.
5   Providing needed products and services.
6   Assisting with money management.
7   Providing the best investment value.

And shareholders rank funds second in providing the other seven services:

 8   Completing transactions accurately.
 9   Completing transactions in a timely manner.
10   Having courteous employees.
11   Providing convenient access to services.
12   Providing financial advice.
13   Providing security and safety for savings.
14   Having the best reputation for service.

Thus shareholders have positive perceptions of specific mutual fund services.

Actual versus ideal services

Mutual funds are perceived best by shareholders in providing services, but the ICI (1994b) concluded they fall short of ideal. Both direct market and sales force funds, but especially the latter, were less than ideal in providing the single service shareholders perceive as most important: accurate processing of transactions and requests. This finding is somewhat surprising.

Direct market funds are perceived by shareholders as better than ideal in providing a variety of funds, offering friendly and courteous employees, applying the benefits of technology, and treating investors as valued customers. Direct market funds are less than ideal in taking responsibility for resolving problems (lowest score) knowledgeable employees, facilitating transactions, and understanding investor needs.

On the other hand, *sales force funds* are a bit better than ideal in providing variety of funds and friendly and courteous employees. Sales force funds are less than ideal in providing knowledgeable employees (lowest score), taking responsibility for resolving problems, facilitating transactions, clear and easy to read printed materials, understanding shareholder needs, materials that facilitate decisions, feelings of being valued customers, and financial advice. These results thus show some interesting similarities but also dichotomies. But direct market funds are much closer to ideal than sales force funds, which suggests sales force funds do not provide what should be their natural advantage – shareholder advice. Direct market funds actually rank better in providing financial advice.

Dziubinski (1999a) also observed that mutual fund service is far from ideal. There is not always a correlation between quality of portfolio managers and quality of fund services, such as telephone representatives. Also, shareholder account statements often leave much to be desired by omitting details like shareholder rates of return, dollar expenses paid, and capital gains and losses from trades. However, a few fund families place a high value on shareholder satisfaction, among them Longleaf (again), T. Rowe Price, and Vanguard.

Direct market and sales force fund services

The ICI (1994b) study also identified overall service factors both direct market and sales force fund investors perceive as keys to investment decisions. Overall, fund family reputations for investment performance and reputation rank first and second, respectively, in decisions to invest. These factors are most important to both direct market fund and sales force fund investors. Overall, recommendations of trusted persons and quality of shareholder services rank first and second, respectively, among the third most important factors. These latter factors are important both to direct market and sales force fund investors. However, fund sales loads and fees are most important to direct market fund investors.

Thus shareholder service is not the most important factor in mutual fund choice, but an important one, nonetheless. Forty percent of shareholders who rate fund service quality as excellent/very good plan to increase their holdings, and 81 percent are likely to recommend them to others.

Shareholders also indicated key services mutual funds need to improve to increase their quality ratings. Direct market fund investors perceive funds need to make transactions and requests easier, improve understanding of shareholder needs, and have more knowledgeable employees. Nonetheless, 74 percent rate fund service quality as excellent/very good. Sales force fund investors perceive mutual funds need to improve understanding of shareholder needs, process transactions and requests more accurately, and have more friendly and courteous employees. Nonetheless, 68 percent rate service quality as excellent/very good.

Overall, the following percentages of direct market and sales force fund shareholders rate the quality of shareholder services as:

Excellent	32
Very good	39
Good	22
Fair/poor	7
	100

Thus 71 percent consider fund service quality as excellent/very good. Also, direct market and sales force funds individually receive high ratings. These findings appear to speak well for quality of fund shareholder service. As noted above, shareholders perceive the quality of fund services superior to other financial service providers. They also give high ratings to the quality of fund services on its own merits, both for direct market and for sales force funds.

Direct market versus sales force fund channels

Mutual fund investors use direct market funds as well as various channels offered by sales force funds. In response to increasing competitive pressure for investor dollars, some no-load funds are becoming 100 percent loaded, others are adding load funds to their offerings, and still others are adding to offerings of multiple share class funds.

The competition has become particularly tough for smaller fund families, with giants Vanguard, Fidelity, and Janus dominating the battle for cash inflow. Investors who buy funds through sales agents now represent two-thirds of all investors. As reported by Whelehan (2000b), 32 percent of fund investors buy fund shares directly from funds or discount brokers, while 68 percent use full-service brokers, insurance agents, financial planners, or banks.

ICI (1994a) determined that shareholder choice of distribution channels depends on perceived investment needs (discussed above) and perceptions of each channel's attributes. The percentages of mutual fund shareholders rating the availability of information from each distribution channel as good/excellent follows:

Direct market funds	81
Full-service brokers	82
Discount brokers	57
Insurance agents	46
Banks	42
Financial planners	85

Direct market funds, full service brokers and financial planners rank highest for mutual fund information.

Further, direct market funds are primarily perceived as providing reasonable fees, but also convenience and information. Full-service brokers and financial planners are perceived as providing investment advice, personalized service, information, and convenience. Discount brokers are primarily perceived as convenient and with reasonable fees and information. Insurance agents are primarily valued as existing relationships, but also for personalized service and convenience. Banks are primarily seen as convenient.

In summary, investors perceive the primary attributes of each mutual fund distribution channel as follows:

1   Direct market funds
   (a)   Low or no fees or commission.
   (b)   Offers funds with solid performance.
2   Indirect market funds
   (a)   Full-service broker: investment guidance and advice.
   (b)   Discount broker: low or no fees or commission.
   (c)   Insurance agent: established relationship.
   (d)   Bank: convenience.
   (e)   Financial planner: investment guidance and advice; established relationship.

Based on shareholder perceptions of investment needs and the attributes of mutual fund distribution channels, ICI (1994a) computed he percentage of shareholders currently using each channel as follows:

Direct market funds	52
Indirect market funds	
Full-service brokers	51
Discount brokers	14

Insurance agents	15
Banks	13
Financial planner	18

Most shareholders use both full-service brokers and direct market channels.

ICI (1994a) also revealed shareholder satisfaction with mutual fund distribution channels used most recently. The percentage of shareholders that expect to use the same channel for their next fund purchase follows:

Direct market funds	93
Indirect market funds	
Full-service brokers	72
Discount brokers	71
Insurance agents	39
Banks	47
Financial planners	68

The results indicate shareholders are most likely to again use direct market funds. Over time, this suggests an increase in market share for direct market funds and loss of market share for indirect market funds, especially insurance agents and banks.

The primary reasons shareholders (more than 20 percent of respondents) give for *not* using particular channels again are dissatisfaction with fund service, performance, advice, fees/expenses and availability, as well as determination that financial guidance is no longer needed. Further, 51 percent indicate they will no longer use full-service brokers.

Assessing shareholder services

As noted, investors rate mutual funds highest in providing services. As seen in table 11, the menu of *model* mutual fund services is extensive, including online services. Online services appear to correlate closely with traditional fund service offerings. As discussed, the key issue is whether particular fund actual shareholder services are actual advantages to particular investors in meeting their investment needs.

Only a particular investor can answer this question. The investor's first step is to review model fund shareholder service quantity (table 11) and list/check those services desired. The second step is to review fund services and compute the percentage of desired services provided. The third step is to review articles assessing fund family service quality (discussed below) and indicate whether quality is excellent, acceptable, or unacceptable. The fourth step is to assess fund overall shareholder services and indicate whether they are excellent, acceptable, or unacceptable. For example, table 11 indicates Vanguard Windsor II (VWII) provides 100 percent of desired services and its service quantity is therefore excellent. Moreover, based on table 12 (discussed below), the quality of Vanguard's shareholder services is identified as excellent. Thus Windsor II's overall shareholder services are excellent. This information is summarized in table 27.

Fund families as service providers

As noted, for investors to identify particular mutual funds that provide needed services, it is important to know which fund families provide the desired quality. Fund families have become increasingly sensitive to the importance of shareholder service. This may be more defensive than proactive to the extent they follow the axiom that mutual funds cannot win investors with shareholder services but they can lose them. They are also generally aware of opportunities afforded by technology to provide additional and improved services. For example, over 60 percent of fund transactions no longer involve human interaction.

A relatively new focus in mutual fund service is investor education, much of which is provided in fund Web sites. This is especially so for major fund families that perhaps fear that the once long-running bull market blinded investors to risk, making their response to serious market downturns problematic. Fund managers wish to prevent a mass exodus from mutual funds when the time comes. These education efforts typically include basic information on investing, diversification, and fund risks and returns over time. Importantly, they show investors how to use their risk tolerances and investment horizons to determine long-term asset allocation among cash, stocks, and bonds, for the purpose of reducing anxiety and smoothing performance over the market's inevitable ups and downs.

As suggested above, surveys have assessed the quality of shareholder service offered by fund families. Investors should refer to recent surveys in making this assessment. For example, Lauren Young (1998a) evaluated the service quality of the twelve largest no-load funds and six largest broker-sold funds, with assets under management ranging from $20 billion to $675 billion. The study is not representative of smaller fund families, but over 55 percent of industry assets are included. Each mutual fund family is evaluated on its (1) customer service representatives – knowledge, ability, professionalism and patience, (2) range of services offered, (3) online services, (4) account statements, and (5) investing information (prospectus).

Overall, Fidelity Investments and the Vanguard Group ranked first and second, respectively, in service quality, the same as the prior year. Fund families with the next highest scores are T. Rowe Price, American Century, and Scudder. For individual services, Fidelity was first in range of services offered and online services, and Vanguard is first in online services and investing information. The only other fund families with top individual scores are Scudder for customer service representatives and Putnam Investment for account statements. It appears biggest is best for service in that Fidelity ranks first and Vanguard second in mutual fund assets under management.

Table 12 provides a guide to twenty-seven shareholder services offered by thirty mutual fund families. Services such as debit cards, wrap accounts, margin loans, funds sold through mutual fund supermarkets, sale of funds in other fund families, brokerage services and fee-based financial advisors are not strictly fund services, but are normally provided by their broker/dealers. Of the twenty-two yes/no questions, Fidelity and Vanguard have twenty and nineteen positive answers, respectively. For sales force funds, Prudential, Scudder and Smith Barney have twenty-one, twenty and nineteen yes answers, respectively. These and other fund families provide a wide range of services.

Whelehan (1999a) surveyed *Mutual Funds* readers to identify favorite mutual fund families. Vanguard and Fidelity rank one, two, respectively, for telephone service, financial planning assistance, educational planning, tax planning and overall favorite family. Investors consider long-term performance, expenses, and sales loads most important in fund selection. The largest complaints are about sales loads and high expenses. The three most important services are knowledgeable telephone representatives, availability of telephone fund exchanges, and twenty-four-hour phone service.

In a study of mutual fund families, Willis (1999a) concluded that "Fidelity best meets the needs of most investors." Fidelity has the best management depth, with seventy-two traders, 242 analysts, and eighty portfolio managers running 283 funds! They provide strong fund performance across a broad range of categories and investment styles. They offer good shareholder service backed up by enormous investment in computers, readable prospectuses, the best online Web site, a leading funds supermarket, and both direct market and sales force funds.

In addition, major mutual fund families normally offer one or more classes of premium service. To qualify, investors must meet minimum levels of assets under fund family management. For example, the minimum at Fidelity is $500,000 and at Vanguard it is $250,000. Premium services typically include teams of experienced customer service representatives, investment newsletters, and seminars with portfolio managers. Ancillary services often requiring larger accounts include estate planning, trusts, portfolio planning and allocation, and management of retirement assets.

CHAPTER THREE

MUTUAL FUND SERVICE ADVANTAGES: PROFESSIONAL MANAGEMENT

Chapter 3 follows chapter 2's theme of mutual fund service advantages, but with the focus on professional management. The first goal is to identify and discuss the distinct professional management service advantages provided by mutual funds generally. Management quality is the single most important element to success in any business. Not surprisingly, then, professional management is an important service advantage of mutual funds generally. Professional management is used here to include services provided by investment advisors, but with a particular focus on portfolio management.

Several subjective influences on the quality of portfolio management are discussed. The issue is not whether funds generally offer professional management, they do, but whether particular services provided are advantages in meeting the needs of particular investors. That is, do actual professional management services of particular funds translate to actual specific service advantages for particular investors?

The second goal is to provide guidelines that facilitate determination of whether particular fund professional management services are actual advantages to particular investors. Vanguard Windsor II is again used to illustrate these services. The treatment is designed to evaluate the background elements of particular portfolio managers. These elements include education, previous investment experience, current tenure as portfolio manager, and assessment of overall background. Everything portfolio managers bring to the table is reflected in attributes of fund portfolios. For example, portfolio manager education and experience influence fund diversification risk by their impact on portfolio management.

Implicit in this general service is that portfolio managers provide a level of skill, expertise, and portfolio performance beyond what investors are able or wish to exercise for themselves. If not, all else equal, why would investors depend on professional managers to manage their money? Of course, the fact investment management companies, in effect, hire themselves as investment advisors may cast some doubt on this assumption. Whether or not particular funds have effective portfolio managers cannot be assumed, but must be assessed on a continuing basis. Investors should accept the general case of professional management, but must verify it in particular cases. This is another example of Reagan's "Trust, but verify."

RESOURCES AND PERFORMANCE OF PORTFOLIO MANAGEMENT

The unprecedented growth in number and size of mutual funds has generated investment management company revenues of about $30 billion a year. This revenue provides much more than that needed to: (1) hire real professional portfolio managers and who apply appropriate analytical methods of analysis and style of portfolio management, and (2) provide essential analysts, support staff, research data, technology, and infrastructure.

Growth of the mutual fund industry has also provided investors with broad choices of fund investment objectives and investment styles, as well as access to additional types of securities, such as derivatives and international securities. Overall, mutual funds are financially positioned to provide a truly professional product, but the ultimate test lies in portfolio performance, the subject of chapter 10. Chapter 10 also includes portfolio attributes of successful portfolio managers. The focus here is the *qualitative* attributes of portfolio managers.

Mutual fund portfolio managers are responsible for the performance of actively managed portfolios, but they too face constraints determined by investment objectives (table 6), investment strategies and limitations, and investment advisor and board policies and directives. At the operating level, if not the strategic level, fund portfolio managers are responsible for security analysis, portfolio investment style, security selection, portfolio asset allocation, securities trading, among others, all of which constrain the degree of diversification and risk.

The down side of active mutual fund portfolio management is that the average fund does not provide the level of *performance* implicit in funds as providers of professional management, if, by this, above average performance is assumed. However, this level of performance cannot be generally assumed. After all, average fund performance cannot be above the average performance of all funds. For any given fund, professional portfolio management may provide above average performance, but this cannot be assumed and should be revisited annually. Thus relative fund performance cannot be assumed but must be identified and revisited on a continual basis.

PROFESSIONAL MANAGEMENT

Family background

Where do successful mutual fund portfolio managers come from? Casual empiricism suggests successful portfolio managers are, not infrequently, children/grandchildren of successful family-owned investment management firms. The notion of going into the family business is an old custom, but it is interesting how strong it is in the dynamic financial services industry, especially mutual funds. This too will change.

Although the industry has become much more complex, McReynolds (1999) reported that "what investors of this generation have learned from their parents will continue to shape the industry as it moves to the next millennium." Unfortunately, this outlook may be too optimistic because family-owned money management firms are increasingly being acquired by larger companies with wider, non-family ownership.

In the meantime, Bamford (1998) explored why it is that succeeding generations have come to join family money management firms. Not surprisingly, perhaps, the common ingredient is dinner table conversation. John C. Bogle, former Vanguard group chairman, believes this exposure is key to family succession in the investment management business. And this exposure is more important than inherited talent, intelligence, and determination – a bit strong, perhaps.

Interestingly, John C. Bogle's son, John Jr., is precluded from Vanguard employment by its nepotism policy. This is a case where success actually worked against family successor management. But this policy has not kept him from fund management. Does Vanguard's policy reflect potential in-house perceptions of unfair hiring or does it reflect an implicit concern about the quality of these hires? In Bogle Jr.'s case, his career has clearly proved the former to be the case.

In the Oberweis fund family business, James Oberweis recalled how he was drawn to the family business. He remembered his father's enthusiasm and dinner table tutoring on investing basics. His father also took him along on visits to companies and meetings with CEOs. In another example, Alexandra Lebenthal is the third generation in Lebenthal & Co., a bond brokerage firm founded by her grandparents. She recalled how her interest as a child was also sparked by dinner table conversation. She also remembers her father's passion for saving and investing. During office visits, her grandmother taught her to write checks properly and how to keep track of client accounts and trades.

Zweig (1995) reported that Shelby Davis of the Davis mutual funds family accompanied his father, a private money manager, on company visits beginning at age twelve. His father advocated long-term investing and taught him the rule of seventy-two to see how long it takes money to double. As reported by Bamford (1998) and Barbee (1997b), the senior Davis's sons Andrew and Chris are the third generation in the family business. Each manages a mutual fund advised by Davis Selected Advisors. The brothers recall their father's dinner table questions and answers concerning investment concepts. He taught them every investor should understand investment basics and the value of long-term investing. Family vacations included company visits, which Andrew and Chris did not fully appreciate until much later. As they grew up, they were paid small amounts to prepare company research reports. The brothers invested these small amounts in the stocks they liked.

These and other persons active in family investment management businesses share the common experience of long-term exposure. To the extent previous generations or two are meaningfully engaged when younger, they are likely grounded in the values, philosophy, and skills that made the family businesses successful. These offspring are also likely dedicated to continuing the family tradition of success in these businesses. Thus portfolio managers with good relevant childhood experiences who join successful family money management firms are likely dedicated to continuing that success for their offspring.

However, this is not to imply that younger family members have singular talents, but that the odds of success may be slightly tilted in their favor. The transition to the next generation may be more reassuring to mutual fund shareholders if it follows the Whitman model, reported in Edgerton (1998b). In this model, the next generation of portfolio managers have already demonstrated their abilities and are acknowledged as co-managers of established funds or managers of new funds. In 1997, Martin Whitman of the Third Avenue Value Fund selected

Curtis Jensen, a former student, not a family member, as successor-to-be. Jensen was installed as founding co-manager of a new Whitman fund, a first for Whitman.

Support for family members as successor fund managers is much stronger when coupled with large family member investment in the funds they manage (discussed below). This congruence contributes to a passion for investing, which generally finds expression in lower portfolio risk and higher tax efficiency. It's their money, too!

Education

Traditionally, portfolio managers joined investment firms immediately out of college, or, perhaps, without college, and worked their way up. The process often included being mentored by senior persons, as in the Whitman case. In another well known example, Michael Price joined Heine Securities following college as a research assistant. Subsequently, Price became Max Heine's protégé, and by the 1980s Price was essentially managing the advisory company and the fund. At Heine's death, the fund had about $2.5 billion in assets, and Price bought the advisory firm for $10 million. And, in one of the amazing stories of the bull market, Price sold Heine Securities to Franklin Resources in 1996 for cash and stock that with incentives was worth $600 million to $800 million. At the time, Price was managing several Mutual Series funds with assets over $17 billion. Much more impressive than the superior returns Price earned on his funds is the return Price earned on his Heine Securities stock, which revealed the immense profitability of investment advisory firms.

Today, major investment management companies generally use educational background as an initial screen in hiring new and recent graduates. Hiring may be a bit less structured in smaller advisory firms. Nonetheless, on Wall Street and beyond, the optimal educational backgrounds for new professional employees are MBAs and CFAs. The CFA designation is a professional certification and may be in progress, pending, or awarded when analysts are hired.

However, it should be noted that not all MBA degrees are equally valued on Wall Street. The most highly valued degrees are those awarded by business schools with best access to Wall Street – those with long-term professional ties and large numbers of graduates employed in the firms.

Many of these school–Wall Street relationships pre-date the growth and importance of MBA degrees. For example, Jay Sanders (1994) determined that the top five undergraduate degrees held by mutual fund managers were awarded by four private and one public universities. At the graduate/MBA level, the top five degrees held by mutual fund managers were awarded by three private and two public universities. The pool of business schools from which MBA graduates are hired has broadened as the demand for persons with advanced degrees has expanded. Nonetheless, the majority of these degree programs remain located in or around major cities, especially Boston, Philadelphia, New York, Chicago, Los Angeles, and San Francisco.

The *CFA charter* (*designation*) is to investment managers what the CPA is to accountants. The CFA designation certifies successful completion of an extensive educational program for current and prospective investment professionals. The Institute of Chartered Financial Analysts (ICFA) has awarded the CFA designation since 1963. The ICFA and the Financial Analysts Federation merged in 1990 and formed the Association for Investment Management and

Research (AIMR), a nonprofit organization of investment professionals and academics. It promotes high ethical, professional, and educational standards for investment professionals. Reilly and Brown (1997) discuss the CFA designation in some detail, including the standard of ethics and professional conduct.

As discussed in AIMR (1999), a bachelor's degree or equivalent is required to enter the CFA study program. A person must pass three six-hour examinations over a minimum of three years to be awarded the CFA charter. The person must also have at least three years' experience as a financial analyst, join a nearby constituent financial analysts' society, demonstrate high ethical conduct, and follow the AIMR code of ethics and standards of practice. Examinations may be taken before satisfying the other criteria, which benefits those just out of college.

The study program includes review material and readings organized around a body of knowledge that focuses on the investment decision process. The curriculum includes ethical and professional standards, financial accounting, fixed income and equity securities analysis, portfolio management, and quantitative techniques. The first examination covers tools and inputs for investment valuation and management, the second covers investment evaluation, and the final examination focuses on portfolio management. Each examination includes ethical and professional standards. Well over 25,000 CFA charters have been awarded.

Brockman and Brooks (1998) even asserted that as the number of CFA designations has increased, perceived market risks have declined and stock prices have increased. The reasoning is that the CFA designation indicates a high level of professional competence and integrity, which increases investor confidence in recommendations of market professionals. This increased competence and integrity in the market leads to lower risks perceived by investors and increased willingness to pay higher prices for stocks. Wow!

Hiring practices

Abigail Johnson (1998), a third generation family member of Fidelity Management & Research, described its approach to hiring and training future portfolio managers. Fidelity is the largest domestic mutual fund family in assets under management. Fidelity seeks young business school graduates who evidence high intelligence, strong analytical skills, ability to ask the right questions, a passion for analysis, exceptional physical stamina, and fondness for company visits.

The persons Fidelity employs enter a grueling process designed to identify those capable of managing large fund portfolios. The process begins with initial assignments as analysts for particular industry segments. Those who demonstrate strong performance in a series of assignments move up to portfolio managers of sector funds, such as Fidelity Select Electronics, that invest in single industries. Performance there and the quality of assistance they provide others determines who advances to the next round as portfolio managers of Fidelity's large, diversified mutual funds, such as Fidelity Growth and Income.

To support the work of its portfolio managers, Fidelity provides up-to-date workstations, access to a global peer network, needed resources, and small group interaction with other managers. Portfolio managers receive a great deal of autonomy, including considerable latitude in portfolio construction, but this autonomy comes with strict accountability for performance. Fidelity's approach to training future portfolio managers would make interesting survivor MBA case studies.

Peter Lynch (1993), Fidelity's former Magellan Fund guru, provides yet another perspective on the Fidelity way of portfolio management. In a nutshell, Lynch believes there are good stocks everywhere and all you really need is the right people to find them. These persons usually begin at Fidelity as raw talent, but with particular characteristics: (1) ability to do independent analysis; (2) ability and willingness to share ideas; (3) fast learners who also think things through; (4) willingness to take risks and ability to accept the mistakes that will be made; and (5) ability to explain why particular stocks have been purchased and why they own them when the market falls.

Janus Capital, the investment advisor to another mutual fund family, appears a bit more traditional in the way it selects and trains future portfolio managers. As discussed in Claire Young (1998), Janus hires future portfolio managers directly out of college or early in their careers, and then grows them from within. Liberal arts graduates are usually preferred, in the expectation they will be big-picture thinkers. However, Janus has also hired science graduates, and one portfolio manager has both an MBA and a CFA designation. This may signal a more contemporary approach.

Janus seeks generalists characterized by (1) demonstrated genuine curiosity, (2) a competitive nature, (3) love of the market and (4) ability to formulate arguments quickly. Examples of demonstrated creativity include non-traditional investment strategies. Janus research stresses analysis of fundamentals to identify superior growth opportunities. This research includes invited in-house presentations by corporate executives and on-site company visits, which Janus believes provide critical insights.

As discussed, MBAs plus CFA designation are increasingly the model for entering the investment management business. This trend is becoming more pervasive with the retirement of senior portfolio managers. As portfolio managers with a model education continue to increase, it will be interesting to see if they provide improved returns. Time will tell, but they are likely to make markets more efficient, and thus make it more difficult to earn above average returns. If so, then highly educated individuals will be needed just to be average.

Continuing education

The likelihood persons with the desired educational and professional certification will, in fact, become portfolio managers also depends on their being able to apply their education, but also to remain current while proving themselves in ever more challenging positions. Success as a portfolio manager requires high tolerance of uncertainty, great self-confidence, ability to accept mistakes, and ability to act quickly, decisively, and rationally (especially when the market is not rational). Portfolio managers are often wrong, but they must not make a habit of it or lose confidence in their vision, objectives, and strategies.

Today's increasingly sophisticated approaches to securities analysis, decision making, and new product development on a global basis call for matching levels of education, as well as continuous upgrading of skills. As reported by Prola (2000) in *Smith Business Online*, "rocket scientists are all over Wall Street." These *financial engineers* create new advanced financial products, such as models for pricing exotic securities. Increased use of financial engineers is visible in the large and increasing employment of academic types with PhD degrees, such as physics and applied mathematics, but with fields in mathematical finance.

These current or former professors must be able to work in the trenches with investment types in developing new advanced financial products and complex investment strategies.

Portfolio manager tenure

An investment axiom states that to be successful portfolio managers need to have experienced both good and bad markets. Another rule of thumb states that the market goes up about two of three years. This has not been the case since 1982. However, this is not to say that past is not prologue. If this rule is a reasonable assumption, then it should not take much more than four years to go through a complete market cycle. This assumes bad markets occur in the third year and take one additional year to stabilize.

Since 1926, the market has experienced losses in a total of twenty years. Further, from 1960 to 1982 the market experienced negative returns in 1962, 1966, 1969, 1973–4, 1981, and 1990. But, as noted, the historical pattern has not been repeated since 1982. Since then, the market has suffered only a small loss in 1990 and a moderate one in 2000. The market even had a positive return in 1987, the year of the October market collapse.

The impact of this extraordinary run of great years since 1982 is that most portfolio managers have not experienced a real 1973–4 type bear market. Sanders (1998) reports that the average portfolio manager now has less than four years' tenure. Thus the average portfolio manager has not seen a complete market cycle, and 1973–4 and 1987 are historical footnotes. For example, a fund advertised whether you want portfolio managers with nineteen years' experience or others who have only managed the "up side of a roller coaster run." However, this is not to say that most portfolio managers are amateurs. As stated by Rekenthaler (1993a): "[T]he average mutual-fund portfolio manager is not some brash kid a few years out of business school, but is instead 43 years of age and will have been in the business for more than a decade. Only 3 percent of all fund managers are in their 20s."

Paluch (1997) examined the tenure of portfolio managers of diversified equity mutual funds for the twenty largest mutual fund families. The fund families with the longest median portfolio manager tenure (with grades) are (1) Merrill Lynch (A+), (2) American Funds (A), (3) Franklin Templeton (A), (4) T. Rowe Price (A–), and (5) Smith Barney (A). Fund giant Vanguard rates only B and the largest fund family, Fidelity, C–. Those fund families with the shortest median portfolio manager tenure are (1) Kemper (D–), (2) Dreyfus (D), and (3) Van Kampen American Capital (D+). Common sense says to invest in fund families known for very experienced portfolio managers.

Tenure and performance

Lemak and Satish (1996) took the next step and analyzed the impact of portfolio manager tenure on mutual fund risk/return performance for ten years ending 1994. Performance of those who managed portfolios for the entire period was compared with that of those with shorter tenure. The fact some portfolio managers survived the entire period in this time of rapid turnover of portfolio mangers, and even funds, implies these are successful managers, at least subjectively. However, those who would have been successful managers may have gone elsewhere based on shorter-term performance.

The analysis provided several results. First, all funds underperformed the S&P 500 Index for the ten-year period. This says a great deal about the difficulty in being above average over time, assuming use of correct benchmark indices. Second, managers with at least ten years' tenure generate only slightly higher portfolio returns than shorter-tenured managers. But, third, their portfolios have less risk. Fourth, investment style has no significant impact on performance for ten-year managers. And, fifth, there is no relationship between portfolio manager investment style and portfolio systematic risk for ten-year managers. Thus all else being equal, very experienced portfolio managers appear to have survived with good reason, especially with respect to risk management.

Phillips (1991) confirmed this general finding concerning the performance of long-tenured portfolio managers. The mutual fund universe was divided into five groups based on length of portfolio manager term of service. Managers with tenure over ten years performed best on a risk/return basis. Fund portfolio quality also generally improved for each additional two years of service. This occurred even though these funds attracted much larger net cash inflows, which may normally be expected to reduce performance.

Mutual fund portfolios with experienced managers have smaller *portfolio turnover* and smaller *expense ratios*, both reflecting *buy-and-hold* strategies. But does smaller portfolio turnover come about from the security of long tenure or does it contribute to achieving long tenure (not being fired)? Phillips (1995) concludes that smaller portfolio turnover does not in itself create star portfolio managers, but it does reflect more patience (and confidence) with portfolio holdings. Long-tenured stars can not only identify undervalued stocks, but have the conviction to stay with them until rewarded.

However, *Mutual Funds* (1998b) reported a discount broker Charles Schwab & Co. study that had opposite results. Over a five-year period, mutual funds less than three years old outperformed older ones across all approaches to portfolio management. But the time period selected could have favored new, less diversified and more volatile portfolios, which suggests the need to use risk-adjusted performance measures. And, probably most important, new funds are small, more nimble, and able to establish large positions in favored stocks. They also have enough net cash inflow to avoid having to sell some favorites prior to making new investments.

Eileen Sanders (1994) disagreed with the preference for older mutual funds. Over a five-year period, funds twenty or more years old were outperformed a bit by younger funds. But the risk levels of both groups were about equal. Older funds understandably held larger cap. size stocks than younger funds, and younger funds outperformed older funds across most all investment styles. Of course, older mutual funds do not necessarily have the most experienced portfolio managers. Unfortunately, portfolio manager tenure is not sufficient to identify funds that are most likely to continue performing well. Portfolio manager tenure should be considered, but perhaps only after selecting funds using measurable criteria.

Marcus study

Assuming long-tenured portfolio managers outperform shorter-tenured managers, how long does it take to attribute this performance to manager skill? This is the real issue, but it is also one that cannot be estimated or confirmed statistically in most cases. In an interesting study, Marcus (1990) evaluated Peter Lynch's management of Fidelity Magellan fund for thirteen years ending 1989. In this case, the fund's superior performance was estimated and confirmed as due to Lynch's skill. But the same could not be said for *any* of the other fund portfolio managers. Magellan's returns were higher than the S&P 500 Index in eleven of thirteen years. But this alone does not demonstrate superior portfolio manager skill. What makes the case is the average margin by which Magellan annually outperformed the S&P 500 Index. This margin was greater than could be explained by chance in an efficient market with as many as 500 portfolio managers. Lynch's performance may be attributed to superior skill in selecting stocks. The fund is fully invested at all times and does not use *market timing*, which Lynch believes to be wasted effort.

The most interesting but also most discouraging finding is that the Magellan fund's *outperformance* of the S&P 500 Index in eleven of thirteen years was insufficient to demonstrate managerial skill. Intuitively, it would seem this is quite enough. However, based on simulated samples of fifty, 100, and 250 portfolio managers, there is a 43.3 percent, 67.1 percent, and 94.3 percent probability, respectively, that this performance was due to chance. Most striking is the 5.9 percent probability that the single best of 500 portfolio managers would outperform the market in thirteen of thirteen years! Again, by chance!

These Marcus findings are also important to judging the validity of mutual fund advertising. The message of fund advertising has traditionally been to the effect that their star portfolio managers beat the market in, say, each of the last five years. What we know from the Marcus study is that what is actually being advertised is chance results. The hype that attends hot funds of the month in investment publications should be viewed for what it is *not*. They are not signals of managerial stock selection skill on a probabilistic basis.

So how long is long enough to establish portfolio manager skill? Based on the Marcus study the answer is a very long time (no pun intended), especially when compared with average portfolio manager tenure. William Bernstein's (1999) statistical analysis of how long it takes is a bit discouraging. A small cap. portfolio manager who outperforms his peers by three percentage points a year for fifteen years would have to do so for 256 years before it could be reasonably concluded that manager skill was the explanation.

Brealey (1990) came to a more practicable finding when he concluded that "[a]s a rough rule of thumb, you probably need at least twenty-five years of fund performance to distinguish at the 95% significance level whether a manager has above-average competence." And by then it is likely that all relevant factors with have changed, including economic and financial market environments, competition, portfolio managers, style of portfolio management, control of advisory firms, fund investment objectives/policies, etc. These studies cast a huge cloud over fund advertising hyping portfolio manager performance. *Caveat emptor.* Let the buyer (investor) beware of false performance prophets from Madison Avenue.

Tenure and herding

McDermott (1999) reported an interesting footnote to the issue of portfolio manager tenure and performance. The safest career move for young (in tenure) portfolio managers is to follow the herd. There is also evidence of *herding* in academic research. One explanation for this is that less tenured portfolio managers are removed more quickly than experienced managers for below average performance and/or for deviation of portfolio profiles from similar types of funds.

Portfolio managers under age forty-five who underperformed the market by at least 15 percent in each of the years 1992, 1993, and 1994 have a 37 percent chance of being fired. But, under similar circumstances, portfolio managers forty-five years and older have only a 17 percent chance of being terminated. Thus following bad performance years, fund advisors, and apparently investors also, tend to stay with experienced portfolio managers of known quality based on long-term track records, more so than managers without established track records.

Portfolio managers as investors

Who would be the better choice for portfolio managers and investment advisors, persons with a small personal investment in their funds or those who have invested the ranch? As noted above, this latter finding is more likely to occur in cases of family owned management companies with family member portfolio managers. Many argue it is human nature to take more care with one's own money than someone else's, the classic case being government spending. If true, portfolio managers and fund advisors who invest significant amounts of personal wealth in their funds may be a bit more likely to generate additional returns, have better control of risk, or both, in their dual roles as investment managers and shareholders. At a minimum, these fellow shareholders share the pain of losses, which may make them more thoughtful and careful in decision making.

The ICI's negative position on disclosure of portfolio managers' investments in the funds they manage is hidden behind the "individual investors are bozos" argument. The Investment Company Institute is the trade association for the mutual fund industry. The ICI argued this information would be of interest to only a few investors. How do they know this? They do not, but this excuse is given for not providing this disclosure. In fact, the information would be of value to mutual fund shareholders in selecting funds. The industry does not want investors to have it. The information is of fundamental importance to effective mutual funds communication.

It is therefore not surprising that Sanders (1998) identified only a few investment advisors who significantly invest with shareholders. These few investment advisors include Davis, Longleaf, Clipper, Brandywine, Weitz, and Tweedy Browne. For example, Longleaf staff must invest in their funds and Tweedy Browne makes a point of it, as well. Moreover, Burton (1998a) identified only twelve portfolio managers who significantly invest in the portfolios they manage: (1) Richard Lawson, Weitz Series Hickory; (2) Ron Baron, Baron Asset; (3) Michael Fasciano, Fasciano; (4) Martin Whitman, Third Avenue Value; (5) David Williams III, Excelsior Value and Restructuring; (6) George Mairs III, Mairs and Power Growth; (7) Ron Muhlenkamp, Muhlenkamp; (8) David Schafer, Strong Schafer Value; (9) Robert Torray, Torray; (10) L. Roy Papp, Papp America-Abroad; (11) David Dreman, Kemper-Dreman Hi-Return Equity A; and (12) Chris Davis, Davis New York Venture A. The amounts invested range from $125,000 (Papp) to $349 million (Davis family). Further, these funds are generally known for providing above average returns.

Family Fund Shareholder Association (1998) examined the issue of director investment for fund giant Vanguard. Former chairman, John C. Bogle, an advocate of directors investing in their funds, has $35.2 million invested in thirty-six Vanguard funds, including one-third in another of his causes, index funds. And, together with current chairman John Brennan, they have over $46 million invested. Eight other directors have a total of $39.5 million invested, but nothing in more than one-third of Vanguard's non-institutional funds. Only one director invests in more than fifteen funds. Interestingly, index fund advocate and researcher Burton Malkiel has less than one-third of his money in index funds. Of course, it should not be assumed directors invest only in Vanguard.

Invest with the investors: an example

As reported by Zweig (1998b), Southeastern Asset Management, headed by Mason Hawkins, Longleaf's investment advisor, has a stated principal to "invest with the investors." Longleaf's staff, directors, and families have over $175 million invested in the three funds they manage. This contrasts with fund advisors that consider funds products to be marketed. Southeastern's managers invest significantly in their funds, and employees are prohibited from investing in any other. This restriction applies also to staff bonuses and profit-sharing payments. The incentive to do well by their funds is further strengthened by senior management's shared ownership in Southeastern Asset Management. Similarly, Davis Selected Advisors has advertised that the $600 million the Davis family, directors, and employees have invested makes them the largest shareholders.

Southeastern Asset Management follows a very conservative investment strategy that considers only stocks selling at 60 percent or less of intrinsic value. Longleaf family funds hold relatively few, but carefully selected, stocks and also hold them for an average of five years. For example, Longleaf Partners fund is characterized by decreasing management fee percentages, infrequent portfolio trading to keep realized capital gains and shareholder taxes low, and an active ban on short-term speculators who can drain assets needed for investing. What's more, the fund also outperformed over 96 percent of all funds over the 1990s.

This behavior contrasts with *hedge funds* that provide extreme examples of investing the ranch. General partners normally must invest most of their personal net worth as protection and commitment to the limited partners. Why? Because, while limited partners invest large sums, they receive only cursory investment and performance information, such as "Up 20 percent this year."

Hedge funds also normally have substantial leeway and flexibility with respect to investment strategies, which often include leverage (borrowing), *derivatives*, short selling, and concentrated portfolios. This may explain why hedge fund investors tend to be relatively sophisticated. Lack of *performance and portfolio transparency* supposedly acts to keeps proprietary models secret. But what it does do is avoid the need to explain what they are doing, why they are doing it, and how well they are doing it. Hedge fund investors are confirmed believers.

Ackermann et al. (1999) analyzed 906 hedge funds and observed that they outperform mutual funds, but with more risk and also higher risk-adjusted returns. However, they are unable to consistently outperform benchmark indices. Overall, hedge funds outperform on a gross returns basis, but generally not so on a net returns basis after payment of incentive payments and administrative costs.

Mutual funds as communicators

If mutual fund investment advisors invest in their own funds, they may be more likely to treat shareholders as owners, such as by having annual shareholder meetings. The general lack of shareholder meetings and other direct communication between mutual fund shareholders and portfolio managers appears wrongheaded. Lallos (1998) stated that shareholder meetings are important if for no other reason than they signal shareholders are owners.

Shareholder meetings are generally collegial and informative and are not automatically scary for fund managers. They provide shareholders with an opportunity to size up portfolio managers, but also to obtain more detail on fund strategies and results. Shareholders are also provided the opportunity to ask questions, which adds to improved mutual understanding.

The real down side of mutual fund shareholder meetings is that there are so few. Zweig (1998b) and Lallos (1998) looked for funds that have shareholder meetings and observed only eight shareholder-friendly investment advisors: (1) Longleaf (again), (2) Acorn, (3) Aquila, (4) Baron, (5) Benham, (6) FAM, (7) Templeton, and (8) Heartland. Further, Zweig identified just nine fund families that "have shown they care deeply about their investors." These select funds led by Longleaf (again) also include (1) Clipper (again), (2) Ariel, (3) CGM, (4) FPA, (5) Nicholas, (6) Numeric Investors, (7) Oakmark, and (8) Torray. It is quite shocking to find so few fund families following the model set by corporate America.

Some few shareholder meetings – and this may be a bit optimistic – actually generate feelings of camaraderie and shared values. This all works to dispel what Purcell (1994a) called the "nameless dread" – that secret information is somehow guiding fund decisions and individual investors do not have access to it. In general, mutual funds should find no significant down side but actually more up side to having shareholder meetings. The funds that do have shareholder meetings appear to be among the more respected and better performers. Maybe this is why they do not have the nameless dread about holding shareholder meetings.

In addition to the general lack of shareholder meetings, too few fund families provide investors with prospectuses and financial reports that are informative, educational, and perhaps even enjoyable to read. In fact, there appears to be a positive correlation between quality of shareholder communication, including shareholder meetings, and long-term fund performance, as well as fewer investor mistakes.

Consistent with this view, Rekenthaler (1996a) stated: "The fact is, companies offering low-cost funds, high-quality shareholder reports, and responsively timed fund promotions put out consistently good products." The reason this is true is that high costs and fad funds decrease fund returns, which leaves managers of poor funds "in no position to offer honest, insightful communications." For managers of poor funds to do otherwise is to reveal just how expensive and badly managed they are.

This potential decision rule for selecting funds was confirmed by Purcell (1993). There is a notable positive correlation between grades assigned equity fund reports by Morningstar, the fund research company, and average returns. If nothing else, the quality of shareholder communication projects the degree of confidence fund advisors have that their funds provide for investor needs.

Shareholder communication: an example

The Oakmark Fund semi-annual report (1998) provides a good example of excellent shareholder communication. Portfolio manager Robert Sanborn, subsequently fired for poor performance in a time of large-cap. fund outperformance, discusses fund performance relative to the market, reviews market performance, and describes and explains substantial portfolio changes, all of which is done with a light touch. His firing was premature and reflected less than solid belief in value investing.

The Oakmark semi-annual report goes the extra mile and details the kinds of investors who should invest in the fund. This is most unusual beyond the typical boilerplate statements. Current and potential Oakmark investors are told they should: (1) review the portfolio's risk/return attributes; (2) be prepared to invest for at least five years (Sanborn's firing evidenced impatience of investors and/or the investment advisor); (3) be able to absorb a 30 percent portfolio decline without changing lifestyle; (4) know that Oakmark portfolio managers and investment advisors invest heavily in the fund; and (5) Oakmark portfolio managers are compensated based only on long-term performance. Unfortunately, the investment management firm and fund shareholders did not follow the investor profile established for the fund. Further, the report reminds critics of particular portfolio holdings that, by the time company problem holdings become public, they have already been factored into portfolio decisions.

Shareholder reports

In an effort to set standards for mutual fund shareholder reports, Sanders (1996b) set four criteria. Shareholder reports should (1) explain performance, (2) set reasonable shareholder expectations, (3) educate investors, and (4) even entertain them. The Oakmark Fund report certainly meets these criteria. The Vanguard family of funds is cited for providing candid discussions of performance, relevant informational topics for investors, and clarity of writing style. The Third Avenue Value fund is also complimented for providing shareholders with non-required quarterly reports in addition to required reports. The reports are lengthy (ten to twelve pages) and are written with humor and candor. The Clipper Fund is applauded for its use of analogy to relate investment topics to the real world, and the Parnassus Fund for candidly explaining the poor performance of several large holdings, not easy to do well.

The prospectus and statement of additional information have traditionally been too lengthy and filled with legal jargon designed to protect funds but not inform investors. They are also too focused on general risk contingencies, rather than detailing real potential and actual specific risks. They do provide more specific coverage of investment objectives, investment style, strategies, limitations, and prohibitions. These documents are generally considered to be less than user-friendly.

The SEC has also worked to improve mutual fund disclosure, especially with pre-testing and final approval of the optional *profile*, a formatted summary prospectus. Investors requesting profiles before making transactions also receive the prospectus with purchase confirmations. They may also request the more detailed statement of additional information, which includes really "good stuff," sometimes in small print.

The SEC's profile was guided by the goal of a document that is (1) concise and written in plain English, (2) more focused on actual risk disclosure, and (3) presented in a simpler and standardized summary format. The ICI (1996b) surveyed investors. Sixty-six percent favored receiving only the profile or the profile plus the option of receiving the prospectus. Another 23 percent preferred receiving both documents automatically. Overall, 70 percent of investors surveyed believed profiles include the "right amount of information," and 79 percent perceived them as at least equal to the prospectus.

The standardized profile provides the following specific mutual fund information: (1) investment objectives, (2) principal investment strategies, (3) principal risks, (4) fees and expenses, (5) investment advisor and portfolio manager, (6) purchase of shares, (7) sale of shares, (8) shareholder distributions and tax information, and (9) other services provided. Fund risk is discussed in plain English and is accompanied by a graph of ten-year annual returns compared with at least one broadly based benchmark index. Tables include fund average annual returns for one, five, and ten years compared with a market index, as well as best and worst quarterly performance for the prior ten years.

The development of the profile, however, does not substitute for well written prospectuses and statements of additional information. Only these documents can properly discuss mutual funds risks in adequate detail. The SEC has improved the prospectus, which must be written in plain English, with legal boilerplate disclosure moved to the statement of additional information. But the continued lack of adequate risk disclosure cannot be overstated.

The Vanguard Group was among the first mutual fund families to provide an easy-to-read prospectus with relevant investor topics. For example, the US Growth prospectus (1997) included plain-talk commentaries on several specific issues: (1) shareholder transaction costs, (2) expenses, (3) financial highlights, (4) investment style, (5) fund trading costs, (6) portfolio market capitalization, (7) portfolio turnover, (8) use of derivative securities, (9) past performance, (10) shareholder distributions, (11) tax considerations in purchasing shares, (12) Vanguard's corporate structure, and (13) information on portfolio managers. Warning flags also mark discussions of market risk, investment objective risk, and risks of derivative securities. Nonetheless, more specific discussion of investment policies, practices, potential risk implications, and performance are needed.

Communication of fund returns

Investors should also be aware that it is most unlikely that they actually earned the annual or annualized returns reported by mutual funds. Investors do not invest annually on a per-share basis, stated most simply as buying one share on January 1, reinvesting any interest/dividends in additional shares, and selling all shares on December 31, without tax consequences. These *time-weighted returns* and issues underlying AIMR's performance measurement standards are discussed in Jacob (1998). While time-weighted returns are appropriate for reporting returns to investors in general and over particular time periods, individual investors would be better served by *dollar-weighted returns*. Arnott (1999) identified only one fund, American Century, as providing this information. Most funds claim it is too difficult or expensive to provide.

To compute dollar-weighted returns, it is necessary to know the dollar value (outflow) of the investment at the beginning of the measurement period, the timing and amounts of cash inflows/outflows during the period, and the value (inflow) of the investment at the end of the period. Dollar-weighted returns are akin to weighted averages. In essence, they adjust time-weighted returns to reflect the returns earned on the varying amounts actually invested at the beginning, during, and end of the period.

For shareholders, a correct question about mutual fund performance is whether they earned the same or better returns on their later much larger dollar fund holdings as they did on their early small dollar holdings. Dollar-weighted returns are also necessary for fund managers to determine whether performance has declined as total assets increased. Do funds earn the same or better returns when assets are large as they did when assets were small (chapter 10)? The answer to this question normally makes it clear why funds do not want to provide the information. Fund managers are paid based on asset size, so it really is not in their interest to close funds to new investors. This explains why some funds become grossly too large for effective portfolio management.

Even when mutual fund managers close funds to new investors, the door is usually not really closed. Current shareholders are usually allowed to add to their accounts. And, similarly, owners of retirement and pension accounts may continue investing. The only way to close funds effectively is to do so before they actually should be closed so current shareholders may continue to invest without harm to their returns.

This may not be easy for mutual funds to implement, however. What often happens to funds is that at the peak of their performance they receive an avalanche of cash from investors chasing hot funds. Subsequently, fund dollar-weighted returns normally decline relative to time-weighted returns. This explains why investors who follow the herd chasing performance often invest just as fund assets increase sharply and subsequent returns decrease. This also explains why the industry is not anxious to provide actual dollar-weighted returns.

To determine the significance of differences between time-weighted and dollar-weighted returns, Lucas (1993) examined ten funds with large differences in cumulative five-year time-weighted returns (higher) and dollar-weighted returns (lower). The differences approximate the foregone returns from chasing performance. Funds with the largest performance differences are characterized by high asset growth (not surprising) and more aggressive (growth) portfolio management (again, not surprising). The differences in five-year total cumulative returns are huge. On average, there is more than a 100 percentage point difference between time-weighted returns (ranging from approximately 118 percent to 165 percent) and much lower dollar-weighted returns (approximately 11 percent to 38 percent)!

Sanders (1997c) examined mutual fund performance over a five-year period to determine how much investor returns were diminished by chasing hot funds, rather than *dollar-cost averaging* – consistently investing a fixed amount of money at set intervals. The returns from dollar-cost averaging are larger than dollar-weighted returns for all types of funds. The funds with the largest differences in returns invest in smaller, growth-oriented companies. Sanders (1997c) also provided a calculator for investors to compute their real returns.

Risk disclosure

Shareholder disclosure should cover the range of risks (chapter 7) to particular funds, as well as their implications under various scenarios. This disclosure is essential because, as stated by

Gillis (1994), "no one risk measure can possibly account for all the risks a fund assumes, [and] any single measure will fail to accurately reflect the risks." This disclosure should include the use of derivative securities for other than hedging portfolio risk as well as securities with limited or no marketability, illiquid private placements, and less liquid emerging markets securities. In addition, comparable disclosure should be provided for fund peer groups and appropriate benchmark indices. It is not enough to say investors could not understand these measures (the investors-are-bozos excuse); they can be provided in understandable ways. The real problem is that investors may understand the risks all too well.

Fund advertising

Quality communication benefits both mutual funds and shareholders. Unfortunately, much fund advertising fails in this regard. Fund advertisements have included incorrect statements and/or misleading messages. For example, advertisements have touted new portfolio managers based on performance data generated by previous managers. Most commonly, advertisements headline fund returns, often short term, without mention of risk (not any). Advertisements frequently state funds rank number one in this, that, or the other comparison and period of time. By slicing fund return and holding period data in enough different ways, funds can often advertise as first in something, sometime. Zweig (2000) even picked out misleading fund advertising in the mountain charts of cumulative dollar returns. The scale was manipulated to make cumulative growth appear more rapid than it actually was.

Phillips (1993b) reported a classic example of mutual fund advertising so misleading it is hard to believe it happened, and, more so, how it happened and no regulatory sanctions followed. Five funds were ranked as performing one through five. These were not the top five performing mutual funds. The small print indicated the rankings were independently derived from performance in separate fund categories. But these categories were artificially narrowed to provide the rankings. Moreover, the first three funds actually represent different load structures for the same portfolio.

Another classic case of misleading mutual fund advertising received Zweig's (1996b) "worst advertising blurb award." The fund, an international portfolio, claimed international markets outperformed domestic markets in each of the last twenty years. This was simply not true. As is usually the case, at least one specific international market did outperform the domestic market each year, but not all international markets.

Zweig (1996c) also discussed factors that can make mutual fund advertisements misleading, even though not normally so on purpose. These include sensitivity of computed annualized returns to measurement periods and inconsistency of actual investor holding periods with those assumed in computing fund annual and annualized returns. Investors should be alert to how abruptly advertised multi-year annualized returns increase when earlier bad year returns are replaced with later good year returns. Lucas (1992b) examined the returns of ten funds that gained the most when October 1987's disastrous returns dropped from the computation of five-year annualized returns. The annualized gains ranged from some ten to fifteen percentage points!

Regnier (1997) examined the effects of replacing October 1987 in ten-year annualized mutual fund returns. The types of funds that most frequently improved risk/return performance are the more volatile small growth, mid-cap. growth, and small blend funds. Those fund types that least frequently improved risk/return performance include the more conservative large value, large blend, and mid-cap. value funds. The investor message is that it is important to check the volatility of fund annual returns before focusing on their five-year or ten-year annualized returns.

As discussed, mutual fund advertising has often been characterized by misleading messages hyping short-term performance to the total exclusion of risk. The irony in bad fund advertising is its implicit failure to recognize that funds themselves benefit from shareholder loyalty. This loyalty ultimately reflects the honesty, trust, openness, vision, and competence conveyed by fund communication, or lack thereof.

In more recent years, fund advertising has shown some selective improvements. Only a few funds cite long-term returns *plus* risk measures and mention of investment objectives and approaches. A very few funds even discuss the types of investors for which the funds are appropriate, and without *any* performance data(!). Effective communication not only educates shareholders, but attracts more patient shareholders. Patient shareholders may favor effective communication, with a long-term focus that minimizes unpleasant portfolio and market surprises along the way.

Effective shareholder communication

Both mutual funds and shareholders benefit from stable asset bases facilitated by effective communication and investor patience. Stable assets reflect control over large redemptions, especially by practitioners of market timing. This stability makes it much easier to practise effective and profitable portfolio management. This is especially so for funds following long-term, low portfolio turnover strategies in search of undervalued securities.

Portfolio turnover is measured by the turnover ratio, which is computed by dividing the smaller of its annual purchases/sales of securities (excluding cash) by average monthly net assets. Large redemptions may require the sale of securities to raise cash, often at inopportune times, which also involves trading costs and lost future returns. Redemptions may also generate untimely realized capital gains and taxable distributions for shareholders. Tax liabilities may occur even if funds' portfolios have losses for the year. Thus funds with effective shareholder communication may be more likely to generate additional long-term returns for their more informed investors.

Effective mutual fund communication also contributes to reducing the convenient Wall Street myth that individual investors are bozos. As stated by Phillips (1996): Clearly, the myth of the dumb individual investor serves Wall Street often and well. It is very convenient to blame every missold fund product on investor demand. Uninformed is not the same as dumb, though. Some of the contributions to this myth may be sour grapes by pension managers who lost 401(k) pension accounts to individual IRA rollover accounts. Individual investors do indeed make many mistakes, but many derive from poor shareholder communication, such as lack of risk disclosure.

And, while on the topic, Wall Street clearly makes its share of mistakes, as well. Moreover, technical market indicators that assume individual investors are wrong when most optimistic or pessimistic appear to demonstrate only chance results. Although all investors have less than complete access to information, this limitation is reduced by effective shareholder communication and continuing improvements in the quality and content of online sources of information and analysis. This is not to attribute quality to the vast amount of online noise that passes for information in some quarters.

Rekenthaler (1993a) examined Wall Street's contention that mutual fund investors panic and sell when the market declines. There is also the claim that inexperienced fund portfolio managers will likewise panic. The first claim is not correct. In fact: "One may even argue that, of the two groups, retail buyers are the wiser. In the fund industry, they've often shown more fortitude than have the professionals." This conclusion is supported by Rea and Marcis's (1996) analysis of stock fund shareholder behavior over the provious fifty years. Shareholders do not liquidate shares *en masse* in any one of the market declines. They are sensitive to stock price movements, but the response tends to be spread over time. Stock fund shareholders are sensitive to long-run trends in stock returns, with fund cash net inflows positive when returns are high and vice versa when returns are low. Thus "stock fund shareholders generally are experienced investors, have long-term investment objectives and horizons, and have a basic understanding of investment risk."

On the other hand, portfolio managers often suffer from quarterly performance anxiety and its implications for employment and end-of-year bonuses. Rekenthaler (1996b) reported a fund manager who admitted "that the previous year was a 'battle' between small investors who are looking ahead with long-term goals in mind and are pouring unprecedented amounts of money into mutual funds, and professional investors who are currently overwhelmed by short-term anxieties." It appears short-term market volatility may reside more on Wall Street than on Main Street. The second claim about average portfolio manager experience is incorrect. As discussed above, the average portfolio manager is forty-three years old, with over ten years' experience in the investment business.

Advisors and subadvisors

Most mutual fund portfolios are managed by in-house portfolio managers with single *lead portfolio managers*. While most funds have single portfolio managers or teams of managers, other funds use subadvisors to manage all or part of their portfolios. This occurs when fund investment advisors subcontract some or all of their roles as portfolio managers to outside firms/persons. Some investment advisors even act as subadvisors to other funds.

Lucas (1992c) determined that subadvisors manage approximately 10 percent of growth-oriented fund portfolios and 30 percent of international fund portfolios. The relationships take several forms. In one form, subadvisors have complete responsibility for portfolio management. This is a very straightforward approach, but it requires close oversight of performance and consistency with investment objectives, policies, and limitations. In a second form, investment advisors provide lead portfolio managers who supervise the portfolios, but also manage some portion of them. They also provide oversight of the one or more subadvisors engaged in managing the remaining portions of portfolios. Vanguard separates portfolio management from fund management in its mutual organizational structure and calls subadvisors portfolio managers or multimanagers. In a third form, investment advisors provide active portfolio guidance, but not actual portfolio management, to one or more subadvisors for all or specific portfolio portions. The use of subadvisors may even be an organizational illusion where distinct management companies and investment advisors have common ownership.

As noted by Rothschild (1994), a few mutual fund portfolios also employ *multimanagers* for their portfolios. These funds diversify portfolio management by investment style, using portfolio managers known for each style. This approach assumes that, at any given point in time, not all styles will be performing equally. In some arrangements, investment advisors periodically rebalance subadvisor portfolio portions back to original allocations. In others, Vanguard being one, assets are periodically moved from poor performing to better performing multimanagers, or one or more is fired and replaced with new ones. If portfolio assets and subadvisors are moved frequently, the resulting portfolio strategy becomes in effect one of timing subadvisor performance.

Proponents of subadvisors argue this arrangement allows investment advisors to hire the best available managers, not just the best in-house talent. Subadvisor fees also tend to be lower than in-house advisory fees. This benefit could very well result from the arm's-length negotiation of fees with subadvisors, which is obviously not present when funds are managed in house. It is also much easier for fund managers to fire subadvisors than in-house portfolio managers.

Lucas (1992c) confirmed this by comparing the average tenure of in-house portfolio managers and subadvisors. The average tenure was 3.9 years for subadvisors and 5.3 years for in-house portfolio managers. In neither case was tenure long enough to enable sound statistical statements to be made about the relative skill of subadvisors and in-house portfolio managers. The general assumption is that subadvisors have not generated higher than average returns, but this is not necessarily bad.

However, both Lucas (1992c) and Rothschild (1994) observed that subadvisors have performance problems. Equity funds managed by subadvisors have both lower average risk/return performance and higher average expenses. One reason for the higher expenses could be fee redundancy. Total management fees could be larger when related in-house expenses and subadvisor fees are totaled. This redundancy could exceed the advantage noted above that subadvisory fees are lower than in-house advisory fees. But this comparison includes only direct costs.

Use of subadvisors can also provide unknown uncertainties to shareholders secure in the management styles of brand name mutual funds and fund families. They may be caught unawares if subadvisors are engaged. This may happen when investment advisors lack in-house talent to manage new fund portfolios, say, international funds. On the other hand, it has been argued that investment advisors should not subject shareholders to these uncertainties. That is, fund families should not organize funds outside their basic competencies. In any case, shareholders may not be aware of these issues within particular fund families.

Investors should therefore determine whether mutual fund portfolios are managed in house or by subadvisors. Hopefully, fund communication goes beyond what is required to make this clear. If subadvisors are used, shareholders need to determine whether they provide performance and expense advantages in meeting their investment needs. Do subadvisors have track records with particular funds or do fund managers make their record managing funds available? Are the qualifications for the selection and continued use of subadvisors made clear and enforced if performance falters?

Stars and multiple managers

Mutual funds provide professional management – this is one of the major service advantages offered by funds. Yet some funds go to great lengths to obfuscate who calls the shots in portfolio decisions. This results in less shareholder disclosure, akin to historical industry practice. Such efforts, however misguided, are misleading. For example, Sanders (1996a) indicated two instances when fund performance faltered after the founders/portfolio managers sold their advisory firms and retired. This also happens very frequently with the short tenure of portfolio managers. They move around like baseball players, some owning the teams. Therefore, it is very common for fund managers to downplay changes in portfolio managers.

The SEC has facilitated this trend towards less portfolio manager disclosure. This may have followed because of growing expenses and risks to fund assets resulting from the star portfolio manager phenomenon. The media stimulated the creation of stars to sell magazines and advertising, but investment advisors were quick to join in and merchandise their stars to attract more assets to manage. For example, Norton's (1998) article in *Barron's* asked readers whether their portfolio chiefs made it into the "top 100". Among the more well known stars of past years are Peter Lynch of Fidelity Magellan fame, John Neff of Windsor Fund fame, John Templeton of international investing fame, and Michael Price and his brand of value investing fame, among others.

The marketing and promotion of star portfolio managers reversed traditional limited disclosure and made star power a competitive tool. And it has worked, as stars are proven magnets for investor dollars. Henderson and Ward (2000) carried star gazing with career summaries to the next level in *Barron's* "The All-century Team."

Nonetheless, the star system has created a major down side for investment advisors and mutual fund shareholders. The competition for stars became fierce and greatly escalated their compensation and opportunities. Portfolio managers have been lured away by huge compensation packages and/or opportunities to create their own investment advisory firms and mutual funds. This mobility is evident in the short average tenure of portfolio managers. The financial implications to fund managers of this mobility have become immense, with bonanzas to stars and increasing cost burdens to fund advisors and shareholders.

There are other factors that have contributed to the diminishing appeal of the star system. As noted, most important, star performance is often fleeting. The short half-life of star performance may be explained by chance results (discussed below) and/or perhaps by idiosyncratic investment styles that worked well in particular market scenarios. This performance problem has been caught up in the media attention to the general failure of funds to outperform passively managed index funds.

Investment advisors have also lessened star power by giving stars less free reign in managing portfolios. Fidelity Investments is such as example. Index funds are the most extreme example of constrained portfolio manager behavior: portfolio management in the usual sense is eliminated. Other constraints include the growing use of rigid asset allocation and particular investment styles.

In sum, investment advisors have increasingly concluded the the financial payoff from stars is less than the cost, when the chance they will leave is factored in. By cost, advisors include the loss of fund assets and advisory fees when stars become mere mortals or when they leave for more lucrative positions. This threat has motivated investment advisors to focus on ensuring the stability of fund assets. Advertising now appears to reflect this theme.

The SEC also joined in the effort to downplay the star system. Mutual funds must disclose portfolio managers in the prospectus or annual reports, but the SEC gave funds a convenient out for disclosure. It is now common for funds to list *multiple managers* – two or more portfolio managers who supposedly share portfolio management. And in many cases the names of analysts were added and backdated to give an appearances of longer-term shared responsibility. Thankfully, such revision of history is now prohibited.

As early as 1994, Rekenthaler (1994b) observed that over 30 percent of funds listed multiple managers, and the number has increased. That this change actually represents a change in the decision process is most unlikely, except by those few funds that have historically used management teams. At the other extreme, other funds have diffused star power by listing all persons who have some related portfolio responsibility. The result has been the addition of security analysts and portfolio assistants to lists of fund portfolio managers. Again, a real change in the decision process is not likely.

But mutual fund advisors have also taken the effort towards portfolio manager anonymity to its logical conclusion. Numerous funds have replaced the names of portfolio managers with the less informative *management team*. This is legally permitted if committees make all portfolio decisions and no one person calls the shots. These must be very unusual decision-making sessions with no lead portfolio manager.

After star portfolio managers leave mutual funds, it is not unusual for shareholders to discover portfolios were solely managed not by them, but also by others now named. For example, Rekenthaler (1992c) reported a particular fund's efforts to calm shareholders after a big star retired. Shareholders were told not to worry because the star had not actually managed the largest fund for a number of years, and the actual (backdated?) manager was still in charge. If so, what was the justification for previously promoting the star as manager of the fund, no less the others? Even worse, Penn (1994) reported cases where shareholders invested with particular portfolio managers only to find out much later the stars (along with Elvis) "have left the building."

Previously discussed Michael Price's departure provided another example of what happens when stars retire from portfolio management. Since the 1980s, Price earned a star reputation and was prominently featured as such in the media and fund advertisements. Initially, his retirement from the Franklin Mutual Series funds had a less revisionist history surrounding his role.

When Price sold his advisory firm to Franklin Resources in 1997, the newly labeled Franklin Mutual Series advertisements featured Price *and* his team. The message conveyed was that Price was still the leader, but he now shared the responsibility. And, most importantly for Franklin, the team was presented as experienced and capable of continuing Price's record of performance. Later, Cullen (1998b) reported Franklin stating officially that Price, now Franklin CEO, was still actively engaged in managing the portfolios of his former funds. But this appeared to be revisionist history when one of Price's former team members, now a portfolio manager, remarked off the cuff that Price was not calling the shots and had not done so in recent years.

As discussed, mutual fund investment advisors have hyped star portfolio managers to increase the assets under management. But it is not just the names of star portfolio managers that are used. Some investment advisors leverage their use of stars by actively engaging them in sales pitches to potential major accounts. They also make wide use of their reputations by assigning them other portfolios to manage, including mutual funds, variable annuity accounts, 401(k) retirement accounts and private accounts. Thus even when used, investment advisors have diffused star managerial focus, which may not be in the interests of investors who bought funds to get these portfolio managers.

Portfolio manager duties: an example

Edgerton (1998a) reported the activities of the now late David Alger of the Alger funds to illustrate the duties performed by star portfolio managers. Alger frankly noted that he ran five mutual funds, but he also managed four variable annuity accounts, four retirement plan portfolios, and seventy individual and pension fund accounts. These eighty-four accounts had total assets of $8.2 billion. Alger estimated he spent 35 percent of his time on marketing, 15 percent on administration, and 50 percent selecting stocks, along with his portfolio managers.

Alger's forthcoming comments reflect the increasing pressure, sometimes self-imposed, for stars to manage larger numbers of diverse types of accounts, plus client marketing. However, it is difficult for investors to assess the totality of portfolio manager activities. The SEC does not require funds to disclose 401(k) and private accounts managed, and most fund families are not anxious to disclose this information. Yet such disclosure is material to shareholder assessment of portfolio managers. It appears focused fund portfolio managers may be a bit more likely than those with diffused responsibility to generate additional shareholder returns.

Mutual fund performance obviously depends on the quality of portfolio management and, for this reason, investors need improved disclosure (chapter 4) about those responsible for performance, including names, education, previous investment experience, tenure, and performance as portfolio managers, investment philosophy and style, personal investment in their funds, and other duties. Shareholders also need information to judge whether portfolio manager compensation incentives are consistent with fund objectives and policies. Further, they need effective communication from portfolio managers through commentaries, interviews, and shareholder reports and meetings.

In sum, do investors have a greater likelihood of selecting funds that will generate additional returns if they are able to evaluate portfolio managers – those responsible for performance? The management literature tells us the answer is yes. Rekenthaler (1994b) concluded that specific portfolio manager disclosure is needed to give investors improved understanding of the investment process. In the meantime, investors should pay close attention to funds with recently named management teams or lists of multiple portfolio managers. Both improved regulatory disclosure and investor pressure from avoiding less than forthcoming funds are needed to correct this problem.

Determination of which particular portfolio managers actually manage mutual funds may not be enough, however. There are often obstacles to gaining this access. Access may be limited by large minimum purchases, such as the $1 million for Gary Brinson's Global Equity fund. Other funds limit access with large load fees or by closing funds to new investors (a good thing generally).

In the face of such obstacles, DiTeresa (1999a) suggested several secret ways to gain access to favored portfolio managers. First, do managers run related mutual funds with easier access? Second, do the managers run alternative types of investments, such as closed-end funds or *variable annuities*? Third, do their funds have smaller minimums for IRA accounts? Most funds do. Fourth, do the funds accept smaller minimum purchases as part of a commitment to automatic investment plans, or as down-payments on larger agreed purchases within a stated time frame? Fifth, are the funds also sold through discount brokers or fund supermarkets that often have lower minimum purchase requirements? Curtis (1998) provided a list of institutional stock funds with no loads and low or no minimum required investments, available from specific discount brokers and supermarkets. Some well known portfolio managers are available. And, sixth, have investors made the case as personable long-term investors with sales representatives or supervisors?

Effective mutual fund disclosure also needs to go beyond portfolio managers. Successful managers, like successful baseball teams, need strong benches. It is a rare manager who can go it alone. To this end, Barbee (1997c) defined the prerequisites for successful portfolio managers: (1) necessary technology and staff, including (2) talented securities analysts; (3) congruence of investment philosophies and approaches between investment advisors and portfolio managers; (4) compensation plans consistent with fund investment objectives and policies; and, finally, (5) effective shareholder communication that promotes investor patience and understanding.

Annual report: an example

Tweedy Browne's annual report (1998a) is an example of effective essential disclosure. This minitext is an excellent and thorough example of effective shareholder communication. The Tweedy Browne propectus (1998b) also provides effective shareholder communication. The annual report includes thoughtful, thorough, and even humorous discussions of: (1) fund performance, both absolute and benchmarked; (2) fund financial characteristics; (3) stock market performance, both current and long-term; (4) advisor philosophy and approach to long-term value investing; (5) what portfolio managers can and cannot do effectively (what works and doesn't work); (6) and news of the management team. Tweedy Browne's, people, philosophy, and team-oriented approach to strict value investing is reviewed by Arnott (1995) and Sanders (1997a).

Nonetheless, improved mutual fund disclosure is called for in general, if only to be comparable with what public corporations must disclose. Fosback (1998b) indicated that this dichotomy is unacceptable. Funds should be required to disclose: (1) how much directors and key fund officials are paid; (2) how much portfolio managers have invested and whether it is increasing/decreasing; and (3) post-portfolio holdings monthly, with a maximum thirty days' lag.

PORTFOLIO MANAGER BACKGROUND

Three benchmarks for evaluating mutual fund portfolio manager backgrounds are education, previous investment experience, and current tenure (table 13). The relative importance of each element depends on the particular circumstances. For portfolio managers with long-term track records, education and previous investment experience are less important. For example, education and previous investment experience must count more for Fidelity's less experienced sector fund managers. These funds are testing grounds for future managers of larger, more broadly based funds.

Each person with portfolio management responsibility should be evaluated. Traditionally, this involved individual portfolio managers. Today, however, mutual funds often disclose only a management team or list multiple managers. In the former case, reference to published interviews (if any) may be necessary to identify actual portfolio managers, although the proper move may be to investor-friendly funds. In the latter case, reference to any published interviews may be necessary to identify which portfolio manager(s) actually call the shots. Again, the proper move may be to friendlier funds. Investors should not have to play Sherlock Holmes to know the identity of the real portfolio managers. The SEC should prohibit this lack of disclosure, which is not practised in corporate America outside mutual funds.

In cases where mutual funds employ one or more subadvisors, the weight of the analysis should focus on the lead portfolio manager. In the case of Vanguard funds, the term *multi-advisors* rather than subadvisors is used, owing to their mutual form of organization. In any other fund family they would be called subadvisors, with a Vanguard lead portfolio manager. If portfolio managers are not explicitly identified, or their portfolio responsibilities are unclear, again, the inclination is to look elsewhere.

Table 13 provides a checklist to determine whether the backgrounds of particular (or lead) portfolio managers are *overall* excellent, acceptable, or unacceptable. Previous management experience is moved up a notch for members of successful investment management families. Vanguard Windsor II is used to illustrate the analysis of funds. The discussion here focuses on portfolio manager background, not performance.

Educational background

Education is the first element in evaluating portfolio manager backgrounds. As discussed previously, the model preparation is an MBA degree, especially from a competitive program, and CFA charter. This is especially true for younger, less experienced portfolio managers. However, for portfolio managers with ten years' or more investment experience/current tenure, education counts for less. The same is true for star portfolio managers with deserved reputations.

Thus, in judging younger portfolio managers, the model MBA plus CFA charter is excellent, MBA *or* CFA charter is acceptable, and anything less is unacceptable. An undergraduate degree is acceptable for portfolio managers with ten or more years' investment experience. For example, Michael J. Walsh, co-manager of Oakmark International Fund, has a master's degree in finance and a CFA charter. He also has a CPA for good measure. His educational background is a model for younger portfolio managers.

As discussed in Vanguard Windsor II's prospectus (1999), James P. Barrow, the very experienced lead portfolio manager, holds a bachelor's degree, which is typical of longer-term portfolio managers. He is a principal in Barrow Hanley Mewhinney & Strauss, and responsible for managing approximately 68 percent of Windsor II's portfolio. Three other persons in two other advisory firms also manage portions of the portfolio. George P. Sauter, Vanguard managing director and index guru, is responsible for Vanguard's core investment in the fund. The latter four portfolio managers hold MBAs from programs with strong ties to Wall Street. Overall, the five Windsor II portfolio managers have excellent education, and more so in light of their long experience.

Previous investment experience

Previous investment experience is the second element in assessing portfolio manager backgrounds. It represents experience prior to current tenure as portfolio manager. This assessment includes both the nature and length of this experience and requires more judgment because there is no single model for experience. Previous experience is especially important for portfolio managers with short current tenure. For example, Purcell (1995) noted that Morningstar, the fund research firm, provides the public record and investment style of rookie portfolio managers.

However, the nature and quality of previous investment experience may act to place less emphasis on length of experience. The best example of previous experience is long-term successful portfolio management experience. Conversely, previous investment experience is less relevant for portfolio managers with long current tenure. In general, less than five years' previous investment experience is unacceptable, five to ten years' experience is acceptable, and ten years or more of experience is excellent. As suggested, these guidelines may be modified based on particular portfolio manager experience.

An example of excellent previous investment experience is provided by Vanguard Windsor II's prospectus (1999). Vanguard Windsor II's portfolio managers have long and relevant previous investment experience. Barrow was a bank portfolio manager for eight years prior to joining his investment advisory company. He has been in the investment management business for some thirty-five years, thirty as a portfolio manager. He has been Windsor II's lead manager for some fifteen of those thirty years. This explains why educational background is less important in his case. The other four portfolio managers average over twenty years' previous investment experience, ranging from some fifteen to thirty years in individual cases. Without question, Windsor II's portfolio managers have excellent previous investment experience.

Current tenure as portfolio manager

Current tenure as portfolio manager is the third element in evaluating portfolio manager background. As in chapter 2, tenure is rarely long enough to state with statistical confidence that performance is due to skill, rather than chance. Therefore, whether portfolio manager current tenure is excellent, acceptable, or unacceptable remains a judgment call. For example, it might be argued that having survived ten years as a portfolio manager is *prima facie* evidence of adequate performance. However, this should not be used as general evidence of adequate performance because more competent portfolio managers are more likely to have changed positions in less than ten years.

At minimum, portfolio managers should have experienced at least one complete market cycle. Historically this was a reasonable requirement, because portfolio managers had longer average tenure, and the market averaged a loss every one of three years or so. But the market has not acted in its historical pattern since 1982. Further, portfolio managers now average less than five years' current tenure. Thus the October 1987 market crash is a historical footnote to most portfolio managers.

Determining how long is long enough to judge portfolio manager performance is therefore statistically even more problematic than it used to be. As a rough guide, less than five years' current tenure is unacceptable, five to ten years' tenure is acceptable, and ten or more years' is excellent. As seen in Vanguard Windsor II's prospectus (1999), the average current tenure of its several portfolio managers is excellent. Barrow, the lead portfolio manager, has over fifteen years' current tenure; a second portfolio manager has over ten years' current tenure, and the other three average nearly ten years each.

Overall evaluation

As identified in table 13, Windsor II's portfolio managers are excellent with respect to education, previous investment experience, and current tenure as portfolio managers. Thus Windsor II's overall manager background is also excellent. This finding is summarized in table 27. In general, only excellence in this criterion justifies continuing analysis of particular mutual funds. However, exceptions may be made with validated information justifying the continuing analysis of funds with acceptable educational background ratings.

CHAPTER FOUR

MUTUAL FUND SERVICE DISADVANTAGES

> There's no doubt that mutual funds have treated their shareholders very well. Nevertheless, they have treated their owners even better.
>
> (*John Rekenthaler, in* **Morningstar Mutual Funds**, *May 28, 1993*)
>
> Money management is the most profitable business in the United States.
>
> (*Arthur Zeikel, Merrill Lynch Asset Management, in* **Money**, *February 1997*)
>
> A low expense ratio is the single most important reason why a fund does well.
>
> (*John C. Bogle, Vanguard Group, in* **Common Sense on Mutual Funds**, *1999*)

This chapter reverses the theme in chapters 2 and 3 concerning mutual fund service advantages. The key issue here is not whether mutual funds generally offer service disadvantage – they do – but whether particular funds offer them as minimum disadvantages in meeting the needs of particular investors. That is, do the specific service disadvantages of particular funds translate to at least minimum specific service disadvantages for particular investors?

The goals of chapters 4 and 5 are twofold. The first goal is to identify and discuss the service disadvantages provided by mutual funds generally. Mutual funds generally provide several major service disadvantages: (1) types of assets, (2) trading costs, (3) shareholder tax planning, (4) regulatory issues, and (5) fund expenses (chapter 5). These disadvantages are covered in detail.

The second goal is to provide guidelines that facilitate determination of whether particular fund services are minimum actual disadvantages to particular investors. This determination of fund performance across these and various other dimensions is a theme throughout the book. Vanguard Windsor II is again used to illustrate these services. Specific guidelines are illustrated for each service disadvantage.

Limits on the types of assets mutual funds can invest in are a general service disadvantage. Mutual funds cannot invest directly in tangible assets. However, there are funds that invest in the securities of firms in most industries that do, such as real estate and precious metals. As a result, it is likely the actual disadvantage of limited assets does not translate to an actual service disadvantage for most investors.

Trading costs are a major service disadvantage of mutual funds. They represent the hidden costs of mutual fund investing and can be the largest shareholder expense. Trading costs are always positive, reflecting market mechanics, market liquidity, and investor trading motivation and investment style. In practice, they include (1) brokerage commission, transaction fees and taxes, (2) bid–ask spreads, (3) immediacy costs, and (4) opportunity costs. Trading costs are also affected by soft dollar arrangements and magnified by portfolio turnover.

The lack of shareholder control over the timing, size, and mix of fund taxable distributions of capital gains and income is a mutual funds service disadvantage. For example, an investor wants to minimize current taxable income, but funds control decisions generating taxable income. A particular fund trades securities infrequently, thereby minimizing capital gains and investor taxable income. On this dimension, the fund actually minimizes this service disadvantage.

There are two approaches shareholders may take to minimize lack of control over tax planning. First, invest in low turnover tax managed funds, which normally include index funds, and, second, follow specific guidelines designed to minimize the problem. The key to investor returns lies both with fund returns and with the percentage of returns that translate to after-tax returns.

Regulatory issues also provide a major service disadvantage of mutual funds. While regulation does much good, much more should be done in the areas of shareholder disclosure and alignment of independent board directors with shareholder interests. The 1940 Act is acknowledged as landmark legislation, but there is growing concern that independent directors are not independent enough as shareholder watchdogs. Most independent directors (1) have only nominal holdings in the funds they serve, (2) are selected by management as known quantities, and (3) are compensated very generously (positive relationship to fund expenses). Fund officers have dual roles as fund managers and officer/principals in investment advisory firms.

Independent directors have allowed fund assets to grow too large and expenses to increase, rarely replace investment advisors, and do not encourage shareholder communication. Shareholders usually do not support independent directors when they do take action. Shares of investment advisory firms outperform the funds they manage.

The need for improved mutual fund disclosure provides other regulatory issues. There is need for improved disclosure concerning specific portfolio manager issues, board of director concerns, and portfolio management issues. Regulatory issues include the SEC's role as regulator and mandate for change, "mutual" mutual fund organizations, new fund products, industry ethics, portfolio pricing, portfolio posting, communication and legal actions, and historical revisionism in past performance.

Mutual fund expenses (chapter 5) are a key element in fund investing. Fund expenses represent a very major service disadvantage of most mutual funds. Mutual funds have traditionally been considered low-cost providers, but what once may have been the case is increasingly less so. In general, fund expenses are too high and increasing. This is reflected in several dimensions: (1) management company profitability and market value, (2) total fund expenses, (3) fund management fees, (4) 12b-1 fees, (5) mutual fund supermarket fees, (6) soft dollar arrangements (at least for commission costs), (7) "other" fund expenses, (8) the relationship of sales loads/fees and expenses, and (9) fund family expenses. Expenses are a certainty of fund investing, but returns are not.

The third goal is to bring forward the assessments of Windsor II's attributes and portfolio background and to summarize them as excellent, acceptable, or unacceptable (table 27).

LIMITED TYPES OF ASSETS

As noted, mutual funds are financial service providers that pool investor monies and invest them in domestic and international equity and fixed-income securities (*financial assets*). However, mutual funds are not allowed to invest directly in *real* (*tangible*) *assets*. Their portfolios may include money market securities, capital market securities, and derivative market securities. *Money market securities* have a maturity of one year or less and include US Treasury bills, negotiable certificates of deposit, commercial paper, Eurodollars, repurchase agreements, and bankers' acceptances. *Capital market securities* have a maturity exceeding one year and include US Treasury bonds, US agency bonds, municipal bonds, asset-backed securities, preferred stock, and common stock. Derivative securities derive total or partial value from claims on underlying securities. They may be used to hedge portfolio risk, substitute for holding the underlying securities, or for speculative purposes. They include *options, warrants, futures contracts*, and *options on futures*. Sharpe et al. (1999) treat these assets.

Tangible assets: fine arts

The *fine arts* represent a broad category of tangible assets in which mutual funds are not permitted to directly invest. As defined here, fine arts are assets sold and auctioned by major auction houses and dealers, such as fine jewelry, art works, antiques, fine wines, antique silver, gemstones, ceramics, rare books, rare coins, stamps and collectibles. *Collectibles* reflect other (non-fine) fine arts that are often whimsical or sentimental, including rare baseball trading cards, antique toys, early comic books and celebrity and historical autographs and memorabilia. Fine arts are also defined as such by being sold in leading galleries and dealers worldwide.

Fine arts are unique assets (only one) or assets explicitly known to be limited in number, unlike commodities, and therefore do not lend themselves to being publicly traded. Their markets are therefore limited to those specific art auction houses and dealer/owners that act as intermediaries and make markets for them. The most active and liquid markets for major fine arts and collectibles are Sotheby's and Christie's auctions in New York, London, and other major cities. Auction markets represent about 25 percent of global fine arts sales. Sotheby's and Christie's issue catalogs detailing their monthly auction calendars. For example, an auction calendar at Sotheby's included Old Master nineteenth and twentieth-century prints, contemporary prints, tribal art, rare wines, pre-Columbian art, and Indian art. Sotheby's and other auction houses also utilize the internet for online auctions and sales.

Reilly and Brown (1997) discussed the Sotheby's Index that includes thirteen areas of art and antiques and auction prices. There are wide ranges in returns and risks among the various assets, but fairly consistent risk/return relationships over sixteen years. Analysis revealed which assets provided abnormal returns for their risk classes. In this case, returns on English furniture were tops and American painting second. The correlations among the various asset returns vary from 0.9 to negative – good portfolio balancers if marketable. The correlation of returns of art/antiques and bonds are generally negative, but they are positive for stocks. Several asset classes, such as Chinese ceramics, are also good inflation hedges. The conclusion, liquidity issues aside, is that art/antiques along with stocks and bonds can generate low-risk portfolios (and look great). The way to control for the liquidity issue is to buy only fine arts/ antiques that are desirable of themselves, without regard to investment attributes.

Non-auction sources and markets for fine arts are galleries and private dealers. They represent the other 75 percent of global fine art sales. Art dealers are generally proprietorships, partnerships, or small privately held corporations. Family ownership and management are traditional, but less so with companies providing online art sites. As with auction houses, art dealers and galleries are increasingly directly or indirectly utilizing the Internet for sales. Some sites exhibit art for sale by dealers, and others act as dealers in selling and/or auctioning art provided by dealers or artists. For example, artumbrella.com (2001) provides an online guide to fine arts sources and services globally, while *art*line.com (2001) provides a portal to leading art galleries and artists worldwide.

As noted above, fine arts are unique or limited and do not lend themselves to being *securitized* (packaged as securities) and publicly traded, such as financial and commodity contracts. That is, fine arts prices are not determined in good markets, such as those for publicly traded financial assets. This was evidenced in the legal charges made by the federal government for fixing commission rates.

So what are good markets? Reilly and Brown (1997) characterized them as providing: (1) accurate and timely price and volume information on market transactions; (2) "liquidity" – ability to buy/sell quickly ("marketability") at prices not substantially different from those of the previous trades, assuming no new market information; (3) "depth" – numerous potential buyers/sellers at prices above/below current prices; (4) "internal efficiency" – low transaction costs, including brokerage fees and bid–ask spreads; and (5) "informational efficiency" – rapid price adjustment to new information, with current prices reflecting all available information. Fine arts markets thus are not good markets.

Tangible assets: real estate and precious metals

As with fine arts, mutual funds are not permitted to invest directly in tangible real estate assets. But they may invest in the securities of firms that do invest directly in real estate. For example, Fidelity's Real Estate Investment Fund purchases shares in two types of *real estate investment trust* (REITs). The first type, equity trusts, have direct ownership interests in real properties, while the second, mortgage trusts, have creditor interests by making construction loans and mortgage loans. There are also hybrid trusts that combine equity and mortgage trusts. The Fidelity Real Estate fund also invests in securities of real estate developers and brokers, and companies with substantial real estate holdings. Howard (1993) reported preferences for REITs that manage properties in-house and own 100 percent of one type of property in one geographic area. This appears to favor better control over property development to diversification.

Real estate investment trusts are cousins of closed-end investment companies that invest in real estate rather than financial assets. They are not taxed as long as they distribute 95 percent of their income. Further, at least 75 percent of their assets and income must be from real estate equity or mortgages. They must have at least 100 shareholders, and their portfolios must be diversified, with no more than 30 percent of income from the sale of properties held for less than four years. A majority of directors must be independent, and managers are often compensated by profit-sharing arrangements.

Real estate investment trusts differ from mutual funds in that they are actual operating companies. They have professional managers (trustees) experienced in real estate who actively oversee the acquisition, management, and sale of real estate properties. REITs assemble portfolios of actual properties, as well as creditor claims on actual properties, and finance the portfolios by selling publicly traded or privately held equity claims against the securitized assets. Some REITS also borrow funds to leverage their returns. The nature and periodic problems of REITs are reviewed in Barbee (1998b).

Total returns from REIT shares are comprised of income from properties and changes in market value of real estate holdings. REIT shares are often used to reduce portfolio risk because their returns are generally not highly correlated with stock and bond returns. For example, Windawi (1995) estimated that only 13.8 percent and 8.6 percent of variability in REIT returns is explained by variability in equity and bond returns, respectively.

Traditionally, shares in precious metal firms have been the classic asset for reducing the risk of stock and bond portfolios, and in the same way as noted for REITs. Again, mutual funds cannot invest directly in tangible assets, which in this case includes precious metals, such as gold and silver. But funds may invest in the securities of firms engaged in the precious metals industry. Fidelity's Precious Metals and Minerals fund is an example of a gold fund. This fund invests primarily in the securities of firms engaged in exploration, mining, processing, or dealing in gold, silver, diamonds, and other precious metals and minerals. There has been very limited fund interest in buying and selling various type of commodities contracts, such as for frozen orange juice (remember the movie *Trading Places*?), soybeans and silver. What limited interest there has been has not been rewarded by good performance.

In conclusion, although mutual funds cannot invest directly in tangible assets, in some cases they are permitted to do so indirectly by investing in the securities of firms that are engaged in tangible assets. However, even indirect investment in fine arts is difficult, because art dealer shares are normally not publicly traded in good markets. To this extent, mutual funds have service disadvantages in providing only financial assets (and not in all cases) to meet a broad range of investor needs or desires. Nonetheless, the issue is not whether mutual funds are limited to financial rather than tangible assets, they are, but whether particular funds minimize this disadvantage in meeting the needs of particular investors. That is, do the actual financial assets of particular funds translate to actual minimum disadvantages in not being able to directly hold tangible assets for particular investors? It is likely this limited asset service disadvantage does not translate to actual disadvantages to most, but certainly not all, individual investors.

MUTUAL FUND TRADING COSTS

As clarified previously, trading costs are the costs associated with portfolio security transactions, not the expenses of managing funds or shareholder transaction costs.

Markets and theoretical trading costs

Price transparency and price discovery are two basic market functions. *Price transparency* reflects the degree to which market makers know the size and direction of current buy/sell orders when they set bid–ask prices. Transparency enhances market liquidity by lowering bid–ask spreads. It also reduces the chance less informed traders are disadvantaged in the prices they pay/receive. Auction markets are inherently more transparent than dealer markets, both pre-trade and post-trade.

Price discovery refers to the process of determining security prices through buyer/seller interactions that incorporate new information. With increased market fragmentation, the issue arises as to where discovery takes place. For example, Hasbrouck (1995) determined that over 90 percent of price discovery for very large capitalization stocks takes place on the New York Stock Exchange. It is expensive for markets to provide price discovery mechanisms for balancing supply/demand in an orderly fashion. Once discovered and publicized, however, it is inexpensive to execute matched buy/sell orders.

Trading costs are the hidden costs of mutual fund investing and can be the largest borne by shareholders. Trading costs are always positive, reflecting market mechanics and liquidity, transaction characteristics, and portfolio manager trade motivation and investment style. Trading costs are implicit in net amounts received or gross amounts paid for trades and, thereby, reduce potential returns by diminishing portfolio value.

Theoretical trading costs represent the difference between trade prices and market prices in the absence of trades. As reviewed in Robert Arnott (1998), these prices are unobservable and, therefore, unmeasurable. Theoretical trading costs include *immediacy* (*market impact*) *costs* and *opportunity costs* (waiting costs), but only the former relates to actual trades. Immediacy costs are included in price concessions given to force immediate trades, and are especially significant in large *block trades*. Opportunity costs largely depend on how much market prices move against traders while they are attempting to minimize immediacy costs.

Traders can reduce immediacy costs by taking advantage of favorable temporary differences between market and equilibrium prices. In so doing, market prices readjust to equilibrium values. The faster this readjustment takes place, the greater the degree of *market resilience* and efficiency. Immediacy costs are also influenced by portfolio management style. They are largest in growth investing, where execution immediacy is key to minimizing opportunity costs. They are lowest in value investing, where trading immediacy is less important.

A "graph" of theoretical trading costs has "cost" on the vertical axis and "available time" on the horizontal axis. Immediacy cost curves decrease from left to right, reflecting decreasing costs as trading immediacy (urgency) decreases. Opportunity cost curves increase from left to right, reflecting the increasing costs of forgone returns as the length of time for trade execution increases. The intersection of the two cost curves identifies the minimum theoretical trading cost, which also identifies the optimal time for executing trades.

There is both evidence and hope that advancing technology will reduce immediacy and opportunity costs. As an example of developments in electronic markets, Espinoza (1999) reported a new "optimal market" system that is set to launch. The system permits institutional investors to trade anonymously, with almost immediate execution and no influence on stock prices. The goal is a market in which institutional investors can buy/sell shares at the best possible prices, thereby increasing returns. It is probably only a matter of time until electronic markets dominate trading. How soon this will happen is another issue, both political and technical.

Types of trading costs

In practice, there are several types of trading costs. These trading costs include (1) brokerage commission, transaction fees and taxes, (2) *bid–ask spreads*, (3) immediacy costs (discussed above), and (4) opportunity costs (also discussed above). Only brokerage commission is easily measurable, but it does not always reflect actual costs (discussed below). Brokerage commission reported as total dollars or average cents per share is reported in the prospectus. Mutual fund trading expenses also include appropriate allocations of overhead costs, equipment, and personnel.

The importance of mutual fund brokerage commission may be seen by dividing dollars of brokerage fees by average annual net assets. Arnott (1993) analyzed brokerage commission in this way, but it does not capture the implicit commission in bid–ask spreads for securities traded in dealer markets, rather than on exchanges. This is especially true for bond mutual funds, because bonds are primarily traded in dealer markets. The average expense ratio of domestic equity funds was estimated at 1.32 percent plus 0.31 percent in brokerage fees. Some fund families are also known for having both small expense ratios and brokerage fees. Vanguard, for example, has average brokerage fees of 0.15 percent.

Mutual fund attributes also impact the size of brokerage commission. Measured by percentage of average annual net assets, international stock funds have average brokerage fees of 0.60 percent, about twice the domestic average. Funds with specialized investment objectives and more aggressive objectives also have above-average brokerage fees. As examples, precious metals funds have average fees of 0.79 percent, aggressive growth funds have average fees of 0.44 percent, and equity-income objectives have the lowest average fees, at 0.19 percent. Brokerage fees are adversely affected by portfolio turnover, but asset size has an even larger impact. Brokerage fees decline as fund asset size increases. Funds also trade securities within the family of funds to save trading costs.

Bid–ask spreads

Bid–ask spreads represent the difference between market maker (dealers and specialists) bid and ask prices. This spread compensates market makers for supplying liquidity by guaranteeing minimum size trades at quoted bid/ask prices. Investors obtain liquidity by submitting buy/sell orders that are matched against market maker buy/sell quotes to effect trades. Thus investor demand for liquidity carries a cost.

Bid–ask spreads are the largest trading cost as measured by differences between current highest bid prices (to buy) and lowest ask prices (to sell). Purchases are made at the high end of ask prices and sales at the low end of bid prices. Mutual funds frequently make large block trades that have larger trading costs than the small trades of individual investors.

Bid–ask spreads are generally held to reflect three types of costs: (1) order processing, (2) inventory holding, and (3) adverse selection. Order processing costs represent market maker fixed and variable costs of doing business, such as stock exchange and clearing fees, back-office expenses and profit. Inventory holding costs (order imbalance costs) reflect the carrying costs of transitory imbalances in optimal levels of market maker inventories due to order flow imbalances, which occur where, for example, sell orders follow upon sell orders. Market makers provide investor-demanded liquidity by adjusting inventory and bid–ask spreads to equilibrate (balance) order flow. The larger the deviations in desired inventory levels, the larger the spreads.

Stated another way, Madhavan and Smidt (1993) discussed market makers as both dealers and investors. As dealers, they adjust bid–ask prices to control fluctuations in inventory. As investors, they seek to maintain long-term positions, while profiting from information about impending order imbalances. The larger the deviations in actual versus desired inventory levels, the larger the spreads.

Motivations for trades

Adverse selection costs (*the costs of asymmetric information with informed traders*) represent market maker losses caused by trading with investors who have asymmetric, insider information. When market makers perceive they are trading with informed traders with private information, they increase bid–ask spreads to cover potential losses. These *information-motivated trades* increase bid–ask spreads, while *liquidity-motivated trades* for routine portfolio rebalancing do not. Trading immediacy is most important in information-motivated trades, where timing is crucial to minimize opportunity costs.

The dollar volume of trades is very sensitive to bid–ask spreads, especially for information-motivated trades. Chalmers et al. (1999) examined these relationships in their analysis of 137 mutual funds for the period 1984–93. The sensitivity of trading volume to bid–ask spreads tends to persist over time, with good portfolio managers attempting to minimize spreads, while others do not. Spread expenses were also computed for 106 funds for the period 1985–99.

Spread expenses are trading costs expressed as a percentage of total assets under management. Average annual spread expenses were estimated at 0.34 percent, but they vary by investment focus and fund asset size. The spread expense is 0.40 percent for aggressive funds, 0.28 percent for conservative funds, 0.31 percent for funds with over $100 million in assets, and 0.40 percent for smaller funds.

Other impacts on trading costs

Brokerage commission is positively related to portfolio turnover and operating expenses, but negatively to asset size. Fortin and Michelson (1998) examined these relationships in an analysis of over 3,400 mutual funds. The relationship between commission and operating expenses suggests that investment advisors do not pass on soft dollar savings (discussed below) as a reduction in fund expenses. Average brokerage commission is 0.30 percent and represents over 22 percent of fund expenses. It is highest for international stock funds, lowest for government and municipal bond funds, and marginally higher than average for no-load equity funds.

There is also a relationship between the number of market makers, trading activity, and reduction in bid–ask spreads. Goldstein and Nelling (1999) examined these relationships for Nasdaq stocks, the centralized market for over-the-counter (unlisted) securities. Trading volume includes both trade size and number of trades. Stocks with high trade volume tend to have more market makers, which lowers bid–ask spreads. Also, large company stocks and those traded most frequently have more market makers and lower bid–ask spreads.

Keim and Madhaven (1997) provided a detailed analysis of mutual fund trading costs for the years 1991–3. Institutional trading costs were estimated based on the particular markets where trades were made, the size of the trades, stock market caps, stock prices, and whether the trades were buys or sells. Trading costs also included commission and market impact costs. Trading costs are economically significant and are related to difficulty of trades and market liquidity. In addition, trading costs are affected by trade initiation and exchange listing. Trading costs vary across institutions and reflect trading ability and investment style. Value investors have lower trading costs than trades motivated by trading immediacy. Trading costs should be considered in connection with the formulation and assessment of investment strategies.

Soft dollar practices

Broker–dealers often provide mutual fund advisors with bundles of research products/services in addition to trade execution. These soft dollar arrangements provide investment advisors with specified dollar amounts of research products/services from broker–dealers in exchange for specified dollar amounts of trading commission. Nearly all broker–dealers use soft dollar (payments) arrangements. The US Securities and Exchange Commission (1998) computed that the average investment advisor allocates $1.70 in commission for each $1.00 of soft dollar payments. The value of research purchased annually with soft dollars is estimated at over $1 billion.

Investment advisors also use *step-out transactions* to reward broker–dealers for the sale of shares without losing opportunities for better execution provided by others. In these cases, investment advisors direct particular broker–dealers to execute trades and others to provide soft dollar payments. Broker–dealers executing the trades "step out" of portions of commission to the broker–dealers making soft dollar payments.

Traditionally, mutual fund investment advisors were deemed as acting with conflicts of interest if trading commission was effectively used to purchase research services/products or if non-competitive prices were paid for those purposes ("paying up"). The regulatory concern was the potential conflict of interest between investment advisor needs for research services/products and fund shareholder rights to "best possible" trade execution. However, the Securities and Exchange Act of 1934 as amended now provides "safe harbor" for these actions if they are disclosed to shareholders. Commission paid in soft dollar arrangements may also reflect the care and skill of particular broker–dealers in effectively executing large and difficult trades.

More recently, the concern about soft dollar arrangements is whether soft dollar payments actually follow regulatory requirements. The SEC (1998) audited seventy-five broker–dealers and 280 investment advisors and mutual funds to find out. The two major categories of soft dollar payments are for research reports (54 percent) and news (13 percent). The three largest sub-categories are general company, general economic, and individual company/sector research.

The majority of soft dollar payments were properly made for research, but 35 percent of broker-dealers provided non-research services/products and 28 percent of investment advisors received them. As noted, payments for non-research items may be lawful with required shareholder disclosure, but virtually none of the advisors provides disclosure.

The positive news in the analysis is that most mutual funds do *not* have soft dollar arrangements, and fewer than 15 percent of fund advisors use them. Nearly all investment advisors with these arrangements disclose them, but the nature of disclosure varies widely. The negative news is that most investment advisors use boilerplate language for disclosure that lacks sufficient information concerning actual policies and practices. Further, the information is generally inadequate for directors to fulfill the legal responsibility they have for reviewing these arrangements. About 50 percent of advisors with soft dollar arrangements disclose them in the prospectus, statement of additional information, and/or annual report. Others make less obvious disclosure in the footnotes to financial statements.

The distortion of soft dollar payments on the accounting for mutual fund expenses is an important disclosure issue. Only about 50 percent of fund advisors making soft dollar payments actually increase ("gross up") fund expenses to reflect them and also make disclosure in financial statement footnotes. However, funds are required to make such disclosure as will allows shareholders to compute actual fund expenses. Soft dollar payments are generally included in reported brokerage commission, which is normally reported only in statements of additional information. The accounting for soft dollar payments understates actual fund expenses and overstates brokerage commission paid. Further, reported commission figures do not note additional amounts paid by not seeking best available trade execution.

The effect of soft dollar payments on mutual fund brokerage commission is significant. Gasparino (1998a) reported investment advisors pay commission of about 6c a share to broker-dealers that provide soft dollar payments. The extent of soft dollar payments is seen when compared with the 3c paid per share without soft dollar arrangements. Moreover, mutual fund directors need to know whether investment advisors are providing funds with the "full benefit" of the soft dollars they receive. If not, this lack of dollar values should be reflected in lowered costs of advisory contracts.

Other soft dollar issues

Another issue related to soft dollar arrangements is whether investment advisors place shareholder interests above the interests of advisor investment management companies. Rekenthaler (1996a) reported a test of the belief that low-expense funds help keep expenses low by funneling more research costs into soft dollar payments attached to brokerage commission. The result was quite the contrary. Funds with low expenses also have unusually low brokerage commission, and those with high expenses tend to have high brokerage commission. This joint expense/commission behavior places additional importance on investing in funds with low expense ratios. Thus it appears cost containment is across the board either good or bad.

The SEC (1998) study concluded there are several regulatory problems with soft dollars: (1) violation of safe harbor by making payments for non-research purposes and without required disclosure; (2) inadequate broker-dealer and investment advisor records of the use of soft dollars for non-research and research/non-research purposes; (3) inadequate investment advisor disclosure to fund directors, including use for non-research purposes; and (4) inadequate broker-dealer and investment advisor internal control procedures to monitor, report, and disclose use.

In summary, soft dollar payments are measured in a way that in other applications violates accounting principles and practice. Improved accounting for soft dollar arrangements is needed, but, optimally, they should be prohibited in the interests of proper disclosure and proper accounting practice, including proper measurement of fund commission and expenses. At a minimum, fund brokerage fees should explicitly reflect competitive execution fees plus the additional cost of soft dollar payments.

As concluded in Rekenthaler (1996c):

> Funds should assign to each trade the going competitive rate for commission, and place the amount in the commission account. All remaining costs should be termed management or operating costs, as appropriate, and calculated into the official expense ratio. It's a simple matter of market efficiency: If investors are to make rational decisions, they need rational tools.

And proper accounting is the tool.

Portfolio turnover and trading costs

As outsiders to mutual fund records, it is difficult for shareholders to interpret the relationship between portfolio turnover and fund trading costs. The portfolio turnover ratio is the measure of portfolio turnover, and it quantifies the frequency of discretionary securities trades. For example, a turnover ratio of 1.00, usually stated as 100 percent, is equivalent to trading 100 percent of securities holdings over the year. But there are nuances to the measure. Ronald (1999b) illustrated how the turnover ratio is the same whether, for example, numerous small trades were made that sum to turnover of 100 percent or whether one large trade summed to 100 percent. Also, the turnover ratio is zero if, for example, all trades are purchases and there are no sales. The ratio is computed using the smaller of purchases or sales.

Portfolio turnover has increased over the years as portfolio managers have attempted to outperform benchmark indices using aggressive short-term strategies. These strategies are the polar opposite of buy-and-hold strategies with little trading. Bogle (1999a) noted fund portfolio turnover increased from 17 percent in the mid 1960s to 85 percent in 1997. Moreover, fund shareholders have contributed to this escalation. Investor turnover was about 8 percent in the 1960s and most of the 1970s, but now it is running at 31 percent. These increases have been accompanied by increased trading costs, greater portfolio risk in efforts to increase returns, and more shareholder taxes on realized capital gains distributions.

Portfolio turnover magnifies the costs of mutual fund trades. All else equal, portfolios with a small portfolio turnover have smaller total trading costs than portfolios with a large turnover. But when is everything equal? As noted above and by Barbee (1999b), the portfolio turnover ratio is not a precise guide to portfolio manager holding periods. The ratio is easily distorted by the ebb and flow of fund assets. For example, assume two portfolio managers sell the same amount of stock a year, but the one with the larger asset growth has the lower turnover ratio because its asset base is larger.

Nonetheless, a method is needed to compute total mutual fund trading costs, and it must include the number of trades measured by the portfolio turnover ratio and trading costs per trade. Such a method facilitates computing and comparing the trading cost effectiveness of alternative funds. That is, the fund with lowest total trading cost per percentage rate of return is most cost-effective. After all, the purpose of portfolio turnover is to enhance or protect portfolio performance.

Trading cost effectiveness is analogous to the amount of portfolio risk per percentage rate of return. In both cases, the smaller result is preferred. That is, smaller risk per unit of return is a good thing, as is smaller trading cost per unit of return. The more effective a fund's trading, the smaller is its trading cost per unit of return. Trading cost effectiveness is particularly useful in comparing trading effectiveness among fund peers and between funds and benchmark indices. The computation facilitates making comparisons of trading cost effectiveness where, for example, one fund has both high returns and high portfolio turnover and high the other has both low returns and low turnover. Market index computations are based on actual index funds to obtain real portfolio turnover data for computations.

Mutual fund portfolio turnover differs along several dimensions, including investment objectives, investment style, shareholder redemptions, market conditions, and expectations. Growth-oriented investment objectives normally have higher turnover than income-oriented objectives, owing to more aggressive portfolio management. Value investment style normally has lower turnover than the growth style. The value style searches for undervalued stocks that normally take some time to attain "fair market value." The growth style searches for stocks with expectations of faster earnings growth rates and rapid price increases. Rapidly changing market conditions and expectations normally imply higher turnover as managers, especially those using short-term strategies, scramble to adjust portfolios to each new reality or perception thereof. The relationship between portfolio turnover and fund performance is discussed later.

As discussed, portfolio turnover magnifies total trading costs: trading cost per trade times portfolio turnover ratio. However, until more recently, neither factor was recognized as contributing significantly to fund costs. Turnover is important because each trade has implications for shareholder distributions of capital gains. Portfolio managers have traditionally focused on portfolio returns and not investor after-tax returns. The reason is twofold. First, portfolio managers are evaluated and compensated on portfolio, not investor, performance. Second, fund managers argue that investor tax brackets and financial situations are too diverse and unknown for them to do anything else. This problem has been addressed by recent offerings of *tax-managed funds*. As discussed below, these funds by their performance demonstrate the importance of portfolio turnover and other strategies that reduce after-tax returns.

Assessing trading costs

Numerous studies have examined theoretical and empirical issues surrounding the size of trading costs, especially bid–ask spreads. Table 14, section A, summarizes trading attributes and notes whether they tend to increase or decrease bid–ask spreads. This section adds specifics to the general chapter discussion of fund trading costs.

In a classic study, Loeb (1983) met the need for measurable trading costs by providing market-determined estimates of round-trip (buy and sell) immediacy costs for combinations of (1) average market capitalization of stocks traded and (2) average dollar block size of trades. These findings are often cited among the useful studies of trading costs.

The Loeb table of trading costs is provided in table 15. The trading costs were derived from "upstairs" dealer market trades, a negotiated market of highly capitalized stock exchange member firms dealing in listed and over-the-counter stocks. This market provides (1) uniform trading costs across publicly traded domestic securities, (2) maximum liquidity, with access to risk capital, and (3) ready markets. Block size trading costs were estimated for a sample of Wilshire 5000 stocks representing unweighted averages of some 1,200 quoted bid–ask spreads divided by stock prices across a number of dealers. As noted, costs were estimated using stock market capitalization and average dollar block size trade.

For example, table 15 reveals round-trip trading costs range from 1.1 percent for the smallest block size trades of large capitalization stocks to 43.8 percent for moderate block size trades of very small capitalization stocks. Trading costs of stocks with market capitalization exceeding $1.5 billion range from 1.1 percent for smallest block size trades to 8 percent for largest block trades. Trading costs of modest size block trades ($250,000) range from 43.8 percent for stocks with the smallest market capitalization to 1.3 percent for stocks with the largest market capitalization.

Loeb's data thus indicate that the so-called invisible trading costs are indeed significant. The data also provide the opportunity to compute the effectiveness of trading costs to determine whether a particular fund's actual trading costs are an actual minimum disadvantage to particular investors in meeting their needs.

The data were collected at the beginning of the long-term increase in stock prices. Therefore, dollar block size trades and stock market values (capitalization) have increased dramatically since then. Nonetheless, the trading cost estimates appear reasonable based on other estimates. In any case, Loeb trading cost estimates are best used on a comparative basis for particular funds or groups of peer funds with the same investment objectives and style parameters, or for one or more of such funds against appropriate benchmark indices.

The Loeb study is among the few that estimated the market impact of trades. As stated in Perold and Salomon (1991), as assets under management grow, the size of trades also increases. The result is larger trading costs and lower returns on portfolios. The effect of more assets under management is an increase in "implementation shortfall" – both higher trading costs and opportunity costs as more orders go unexecuted. With respect to trading cost effectiveness, there are diseconomies of scale from the increased costs of larger block trades. As noted, as assets under management grow, block trades increase in size, and portfolio returns decrease, owing to wealth lost by trading. Although returns decrease, wealth continues to increase until the costs of additional trading equal the opportunity costs of not trading. Asset growth beyond this point leads to increases in unexecuted trades, larger opportunity costs, and lower portfolio returns.

The nature of investment advisory fees is also important. If expense ratios are fixed, dollar amounts of fees increase as assets increase. However, shareholder wealth suffers from asset growth as the opportunity costs of implementation shortfall increase. This creates a conflict between the interests of shareholders and those of fund advisors. The problem is reduced with incentive-based management fees. Investment advisors lose revenue if assets increase beyond the wealth-maximizing amount and shareholders do not suffer implementation shortfall. Performance fees thus provide incentives for fund advisors to limit asset growth, but they are seldom used.

There are also disadvantages to incentive-based investment advisor compensation schemes. Brown et al. (1996) analyzed the performance of managers of 334 growth-oriented mutual funds for the period 1980–91. Fund managers who perform poorly during the first half of the year tend to increase portfolio volatility during the second half to increase returns and earn any incentives. This behavior has become stronger as investor awareness of fund performance has increased, especially for newer funds and funds that have been consistent winners and losers in past years. The results suggest a tournament in which funds compete for additional assets based on relative performance. By focusing so much on annual performance assessment, this tournament can provide adverse incentives to fund portfolio managers. Portfolio managers are encouraged to change managerial objectives from long-term to short-term to salvage annual performance. Longer-term approaches to managerial compensation could provide great benefits to both fund managers and shareholders. The savings in trading costs alone would be enormous.

Loeb trading costs

As noted, portfolio turnover magnifies the size of mutual fund trading costs. Loeb's trading cost data provide the costs of round-trip trades. Multiplying trading costs by the volume of trading (portfolio turnover) provides estimates of fund trading costs:

$$TC = LTC \times PTO$$

where TC = trading cost (%) and LTC = Loeb's trading cost per round-trip trade (%). To identify Loeb's trading cost, the average market capitalization of stock portfolio holdings and average dollar size of stock holdings is required, the latter assumed as dollar block size owing to data limitations. For example, table 40a identifies Vanguard Windsor II's portfolio turnover as 30 percent and provides data for computing its trading cost. Windsor II's median market capitalization of portfolio holdings is \$25,916 million and its average security holding (and assumed average block size trade) is \$107,693,728. The average block size trade is approximated by dividing the portfolio's total net assets (\$30,908.1 million) by the number of stocks held (287). Windsor II's capitalization is over \$1,500 million, and its average block size trade is over \$20 million.

Thus by referring to table 15, its round-trip trading cost is estimated as 8 percent. This cost is high because of its large block size trades, not because of its holdings of large market capitalization stocks. As identified in table 14, the former is positively associated with bid–ask spreads and the latter, negatively. Thus:

$$LTC = 8\%$$
$$TC = 8\% \times 31\%$$
$$= 2.48\%$$

To determine how Windsor II's trading cost compares with the benchmark index, the same steps are followed for the Vanguard 500 Index, for which data are available in table 41a. The index fund's Loeb trading cost is also estimated at 8 percent, but its portfolio turnover, as an index fund, is only 5 percent. Thus:

$$LTC = 8\%$$
$$TC = 8\% \times 5\%$$
$$= 0.40\%$$

To determine how Windsor II's trading cost compares with those of its peer group, the same steps are again followed, for which data are available in table 42a. The peer group's Loeb trading cost is estimated at only 5.9 percent, but this advantage is lost by its higher portfolio turnover of 70 percent. Thus:

$$LTC = 5.9\%$$
$$TC = 5.9\% \times 70\%$$
$$= 4.13\%$$

Trading cost effectiveness

The next step is to determine whether Windsor II's portfolio performance relative to the index fund justifies its larger trading cost. That is, how much does Windsor II pay in trading costs per unit of rate of return? The smaller its computed trading cost effectiveness, the more cost-effective its trading. The three-year annualized return is used to normalize fund returns. Trading cost effectiveness is computed by dividing the fund's trading cost by its three-year annualized return:

$$CE = TC/ROR$$

where CE = cost effectiveness (of trades) and ROR = three-year annualized return. Table 40a identifies Windsor II's three-year annualized returns as 24.13 percent. Its trading cost effectiveness is computed by dividing its trading cost by its return:

$$CE = 2.48\%/24.13\%$$
$$= 0.103\%$$

Next, table 41a identifies Vanguard 500 Index's returns as 28.16 percent and its cost effectiveness is computed as follows:

$$CE = 0.40\%/28.16\%$$
$$= 0.014\%$$

Thus Vanguard 500 Index's trading is much more cost-effective than Windsor II's: 0.103 percent versus 0.014 percent. There are two reasons for this difference: its trading cost is much lower owing to lower portfolio turnover and its annualized return is much higher.

Next, table 42a identifies the peer group's returns as 19.74 percent, and its cost effectiveness is computed as follows:

$$CE = 4.13\%/19.74\%$$
$$= 0.20\%$$

Breakeven rate of return

To be as cost-effective as the index fund, Windsor II's annualized return must be large enough to equate its cost effectiveness with the index fund, given its much larger trading cost. How large must the fund's breakeven return be and is this likely to occur? Windsor II's so-called *breakeven return* is computed as follows:

$$B/E\ ROR = TC\%/CE\ goal$$

where B/E ROR = breakeven return (equally cost-effective return), TC = trading cost, and CE goal = cost effectiveness goal (smallest). Using the above data, Windsor II's breakeven return is computed by dividing its trading cost by the index fund's trading cost effectiveness:

$$B/E\ ROR = 2.48\%/0.014\%$$
$$= 177.14\%$$

This finding makes the point: index fund (low turnover) trading is much more cost-effective than fund trading in general. This conclusion also generally holds even if the index fund's returns are lower than the fund's returns. The reason, again, is lower portfolio turnover. Large-cap. *value* funds are likely to have smaller cap. size holdings and smaller block size trades than large-cap. blend (value and growth) index funds. However, the key difference is likely to be portfolio turnover, and the return Windsor II must earn to compensate for this difference is simply beyond all probabilities.

Next, for the large-cap. value peer group to be as cost-effective as Windsor II, its annualized returns must be large enough to equate its cost effectiveness with Windsor II, given its larger Loeb trading cost. How large must the peer group's return be and how likely is this to occur? The peer group's breakeven return relative to Windsor II is computed by dividing its trading cost by Windsor II's trading cost effectiveness:

$$B/E\ ROR = 4.13\%/0.103\%$$
$$= 40.1\%$$

This compares with the large-cap. peer group's three-year annualized returns of 19.74 percent. Funds in the same large-cap. category are likely to have similar cap. size holdings and block size trades. In this case, the key can only be portfolio turnover, and the return the peer group must earn to compensate for this difference is most unlikely, especially for average performance. This finding makes the point: low portfolio turnover is much more cost-effective for funds and fund groups with the same investment style.

Table 14, section B, provides a comparative summary of Loeb trading costs, trading cost effectiveness, and breakeven rate of return for equal cost effectiveness for Windsor II relative to the Vanguard Index 500 fund. The first step is to enter the computed trading costs of Windsor II and Vanguard 500 Index. The second step is to enter the trading cost effectiveness of each fund. The third step is to enter the computed return Windsor II needs to be as cost-effective as Vanguard Index 500. And the fourth step is to judge Windsor II's Loeb trading cost as excellent, acceptable, or unacceptable in table 14, section B.

In the case of Windsor II and the Vanguard 500 Index, the index fund wins all comparisons and the magnitude of the difference in cost effectiveness suggests unacceptable performance for Windsor II. This is the usual outcome when comparing managed funds with passively managed index funds. Normally, index funds are expected to be unattainably more cost-effective. Thus it is more reasonable to compare Windsor II with its peer group, which is more directly the fund's competitor. In this case, the differences in cost effectiveness identify Windsor II's performance as excellent in table 14, section B. These results are summarized in table 27.

Other trading cost estimates

Trading cost estimates vary, owing to differences in samples and methods, but also to difficulties in measuring some costs. For example, Bogle (1994) estimated that mutual fund trading costs range from 0.5 percent to 2 percent, which converts from 1 percent to 4 percent on a round-trip (buy and sell) basis. This approximates Loeb's costs for small to above-average block size trades of large capitalization stocks. In another study, Jones et al. (1990) estimated bid–ask spreads on round-trip trades. The 1982–8 average spread on S&P 500 stocks was 1.84 percent, versus 2.68 percent for non-S&P 500 stocks. These estimates are similar to Loeb's small to medium block size trades of large capitalization stocks.

Dziubinski (1998b) reported the unusual case of a mutual fund disclosing its trading cost estimates. John Bogle, Jr. (son of Vanguard's Bogle), former manager of Numeric Investors' Growth and Value, provided hard evidence that trading costs increase with asset size. The larger fund assets are, the harder it is to execute entire trades at good prices, or even on the same days.

As reported in Rowland (1998), Bogle Jr. breaks trading costs into four elements: commission, bid–ask spreads, the market impacts of trading, and opportunity costs, the latter the costs of not trading at desired prices. Mutual fund trading costs vary by investment style. Small-cap. growth stocks are more costly to trade than large-cap. value funds, and the difference increases sharply with fund asset size. The asset breakpoint size for small growth funds is $800 million. Trading costs are about 75 basis points for large-cap. value funds and 325 basis points for small-cap. growth funds with assets of $2.2 billion. Analysis of about 33,000 trades determined that trading costs reduced returns by as much as eleven percentage points a year! This incredibly high estimate is explained by Bogle's portfolio turnover rates of 300–600 percent.

Atkins and Dyl (1997) examined mean and median Nasdaq stock bid–ask spreads. For the period 1983–91, mean and median bid–ask spreads were 5.14 percent and 3.75 percent, respectively. They were larger in 1991, with mean and median bid–ask spreads of 7.15 percent and 5.0 percent, respectively. This contrasts with mean and median NYSE stock bid–ask spreads. For the period 1975–89, mean and median bid–ask spreads were 1.38 percent and 1.03 percent, respectively. In 1989, mean and median bid–ask spreads were 1.48 percent and 0.99 percent, respectively. The cost advantage of NYSE trading is very evident.

And, finally, Chalmers et al. (1999) analyzed the "operating efficiency" of mutual fund trading practices. The sample included 137 funds for the years 1984–91. Operating efficiency is measured by fund ability to manage both bid–ask spreads and capital gains/losses. Operating efficiency was positively related to risk-adjusted returns. Funds can enhance returns by managing trading costs. The average bid–ask spread is forth-four basis points and the average expense ratio is 1.08 percent. Nonetheless, operating efficiency is less important than the ability to select good stocks. Over time, funds with operating efficiency tend to stay efficient and, conversely, inefficient funds tend to stay that way.

The study also determined that load and no-load mutual funds have equal bid–ask spreads (0.34 percent), conservative funds (0.28 percent) have smaller bid–ask spreads than aggressive (0.40 percent) funds, and larger funds (0.31 percent) have smaller bid–ask spreads than smaller (0.40 percent) funds. Brokerage commission is smaller for load funds (0.26 percent) than for no-load funds (0.32 percent), conservative funds (0.25 percent) have smaller commission than aggressive (0.32 percent) funds, and smaller funds (0.32 percent) have smaller commission than larger (0.27 percent) funds. And, finally, expense ratios are smaller for load (1.01 percent) than for no-load (1.13 percent) funds, smaller for conservative (1.01 percent) than for aggressive (1.14 percent) funds, and smaller for larger (0.95 percent) than for smaller (1.28 percent) funds.

Tobias (1999) reported the smallest estimate of round-trip trading costs of 1 percent. All in all, Loeb's trading cost estimates appear ballpark, at least for comparative use, and especially for other than largest block size trades of largest capitalization stocks. A trading cost estimator is located at PersonalFund.com (1999).

Trading costs and asset size

Bogle Jr. (1997) noted that mutual fund assets need to be large enough to defray the fixed costs of management and shareholder services, but at some point average costs cease to decline with increased asset size. Optimal asset size varies by investment style. In general, funds show their best performance when they are relatively small. Opportunity costs of trading increase as funds get larger and their trades get larger. Also, small-cap. funds have higher trading costs than large-cap. stocks, owing to the higher costs of trading small-cap. stocks. It is difficult for small-cap. funds to sustain profitability when assets are over $500 million. Funds with high portfolio turnover should close before small-turnover funds because of larger trading costs.

A final note

Theodore R. Aronson, Aronson & Partners, mutual fund advisor and portfolio manager, graphically described the importance of trading costs in Welling (1998):

[The] problem of money chasing a fabulous sexy record is often exacerbated, when it crashes or falls out of favor, by transaction costs. But, it's hard to get your hands around trading costs. . . .

The commission . . . are just the tip of the iceberg. . . . Commission are trivial. But below the water level, there's another cost that most professional investors understand – the spread between what somebody wants to get and what somebody wants to pay. Think of an illiquid stock. The market makers and specialists have to make money. Below that, there is yet another level of transaction costs for significant institutional money. An institution might step up to the trading post and want to buy a lot more than what's offered. Its buying is going to "impact that stock." Push it higher to buy or lower to sell. What's more, there's the notion of opportunity cost. This gets hairy – makes your eyes glaze over. But it's the price you pay for basically not being able to do what you wanted to do, when you wanted to do it. Which is the fancy way of saying you have to wait to do the trade. . . .

But when you add up the commission, spreads, the impact from buying or selling more and throw in this trend or opportunity cost, you find true transaction costs measured in whole percentage points, not basis points. What is germane about this? If the majority of investors are invested in the stock market through mutual funds, these costs can very much impact their total returns. They are astronomical. They are the difference between the theoretical paper results you hire a manager to get and what you actually end up with.

SHAREHOLDER TAX PLANNING

Tax planning is an essential element of the investment process, for both taxable individual and company accounts. A major mutual fund service disadvantage is lack of direct shareholder control over the timing, size, and types of taxable distributions. However, the issue is not whether mutual funds generally limit shareholder tax planning, they do, but whether particular funds minimize this lack of control in meeting the needs of particular investors. That is, do the actual taxable events of particular funds translate to actual minimum taxable event disadvantages for particular investors? This problem arises from the nature of mutual funds as registered investment companies (discussed below) that must follow prescribed formulas for distributions. This is not to say, however, that investors themselves cannot incur realized capital gains and losses by selling fund shares in taxable accounts. Investors can and do, which gives them the ability to ameliorate fund limitations on shareholder tax planning.

Mutual fund shareholders may follow one and/or two basic approaches to minimize their lack of control over fund distributions. The first is to purchase low turnover tax-managed funds, which normally include index funds, and the second is to follow guidelines designed to minimize the problem. But first it is useful to discuss mutual fund tax efficiency.

Tax-efficient funds

In this context, *tax efficiency* refers to the percentage of pre-tax mutual fund returns that translate to shareholder after-tax returns. Of course, this applies on a current basis to taxable portfolios and not to tax-exempt portfolios or those with deferred tax features. Funds and financial publications are increasingly recognizing the importance of tax efficiency. For example, Ronald (1999a) discusses tax efficiency and provides a checklist applied below.

Table 16 lists the efficiency of the 100 largest stock funds, as measured by percentage of returns translating to model shareholder after-tax returns. Efficiency ranges from 98 percent to 76 percent, which appears quite good until it is noted these are just the largest funds. Sanders (1997) examined the tax efficiency of the top fifty equity mutual funds over the last five years. The most tax-efficient funds lost an average of twenty-seven *basis* points to shareholder taxes and the least efficient lost an average of nine *percentage* points. The latter loss has a much larger effect on returns than expense ratios! There is no clear pattern of tax efficiency among large-cap. and small-cap. funds.

Traditionally, mutual fund portfolio managers have given little, if any, attention to tax efficiency. The standard defense is they should not be constrained by such considerations in managing portfolios, and, besides, shareholder tax issues and brackets are too diverse to do so effectively. Moreover, portfolio manager compensation has traditionally been based on fund returns, not shareholder after-tax returns. This is changing as investors force the issue by investing increasingly greater amounts in tax-efficient index funds and tax-managed funds (discussed below).

The Vanguard mutual fund family was first to provide information on tax efficiency across a broad range of funds. Other industry leaders are sure to follow. This disclosure has led to a debate about how to measure after-tax returns. Vanguard uses the "pre-liquidation" method that assumes distributions are taxed, but shares continue to be held. That is, this method does not incorporate capital gains tax upon assumed sales of shares. The other approach, the "post-liquidation" method, incorporates taxes on distributions and assumed sale of shares. This method provides only a very small advantage for tax-efficient funds. Not surprisingly, Vanguard, the leader in tax-efficient index funds, advocates the pre-tax method, and Fidelity, the managed fund leader, advocates the post-tax method. Another advantage of determining a mutual fund's tax efficiency is that it tends to be a good indicator of future tax efficiency.

Tax efficiency and portfolio attributes

As noted in Dziubinskyi (1997), tax efficiency ratings are more useful if used in conjunction with portfolio turnover, changes in portfolio managers, net cash inflows, and after-tax returns. Two-thirds of highly tax-efficient funds three years ago continue to have above-average or better efficiency ratings. And three-fourths of tax-inefficient funds continue to have below-average or worse ratings. This consistency is good news to long-term investors with tax concerns.

Although funds with high portfolio turnover tend to be less tax-efficient, the relationship is not linear. Some funds actually become more tax-efficient by increasing turnover. They do this by offsetting realized capital gains by taking capital losses. However, when increases in turnover are preceded by changes in portfolio managers, the result is less tax efficiency. The first thing new managers usually do is make numerous portfolio changes. This is less likely to happen in those cases where investment objectives and investment styles are defined to limit portfolio manager flexibility.

Mutual funds with ample net cash inflows from new shareholder investments are likely to be more tax-efficient than funds with small or negative cash inflows. They are able to meet redemptions and other needs from incoming cash flows rather than the sale of securities. This, of course, limits the need to sell securities and realization of capital gains. Net cash inflows from new shareholders also assist current shareholders by proportionately sharing in distributions from realized and/or forthcoming capital gains.

The choice of mutual funds sometimes involves tradeoffs because tax-efficient funds are often more aggressive. Rekenthaler (1994a) examined fund tax efficiency by investment objective, and significant percentage differences were indicated:

Municipal bond	96
Small company	80
World stock	75
Growth	70
Growth and income	70
Balanced	65
Corporate high-quality bond	55
World bond	55
Corporate high-yield bond	50
Government Bond	50

Note that taxable bond funds are terribly tax-inefficient and tax-exempt bonds are most tax-efficient. These differences suggest that fund investment objectives provide a good place for investors to begin if tax considerations are important.

Sanders (1997) examined the tax efficiency of mutual funds by investment style. Growth funds are only slightly more tax-efficient than value funds, but not by much and not at all times. Also, there is no clear pattern of differences in tax efficiency between large-cap. and small-cap. funds. Tax efficiency also varies by type of assets. More specifically, Lallos (1994) identified growth funds are 86 percent tax-efficient versus 81 percent for value funds. Growth funds tend to let their gains run, while value funds harvest them at set "trigger points." Moreover, the potential capital gains tax liability of growth funds is 11 percent, versus 16 percent for value funds. This is true although value fund portfolio turnover is only one-half that of growth funds. Growth funds also realize losses more rapidly than value funds, while value funds are more patient in waiting for losers to become winners. The results thus indicate growth funds are more tax-efficient than value funds, both looking back and looking to the future.

Finally, as stated by Sanders (1995b): "While tax considerations shouldn't be the main driver in an investment decision, they do merit attention." Tax efficiency is a necessary but not sufficient condition to enhance shareholder after-tax returns. After all, funds with no returns are very tax-efficient. Shareholder after-tax returns, the real focus here, are determined by pre-tax fund returns *and* fund tax efficiency.

The impact of portfolio turnover on mutual fund tax efficiency is summarized in Welling (1998) by Theodore Aronson's statement that "if you crunch the numbers, turnover has to come down, not to low, but to super-low, like 15–20 percent, or taxes kill you. That's the real dirty little secret in our business. Because mutual funds are bought and sold with virtually no attention attached to tax efficiency." Nonetheless, some high-turnover mutual funds are tax-efficient because they use *gains/loss management*, where capital losses are realized to offset realized capital gains. This is most practicable when markets are volatile, creating numerous gain/loss opportunities. Evensky (2000) recommends investing only in funds that practise HIFO ("high cost in, first out") in deciding which particular shares to sell. This tax strategy sells stocks with the highest costs, which minimizes current capital gains and maximizes tax deferral.

Table 17 illustrates the impact of portfolio turnover on the percentage of realized capital gains. It ranges from 33 percent for 16 percent turnover up to 82 percent for 150 percent turnover. Thus the impact of turnover on shareholder taxes is very significant, but it is not the sole determinant. Further, table 18 illustrates the percentages of inflation-adjusted mutual fund returns that shareholders pay as taxes. Based on the assumptions, taxes are 58 percent of bond fund returns, 14 percent for low-turnover stock funds, and 43 percent for high-turnover stock funds. Thus type of security and portfolio turnover both have significant implications for shareholder taxes.

For many mutual funds, portfolio turnover is the largest source of low tax efficiency. Its importance was effectively demonstrated in Jeffrey and Arnott (1993). Portfolio turnover, the very activity intended to enhance portfolio performance, also creates taxable distributions to an unexpected degree. The key question is whether the expected economic benefit from portfolio turnover is large enough to cover the fees, trading costs, and taxes on realized capital gains that turnover generates. In general, the answer is "no." Analysis of seventy-one mutual funds and a S&P 500 Index fund gave no indication that turnover adds enough value to cover realized capital gains taxes. In fact, the evidence is quite to the contrary. Thus while the industry standard is to manage taxable portfolios as if they were tax-exempt, the practice is "inherently irresponsible." On the other hand, the tax deferral provided by unrealized capital gains increases the present value of investor terminal wealth and is under portfolio manager control.

Conventional wisdom considers portfolio turnover ranging from 1 percent to 25 percent as low and of minor consequence. The reality is quite different. Portfolio turnover of 25 percent incurs over 80 percent of the taxes incurred at turnover of 100 percent. It is therefore essential that funds desiring to be tax-efficient should limit turnover in the low ranges. Most of the tax damage has already been done by the time turnover reaches average levels, say, 80 percent.

Tax efficiency and fund families

There are differences in tax efficiency not only among mutual funds but among fund families, as well. Dziubinski (1997) computed the tax efficiency of diversified equity mutual funds in the twenty largest fund families. Eleven families have at least one of three characteristics of tax-efficient funds: net cash inflows, moderate portfolio turnover, and few changes in portfolio managers. Only T. Rowe Price has all three characteristics. Five families, including Vanguard, provide moderate portfolio turnover and few portfolio manager changes. Another five families, including Merrill Lynch, provide large net cash inflows. However, Fidelity has none of these characteristics.

Tax efficiency and cash flows

It should be noted that mutual fund managers have limited ability to control cash inflows. This is important because stable net cash inflows are important to effective portfolio management and tax efficiency, including adequate cash to meet shareholder redemptions. Santini and Aber

(1996) analyzed 127 mutual funds for the years 1974–85 for the effects of manager-controlled policies on cash inflows–load/no-load, sales commission structure, minimum required investment, and expenses. Fund policy variables under management control contributed almost nothing to explaining variability in new cash inflows. This apparently reflects a competitive equilibrium where individual funds cannot attract large new cash inflows through minimum investment requirements, expense ratios, load versus no-load status, or load structure. Individual funds are unable to sustain differences in these variables to generate additional cash inflows. Surprisingly, fund performance does not influence cash inflows. This leaves fund marketing and advertising as possible, but untested, influences.

The relationship between no-load and load mutual funds and new cash inflows was examined. Fund cash inflows are not influenced by whether they are load or no-load funds. There appear to be clienteles for each type of fund. The no-load feature itself is all-important to no-load investors. Fund expenses are not an important consideration for these investors. There is also a positive relationship between minimum required investment and rate of new cash inflows for no-load funds. This reflection of cost-conscious investors does not hold for load funds. Load funds have smaller minimum investment requirements, apparently to encourage sales efforts.

However, there is a positive relationship between both no-load and load fund expenses and cash inflows. Expenses are increased during periods of major cash inflows, but are not reduced during major cash outflows. Variations in loads do not act as a significant deterrent to new cash inflows. The purchase requirements at which reductions in loads begin do not provide greater incentives for investors to invest. In fact, investors appear to invest more in funds where the smallest loads are at the highest minimum purchase requirements. Load fund investors do not seek reduced loads, but appear to place more value on advice than its price.

Mutual funds that practise tax efficiency apply a number of strategies. Sanders (1997) analyzed the tax minimization strategies of eleven tax-efficient mutual funds. The funds employ from one to six strategies. Five funds use low turnover, low-yield stocks, gain/loss management, and derivatives/short sales. Derivatives and short sales are used to defer realization of taxable gains. Three funds use only municipal bonds. Two others use low turnover, gain/loss management, derivatives/short sales, and indexing. And one stock/bond fund applies all six strategies: low turnover, low-yield stocks, gain/loss management, derivatives/short sales, indexing, and municipal securities. Overall, nine funds include low turnover, gain/loss management, and derivatives/short sales among their strategies.

Several general conclusions may be made concerning mutual fund tax efficiency. Equity fund efficiency is relatively consistent over time. Tax-efficient funds are more likely to remain efficient, and the same pattern exists for less tax-efficient funds. Tax-exempt bond funds are much more tax-efficient than stock funds. Stock funds are much more efficient than taxable bond funds, owing to the latter's large income distributions. Growth funds are only slightly more tax-efficient than value funds, and the advantage is inconsistent over time. The tax efficiency of large and small capitalization stock funds is not significantly different.

Tax efficiency strategies

It is thus essential that mutual funds use strategies designed to maximize shareholder after-tax returns. Such strategies include: (1) realizing available portfolio tax losses (*tax-loss selling*), subject to net tax savings exceeding trading costs and profits lost from being temporarily out of the market; (2) using derivatives rather than stock trades to tilt portfolios based on short-term forecasts, assuming the ability to make accurate forecasts; (3) offering passively managed index funds with turnover under 5 percent; and (4) limiting portfolio trades (and taxes) in the name of diversification. The types of funds that are inherently less tax-efficient include cyclical stocks (volatility causes higher turnover), small company stocks (volatility and taxes on take-overs), and sector funds (limited diversification).

Estimated tax liability

Mutual fund tax efficiency and shareholder after-tax returns are historical data, but what is needed is a method of anticipating future realized capital gains and distributions. Purcell (1993) and Rekenthaler (1993b) reported Morningstar's method of anticipating future tax efficiency by computing "current (potential) capital gains tax liability" or "estimated tax liability." This method focuses on the realized/unrealized capital gains currently built into fund net asset values. This potential tax liability is calculated as the sum of unrealized capital gains/losses, undistributed capital gains/losses and income, less *tax-loss carryforwards*, all expressed as a percentage of net fund assets. Negative estimated tax liability represents greater realized losses than gains, but provides an offset to future realized capital gains.

A more hands-on approach to computing estimated tax liability is suggested in Zweig (1999b). Investors should access form N-30D at the SEC's Web site (www.sec.com) and locate a mutual fund's latest annual and semi-annual reports. Then calculate the sum of net unrealized capital gains, undistributed investment income, and undistributed capital gains. If the total exceeds 15 percent of total net assets then it should be assumed there is a significant tax overhang for both current and new shareholders.

Mutual funds with high portfolio turnover that regularly distribute capital gains are less likely to have sizable unrealized capital gains built into net asset values. The implication for new shareholders is a small estimated tax liability. Conversely, it is the very funds that have been most tax-efficient in the past that have large unrealized capital gains built into net asset values. The implication of this for new shareholders is a large estimated tax liability.

The keys to estimated tax liability are the extent of fund asset growth from capital appreciation and from future net cash inflows. Funds that focus on growth are more likely to generate capital gains than funds focusing on income or undervalued stocks. But the worst combination for new shareholders is, of all things, a history of large unrealized capital gains plus small portfolio turnover. These funds have been most tax-efficient by carrying unrealized capital gains in net asset values. Future fund sales/redemptions and resulting net cash inflows/outflows also impact future tax liability. If net cash inflows are negative, shareholder estimated tax liability is spread over fewer shares (more tax per share), but the reverse is true if outstanding shares increase.

However, having considered estimated tax liability, Barbee (1997a) discovered only an indirect relationship between estimated tax liability and future tax efficiency. Funds with large unrealized capital gains are not necessarily less tax-efficient. This can happen if net cash outflows from redemptions do not force liquidation holdings with unrealized capital gains. This finding reasserts the importance of net cash inflows to tax efficiency. Moreover, capital gains will be realized only gradually if portfolio turnover is low.

Mutual fund shareholders can also take steps to avoid large unexpected capital gains distributions. These include investing in funds with consistent investment styles and strategies, narrowly defined investment guidelines, histories of long-tenured portfolio managers, and consistency in distributions and portfolio turnover. Together, these and the other strategies provide an approach for minimizing tax surprises and provide an incentive to invest after capital gains distributions.

Fund tax losses

Mutual funds that reflect negative tax liabilities have tax-loss carryforwards from net realized capital losses. The carryforwards may be offset against future taxable realized capital gains for up to eight years. To the extent future realized capital gains are offset by loss carryforwards, they do not have to be distributed as taxable income to shareholders. For example, Murphy (1999) reported that in 1998 the Templeton Developing Markets fund had $123 million in tax-loss carryforwards plus a concurrent rebound year return of 18.7 percent! No taxable distributions were required and all realized capital gains were included in net asset value. Fund tax-loss carryforwards are normally reported in footnotes to the financial statements in annual and semi-annual reports.

Mutual fund shareholders can also initiate share redemptions/exchanges to take advantage of current capital losses in their accounts and save taxes. Mutual funds that reflect negative tax liabilities have tax-loss carryforwards from net realized capital losses. The carryforwards may be offset against future taxable realized capital gains. Net losses over $3,000 may also be used to offset realized capital gains from other assets. Remaining net losses exceeding $3,000 may be used as tax-loss carryforwards in maximum amounts of $3,000 for each of the next fifteen years.

One of the worst aspects of mutual fund taxation is that realized capital gains can trigger taxable distributions even if fund net asset values declined owing to unrealized capital losses. Amy Arnott (1998) reported an international fund that distributed realized capital gains of about 21 percent of net asset value, but had a 38.5 percent loss for the year. This provided a double whammy – negative returns plus a tax bill. A $10,000 January 1 purchase was worth $6,150 at year end, coupled with a $1,300 capital gains distribution!

Lauricella (1999) reported another example of poor mutual fund performance, huge cash outflows, large capital gains distributions, lost profit opportunities, and shareholder taxes. The fund's poor performance led to major redemptions that reduced assets from $1.5 billion to $900 million. To raise cash, stocks were sold with losses and gains, the latter not yet having reached target (sell) prices. The net result was huge realized capital gains and the fund's largest capital gains distribution. This was bad enough, but what was worse was that per-share distributions were much larger, owing to the decline in shares outstanding. The result was a decline in fund value and huge shareholder tax bills from a historically tax-efficient fund.

Index funds and tax efficiency

Index funds are normally more tax-efficient than actively managed funds. Their efficiency attributes were later applied to the development of even more tax-efficient so-called tax-managed funds (discussed below). Theodore Aronson summed up the tax advantage of index funds in Welling (1998): "The costs of our active strategies are high enough without paying Uncle Sam. Active is the operative word. Capital-gains taxes, when combined with transactions costs and fees, make indexing profoundly advantaged, I'm sorry to say."

It is easy enough to find index funds, but this does not necessarily also equate with tax efficiency. Not all index funds are tax-efficient. Barbee (1997b) analyzed the tax efficiency of several index funds and fund categories. The efficiency percentages range from 64 percent to 96 percent:

Wilshire Target Small Growth Investors	75.0
Vanguard Index Short-term Bond	63.8
DFA US six to ten small company	85.8
Average US diversified equity fund	88.6
Average hybrid fund	84.5
Average bond fund	65.1
Vanguard 500 Index	95.9

The least tax-efficient index funds are bond, short-term bond, and small capitalization funds, while large capitalization index funds are most tax-efficient.

The tax efficiency of index mutual funds also depends on the breadth of the particular benchmark index, the frequency of actual index composition changes, and whether the market has delivered large unrealized capital gains. As reported by Lucchetti (2000), market-inclusive index funds that hold thousands of stocks are not concerned about replacing stocks that have increased in value. These stocks cannot outgrow the index because the index is the market. This is not the case, however, for narrower breadth index funds, such as small-cap. funds. When stock market caps outgrow size categories, they are replaced in the actual indices. When funds replace these stocks in their portfolios, any unrealized capital gains are realized and distributed to shareholders. These distributions can be quite high when the market has driven up prices over a number of years. Contrary to usual thought, some types of and particular index funds should be favored in tax-deferred accounts, not taxable accounts.

Tax-managed mutual funds are relatively new and are finding a response in the growing demand for these funds. They are not designed simply to minimize shareholder taxes, but to *maximize* shareholder after-tax returns. As discussed above, the key is to focus on shareholder after-tax returns, not just tax efficiency. To do this, Penn (1994) recommended investors learn the basics of fund taxation, fund attributes that affect tax efficiency, and focus on after-tax returns. It is important to note that length of investment horizon determines how important the deferral of capital gains taxes is to particular investors. The longer investors hold fund shares, the greater the time value advantage of deferring capital gains taxes. That is, the present value cost of a dollar of deferred taxes is less than current taxes. Those with ten-year horizons benefit from funds that defer realizing capital gains. They are able to reinvest amounts that would otherwise be paid in taxes. Investors with short investment horizons, say two to three years, benefit much less from deferral of capital gains taxes. The present value benefit of deferred taxes is much less.

Table 19 provides investor guidelines for selecting tax-efficient mutual funds. The first step is to identify the number of attributes of tax-efficient funds provided by particular funds. The second step is to compute the percentage of actual attributes provided by particular funds relative to the total number of model attributes. The third step is to determine whether particular funds are more tax-efficient than their category peer groups, with an absolute goal of 90 percent tax efficiency. The fourth step is to identify the overall tax efficiency of particular funds as excellent, acceptable, or unacceptable. With the exception of checklist item 16, this is done on an absolute basis with no comparison to other funds. Vanguard Windsor II satisfies ten of the sixteen attributes of tax-efficient funds (67 percent), including that its three-year tax efficiency is higher than its category (tables 40b and 42b). The fund's 88.7 percent tax efficiency does not quite satisfy the goal of 90 percent tax efficiency. Windsor II's overall tax efficiency is therefore judged acceptable. This finding is summarized in table 27.

Tax-managed funds and large capitalization index funds are normally more tax-friendly than other funds. Boitano (1999) verified this for domestic tax-managed equity funds, where the average difference between pre-tax and after-tax returns is only 0.28 percent, but 1.68 percent for regular funds. Barbee (1999c) examined the behavior of the Vanguard Tax-managed Capital Appreciation fund. The fund (1) uses a sampling program to match the sector breakdown and median market capitalization of the Russell 1000 index, (2) discards higher-yielding stocks, (3) imposes two-tier sales transaction (redemption) fees, (4) provides above-average before-tax risk-adjusted returns, and (5) provides after-tax returns in the top quarter.

Thus tax efficiency is a key to determining whether a particular mutual fund's actual service disadvantage of lack of investor control over tax planning is an actual minimum disadvantage to particular investors in minimizing taxable income. But, again, tax efficiency contributes to investor after-tax returns, but it is *not* the sole factor.

Investor tax guidelines

There are several guidelines for mutual fund investors to lessen the negative impact of lack of control over tax planning. These guidelines are only elements in overall tax planning and include only those with direct application to mutual fund shareholders. Further, they generally apply to holdings in taxable accounts. To the extent possible, investors should invest in tax-deferred rather than taxable accounts to benefit from ongoing tax-free compounding of distributions.

The following shareholder actions in taxable accounts have potential capital gain/loss tax implications: (1) sale of fund shares, (2) exchange of shares from one fund to another in the same/other family, and (3) depositing/writing checks drawn on equity/bond fund accounts. Capital gains treatment is determined by how long funds hold securities, not how long investors hold fund shares. Fund capital gains distributions are realized capital gains net of realized capital losses. Fund dividend distributions of ordinary income are dividends and interest income net of operating expenses, and realized short-term capital gains net of realized short-term capital losses.

The Internal Revenue Service allows consistent use of one of four methods to calculate gains/losses. Investors should determine the best methods for minimizing taxes. How to determine the "cost basis" for each of these four methods is illustrated in Ronald (1998b).

The IRS default method is "first in, first out," where the first holdings of particular securities are assumed sold first. This method is usually least desirable in rising markets because it maximizes capital gains and taxes. The "specific share" method is flexible and usually most advantageous to investors, but requires meticulous records and written fund confirmations. In this method, shares are selected to minimize/maximize capital gains/losses. The "single category" method averages the costs of the various holdings of particular securities. Shares sold are assumed to be those held for the longest time. This method is normally used by mutual funds that compute shareholder gains/losses. It is computationally the easiest for funds and investors.

The "double category" method divides all holdings of particular securities into two groups and averages their costs. The first group includes securities holdings qualified for long-term capital gains/loss treatment, and the second includes holdings qualified for short-term treatment. Investors can normally reduce taxes by computing capital gains from the first group and losses from the second. But they do have to instruct their funds how many shares from each category they wish to redeem.

Table 20 provides mutual fund investor guidelines for minimizing taxes. This guide does not provide suggestions for minimizing taxes on investing, in general. It focuses on those issues that have specific application to mutual fund investors. However, it should not be forgotten that eligible mutual funds are not themselves taxed, only the distributions they make are taxed at the investor level. And investor-initiated trades/exchanges have potential tax implications, as well.

Before turning to the next section, it is useful to illustrate the effects of the variables discussed (with one exception) to this point on mutual fund returns (table 21). These variables are portfolio turnover, active (versus passive) portfolio management, fund expenses, shareholder taxes, and survivor bias in the data. *Survivor bias* refers to the upward bias in historical aggregate mutual fund returns due to the omission of funds that disappeared during the period. This is not a minor issue. For example, Carhart (1997) determined that no less than one-third of stock funds disappeared between 1962 and 1993. Inclusion of returns on these lost funds reduces reported historical aggregate fund returns.

Table 21 indicates the huge impact these variables have on after-tax shareholder returns. As a class, no-load index funds provide only 89 percent of the returns of the Wilshire 5000 stock index. This index represents the stock market as measured by the largest 6,500 publicly traded firms. The results are worse for managed mutual funds. No-load managed funds and load managed funds earn 76 percent and 73 percent, respectively, of the Wilshire 5000's returns. On a more realistic basis, if no-load index funds are used as the market surrogate the results improve. No-load managed funds and load managed funds earn 85 percent and 81 percent, respectively, of no-load index fund returns. These results indicate that mutual funds do not come close to earning the advertised and reported returns for their shareholders once adjusted to reflect after-tax returns.

Barbee (1999a) examined survivor bias in mutual fund returns for a five-year period. Survivor bias increased the returns on mid-cap. blend, small-cap. value, large-cap. value, and mid-cap. growth funds by about one percentage point, but did not increase large-cap. blend returns. However, survivor bias increased small-cap. growth returns by 1.7 percentage points. These and other reported findings of survivor bias of 1.5 percentage points support the conservative 1 percent survivor bias assumed in table 21.

REGULATORY ISSUES

The major issue in mutual fund regulation is whether mutual fund independent directors are sufficiently aligned with shareholder interests. As noted below, the SEC may share in this shortcoming. The issue is not whether mutual funds generally follow regulatory disclosure requirements, they do, but whether regulation is aligned with shareholder owners and whether particular funds go beyond the required minimum disclosure in meeting the needs of shareholders.

That is, do the actual disclosures of particular funds translate to actual minimum disclosure disadvantages for particular investors? Following this discussion, attention shifts to disclosure issues relevant to investors making more informed choices. There are numerous disclosure issues needing attention, but there are also funds that are more forthcoming than legally required. But no funds disclose close to what shareholders need to be empowered as real owners. Some other regulatory issues are also discussed.

Board effectiveness

In this regard, Tam (1999c) reported a study that ranks 138 mutual fund boards of directors by their effectiveness. Two equally weighted criteria are used: first, board structure, measured by the number of independent directors and their compensation; second, investment performance, measured by consistency, risk, costs, and *style drift*. The top ten boards are: (1) Nicholas Funds, (2) Alleghany Funds, (3) Alliance Capital Management, (4) Ariel Capital Management, (5) BT Funds, (6) Accessor Funds, (7) Global Asset Management, (8) Harbor Capital Management, (9) Vanguard Group, and (10) Glenmede Trust. The boards of less known funds are well represented, but those large fund families with household names, much less so.

Next, Tufano and Sevick (1997) described the composition and compensation of mutual fund boards of directors and examined the relationship between board structure and the fees charged shareholders. A useful review of board's legal responsibilities and their independence and effectiveness is also provided. Shareholder fees are lower when boards are smaller, have a larger proportion of independent directors, and directors serve a large proportion of investment advisor funds. Some evidence suggests a positive relationship between independent director compensation and shareholder fees.

Mutual funds have economies of scale, with fees inversely related to fund size. However, these economies are limited at the investment advisor level. Fees also vary by fund investment objectives, means of share distribution, and shareholder clientele. There is also a positive relationship between fund age (experience) and shareholder fees. This could reflect the greater reputations of established funds. But there is only a weak link between fund performance and fees.

Independent directors and fees

Mutual funds with larger boards but a smaller proportion of independent directors tend to charge shareholders larger fees. But the reverse holds for boards with larger proportions of independent directors. Board structure also appears more important in explaining fee differences between fund families than within. Surprisingly, funds with independent directors who sit on a larger proportion of investment advisor fund boards have lower fees. This breadth of oversight appears to give independent directors more leverage in negotiating with fund advisors. This benefit is much stronger in negotiations with third-party service providers than with fund advisors.

However, in interpreting the impact of board structure on fund fees, it should be noted that the law only requires fund fees to be "not excessive." Also, the nature of fund board structure is partly defined by law. Directors also have legal oversight responsibilities not directly related to fees. Fund advisors also influence fees by the types of boards they select. In this case, changing the board structure will not necessarily lower fees.

Independent directors and shareholder interests

The 1940 Act is acknowledged as landmark legislation that has generally served the interests of mutual fund investors. And it has done this over the years with a minimum number of scandals. Thus it would appear the totality of state and federal regulation assures the primacy of fund shareholders as legal fund owners. This is not always an easy hypothesis to test, however, as differences in the letter and spirit of the law may be very subtle, especially where reasonable persons may well differ.

Nonetheless, since the 1980s there has been growing concern that mutual fund independent (disinterested) directors are not independent enough as watchdogs of shareholder interests. As fund outsiders, they carry *the* major legal responsibility for ensuring the primacy of shareholder interests. One way to encourage independent directors in this mission would be to require they comprise 60 percent of the board, not 40 percent. A second way would be to take steps to ensure independent directors are competent and effective in protecting shareholder interests. In these ways, independent director and shareholder concerns might prevail in issues, discussions, and votes.

The issue of director competence and will is thus very important to mutual fund shareholders. In fact, an analysis of fund boards by Phillips (1997) indicated a direct relationship between the quality of fund directors and the quality of the funds they oversee. Some funds are known for active and visible boards of directors whose counsel is valued. Other funds prefer not to showcase directors, but rather keep them as invisible as the law allows. It appears strong directors are hallmarks of strong, well managed funds and vice versa – a chicken-and-egg relationship.

Aligning directors with shareholders

An important public policy and mutual fund shareholder issue is how to ensure that fund directors are aligned with shareholder interests. Several arguments are offered. First, independent directors would be more aligned with shareholder interests if they invested significant proportions of personal financial assets in the funds they serve, along with adequate shareholder disclosure. This would work to motivate independent director alignment with shareholders at least on a financial self-interest basis. The same argument also applies to fund managers and portfolio managers and their alignment with fund shareholder interests.

Currently, mutual funds must report only director investments in excess of 1 percent of fund assets, and only in the statement of additional information. The likelihood of this occurring is greater in small than in large funds because of the huge differences in absolute dollars involved. However, in any case, the general finding is that most independent directors have only modest personal financial holdings. For example, Bogle (1999a) computed that the average independent director has only $30,000 invested in all funds served. The question then arises whether funds should set (with SEC oversight) minimum *dollar* investment requirements for independent directors? And, in either case, should these holdings be disclosed annually in the prospectus?

Another advantage of significant investment by independent directors, and also by fund managers and portfolio managers, has to do with closing funds to new investors before they become too large to maintain past performance. As discussed in Zweig (1996a), growth in fund assets has both performance and potential conflict of interest implications for independent directors. Fund performance tends to decline as cash inflows exceed the ability of portfolio managers to apply strategies that worked well with small asset bases. The break point appears to be $1 billion in assets.

The very success that attracted large cash inflows becomes the reason why mutual fund performance becomes less sustainable as size increases. Shareholders thus do best when fund assets are optimal size, but investment advisors do best when funds are beyond this size – the dollar amounts of advisory fees increase with asset size. Phillips (1993) determined that once funds achieve the critical asset size of $50 million to $200 million, they become licenses to print money for investment advisors. Accordingly, investment advisors do not want to kill the goose that continues to lay golden eggs. The penalty for seeking large returns but coming up short of market returns is often considered more problematic than approximating market returns by *closet indexing*. This strategy is usually supported by marketing and advertising, which increases fund expenses. This effort includes advertising, broader and more costly uses of distribution channels, and focuses on maintaining asset size and attracting new shareholders.

This issue of optimal mutual fund size is analyzed in Collins and Mack's (1997) study of all 533 mutual fund complexes (families) for the years 1990–4. Two types of scale economies are considered: average fund and by type of fund. Significant economies of scale were indicated, but note that recent trends towards providing capital-intensive retirement services may require these savings. Two groups of fund families were identified. The smallest group of families with assets of $100 million or less may not survive owing to its smaller scale economies. Typically, only one or two types of funds are offered. Much greater scale economies could be achieved by adding new types of funds. The second group of fund families, the average family, has achieved higher but less than optimal scale economies. Typically, all three types of funds are offered: stock, bond, and money market.

Optimal scale economies are achieved with mutual fund family assets of $20 billion to $40 billion, but, beyond this, scale economies decline. Fund families offering bond funds achieve efficient scale with assets between $6 billion and $8 billion, while money market funds achieve efficient scale with assets between $10 billion and $12 billion. However, equity funds achieve scale economies at much lower asset sizes, $600 million to $800 million. This lower size may explain why smaller stock funds charge higher fees and why many fund families offer only stock funds. And, counter to the justification for 12b-1 fees, they act only to increase expenses. These findings certainly give impetus to concern about the failure of most fund families to close funds at more cost efficient asset sizes.

Latzko (1999) analyzed scale economies for individual mutual funds using a 1997 sample of 2,610 funds with average assets of $857.3 million. Significant economies of scale exist in all but three investment objectives: convertible securities, micro-cap stocks, and S&P 500 index funds. Adjusted for investment categories, funds exhibit significant scale economies across all five asset sizes, but the rapid decline is exhausted at assets of about $3.5 billion.

Whether or not mutual funds close to new assets before they get too large to continue the successful application of their investment styles may be an effective test to determine whether funds consider shareholders as customers or owners. In what has to be one of Fundom's greatest ironies, Kelley (1995b) calculated that two-thirds of closed funds outperform their investment objectives since closing. This better performance makes the point that if fund shareholders were considered owners and not customers, fund closings would be a routine element of investment strategies. The small Merger Fund is a case in point. The fund is often closed to minimize taking in more assets than can profitably be used in merger arbitrage.

Second, mutual fund independent directors would be more aligned with shareholder interests if they were not handpicked by fund investment advisors. Shivdasani and Yermak (1999) determined that fund directors are less likely to monitor aggressively when CEOs are involved in the selection process. The results are fewer outside independent directors, more outside directors with gray area conflicts of interest, and boards where independent directors are a minority. It is not unlikely that independent directors selected by fund advisors are implicitly more concerned with management than with shareholder interests. They know who is responsible for their appointments, and board tenure tends to be long-term, and in many cases to carry generous fees and retirement annuities based on years of service. Typically, initial slates of independent directors are selected from former business relationships or acquaintances and personal friends. Later, independent directors may include academics or individuals adding public visibility and prestige. Independent board members typically include lawyers, retired and active executives, academics (maybe), and visible former public officials. They share one common characteristic – no previous mutual fund experience. Moreover, shareholders receive one slate of nominees for independent directors and not their slate.

The fact that independent directors rarely take on or attempt to fire mutual fund investment advisors provides indirect evidence of tacit *quid pro quo* understandings with management. This is not surprising, but it has nothing to do with ensuring the primacy of shareholder interests. Independent directors might be more inclined to replace investment advisors if the law gave them sole authority and 60 percent of directors were independent. There is more courage in a crowd. Mutual fund directors serve with a great deal of anonymity facilitated by the requirement they be identified only in the statement of additional information.

The implications of lack of strong independent directors is implicitly seen in negative correlations between advisory fees and other expenses, including 12b-1 fees, and the returns provided by mutual funds. In this context, shareholders have effectively become financial service company customers, not fund owners. Moreover, most investment advisory firms generate larger returns than the funds they manage. Bogle (1997b) reported that investment advisors enjoy pre-tax profit margins of 35–40 percent, which approximates 50–60 percent exclusive of marketing expenses designed to increase fund size and total management fees.

Marketing and distribution costs are included in fund operating expenses, usually as 12b-1 fees.

Sivy (1998) looked beyond profit margins to T. Rowe Price's shareholder returns and earnings growth. Share prices of this largest publicly traded investment advisor have increased fourteenfold since 1990–1, compared with three and one-half times for the DJIA. Over the past five years, earnings have increased at an *annualized rate of return* of 27.5 percent. Has any fund performed better risk adjusted? McGough (1998) examined the returns of seven other investment advisors for the years 1994–8. The lowest returns averaged only about 7 percent, but for the other six advisors annualized returns ranged from about 20 percent to 29 percent.

One of the great ironies of mutual funds is that when independent directors do act, shareholders usually do not support them. For example, in three recent cases, shareholders voted with management when directors moved to replace them. Further, Regnier (1999b) reported a case where independent directors accused the advisor/portfolio manager of deviating from the fund's stated investment style, delegating portfolio duties, and ignoring an ethical issue. However, the real concern was apparently poor fund performance. After directors voted to oust the investment advisor, management called for a proxy vote and was supported by owners of 90 percent of shares voting. But by then 70 percent of shareholders had already voted with their feet and redeemed shares. As it stands now, shareholders generally back management rather than directors. Talk about supporting your independent directors when they do stand up for shareholders!

The lack of proxy support for mutual fund independent directors may partly reflect investor emphasis on investing with star managers. To the extent that shareholders are attracted to funds with star portfolio managers, it is not surprising they continue to support the stars as long as they remain confident in them. If so, it suggests that director efforts to remove investment advisors would be more successful if strongly anchored on fund performance, assuming most shareholders are still invested.

On the positive side, Simon (1993) reported a case where mutual fund directors successfully took on a fund's investment advisor. The investment advisor had announced plans to impose sales loads of 5.75 percent on two funds, but independent directors were convinced this action ignored shareholder interests and refused to approve new loads. The investment advisor then announced it was selling the funds to another advisory firm, but the board voted to sell the funds to a third advisor. Simon stated: "The . . . directors' revolt was an extraordinary event in the fund industry – not because . . . [the board] overreached their authority, but rather because they *exercised* it." The sad commentary about this incident is that it was reported at all. If such board behavior were commonplace, as it should be under law, it may have only been given passing notice.

Lack of shareholder support for mutual fund independent directors could also reflect lack of effective communication. This could underlie the problem independent directors have in gaining shareholder support to remove investment advisors. Certainly, there is little evidence that directors are encouraged to communicate with shareholders, and vice versa. It is not surprising, then, when independent directors state they never (or almost never) hear from shareholders.

However, Dziubinski (1998a) stated that shareholders must accept some blame for lack of communication by not acting more proactively. In most cases, when shareholders get upset they simply redeem their shares. This is easier than expressing what (little) power they do have by voting proxy statements and communicating their concerns, including requests for annual shareholders' meetings.

Should mutual funds be at least encouraged to improve shareholder–director communication? As stated above, information about directors usually appears only as required in the statement of additional information. Disclosure of director email addresses would go a long way toward improving at least one-way shareholder communication. Thus far, there is no suggestion (yes or no) that independent directors favor this. But independent directors would feel a greater sense of independence if provided with small offices and staffs, along with consultants and legal counsel. This would reduce dependence on data provided by management.

On a positive note, not all investment advisors control the process for nominating new independent directors once the initial directors have been named. In these cases, independent directors act as nominating committees for new independent directors. In some few cases, it has been said management is well advised to keep its hands off the nominating process. Moreover, it would be easier for independent directors to be independent if they received advice from consultants and legal counsel of their own choosing. This is important because directors get most of their information from management. Should funds be encouraged to disclose prior management/independent director relationships annually in the prospectus?

Third, mutual fund independent directors would be more aligned with shareholder interests if board fees and annuities did not result in subconscious or tacit melding of financial interests with fund management. Many independent directors are paid very handsomely and receive generous retirement benefits for a limited amount of work. Most independent directors receive what amounts to lifetime annuities. Simon (1993) reported that independent directors generally make $1,000–$10,000 for each fund they serve and lesser amounts for each board meeting (four to twelve annually) attended, and perhaps also for each committee chaired and committee meeting attended. And, in two-thirds of fund families, one board serves all funds. Annual fees have been reported totaling $100,000 to over $350,000. As Simon stated, "Not bad for a part-time job."

Bogle (1997b) computed that the independent directors of the ten highest-paying fund families receive average annual fees of $150,000. This contrasts with an average of $78,000 paid annually to directors of the ten largest Fortune 500 companies. Some investment advisors also pay affiliated directors fees in addition to their managerial compensation. It is not human nature to nominate troublemakers, and independent directors know this full well. And then, there is that pension.

Potential conflicts of interest are increased by the common industry practice of one board serving all family funds. This is certainly convenient and efficient for investment advisors and directors. Independent director compensation even appears more reasonable (not much) when computed on a per-fund basis. Tam (1999b) reported that one major fund family pays independent directors $190,000–$200,000 to supervise 259 funds. The highest-paid board member of another fund family receives $406,000 for supervising ninety-eight funds. And Dziubinski (1998a) reported a director of one fund family who was paid nearly $340,000 in 1996 for serving as trustee for fifty-five funds. Yet another fund family pays independent directors $70,000 for supervising 101 funds. This latter pay scale is more in line with independent director compensation in major corporations.

More important than convenience and efficiency is the question of how effective can independent directors be in oversight if they serve numerous funds? Most every fund has unique disclosure and performance issues. And then, there is that issue of fund expenses. There is empirical evidence of a positive relationship between director fees and fund expenses. Mulvihill (1996) computed that the average expense ratio (excluding 12b-1 fees) of domestic equity funds that pay directors more than $100,000 is 1.06, compared with 0.91 percent for those funds paying directors less than $25,000. For taxable bond funds the expense ratios for the same salaries are 0.89 percent and 0.66 percent, respectively. Again, the fact that directors rarely move to change investment advisors provides indirect evidence of at least potential problems. Thus should funds be encouraged to disclose individual director fees and benefits in the prospectus, including the number of funds served, rather than just in the statement of additional information?

Fourth, in an argument that compounds the implications of numbers two and three, mutual fund independent directors would be more aligned with shareholder interests if fund managers did not have dual management roles. Unfortunately, this dual role underlies mutual funds as externally-managed shells and magnifies the probability and implications for misalignment of independent directors with shareholder interests.

The dual role of fund managers is seen in the fact that fund board chairs normally hold similar positions in management companies that act as investment advisors and usually more to funds. This provides an important reason why independent directors should serve as board chairs. This same duality generally also applies to other fund officers and affiliated (inside) directors. Fund shareholders may not be sufficiently concerned or aware of this duality and its greater potential for favoring management interests. The significance of this is increased when it is noted that management companies normally provide directly/indirectly most, if not all, administrative, investment, and distribution services. These services are normally "marked up" to funds and continue to increase in absolute and/or relative terms.

Another important implication of duality in mutual fund manager roles is perhaps unique to the investment company world. Fund managers pay themselves as investment advisors and managers before shareholders are paid a cent. Therefore, given human nature, whose asset values are fund managers attempting to maximize? Is it their investment management company assets or shareholder-owned fund assets? Again, it is only necessary to look at the profitability of investment advisors to know the answer. Returns on investment advisory firms normally exceed those on the funds advised. Should funds disclose these dual management relationships in the prospectus, along with overall compensation and investment advisor ownership interests?

As discussed above, there is also indirect empirical evidence of the cost implications of these several arguments on the primacy of shareholder interests. Table 23 shows that mutual fund expense ratios increased by 33 percent from 1986 to 1999, and table 25 shows that management fees alone increased by nearly 90 percent from 1920–30 to 1995–6. While funds were much smaller in 1920–30 and offered many fewer services, the key point is that investment advisors have not and do not significantly share the cost savings from economies of scale as they advise more and larger funds. Fund shareholders do have legal authority to challenge advisory fees and sue both investment advisors and directors for "breach of fiduciary duty." But the fact remains that the costs of legal action are typically larger than individual losses, unless shareholders combine in class-action suits.

To make matters worse, increased mutual fund management fees and expenses have generally not been offset by commensurate increases in performance. In most years, actively managed funds underperform comparable index funds, often before and generally after shareholder taxes. In the latter case, advisory fees and expenses are larger than the value added by active portfolio management.

The SEC as regulator

Clark (1999) identified ten areas for needed improvement in SEC regulation of mutual funds. The basic problem is that the SEC operates within an environment of political give-and-take. The SEC, its priorities, and its budget are subject, in varying degrees, to Congress, the White House, the industry, and the media in serving shareholders, but also to the regulatory perspective, vigor, and independence of SEC staff. Clark simplified the constraints facing the SEC as follows:

1 "We're [SEC] overwhelmed." Resources are inadequate in the face of rapid industry and technology growth.
2 "We're a political football." Congress and the White House are sensitive to the industry.
3 "Our talk is cheap." "Jawboning," rather than ordering, is the preferred and often most feasible way of effecting change.
4 "We put the fox in charge of the henhouse." Agency leadership often comes from Wall Street, and the industry is partly self-regulating (NASD).
5 "Our arbitration system favors the big boys." Court action is prohibited and the SEC is not proactive in ensuring fairness of NASD's management of the arbitration process.
6 "We allow insider trading – every day." Selective (insider) disclosure to institutional investors/ analysts acts to disadvantage individual investors.
7 "The Internet befuddles us." Electronic trading and communication have grown beyond its ability to regulate.
8 "We make stock fraud too easy." Regulation and disclosure is inadequate to limit small company stock fraud.
9 "We'll steamroll shareholders when we have to." Protection of small investors is sometimes a victim of lessened regulatory burden and competing interests.
10 "Kickbacks? We look the other way." Conflicts of interest and hidden payments practices are often met by calls for change and better disclosure.

As examples of the last point, brokers continue to receive larger commission by selling in-house mutual funds. Some investment advisors arrange broker "support payments" for selling their funds. And SEC findings of abusive soft dollar practices called only for improved disclosure. Clark's headlines are oversimplified, but they make the point that the SEC can only do so much with its budget and within the political environment in which it operates. But agency leadership is essential.

On the other hand, Clark's banners may not be oversimplified when related to the public interest served by mutual fund independent directors. In Bullard (2000b), a former SEC staffer reported on a conference attended by SEC officials and mutual fund directors. The conference followed the issuance of proposed regulations that would require 50–75 percent of fund directors be independent. The SEC had also voiced interest in improving regulation in several other areas benefiting fund shareholders.

However, the conference proved disappointing from the standpoint of improved disclosure to shareholders. Participating mutual fund directors generally ignored the SEC issues and focused instead on better protection for directors from shareholder lawsuits, not shareholder protection. The conference is perhaps best characterized by the important topics ignored: (1) misleading advertising concerning the sustainability of returns; (2) the impact of fees and expenses on returns; (3) personalized statements of fund expenses; (4) disclosure of hidden expenses, such as brokerage commission; (5) more frequent disclosure of portfolio holdings; (6) the use of quantitative risk measures; (7) improved proxy voting records; (8) disclosure of fund earnings not distributed; and (9) disclosure of shareholder after-tax returns. All of these issues should be implemented. In spite of the proactive efforts by former SEC chairman Arthur Levitt, the regulation of mutual funds through effective disclosure remains yet a goal, not a reality.

Shareholder protection

To assist mutual fund shareholders, Updegrave et al. (1994) identified several questions they need to answer to protect themselves. These are also questions the industry and SEC should provide answers. First, is the fund as safe as it says it is? How are derivatives used (restricted in money market funds) and what are the actual risks? Should there be improved disclosure and restricted use of risky derivatives? Second, does the portfolio manager place his/her interests above shareholder interests? Has the fund adopted the ICI code of ethics on portfolio manager personal trading? Should returns on personal trades be disclosed? Should personal trading be barred?

Third, how much does the fund actually cost? Invest only in no-load funds and avoid multiple share classes. Should all fees and expenses be combined for ease of comparison? Fourth, who is actually managing the portfolio? Who is calling the shots when team managers are cited? Should real portfolio managers be disclosed and more information provided (duties and portfolio allocation) where team managers are actually used?

Fifth, are the fund's net asset values accurate? Are portfolio holdings (especially municipal bonds) priced at actual or appraised values? Should the method used to price less liquid securities and how these estimates compared with actual sales prices be disclosed? Sixth, who is looking out for shareholder interests? Should funds have shareholder ombudsmen and should SEC efforts be supplemented by a self-regulatory agency?

Mandate for change

The actual role of independent directors should thus be to fulfill their explicit legal mission as shareholder watchdogs. The model for director activism is alive in corporate America's not too recent emphasis on the creation of shareholder value. To accomplish this for mutual funds, a renaissance is needed in the *actual* mission of mutual fund governance, including impetus from public reassessment of the industry. The desired result is simply to attain the letter *and* the spirit of the 1940 Act. Such a result should also include the bonus of a more price-competitive industry.

As the industry stands today, however, it is unlikely that the major mandate of the 1940 Act is being achieved: mutual fund shareholders are *owners* and independent directors are their voice and watchdogs. The primary, active mission of fund boards is to ensure the primacy of shareholder interests. Both public and investor interests are adversely affected when mutual funds are managed in the interest of investment advisors or subjected to inadequate "independent scrutiny."

This 1940 Act imperative came at a time industry survival required renewed investor confidence, severely lacking following the 1929 crash, subsequent depression and closed-end fund scandals. However, this imperative has grown faint since 1982, during which time market performance and industry growth have created an environment of plenty and the illusion of indefinite growth and prosperity. During this period, it has been easy for fund management to rationalize placing their interests ahead of shareholders and for independent directors, and shareholders for that matter, to go along implicitly.

"Mutual" mutual funds

Bogle (1999a), the industry's most active critic, has argued that change is needed in mutual fund organizational structure if shareholder value is to be enhanced. As discussed, mutual funds are normally shell organizations managed externally by various service providers. This organization guarantees separation of fund control and ownership and is implemented by the dual roles of investment advisors as fund managers. Investment advisors serve both their own shareholders/principals and those of the funds they serve as investment advisors. Fund shareholders, therefore, get their returns only after investment advisors receive their returns for portfolio management and directly/indirectly providing any other services. This is the built-in conflict of interest discussed above.

Traditionally, investment management companies were founded and managed by individuals, much like small, family-owned businesses. Over time, many of these firms evolved or acquired their ways into larger organizations or were acquired by larger organizations, usually with broader ownership. A small number of corporations have become publicly traded. More recently, as discussed, other financial institutions have noted the profitability of fund management and are increasingly acquiring investment advisors as elements in financial service conglomerates.

Bogle (1999a) noted that investment management companies sell for an average of 4 percent of the assets under management. The management companies in the then $5 trillion business are, therefore, worth approximately $200 billion. For example, Hechinger (1999) separately estimated that Fidelity, the largest manager of mutual funds, is worth about $30 billion. To justify the $200 billion industry value, investment advisors are assumed to earn 17 percent on investment before taxes and 12 percent after taxes. A 17 percent annual return provides $34 billion above actual cost of fund services. Most of this $34 billion would accrue to mutual fund shareholders if mutual internal organizational structures like Vanguard's were adopted. Under this structure, the shareholder-owned funds are managed *internally* (not externally) at cost, and the profits that conventionally go to external service providers are rebated to fund shareholders in reduced expenses.

Bogle (1999a) believes mutual funds should be organized and operated as truly mutual organizations without separation of ownership and control and without external service providers.

In this way, the Vanguard way, necessary fund services are provided at cost by funds themselves. Several important advantages are claimed for this mutual style of organization: (1) single focus on enhancing shareholder value as owners, not customers; (2) enhancement of shareholder value by (3) avoidance of trendy funds-of-the-month designed to gather assets, and (4) provision of educational advertising and marketing, rather than costly and aggressive advertising and marketing designed to attract new shareholders and paid for by current shareholders; (5) *provision of fund services at cost;* (6) more reasoned acceptance of index funds as lower-cost investment vehicles; and thus (7) no need to pursue more risky investment strategies to compensate for higher expenses. For a different slant, Fund Family Shareholder Association (2000) provided an inside look at the compensation plan that underlies the organization.

In this mutual form of organization, outside investment advisors are hired to manage all or some portion of fund portfolios. These portfolio managers are called multi-advisors, not sub-advisors in the usual sense where fund investment advisors and funds are separate organizations.

New product issue

Another issue largely ignored during this period of plenty is the growing complexity of securities markets, such as exotic types of bonds, greater use of derivative securities of all shades of risk, and the popularity of volatile emerging-market securities. There are also competitive forces causing some fund families to develop new funds based on shaky premises, and to undertake more dangerous and less well understood strategies to enhance returns and gather investor assets.

Kelley (1995a) saw this problem with some new single-state municipal bond funds with income exempt from particular state income taxes. The funds were designed and marketed to investors in either one of two states without income taxes. The funds were successfully offered, but fund managers admitted investors did not know what they were getting. The result of these and other forces is that fund shareholders are being subjected to risks many of them are unaware of, still less understand. And all of this is happening within the context of a market priced at never-seen-before levels. The overall investment climate thus couples increased fund risks with increased market risks.

Industry ethics issues

Mutual fund ethics and integrity issues continue to come to the attention of regulators, the industry, and investors. Lucchetti (1999d) reported that 74 percent of asset managers consider portfolio manager personal trading a matter of "high concern." And these are senior industry executives! Also, 80 percent of asset managers are equally concerned about insider trading for personal or mutual fund accounts. In addition, they are concerned about misleading advertising and fraudulent financial reporting and, to a lesser degree, soft dollar payments and customer gifts. Some funds restrict portfolio manager participation in initial public offerings and private placements. However, only 20 percent of the respondents publish their ethics guidelines.

Mutual funds are required to have ethics codes with trading guidelines prohibiting the use of insider information for personal gain. Further, the ICI recommends that ethics codes include the following compliance procedures: (1) all trades must be approved in advance, (2) all trading activity is monitored following approval, (3) records of trading activity are provided to compliance staff, (4) personal holdings are disclosed annually, and (5) employee certification of compliance with the ethics code. The major fund families have adopted these guidelines, but they are not routinely included in the prospectus. Some funds provide them upon request and others provide only verbal summaries.

Fidelity Investments provides an example of one fund family's approach to ethics and personal trading. Pozen (1994), then general counsel and managing director, reported that Fidelity takes its fiduciary responsibility very seriously. Fidelity has a code of ethics and a compliance staff to enforce it. This staff and internal and external auditors make semi-annual reports to the board's audit committee, which comprises only independent trustees. Fidelity follows SEC guidelines and allows fund managers to make personal trades as long as safeguards against conflicts of interest are in place.

However, Zweig (1995, 1996b), Misra and Zweig (1996), and Gasparino (1998c) noted five cases where mutual fund portfolio managers were reported to the SEC for possible violations of personal trading rules. They involved "front running" – buying first for portfolio manager portfolios and then for fund portfolios to drive up prices, but also violation of personal trading rules, and failure to report personal trades. On the positive side, these few cases certainly do not represent an epidemic. Further, in three cases the fund advisors alerted the SEC, and in the other case the advisor strongly denied the allegations. In all cases, no shareholder money was lost.

Portfolio pricing issues

Mutual fund directors have ultimate responsibility for pricing portfolio securities. Pricing is delegated operationally on a day-to-day basis, but remains subject to regulation, fund policy, and board oversight. Prices used are normally last trade prices for exchange-listed securities and midpoints of most recent bid–ask spreads of unlisted securities. This is called *market value pricing*. But, in the case of illiquid or less liquid securities, "good-faith estimates" must be made, using one of several accepted valuation methods. This is called fair-value pricing, which is usually discussed in the statement of additional information. As a result, measured fund performance may reflect pricing estimates as well as actual market prices. Fair-value pricing by its nature is difficult to employ consistently in all applications, both within a given portfolio and among different portfolios.

Fair-value pricing finds its most common use in situations involving (1) adjustment of market prices for time differences among global markets, (2) holdings of less liquid and illiquid portfolio securities, (3) halts in exchange trading with no closing prices, (4) differences in pricing methods, and (5) anything else making closing prices problematic. When proven to be inaccurate measures of market values, fair-value prices can lead to sudden and large writedowns of security values. These writedowns have been especially troublesome in respect of funds with less liquid bond and municipal bond holdings.

With the growth of global investing, time zone differences more frequently dictate "fair value" estimates of international security prices at close of US trading. This is especially so when earlier international market closing prices differ markedly from after-hours trading prices. This means international prices are either too high or too low for use at the close of US trading. Application of fair-value pricing limits the potential for *arbitrage profits* in this case arising from stock price discrepancies in domestic and international market prices due to differences in global time zones. Fair-value pricing can resolve these pricing discrepancies and reflect them in the computation of portfolio values and net asset value. In this way, fair-value pricing reduces the potential for arbitrage to impose additional trading and portfolio adjustment costs on long-term shareholders.

Pozen (1998a), Arnott (1997), and Sanders (1998a) described and commented on how Fidelity Investments used fair-value pricing when lower prices at the close of Hong Kong trading rebounded sharply in after-hours trading. At the close of US trading, Fidelity estimated Hong Kong prices at about 10 percent higher than actual closing prices. This proved too conservative, as Hong Kong prices increased about 14 percent the next trading day.

The pricing issue is very important for mutual funds. Funds portfolios were designed to engender confidence based on accurate, daily pricing of each holding. This implies that daily fund net asset values correctly reflect realizable portfolio liquidity. This assurance has become less so as funds increasingly hold illiquid derivatives, less liquid small capitalization domestic securities, and international securities trading in less liquid markets. The realized lack of "easy liquidity" in these cases is often forced by redemptions that result in large, unexpected overnight reductions in net asset value.

Fair-value pricing is sometimes criticized for violating the sacrosanct nature of net asset value. After all, two funds acting in good faith may well price the same illiquid securities a bit differently. Fair-value pricing is nothing new, but, as mentioned, its use has become more prevalent as funds hold more illiquid and less liquid securities and trade in less liquid global markets. Thus there are several reasons why the SEC should require explicit disclosure of potential and actual uses of fair-value pricing, including the estimation methods used and explicit pricing implications.

Rekenthaler (1994b) and Phillips (1994) made several recommendations concerning the pricing of illiquid and less liquid securities. First, there is a need to standardize definitions of derivative securities and to disclose clearly their use and risk. Second, the legal definition of *restricted securities* should be broadened from *private* and illiquid *securities* to include secondary market liquidity. Many derivatives are illiquid if held in large amounts. Third, develop closed-end vehicles with no redemption pressures to invest in illiquid and less liquid securities. These securities include emerging market debt and equity securities, very small (*micro-cap*) capitalization stocks, *collateralized mortgage obligations* (CMOs), and *inverse floating rate notes* (IFRNs). Mutual funds that invest in securities of developing countries are called *emerging market funds*. Fourth, require delayed monthly online portfolio postings to monitor *window dressing* as well as illiquid and less liquid securities with potential for pricing surprises when sold. Fifth, reduce the legal maximum of net assets that may be invested in illiquid securities from 15 percent to 5–10 percent.

Portfolio posting issues

Monthly lagged online postings of mutual fund portfolios is consistent with treating shareholders as owners, not customers. Arnott (1996a) even stated that two to four-week lagged

portfolio postings should be adequate to protect shareholder interests from day traders, speculators, and short-term market timers. And it does make it easier for investors to observe and
monitor portfolio liquidity and performance.

Use of frequent online portfolio posting also implicitly assumes, and correctly so, that some
portfolio managers *dress up* portfolios prior to required disclosure. Some portfolio managers sell
securities with losses and those with questionable liquidity and risk relative to fund investment
objectives and policies and replace them with higher-quality securities. Musto (1999) also
noted that online portfolio disclosure should reduce the time available for portfolio managers to
make short-term bets on the ongoing direction of security prices between required disclosure
dates.

Some portfolio managers also engage in *portfolio pumping* to get a quick performance boost
on the last trading day before required *portfolio postings*. Additional shares of less liquid, small
capitalization stocks are purchased on the last day to push up prices of total holdings of these
stocks. For example, Zweig (1997c) reported large-cap. funds beat the S&P 500 Index by 0.53
percentage points on the last trading day, and small-cap. funds beat their index by 1.03
percentage points. And, over the period 1985–95, 90 percent of 1,550 funds beat the market on
the last day of the year at least once. Portfolio pumping can be enhanced by buying call options
that increase in price as small-cap. stock prices are driven up, and also by reducing cash assets
to buy additional shares. Manipulation of share prices is illegal, but it is not easy to prove.

Window dressing and portfolio pumping are two strategies used to dress up portfolios and
performance at portfolio disclosure dates. Bullard (2000a) noted these and others that may be
disclosed by online portfolio posting. These strategies include window dressing and portfolio
pumping to enhance performance, but also style drift, whereby actual and stated portfolio
objectives and investment styles differ. This may be done between disclosure dates in efforts to
outperform *stated* peer competitors. As noted, funds must invest only 65 percent of assets
consistent with their names. But this could be reduced between required disclosures. Minimize
style drift by investing only in funds with clear statements and explanation of investment
objectives and investment styles.

However, Zweig (1998c) observed frequent portfolio postings might actually have the
effect of increasing window dressing. Portfolio managers may become less patient in holding
undervalued securities that have yet to move up. Another issue is psychological. Online posting
might cause portfolio managers investors to "ride" poor performing securities too long rather
than be proved "wrong."

Another argument for not posting monthly mutual fund portfolios online applies to shareholders who buy funds to get professional portfolio management, especially portfolio managers with unique approaches. Frequent posting could deny these latter portfolio managers
the relative performance advantage they would otherwise have obtained. Second-guessing
portfolio managers by frequent portfolio reviews, even assuming shareholders are competent
to do so, is inconsistent with paying for professional management. Shareholders should focus
on what portfolio managers do with their portfolios by reviewing performance over time, at
most quarterly, and not portfolio details. Moreover, even if monthly postings contain valuable
information, would individual investors be able to act in time to profit from it?

However, an argument supporting frequent portfolio postings may be made for mutual fund
shareholders who buy load funds or pay financial planners for advice. In such cases, advisors
have a fiduciary duty to seek out all relevant information available for advising clients. The

one-size-fits-all solution to frequency of portfolio postings would provide both detail and summary online portfolio postings and let shareholders and advisors choose which one or both or any they want. Such disclosure would also treat shareholders more like owners than customers. Concerns about market timers and day traders making use of the information could be solved by providing portfolios lagged by a month.

Interestingly, the SEC is considering a quite radical position on frequency of portfolio postings. This proposal has the goal of "doing better with less." Individual fund investors would be provided with more useful information than is currently provided twice yearly or would be provided by more frequent online portfolio postings. This more useful information would include streamlined postings of largest holdings, along with visual and written explanations of how these holdings contributed to performance. Of course, complete portfolio postings would also be available online or upon request.

Shareholder litigation issues

Mutual funds also face increased litigation in recent years. There have been numerous shareholder class-action suits against investment advisors for charging excessive management fees and expenses. There have also been suits charging advisors with misleading investors as to their intentions concerning investments in risky derivatives and/or illiquid securities, and with failure to disclose the risks adequately.

Ineffective communication with inadequate or inaccurate disclosure may underlie some litigation. Litigant shareholders may well have perceived, implicitly or explicitly, and perhaps correctly so, that the claimed improper disclosure reflects a view of them as customers rather than owners. A more enlightened view of shareholders as owners with legitimate information needs would likely reduce the frequency of legal action.

Poor mutual fund performance along with legally required disclosure does not provide grounds for legal action. Shareholders are responsible for assessing investment risks, but fund disclosure must be legally sufficient to make such assessments possible. Arnott (1995) stated: "Shareholders can expect fund management to live up to its promises, but before mailing off their checks, investors should take time to understand just what those promises are." And this requires forthcoming disclosure.

Historical revisionism issues

There are three methods for mutual fund advisors to get rid of poor-performing funds: liquidate them, sell them to other advisors or firms, or merge them into previously established or newly created family funds. In the latter case, the SEC once allowed the performance histories of non-fund portfolios to be included in the prospectus or sales literature of new mutual funds for up to one year. Now, newly created funds may incorporate the performance histories of portfolios converted to mutual funds, as long as they are "not misleading." As stated by Zweig (1998b): "Which came first, the fund or its performance?" These backdated histories actually come before the newly created funds to which they become attached. Backdated histories from bank commingled trust accounts, limited partnership portfolios, composites of insurance company "separate accounts," and advisor incubator portfolios have been attached to new mutual funds.

Investment advisors use incubator portfolios to flight-test investment ideas and/or portfolio managers. These portfolios are funded by management, limited in size, and pretested for a year or so to see if they warrant being converted to mutual funds. If converted, the performance histories of the incubator funds may be attached to new mutual funds as long as they share substantially similar investment objectives, policies, and strategies. This is not a difficult requirement to meet.

Incubator portfolios that do not perform well are simply liquidated and not converted to mutual funds. The relative frequency and investment objectives of portfolios converted versus those liquidated may be more relevant than knowing that a particular portfolio was flight-tested. This information could provide investors general insight on the motivation and competence of particular investment advisors in pretesting portfolios. Are pretested portfolios consistent with the investment advisor's competencies and philosophy in managing funds, or are they designed to catch some new wave in funds and accumulate assets to manage?

There is nothing inherently wrong with flight-testing portfolios, but the SEC's implicit assumption in allowing backdated performance histories to be attached to new mutual funds is that the is no significant difference in managing the two different types of portfolios. That is, managing non-mutual fund portfolios is equivalent to managing real mutual funds. This is a real stretch, especially if the SEC wants to be proactive about improving shareholder disclosure. As an example, Sanders (1998b) identified a fund that opened in October 1996 and advertised its returns since July 1989, when it was a subadvisor-managed asset pool.

In addition, Arnott (1997) concluded there are significant differences in managing private portfolios and real mutual funds. Private accounts have different investment and regulatory environments, such as not being subject to the 1940 Act, and much less public scrutiny. Private accounts have no directors providing oversight, no diversification requirements, no borrowing limitations, and no daily net cash outflows or inflows to impact portfolio management. Conversion to mutual funds may also involve subtle or not so subtle differences in investment objectives and/or investment styles, as well as changes in organizational structure and culture.

In addition to allowing past performance histories to be attached to new mutual funds, the SEC has also permitted a second form of historical revisionism. Portfolio managers of old mutual funds have been permitted to attach their performance histories to new mutual funds under different investment advisors. Approval requires portfolio managers be able to prove they were solely responsible for performance of the former funds. For example, Zweig (1997a) reported a case where the portfolio manager of a new mutual fund proved she had complete control of the former fund's investment portfolio.

Nonetheless, approval of attaching portfolio manager histories to new mutual funds implicitly assumes that the organizational structure and climate of the old and new funds and investment advisors are the same. But no investment advisors manage money in the same exact ways. This is especially so if the portfolio manager's former investment company is known for its strong bench support, such as Fidelity. It could well be that the portfolio manager in question serves as securities analyst, portfolio manager, and marketer in new and/or smaller fund environments. If particular portfolio managers can strongly demonstrate the equivalence of past and new mutual fund roles, the evidence should be documented in caps in the prospectus. But the best solution is to exclude historical revisionism in shareholder communication.

In conclusion, Fosback (1997) indicated that the liberalization of SEC policies is too permissive. As discussed above, historical revisionism has been applied to fund performance in several ways: (1) historical portfolio manager performance records may be applied to new funds if former and new funds have similar investment objectives and policies; (2) historical fund performance records may be applied to new share classes of existing funds, and (3) new mutual funds may adopt historical performance records of various non-fund accounts if converted to mutual funds.

Shareholder interests: a final note

To conclude this discussion of mutual fund shareholder interests and fund disclosure, Phillips (1997) provided a brief historical note on the underlying issue – treatment of mutual fund shareholders as owners:

> The tradition of investors as empowered shareholders, funds as investment companies, and independent directors as shareholder representatives has served all parties well. Are these principles any less important today? At every step, we must be reminded that investors are shareholders and that this protection is what ensures the industry's future.

So what can mutual funds do to better serve shareholders? Zweig's (1998a) list provides a start, which restated as needed improvements, follows:

1   Reduce expenses by truly sharing economies of scale.
2   Improve performance by limiting asset growth through fund closings.
3   Improve after-tax returns through tax management.
4   Reduce trading costs by reducing portfolio turnover.
5   Reduce portfolio manager turnover through increased personal investment.
6   Reduce guaranteed middling performance by eliminating the herd mentality in portfolio management.
7   Represent shareholder interests in the selection of truly independent directors.
8   Treat shareholders as owners in the communications they receive.
9   Practise broad investment styles and strategies rather than marketing new funds.
10 Regain simplicity of focus on investor needs rather than the confusion of multiple share classes.

ASSESSING FUND DISCLOSURE

Table 22 provides an investor checklist of model fund disclosure. Some of these issues are also discussed in Sanders (1998c). The table is organized into three categories, each of which reflects a general area for disclosure. The first concerns portfolio manager disclosure, the second director disclosure, and the third portfolio disclosure.

The investor's first step is to search for the individual disclosure items in a particular fund's semi-annual and annual reports, prospectus, and statement of additional information. The second step is to divide the number of disclosure items found by the total number of disclosure issues in table 22. The third step is to assess the fund's overall disclosure and indicate whether it is excellent, acceptable, or unacceptable. For example, Vanguard Windsor II's disclosure provides fewer than 20 percent of the desired table 22 attributes, and its overall performance is therefore unacceptable in an absolute sense. But its overall disclosure relative to other funds is acceptable. Vanguard does a better job at disclosure than most fund families, which may not be a strong endorsement for the industry. This latter performance is summarized in table 27.

CHAPTER FIVE

MUTUAL FUND SERVICE DISADVANTAGES: EXPENSES

Mutual funds have traditionally been perceived as low-cost providers. Citing mutual fund expenses as a general service disadvantage may be counter to what many investors have been led to believe, but what once may have been the case has become increasingly less so. Mutual fund expenses are increasingly recognized as a significant general service disadvantage. This is an important issue because, after all, expenses are the single most important controllable variable for fund investors. But it may well be that fund expenses, no matter how large, may be less than the cost to investors of buying equivalent portfolios directly in the market.

The issue is not whether mutual funds generally have expense disadvantages, they do, but whether particular mutual funds minimize expenses in meeting the needs of particular investors. That is, do the expenses of particular funds translate to minimum disadvantages for particular investors? The issue of expenses relative to fund performance is discussed later.

While investors cannot control the performance of funds they purchase, they can control expenses indirectly by the choices they make – by selecting only low-cost funds. This is important because, in aggregate terms, mutual fund expenses are not insignificant by any means. Zweig (1997b) estimated fund shareholders pay $26.7 billion in fees on assets of $3.2 trillion. Of this, 20 percent, or $5.3 billion, represents annual overcharges. And what are these expenses? Zweig also graphically answered this question:

> What are expenses anyway? Again, we're not talking about sales commission or "loads." Rather, the . . . money that fund sponsors siphon out of your account to pay for day-to-day operations. Your fund has a board of directors, which hires an investment manager to run the money; a transfer agent to process the transactions; a custodian to hold the assets in safekeeping; accountants to check the books; and lawyers to keep everybody honest. The fund may also pay an annual fee to brokers and financial planners who help peddle its shares. By far the biggest of these charges is the management or advisory fees charged by the investment manager; it usually accounts for at least 60% of a fund's total expenses.

The industry response to this challenge has been silence.

MUTUAL FUNDS EXPENSES: NATURE AND PROS AND CONS

The issue here is not that fund expenses *per se* are bad, but that their size suffers from lack of effective cost competition in the industry. As reported in Oster (2000), John Brennan, Vanguard chairman, states that investors "are not shopping on price." And shop they should. The return of fund performance to historical levels should make investors more cost-conscious. But at what cost should these services be provided? The only certainty in mutual fund investing is shareholder expenses/fees, not shareholder returns.

However, fund shareholders must bear some of the blame for increasing fund expenses. They desire particular services associated with fund ownership and these services cannot be provided free. Also, the unsurpassed bull market seems to have made investors indifferent, if not unaware, of continuing increases in expense ratios readily imposed by investment advisors. In particular cases, increases may not seem like much unless translated into dollars. And, despite calls to provide this information in dollar amounts on shareholder account statements, the industry has no desire to do so.

The lack of price competition, investor desire for more services, and apparent investor indifference to increasing expense ratios have also made it possible for fund investment advisors to benefit further as fund asset bases increase. The additional dollars investment advisors receive as asset bases increase is further magnified by economies of scale resulting from this increased asset size. This is seen by the fact that few funds are closed to new shareholders. The dollars earned from economies of scale dwarf those from increasing expense ratios, and together these two sources of revenue generate huge returns to investment advisors, their principals, and officers. Those who benefit most from scale economies are investment advisors, not fund owners (shareholders). The prices received from the sale of investment advisory firms certainly reflect profits from scale economies, but these savings are not reflected in the expenses shareholders pay.

As noted by Purcell (1995), equity funds have hidden higher dollar expenses behind increasing asset size on the premise that shareholders will not notice if expense ratios remain constant. Fund expense ratios must decline proportionately with mutual fund asset growth rates if actual dollar expenses are not to increase, something that generally does not occur. However, these larger dollar expenses will appear as larger expense ratios if fund assets decline. Although large funds have lower average expense ratios than smaller funds, the reductions are not proportionate to the rate of asset growth and the benefits of scale economies provided. This is another reason why fund shareholders need to compute the dollar amount of expenses and why funds do not wish to provide the information. In fact, some funds benefiting most from economies of scale have the largest expense ratios.

There may also be a more insidious reason why mutual fund expenses have risen. Competition in the mutual funds industry also has much more to do with advertising and marketing than with price competition. While market stock indices have increased dramatically over time, during many of these years most funds have not done as well. As a result, funds appear to be giving greater attention to advertising and marketing than performance in efforts to maintain assets. Bogle (1999b) stated: "What we need in the mutual fund industry is far more focus on the management of shareholder interests and far less on the marketing of fund shares." This misalignment has several negative implications: (1) increased marketing and fund expenses,

(2) larger portfolios making it more difficult to earn above-average returns, (3) increased hype reducing investor awareness of risk, and (4) perception of fund shareholders as customers rather than owners.

This is not to say, however, that there are not valid external pressures working to increase mutual fund expenses. Funds are more than ever competing for broker sales force and super-market distribution and this increases distribution expenses. This pressure includes traditional no-load funds as well as load funds. There has also been tremendous investor demand for supermarket listed funds, which, as discussed below, increases fund expenses. These pressures on fund expenses, including 12b-1 fees, are especially felt by new, small funds.

Bogle and Phillips on expenses

Over the years, John C. Bogle has been the industry champion and advocate of low-cost mutual funds. This has been his major concern about fund investing. In Bogle (1998), the arguments that fund expenses are "grossly excessive" are summarized in no uncertain terms:

1   Fund expenses are high and increasing at an increasing rate.
2   Fund assets have increased by 6,650 percent and expenses by 8,470 percent over the past 17 years.
3   The cost savings from fund economies of scale are not passed on to shareholders.
4   Many fund management companies are earning excessive returns on increasing asset bases.
5   Independent fund directors should be reducing, not increasing, expense ratios.
6   Funds that underperform in increasing asset environments tend to increase expenses, especially for marketing and advertising.
7   In periods of "normal" returns, a 2.5 percent expense ratio consumes 50 percent of investor net "real" return.
8   Fund expenses are the critical third element in fund performance, along with risk and return.

In a companion piece, Umphrey (1998) made an unsuccessful effort to counter Bogle's broadside. The fault lies with investors, not the fund industry. Offerings of new, smaller funds reflect investor demand for more choice and outweigh any expense concerns. More than ever, it is also costly to provide superior, technologically based shareholder services. Fund share-holders see expenses as just one element in fund selection and one that is more than compen-sated for by consistent, superior fund performance. Thus investor choice is the determinant of high expense ratios, but not to worry, because performance takes care of them. Even given that investor choice is to blame, superior fund performance is certainly not a given.

The concern about mutual fund expenses also been repeatedly voiced by Don Phillips, former president of Morningstar, the fund research firm. Zweig (1997b) quoted him as saying: "I'm beginning to despair about the future of mutual funds as a low-cost option for investors." Fund expenses and loads can eat up all or a significant proportion of the historical *equity risk premium* of equity returns over bond returns. Or, from another perspective, such charges would be equivalent to paying an accountant 20 percent of income for preparing tax returns. Even some fund managers have voiced concern. For example, Ralph Wanger, co-manager of the Acorn Fund, stated: "Unless fees come down, investors will get tired of being hosed, and they will find another way to invest." The fund then went on to increase its expense ratio.

To place mutual fund expenses into perspective, shareholders should multiply the dollar amount invested in each fund by its expense ratio. As an example of how easy it is to reduce expenses, Rekenthaler (1997) began with a $300,000 portfolio of six sample funds that had $2,754 in expenses. Then he reduced expenses to $1,704 by substituting five comparable funds for three original ones. This simple exercise illustrates how many actual dollars investors pay in expenses, and is more revealing than comparing apparently small expense ratios. This is why fund managers are so against providing total expenses for each shareholder account.

Trends in fund expenses

Trends in mutual fund expenses are up. For example, Zweig (1997b) reported that from 1986 to 1995, *management* (*advisory*) *fees* increased nearly 12 percent and overall expenses climbed 22 percent. And some of the largest fund families charge fees that are at least 75 percent higher than peer averages. In 1960, 73 percent of investment advisors paid fund bookkeeping expenses and 11 percent paid transaction expenses, yet average net profit margins were 18 percent. Today, most investment advisors charge shareholders for these and other expenses. Moreover, 56 percent of all bond and stock funds with ten-year records have actually increased expenses, yet average investment advisor net profit margins are 25 percent or higher. As an example, prior to its acquisition, Michael Price's Heine Securities had net income of $62.5 million on revenue of $95 million, a 65.8 percent net profit margin! This explains why Price may ultimately receive as much as $800 million from its sale.

The consistent upward trend in mutual fund expenses is seen in table 23. Mutual fund expense ratios increased by 38 percent from 1986 to 1999. As mandated by the SEC, the expense ratio is defined in the prospectus as *total operating expenses* divided by average total assets. The components of the expense ratio are management fees, 12b-1 fees (if any), and "*other*" *operating expenses*. These expenses are detailed below and also summarized in Ronald (1998a).

Table 24 provides examples of mutual fund expense ratios and component expenses. The tables provide comparisons of expense ratios both within and among selected fund families, including multiple share classes. In particular, note Windsor II's 0.41 percent expense ratio (table 24a). This fund serves as an example in the following chapters, where its performance along numerous dimensions is compared with its peer group and the S&P 500 benchmark index. Windsor II's expense ratio is excellent (small) when compared with its peer group's expense ratio of 1.31 percent (table 42a). Comparison with the market is not valid in this case because the S&P 500 Index is not an actual fund. The Vanguard 500 Index Fund is often used as a surrogate for its benchmark index in the following chapters. The Vanguard 500 Index Fund mimics the index's performance, less its small expense ratio of 0.19 percent (table 24a). Windsor II's excellent overall expense ratio is summarized in table 27.

The trend towards higher mutual fund expenses also applies to new funds. Rekenthaler (1996d) calculated that the average management fee of new domestic stock funds is 0.75 percent. Then, by adding forty basis points for 12b-1 fees and other expenses, average expense ratios are 1.20 percent. Load funds are also paying brokers more for distribution. It is routine for new funds to add 0.25 percent annual 12b-1 fees for "Schwab-type" distribution.

Mutual fund expenses take an entirely new and significant dimension when expressed as percentages of fund gross income, which is the corporate model for analyzing expenses on the income statement. Bogle (1994) determined that expenses consume 54 percent of stock fund gross income, 24 percent for balanced (stock and bond) funds, 12 percent for bond funds, and 18 percent for money market funds. Expenses thus consume a large percentage of gross income, even for money market funds. These percentages indicate just how important it is for investors to convert expense ratios into dollars, and to relate them to fund dollars of revenue.

Management fees

The size of fund investment advisory fees (management fees) is questioned and illustrated in Green's (1998) article "Do these [two] guys deserve $60 million a year?" The particular fund has a history of high returns (and risk) that have since deteriorated. It also has a $16 million advertising budget, exceeded only by the three giant fund companies, including supersize Fidelity.

Investment advisors charge advisory fees for portfolio management and normally also "other" operating expenses for other external services provided. Both may be included in management fees or listed separately. These are generally the largest expenses, excluding 12b-1 fees. The few funds that also borrow to invest, such as the Merger Fund, report interest expenses in the prospectus or annual report. Any interest expenses for administrative costs are provided directly and/or indirectly by investment advisors and, if indirectly, by one or more affiliates and/or unaffiliated firms. These services may include administrator, transfer agent, custodian, and distributor non-12b-1 expenses. Many funds, especially money market funds and bond funds, have "all inclusive" service contracts with investment advisors. Table 25 reports the significant increases in contractual minimum management fees that have occurred. Overall, management fees have increased by nearly 90 percent from 1920–30 to 1995–96.

Further, Bogle (1994) reported management fees ranging from 0.50 to 1.0 percent of average total assets, with investment advisor profit margins often exceeding 50 percent. Advisory contracts may provide financial incentives/penalties based on portfolio performance, usually measured against benchmark indices. However, incentives for portfolio management performance are less often used because most funds fail to outperform their benchmark indices, especially the S&P 500 Index. In fact, Zweig (1999a) reported that only 2 percent of domestic stock funds tie their fees to performance. Some fund advisors advertise higher returns enhanced by temporary *fee waivers* on management and perhaps other expenses, as well. Bond funds often do this because yield is so important to returns. Investors should review prospectus footnotes to determine whether fees are being waived and for how long this will be done.

On a positive note, some mutual fund advisors actually decrease management fee rates as assets increase beyond specified break points. For example, Vanguard US Growth fund pays 0.4 percent management fees (advisory only) on the first $25 million of assets and decreasing percentages at higher break points, down to a minimum of 0.1 percent on assets over $2.5 billion. The agreement does not provide for incentives or penalties based on fund performance.

Portfolio manager compensation is a major component of management fees, but in the larger scheme of things does not represent an obstacle to reduced expenses. *Mutual Funds* (1999c) reported that portfolio managers of large funds are paid the most and those of new funds the least. While portfolio manager compensation continues to skyrocket, several forces are damping the trend. One is that actively managed fund performance has trailed the S&P 500 Index, making passively managed index funds more attractive. And, as discussed, the star manager syndrome has cooled and many funds have taken steps to downplay its importance. Even so, a $1 billion fund with 1.25 percent total expenses and 0.75 percent management fees could easily pay its portfolio manager $1 million. The $1 million is only 13 percent of management fees and 8 percent of total expenses. This suggests that investment advisors have no financial reason to be "pay wise and performance foolish" in compensating skilled portfolio managers. Nor should they blame increased fund expenses on portfolio manager pay.

Rekenthaler (1993a) noted that the expenses of mutual funds with star portfolio managers are often higher than other funds. Investors apparently are willing to pay more on the assumption they will earn more. However, fund expenses are generally related to fund distribution channels and organizational structure, not portfolio manager skill. Moreover, funds with star portfolio managers are often older and larger, which may reduce expense ratios. In this case, it makes more sense to invest with experienced portfolio managers relative to less experienced managers guiding smaller, more costly funds.

12b-1 fees

As noted, rule 12b-1 allows investment advisors to use mutual fund assets to pay distribution expenses, including sales commission, *customer servicing fees*, administrative services, and advertising and sales promotion. Rule 12b-1 fees may not exceed 1.0 percent, including maximum 0.25 percent annual servicing fees. Servicing fees are trailing commission paid for "continuing customer service" to investors, such as responding to inquiries and providing advice and information.

Commission is by far the largest component of these expenditures, followed by administrative expenses, and advertising and promotion. Investment Company Institute (2000) surveyed fund use of 12b-1 fees and reported several findings. First, 63 percent of 12b-1 fees pay broker-dealer compensation and related expenses. These fees include payments to broker-dealers for sales of fund shares; reimbursements to distributors for financing charges from advances made to broker-dealers for sales of shares; and compensation of in-house personnel. Second, 32 percent of 12b-1 fees pay administrative services. These services include compensation to third parties for record keeping and other services provided current fund shareholders. And, third, 5 percent of 12b-1 fees pay advertising and other sales promotion activities. These fees include expenses for printing and mailing prospectuses and sales material to prospective investors.

As a specific example, the Franklin Mutual Series Fund prospectus (1998a) stated 12b-1 fees are used to pay: (1) distribution or customer servicing fees paid to securities dealers or others with fund servicing agreements, distributors, or affiliates, (2) *pro-rated* portions of distributor overhead expenses, and (3) expenses of printing prospectuses and sales publications, preparation and distribution of sales literature, and advertisements.

While 12b-1 fees are technically expenses, they are continuing loads from the shareholder perspective. Only some few fund families close funds to limit asset growth, and when they do it is often after they are already much too large. And, when they do, exceptions are usually made for current shareholders and retirement accounts. Even so, most mutual funds continue to impose 12b-1 fees even after they close.

Cullen (1998) identified sixty funds that limit access, but nonetheless continue to charge 12b-1 fees. No-load funds argue they need the fees to continue marketing to current shareholders. Load funds argue they need the fees to be reimbursed for advance and trailing commission paid to brokers. As discussed below, these are not the reasons given when the fees were originally proposed. Thus, open or closed, funds continue to charge current shareholders 12b-1 fees. Funds generally grow too large to maintain the level of returns, but investment advisors find them too profitable to shut down.

Supposed need for 12b-1 fees

Before the SEC approved the use of 12b-1 fees, no-load funds argued they were needed to be able to compete with load fund distribution networks. The results would be increased asset size, lower operating expenses through scale economies, and sharing of savings with shareholders. And load funds soon realized that 12b-1 fees could enhance their marketing, as well. These funds observed they could appear more like no-load funds by partly or completely substituting 12b-1 fees for large front-end loads, while continuing to pay sales commission and provide continuing customer service. It was argued that trailing commission would not only encourage new sales, but also help keep shareholders invested and investing more. Again, the results would be increased asset size, lower operating expenses through economies of scale, and sharing of savings with shareholders. That was then.

The bottom line is that 12b-1 fees have not fulfilled their purpose. Investment advisors have benefited from the larger asset bases with larger dollar amounts of advisory fees, expense savings economies of scale, and 12b-1 revenue. The same cannot be said for shareholders. They have not significantly shared in the 12b-1 bonanza. As reported by Clements (1992), this is particularly true for those fund shareholders who originally paid large front-end loads and are now being charged 12b-1 fees.

Impacts of 12b-1 fees

Rekenthaler (1992b) determined that pure no-load *stock funds* with assets over $500 million have the lowest average expense ratios of 0.80 percent. Those with front-end loads have the second lowest average expense ratios of 0.97 percent. No-load funds with 12b-1 fees rank a distant third, with average expense ratios of 1.37 percent. Back-end funds are last, with average expense ratios of 1.79 percent. The same ranking applies to stock funds with assets less than $500 million.

Rankings of *bond funds* with assets over $500 million are the same as stock funds. The average expense ratios are 0.51 percent, 0.78 percent, 0.83 percent, and 1.66 percent, respectively. The same ranking applies to bond funds with assets less than $500 million. Phillips (1995) calculated that bond mutual funds with 12b-1 fees have an average expense ratio of 1.10 percent versus 0.64 percent for funds without them. Moreover, as noted, bond funds with 12b-1 fees attempt to overcome higher expenses by assuming more portfolio risk. The net result is that funds with 12b-1 fees have lower returns, higher expenses, and more risk. This is not much of an endorsement. The irony is that 12b-1 fees were supposed to benefit shareholders.

The imposition of 12b-1 fees has also encouraged mutual funds to adopt more risky strategies to compensate for the additional expenses they represent. This is especially true for bond funds, because 12b-1 fees have a much greater relative impact on portfolio yields. Rekenthaler (1992a) described the strategies funds use to offset imposition of 12b-1 fees. These strategies include the (1) sacrifice of portfolio quality for more yield, (2) lengthening of portfolio maturities for higher yields and more return volatility, (3) purchase of bonds selling at a premium to pad reported yield while writing off premiums against net asset value, and (4) sale of call options to bolster short-term capital gains by giving up increased net asset value when interest rates fall. In addition to everything else, 12b-1 fees have also perverted bond fund risk profiles.

Further, as discussed in *Mutual Funds* (2000b), some mutual funds even account for 12b-1 fees in ways that avoid disclosure. These funds pay 12b-1 fees from their investment advisory fees, which are charged against fund assets. In this way, 12b-1 fees are not separately disclosed. But, because the 12b-1 plans have been approved, the investment advisor can defend this action against charges that management fees are spent on marketing.

Fund supermarkets and expenses

In 1992, discount broker Charles Schwab & Co. introduced the first mutual funds supermarket. Online discount brokers sell hundreds of no-load funds with *no transaction fees* (NTF). They also provide one consolidated statement of all transactions and account information. This business has grown tremendously and is dominated by Schwab, Fidelity Funds Net, and Jack White & Co. Corman (1997) reviewed supermarket costs and other issues.

Although supermarkets claim they do not impose transaction fees, there are explicit limitations. Fees are typically waived only on shares held for ninety to 180 days, and longer limits apply to individual investors than financial advisors. Fee waivers may also apply only to a limited number of annual trades. Account minimum purchase requirements range from $1,000 to $25,000, which may be lower than offered by some funds directly. Some supermarkets offer only their private-label brands of index funds and money market funds, which normally serve themselves better than fund shareholder customers.

Supermarkets: con

Mutual fund supermarkets do not explicitly impose transaction fees on investors, but investors pay them indirectly. Transaction fees end up in the expense ratios of funds listed on supermarkets.

Supermarkets do provide some customer services normally paid by mutual funds, but there are some additional add-on marketing costs, as well. Funds may normally reduce supermarket fees through soft dollar arrangements (discussed below), in which funds provide supermarket broker-dealer affiliates with specified amounts of commission in return for research products and services.

Supermarket mutual funds both with and without 12b-1 fees have higher expense ratios than independent funds. Overall, Regnier (1997) determined that supermarket funds have an average expense ratio of 1.3 percent, versus 1.08 for independent funds. These higher expense ratios reflect fund fees paid to supermarkets, which range from 0.25 to 0.35 percent or even 0.4 percent of sales. Large fund families pay fees close to 0.25 percent of assets and smaller families and new supermarket funds pay 0.35 percent or more. Newly listed funds also pay supermarket "set up" fees of $12,000, or more. As noted, supermarkets provide some customer services normally paid by mutual funds.

Mutual funds vary in the approach used to pay supermarket fees. For example, no-load funds may impose 0.25 percent 12b-1 fees on shareholders. In this case, any supermarket fees in excess of 12b-1 fees are charged to fund operating expenses. This may be done because supermarkets pay certain bookkeeping and shareholder services that funds would otherwise pay. Funds that do not impose 12b-1 fees to pay supermarket fees charge them to operating expenses. Supermarket funds with no 12b-1 fees have average expense ratios of 1.24 percent versus 1.0 percent for independent funds. This is equivalent to adding 0.25 percent 12b-1 fees. Supermarket funds both with and without 12b-1 fees must also bear any costs associated with supermarket conferences, cooperative advertisements, and publications. Some funds have even felt it necessary to increase advertising to maintain distinct images in the maze of supermarket choices (just like grocery brand names).

As discussed in Ward (1998), brokerage firms and mutual fund supermarkets are increasingly using their leverage to charge fund managers part of their distribution costs in return for shelf space and priority sales efforts. This is in addition to commission and 12b-1 fees. The payments are made at the corporate level, not at the sales level. Fund managers can reduce these charges by providing securities trades.

Wolde (1999) summed up the disadvantages of mutual fund supermarkets to investors: (1) reduced mutual fund performance by facilitating short-term traders; (2) slower transmission of fund shareholder information by limiting direct access and delayed mailings; (3) outdated online information; (4) limited online fund information and news; (5) longer holding periods for avoiding redemption fees imposed on individual investors than on financial advisor clients; (6) private label money market funds have below-average returns; (7) higher 12b-1 fees for listed funds; (8) poor-performing funds also listed; (9) private-label index funds have above-average expenses; and (10) most funds listed are available only as Class A shares. Supermarkets deny these claims and cite evidence of excellent service, such as twenty-four-hour online access.

Differences in the way mutual funds pay supermarket fees do not differentially impact supermarket investors – the bottom line is, they pay the fees in any case. So do fund supermarkets really impose NTFs? Barbee (1998c) answered the question in this way: "Investors who really care about costs have Vanguard, those who value choice and convenience have Schwab." There is no shareholder free lunch in mutual fund distribution.

Supermarkets: pro

On the positive side, mutual fund supermarkets do provide service advantages to individual investors. First, individual shareholders can gain access to portfolio managers who manage only institutional accounts, such as company pension plans. These plans provide portfolio managers with consistent (and large) net cash inflows, which make it easier to implement well defined long-term strategies. Supermarkets normally reduce minimum purchase requirements for these listed institutional funds to $1,000–$10,000. So why are institutional funds willing to take on smaller, less cost-effective retail accounts? The major reason is that they do not service these accounts. Supermarkets provide the services and supply funds with large asset pools managed with economies of scale. Nonetheless, supermarkets do not absorb these costs.

Second, institutional mutual funds have lower average expense ratios than retail funds. Lower institutional fund expense ratios fees reflect the leverage large institutional clients have in choosing funds, but also the economies of scale these accounts offer fund managers. The tradeoff for institutional fund managers is huge and growing amounts of money to invest in return for very low expense ratios. Institutional fund managers thus earn high returns from the economies of scale provided by huge and increasing asset bases, and institutional fund share-holders get lower expense ratios. For example, Barbee (1997c) reported that institutional funds have average expense ratios of 0.94 percent versus 1.54 percent for comparable retail funds. This difference also explains most of the average performance advantage institutional funds have over retail funds. And, as stated by Kelley (1996a), "The real source of extra gains isn't in the pedigree [Ivy League portfolio managers] – most of it's in the expenses."

Third, mutual fund supermarkets provide twenty-four-hour customer service along with convenience and access to numerous funds. Harris (1997) examined services offered by thirteen supermarkets and rated them by breadth of products, transaction prices, mutual funds quantity/quality, cash management, advisory services, research, and variable annuities. No single best supermarket was identified, but there are different bests, depending on investor needs. For example, Fidelity, Schwab, Waterhouse Securities, and Jack White rank A in the number of funds offered. But only Prudential Securities and Smith Barney rank A in quality of funds sold.

Twenty-four-hour customer service is a convenience to busy investors, but it also facilitates excessive online day trading. Online trading has grown tremendously and is fueled to no small degree by so-called "investors" who enjoy the game and trade on market "noise." *Day traders* and others with intra-day holding periods may suffer from "illusions of control," where active trading is confused with market control. Short-term trading adds to concerns that supermarkets may be indirectly imposing additional costs on funds and fund shareholders. Short-term redemptions can increase fund portfolio turnover and trading costs, with increased capital gains taxes and reduced returns to shareholders.

"Other" operating expenses

"Other" operating expenses are those incurred and paid directly by mutual funds. The amounts paid depend on the extent to which investment advisors directly and/or indirectly provide all service functions. If all expenses are included in advisory contracts, "other" operating expenses will be correspondingly small, and vice versa. Excluding 12b-1 fees, these expenses are typically the smallest, often ranging from 0.2 percent to 0.3 percent. At a minimum, these expenses might typically include: (1) taxes, if any, (2) legal and auditing fees, (3) independent directors' fees and expenses, (4) non-advisory personnel expenses, (5) insurance premiums, and (6) trade association dues. For example, the Franklin Mutual Series Fund prospectus (1998a) listed these expenses plus custodial and net asset value calculation expenses, the latter a typical transfer agent service.

Expenses, loads, and 12b-1 fees

Mutual funds increasingly use 12b-1 fees, fund supermarkets and multiple share classes, all of which contribute to continuing cost increases to fund shareholders. Cost-conscious investors find it increasingly difficult to sort out the implications of these developments. To this end, Malhotra and McLeod (1997) generated a framework for determining the relationship of fund loads, 12b-1 fees, and other variables with fund expense ratios. Differences in expense ratios were calculated across 1992 and 1993 samples of equity and bond funds. In 1993, for example, average equity fund expense ratios are 1.27 percent versus 0.88 percent for bond funds. The relationship between 12b-1 fees and expense ratios was also examined. Funds were first categorized as load or no-load funds and then again as funds with or without 12b-1 fees. Equity load funds have average expense ratios of 1.31 percent versus 1.22 percent for no-load funds. And funds with 12b-1 fees have average expense ratios of 1.42 percent versus 1.12 percent for those without them. The analysis explained approximately 45 percent of the variability in expense ratios.

Sanders (1995a) noted similar results for equity mutual funds. No-load funds have average expense ratios of 1.11 percent versus 1.62 percent for load funds. Thus, to identify stock funds most likely to have low expense ratios, investors should focus on older, larger, no-load funds with no 12b-1 fees.

These findings deflate the myth that no-load funds cost more than load funds over time. The myth is based on the argument that funds sold by sales agents grow larger, which provides scale economies, leading to smaller fund expense ratios. This reduction in expense ratios has not happened, and the situation has worsened with addition of 12b-1 fees to fund expenses. Further, no-load funds have less risky portfolios and higher load-adjusted returns for all investment horizons less than ten years (equal for ten years).

The study's statistically significant conclusions for *equity* mutual fund expenses follow: (1) large funds have smaller expense ratios than smaller funds, owing to economies of scale, (2) funds with negative asset growth have larger expense ratios, (3) funds with high portfolio turnover have higher expense ratios, (4) funds with high current yields have lower expense ratios, (5) funds with 12b-1 fees have higher expense ratios, (6) older funds have lower expense ratios, and (7) funds in families have lower expense ratios. However, the inconsistent relationship of size of front-end loads and expense ratios is not significant. And not significant are the positive relationship of the cash ratio to expense ratios, the positive relationship of income funds to expense ratios, and the negative relationship of growth funds to expense ratios.

Load *bond* mutual funds have average expense ratios of 0.96 percent versus 0.73 percent for no-load funds. And bond funds with 12b-1 fees have average expense ratios of 1.06 percent versus 0.68 percent for those with none. The analysis explained about 34 percent of the variability in expense ratios. Thus, to identify bond funds most likely to have low expense ratios, investors should focus on larger funds with long maturity portfolios, very low or zero loads, and no 12b-1 fees. However, *high-yield bond funds* tend to have higher expenses, loads, and 12b-1 fees than other bond funds.

The study's conclusions for *bond* mutual fund expense ratios follow: (1) funds with high sales loads have larger expense ratios, (2) funds with long maturity portfolios have larger expense ratios, (3) funds with 12b-1 fees have larger expense ratios, (4) funds with negative asset growth have larger expense ratios, (5) large funds have lower expense ratios, (6) high-yield funds have higher expense ratios, and (7) older funds have lower expense ratios. However, the positive relationship of fund families to expense ratios is not significant. Nor is the positive relationship of portfolio systematic risk (beta) and expense ratios.

Dellva and Olson (1998) also examined mutual fund loads/fees and expenses, using 1987–92 samples of over 500 *equity* mutual funds. Three questions were asked. First, are higher fund loads/fees justified by reducing operating expenses or improving performance through more effective research? Second, do front-end loads and back-end loads induce fund shareholders to stay invested, thereby reducing fund expenses and trading costs? Third, do funds with 12b-1 fees attract more assets by paying sales commission and advertising, thereby reducing fund expenses through economies of scale?

The study reached several conclusions. Larger mutual funds have substantial economies of scale and smaller expense ratios. Expense ratios are higher for (1) new (small) versus old funds, (2) funds with high versus low portfolio turnover, and (3) international versus domestic funds. Funds with 12b-1 fees have smaller unit costs, but the savings are not shared with investors. Funds with front-end loads have lower expense ratios than those with back-end loads, including redemption fees. Finally, back-end loads and 12b-1 fees are hidden deadweight costs to shareholders that provide no shareholder benefits.

The study also determined that the average mutual fund expense ratio increased from 1.26 percent in 1987 to 1.46 percent in 1992. Further, 63 percent of funds impose 12b-1 fees, deferred loads or redemption fees. Further, 48 percent of funds impose 12b-1 fees, 9 percent impose deferred loads, and only 7 percent impose redemption fees. Small funds have higher expense ratios than large funds. And small funds tend to use fees while large funds tend to use front-end loads.

Expenses, loads, and fund families

Mutual fund expenses also differ among mutual fund families. Table 26 ranks the 100 largest fund families by average sales loads plus expenses for the last five years. Each family is ranked in four fund categories: large company, small company, global, and bond funds. Vanguard ranks first, reflecting its low-expense philosophy, with two "one ranks" and two "two ranks." No other family with funds in all four categories comes even close. Fidelity Investments, the largest fund family, ranks forty-second, and Schwab, the largest supermarket, ranks eighth. Merrill Lynch, the large retail broker and fund sponsor, ranks fifteenth. And Longleaf ranks fourteenth. This latter finding does not appear as investor-friendly as discussed earlier.

Expenses and fund asset size

A related issue (noted above) is whether mutual fund families impose smaller expense ratios as funds increase in size. Interestingly, Kelley (1996b) noted that expense ratios decline more while funds are growing from small to mid asset size than they do once they are large. Large funds have lower expense ratios, but they are not reflective of actual savings from economies of scale. This is the bonanza of money management. Rekenthaler (1996b) expanded the analysis to international funds, and found their expense ratios to be particularly lethal. This says nothing about higher brokerage fees and bid–ask spreads in international markets. Vanguard's international funds also have below-average expense ratios.

Kelley (1996b) examined the relationship of mutual fund asset size and expense ratios among fund families. The mutual fund families that lower expense ratios as assets increase are (1) T. Rowe Price, (2) Oppenheimer, (3) Merrill Lynch A shares, (4) Scudder, (5) Janus, and (6) the former Dean Witter. However, Dean Witter has by far the highest expense ratios for all asset sizes. The families that do not lower expense ratios as assets grow are the already lowest-cost (1) Vanguard, (2) Fidelity, (3) Twentieth Century, (4) Putnam A shares, (5) American funds, and (6) Dreyfus. Also, the different multiple share class 12b-1 fee structures for load funds may well offset other expense reductions. Vanguard's very small expense ratios are easily the lowest compared with small asset size funds, but somewhat less so compared with large size funds. Investors should not only buy funds with low expense ratios, but also only those that reduce expense ratios as assets grow.

Expenses, fund size, and investment style

The relationship between mutual fund asset size and expense ratios also varies by investment style and portfolio cap. size. The relationship of fund asset size and returns is discussed later. Barbee (1998a) asked the question "Does asset size matter?" for fund expenses. The answer is "Yes." Large cap. funds lower expense ratios as they increase in size, but value funds decrease them more sharply than growth funds. In fact, large cap. value funds have the lowest expense ratios. Expense ratios also fall for small/mid-cap. funds as they increase in size, but again more so for value funds than growth funds. Small/mid-cap. growth funds have the least friendly expense ratios.

The industry case

The mutual fund industry has undertaken research to prove that mutual fund expense ratios have actually declined. The ICI's Rea and Reid (1998) analyzed equity mutual fund loads, fees, and expenses to counter general evidence of increasing expenses. The analysis was performed using "total shareholder costs," which include loads, fees, and expenses. Sales loads and deferred loads are annuitized and added to annual expense ratios. Annual total cost ratios are computed and then weighted by each fund's share of total new fund sales. This gives most weight to very large, relatively low-cost funds in large fund families, which receive the greatest share of new cash inflows.

The major finding of the study is that between 1980 and 1997 mutual fund total costs declined by more than one-third, from 2.25 percent to 1.49 percent. Overall, the reduced size and use of front-end loads more than compensated for increasing 12b-1 fees, which represent 37 percent of total distribution costs. Further, load fund shareholder cost ratios fell from 3.02 percent to 2.11 percent, but they *increased* for no-load funds from 0.78 percent to 0.89 percent.

Economies of scale were also indicated in that mutual funds that grew the most in asset size generally have the largest reductions in expense ratios. This is as it should be, because constant expense ratios increase dollar amounts of expenses as fund assets grow, but the reductions were not proportional to asset growth. Average expense ratios range from 1.25 percent for funds with assets less than $250 million to 0.64 percent for assets over $5 billion. Similarly, the average expense ratios of new funds range from 1.25 percent to 0.76 percent, and for old funds from 1.23 percent to 0.61 percent.

The contra industry case

To counter the industry results, Barbee and Cooley (1999) credited investors for most of any cost reductions, not the industry. About 50 percent of the expense reductions resulted from investors shifting assets from higher-cost load funds to large, lower-cost no-load funds, such as Vanguard 500 Index Fund. Moreover, both load and no-load investors increasingly shifted assets to lower-cost versions of load and no-load funds, respectively. Load fund total costs were reduced by the partial or complete substitution of 12b-1 fees for front-end load funds.

To evaluate the ICI study, the same asset-weighted methodology was used to compute total costs over the period 1984–98. Total shareholder costs of load funds declined by 25 percent, but no-load fund costs declined less than 10 percent. However, excluding the largest load fund, average total shareholder costs declined by only 15 percent, and expense ratios actually increased from 0.76 percent to 0.88 percent. Excluding Vanguard and Fidelity, no-load fund shareholder costs actually increased a bit. So who are the heroes in the cost saga? If there are any, it is certainly not the industry, but those investors who voted for lower-cost funds with their dollars.

The ICI analysis calculated average annual asset-weighted total shareholder costs, which weighs the lower expense ratios of huge funds more heavily. The other option is to use average total fund costs, on the grounds that industry cost behavior is reflected in fund unit behavior, not weighted fund unit size. The choice of weighted rather than unweighted costs is an important determinant of industry study findings. Moreover, the findings are influenced by the methods used to annualize total costs and estimate shareholder holding periods. For example, high redemption rates decrease effective holding periods and increase total cost ratios. These factors are key to determining whether shareholder total costs increased or decreased, especially since unweighted average fund expense ratios increased.

To conclude this discussion, Norman Fosback, another industry critic, reviewed the ICI study and summed up what he believed to be "the reality" of mutual fund expenses. Fosback (1999b) reported that the average equity fund has an expense ratio of 1.40 percent versus a capitalization-weighted average of about 1 percent. The latter computation is based on the asset size of each fund, not each fund equally. Assuming funds earn about 10 percent a year over the long term, then, depending on which expense ratio is used, somewhere between 10 percent and

14 percent of fund returns goes to pay investment advisor expenses and profit. The ICI study puts a good face on expenses in concluding that shareholder costs have declined over 30 percent since 1980. One problem with the ICI study is that shareholder transaction behavior relies on estimates from a sample of fund accounts opened twenty-five years ago. Further, the largest constraint on fund expenses has not been the industry's move to lower costs, but rather investor migration to lower-cost funds.

Removing the study's biases, Fosback stated that it appears "shareholder costs actually increased modestly over the last two decades. But leaving aside whether costs are down a little, flat, or up somewhat, the real scandal here is that expenses levied on shareholders, as a percent of assets under management, haven't declined dramatically."

Over the last twenty-five years, equity mutual fund assets have increased a hundredfold and the number of funds has increased about tenfold. That is, the average fund has grown ten times in size. But where are the economies of scale that resulted? They are there, but shareholders have not significantly benefited from them. In the past, fund expenses declined with asset growth, but this is now the exception. Fosback (1999b) concluded: "The fund industry has simply gotten fat in the bull market, and with a tiny handful of exceptions . . . , most fund families have gone willingly along for the ride, content to fatten their profits at the expense . . . of the shareholders who have entrusted their wealth to them." And fund directors have gone along.

MUTUAL FUND ATTRIBUTES AND PORTFOLIO MANAGER BACKGROUND

Table 27 provides an overall assessment of Windsor II's fund attributes and portfolio manager background discussed to this point. These attributes are (1) loads/fees, (2) overall shareholder service, (3) portfolio manager background, (4) Loeb trading cost, (5) tax efficiency, (6) shareholder disclosure, and (7) expense ratio.

The overall assessment of the background of Windsor II's portfolio managers is excellent and the fund attributes are overall excellent/acceptable. Three attributes are summarized as excellent and three as acceptable. Two attributes are assessed relative to Windsor II's peer group category and the average fund.

CHAPTER SIX

LONG-TERM INVESTING IN MUTUAL FUNDS AND STOCK/BOND PORTFOLIO ALLOCATIONS

> What do you consider to be humanity's greatest discovery? Compound interest.
>
> (*Albert Einstein*)
>
> There is more to lose by missing a bull market than there is to be gained by dodging a bear.
>
> (**Gerald Perritt, Perritt Investments, in** Worth, *July–August 1994*)
>
> Uncertainty is the only certainty. Long-term investors diversify. Short-term investors look for gurus. There are no gurus.
>
> (**Harold Evensky, Evensky Brown & Katz, in** Money, *year-end 1998*)
>
> Investing is a marathon, not a sprint.
>
> (*Jason Zweig, in* Money, *July 1998*)
>
> Spend less time studying your investments and more time studying yourself.
>
> (*Jason Zweig, in* Money, *November 1998*)
>
> Don't think you know more than the market. Nobody does.
>
> (*John C. Bogle, Vanguard Group, in* **Common Sense on Mutual Funds: New Imperatives for the Intelligent Investor,** *1999*)
>
> If you're investing for retirement, you're interested in how much money you'll have to live on when you retire. You can't eat ACR [average compound return].
>
> (*William Sharpe, Financial Engines, in* Bloomberg Personal Finance, *March 1999*)

There are several goals in this chapter. First, the historical case for reduced risk and higher returns in long-term equity investing relative to bonds is considered and illustrated. Second, the reasons why buy-and-hold investing is a better choice than market timing are explored. Third, time diversification and its reduced risk to long-term returns, but increased risk to long-term portfolio values, are considered and illustrated. Fourth, investor risk behavior based on modern finance utility theory and its behavioral shortcomings are discussed. Fifth, the investment process consisting of investment policy and investment management and their elements are defined. Sixth, the investment policy elements of identifying investor risk preferences, portfolio investment objectives, and passive asset allocation are discussed. The importance of passive asset allocation is described. An empirically consistent investor risk test is discussed and the process of matching identified risk category to portfolio investment objectives and passive stock/bond asset allocations are described. Finally, stock/bond allocations are identified.

History has made the case for long-term investing in equities relative to bonds. Equity returns stabilize as the investment horizon lengthens, but bond returns do not. And it has shown that the odds favor a long-term buy-and-hold strategy relative to market timing. Market timing suffers from lags entering/exiting the market, which subject it to missing the few market surges that explain market returns.

Both cross-sectional and time-series diversification reduce the long-term uncertainty of portfolio returns, but market timing reduces short-term uncertainty at the expense of long-term uncertainty. Time diversification states that equity returns are more stable (less risk) as the investment horizon lengthens. But this result is based on a historical sample of one, and nothing guarantees that the future must be like the past.

But there is a less obvious fallacy in time diversification. Historically, rates of return stabilize (less risk) as the investment horizon lengthens, but the magnitude of potential risk to wealth increases. As the investment horizon lengthens, time diversification has a larger probability of not achieving a given portfolio value (wealth shortfall).

Investor risk preference as defined by various utility models in modern finance theory are attacked in behavioral finance as not describing actual investor behavior. Several such behaviors have been identified that are inconsistent with the assumptions of purely rational investors.

The investment process includes investment policy and investment management. Investment policy requires the identification and statement of investor risk preference, portfolio investment objective, and passive asset allocation. The latter includes determining the amount in the out-of-portfolio cash reserves (cash bucket) and portfolio stock/bond allocation, along with annual *portfolio rebalancing*. Investment management is the active implementation of investment policy. It includes identification and implementation of active portfolio allocation (market timing), investment style allocation, mutual fund selection and allocation, and performance evaluation.

Investor risk preference is identified by an empirically determined categorical risk test. There are no validated modern or behavioral finance models that measure investor risk tolerance scientifically, especially if investor ability and willingness to participate are considered. The identified risk category is validated by investor major life influences.

Investor risk preference is next matched to the appropriate portfolio investment objective, validated using objective subcategories, and also matched to a passive stock/bond portfolio allocation.

Passive asset allocation has been identified as the single most significant variable explaining variability in portfolio returns, relative to active portfolio allocation (market timing) and security selection.

A 20/80 stock/bond passive asset allocation has been approximated by a Markowitz-type portfolio optimizer model as the low-risk passive allocation. The five-year US Treasury bond was most efficient for bond allocations, but, later, global stock/Treasury securities portfolios with maturities from one to three years were most efficient.

Four normalized model portfolios with broad security allocations are presented as examples of long-term investing. Three models present stock allocations and one presents both stock and bond allocations.

A Markowitz-type optimizer identified the most efficient, including minimum risk, portfolio allocations for (1) small-cap. stock/bonds, (2) large-cap. stocks/bonds, (3) domestic large-cap./international large-cap. stocks, and (4) domestic small-cap./international small-cap. stocks. These assist in designing normalized portfolio allocations.

Normalized portfolio risk was reasonably close to that of future realized optimized portfolios. This is good news, because optimized portfolio allocations are very sensitive to model inputs and forecast errors. Over short to intermediate time periods, normalized portfolios must underperform future realized optimized portfolios because of uncertain transitory market developments. Normalized portfolios outperformed simpler 100 percent S&P 500 Index portfolios in twenty of twenty-seven market/economic scenarios.

LONG-TERM EQUITY INVESTING

The return on equities

The case for long-term equity investing has been made many times, but most effectively in Siegel (1998). As seen in table 28, the annualized *real rate of return* on equities has been 7 percent since 1802. Further, this return has been extremely stable over the 1802–70, 1871–1925, and 1926–97 subperiods: 7 percent, 6.6 percent, and 7.2 percent, respectively. This stability reflects *mean reversion* (*reversion to the mean*) of returns, whereby short-term fluctuations (volatility) in returns then offset to produce far more stable (less risky) long-term rates of return. This pattern has also been noted in other major countries. Thus the data indicate that patience is a virtue in long-term equity investing.

Why has the long-term annualized real rate of return on stocks been 7 percent? The basic answer is that over time stock returns reflect the earnings growth of US corporations. The specific answer is that, for well over a century, inflation-adjusted current *dividend yields* plus annual earnings growth rates have approximated 7 percent. However, over shorter periods of time, returns have fluctuated widely and wildly owing to changes in price–earnings ratios, the price investors are paying for a dollar of earnings. The long-term nominal median price–earnings ratio approximates 14, and its normal range extends from 8–10 to 20–1. The normal real rate of return of 7 percent is, therefore, the return from basic economic activity. Deviations are attributed to short-term changes in dividend yields and earnings growth accompanied by overly optimistic/pessimistic investor behavior, reflected in larger/smaller than normal price earnings ratios.

Unfortunately, the history of returns on fixed-income securities has not been as steady. Also as noted in table 28, annualized real rates of return on Treasury bills have fallen from 5.2 percent to 3.2 percent to 0.60 percent over these same three subperiods. Similarly, real annualized rates of return on Treasury bonds have declined from 4.8 percent to 3.7 percent to 2 percent over these same subperiods. Thus over time, the real returns on fixed-income securities have dropped significantly, which contrasts significantly with equity returns.

Stocks versus bonds

The history of returns on stocks and bonds tells us bonds are best for reducing portfolio risk, but not for generating positive, inflation-adjusted returns. This is what stocks do best over the long term, with numerous pitfalls along the way. The case for equities is strengthened because there has never been a negative annualized rate of real return over *any* single period exceeding seventeen years. Although stocks are more risky than fixed-income securities in the short run, their *worst* five-year annualized return is only slightly larger than the worst five-year annualized return of fixed-income securities. And, further, the *worst* ten-year performance of stocks is better than the worst ten-year performance of fixed-income securities.

As the holding period increases, the probability that stocks will outperform fixed-income securities increases. Stocks outperform fixed-income securities nearly 80 percent of the time for ten-year periods, over 90 percent for twenty-year periods, and nearly 100 percent for thirty-year periods. However, over one and two-year periods, stocks outperform fixed-income securities only about 60 percent of the time. Moreover, this is also seen in Yoo's (1998) 1871–1998 analysis of monthly returns on the S&P 500 Index. Nearly 40 percent of monthly returns were negative, but less than 2 percent of ten-year returns were negative.

Updegrave (1999a) reported Martin Leibowitz's, TIAA/CREF chief investment officer, findings on the issue of long-term stock/bond returns. The chances of bonds outperforming stocks may be larger than is usually assumed. After all, there has been only "one history of US capitalism since 1800." Stocks are the "odds-on favorite" to outperform bonds over the long run, but the probability this will not happen is "surprisingly high." In some cases, the probability is as high as 21 percent over thirty years and about 15 percent over forty years. Even the 10 percent textbook stock return has not been achieved in nearly 50 percent of ten-year rolling periods since 1926. One study reported that investors who buy stocks with P/E ratios of 21 or more receive annualized returns of only 6.9 percent over the next three years and only 4.8 percent over the next ten years.

Based on histories of long-term returns, it appears that approximately 40 percent of the time investors need to guard against actions that will reduce the long-term superiority of equities. Findings in McInish et al. (1993) are consistent with the notion of constancy in equity holdings. Analysis of 3,000 households revealed a negative relationship between risk aversion and both net worth and income. That is, individual investors would have more wealth at retirement if they held to less conservative (less risk-averse) investments. Alexanian (1993) confirmed this constancy, but adds the importance of starting investing early to benefit from the power of compounding. Also, the risk in long-term investing is not the potential for loss,

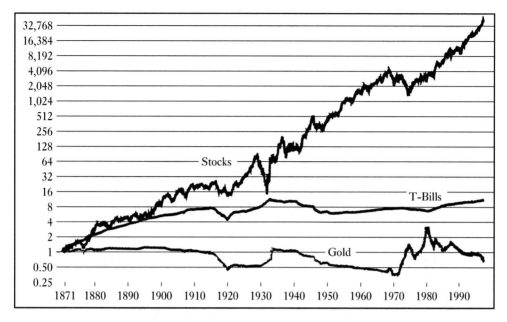

Figure 6.1 Stocks, Treasury bills, and gold: total return after inflation, 1971–97. Total return index of NYSE common stocks, three-month Treasury bills, and gold bullion, all deflated by the consumer price index. Each horizontal line represents a doubling. Source: reprinted with permission from "You just Can't do Better than Stock Funds," *Mutual Funds*, July 1998, p. 25.

but rather the failure to reach financial goals. In fact, "the greatest danger in long-term investing is *not to be* invested. . . ."

Siegel (1998) makes the all-weather case for constancy in equity investing: "There is no compelling reason for long-term investors to significantly reduce their stockholdings, no matter how high the market." This belief in equity investing is echoed in figure 6.1, which portrays the 1871–1997 annualized real returns on NYSE stocks and ninety-day Treasury bills. Consistent with Siegel, Mutual Funds (1998) concluded: "Notwithstanding both great and small bear markets one of the most interesting findings . . . is the virtual constant rate of long-term growth by stocks over the last 127 years." To the extent that wealth is increased by long-term compounding of returns, long-term wealth is also diminished by compounding annual fund expenses. This reverse analogy provides a reminder of the importance of expenses as well as returns to long-term investment success.

Plain-speaking Ted Aronson, Aronson & Partners and portfolio manager, placed long-term stock returns in perspective, both as to consistency and reality, for individual investors. In a frank interview with Welling (1998), Aronson stated:

> It's easy to say, 24 years later, that those low single-digit P/Es, the Dow's 6 percent yield, meant you should buy and hold for the next 24 years. But nobody wanted stocks then. . . . [E]veryone has forgotten that after the horrible experience of '29, it took you a mere 18 years to get back to even. This attitude that if you buy stocks for the long run there is no risk is so laughable.

In an interview with Zweig (1999), Aronson held forth on the returns investors actually get: "I love equities, I'm not a weirdo and I don't live in a bomb shelter. But in a real sense, the compounding of stock returns is a fraud. It really is. No one has ever gotten those returns." The published returns include stocks that later went bankrupt, stocks not included that later went bankrupt, money taken out of the market, dividends not reinvested, poor market timing, and panic sales. Aronson concluded that: "They [investors] didn't buy and hold, they bought and sold. That's why this religious belief that stocks return 9 percent or 10 percent or 11 percent over the long run is just . . . guano." Ouch!

MARKET TIMING VERSUS BUY-AND-HOLD STRATEGIES

These findings suggest a potential advantage in long-term investing, but could these returns be improved through effective market timing? In its simplest and most effective case, market timing involves investing 100 percent in equities just as the market is poised to turn up and, conversely, investing 100 percent in cash assets, such as money market funds, just as the market is poised to decline.

Cash assets are marketable short-term securities with low price volatility that can quickly be converted to cash. The effectiveness of market timing has been long debated, including numerous empirical studies that tested whether portfolio managers can correctly call turns in the market and adjust portfolios accordingly. If so, this strategy still bears the burden for more frequent trading and its implications for greater trading costs and taxes on realized capital gains.

Market timing: empirical studies

In general, market timing is not supported by empirical studies. For example, Treynor and Mazuy (1966) and Fabozzi and Francis (1979) concluded that mutual funds are unable to time the market and adjust their portfolios accordingly. The latter study also reported that fund portfolio managers neither reduce portfolio systematic risk (beta) in bearish markets nor increase it in bullish markets. Kon and Jen (1979) observed that many funds exhibit superior timing ability, but none can do so consistently. And Kon (1983) observed instances of significant positive timing ability and/or performance, but not in general. Overall, findings are consistent with efficient markets – portfolio managers do not exhibit special information relative to unanticipated market returns.

In other studies, Veit and Cheney (1982) noted that mutual funds do not consistently change portfolio risk along with their timing strategies. Henriksson (1984) tested fund market-timing ability over two time periods. No such ability existed in either period. Further, funds with the ability to select stocks have negative market timing ability. Chan and Chen (1992) tested *asset allocation funds* to determine whether they can time the market by changing portfolio mix in anticipation of market changes. They evidence no such ability. Chang and Lewellen (1984) presented the most damaging results for traditional security analysis and market timing. Mutual funds are neither skilled market timers nor skilled stock selectors and, therefore, are unable to outperform a passive strategy.

Jeffrey (1984) analyzed quarterly returns for the S&P 500 Index and Treasury bills for the years 1926–82. The data indicate inability to time the market over the long term. In fact, the risks of trying to time the market outweigh the rewards. The maximum downside risk is more than twice as large as the maximum upside potential. With 50 percent timing accuracy, the best-case scenario is a return twice that of a buy-and-hold strategy, but the worst case is much worse.

The reward/penalty for good/bad timing is not symmetrical but negatively skewed. The maximum downside risk is more than twice as large as the maximum upside potential. From 1975 to 1982, for example, 100 percent market timing accuracy added ten percentage points to average returns, but zero percent success subtracted eighteen percentage points. The advantage of being invested 100 percent is not just that there are more positive return quarters than negative, but most positive returns are compressed into just a few periods.

These general findings were consistent with Sanders's (1996b) analysis of twenty years of quarterly returns for the S&P 500 Index and Treasury bills. Market timing requires 65 percent accuracy to outperform the market average. How many persons can call each market turn correctly two out of three times, and do so consistently? Please get their e-mail addresses. The S&P 500 also outperformed Treasury bills in fifty-six of eighty-six quarters (65 percent). This is important because poor timing usually means missing more bull markets than bear markets, which precludes compounding more frequent bull market returns.

Sanders also reported a 1901–90 finding that market timers require 69 percent accuracy to beat a buy-and-hold strategy. Further, 100 percent accuracy in timing bear markets *and* 50 percent accuracy in timing bull markets underperforms a buy-and-hold strategy. Thus perfection in avoiding downside risk in not enough to offset fifty–fifty chances of timing bull markets.

Thus the general finding is that the odds are strongly stacked in favor of buy-and-hold portfolio managers, not market timers. As would be expected, Chandy and Reichenstein (1993) observe that market timers generally enter the market after it starts to rise and exit after it starts to fall. This lag exposes portfolios to the real risk of not being invested when the market surges. This is most important, because all gains in the S&P 500 Index were concentrated in only fifty-five months, just 7.1 percent of the total! Further, the long-term return advantage of stocks over Treasury bills was concentrated in only 3.5 percent of the months. Theoretically, market timers could lose 100 percent of the long-term return advantage of equities despite holding them 96.5 percent of the time!

Phillips (1991) examined the performance of three market-timing mutual funds over a five-year period. Fundamental analysis has more potential for increasing stock returns than market timing. But market timing appears to have a strong following. As Phillips stated: "Despite the overwhelming evidence against timing, it – like alchemy before it and astrology to this day – still boasts devoted followers."

The negative finding for market timing is confirmed by the practices of investment icons such as John Templeton, Warren Buffett, and Peter Lynch, but also by the fact that not one top-performing mutual fund times the market. Moreover, Sanders (1996a) reported Tom Mathers, former long-term fund advisor/manager, as saying, "Market timing is a fraud as far as I'm concerned. I don't think there's anybody who can really do it. . . . Wall Street is paved with the bones of market-timers." The conclusion must be that the ability to time the market correctly and consistently is rare indeed, which favors a diversified long-term strategy.

William Bernstein on market timing

William Bernstein (2000b) applied a (*Markowitz-type*) *mean variance optimizer* to indicate empirically just how difficult it is to successfully time the market. *Factor models* are used to explore how market and fund attributes change in importance in explaining the performance of domestic equity markets in each of the last three decades of the twentieth century. Factors include variables that are both in common and unique (unexplained) to securities. Three factors are defined and measured, using four asset classes and three market indices: (1) the market factor – difference in returns between the broad market and short-term Treasury bills, the risk premium; (2) the size factor – the difference in returns between small-cap. and large-cap. stocks; and (3) the value factor – difference in returns between value and growth stocks.

The results are very illuminating in explaining which factors contribute positively and negatively to market performance. The 1990–2000 factor returns indicated that market returns were very positive. Size and value factor returns were negative. Large-cap. growth was the winning investment style. But the 1980–9 factor returns were different. The market factor had the largest positive returns, but it was less strong than during the succeeding decade. Value factor returns were also positive, but size factor returns trailed greatly. Large-cap. value stocks prospered. During the 1970–9 decade, value factor returns were by far the largest. Returns to the size factor were positive, and market returns trailed. Small-cap. value was the winning combination.

For all three decades, there was a strong negative relationship between market and value factors, with value factors always located on the efficient frontier. But the size factor is not on the efficient frontier. So will any of these scenarios be repeated and, if so, which ones and when? What we have here is an actual historical demonstration of why market timing is not recommended.

There is also a lack of market timing ability among international mutual funds. Kao et al. (1998) analyzed ninety-seven funds with at least five-year returns. The portfolio managers have good stock selectivity and overall performance. And, consistent with domestic studies, there is a negative correlation between stock selection skills and market timing. A summary of findings from other studies is also provided.

Undervalued stocks and market timing

Prompted by the volatility of equity markets, Volkman (1999) investigated the ability of 332 mutual fund managers to select undervalued securities and time major market movements before and after the October 1987 market crash. On average, there is no evidence that fund portfolio managers have the ability to select undervalued securities. But they do have a negative ability to correctly time the market during periods of high volatility. However, some funds have the ability either to select undervalued securities *or* to time the market, but few can do both. There is a high correlation between fund performance both before and after the 1987 crash, which indicates persistence in timing both before and after the crash.

Interestingly, mutual fund portfolio manager compensation is positively related to ability to time the market. Highly paid fund managers exhibit better market-timing skills than lower-paid managers, but no ability to select undervalued securities. Moreover, managers who receive incentive fees perform slightly better than those without fee incentives. They also exhibit more ability to select stocks, but no additional market timing ability. Managers paid with incentive fees also make greater efforts to time the market during periods of high volatility, which leads to increased portfolio risk.

Large funds demonstrate more ability to select undervalued securities than small funds, but they do not exhibit more ability to time the market. Stated fund risk objectives do not affect the ability to select undervalued securities, but they do affect market timing ability. The percentage of funds with positive timing ability increases as stated objectives becomes less risky.

To sum up, mutual fund portfolio managers have several problems in efforts at timing the market: (1) inability to predict near-term stock returns, which (2) exposes portfolios to unnecessary risks; (3) inability to overcome advisory costs, taxes, and trading costs; (4) exposure to the risk of missing market surges and, therefore, (5) reduced long-term returns due to limited equity investing.

Sanders (1997c) examined the usefulness of other options when bear markets appear imminent. One option is to buy funds in categories that have performed relatively well in past market declines. However, four market declines reflected inconsistent performance across fund categories – too inconsistent for effective use. The second and best option is to build diversified portfolios using asset allocation, including *equity style allocation*.

Cross-sectional and time-series diversification

Chandy and Reichenstein (1993) also noted several other problems with market timing. The first is the general inability of investors to correctly forecast short-term stock returns. This problem alone suffices. Second, timing involves sharp changes in allocations, which subject portfolios to unnecessary risks. For example, Samuelson determined that a fifty–fifty stock/bond portfolio is much less risky than one of 100 percent stock 50 percent of the time and 100 percent bonds the remaining 50 percent of the time. This may be explained in the context of *cross-sectional diversification* (at a given point in time) and *time diversification* (across time). The certain benefits of diversification in an uncertain world are too important to ignore.

Together, both types of diversification reduce the long-term uncertainty of portfolio returns, but market timing requires portfolios to be either 100 percent cash or 100 percent stock at any point in time. By not being cross-sectionally diversified in the short run, market timing increases the uncertainty of portfolio long-term returns. For example, a timing strategy that currently calls for 100 percent cash makes short-term returns certain, but in so doing it increases the uncertainty of long-term returns. This arises from the difficulties discussed above and below.

Third, examining market timing returns after the fact ignores the opportunity cost of market timing before the fact. For example, the 100 percent cash strategy assumed above runs the risk of missing a surge in stock prices while being out of the market.

Fourth, market timing generally reduces average exposure to equities, which generally reduces long-term portfolio returns. As discussed in the previous section, market timers generally enter/exit the market with lags and thereby expose portfolios to the risk of being out of the market when it surges. For example, from 1926 to 1990, the S&P 500 Index had average monthly returns of 0.80 percent. But the best 7.1 percent of the months had average returns of 11.26 percent, and the remaining 92.9 percent had nil returns. The best annual returns were concentrated in 34.5 percent of the years, and only some 1 percent of the days.

Chandy and Reichenstein (1993) generalized these findings: a great year generally consists of a few market spurts surrounded by mediocrity. Thus "an investor who misses a few bull stampedes may miss the long-run advantage that stocks have historically provided." Further, Investment icon John Neff, retired manager of Vanguard Windsor fund, outperformed the market by an average of three percentage points a year over thirty-one years. As reported by Zweig (1997b), a considerable portion of Neff's cumulative outperformance came in just two years, 1975 and 1976. This certainly illustrates the danger of being out of the market when it surges.

TIME DIVERSIFICATION

Returning to the earlier discussion, Peter Bernstein (1996b) summarized Siegel's (1998) case for long-term equity investing as follows: (1) no negative returns in over 169 rolling twenty-five-year holding periods; (2) annualized real return of 7 percent since 1802, with only a 2.6 percent standard deviation; and (3) stocks outperformed long-term bonds in 85 percent of the years by an average of 3.1 percentage points. Bernstein concluded: "Siegel makes the most complete case for common stocks that anyone has ever made. . . . In the face of all that evidence, only a fool would tell you investing in stocks over the long run is a bad idea."

Jones and Wilson study

Jones and Wilson's (1995) analysis of time diversification involved the construction of tables to assess the probability of achieving minimum annualized rates of return, both nominal and inflation-adjusted, over horizons (holding periods) ranging from one to forty years. The cumulative probabilities in table 29 are based on log-normal probability density functions for single-year and multiple-year horizons. The data used are means and standard deviations of realized nominal returns for 1871–1993 and 1926–93. As seen in table 29, the probability of earning *at least* Siegel's 7 percent annualized *real* return ranges from 49 percent for one-year and five-year periods to 47 percent for twenty-year and thirty-year periods. The probability of earning *at least* the textbook 10 percent annualized *nominal* return is 48 percent for one-year periods, 42 percent for ten-year periods, 39 percent for twenty-year periods, and 37 percent for thirty-year periods. However, the probability of earning *at least* a 5 percent annualized *nominal* return is 58 percent for one-year periods, 67 percent for five-year periods, 74 percent for ten-year periods, 81 percent for twenty-year periods, and 86 percent for thirty-year periods. The probability of earning *at least* a zero annualized *nominal* return is 68 percent for one-year periods, 85 percent in five-year periods, 93 percent in ten-year periods, 98 percent in twenty-year periods, and over 99 percent in thirty-year periods.

Several general findings should be noted. First, the probabilities apply to annualized rates of return, not total cumulative returns. Second, it is interesting that historically investors have a *minimum* 64 percent probability of breaking even, both real *and* nominal, in all holding periods.

And, third, there is a *minimum* 67 percent probability of earning a 5 percent annualized *nominal* return in all holding periods of five or more years.

Table 29 illustrates Jones and Wilson's (1995) statement that these probabilities reflect "the outcomes of the 'past happening over and over again' in random order." But, most important, "the returns might (or might not) relate to any possibilities of future return outcomes." Thus such evidence must be taken on the understanding that there can be no proof the distribution of future returns must be the same as for past returns.

Peter Bernstein's studies

With respect to the discussion above, Peter Bernstein (1996b) stated that "only a fool" would disagree with Siegel's (1998) findings, but then added: "The case for stocks is just too pat." Then Bernstein (1997b) elaborated on this point along three dimensions. First, and also noted by Jones and Wilson (1995): "Nobody can claim that the distribution of future returns in stock market must be the same as the distribution of historical returns." That is, quoting Samuelson, "We have only one sample of the past."

Second, the case favoring equities over bonds may not be as strong over the next twenty-five years. Stocks' greater volatility and the increased attractiveness of bonds at today's valuations weaken the long-term case for stocks. Martin Leibowitz, Chief Investment Officer of TIAA/ CREF, supported this view in Zweig (1996):

> Thinking stocks will always whack fixed-income assets because they always have in the past is like concluding that Cal Ripken, Jr. will start at shortstop [third base] for the Orioles forever because he hasn't missed a game since 1982 [until 1998]. Someday the streak will end. [It has.] In fact, . . . there is a 19 percent likelihood that stocks will underperform bonds over even a thirty-year period, based on valuations similar to those in today's market [yet to be seen].

Third, the market psychology that considers stocks to be risk-free long-term investments at any level of valuation is contrary to logic and history.

However, Peter Bernstein (1997b) appeared to think otherwise in stating that stock returns regress to their long-term means, but bond returns were more unpredictable because they offer unexpected inflation surprises. Bernstein concluded this point:

> A strange and unexpected conclusion emerges. Stocks are fundamentally less risky than bonds, not only because their returns have been consistently higher than those of bonds over the long run but also because less uncertainty surrounds the long-term return investors can expect on the basis of past history.

The key to Bernstein's point is the phrase "on the basis of past history." This phrase introduces the attack on so-called *time diversification*. This concept advocates long-term equity investing with its declining standard deviation of annualized returns as the investment horizon lengthens. It promises to average out single-period risks over longer horizons, much as diversification averages out risk over a number of securities. Thus, as the argument goes, time diversification is the route to stable long-term returns with reduced risk.

Samuelson's studies

Samuelson, in Burton (1998), summed up the fallacy in assuming long-term returns on stocks are somehow assured:

> Many people now believe that if they simply hold stocks long enough – 10, 20, 50 years – they will not, cannot, lose money . . . and are assured of making the long-term historical average annual return from stocks.
>
> This new dogma is a fallacy. . . . [W]hile it's likely that over the long term stocks will fare better than other assets, to invest on that assumption is dangerous. Risk does not go to zero over long periods. . . . [W]hen stock prices do turn down (as inevitably happens . . .) your optimistic equity exposure can overwhelm your gut-level risk tolerance, leading to poor short-term judgments and even outright panic.

Further, Samuelson noted, as "you generate new histories of how the future can look using the same probabilities as applied in the past, it is not the case that serious losses are squeezed away. Serious losses . . . may stay the same, get worse, or get lessened. . . ."

These arguments aside, studies by Samuelson (1974, 1989, 1990, 1994, 1997) and others have also focused on the less obvious, but key, fallacy of time diversification. As summarized in Bodie et al. (1999), time diversification assumes that rates of return over successive periods are statistically independent, with the result that longer-term investment horizons have less risk. The problem is not that long-term returns do not stabilize, which historically they have, but that the risk to *wealth* increases as the horizon lengthens. That is, the risk to average *rates* of return decreases as the holding period lengthens, but the risk to *dollar* returns increases.

Risk of time diversification

The risk behavior of portfolios over time is seen historically in figure 6.2. This figure shows that holding equity portfolios over the long term decreases the risk of losing money. However, not shown, increasing the investment horizon does not reduce all the risks of equity investing. A long investment horizon decreases the probability of losing money, but it does not decrease the variability of portfolio values. That is, the range of possible portfolio values increases as the investment horizon lengthens. In the retirement portfolio context, periodic net withdrawals during retirement dramatically increase the risk of shortfalls in terminal wealth just as periodic additions decrease it.

Moreover, table 30 illustrates the impact of portfolio risk/return parameters on the probability of not achieving various levels of terminal portfolio value. The probability of wealth shortfall increases over time, and this holds for both high-risk and low-risk portfolios. However, low-risk portfolios have a *smaller* probability of *not* achieving relatively small portfolio values (better outcome) than high-risk portfolios. But, beginning at some relatively large portfolio value (here $110,000), high-risk portfolios have a *larger* probability of achieving relatively large portfolio values (better outcome) than low-risk portfolios. Thus time diversification's focus on decreasing risk over time is flawed if different amounts of wealth are at risk, which is the typical case. This is an important consideration for retirement portfolios.

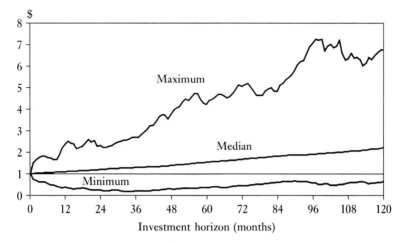

Figure 6.2 Results of a dollar invested in the S&P 500, 1871–1998. Source: calculations by Peter Yoo based on data from Robert Shiller. Reprinted with permission from Peter Yoo, The Long and Short (Runs) of Investing in Equities, *National Economic Trends* (Federal Reserve Bank of St. Louis), October 1998, p. 1.

Sanders (1997a) also determined that increasing the number of domestic equity fund holdings reduces the range of returns over five years and increases the probability of reaching given portfolio values. Most of this potential benefit is achieved in portfolios of seventeen funds, but the largest incremental benefit is by increasing fund holdings from one fund to three. The benefit also varies by investment style. Small-cap. value and blend funds have the widest range of performance and benefit most from increasing fund holdings.

McEnally (1985) effectively summarized the case against time diversification:

> It is no accident that the standard deviation of annualized *rates of return* decreases with the length of the investment horizon while the standard deviation of *total returns* increases with the horizon. Common stock returns, and returns of other primary securities, are well behaved in a statistical sense. That is, they are approximately "independently and identically distributed" over time.

But "[a]s the investment horizon lengthens, the deviation of average periodic returns from the expected periodic return gets smaller and smaller. But, this effect is more than offset by multiplying the smaller and smaller deviations by more and more occurrences." That is, "[a]s long as the focus is on total returns over the investment horizon, risk uniformly increases with the length of the horizon."

More recently, various studies have reported problems with the arguments against time diversification. Fisher and Statman (1999) take a behavioral approach (discussed below) and find risk and return are inadequate descriptors of the world of financial choices. Kritzman (1994) held that Samuelson's argument is not a general refutation of time diversification, but only under his assumption that risk aversion does not change with wealth. Stay tuned, more to come in this debate.

INVESTOR RISK PREFERENCES: THEORY

Investor risk preference is an integral element of portfolio theory. Theory assumes investors choose the asset with the lowest risk among those offering equal returns, and they choose the asset with the highest return among those offering equal risk. These choices assume investors are *risk-averse*, that is, they receive more utility from a certain (riskless) return than from an uncertain return of equal expected value. The so-called *certainty-equivalent return* is the certain return that provides investors with utility equivalent to the expected value of an uncertain return.

As reviewed in Kritzman (1995, 1998), the utility concept originated by Bernoulli in 1783 held that asset value is determined not by its price, but by the *utility* (satisfaction) it provides. And the amount of utility it provides depends on a person's particular circumstances. While persons prefer more wealth to less, they receive smaller and smaller utility increases with each additional increment of wealth – *diminishing marginal utility of wealth*. Utility is measured by the natural logarithm of wealth, which assumes investors have constant relative (percentage) risk aversion. That is, investors prefer the same portfolio allocation mix (percentages) for all size portfolios.

Markowitz's (1952, 1961) portfolio theory assumes diminishing marginal utility and risk aversion. As described in Reilly and Brown (1997), Markowitz makes several assumptions. First, investors use a probability distribution of expected one-period returns to consider each investment alternative. Second, they use indifference curves reflecting diminishing marginal utility of wealth to maximize one-period utility. Third, they use the variability of expected returns to measure portfolio risk. Fourth, they make decisions *solely* on the basis of expected returns and risk, as reflected in their indifference curves. And, finally, investors are assumed risk-averse and prefer higher versus lower returns for a given risk level. The investor's optimal portfolio is identified in risk/return space by the highest indifference curve tangent to a linear set of efficient portfolios.

Later developments in utility theory, reviewed in Alexander and Francis (1986), consider investors may be risk-averse, but they may also be risk-neutral or risk-seeking. The more concave the utility function with increasing wealth, the more risk-averse the investor. Risk-averse investors reject a fair game, but risk-neutral investors are indifferent and risk-seeking investors accept it. Risk-averse investors reject a fair game because they receive more utility from a certain return equal to the expected return of the game. Risk-neutral investors are indifferent because they receive equal utility from a certain return equal to the game's expected return. And risk-loving investors accept the fair game because they receive less utility from a certain return equal to the game's expected return.

Risk aversion is further delineated as to whether utility increases, remains constant, or decreases as an *absolute* or *relative* (percentage) function of increases in wealth. Chow (1995) described investor expected utility as having three dimensions: (1) expected return, (2) absolute risk (variability), and (3) relative risk (*benchmark tracking error*). The bottom line is that actual investors may be more/less risk averse than assumed by Bernoulli.

INVESTOR RISK PREFERENCES: BEHAVIORAL

In recent years, *modern finance* has come under increasing attack by students of cognitive psychology and *behavioral finance*. "Behavioral finance" refers to the application of psychology to financial behavior. Supporters of behavioral finance do not believe that the assumptions of modern finance describe actual investor behavior. For treatments of behavioral finance, see Shefrin (2000), Statman (1995a, 1995b), and Woods (1995).

The prevailing wisdom of modern finance is that markets are highly efficient and prices determined by rational investors. (Here, Gray's 1997 footnote comes to mind, albeit tongue-in-cheek: "Rational behavior is often defined as that which maximizes expected utility. This definition . . . allows all behavior to be rational.") Now, these assumptions are being questioned by behaviorists who believe that irrational investors also determine market prices. For example, how does one explain the frenetic activity of day traders? These persons evidence too much self-confidence or why else would they trade so often without any thought of diversification?

Modern finance agrees investors do not always behave rationally, but asserts that there is no evidence that this behavior affects prices. Efficient markets theory predicts there will be *anomalies* (exceptions to the theory), but they are generated by chance. But, more generally, the cost of active portfolio management makes markets too efficient to generate consistently abnormal returns. However, both sides of the debate agree on a low-cost buy and hold strategy. And this is what passive asset allocation is all about.

More precisely, modern finance is criticized for considering what investors should do, rather than what they actually do. The "should" means that economic agents optimize their actions subject to rational models without error, such as that which describes investors as maximizing expected utility. It is assumed that investors use expected returns and standard deviations derived from estimates of probability distributions of returns to assess assets. Investors also display no systematic biases (consistent mistakes) when assessing true asset probability distributions.

Behavioral finance does not believe all economic decisions can be described by equilibrium conditions. As noted, investors behave less than fully rationally some of the time. For example, Kahneman et al. (1982), the godfathers of behavioral finance, observed that investors are not consistent in how they treat economically equivalent choices if the choices are framed (presented) in significantly different contexts. These *framing effects* are present in several types of investor behavior. Investors do not act the same way in choices involving large gains versus large losses. They are risk-averse in preferring certain large gains to slightly larger expected gains with much more risk. However, they are not risk-averse in appearing to prefer large expected losses to slightly smaller certain losses. Investors also appear to overestimate the probability of unlikely outcomes, such as Internet stock earnings, and underestimate the probability of more likely outcomes. Investors also appear to overreact to good and bad news. They bid up the prices of stocks reporting unexpectedly good earnings beyond fair value and, conversely, push down the prices of stocks reporting unexpectedly bad earnings below fair value. Thus exploring what *cognitive psychology* has to offer investing promises improved understanding of behaviors that do not fit standard finance paradigms. For example, there are anomalies to *efficient markets* theory, a keystone of modern finance.

DeBondt and Thaler study

As discussed in DeBondt and Thaler (1995), modern finance holds that investors are risk-averse expected utility maximizers (as in Markowitz, above) and unbiased Bayesian forecasters

– that is, investors make rational choices based on rational expectations. Behavioral finance has two basic criticisms of modern finance. The first criticism is that its assumptions are sometimes false and, second, its set of assumptions is incomplete. This means, for example, that real investors may *not* (1) have single-period decision horizons, (2) always be risk-averse, (3) measure risk as volatility, and (4) rely only on the risk/return paradigm to make decisions. What it does mean is that actual investor behavior (Gen-X, for example) is more complex than assumed for the *economic man* of modern finance.

Several investor behaviors have been identified that are inconsistent with the principles of modern finance. The result is that it is no longer enough to argue that theory should be judged only by its predictive ability, but rather also by the realism of its assumptions. First, investors reflect *overconfidence*. Real-world investors overestimate their knowledge and its reliability. Investors are more confident of their predictions where they have self-declared expertise, such as market timers. Second, investors use the *representativeness heuristic* (decision rule) in making probability judgments. This heuristic induces investors to make probability judgments that depend too much on recent outcomes, such as market declines, and not enough on basic market outcomes, such as the preponderance of up markets over time. This heuristic thus leads investors to make forecasts that are too extreme, given the predictive value of available information.

Third, investors use *prospect theory*, a behavioral theory of decision making under uncertainty. Prospect theory states that investors are *loss-averse* and therefore treat gains and losses differently. They focus on changes in wealth, not levels of wealth, and losses are weighted approximately twice as much as gains. Loss aversion implies that decisions are sensitive to the way alternatives are framed. That is, investors use *mental accounting* to frame alternatives. For example, investors are more likely to sell securities with losses if they are considered elements in larger portfolios. But, if they consider securities separately, risk-averse investors are less likely to sell and realize losses. Mental accounting may also be used to instill control. As discussed below, mental accounting is used to identify two separate portfolios – one for meeting cash needs over the next six years, and the second for long-term investment using asset allocation. In this case, mental accounting prevents the investment portfolio from being too conservatively managed because of overhanging concern about liquidity needs. And it places the investment portfolio off-limits to spending, which is provided for in the first portfolio.

Fourth, investors are influenced by fashions and fads that pressure them to conform. This is seen in the herding behavior of some portfolio managers, who feel more secure performing like the market than risking failure by attempting to beat the market. This is also seen in the herding behavior of investors who flock to the latest guru of the month. Fifth, investors feel *regret* (remorse) for decisions that lead to bad outcomes. Investors minimize future regret by shifting decision-making responsibility to others, such as market gurus noted above. They also avoid regret by making conventional decisions, such as investing in popular blue chip and *glamour* securities rather than unpopular, undervalued securities. This may explain any abnormal returns in value investing.

DeBondt and Thaler (1995) explained that two axioms of modern finance must be systematically violated to establish the need for behavioral finance. First, the rational behavior underpinning modern finance must be systematically violated and, second, financial markets cannot be relied upon to eliminate evidence of irrational behavior. Such evidence is present in anomalies not explainable under the modern finance paradigm.

Anomalies

Active portfolio management and trading is the first anomaly. In rational models, differences in private information may create disagreement among investors, but does not generate trading if rationality is common knowledge. In reality, investors act assuming their interpretation of information is correct. And institutional investors trade more often than individual investors. Overconfidence explains both why portfolio managers are hired and why they trade so much.

The second anomaly is *contrarian strategies*. Contrarian strategies (discussed in a later chapter) include various measures for identifying out-of-favor stocks. The general behavioral explanation for the success of these strategies lies in a combination of biased forecasts of profits and misperception of risks. The purchase of "irrationally underpriced" securities requires strong conviction because unconventional choices cause regret if wrong.

Asset pricing and investor sentiment is the third anomaly. Modern finance holds that asset prices are equal to their intrinsic values. This hypothesis is not generally easy to test because only market values are observable. However, closed-end funds provide an interesting test of market efficiency. That is, why do shares in these funds usually sell at a discount to net asset value? If investors are rational, they would only buy them at a discount. Behavioral explanations revolve around various tests of investor optimism/pessimism over time.

The fourth anomaly is the *equity premium puzzle*. Why are there such large differentials between stock returns and risk-free interest rates, and are the differences consistent with rational models? One explanation for large equity premiums is that investors are extremely risk averse. A behavioral explanation under prospect theory includes loss aversion and mental accounting. Loss aversion is consistent with prospect theory in which disutility of losses is about twice that of gains. Mental accounting is seen in the frequency of portfolio evaluation. The more often portfolios are evaluated, the greater the chance of regret due to negative returns. This combination of short horizons and loss aversion is called *myopic loss aversion*. There is less regret in long-term returns because they are predominantly positive.

Investor overconfidence

The finding that investors may be overconfident should not be surprising. Most persons tend to overestimate their knowledge and abilities, especially in areas where they think they have some expertise. After all, do you know anyone who is not a self-proclaimed above-average driver? This behavior can be very costly in investing. As an example, Sturm (1999) reported male investors doing their guy thing are generally more (too) confident than women. This behavior leads males to trade excessively and, not unexpectedly, lower performance. Rowland (1999) reported that men have a higher portfolio turnover than women: 77 percent and 53 percent, respectively. Both are too high. But men tend to feel more competent (overconfidence) than women in financial matters, and this false sense leads to more trading.

Moreover, Lowenstein (1994a) reported that novice women investors are cautious and fact-oriented. Women prefer to research investments and are more risk averse than men. Women portfolio managers more often manage fixed-income and international funds, where they have had more opportunities. But they are equal to men in performance. Several variables explain differences in portfolio manager performance, but gender is not one of them.

Overconfident investors often forgo long-term buy-and-hold strategies in the belief they can beat the market short-term. But Clements (1998) reported this belief false and noted why bad things happen to overconfident investors. Overconfident investors (1) ignore trading costs and trade too much; (2) react to short-term market noise and trade for other than liquidity needs; (3) get caught up in trading activity and "confuse bull markets with brains"; (4) bet too much on initial public offerings, hot stocks, and narrow industry sectors; (5) sell winners too soon, but also keep losers too long rather than admit mistakes; (6) compound investment mistakes with yet more trading; and (7) have the ability to forget past mistakes and their implications.

However, overconfidence does have a positive side if it makes conservative investors invest in equities. For example, Clements (1999a) reported that stock winners sold the previous year outperform losers they held on to during the next year. While investors hold on to losers to avoid regret at having to admit bad decisions, this behavior may also have good endings. It may prevent them from selling stocks at low prices and, in effect, waiting for prices to rebound. This assumes that the original purchase decisions were correct and the reasons for buying have not changed. Usually, however, the original decisions were wrong. Nonetheless, rather than reacting to news that has already been incorporated in stock prices, it is better to rethink why stocks were purchased and whether original decisions continue to be correct.

Cognitive dissonance

Goetzmann and Peles (1997) see evidence of *cognitive dissonance* in investor memories of past performance. Memories are consistently better than actual fund performance. Investors are distressed by discrepancies between the empirical evidence and past choices, and they alter their beliefs to reduce discomfort. An *endowment effect* is also present in investor belief that securities owned are better than those not owned.

Behavioral finance also observes that exaggerated investor behavior in bull and bear markets is analogous to manic depressive illness. Clements (2000b) reported several psychological shifts contributing to exaggerated market prices both on the up side and on the down side. On the manic side there is the house money effect, where investors take additional risks with paper money winnings (the house's money), knowing they will still be ahead. Second, there is the greater fool effect, where the more the market goes up the more investors extrapolate to the future in the implicit belief that someone will also buy at those prices. Third, there is the confusing-a-bull-market-for-brains effect (noted above), where investors become even more overconfident and trade more, knowing how skillful they are.

When markets inevitably fall (surprise, surprise), bull market mania is destroyed, but exaggerated behaviors continue, this time on the depressive down side of the market. First, there is the "real money" effect, where investors take fewer risks (more risk averse) with what is left after losses. Second, there is the "I'm a fool" effect, where the more the market goes down the more investors extrapolate the implicit belief that no on will buy at these prices. So sell now! Third, there is the "How could I have been so stupid?" effect, where investors become (even more) insecure and trade less, not knowing what to do. Should I sell, or what?

Investor overconfidence as a theory

In recent years, anomalies have challenged the modern finance view that securities are rationally priced to reflect all public information. Daniel et al. (1998) stated these exceptions include: (1) event-based return predictability, with public event date stock returns having the same sign as subsequent long-term abnormal performance; (2) short-term returns, with positive short-term autocorrelations of stock and market returns; (3) long-term reversal of returns, with negative autocorrelations of short-term returns separated by overreaction; (4) high volatility of asset values relative to their fundamentals; and (5) short-term post-earnings announcement stock prices drift in the direction of earnings surprises, but abnormal stock price performance is in the opposite direction of long-term earnings changes.

Daniel et al. (1998) developed a theory that makes it possible to explain the above anomalies based on imperfect, not perfect, investor rationality. This theory is based on investor over-confidence and variations in confidence arising from *biased self-attribution*. The premise of overconfidence is derived from cognitive psychology, which shows that persons attribute good outcomes to their own abilities and bad outcomes to externalities. In fact, DeBondt and Thaler (1995) concluded that investor overconfidence is "perhaps the most robust finding in the psychology of judgment."

Overconfidence causes stock prices to overreact to private signals and to underreact to public signals. Experts tend to be more overconfident than relatively inexperienced persons. Overconfidence is stronger for judgment tasks and tasks with delayed feedback. Fundamental analysis of securities requires judgment about open-ended issues with delayed and noisy feedback. Thus investors believe themselves more able to value securities than they actually are and underestimate forecast errors. Individuals tend to overestimate their abilities and perceive themselves more favorably than others perceive them.

Biased self-attribution is consistent with several behaviors. First, and most important, stock prices overreact (investor *overreaction*) to private information signals and underreact to public signals. Positive return autocorrelations can result from continuing overreaction followed by long-term correction. Short-term positive autocorrelations can thus be consistent with long-term negative autocorrelations. This overreaction–correction pattern is consistent with long-run negative autocorrelations in stock returns, excess volatility, and signal-dependent volatility.

Second, the phenomenon of public event stock price reactions having the same signs as post-event long-term abnormal returns is due to market underreaction only if events are chosen in response to market mispricing. Rather, this predictability may arise when public events cause continuing price overreactions. For example, post-earnings announcement *price drift* may reflect continuing overreaction of earnings announcements to pre-event information. Third, price variability arising from unpredictable (noise) trading reflects investor misinterpretation of real new private information. These trading mistakes are correlated with fundamentals. Predictions about the dynamic behavior of stock prices depend on the particular errors made, and these biases explain several anomalous price patterns. Fourth, noise investing implies long-term price reversals and short-term price *momentum*. These price movements are reconciled. Overconfident informed investors lose money on average, and rational investors may not predominate in the long run. Risk-averse investors may underestimate risk and allocate more wealth to risky, high-expected-return assets. Overconfident investors with real information signals may exploit information more effectively. Thus overconfident investors may earn larger returns than rational investors.

Finally, investor overconfidence has more severe impacts in less liquid markets and assets. Large stocks tend to be more rationally priced through arbitrage in liquid markets. Given overconfidence about private information, the predictability of returns is strongest in stocks with the largest information asymmetries, which implies that small-cap. stocks are priced less efficiently. Both individual and professional investors may be overconfident. Uninformed investors could be interpreted as *contrarian* investors.

A final note

To sum up, Fraser (1999) and Zweig (1997c) reported several basic truths concerning investor behavior. First, investors are more averse to losing money than forgoing potential gains. Second, investors prefer certainty to uncertainty and will accept somewhat lower returns to get it. Third, investors facing uncertainty prefer many small risk exposures to a few large ones. Fourth, investors judge the probability of actions by the ease with which they come to mind, such as the October 1987 crash. Fifth, investors take risks to avoid certain losses, but prefer certain gains to taking risks for more gains. Sixth, investors have more regret for bad outcomes arising from actions taken than for those not taken. This fear of regret is called the "*status quo* bias." For example, rather than buying more stock when the market falls, investors let inertia take over, fearing more regret if new actions have bad outcomes. Seventh, investors purchase managed mutual funds in the hope (small probability) of large returns, rather than index funds with a near certainty of "only" market returns. Eighth, investors suffer from the *illusion of control*, which leads them to make decisions without fully understanding the odds. The more investors think they know, the larger the gap between what they actually know and what they think they know. So much for experts! Ninth, investors anchor views of stock values to historical prices. For example, investors see current prices as bargains, when in fact company fundamentals have changed for the worse. And, finally, investors use mental accounting to set up separate accounts for different objectives. This causes them to take the wrong risks, such as avoiding market risks and ignoring inflation risks in retirement accounts.

In the debate between modern finance and behavioral finance, there does appear to be some agreement concerning the implications for investors. As reported in Clements (2000c), Thaler stated that the validity of behavioral finance does not depend on investors being able to beat the market. Investors are overconfident and trade too much, but this could make stock prices both "wildly irrational" and "unpredictable." The market may be crazy and not entirely efficient, but this does not mean you can beat it. The best advice: buy and hold. Professor Rubinstein agrees that investors are overconfident, which causes active portfolio managers to spend too much on research and thereby increase market efficiency. Professor Sharpe bridges the gap and states that, no matter which theory is correct, investors should act as if markets are efficient. The best advice: buy and hold.

INVESTMENT POLICY AND INVESTMENT MANAGEMENT

Before discussing the practical identification of mutual fund investor risk preferences, it should be noted that this is the first step in the investment process. For discussion of the investment process, see Fogler and Bayston (1984), Sharpe (1984b), and Maginn and Tuttle (1990). As discussed in Gibson (1996), there are two major components of the investment process: investment policy and investment management. These issues were approached from the investment advisory point of view, while the focus here is directly on individual investors. The purely investment issues are the same in either case. *Investment policy* as defined here includes the identification of investor risk preferences, portfolio investment objectives, and passive asset allocation.

Passive asset allocation includes the identification of normal long-term stock/bond portfolio allocation, including the frequency of portfolio rebalancing. Asset allocation in both its active (discussed below) and its passive versions is treated in Sharpe (1987a, b, 1990), Perold and Sharpe (1988), Arnott and Fabozzi (1992), Gibson (1996), and William Bernstein (1995, 1997b).

A prerequisite to passive asset allocation is determination of the amount and allocation of the so-called *cash bucket*. The account is managed separately from the investment portfolio to meet anticipated and unanticipated cash needs for a defined number of years. These cash assets are usually included in investment portfolios, but not here. The use of mental accounting in separating the cash bucket and investment portfolio makes it possible to manage the investment portfolio along a single time line, the long-term investment horizon, without concern for cash needs along the way.

Mental accounting does not provide optimal portfolio efficiency (neither do efforts at optimization), but provides more psychological ease in framing the solutions of two problems into separate portfolios: (1) cash reserves for anticipated or unanticipated living expenses for the next defined number of years, and (2) a passively managed investment portfolio to grow the assets needed for long-term needs in a way that is comfortable to investor risk tolerances.

Peter Bernstein (1997a), student of risk, agrees with preparing for contingencies that justify use of the cash bucket. He stated:

> What should your own concept of asset mix be? The answer is a matter of gut, not statistics. Keep enough money outside the stock market to be certain that you will have the courage to hang in when the inevitable crashes occur. That is an unscientific solution to a critically important question, but my long experience has taught me that the biggest risk of all – and the risk that is imperative to manage ahead of time – is the risk of chickening out in the terrifying moments when opportunities are the greatest.

Investment management represents the active, ongoing process of implementing investment policy. Its elements include active portfolio allocation, investment style allocation, security selection and allocation, and performance evaluation. *Tactical (active) asset allocation* identifies portfolio asset allocations based on a form of market timing (a bad idea) designed to profit from short-term market conditions. *Strategic (passive) asset allocation* identifies relatively constant portfolio asset allocations based on long-term market conditions. (*Investment) style allocation* identifies equity style allocation classified by combinations of value/growth and cap. size, including specialized mutual funds. It also identifies debt securities allocation classified by combinations of effective maturity and credit quality.

Fund selection and allocation identify the particular mutual funds and proportions appropriate for each identified style allocation. *Performance evaluation* compares portfolio performance relative with standard market indices, but especially with benchmarks consistent with the portfolio's investment objective and style allocation. Investment management is discussed later.

INVESTMENT RISK

The next section deals with investor risk preference (tolerance), but first it is important to remember that risk is in the eye of the beholder and this perception changes from time to time. There are different types and measurements of risk. As measured historically, risk often focuses on portfolio risk (mutual funds) as well as security risk. Of course, it would be nice (and very profitable) to be able to identify future risk accurately, but, in general, past risk provides a "darkened window" on to future risk. Nonetheless, past risk has generally been a more accurate estimate of future risk than past returns have been as estimates of future returns.

What is it?

But, to begin, what do mutual fund investors think risk is? ICI (1996) surveyed mutual fund investors and reported that 57 percent define risk as the chance of losing some part of the *original* investment. Other investor definitions of risk are: (1) not keeping pace with inflation (47 percent), (2) decline in portfolio value (46 percent), and (3) not having enough to achieve long-term goals. While 66 percent of investors strongly agree that investing in mutual funds involves some degree of risk, 58 percent are comfortable with the overall risk of fund holdings. Performance (75 percent) and risk (69 percent) are the most frequently used types of information prior to fund purchase. In order, the next most frequently used types of information are investment goals, portfolio securities, and fees and expenses. Hopefully, concern about fund fees/expenses (43 percent) will become more important.

Mutual fund investors are primarily long-term investors. At least, they think of themselves this way. Only 4 percent of investors have investment horizons less than one year, 33 percent have horizons of one to five years, 28 percent have horizons of six to ten years, and 34 percent have horizons over ten years. Further, 73 percent have no concern about short-term fluctuations in long-term portfolio values. Agreement with this statement ranges from 59 percent for investors with investment horizons less than one year to 68 percent for investors with horizons of one to five years, 69 percent for those with horizons of six to ten years, and 85 percent for those with horizons over ten years. If only portfolio managers were so wise and investors followed their statements.

Finally, mutual fund investors appear to have a basic understanding of the risk in investing. Over 60 percent strongly agree that investing in stocks and bonds involves some degree of risk. Further, 57 percent shop around before buying funds, and 58 percent are comfortable with the overall portfolio risk levels. To make risk assessments, 57 percent of investors use the standard deviation, 70 percent use beta, and 48 percent use duration for bond funds. Duration reflects the average maturity of the stream of payments generated by a bond. Thus fund investors see themselves as long-term investors who know risk is involved and who use quantitative measures to assess risk. These are welcome findings, but a serious bear market might find them undergoing major behaviorally induced revision.

Risk is the other side of return. Returns comprise two elements, the periodic payment of interest or dividends (*yield*) and change in asset values over a period of time (capital gains/losses). All investment decisions involve a trade-off between risk and return. The *capital asset pricing model* (CAPM) posits that return and risk are positively related – higher return carries higher risk. Investors cannot expect higher returns without being willing to assume larger risks. Empirical tests of the CAPM generally find that the trade-off relationship between expected return and risk is an upward, positively sloped straight line. The general nature of this trade-off was also confirmed behaviorally in Baker et al. (1977).

Moreover, in this portfolio context, relevant risk is not an asset's own risk, but its effect on portfolio systematic risk. Bearing systematic risk does not command a risk premium. Investors are rewarded only for assuming risk that cannot be eliminated through diversification. Thus investors are not rewarded for bearing unsystematic risk. Empirical evidence indicates that markets price securities based on a linear relationship between systematic risk and return. The role of unsystematic risk in the market pricing mechanism is small, at best.

Risk has many faces, reflecting the sources of the risk. All of the relevant types of risk are brought together in the market's asset pricing mechanism. As suggested above, capital theory repackages individual sources of risk into two general types, which together sum to *total risk*: general risk plus specific risk, or, as stated above, systematic (market) risk plus non-systematic (unique) risk. Systematic risk is caused by broad market factors that impact most all securities, such as monetary policy, tax policy, inflation, economic outlook, and market outlook. Conversely, unsystematic risk is caused by residual factors not captured in systematic risk, such as a company's financial strength, earnings outlook, management skill, brand recognition, and competition.

Types of risk

Traditionally, risks have been described along several dimensions widely used in investments. These risks include interest-rate risks, market risks (as defined above), inflation risks, business risks, financial risks, liquidity risks, and the risks of international investing. International risks include exchange-rate risk and an inclusively defined country risk. These risks affect the volatility of security prices in the following ways:

1 *Interest-rate risk:* increased volatility of security returns derived from changes in interest rates. Rate increases (decreases) are associated with decreases (increases) in stock and bond prices, but the impact directly affects bond prices and yields.
2 *Market risk:* increased volatility of security returns derived from changes in the overall level of financial markets (systematic risk as defined above). Risk increases (decreases) are associated with decreases (increases) in security prices, but primarily stock prices.
3 *Inflation (purchasing power) risk:* increased volatility of security returns derived from changes in the rate of inflation. Risk increases (decreases) are associated with increases (decreases) in bond yields with decreases (increases) in bond prices to compensate for loss (gain) of purchasing power.

4   *Business risk:* increased volatility of a particular security's returns derived from changes in the risk of the particular business. Risk increases (decreases) are associated with decreases (increases) in security prices.

5   *Financial risk:* increased volatility of a particular security's returns derived from changes in firm risk due to the firm's proportionate use of debt financing. Risk increases (decreases) are associated with decreases (increases) in security prices due to increases (decreases) in the proportion of debt in the capital structure and associated increases (decreases) in earnings variability. A related concept is *operating leverage* – derived from changes in firm risk due to a firm's proportionate use of fixed assets as seen in proportion of fixed costs to total costs.

6   *Exchange (currency) risk:* increased volatility of security returns derived from changes in the risks of operating internationally due to changes in the conversion rates of international earnings into dollars. Risk increases (decreases) are associated with decreases (increases) in security prices that recognize earnings losses (gains).

7   *Country (political) risk:* increased volatility of security returns derived from changes in the risks of firms operating internationally due to changes in the ability to convert international earnings into dollars. Risk increases (decreases) are associated with decreases (increases) in security prices that recognize earnings losses (gains).

8   *Liquidity risk:* increased volatility of security returns derived from changes in the liquidity of markets in which securities are traded. Risk increases (decreases) are associated with decreases (increases) in security prices received and increases (decreases) in prices paid.

Measures of risk, especially those associated with developments in capital theory, focus on dispersion of returns around expected (likely) outcomes. Risk is assumed to derive from variability in investor returns. Or, in other words, by the chance that returns on investments will differ from expected returns. They take several forms, depending on the type of risk being measured. Some basic measures include standard deviation of returns, beta, and *R squared* (R^2). Others developed for measuring mutual fund risk include *CDA Rating*, *Morningstar (star) Rating* (star system), and Morningstar Risk (also in conjunction with Morningstar Return). These measures are discussed later.

However, ICI (1996) computed that only 26 percent of recent mutual fund buyers use any quantitative risk measure. The measures most commonly used by these investors are standard deviation, bond portfolio duration, and beta. Investors that use these measures have larger incomes, seek long-term portfolio growth, and are more likely to own stock, bond, and money market funds.

INVESTOR RISK PREFERENCES: APPLIED

The first and best advice investors should receive is to know their risk tolerance. It is critical for investors to understand, realistically, their risk tolerances, or, in the case of investment advisors, their clients' tolerances for the risks of long-term investing. Nothing is more essential and nothing is harder to determine correctly. There is no modern and/or behavioral finance model that assures correct management of investor risk tolerances, especially if investor ability or willingness to participate in the process is considered. As discussed above, investor behavioral issues should be considered. For example, investors' judgments may be influenced by real-time market noise that provokes a too confident view of actual long-term risk tolerances, even if they are not conscious of or willing to admit it. Thus identification of investor long-term risk tolerance needs to be separated from short-term risk tolerance based, for example, on the performance of Internet stocks. Identification of investor risk preferences should focus on the long term, in both good and bad markets, and, if the desire is to be particularly conservative, especially the latter. For example, Meyer and Phillips (1993) concluded that investor risk tolerance and investment time horizon are the two most important constraints in building portfolios. Investors must also understand that investment decisions involve risk/return trade-offs, and, over time, there are no free lunches – the desire for high return comes with commensurately high risk.

Investor risk test

Real-world individual investors are thus probably best served today by an understandable and practical approach to identifying long-term risk tolerance. Numerous risk tests exist, many of which are long and test investor knowledge perhaps more than investor preferences. Representative risk tests are provided in Peers (1987), Fidelity Investments (1988), Heckman (1988), LeBaron et al. (1989), *Fortune* (1989), Roszkowski and Snelbecker (1989), Power (1990), Rowland (1990), Comrey (1992), Fidelity Investments (1995), Hube (1998), and Lowenstein (1998b). As suggested above, there is no single validated scientific model for identifying investor risk tolerances. No operational model is known to correctly blend modern finance theory and investor behavior to measure the rational/irrational, interactive, illusive, and dynamic influences on investor risk preferences.

As a result, the second best approach may be to use an empirically tested questionnaire to determine investor risk tolerances categorically. In this way, identified risk categories may be matched to appropriate portfolio investment objectives. To this end, over the last decade, several risk tests were administered in combinations of three to some 1,000 persons. This made it possible to identify the particular tests that are most consistent in the investor risk categories they identified. Among the tests, three, but especially two, are most consistent in identifying risk categories. Of the two, the shorter test was selected for use here because its record of consistency was at least equal to that of the other. This test is presented in table 31.

Validation of risk test results

After an investor's risk category has been identified, but before matching it to a portfolio investment objective, it should be validated by self-analysis of major life influences on risk tolerance. For the risk test and self-analysis results to be consistent, the test must implicitly incorporate various life influences on long-term risk tolerance. If the risk test and self-analysis both identify the same risk category, the next step is to identify the appropriate portfolio investment objective. If not, the differences should be reconciled by judging which risk category is ultimately most comfortable. For example, if the test says moderate risk and self-analysis implicitly says modest risk, judgment is the final arbiter as to which category best represents the investor's long-term risk tolerance.

Judgment includes determining whether the expected long-term returns generated by the comfortable risk category will be adequate to meet lifetime goals, such as retirement income or travel. Conservative portfolios may not generate the wealth needed to achieve goals, and risky portfolios may not as well, owing to greater risk to wealth over time. To determine the portfolio allocation with the greatest chance of achieving their goals, investors should use probabilistic financial planning programs such as Financial Engines (2000), discussed below. Run-of-the-mill financial planning programs are not sophisticated enough and run the risk of identifying portfolios that will not achieve goals. No portfolios achieve goals with 100 percent certainty, so investors should make sure the odds are in their favor.

As reported in Clements (2000a), the best way to begin the process of determining the appropriate portfolio allocation is *not* to determine risk preferences. A more appropriate process is to: (1) specify financial goals and the amounts required; (2) understand the implications of portfolio allocation and composition and the remaining investment horizon for achieving goals in an uncertain world; (3) select appropriate portfolio allocation; (4) compare the allocation with that which best meets risk preferences; and (5) reconcile any differences on the side of probabilities or preferences and/or reduce financial goals, but be aware of the trade-offs in each choice.

Three major life influences on investor risk tolerance are: (1) *family background core values* (environment), (2) *psychological risk instincts* (genetic), and (3) *socioeconomic characteristics* (demographic), including stage in the investment life cycle. For example, some persons are genetically disposed to safe securities and others to aggressive growth stocks. Some persons have been trained at home to save and invest and others to earn and spend. And some persons have socioeconomic traits that favor high dividends and others that favor capital gains. These are just a sampling of the numerous types and combinations of influences. Such factors help explain why we are as we are. Each person is unique and spends his/her life proving it.

Validation of investor risk category

The validation of investor risk category is eased by factor constructs identified in Baker and Haslem (1974b). Three factors were most important in explaining investor perceptions of what is important in making equity decisions. In perceived order of importance, they are (1) dividends, (2) future expectations, and (3) financial stability (risk). The analysis indicated two distinct types of investors: (1) those who seek dividend income and (2) those who seek capital gains. This suggests that equity securities with particular attributes attract particular "investor clienteles."

Investor preferences for *dividends* are significantly positively correlated with interest in dividend income, older investors, female investors, and service workers. Conversely, dividends are significantly negatively correlated with acceptable risk of loss, interest in capital appreciation, and level of family income. Investor preferences for *future expectations* are significantly positively correlated with interest in capital appreciation, portfolio size, and housewives or retired or non-employed adults. And investor preferences are significantly negatively correlated only with interest in dividend income. Investor preferences for *financial stability* are significantly positively correlated with older investors, interest in dividend income, level of expected annual returns, and female investors. Stability is significantly negatively correlated with level of education and interest in capital appreciation.

Baker et al. (1977) reported several findings. First, there is a strong positive relationship between acceptable risk levels and expected total returns. Consistent with theory, the contour of this relationship reveals a no free lunch positive linear to slightly risk-averse risk/return trade-off. Second, there is an extremely negative relationship between acceptable risk levels and interest in dividend income. Low-risk investors prefer dividend income because of its greater certainty relative to capital appreciation. Third, there is a strong positive relationship between acceptable risk levels and capital appreciation. These findings infer the overwhelming influence of capital appreciation in total return expectations. Finally, the existence of both dividend and capital gains investors also suggests clientele effects for stocks with preferred attributes.

Baker and Haslem (1974a) analyzed socioeconomic variables for their influences on investor preferences for expected dividend yield, expected price appreciation, share marketability (liquidity), and share price stability. Five important socioeconomic variables were identified. Preferences for expected *dividend yield* are significantly related to older investors, female investors, dependent decision makers, separated or divorced or non-employed investors, and those with lower family incomes. Preferences for *expected price appreciation* are significantly related to younger investors and independent decision makers. Preferences for (high) *marketability* are significantly related to older investors, And, finally, preferences for (high) *share price stability* are significantly related to female investors and those with less education. Overall, the most important variable is investor age, followed by gender, dependent/independent investment decision maker, marital status, education, and family income.

Investors are often portrayed as following an investment life cycle in which their risk/return preferences, and thus their investment objectives and portfolio allocations, are influenced by their stage in the cycle. Many model portfolios use age as the primary or sole determinant of investor stage in the cycle. Older investors are assumed to prefer less risky, income-focused investment objectives to more risky capital gains objectives. However, Baker et al. (1979) rejected the age-only life cycle model. Socioeconomic attributes in various combinations identify actual stage in the life cycle. Attributes were identified for investors interested in dividend income, future expectations (of industry, firm, management and *risk/return performance*), and financial stability (risk).

Investors most interested in *dividend income* are older investors, those with lower family incomes, and the separated or divorced or non-employed. Those most interested in *future expectations* have larger portfolios and at least some college education. Investors interested in *financial stability* are older, with at least four years of high school, and any marital status and level of family income. Age is the most important attribute of stage in the cycle for investors interested in dividend income and financial stability, but it is an incomplete description of investment cycle behavior. The other identified attributes, in various combinations, are important as well.

Table 32 provides a summary checklist of investor socioeconomic characteristics associated with interest in dividend income (less risk) and capital appreciation (more risk). It provides assistance in determining whether investor socioeconomic characteristics favor dividend income or capital appreciation. For example, dividends are favored by older persons, females, service workers, those with lower family incomes, separated or divorced or non-employed persons, those with less education, and dependent investment decision makers.

Risk test and self-analysis validation: example

To illustrate the risk test and self-analysis validation process, the responses of "Kate," who recently embarked on her career, may be helpful. Her responses to the table 31 risk test totaled nine, which identifies her as a moderate risk taker. She was asked to validate this finding through self-analysis of family background core values, individual risk instincts, and her socioeconomic characteristics. Kate's abridged responses follow:

Family background core values
My family background was quite conservative. To earn my modest allowance, I had to perform chores. No exceptions were made. As a result, I saved as much as possible "just in case."
   My father never really discussed financial matters, but I think he primarily bought bank CDs. Both parents emphasized saving and spending money wisely.

Psychological risk instincts
My "comfort zone" lies in taking reasonable risks to earn solid long-term returns. But, at the present, I am being conservative to build a cash reserve. Later, as I advance in my job and begin to earn "real money" I will invest more aggressively than now.

Next, Kate reviewed her socioeconomic profile in table 32 to determine whether it identifies a preference for lower-risk dividends or more risky capital gains. She responded positively to (expected) larger portfolio, higher education, younger investor, and (expected) independent decision maker. Only her gender suggested a preference for dividends. Kate's abridged self-analysis follows:

Although my family background suggests modest risk, my own instincts and socioeconomic characteristics favor moderate risk. My conclusion is that I am a *moderate risk* investor. I am comfortable with this for the future because I majored in finance and studied the dangers in short-term investing compared to long-term investing.

Thus Kate's self analysis and socioeconomic profile are consistent and identify her as a moderate risk investor.

PORTFOLIO INVESTMENT OBJECTIVES AND THE CASH BUCKET

After the investor risk category has been identified and validated, it should be matched with the appropriate portfolio investment objective in table 34. The table includes four investor risk categories that are matched to particular portfolio investment objectives. In addition, the table includes a fifth "no risk" category that is matched to the capital conservation investment objective, in which no decline in value is acceptable. This no-risk category is described above as the cash bucket.

Nature of the cash bucket

The cash bucket is managed separately from the investment portfolio to meet cash needs for a defined number of years. The cash bucket should include assets equal to estimates of future or potential cash needs, such as emergency reserves, retirement income, house purchase, college tuition and other needs and desires, within the next two market cycles, or six years. The cash bucket should be refilled from the investment portfolio each year, preferably when rebalancing to desired allocations.

The very short-term component of the cash bucket should be invested in taxable and/or tax-exempt money market funds, as appropriate to the portfolio's tax status. The longer-term component should be invested in taxable and/or tax-exempt short/intermediate-term bond funds of comfortable quality, such as US Treasury securities. For this purpose, short-term bond funds offer the advantages of higher returns than money market funds, but with little price sensitivity to changes in levels of interest rates.

The use of more than one type of mutual fund in the cash bucket is suggested if the account is large because small yield differences can be significant when compounded over time. However, unless the amounts are sizable, keeping it simple, as discussed above, is recommended. With this in mind, DiTeresa (1998) recommended a more aggressively invested cash bucket. In place of money market funds for the shortest-term component of the cash bucket, invest in high credit quality ultra-short bonds and funds that invest in US Treasury bills, mortgage-backed securities, and corporate bonds with an average duration of six months. The very short maturity precludes significant losses from increasing interest rates. For the longer-term component, invest in short-term municipal bond funds (for taxable accounts) with durations up to three and a half years. If cash withdrawals are made on specific dates, funds that invest in high credit quality floating prime rate bank loans could also be used. These funds usually limit redemptions to once a quarter.

To implement the cash bucket, investors need to select mutual funds of the type discussed above for the purpose. This decision may be made simply or less so, depending on the investor, but simple is often not far from optimal. The simplest approach is to use money market and short to intermediate-term bond funds offered by the fund family that provides the investor's core fund investment in the stock/bond portfolio. This provides ease in exchanging cash back and forth between the cash bucket and investment portfolio as needed.

To validate this approach, investors should review Morningstar (2000) reports and ratings of potential mutual funds for the cash bucket. In most cases, credit quality is not a critical issue, but the review will identify funds that provide investor comfort with respect to duration and credit quality. It is also important to select money market funds offered by major fund families to increase the likelihood that fund losses will be made good.

In any case, cash buckets constrain assets dedicated to investment portfolios and to that extent they do not contribute to optimal overall portfolios. This is a case where mental accounting is especially useful to investors – knowing future cash needs will be met and allowing investment portfolios to be managed along the same long-term time line with appropriate stock/bond allocations.

Years' needs in the cash bucket

The dollar amount in the cash bucket should include cash needs projected for the next six years, or two market cycles. This appears quite conservative, but six years is not all that conservative. Historically, the market may be expected to decline in one of every three to four years. In fact, the prices of large capitalization stocks have fallen in about 27 percent of the last seventy-three years. Stock prices have declined 20 percent or more nine times since World War II, by an average of 30 percent. The largest decline was 48 percent that began early in 1973 and lasted two years. The market has not experienced anything like this frequency or size of decline in the years since 1982, but it is prudent to make a conservative assumption.

Two market cycles of three years each are considered appropriate in the hope that six years will permit one late or two early market declines to work out without reducing the investment portfolio to meet cash needs, especially at inopportune times. Of course, the number of years' expenses in the cash bucket may be adjusted as needed to fit particular investor circumstances. But prudence suggests no less than four years, with average bond fund *duration* not exceeding three years, which limits losses to about three percentage points for each percentage point increase in interest rates.

Clements (1999b) reported a more conservative cash bucket, with seven to nine years' cash bucket invested in short to intermediate-term bonds. However, Lowenstein (1998a) reported a less conservative approach, with just two to four years' needs invested in short-term assets.

Managing the cash bucket

There are numerous approaches to the management of the cash bucket. DiTeresa (1999b) reported an approach modified here to be consistent with a cash bucket containing money market and short-term bond funds and an investment portfolio with only stock/bond allocations. First, exchange all stock and bond fund distributions to the cash bucket to minimize the amounts needed to replenish it. Second, if additional cash is needed to replace one year's needs in the cash bucket, take it from the investment portfolio at the annual rebalancing. When both stocks and bonds have increased for the year, first use bonds and then stocks, as needed, to replenish the cash bucket. But, in any case, do not take out more than the annual increase in stock value. If both stock and bond values are down, use only bonds to replenish the cash bucket.

And never use stock to replenish the cash bucket when its value is down for the year. In that case, use future increases in stock value to funds to replenish bonds and rebalance the stock/bond allocations. But, again, do not use more than the annual increase in stock value. This approach, except for requiring six to eight years' cash needs in the cash bucket, is recommended for the six-year cash bucket discussed above.

Matching risk categories to portfolio investment objectives

As seen in table 34, there are five risk categories, including one no-risk category and four with risk categories. The no-risk category is matched to capital conservation and is represented by the out-of-portfolio cash bucket. The other four risk categories are matched to particular portfolio investment objectives:

1   No risk matches with *capital conservation* (cash bucket).
2   Low risk with *income* investment objective.
3   Modest risk with *growth and income* investment objective.
4   Moderate risk with *growth* investment objective.
5   High risk with *aggressive growth* investment objective.

Thus Kate's risk test score is 9 and is identified as moderate risk, which is matched to the growth portfolio investment objective.

Matching portfolio investment objectives to subcategories

Next, the four risky portfolio investment objectives are matched to two subcategories of investment objectives. The subcategories include twenty-one investment objectives that in turn are matched to thirteen CDA/Wiesenberger (1998) investment objectives. The CDA/Wiesenberger fund investment objectives are particularly useful because they report the total risk (standard deviation of returns) of each objective. The risk data are very helpful in providing a quantitative dimension to the four risky portfolio investment objectives. These subcategories are typically used to describe mutual fund investment objectives, but here they are used to identify particular types of funds generally associated with the four risky portfolio investment objectives.

The table 33 matching of overall portfolio investment objectives to the two subcategories of investment objectives is based on empirical risk/return attributes and investment experience. There is no pretense the matches are perfect, but they are adequate to provide investor guidance in designing portfolios for each portfolio investment objective. This approximation may not actually be a limitation in practice, where too much assumed precision can be misleading with respect to outcomes. In the uncertain world of investments, there is always a difference between expected and realized risk/return outcomes. And, frequently, the difference is substantial, and, not uncommonly, with signs opposite from those expected.

Validating portfolio investment objectives

Once investor risk categories have been matched to portfolio investment objectives, their correctness should be validated. This involves review of table 33 to ensure that identified risk categories and portfolio investment objectives relate comfortably with the CDA/Wiesenberger and chapter 2 subcategories of investment objectives. If not, the identified risk category and overall portfolio investment objective should be revisited. Kate validated that she was comfortable with both her identified moderate risk category and her growth portfolio investment objective and its subcategories.

PASSIVE PORTFOLIO ALLOCATION

The evidence

The importance of passive asset allocation was recognized in Brinson et al.'s (1986) study. Data for ninety-one large pension plans were analyzed for the years 1974–83 to determine the relative importance of passive asset allocation, active asset allocation (market timing), and security selection on portfolio risk/return. Passive asset allocation was identified as the single most important variable explaining variation in portfolio returns. It alone explained 93.6 percent of the variation. Passive asset allocation plus active asset allocation explained 95.3 percent of the variation, and passive asset allocation plus security selection explained 97.8 percent.

Pension fund returns averaged 9.01 percent, but passive asset allocation returns alone were 10.11 percent. The difference reveals that active asset allocation and security selection *reduced* average total returns by 1.10 percentage points! More specifically, returns from passive asset allocation plus market timing averaged 9.44 percent, while returns were 9.75 percent for passive asset allocation plus security selection. Of the 1.1 percentage point loss from market timing and security selection, 0.66 percent was due to timing, 0.36 percent to security selection and 0.07 percent to other factors. Thus passive asset allocation is the single positive variable explaining variation in portfolio returns. These findings provide more evidence of reduced returns from market timing and support for passively managed portfolios.

If later research proves asset allocation less important, asset allocation will, nonetheless, remain significant in explaining variability in portfolio returns. In fact, the above results were confirmed in Brinson et al.'s (1991) 1977–1987 analysis of eighty-two large pension plans. Asset allocation explained 91.5 percent of variability in portfolio returns. Average portfolio returns were 13.41 percent, but 13.49 percent for passive asset allocation alone. Returns were 13.23 percent for passive allocation plus active asset allocation and 13.75 percent for passive allocation plus security selection. Thus, again, passive asset allocation is the single major variable explaining variation in sample returns. However, this time security selection makes a small positive (rather than negative) contribution to total portfolio returns, while active asset allocation continues to reduce average total returns.

The Brinson et al. findings are often criticized for questions the studies never intended to address. For example, Paluch (1997) and Arnott (1997) revisited asset allocation and provided different slants on the argument. To clarify, Ibbotson and Kaplan (2000) examined fund and pension asset allocation for what it is and what it is not. A sample of ninety-four balanced funds with ten years of monthly returns ending 1998 was analyzed. By moving cash assets into the cash bucket, the funds were allocated as follows: 43 percent large cap. stocks, 14 percent small cap. stocks, 2 percent international stocks, and 43 percent domestic bonds.

The first issue is the one Brinson et al. addressed: What percentage of the variability in returns over time is explained by asset allocation? The answer is about 90 percent. The second issue is how much of the variability in returns among funds is explained by differences in asset allocation? If all funds invested passively, using the same asset allocation, there would be no variation among funds. If the same funds then varied asset allocation, all of the differences in funds would be due to asset allocation. Asset allocation explains 40 percent of the variability of returns among funds. The remaining 60 percent of variability is explained by asset class timing, style within asset classes, security selection, and fees.

The last issue is what portion of the level of returns across funds is explained by returns to asset allocation policy? A fund that followed its asset allocation policy and invested passively would have a ratio of 100 percent, while a fund that outperformed its policy would have a ratio less than 100 percent. On average, asset allocation explains a bit more than 100 percent of the return level across funds. Funds are not adding value above their benchmark asset allocations owing to timing, security selection, management fees, and expenses.

Updegrave (1999b) continued the discussion and reported implications of these results. There is no single right percentage because the influence asset allocation has on returns depends on the type of investor. For investors who maintain passive asset allocations invested in index funds, asset allocation will dominate returns. For investors who time the market and actively manage asset allocations invested in index funds, timing will dominate returns. And, for investors who maintain passive asset allocations but actively manage securities within the classes, selection ability will dominate returns.

Bogle (1999) built on the importance of asset allocation in an analysis of pension plan and mutual fund returns. Returns failed to outperform market indices even before expenses were deducted. This failure reflected trading costs and poor stock selection. When fund expenses were taken into account, they accounted for over 90 percent of the shortfall in fund returns. Thus asset allocation is the key to explaining variation in fund returns, and expenses are the largest proportion of the amount by which fund returns are less than market index returns.

However, Lee and Rahman (1991) examined the timing and security selection ability of mutual fund portfolio managers over the period 1977–84. The findings indicated some evidence of both timing and selectivity ability at the individual fund level. To the extent that this is correct, asset allocation is less important relative to stock selectivity, and market timing. Of the sample of ninety-three mutual funds, only twenty-four have significant positive or negative selection ability. Of these twenty-four funds, fourteen have significant security selection ability, and sixteen have significant timing ability. Only ten funds have both significant selection and timing ability. Four funds exhibit significant selection ability and no timing ability, while five funds have significant timing ability and no selection skill. Selection and timing skills are certainly not widely distributed among mutual fund portfolio managers.

Domestic hybrid funds

Before proceeding, it should be noted there are several types of mutual funds that apply versions of stock/bond asset allocation to provide full diversification in one portfolio. *Domestic hybrid mutual funds* are designed to simplify decision making for long-term investors and pension plan participants. This class of funds provides consolidated stock/bond holdings along with security selection and asset allocation. These funds are best used as total portfolios, otherwise the risk-moderating stock/bond asset allocations do not apply to total portfolios. However, they have not yet become as popular as expected.

Earlier hybrid mutual funds come in two basic wrappers: balanced funds and asset allocation funds. Both types precede this classification scheme, and include stock and bond allocations. *Balanced funds* are the original asset allocation funds. These funds normally use strategic (passive) asset allocation with relatively constant long-term stock/bond allocations, along with portfolio rebalancing. These funds are designed for conservative investors with long-term investment horizons. Allocations approximate standard 60/40 mixes of stocks and high-quality bonds, but they vary by fund and may be tilted by investment style based on broad market themes. Investors should determine how widely asset allocations may vary, with a range of five to ten percentage points for larger allocations being reasonable.

Earlier *asset allocation funds* employ tactical asset allocation (a form of market timing), with changes in asset classes dictated by short-term market forecasts. Risk limitations are normally defined as appropriate to fund objectives, such as permissible allocations of stocks/bonds, domestic/international stocks, small-cap./large-cap. stocks and high/low bond quality. More recent versions of asset allocation funds include *life-stage funds*, also called life-cycle and lifestyle funds. As discussed by Lowenstein (1994b), these funds differentiate themselves from asset allocation funds by using asset allocation as a planning tool, not just as an investment objective. Funds are designed to match specific investor investment horizons and risk preferences, which are identified for specific investors through the use of planning tools. For example, Putnam Lifestage Funds offer growth, income, and blend funds. Lifestyle funds also normally have more narrowly defined investment objectives than asset allocation funds.

Consistent with earlier asset allocation mutual funds, life-stage funds typically employ or state potential use of tactical asset allocation, a form of market timing. This strategy is applied to broad allocations of defined classes of bonds and stocks. For example, Fidelity Asset Manager Growth has a risk-neutral mix of 70 percent equities, 25 percent bonds, and 5 percent cash assets. However, 50–100 percent of assets may be allocated to stocks and up to 50 percent in bonds and money market securities. These wide ranges strongly suggest actual or potential tactical asset allocation. Broad allocation ranges provide broad risk/return parameters, which may be inappropriate for conservative long-term investors.

Lifestyle mutual funds also hold securities with wider ranges of investment quality than balanced funds. These holdings might include small-cap. stocks, international stocks, and high-yield bonds. Bond allocations often include high-quality bonds, but high-yield bonds are also frequently held. These bonds are not investment grade, but as diversified holdings they are not inconsistent with long-term portfolios. But, while Brenner (1999) reported an 83 percent increase in life-stage offerings in pension plans, there has been only a 15 percent increase in assets.

Lowenstein (1994b) also identified *target maturity funds* as a new model of life-stage mutual funds. These funds are designed with targeted maturity dates. Investors select the funds that match their investment horizons. Fund portfolio holdings and allocations become more conservative as the stated target dates approach. Stock allocations are reduced and bond and money market fund allocations increased. For example, Wells Fargo Stagecoach LifePath Funds asks investors to select funds that mature closest to the date of their investment horizons when they will need cash. The Wells Fargo funds began with Lifestage 2000 and continued with ten-year interval target dates up to Lifestage 2040. But conservative portfolios are not always best for retirees. Life expectancy at normal retirement age calls for long-term strategies that provide growth to offset inflation.

Life stage funds also include a few exclusively bond mutual funds. *Strategic income bond funds* are based on the low correlations among US Treasury bonds, international government bonds, and high-yield (junk) bonds. This approach could be a good way to allocate bonds in an overall asset allocation portfolio. For example, Lucas (1992) examined the T. Rowe Price Spectrum Income fund. There is a negative correlation between international bond fund returns and high-yield bond fund returns. Also, the market forces explaining variability in T. Rowe Price GNMA fund returns only negligibly explain variability in high-yield bond fund returns.

Funds of funds are another type of domestic-hybrid mutual fund. These funds do not hold individual securities but invest only in other mutual funds. Funds of funds that invest only in funds in their own fund families normally do not impose additional loads, but those that invest in funds in other fund families do. Investors should not invest in the latter types of funds of funds. For example, T. Rowe Price Spectrum Growth Fund invests only in other Price family funds, while its lifestyle Personal Growth Fund invests only in individual securities. Some pension plans now offer tailor-made funds of funds. For example, one plan allows participants to choose from eight different life-stage funds, each of which contains different allocations of five managed asset pools. As discussed, low expenses are essential to successful mutual fund investing. Lowest-cost funds of funds normally hold low-cost index funds, but low-cost funds of funds may also be in the same fund families and in funds catering to institutional investors.

Barbee (1998a) reviewed these issues and concluded: "Lifecycle funds may have all the limitations of prepackaged goods, but they're nonetheless a useful proxy for the real thing." But portfolio manager David Dreman (1998) was less kind. The popularity of tactical asset allocation may be traced to the 1987 market crash and the 1990 market decline that caught portfolio managers unawares. While advocates consider this strategy more sophisticated than simple market timing, others correctly consider it another form of market timing.

The performance of 185 tactical asset allocation mutual funds was compared with buy-and-hold strategies and equity mutual funds over the years 1985–97. This bull market period included the two noted market declines, which make it ideal for testing and proving tactical asset allocation. Tactical asset allocation funds failed the test. Over this period, the S&P 500 Index increased 734 percent, average equity funds increased 598 percent, and tactical asset allocation funds increased 384 percent. Dreman concluded: "Tactical asset allocation has obviously not set the world on fire. In fact, it's downright awful, even in the periods where asset allocators claimed they swept the field. The prosecution rests."

PASSIVE ASSET ALLOCATION: STOCK VERSUS BONDS

Asset allocation is diversification under another guise, and the latter is risk management under another guise. As stated by Peter Bernstein (1997a):

> Diversification, the crown jewel of investment management, is rooted in the recognition that certain investment decisions will be wrong. . . . Diversification begins with a search for investments with high expected returns but . . . low covariance. That is, we seek investments that do not move up and down together. If the covariances are low enough, a small number of holdings will suffice for meaningful rewards at acceptable levels of risk.

Risk management in the form of diversification (asset allocation) is the next step following identification of investor risk tolerance. Risk management incorporates investor risk tolerances in the selection of portfolio allocations that avoid the risk of being wiped out, such as a replay of October 1987. The power of diversification is seen in stock/bond allocations along the efficient frontier. By moving from 0/100 stock/allocations to assumed higher-risk 20/80 stock/bond allocations there is both an increase in return *and* a reduction in risk – the free lunch does exist in particular risk/return combinations.

Peter Bernstein also reported the power of diversification in a portfolio comprised of small-cap. stocks and bonds compared with one of large-cap. stocks and bonds. This example provides evidence of diversification, because the first portfolio carries a higher percentage of more volatile stocks with higher returns, yet has no more risk than the second portfolio with a smaller proportion of lower-risk and return large cap. stocks. This power continues to be seen in global portfolios as well. Since 1986, return covariances among thirteen international markets have been remarkably low. A portfolio of 85 percent S&P 500 Index and 15 percent of equal parts of thirteen international market indices provides both larger returns and lower risk than a portfolio of 100 percent S&P 500 Index. So much for those who decry the use of small cap. stocks and global stocks in portfolios as more risky.

Matching investor risk category and portfolio investment objective to passive stock/bond allocation

Table 33 presents the passive domestic stock/bond allocation that corresponds to each previously identified investor risk category and portfolio investment objective. Bonds as used here are sources of regular income and have a moderating influence on portfolio risk. Bonds are not substitutes for stocks *per se*. They are one element in asset allocation, of which different stock/bond proportions provide different annualized returns, percentages of worst annual losses, and percentage of years with losses. The allocations reflect market experience and well reasoned model portfolios.

It is interesting that differences in average returns between consecutive investment objectives are consistently one percentage point. But differences in worst annual losses between consecutive objectives are consistently seven or eight percentage points. And differences in percentage of loss years between consecutive objectives are only one or two percentage points, except for four percentage points between growth and aggressive growth objectives. This signals a jump in risk for the more aggressive objectives.

Thus Kate's moderate risk and growth portfolio investment objective matches a 60/40 stock/bond allocation. As suggested, these are normal long-term allocations, but alterations may be desirable, owing to changes in investor circumstances affecting risk tolerance and possible long-term shifts in the market – allocations are not written in stone, but neither should they be changed in emotional response to transitory developments.

Minimum risk stock/bond portfolio allocation

In table 33 the low-risk category and its income portfolio objective are matched to the 20 percent stock/80 percent bond allocation. To validate this domestic allocation, it is compared with William Bernstein's (1995) efficient minimum risk stock/bond allocation. These and subsequent Bernstein citations should be checked for any online updates. Markowitz-type mean variance optimizer with rebalancing identified the 1926–94 efficient frontier of a portfolio comprised of the S&P 500 Index (large cap. stocks) and twenty-year US Treasury bonds. A portion of the stock/bond allocations along the efficient frontier follows (percent):

Stock/bond allocation	Annualized returns	Standard deviation
20/80	6.2	8.5
10/90	5.6	8.3
0/100	4.8	8.6

The 10/90 stock/bond allocation is the *minimum risk portfolio*, but the slightly more assertive 20/80 stock/bond allocation has the largest return, with a standard deviation of mean returns (risk) *below* the 0/100 stock/bond allocation. It also has the lowest risk per unit of return among bond-dominated allocations. For these reasons, the 20/80 stock/bond allocation is presented in table 33 as the low-risk domestic portfolio, But again, this is not the literal minimum risk portfolio. The use of twenty-year Treasury bonds implies that investors wish to ground their mutual fund portfolios with bonds of the highest credit quality.

PASSIVE ASSET ALLOCATION: PORTFOLIO REBALANCING

Portfolio rebalancing is important because it reduces portfolio risk and works to prevent portfolio disasters, which implies a form of insurance with costs. For example, Bogle (1999) observed that stocks fell 61 percent from 1929 to 1932, bonds gained 16 percent, and portfolios with 60/40 stock/bond allocations lost 30 percent. Bonds thus moderate losses and provide more stable interest income. Rebalancing is an implied contrarian approach, where particular asset types are sold when the market is most optimistic about them and purchased when the market is most pessimistic about them. It could also be considered a form of market timing where the calendar calls the shots, not investors.

The concern about rebalancing frequency applies to taxable portfolios, where optimal asset allocations should be traded off against the tax implications of rebalancing.

Rebalancing frequency

To determine the most profitable rebalancing frequency, Arnott and Lovell (1993) analyzed the 1968–91 before-tax performance of a 50/50 stock/bond portfolio. Annual rebalancing generated 9.02 percent annual returns, while quarterly and monthly rebalancing earned 9.12 percent and 9.16 percent returns, respectively. The returns were then adjusted for trading costs, but the rankings remained the same. However, the tax implications of rebalancing frequency were not calculated.

William Bernstein (1995) analyzed rebalancing strategies for tax-deferred portfolios and concluded that there is probably no way to determine the optimal frequency in advance. Rebalancing tax-deferred portfolios every year or two probably works as well as shorter intervals. More definite recommendations can be made for taxable portfolios, which should be rebalanced infrequently, at most annually and every three to five years is probably optimal. Further, William Bernstein's (1996b) 1988–94 analysis of five international and domestic asset indices revealed no single best rebalancing frequency. Quarterly rebalancing was best in four cases, and monthly and annual rebalancing were each best in three cases.

Sanders (1997b) illustrated the need for rebalancing to maintain anything near desired asset allocations over time. Over the past twenty years, an allocation of 10 percent cash, 30 percent bonds and 60 percent stock would have grown to 3 percent cash, 13 percent bonds, and 84 percent stock. This represents major changes in the beginning asset allocations. However, reallocation does have a cost, and the cost is highest in bull markets that have few downdrafts. Annual rebalancing of the above portfolio would have reduced returns by 0.80 percentage points per year, assuming no transaction costs and no taxes. But it would also have reduced the standard deviation of returns by 1.3 percentage points per year.

In a taxable account, annual rebalancing would have reduced returns by one percentage point per year. As long as the stock market trend is positive, rebalancing has costs. Nonetheless, an investor who rebalanced annually for twenty years beginning in the 1970s would have outperformed the investor who did not rebalance by some forty basis points per year. Sanders reported studies advocating rebalancing when actual asset allocations deviate by about seven percentage points from desired allocations. Using the initial illustration above, this rebalancing rule would have decreased returns by 0.70 percentage points per year and reduced portfolio risk by 1.20 percentage points per year, assuming no transactions costs and no taxes.

DiTeresa (1999a) constructed a portfolio of five index funds to test for rebalancing frequency. Over five years, rebalancing lowered both risk and return, but the frequency made little difference. The non-rebalanced portfolio was 92 percent tax-efficient, the portfolio rebalanced every eighteen months was 89 percent tax-efficient, and the portfolio rebalanced every three months was 86 percent tax-efficient. Thus portfolios should not be rebalanced any more often than every twelve to eighteen months.

Finally, William Bernstein (2000a) summarized and illustrated the importance of rebalancing on portfolio returns (excluding taxes and transactions costs). The more volatile portfolio assets, the greater the benefit of rebalancing on portfolio returns. The lower the correlation among portfolio assets, the greater the benefit from rebalancing on returns. And the smaller the differences in asset returns, the greater the benefits from rebalancing on returns. For the assumed portfolio, the difference in annual returns based on rebalancing quarterly versus every four years is only eighteen basis points. But, by rebalancing only every four years, portfolio allocations become seriously out of balance and more risky over time.

Commonsense rebalancing

Because there is no single optimal rebalancing interval, a consistent commonsense approach is needed to determine by how many percentage points actual allocations must deviate from desired allocations before rebalancing. Setting the *rebalancing threshold* requires judgment, because strong empirical evidence is lacking. One rule of thumb is to rebalance portfolios only when the largest asset holdings are five to ten percentage points from the desired allocations. Whether to use five or ten percentage point thresholds depends on the relative size of equity allocations in passive stock/bond portfolio. While allocations may appropriately be reviewed monthly or quarterly, especially in fast-moving markets, a second rule of thumb is not to rebalance more than once every twelve to eighteen months, to ease the tax burden. Less systematic rebalancing could be "closet market timing." A third rule of thumb is to "rebalance by not rebalancing." That is, invest new monies in asset holdings assets below the desired allocations. A fourth rule of thumb is to refill the cash bucket from new monies available and then from asset holdings larger than desired allocations.

PASSIVE PORTFOLIO ALLOCATION: BONDS

William Bernstein (1995) also determined the most efficient (least risk for given return) portfolio allocation of US Treasury securities and the S&P 500 Index. A Markowitz-type optimizer with rebalancing identified the 1926–94 efficient frontiers of three domestic portfolios comprised of the S&P 500 Index and thirty-day Treasury bills, five-year Treasury bonds, or twenty-year Treasury bonds. With a clear choice, active domestic asset allocation can focus on investment style allocation and fund selection and allocation, the selection of Treasury security and its allocation already defined. Of course, this assumes that the highest bond credit quality is desired.

In table 33, the bond allocation runs from 20 percent to 80 percent of the portfolio. For example, the 80/20 stock/bond allocation matches the high investor risk category and its aggressive growth portfolio investment objective. The optimizer determined that portfolio allocations of stock/five-year Treasury bonds are more efficient than any allocation of stock/twenty-year Treasury bonds. And five-year bonds are also more efficient than Treasury bills for all allocations of at least 15 percent. Thus Treasury bills do not automatically provide the most efficient minimum-risk allocations of stock and Treasury obligations. The use of five-year Treasury bonds is suggested for all stock/bond allocations in table 33, which again assumes investors want the highest credit quality.

How well does a 20 percent bond allocation fit with how bond mutual fund managers invest for themselves? Zweig (1997a) reported that Ian McKinnon, Vanguard's fixed-income leader, typically keeps 20 percent of his personal portfolio in bonds. But this self-described moderate risk investor now holds a 35 percent bond allocation, owing to market risk. Maintaining a reasonable bond allocation makes sense because bonds tend to zig when stocks zag. Also, well managed bond funds with controlled duration generate relatively predictable returns, and occasionally higher returns than stock funds.

Several other points should be noted when investing in bond mutual funds. First, bond funds are not tax-efficient because they generate large taxable interest distributions. They are normally best held in tax-deferred accounts or as tax-exempt municipal bonds. Second, investors should focus on total return, not yield. Yield is only one element of total return and the stated yield is susceptible to manipulation. Third, buy intermediate-term bonds to minimize the impact on price of large increases in interest rates. That is, they have modest durations. Fourth, "control the controllable" and buy only low-cost funds. Expenses account for most of the differences in bond fund performance. And, fifth, buy funds with broadly diversified portfolios of the desired credit quality, unless only Treasury securities are held.

ACTIVE PORTFOLIO ALLOCATION: MARKET TIMING REVISITED

As noted, investment management is the next step in the investment process. It includes the identification of active portfolio allocation, investment style allocation, fund selection and allocation, and performance evaluation. Also, as discussed, active portfolio allocation identifies maximum/minimum equity/debt proportions for market timing efforts to profit from anticipated short-term changes in market conditions. These efforts could also be applied to investment style allocations. As discussed, such efforts generally fall into the "market timing trap," with results favoring long-term passive asset allocation.

However, Fisher (1998) discussed market timing as a contrarian indicator, to be implemented when everyone says not to do so. Market timers attempt to move significant amounts of portfolio holdings into cash or defensive securities to avoid market declines. Some timers do so daily, others periodically, and others use defensive securities, such as bonds, index puts, utilities, and gold stocks. There are some twenty signals of coming bear markets, including both high inventories and short-term interest rates, excessive dollar inflows from overseas with a strong dollar and reversal and inverted yield curves. Nine rules for timing are also presented, but first it is important to do the following: "[A]fter you've spotted one of these signals, wait until almost no one is bearish. If you talk bearishly and all your friends ridicule you, we're close to a bear market. . . . Oh, and when you see it, call me – I want to see it too."

PASSIVE INVESTMENT ALLOCATION: MODEL PORTFOLIOS

Before beginning, it may be useful to provide a general guide to successful long-term mutual fund investing prior to consideration of asset allocation and investment style allocation. But, first, see Bogle (1991) for data supporting passive asset allocation and evidence of the difficulty in making accurate market forecasts. The rules of successful long-term investing are simple, but not easy to follow when the market is crashing or technology stocks are out of sight. The first is to invest early, consistently and let compound interest work. Small amounts invested early and consistently often overcome much larger amounts invested later. Second, there will be times when madness (or irrational behavior) grips the market. You may likely be psychologically unable to act, even if you are able to communicate with your funds, until most of the short-run damage has been done. Say to yourself: "I will not act upon my fear, which will cause me to sell after the market has already fallen, only to buy in again later after the market has moved up from the bottom." The wealth lost from this misbehavior is much larger than one would think. Third, exercise control and buy funds with low fees and expenses, low portfolio turnover and trading costs, long-tenured portfolio managers, significant advisor, director and portfolio manager investment, well defined objectives and strategies, tax-managed portfolios, and shareholder communication and director actions that treat shareholders like owners. Fourth, keep your portfolio diversified, relatively simple, and stay the course. And, finally, do not read the *Wall Street Journal* every day to see what the latest market noise has done to your portfolio.

The existence of periodic market madness leads to consideration of whether investors should be invested during such times. What should investors do when markets are characterized as speculative bubbles? Should they stay with their basic portfolio allocations or stay out of the market until it crashes? McQueen and Thorley (1994) examined what rational investors should do during these times when *rational speculative bubbles* cause stock prices to deviate from fundamental values without assuming irrational investors. Investors realize that prices exceed fundamental values, but they also believe the chances are good that the bubbles will continue to expand and generate high returns. The probability of high returns exactly compensates them for the probability of crashes.

The model demonstrates that it is rational for investors to stay invested during market bubbles. The reason for this is duration dependence, a unique implication of bubbles. Specifically, as the length of runs of positive abnormal returns increases, the probability the runs will end (crash) decreases. So what is the answer? Diversify your portfolio, stay invested, and maintain a full cash bucket.

Model stock/bond portfolio allocations

Table 35 presents model stock/bond allocations for each set of investor risk category and portfolio investment objectives. These portfolio allocations by William Bernstein (1995), Siegel (1998), Gibson (1990), and Haslem do not purport to be optimal, but are representative of efforts to find portfolio allocations that work in a variety of scenarios. In general, these model portfolios are allocated between large-cap. and small-cap. domestic and international equity securities, but not by value/growth investment style. Exceptions are Siegel's and Gibson's single domestic/international allocation, and the latter's use of equity REITs and precious metals. These model allocations all call for portfolio simplicity as an element of success in the face of future market uncertainties. Investment style is discussed more fully later.

To provide empirical evidence on approaches to asset allocation both within and outside retirement accounts, analysis of educator retirement accounts held by TIAA/CREF is interesting. But, first, Bodie and Crane (1997) defined a menu of "generally accepted investment principles": (1) investors should have emergency funds (a cash bucket) outside retirement accounts invested in short-term safe assets; (2) retirement accounts should be primarily invested in equities and long-term fixed-income securities; (3) the allocation to equities should decline as investor age increases; (4) the allocation devoted to equities should increase with wealth; (5) tax-advantaged securities should be held outside retirement accounts; and (6) investors should diversify across asset classes, and equities should be diversified by industries and companies.

Analysis of TIAA/CREF accounts data generally agreed with these principles, with exceptions. Cash assets held vary with wealth, but not by age. The proportion of tax-exempt bonds increases with wealth, but not by age. Adjusted for age and wealth, there are substantial differences in the proportions of assets invested in equities. And some evidence suggests that older investors tilt retirement accounts towards taxable fixed-income securities. Sample total portfolio allocations (without cash buckets) include those for investors age twenty-five to forty-four: (1) cash, 18 percent; (2) tax-exempt bonds, 1 percent; (3) taxable bonds, 32 percent; and (4) equity, 49 percent. These portfolios are more aggressive than those of investors age sixty-five and older: (1) cash, 19 percent; (2) tax-exempt bonds, 5 percent; (3) taxable bonds, 40 percent; and (4) equity, 36 percent. The major differences lie with taxable bonds and equities.

These findings may be compared with the types of mutual funds held by participants in 401(k) pension plans. VanDerhei et al. (1999) determined that participants in their twenties are 69 percent invested in stock funds, 12 percent in balanced (stock and bond) funds, 9 percent in bond funds, and 10 percent in money market funds. Participants in their sixties invest 50 percent in stock funds, 15 percent in balanced funds, 18 percent in bond funds, and 17 percent in money market funds. These allocations are more aggressive than those conservative faculty types in TIAA/CREF retirement plans.

Before continuing it is important to recall the importance of mutual fund expenses. Bogle (1999) demonstrated that investors can earn higher returns despite reducing the proportion of equities in their portfolios. For example, assume returns of 7 percent on stocks and 6 percent on bonds, an 80/20 stock/bond allocation, and stock expense ratios of 2.2 percent. The portfolio return is 5 percent. But, by changing to funds with 0.2 percent expense ratios and a less risky 20/80 stock/bond allocation, the return is 6.2 percent. Or, without changing the stock/bond allocation, low-cost funds generate a portfolio return of 6.6 percent versus 5.0 percent with the high-cost funds.

Model large-cap./small-cap. domestic/international stock portfolio allocations

William Bernstein (1995) also identified the most efficient and minimum-risk allocations of (1) large cap. stocks/bonds, (2) small cap. stocks/bonds, (3) domestic large cap. and/international large cap. stocks, and (4) domestic small cap. and international small cap. stocks. These two-asset-at-a-time findings are useful ballpark allocations, prior to discussion of value/growth investment style allocations. These allocations are also reflected in Haslem's model portfolio.

To begin, Bernstein's Markowitz-type optimizer (Bernstein's model based on Markowitz) identified the 1926–94 efficient frontiers for portfolios of the S&P 500 Index and twenty-year US Treasury bonds, then the S&P 500 and five-year Treasury bonds, and, lastly, S&P 500 and thirty-day Treasury bills. In the first portfolio, the minimum risk portfolio allocates 10 percent to large cap. stocks and 90 percent to twenty-year Treasury bonds. The same minimum risk allocation is observed when five-year bonds replace twenty-year Treasury bonds. More important, this second portfolio is more efficient than the first portfolio at all allocations. Moreover, for all returns over 6 percent, the second portfolio is more efficient than the third portfolio using Treasury bills.

Next, the optimizer was applied to portfolios of small-cap. stocks and five-year Treasury bonds and then to portfolios of the S&P 500 Index and five-year bonds. The efficient frontiers of these two portfolios almost overlap, but the small cap. portfolio has a small efficiency advantage at returns above 8 percent. More important, for any given risk/return combination, portfolios with small-cap. stocks require a larger allocation of bonds than portfolios with large-cap. stocks and bonds. For example, a portfolio with a 100/0 large-cap. stock/bond allocation has almost the same risk/return attributes as a portfolio with a 60/40 small-cap. stock/bond allocation.

Before discussing the results of optimizing domestic/international stock allocations (both large-cap. and small-cap.), these portfolios are significantly affected by whether international or domestic stocks are outperforming. This has been especially so in the flip-flop of relative values of US and Japanese stock markets. In any case, long-term global economic growth dictates a smaller percentage of the global portfolio for the United States. These ups and downs have also been reflected in numerous applications of Markowitz optimizer models.

Depending on whether the United States or Japan is gaining share of global market value, *efficient minimum-risk global portfolios* range from 60–80 percent domestic large capitalization stocks to 40–20 percent international large capitalization stocks. For example, a fund advertisement illustrated the efficient frontier of large capitalization international and domestic stocks for the years 1970–95. The highest-risk portfolio is 0/100 domestic/international stock and the minimum risk portfolio is 80/20 domestic/international stock.

William Bernstein (1996a) optimized the 1973–94 allocations of domestic and international large-cap. stocks. The S&P 500 Index was used for the domestic allocation and the MSCI (EAFE) Index for the international. The later is commonly used as the benchmark index for large-cap. international funds. The minimum risk portfolio ranges from 75 percent to 95 percent large-cap. domestic stock, with a slight risk advantage to the 80/20 domestic/international large-cap. stock allocation. Portfolio risk increases significantly as international allocations reach 50 percent and beyond.

As discussed in Barbee (1997, 1998b), the 80/20 domestic/international large-cap. portfolio mix differs from the traditional minimum risk portfolio of 70/30 S&P 500 Index/EAFE portfolio (discussed later). The best risk reduction for the S&P 500 Index is provided by its small correlation of returns with Latin America (0.03) and Japanese (0.07) markets. European markets provide the least risk reduction (0.28 correlation). However, for the last twenty years international diversification provided no benefit, but also no huge disadvantage. Much of the EAFE's poor performance was caused by Japan, which represents 25 percent of the index. Nonetheless, the minimum risk global large-cap. stock portfolio for the last ten years is 80/20 S&P 500 Index/EAFE.

Next, William Bernstein (1995) optimized allocations of domestic and international small-cap. stocks. The minimum risk portfolio approximates a 60–70 percent domestic small-cap. stock allocation, with the actual minimum risk portfolio a 65/35 domestic/international small-cap. stock allocation. In this case, the relatively large proportion of international small-cap. stock is due to low correlations of returns among various international countries.

In summary, William Bernstein's (1995, 1996a) Markowitz-type optimizer identified the following minimum-risk portfolio allocations:

1 Domestic large-cap. stock versus long-term US Treasury bonds: stock 10 percent and bonds 90 percent (least efficient of the stock/bond portfolios).
2 Domestic large-cap. stock and five-year Treasury bonds: stock 10 percent and bonds 90 percent (most efficient at returns over 6 percent).
3 Domestic large-cap. stock and thirty-day Treasury bills: stock 5 percent and bills 95 percent (most efficient at returns of 6 percent and less).
4 Domestic large-cap. stock and international large-cap. stocks: domestic 80 percent and international 20 percent.
5 Domestic small-cap. stocks and international small-cap. stocks: domestic 65 percent and international 35 percent.

These portfolio allocations involve two assets.

Bernstein's model portfolio

William Bernstein's (1995) portfolio in table 35 is a simplified version of his original "conventional coward's portfolio." This simplified portfolio has the same percentage allocations for stocks as the "academic coward's portfolio" has for value style index mutual funds in William Bernstein (1997a). The allocations in the simplified conventional portfolio follow (percent):

Domestic large capitalization stocks	25
Domestic small capitalization stocks	25
International large capitalization stocks	25
International small capitalization stocks	25

In the original conventional coward's portfolio, the 25 percent international large-cap. stock allocation is represented individually by Europe (10 percent), emerging markets (10 percent) and Asia (5 percent); the 25 percent international small-cap. stock allocation is represented by Europe (20 percent) and Japan (5 percent). This portfolio allocates 25 percent to international large-cap. stock. In reality, domestic large-cap. stocks tend to earn over 25 percent of their earnings overseas, which means the domestic large-cap. stock allocation is effectively less than 25 percent and the international large-cap. stock allocation accordingly more.

Model portfolios versus optimized portfolios

The table 35 model portfolio allocations are much broader (and fewer) than unconstrained optimized global portfolios with numerous security types. Nonetheless, based on 1988–94 data, Bernstein's simplified portfolio allocation was only some 0.5 percent more risky than future *realized* optimized global portfolios for any given return. It is probably not too hopeful to expect this simple *normalized portfolio* to perform reasonably well in a long-term passive strategy, unless major permanent shifts in the market occur.

The use of broadly allocated optimized portfolios may well be desirable to the extent that they are not significantly less efficient than future realized portfolios. This is especially so because optimized allocations are *very* sensitive to input changes as compounded by *real* difficulties in making accurate forecasts. Thus, in general, it appears to be sensible not to attempt too much precision or cleverness in an imprecise and uncertain world. This is good news for simplicity in portfolio construction.

Sensitivity of optimized portfolios

To see how sensitive optimized portfolios are to changes in parameters, Chow et al. (1999) generated an optimized portfolio using eight asset classes and full-sample risk parameters and compared the allocations with those generated using out-of-sample riskier parameters. In general, the regular portfolio contains primarily domestic equities (25 percent), emerging-market equities (16 percent), international bonds (26 percent), and high-yield bonds (22 percent). The riskier portfolio reduced domestic equities to 2 percent, reduced total equities from 41 percent to 13 percent, increased commodities from 3 percent to 12 percent, and increased bonds from 56 percent to 69 percent of the portfolio.

The broad portfolio allocations also attempt to smooth out differences in forecast and future realized optimized allocations due to short to intermediate-term (transitory) market developments. Nonetheless, at any given point in time, normalized portfolios must be less efficient than future realized optimal portfolios. Moreover, market developments guarantee that, for periods of, say, one to five years or more, normalized portfolios will underperform future realized optimized portfolios that contain more specific security types.

Recent history has provided numerous examples of multi-year transitory market developments. The 1970s witnessed booms in real estate and gold. The late 1970s and early 1980s saw a bond bear market, and the 1980s also saw a greatly overvalued Japanese stock market. The 1990s witnessed a bull market in domestic large-cap. stocks, and the opposite for small-cap. stocks. The decade also witnessed the speculative excesses of dot-com IPOs and Internet stocks and technology companies, both with and without real earnings. Each of these assumed trends at the time has proved less than long-term in duration.

More specifically, table 36 provides a 1994–8 snapshot of security types, some of which performed well and others that did not. For example, the S&P 500 Index had five-year annualized returns of nearly 24 percent, while small Japanese stocks averaged losses of nearly 13 percent. Thus there are winners and losers at any point in time, but at some point winners become losers. And those investors who attempt to catch the wave are doomed to failure over time. Broadly allocated portfolios are for patient investors who control the urge to market time, and do not extrapolate transitory market conditions to the end of time.

Nonetheless, some claim that over the last twenty years there has been no risk reduction from adding international securities to domestic portfolios. Barbee (1998b) examined US stock funds and international stock funds and observed they both moved together and apart over this period. Traditional twenty-year optimized portfolios identified the minimum risk allocation as 80/20 domestic large-cap./international large-cap. stocks. But, over the last ten and twenty years, international stock diversification has neither reduced nor increased portfolio risk. Nor did adding international stocks, bonds, real estate funds, or gold funds protect portfolios from sudden market declines.

Thus it sometimes takes many years for traditional portfolio risk reduction assets to regain historical relationships. But who would suggest that the next twenty years of global economic growth do not call for a significant international stock allocation? Certainly not William Bernstein (1998b), who states that the so-called "death of diversification" will go the same way as the "death of equities" proclaimed in 1979, just three years before the beginning of the longest-running bull market. See Markman (2000) for a vivid argument that asset allocation and diversification are "the source of the [mutual fund] industry's dysfunction."

William Bernstein (1998a) used a Markowitz-type optimizer to determine how well normalized portfolios performed under twenty-seven different financial and economic scenarios. A twelve-index portfolio was created using reasonable allocations and baseline inflation-adjusted returns. Adjustments in returns were made to reflect different combinations of scenarios: high/low/normal inflation, high/low/normal international stock returns, and high/low/normal small cap. returns. The normalized portfolio for each scenario was optimized quarterly from July 1988 to September 1997 against an unconstrained efficient portfolio representing all twenty-seven scenarios, along with the S&P 500 Index.

The findings were generally supportive of reasonably allocated normalized portfolios. In the twenty-seven scenarios, the normalized portfolio was more efficient than the S&P 500 Index twenty times, about the same twice, and less efficient five times. It is interesting that the normalized portfolio is much *more* efficient than the 100 percent domestic large cap. strategy when the scenario is normal in all three dimensions: inflation, international stock returns, and small cap. returns. Thus there appears to be a limit to efficient portfolio simplification.

The few scenarios in which the S&P 500 Index was more efficient than the normalized portfolio may be characterized as: (1) low inflation, high international returns and low small cap. returns; (2) low inflation, low international returns and low small cap. returns; (3) low inflation, low international returns and normal small cap. returns; (4) low inflation, high international returns and low small cap. returns; and (5) normal inflation, low international returns and low small cap. returns.

The 1990s reflect scenario number one, which is also the worst case for the normalized portfolio: low inflation, low international returns, and low small cap. returns. However, the late 1970s to early 1980s were all highs: high inflation, high international returns, and high small cap. returns. The mid-1980s were normal inflation, high international returns and normal small cap. returns, and the mid-1960s were low inflation, normal international returns, and high small cap. returns. These latter three (earlier) scenarios all favor normalized portfolios.

Full optimization portfolios

William Bernstein (1995) performed a 1973–94 "full optimization" of fourteen types of securities to determine the reasonableness of the portfolio allocations. The identified global minimum risk portfolio was quite unreasonable for use as a normalized long-term portfolio: US Treasury bills (87 percent), high-yield bonds (2 percent), international bonds (9 percent), and natural resources stock (1 percent). This allocation provides higher returns and lower risk than a 100 percent Treasury bill allocation – another diversification miracle.

Moreover, *unconstrained optimized allocations* are *not* recommended for general use in long-term portfolio allocations. To see this problem, one has only to look at the asset allocations identified by different providers for the same investment objective. Optimized portfolios are *very* sensitive to the number and nature of the fund asset classes included, as well as forecast inputs of expected returns, standard deviations of mean returns, and cross-correlations of each pair of assets. Input forecasts are generally based on historical data, which usually are off the mark, and often significantly so, relative to their realized values in future optimized portfolios.

The major problem in the unknowing use of optimized portfolio asset allocations is best summed by Updegrave (1999b): "The illusion of certainty that comes out of these programs is an extremely dangerous one." Some cynics even call portfolio optimizers "mistake maximizers." The point is that the use of portfolio optimizers requires judgment and the realization that historical asset relationships are generally imperfect guides to future realized optimal portfolio allocations. This is seen in an example from Makoff (1995). Using six asset classes and, first, applying three-year annualized returns and, second, comparing the results with five-year annualized returns, the optimizer for the same approximate risk level doubled the bond proportion, halved the small cap. proportion, and eliminated nearly all international stocks. Thus again, forecast optimized portfolio allocations are usually quite different from future realized optimized allocations. Portfolio optimization is very useful for computations that go beyond arithmetic, such as determining the impact of one change on asset allocation. It is a useful as a tool for testing various assumptions, but very dangerous as the solution.

To deal with these problems and to ensure broad portfolio diversification, *constrained optimized allocations* are often used to ensure minimum and maximum allocations of particular asset type. This places judgment back into the process and prevents weird optimized allocations that differ greatly from perceived normal allocations. This behavior is consistent with the use of normalized portfolio allocations only when it is pursued rationally, empirically, and for the long term. Otherwise it can easily be a disguised effort at market timing.

Michaud (1998, 2000) provided an alternative to traditional portfolio optimization techniques. The need for change is due to the historically poor performance of professional investors. This performance is due not to market efficiency but to deficiencies in the practice of asset allocation. Asset managers attempt to achieve efficient portfolios by using Markowitz-type optimizers to find portfolios that best increase returns relative to risk.

There are serious limitations with optimizers for real-world asset allocation. Portfolio optimizers use risk estimates and return forecasts as inputs to generate efficient portfolios. But small input errors lead to large optimization errors and, thereby, reduced value in practical applications. These limitations are due to conceptual faults not in Markowitz efficiency but in its implementation. Too much emphasis is placed on assets with the highest returns and lowest risks. Such assets are unlikely to have these extreme values in the future. And constrained optimizers that eliminate extreme portfolio allocations have not performed well, either.

Michaud's approach includes eight steps for increasing the usefulness and value of optimized portfolios. This approach is based on understanding the true nature of asset returns that have occurred only once and in only one fashion. The use of resampling provides replays of history many times to get a better estimate of the true nature of returns. Properly averaging the generated optimized portfolios provides very different sets of optimal portfolios. These portfolios lie on the "resampled efficient frontier" and individual portfolios are "resample efficient." These portfolios do not reflect large allocation changes from small input changes and are often more consistent with investor expectations.

A major bonus with Michaud's approach is a statistical test to determine how often to rebalance resampled portfolios. The test reduces trading to balance portfolio allocations by about 50 percent. The reason for reduced trading is that particular portfolios may look very different from optimal portfolios, but have very similar investment values. Michaud concluded: "Optimization is like surgery; it is a fault-intolerant process. If you don't have to rebalance a portfolio, don't do it."

Normalized portfolio allocations: bonds

William Bernstein (1995) also suggested simple bond allocations for the simplified conventional portfolio in table 35: 50 percent in each of five-year US Treasury bonds and international bonds. However, as discussed previously, investors concerned about credit quality or maximum simplicity would do well simply to invest 100 percent of the bond allocation in five-year Treasury bonds.

However, in William Bernstein (1997c), the focus on five-year US Treasury bond maturities was shortened. Stock/bond mixes were optimized for the years 1970–97 using the simplified conventional portfolio in table 35. The global stock portfolio was divided equally among large-cap. domestic stock, small-cap. domestic stock, large-cap. international stock, and small-cap. international stock. The Markowitz-type optimizer computed efficient frontiers for allocations of global stocks and each of several maturities of US Treasury securities. For example, the least efficient portfolios (ranked from worst to best) at 10 percent returns allocate twenty-year Treasury bonds with global equities, five-year Treasury bonds with global equities, thirty-day Treasury bills, and, finally, one-year Treasury bills with global equities.

More specifically, the thirty-day Treasury bill/global stock portfolio is most efficient for very risk averse investors and returns below 8 percent. The one-year Treasury bill/global stock portfolio is most efficient at returns over 8 percent. Global stock/bond portfolios with allocations of one-year Treasury bills and with five-year Treasury bonds are approximately equally most efficient over the vast middle range of allocations. The conclusion is that the most efficient global stock/Treasury security portfolios have bond allocations with maturities in the one to three-year range, but more so, one year, over the broad range of returns. This appears in the spirit of the findings in Gluck (1995), where it is reported that all bond funds, except high-yield bond funds, produce the same general risk reduction. Thus the implication is that it is not necessary to include more than one type of bond in the bond component of the stock/bond asset allocation.

The broadly based, simplified portfolio allocations discussed and illustrated in table 35 reflect the empirical finding that, given short to intermediate-term market uncertainties, simplicity in portfolio design is generally a good thing. Normalized portfolios are more likely to outperform frequently optimized portfolios using numerous security types over the long term. In general, long-term success in investing lies in a stable, coherent strategy of broad portfolio asset allocations of domestic and international stocks and bonds. As discussed above, portfolio allocation is much more important to portfolio performance than either stock selection and/or market timing. Simple is good, long-term!

THE (FINANCIAL) ENGINE THAT COULD

Financial Engines

One of the most useful Internet developments is investment Web sites designed to help investors assess their long-term portfolios with respect to accomplishing objectives, such as retirement income that lasts a lifetime. Caution is needed, however, because the sites are not generally sophisticated enough to avoid giving poor planning advice. The most sophisticated of these is Financial Engines (2000), a portfolio planning company built on Professor Sharpe's Nobel-winning contributions to portfolio theory. This development and its portfolio model are reviewed in Peltz (1999a). The model was designed initially for millions of employees in self-directed retirement plans without access to investment advice, still less sophisticated advice. The company is gradually broadening its target markets to other types of investors.

Financial Engines is a real-time online model that designs portfolios consistent with investor risk tolerances, financial situations, investment horizons, and future financial needs. The site also provides educational information. It attempts to make a connection between the investor's current financial situation and a defined financial goal. The investor inputs financial information and data, which the model analyzes to determine the probability the goal will be achieved. To design the investor's best portfolio allocation, the model computes thousands of potential economic scenarios based on fifteen asset classes and historical inflation-adjusted rates of return. For example, assume the model determines that an investor has a 70 percent chance of achieving an annual retirement income of $100,000 by age sixty-five. The investor can then tweak the inputs to explore ways to improve the probabilities, such as by taking on more risk, saving more, and/or working longer. The investor finds that, by increasing portfolio risk by

40 percent and working two more years, there is an 85 percent chance of achieving $100,000 per year at age sixty-seven. The model lets the investor make the risk/return trade-offs that are involved in achieving financial goals. The site is at www.financialengines.com.

Financial Engines: example

William Bernstein (1999a) reviewed the Financial Engines model and created a model portfolio for an assumed investor. The investor is fifty years old, with a $1 million portfolio, to which no additional contributions will be made. An annual income of $60,000 is needed, beginning at age sixty-five. The results are in table 37. The next to last row indicates the forecast chance of success, based on various portfolio asset allocations. The chance of meeting the goal is not improved significantly by taking on more risk than level 1.3, where 1.0 is average. The worst forecast annual loss is 11 percent at this risk level. The forecast portfolio with the smallest annual loss is invested 100 percent in short-term bonds, and the one with the largest annual loss is invested 100 percent in the Russell 2000 Index of small cap. stocks. The model favors index funds, and correctly so, for low costs, low portfolio turnover, and zero cash.

Because the model is a Markowitz-type optimizer, it is easy to get strange portfolios, because allocations are very sensitive to input changes. But, for example, several portfolios in table 37 appear quite reasonable in that they allocate 25 percent each to the S&P 500 Index and Wilshire 4500 index, which together represent 100 percent of the domestic stock market. As noted, index funds generally provide the most reasonable portfolio allocations, especially if the allocations are not redundant in their holdings. If the forecast indicates the financial goal is not likely to be met, the investor adjusts personal inputs in an effort to generate alternative portfolio allocation forecasts that are more likely to meet the financial goal. Financial Engines is a powerful tool for identifying, implementing, and reviewing long-term asset allocation portfolios of the type discussed above.

CHAPTER SEVEN

PORTFOLIO DIVERSIFICATION RISK AND EQUITY STYLE ALLOCATION

Inactivity [buy and hold] strikes us as intelligent behavior.
(*Warren Buffett, in* **Annual Report of Berkshire Hathaway,** *1996*)

This new system . . . categorizes funds by their contents [categories], not by their wrappers [investment objectives].
(*Catherine V. Sanders, in* **Morningstar Investor,** *November 1996*)

Don't confuse brilliance with a bull market.
(*Ted Aronson, Aronson & Partners, in* **Money,** *February 1999*)

There are several goals in this chapter. The first is to discuss the concept of portfolio diversification constraints and their degree and risk. These constraints are measured among funds and their peer group categories and benchmark indices based on the attainable global degrees of diversification and risk.

The second goal is to discuss the issues concerning the classification of mutual funds and those concerning equity style allocation and style analysis. The importance of equity style allocation to portfolio returns is discussed, along with the use of style analysis to generate custom style benchmark portfolios to assess fund performance.

The third goal is to discuss Vanguard Windsor II's diversification risks as constrained based on global attainable degrees of diversification and to summarize them as excellent, acceptable, or unacceptable (table 52).

As seen in table 38, the diversification constraints include fund category (as modified here), method of security analysis, method of portfolio management, investment style, cash asset allocation, geographic concentration, asset sector concentration allocation, market liquidity, returns distribution, industry sector concentration, security concentration, and Value Line safety and timeliness concentration (as modified here).

DIVERSIFICATION CONSTRAINTS CONCEPT

It may be noted that the concept of diversification contraints could be considered a broader definition of investment style. That is, the constraints could quite correctly be considered descriptors of the results of portfolio manager actions. However, there is not an optimal investment style for the purposes of comparing fund performance. Diversification risk has the advantage of an attainable global degree of diversification against which the risk attributes of particular funds may be evaluated. Attainable degree of diversification reflects the fact that not all global assets are priced in markets. The assessment also works to allow comparisons of diversification risk among fund portfolios, their peer groups, and benchmark indices.

Before discussing diversification risk, it is important to determine whether the *actual* investment objectives of particular mutual funds are consistent with investor portfolio investment objectives. To recap Chapter 6, investor risk category is identified (table 31), validated by self-analysis, and confirmed by socioeconomic characteristics (table 32). Investor risk category is then matched to the appropriate portfolio investment objective and validated using the subcategories of portfolio investment objectives (table 34). The identified portfolio investment objective is then matched to the appropriate passive stock/bond asset allocation (table 33).

Table 38 is a more operational version of table 6, in which the potential investment objective constraint is replaced by the more useful Morningstar category, or simply category (discussed below). This concept provides more accurate classification of domestic equity fund investment styles, including category peer groups. The category is also a combination of the investment style in table 38. The latter allows portfolios to be compared based on both their value/growth style and their large-cap. to small-cap. style. Further, the potential quality concentration constraint is replaced by Value Line's concepts of portfolio safety and timeliness. These potential quality constraints are measurable and provide more accurate identification of portfolio quality concentration.

CLASSIFICATION OF MUTUAL FUNDS

As seen in table 38, the Morningstar category constraint is used to classify equity mutual funds. It is important that mutual funds be properly classified so that if a fund is, for example, classified as "growth," it should in fact be a growth fund. This is the problem Morningstar (1998b) attempts to correct with its category and investment style classification concepts (discussed below). However, the problem is wider than this because of the various classification schemes used by various other data providers, such as CDA/Wiesenberger, Lipper Analytical, Micropal, and various financial publications.

Renberg (1999) identified seventeen different data providers, with the number of fund classes ranging from three to ten. For example, Morningstar has nine categories of domestic equity investment styles, CDA/Wiesenberger has three, Investment Company Institute has four, the SEC has six, Moody's has eight, and Standard & Poor's has nine. Most providers classify funds by either investment objective or primary type of security.

Causes of misclassification

Misclassification of mutual funds is caused by several factors, but the major underlying one is the ambiguity of the industry's classification scheme (table 7). For example, what is the precise difference between growth funds and growth and income funds? Such ambiguities have several basic implications. One is that different fund sponsors may, in good faith, classify any given new fund differently. There is also *style drift* as portfolio manager investment styles evolve. This often happens following changes in portfolio managers, but also with new funds without historical style precedents. Fund advisors also have less leverage to prevent style drift if portfolio managers become stars. Advisors do not want to risk the large asset bases stars have attracted, which often follows when stars go elsewhere. The irony in this is that the stars are at least partly the creations of fund advertising and promotion.

Portfolio manager style versus classification

New portfolio managers of old funds and portfolio managers of new funds may thus be more likely to follow their style rather than stated investment objectives. Other implications of classification do not result from differences in judgment, but are purposeful. With the large number of funds, fund sponsors want to differentiate their products and attract cash inflows. The classification scheme's ambiguity gives fund advisors enough wiggle room to classify funds where they are most likely to perform relatively well. Fund advisors want five-star funds that attract enormous net cash inflows and bring the benefits of scale economies. And portfolio managers want to be five-star managers to enhance their compensation and marketability.

These desires provide the motivation for portfolio managers to take on more risk to improve relative performance, such as concentrating in few industry sectors and/or securities, timing the market, and by window dressing. Another implication is also purposeful. The providers of mutual fund data want to differentiate their classification products to become or continue to be leading data providers. To this end, marketing considerations may dictate what otherwise would be more statistically correct classification schemes.

Evidence of misclassification

The result of all of these issues is widespread evidence of mutual fund misclassification. In a thorough study, DiBartolomeo and Witkowski (1997) examined 748 equity funds and 40 percent of them were misclassified based on their prospectus investment objectives. Of the 298 misclassified funds, 60 percent should have been classified in more aggressive objectives. This suggests funds advisors are gaming stated investment objectives to enhance relative performance and generate high ratings. That is, stated investment objectives are often more conservative than actual risk/return profiles. Bailey and Arnott (1986) classified funds as value or growth, using cluster analysis. The study included fifty-nine equity portfolio managers and ten years of quarterly returns. One cluster included thirty-seven growth managers and a second had twenty-one value managers. Interestingly, the results are consistent with subjective classifications in a majority of cases.

Monitoring style drift

There is a growing trend for investment advisors to actively monitor their mutual funds for style drift. The desire is to control risk by applying consistent investment styles to broadly diversified portfolios. Investment advisors often want their funds invested as stated in the prospectus, as prescribed, and/or as advertised. This focus is more conducive to team management than to star management.

Edgerton (1998) identified three approaches to maintaining style consistency using *style enforcement*. First, the Vanguard Group compares each portfolio's actual investing style against its *benchmark style index*. This is especially important for fund families like Vanguard that make wide use of outside portfolio managers. Second, T. Rowe Price monitors portfolio style through a committee comprised of the chief investment officer and senior portfolio managers. Each fund's trading activity is reviewed weekly. Third, the Putnam family classifies each equity fund into one of three style groups. Each group's investment officer reviews its fund portfolios for style consistency. Both Vanguard and Putnam funds are known for style consistency.

EQUITY STYLE ALLOCATION AND STYLE ANALYSIS

Equity style allocation

The importance of asset allocation among major asset classes originated with the Brinson et al. studies discussed previously. It may also be recalled that a cash bucket along with passive asset (stock/bond) allocation with periodic rebalancing is recommended. *Equity style allocation* involves the apportionment of investment styles (variously defined) within the equity allocation determined by stock/bond asset allocation. As used here, neither equity allocation nor passive asset allocation has anything to do with market timing. Equity allocation is always fully invested, while some advocate basic tilts and/or periodic shifts of investment styles.

The importance and practice of equity style allocation are reported in Klein and Lederman (1995), with twenty-two chapters by leading practitioners (editors cited owing to chapter overlap). The potential returns from asset allocation and equity allocation were examined for the fifteen-year period 1980–94. Optimal asset allocation produced annualized returns of nearly 32 percent versus over 13 percent for 60/35/5 stock/bond/cash portfolios. Thus the pickup from optimal asset allocation was nearly nineteen percentage points. Optimal equity allocation produced annualized returns of nearly 30 percent versus nearly 14 percent for the Wilshire 5000 Index of the domestic stock market. Thus the pickup from optimal style allocation is nearly sixteen percentage points. These findings indicated that equity allocation rivals asset allocation in importance!

Style analysis

Style analysis (*performance attribution analysis and equity style management*) is based on the premise that portfolio managers should be evaluated based on the style of securities they hold. To do this, *custom benchmark indices* (*custom style benchmarks*) are designed to reflect the characteristics of portfolio manager investment styles. These benchmark indices are most effectively constructed from combinations of indices that together best match past portfolio returns.

The growing importance of style analysis reflects the desire of large, usually institutional, investors to understand the whys of performance to better evaluate portfolio managers, both absolutely and relatively. It extends the hows of long-standing performance evaluation measures to the whys of investment style measures. Investment style has various qualitative definitions, but, quantitatively, it is the set of prominent investment characteristics persistently exhibited by the manager's portfolio. These characteristics are measurable financial variables that significantly correlate with portfolio returns.

Style analysis is thus the process of identifying portfolio manager investment styles for the purposes of performance evaluation. The results are the customized benchmark indices noted above. This process and its developments are summarized in Sharpe et al. (1999) and Bodie et al. (1996). Antecedents and developments in style analysis are discussed more fully in Fama (1972), Sharpe (1978, 1982, 1988, 1992), Fogler (1990), Ankrim (1991), Higgs and Goode (1993), Richard Bernstein (1995), Singer and Karnosky (1995), and Bailey (1996).

Style analysis was moved front and center when Sharpe (1992) determined that *style exposure* explains about 90 percent of variations in average monthly equity fund returns and stock selection only 10 percent. The implication is that equity style, not stock selection, is the more critical issue of the two. A two-dimensional definition of domestic equity fund characteristics was used: market capitalization and style. This led to four classes: large-cap. value, large-cap. growth, mid cap., and small cap. The ratio of book value to market price was used to classify stocks as value or growth.

Other studies classify stocks as value or growth using multivariate approaches that include various market capitalization size and growth/value characteristics, such as dividend yield, earnings yield, forecast of earnings growth rates, and book value/market price ratios. As noted, style analysis is also used to design custom style benchmarks that reflect a particular portfolio manager's investment style. Manager skill is measured as the ability to earn abnormal returns to a custom benchmark index on a consistent basis. These added returns, if they exist, represent the *value of active management* – a scarce commodity.

The emergence of style management has been shaped by Malkiel (1995) and Fama and French (1992), among others. Malkiel's study determined that mutual funds do not outperform the market in general. Evidence indicated the predictability of fund returns from period to period, especially during the 1970s, but persistence in returns broke down during the 1980s. Predictable patterns in returns indicate flaws in the *random walk* theory (weak form) of efficient markets. Fama and French observe that market capitalization and B/P ratios explain much of the differences in returns and in estimating future returns. These two variables are widely used in characterizing investment style along the two dimensions of large-cap. versus small-cap. size and value versus growth.

Determining portfolio manager style

As reported in Klein and Lederman (1995), there are three approaches to determining *portfolio manager style*. The first is to rely on the portfolio manager's own assessment. However, managers characterize their styles as one of several styles rather than as one style mix. The second approach uses factor models to evaluate the fundamental characteristics of portfolio holdings. This approach requires the collection of holdings over multiple periods and is time-consuming, costly, and complex to implement. The third approach is style analysis, which has been incorrectly criticized for implying that portfolios hold securities with styles not actually held. However, the purpose of this analysis is to identify effective portfolio style exposure, not specific security exposure. The proportions of style indices collectively represent the portfolio manager's style exposure with no overlap among indices.

To determine portfolio manager style, performance is attributed (thus attribution analysis) to the mix of investment styles (thus style analysis) that best characterize manager historical returns and security selection. Custom benchmark indices are normally developed that replicate portfolio manager investment style plus return premiums for variance not explained by style.

Performance assessment

Custom-designed benchmarks have proven better at explaining past performance than standard market indices or peer group assessments. The objective is to generate returns (thus "returns-based style analysis") that compensate for style exposure plus securities risk within each style. While attention should be given to manager style drift over time, managers typically operate within relatively tight style domains. Custom style benchmarks provide methods to assess manager ability to add value (thus "value added management") within identified styles, and form the basis for future performance assessments.

With investment style being very important in explaining differences in returns, it appears that *neutral equity style* portfolio management should be reexamined. This approach ignores the potential gains from style management and focuses only on stock selection, the less important of the two. The neutral style thus generates index-fund-like returns plus/minus small amounts from stock selection.

If a style-driven process is necessary to generate added returns from active management, then the first issue is to determine what that style is. For example, should *portfolio style tilt* towards a particular investment style, such as growth or value *and* large cap. or small cap.? If so, should *static tilts* (constant) or variable style tilts be implemented? For example, static value tilts imply that value funds outperform (risk-adjusted) growth funds over time. This important issue and the implications for equity style management are discussed later – that is, what works to generate abnormal returns.

Portfolios with particular style tilts may have different portfolio managers for each. For example, if two or more investment styles are desired, each type of manager may be allocated specific proportions of the portfolio. These proportions are changed periodically as fund policy or outlook changes. Another approach is to have a neutral equity style (indexed) core portfolio of specified proportions, say 67 percent, and value and/or growth style managers for the remaining 33 percent, depending on fund policy and/or outlook changes. At this point, it is enough to say that fund value style is less risky than growth along several dimensions.

Morningstar on style analysis

Morningstar in turn reviewed style analysis, which Rekenthaler (1996b) described as, first, attempting to determine the custom blend of multiple market indices that best explain mutual fund returns. Then, once fund style is described by its customized index benchmark, the second step is to grade portfolio manager performance. To do this, actual fund returns are divided into two components: one called "style," which equals benchmark returns, and, a second called "selection," which is attributed to any positive/negative residual returns. For example, if actual returns less benchmark returns are negative, this negative "residual return" is represented as "poor security selection." Conversely, a positive residual is interpreted as "good security selection."

Rekenthaler (1996c) critiqued style analysis by comparing it with what Morningstar already knew about developments in specific funds. The basic appeal of style analysis is that it explains how funds have been managed. This is not new information in most cases. Moreover, what style analysis does not say is also not new information in most cases. That is, style analysis misses major changes in actual fund styles. Style analysis appears to work best with portfolio managers with consistent investment styles.

Another appeal of style analysis is that it determines whether portfolio manager ability to select securities has added to returns. These returns are in fact residuals not explained by style. But, if style analysis does not fully measure investment style, then residual returns are not likely measuring value added/subtracted by security selection. Morningstar's conclusion is that attribution models are at best research supplements, not substitutes for hands-on analysis. This conclusion becomes a bit more overstated as style analysis continues to get more sophisticated. Again, the case for equity style management is made in Klein and Lederman (1995).

Financial Engines and style

More recently, Financial Engines (2000) has contributed to the development of style analysis and its usefulness in assisting investors to optimize retirement portfolios. Mutual fund investment style describes the types of investments made and is the most important factor influencing potential future performance. For example, funds that invest in small-cap. stocks tend to perform the way small-cap. stocks perform. Once fund style has been identified, the future performance of underlying asset classes may be estimated. This mapping of specific portfolio assets on to long-term asset classes has more predictive power than using fund performance history. To make these long-term projections of asset classes, both individually and in relation to each other, historical and forecast data derived from current market conditions are used.

Fund-specific attributes

Style analysis, in itself, cannot fully explain mutual fund risk/return behavior. The unexplained portion of fund risk/return behavior depends upon how funds are managed. *Fund-specific attributes* have major impacts on fund risk/return performance. These attributes include expense ratios, front-end loads, portfolio turnover, trading costs, taxes, past performance, and performance consistency. These factors are analyzed over time to determine which has the most influence on specific fund performance. However, past performance is only of limited use in estimating future performance. Nonetheless, long-term versus short-term performance history carries more weight, as does consistent versus inconsistent performance.

Thus mutual fund future risk/return performance depends on investment style and fund-specific attributes. This explains why funds that frequently change investment style, hold concentrated portfolios, and time the market carry more risk than broadly diversified portfolios with consistent investment styles. As a footnote to this discussion, it is interesting that risk/return relationships are not always consistent as risk increases. Purcell (1994a) examined this relationship for bond funds, domestic equity funds, sector funds, and international equity funds using ten-year annualized returns. There is a consistent positive relationship between bond fund risks and returns, and a strong positive relationship for domestic equity funds. Equity fund returns first increase, then flatten out at mid-risk levels, and increase again at high-risk levels. But there is an overall negative risk/return relationship for sector funds. Returns first decline with increases in risk, then increase, only to decline again at mid-risk, but especially at high-risk, levels. International equity funds have a slightly negative overall risk/return relationship. Returns are relatively flat as risk increases, but returns decline as risk moves from average to high. But limited observations at extremes may have impacted the results.

Ibbotson on style

Ibbotson Associates, a Chicago investment research firm, has also contributed to the development and application of style analysis. Roger Ibbotson (1997) reported they can predict which particular funds will do better than style-adjusted benchmarks, but not which style will perform best. Thus investors should diversify across investment styles. The key to portfolio outperformance is not to rely on professional portfolio managers, because, on average, they underperform the benchmark index, net of expenses/fees. Moreover, if markets are completely efficient, stock prices reflect their true value, and portfolio managers cannot profitably buy/sell so-called under/overvalued stocks. But no one (not literally true) believes markets are "that" efficient. Most investors believe star portfolio managers do exist, and somehow they can be identified by their track record. But it is not sufficient to select funds based on portfolio managers whose funds had superior past performance. As noted above, it is mutual fund investment style, not stock selection ability, that explains over 90 percent of variance in returns. Portfolio manager skill is a small residual of investment style in explaining this variation.

The Ibbotson approach measures portfolio manager contributions to returns as mutual fund returns less those on custom style benchmarks. Performance benchmarks are computed that best explain previous monthly performance. The calculation is based on weighted combinations of benchmarks for large-cap. growth, small-cap. growth, large-cap. value, small-cap. value, international stocks, bonds, intermediate-term bonds, and cash. If fund performance is larger than median fund performance in given styles, the funds are classified as winners or, conversely, losers.

Analysis of over 3,100 funds demonstrated that 54 percent of style winners repeat the next year, and a majority of winners repeated in thirteen of sixteen years. This so-called *style performance persistence* can be statistically demonstrated only by adjusting for investment style and not by using raw performance data. Funds with repeat year-to-year style performance include Putnam Voyager A, IDS New Dimensions A, Neuberger & Berman Partners, AIM

Constellation, and Guardian Park Avenue. The approach is being improved by using longer periods to define winners and evaluate future performance. Also, the definition of what makes a winner can be drawn more narrowly. Based on three-year style-adjusted fund performance, 42 percent of funds in the top quartile repeated their quartile performance and 62 percent were in the top half.

Performance attribution models go beyond the approach used here, which is to assess mutual funds using more investor-friendly methods and measures. Nonetheless, as discussed, sophisticated Ibbotson-type models are "out there." These advanced models are most often used in the world of institutional portfolio manager selection and assessment. For example, a pension sponsor may want to know how well each of several investment advisors performed, and why. For example, the model may assume portfolio performance is due to *common factors*, such as systematic risk (beta) and market capitalization (large-cap. versus small-cap.), and "sector factors," such as industrial versus non-industrial securities. One manager's high *relative* performance may be explained by positive "beta bets" on the direction of the market that offset poor "cap-size bets" and "sector bets."

DEGREE OF CONSTRAINED DIVERSIFICATION AND RISK (TABLE 38)

Table 38 provides the structure for analysis and discussion of Windsor II's degree of diversification and risk relative to attainable global diversification. But first it is important to identify how Windsor II's degree of diversification was identified for each potential constraint. Then, it is important to identify how Windsor II's degree of diversification for each potential constraint was assessed as to risk. In other words, it is important to know how table 38 was prepared.

Identification of degrees of constrained diversification

As noted, attainable diversification refers to the attainable degree of global diversification. Constrained diversification refers to the actual degree of diversification versus attainable global diversification. Constrained diversification precludes funds from achieving attainable global diversification, as reflected in the various actual potential constraints on fund portfolio management. However, as discussed previously and below, the degree of diversification can result in either high or low diversification risk, depending on the constraint.

The identification of Windsor II's actual versus attainable global diversification for each constraint in table 38 is based on information in Windsor II's prospectus (1999a). In table 6, Windsor II's *growth investment objective* constrains attainable global diversification. This stated objective primarily seeks long-term capital growth and, secondarily, dividend income. Fund investment objectives are legally "fundamental" and change requires shareholder approval of a majority of shares voting.

As noted, in table 38, Windsor II's investment objective is replaced by its Morningstar category, large-cap. value. This category constrains attainable global diversification. Windsor II's cap. size investment style is identified by its stated focus on large-cap. and mid-cap. stocks. Windsor II's value/growth investment style is value based on its stated use of below-average *price–earnings* (P/E) *ratios* and above-average dividend yields (D/P) in selecting stocks. Windsor II's investment strategy is not fundamental and change requires only board approval.

Windsor II's *fundamental method of security analysis* constrains attainable global diversification. Portfolio decisions are based on analysis of securities and their prospects, but also of the stock market and the economy. Value/growth investment styles (discussed above) are two major variants of fundamental analysis, which is the primary method for identifying undervalued and overvalued securities. Value analysis looks for undervalued stocks relative to intrinsic value, and growth analysis looks for undervalued stocks relative to prospects for earnings growth. Use of technical analysis, the other major method, was discussed previously and in the later discussion of the market and economic outlook.

Fundamental analysis includes both active and passive portfolio management, but applied differently. Windsor II's stated use of *active portfolio management* constrains attainable global diversification. Fundamental analysis is identified in the fund's use of traditional research methods and securities selection, which is managed by a lead portfolio manager and subadvisors. Index funds do not require active portfolio management in the traditional sense, but they do require it in the statistical sense. Passive (index) portfolios are managed to match the performance of benchmark indices, less expenses. In some few cases, index funds have outperformed benchmark indices, gross of expenses. In these cases, the net effect is the same as further reduced expenses. Moreover, some portfolios, especially retirement vehicles, are both actively and passively managed. The core portfolio is indexed and the balance actively managed to enhance index returns.

Windsor II's *domestic geographic concentration* constrains attainable global diversification. This is identified in Windsor II's stated policy of limiting international securities to 20 percent of assets. This constraint reflects the fact that international securities are subject to additional types of risk. Windsor II's *stock asset allocation* constrains attainable global diversification and is seen in its predominant holding of stocks, not stocks and bonds. These allocations are consistent with Windsor II's stated investment objective, which cites only domestic stock.

Windsor II's *high market liquidity* constrains attainable global diversification. The fund's non-representative high portfolio liquidity is based on its holdings of very marketable large-cap./mid-cap. stocks that trade in very liquid, low trading cost, markets. In addition, derivatives may not be used for speculative purposes, which precludes those with low liquidity. Deposits on futures contracts are limited to 5 percent of assets, and total contracts may not exceed 20 percent of assets. Restricted and illiquid securities may not exceed 15 percent of assets. Restricted securities are not sold through public offerings and do not require SEC registration. They are "unregistered" and sold direct to investors. Restricted securities must be held at least one year and restrictions (thus restricted securities) limit their sale. Strictly speaking, illiquid securities are assets for which there are no current markets *per se*.

Windsor II's *small cash allocation* constrains attainable global diversification, based on its policy of holding cash reserves of about 5 percent. Historically, average mutual fund cash ratios range from about 5 percent to 10 percent. The cash allocation is used for operating purposes and to provide liquidity to meet shareholder redemptions, which can occur quickly in turbulent markets. But, as noted by Lucchetti (2000), the industry trend is to smaller cash balances, which is expected in a long-term bull market. But, also there is a growing belief that funds are being paid to manage stocks, not Treasury bills. Windsor II's cash allocation is consistent with its policy (noted above), but also with its long-term investment horizon and low portfolio turnover. The fund does not vary its cash assets based on market timing strategies, nor does it want market timers among its shareholders. These short-term investors are explicitly discouraged from investing.

In addition to traditional uses, Windsor II's cash assets may also be invested in stock futures to simulate full investment, while maintaining cash assets to meet redemptions. Separate cash accounts are maintained for obligations underlying futures contracts. In addition, borrowing for emergency or temporary purposes may not exceed 10 percent of assets, and no additional investments may be made if borrowing exceeds 5 percent of assets.

Based on separation of the cash bucket and investment portfolio, the implication is that funds held should use cash reserves only for operating needs, not for market timing purposes. The cash bucket takes care of investor cash needs while the investment portfolio takes care of investing needs.

Windsor II's *dividend and capital gains returns distribution* does not constrain attainable global diversification. The fund's stated objective is capital gains plus some dividends, not simply growth or income. Windsor II's capital gains/dividend allocation also provides more stability of returns than only capital gains. Windsor II's *broad industry sector concentration* also does not constrain attainable global diversification. Its portfolio represents very diverse industry sector holdings. This is consistent with Windsor II's long-term investment horizon with low portfolio turnover that promotes broad industry diversification. No more than 25 percent of assets may be invested in single industries. Windsor II's *broad security concentration* similarly does not constrain global diversification. Its holdings of individual securities are diverse and consistent with the fund's long investment horizon and low portfolio turnover. But, also, as to 75 percent of its assets, the fund may not invest more than 5 percent in single companies, or buy more than 10 percent of the voting shares of single companies. Windsor II's portfolio *quality concentration*, as measured in table 38 by Value Line safety and timeliness quality ratings, are computed and discussed below.

Overall, Windsor II's portfolio is stated to be subject to market, objective, and manager risks. Restrictions and limitations on fund investments and other topics are discussed in detail in Windsor II's statement of additional information (1999b).

Assessment of diversification risk

As noted, the degree of diversification can result in either high or low relative diversification risk, depending on the constraint. The assessment of Windsor II's diversification risk for each constraint in table 38 is based on comparison with same constraint in attainable global diversification. Global investing provides the largest degree of attainable diversification for each constraint, but *not* necessarily the smallest diversification risk. This interpretation is made qualitatively, but based on empirical diversification risk relationships. The results may be sensitive to particular mutual funds, their peer group categories, and benchmark indices.

Of the fourteen individual constraints in table 38, eight represent direct comparisons of Windsor II's constraints versus large-cap. value funds in general. Windsor II's *Morningstar category* is large-cap. value, which has a smaller degree of diversification (more constrained) than large-cap. blend (value plus growth) funds, but less diversification risk. Windsor II's single focus on value stocks also has a smaller degree of diversification (more constrained) than blended growth and value funds, but less diversification risk. In table 6 terms, Windsor II has multiple *investment objectives* (growth and income), with a larger degree of diversification (less constrained) than single-focused funds, but less diversification risk.

Windsor II's *method of security analysis* focuses on fundamental analysis, which has a smaller degree of diversification (more constrained) than fundamental analysis plus technical analysis. It follows that this focus also has *more* diversification risk. Windsor II's *method of portfolio management* focuses on *active* management, which has a smaller degree of diversification (more constrained) than active plus passive management. Again, it follows that this single focus has *more* diversification risk. Windsor II's *value investment style* has a smaller degree of diversification (more constrained) than the use of both value and growth (blend) investment styles. But its value focus has *less* diversification risk than the use of both styles. Also, Windsor II's *large-cap. investment style* is less diversified (more constrained) than a portfolio including representative cap. sizes. But its large-cap. focus has *less* diversification risk. Large-cap. stocks are generally less risky than small-cap. stocks. Windsor II's *cash asset allocation*, represented by its cash ratio, is less diversified (more constrained) than portfolios with average or larger proportions of cash assets. This small cash ratio has *more* diversification risk because cash assets are less risky than common stock. Windsor II's *domestic geographic concentration* is less diversified (more constrained), with *more* diversification risk, than global portfolios. Windsor II's *stock/bond asset allocation*, represented by its proportion of stock holdings, is less diversified (more constrained) with *more* diversification risk than funds with larger relative holdings of representative bonds. Windsor II's *market liquidity*, as measured by its large-cap. stock focus, is less diversified (more constrained) with *less* diversification risk than funds with representative market size portfolios. Large-cap. markets are generally more liquid, with smaller trading costs, than small-cap. markets.

Windsor II's *returns distribution*, represented by its proportions of dividend income and capital gains, is more diversified (less constrained) with *less* diversification risk than funds that focus on one or the other income source. Windsor II's returns include more stable dividend income relative to less stable capital gains, especially as compared with funds with a single focus on capital gains. Windsor II's *industry sector* and *security concentration* are both well diversified (less constrained) with *less* diversification risk. The portfolio invests broadly in diverse industries and a large number of securities, respectively.

Windsor II's *quality concentration* is represented by its Value Line safety rating and timeliness rating as identified in table 38. The fund's portfolio safety rating (portfolio financial quality) is less diversified (more constrained) with *more* diversification risk than funds in its category peer group and the benchmark index. The fund's low safety risk is unacceptable. Further, Windsor II's timeliness risk is less diversified (more constrained) than funds in its category and the benchmark index. The fund's timeliness risk is mixed but acceptable, with more risk than the market index and less risk than its category peer group.

Again, it is important to note that if table 38 included other than Windsor II examples for comparison with particular mutual funds, the degree of diversification and risk most likely would change. For example, as noted, if a fund's focus was solely income, rather than income and capital gains, the fund would be less diversified (more constrained) but with *less* diversification risk. Nonetheless, the examples were selected to provide generally applicable diversification risk assessments for funds, such as Windsor II, for which direct category and investment style comparisons can be made.

As computed in table 38, only 27 percent of Windsor II's diversification constraints match up with attainable global diversification. These three constraints also have less relative risk. This more theoretical assessment finds Windsor II unacceptable as a fund providing attainable global diversification. A more applied approach follows, one that compares Windsor II's degree of diversification and risk with its peer group category and its benchmark index.

MORNINGSTAR CATEGORY AND INVESTMENT STYLE BOXES

As previously reported in table 6, mutual funds are classified by investment objectives to determine peer groups. However, these classifications are too broad to ensure that funds with the same objectives do in fact invest the same way. Also, the management of portfolios often drifts to where stated investment objectives or investment style are not accurate. For example, DiTeresa (1998c) reported claims that Third Avenue Value and American Century–Twentieth Century Ultra are both growth funds. But in fact Third Avenue is a small-cap. value portfolio, and Twentieth Century Ultra is a mid-cap. to large-cap. growth portfolio. This illustrates the flaw in using prospectus investment objectives to identify how funds actually invest.

This flaw also presents problems for investors using chapter 6 type asset allocation portfolios. For example, investment in misclassified funds can result in too much *actual* investment in large-cap. value funds relative to the portfolio's *desired* allocation. Further, misclassified funds can generate inappropriate risk/return profiles. Online sites, such as Morningstar (2000b), are available to x-ray fund portfolios to determine actual allocations and avoid portfolio overlap.

Investment style box

To solve the ambiguity of investment objectives in describing how mutual funds actually invest, Morningstar developed the concept of the *investment style box* (Morningstar, 1998b). Morningstar is a Chicago firm that publishes mutual fund analysis, ratings, commentary, and more. The concept was created in 1992 to determine how funds actually invest, rather than how prospectus investment objectives state they invest. The Morningstar category identifies the actual investment objective of each *domestic* equity mutual fund as determined by the *equity style box* and measured over the past three years. On the other hand, the investment style box identifies the actual investment objective of each domestic equity fund as determined by the equity style box and measured currently.

The investment style box is useful for determining how stock and bond mutual funds actually invest relative to peer groups of funds in the same category and to benchmark indices. Category peer groups are used to benchmark fund performance relative to the appropriate benchmark index. The S&P 500 Index usually serves as the benchmark index and is the choice here. This choice is obviously more appropriate for large-cap. funds than small-cap. funds.

The investment style box also facilitates designing mutual fund portfolios that are diversified by investment style with minimum *style overlap*. For example, over the last three years, DiTeresa (1999) observed that mutual funds that maintain style purity have less total risk and higher returns than funds with style drift. Because cash and bond holdings are excluded in determining equity fund investment styles, investors should also review cash and any bond allocations. These assets dilute style purity compared to funds with the same equity proportions. Funds most likely to remain style purists apply consistent approaches to investment style (obviously), but also to stock selection and portfolio turnover (low). However, as discussed previously, style purity may constrain the future fund performance of currently high-performing funds.

Barbee (1999a) suggested four hands-on rules of thumb for preventing or reducing style overlap: (1) invest only in one fund for each portfolio manager; (2) invest in only one fund in any *boutique* (specialty niche) fund family; (3) avoid funds with similar industry sector weightings; and (4) avoid funds with similar security holdings among the largest holdings.

However, style purity is not a guaranteed way to high performance. Wolper (2000) noted that style drift may also reflect portfolio manager success as, for example, small-cap. stocks increased in price and became mid-cap. stocks. If these stocks are still undervalued, it does not make sense to sell them just because their prices have increased beyond the small-cap. category. There are also some eclectic portfolio managers, like Fidelity's Peter Lynch during his Magellan fund tenure, who invest well across the board. The key is to identify portfolio managers who mimic Lynch's long-term performance. Not likely.

Equity style box

The equity style box is a nine-cell grid (3 × 3 matrix) used to determine the category and investment styles of domestic equity funds. The equity style box classifies funds in one of nine combinations of value/blend/growth and small/mid/large-cap. size: large-cap. value, large-cap. blend, large-cap. growth, mid-cap. value, mid-cap. blend, mid-cap. growth, small-cap. value, small-cap. blend, and small-cap. growth. Blend incorporates both value and growth investment style characteristics.

Morningstar categories differ for other types of equity funds. In these cases, categories are defined rather than determined using the equity style box. There are seven categories of US specialty funds (sector funds): communications, financial, health, natural resources, precious metals, real estate, and utilities. There is also one category of domestic hybrid securities (bonds and stocks). The latter include balanced funds and asset allocation funds. On the other hand, investment style identifies the actual investment objective of each fund as determined by the same type of equity style box discussed above and measured *currently*.

Morningstar categories also differ for international equity mutual funds. The categories are defined rather than determined using the equity style box. There is one fund category each of international stock, world stock, diversified emerging markets stock, and international hybrid. There are also five categories of regional stock funds: diversified Pacific/Asia stock, Europe stock, Japan stock, Latin America stock, and Pacific/Asia (ex-Japan) stock. On the other hand, investment style identifies the actual investment objective of each fund as determined by the same type of equity style box discussed above and measured *currently*.

Regnier (1997b) reported that equity style boxes are unreliable guides to international equity mutual fund categories. International value funds are likely to be as diversified as international growth funds. Value and growth remain important, but valuation issues drive most decisions concerning fund country allocations and stock selection.

Fixed-income style box

As discussed by Lowenstein (1997), Morningstar bond mutual fund categories are defined rather than determined using the *fixed-income style box* (figure 7.1). On the other hand, each bond's *current* actual investment style is determined using the style box. This differs from the process used on domestic equity funds, where the three-year category and current investment style are determined using style boxes.

The fixed-income style box is a nine-cell grid (3 × 3 matrix) used to determine investment styles of bond funds. The style box classifies funds in one of nine combinations of short/intermediate/long duration and high/medium/low credit quality: short-term high-quality, intermediate-term high-quality, long-term high-quality, short-term medium-quality, intermediate-term medium-quality, long-term medium-quality, short-term low-quality, intermediate-term low-quality, and long-term low-quality.

There are seven defined Morningstar categories of *high-quality bond mutual funds*: intermediate-term bond, long-term bond, short-term bond, intermediate-term US government bond, long-term government bond, short-term government bond, and ultra-short maturity bond. There are two categories of *international bond funds*: international bond and emerging market bond.

Risk	Investment style			Median market capitalization
Low	Value	Blend	Growth	
○	Large-cap. Value	Large-cap. Blend	Large-cap. Growth	Large
Moderate ○	Mid-cap. Value	Mid-cap. Blend	Mid-cap. Growth	Medium
High ◎	Small-cap. Value	Small-cap. Blend	Small-cap. Growth	Small

Figure 7.1(a) Morningstar equity style box. Within the equity style box grid, nine possible combinations exist, ranging from large-cap. value for the safest funds to small-cap. growth for the riskiest. (Domestic funds are measured relative to the S&P 500; international funds are measured relative to MSCI EAFE, with P/C used in place of P/E.) Market capitalization for stocks. Large-cap.: 250 biggest stocks. Mid-cap.: 750 next biggest stocks. Small-cap.: smallest 4,000 stocks of the top 5,000. Investment style for stocks. (1) Rank stocks in each market-cap. group by P/E ratios. (2) Find asset-weighted median P/E for each market-cap. group, or point where half of assets are in stocks with higher P/Es and half in stocks with lower P/Es. (3) Calculate P/E score for each stock by dividing its P/E by median P/E. (4) Repeat steps 1 through 3 using P/B ratios. Source: reprinted with permission from Peter DiTeresa, Refining Morningstar's Style Box, *Morningstar Fund Investor*, December 1998, p. 9.

Risk	Duration			Quality
Low	Short	Intermediate	Long	
○				
	Short-term High Quality	Interm-term High Quality	Long-term High Quality	High
Moderate				
○	Short-term Medium Quality	Interm-term Medium Quality	Long-term Medium Quality	Medium
High	Short-term Low Quality	Interm-term Low Quality	Long-term Low Quality	Low
◎				

Figure 7.1(b)   Morningstar fixed income style box. Within the fixed-income style box grid, nine possible combinations exist, ranging from short maturity or duration-high quality for the safest funds to long maturity or duration-low quality for the riskiest. Low: BB or lower. Medium: BBB through A. High: AA or higher. Duration (taxable open-end funds). Short: less than three and a half years. Interim: greater than or equal to three and a half years, less than or equal to six years. Long: greater than six years. Duration (mini-bond funds). Short: less than four and a half years. Interim: greater than or equal to four and a half years, less than or equal to seven years. Long: greater than seven years. Market capitalization for funds. (1) Rank fund's holdings by their market caps. (2) Find middle 20 percent of assets, or point where 40 percent of fund's assets are in larger caps. and 40 percent in smaller caps. (3) Fund's market cap. is asset-weighted average of that middle 20 percent. Large cap.: market cap. $\geq$ 250 largest US stocks. Mid cap.: market cap. < 250 largest US stocks and $\geq$ 1,000 largest US stocks. Small cap.: market cap. < 1,000 largest US stocks. Investment style for funds. (1) Rank fund's holdings by their P/E scores. (2) Find middle 20 percent of assets, or point where 40 percent of fund's assets are in stocks with higher P/E scores and 40 percent in stocks with lower scores. (3) Relative P/E is asset-weighted average of that middle 20 percent. (4) Repeat for P/B ratios. (5) Add relative P/E and relative P/B for fund's valuation score. Growth: valuation score > 2.25. Blend: valuation score $\geq$ 1.75 and $\leq$ 23.25. Value: valuation score < 1.75. Source: as figure 7.1(a).

There are also three defined categories of *municipal bond – national funds*: municipal national intermediate-term, municipal national long-term, and municipal national short-term. Last, there is one category each of *high-yield* bond (low credit quality), *convertible bond*, and *multisector bond*. National funds offer geographic diversification. Single-state municipal bond funds provide residents with income (but not capital gains) that is exempt from both state and federal taxes. Chung (1999) advised investors in high tax rate states to choose funds dedicated to their resident state obligations. Otherwise, they are advised to buy national municipal bond funds.

Maturity of the fixed-income style box is determined by portfolio duration to reflect the relative sensitivity of portfolio values to changes in levels of interest rates. The portfolio values of bond funds with short duration are less sensitive to changes in interest rates. Duration of from one to three and a half years is defined as short-term maturity, from three and a half years to six years is intermediate-term maturity, and six years or over is long-term maturity.

The credit quality of taxable bond funds is defined by average portfolio credit rating: credit ratings below BBB are defined as low credit quality, BBB to AA credit ratings are defined as average credit quality, and credit ratings of AAA and higher are defined as high credit quality. Duration and credit quality definitions for municipal bond funds are summarized in figure 7.1.

Category and investment style processes

Figure 7.1 summarizes the Morningstar process for determining the categories (style boxes) and current investment styles (style boxes) of domestic equity mutual funds and current investment styles of other equity funds. The first step computes and categorizes each fund's relative market capitalization as large, mid, or small. This step is also discussed in Regnier (1997e). Each fund's market capitalization size is determined by its relative market size to avoid style changes caused by absolute changes in market capitalizations. Large-cap. funds have relative weighted capitalizations equal to or larger than the 250 largest stocks. Mid-cap. funds have relative capitalizations smaller than the 250 largest stocks and equal to or greater than the largest 1,000 stocks. And small-cap. funds have relative capitalizations less than the largest 1,000 stocks.

The second step computes each fund's investment style and categorizes it as value, blend, or growth. This process is also summarized in figure 7.1. Relative P/E and P/B ratios are used to avoid style changes caused by absolute changes in these measures. Domestic equity funds are measured relative to the S&P 500 Index. International stock funds are measured relative to the MSCI (EAFE) and the *price-to-cash flow* (P/C) *ratio* is used in place of the P/E ratio. For each measure, 1.00 represents the category average. If the sum of the fund's relative P/E and P/B scores is larger than 2.25, the fund is categorized as growth. If the combined scores are less than 1.75, the fund is categorized as value. Finally, if the combined scores are between 1.75 and 2.25, the fund is categorized as blend, which represents a portfolio of growth and value stocks and/or stocks that have both characteristics.

It is important to note that table 38 replaces table 6's portfolio investment objective with the Morningstar category. The category applies because Windsor II is a domestic equity fund. As discussed, the category provides a more accurate measure of basic investment style for individual domestic equity funds, their category peer groups, and benchmark indices. The category provides a more accurate basis for determining if whether Windsor II's degree of diversification and risk for each constraint (table 38) is more, equally, or less risky than its category peer group and benchmark index. This process identifies whether Windsor II's overall diversification risk is excellent (relatively low risk), acceptable (equal risk), or unacceptable (relatively high risk) relative to its peer group category and the S&P 500 Index or its fund surrogate.

Thus to recap, there are two major uses for the nine-cell grid-style box concept illustrated in figure 7.1. As discussed in Ronald (1999d), the first use of the equity style box is to determine the *basic* investment style of domestic equity funds identified by Morningstar category. The second is to determine the *current* investment style identified by the equity style box for equity funds and by the fixed-income style box for bond funds. These two classifications make it possible to compare the degree of diversification and risk for particular funds based on each of the diversification constraints described in table 38.

Morningstar categories: recap

To recap, Morningstar categories supersede traditional investment objectives and explicitly or implicitly incorporate or supplement the following diversification constraints: (1) fundamental (only) method of security analysis, including active (only) portfolio management; (2) investment style, including value/growth and large/mid/small cap; (3) cash/non-cash asset allocation; (4) international/ domestic geographic concentration; (5) stock/bond asset allocation; (6) portfolio market liquidity; (7) income/capital gains returns distribution; (8) industry sector concentration; (9) securities concentration; and (10) portfolio safety and timeliness concentration. Overall, mutual fund diversification constraints and risk reflect investment advisor choices of categories and investment style and portfolio manager choices in advancing these goals (as further constrained by policies, strategies, restrictions, and limitations) relative to attainable global degrees of diversification and risk.

Morningstar's (1998a, b) category concept is widely used and available in binder, CD-ROM, and online forms. While Sharpe et al. (1999) noted several caveats with the Morningstar investment style concept, they acknowledge its overall usefulness. Haslem and Scheraga (2001a, b) identified methodological problems with Morningstar's categorization of large-cap. funds as either value or growth. Nonetheless, style boxes remain very useful and readily available, along with other tools for fund analysis and selection.

MORNINGSTAR STAR RATINGS AND CATEGORY RATINGS

Morningstar (star) ratings and Morningstar Category ratings are described in Ronald (1999b). Morningstar Ratings are critiqued by Blume (1998) and Sharpe (1998), but defended by DiTeresa (1998d). Morningstar star ratings (one to five stars) are long-term measures of risk-adjusted performance – quantitative measures of how well fund returns have compensated for risk. The measure gives equal weight to risk and return. The calculation is based on each of the past three, five, and ten years relative to one of four broad fund groups: domestic stock, international stock, taxable bonds, and municipal bonds.

Morningstar star ratings

Regnier (1997a) reported that Morningstar (star) ratings now reflect four rating groups: domestic equities, fixed-income bonds, international equities, and municipal bonds. Lallos (1997a) determined that the percentage of four and five-star funds ranges from 70 percent for municipal bonds to 44 percent for international stock funds. Star ratings are also quite successful at separating long-term winners from long-term losers. But, like most tools, the star system should be used in conjunction with other risk/return measures.

However, Ronald (1999b) also reported that Morningstar star ratings are less useful than Morningstar Category ratings for investors seeking to diversify. Category ratings compare mutual funds risk/return tradeoffs with peer groups. Category ratings are also risk-adjusted, but differently from star ratings. They focus only on funds in the same categories, such as a small-cap. value fund and its category peer group of small-cap. value funds. The calculation is based on the last three years because most funds have not been in business for five to ten years. Unlike star ratings, the calculation excludes sales loads to avoid overly penalizing fund performance over short time spans.

Morningstar process

Arnott (1996) discussed the Morningstar analysis approach in the context of improvements made. The improvements are summarized as follow: (1) improved both types of one-page fund information summaries; (2) separated domestic and international equities in "star rating system"; (3) adopted category (style box) scheme for domestic equity funds; (4) added comparisons of fund loads and expenses to categories; (5) added details of total assets and load fees for each share class; (6) added portfolio performance measures relative to the market over the past three years; (7) listed fund supermarkets offering fund shares; and (8) added summary of research and commentary on equity, fixed income and international funds. Investors should review the variety and depth of information provided, for example, in tables 41–3.

To be well diversified domestically, investors should hold funds across all nine domestic equity fund Morningstar categories (figure 7.1). For global diversification, add the value/ growth and cap. size investment styles of the international stock category, securities, and those desired for the passive bond allocation. But do not overweight large-cap. funds. This is easy to do. Barbee (1999c) reported that large-cap. funds hold similar stocks because large-cap. stocks and large-blend stocks are only 6 percent and 1 percent, respectively, of all stocks. Also, do not hold shares in more than one fund managed by a single portfolio manager. Portfolio managers tend to have their own investment styles and strategies, which they apply generally.

MUTUAL FUND RISK

Risk and risk measures

Risk has traditionally been the stepchild of investment returns. But this changed when portfolio theory and statistical analysis provided the means to measure risk. Now both risk and return are considered in making investment decisions. One of the wonderful ironies of risk's traditional role is that it provides a more accurate indicator of future returns than do past returns. Risk is generally a more consistent investment attribute than returns. For example, Rekenthaler (1994c) analyzed equity fund risks and returns over a five-year period to determine whether risk or return is the best predictor of future returns over succeeding five-year periods. The results are clear: past returns do a very poor job of predicting future returns. The standard deviation of mean returns not only does a better job of predicting returns, but it is also a better predictor of risk. Risk, return, and risk/return measures for use in assessing fund performance have been further discussed previously.

Bogle (1999) added to the irony of the risk versus return story in no uncertain terms: "There is no way under the sun to forecast a fund's future absolute returns based on its past record." However, highly probable forecasts can be made for funds with unusually high expenses and superior past returns. The former will continue to underperform and the latter returns will likely regress towards, and usually below, mean market returns over time. Analysis of growth and growth and income funds with returns in the top quartile during the 1970s to 1980s and from 1987 to 1997 indicated that 99 percent of fund returns reverted to or below mean market returns.

However, past performance can provide useful information when based on comparisons with other mutual funds in the same category. Consistency of past relative returns is important because risk measures, notably the standard deviation, test the volatility of past returns. And if past risk is often a good guide to future performance, so must past relative returns.

Morningstar Risk

Morningstar Risk is geared to the notion that investors care about the risk of losing money. As described by Arnott (1998a), Morningstar Risk incorporates the frequency and amount by which fund returns did not exceed Treasury bill rates for each of four asset classes, including domestic equity funds. Morningstar Risk is a more consistent measure than standard deviation and beta because Treasury bills fluctuate less than market or fund returns. However, it does not allow comparisons between classes, such as stocks and bonds, and, like other risk measures, Morningstar Risk says nothing about future returns, portfolio manager changes, portfolio credit quality, and other descriptive attributes of funds and their portfolios.

Morningstar Bear Market Rank

Morningstar Bear Market Rank is another risk measure. As discussed in Barbee (1997b), bear market rank is a longer-term historical measure, one that changes only gradually. It is a convenient way to assess risks among funds as well as for particular funds over time. For stock funds, a bear market month is one in which the S&P 500 Index declined by more than 3 percent during the last five years. For bond funds, a bear market month is one in which the Lehman Brothers Aggregate Index lost more than 1 percent during the last five years. To compute the rank for particular funds, performance during each bear market month is totaled to obtain total bear market return. Funds are then placed in deciles based on their ranks. The best rank is 1 and the worst, 10. Again, this is a historical measure that says nothing about future returns and risks.

Increases in bear market rank act as a red light to determine why risk has increased. As discussed by Barbee (1997a), increases in bear market rank may reflect: (1) increases in portfolio P/Es ratios; (2) increases in industry sector concentration, such as technology; (3) increases in security concentration, such as more volatile stocks; (4) increases in portfolio turnover; (5) increases in beta (systematic risk) and/or standard deviation of mean returns (total risk); (6) changes in portfolio managers; and (7) portfolio style drift, among others.

Downside risk

Downside risk is a more recently developed risk measure that uses semi-variance rather than standard deviation of mean returns. Merriken (1994) described the semi-variance as appropriate because it focuses only on downside risk, that portion of variance that causes asset returns to fail to meet target returns. Investors are averse to any risks that may cause shortfalls in returns, and are less concerned with volatility that causes returns to vary above minimum acceptable rates. The implication is investor preference for skewed returns with higher probabilities of upside performance. This measure makes a great deal of intuitive sense and facilitates making downside risk/return tradeoffs.

Risk disclosure

Mutual fund risk measures are treated inadequately in shareholder communication, the latter discussed previously. Makoff (1995) noted the sad fact that the SEC has chosen not to require funds to provide the menu of risk measures that together allow investors to gauge fund risk along relevant dimensions. This failure is partly resolved here by the concept of constrained diversification and diversification risk, each of which focuses on a particular risk exposure, such as market liquidity.

Stevens and Lancellota (1995) discussed the mutual fund industry's view on appropriate risk disclosure, the approach adopted by the SEC. The industry stated that investors "must understand all dimensions of risk . . . and opposes any requirement that funds report a single, standardized, numerical risk measurement." But, instead of a cohesive mix and explanation of risk measures, the SEC requires only that equity funds provide one-year, five-year, and ten-year annualized returns plus "a bar graph reflecting the fund's total return over each of the past ten years . . ." For bond funds, this "improved" risk disclosure requires a bar graph of portfolio duration.

FUNDAMENTAL ANALYSIS: VALUE VERSUS GROWTH INVESTMENT STYLES

Value and growth are the two major variants of fundamental analysis, which is the primary method for identifying undervalued and overvalued securities. Technical analysis, the other major method, is discussed later for timing the implementation of buy/sell decisions. Willis (1999) reviewed the history of value investing along with criteria for identifying undervalued stock. Sorensen and Thum (1992) showed that the returns from value investing depend to a large extent on how it is applied, and include a glossary of related approaches. Sivy (1999) discussed tools of the trade for analyzing growth and value stocks, including a guide to basic terms. Wang (1997) discussed growth and value investing and criteria for identifying them. Asness et al. (1999) summarized the investment styles of leading funds.

Approaches to value investing

Hester (2000) reported five value investing measures called the "greatest investing strategies of all time." This "understatement" refers to *PEG ratios*, *price-to-sales* (P/S) *ratios*, P/C ratios, *earnings surprises*, and *stock repurchase plans* (buybacks). Peters (1993) compared the performance of portfolios with low PEG ratios to high PEG ratios for thirty quarters ending 1989. The PEG ratio is measured here by dividing the P/E ratio estimated using forecast earnings per share for the next twelve months by the expected growth rate of earnings per share for the next five years. A dollar invested in the low PEG ratio portfolio returned $15.36 and a dollar invested in the high PEG ratio portfolio returned $1.80. Here the PEG ratio is based on the fund portfolio's current P/E ratio and its last three years' earnings growth rate (for example, table 42a). Other studies have confirmed the value of the PEG ratio, including its use in small-cap. portfolios. Hester (1998) also discussed an improved PEG ratio that appears to perform better. This PEGY ratio adds the dividend yield to the expected earnings growth rate in the denominator.

On the other hand, O'Shaughnessy (1996) concluded that the P/S ratio is the best predictor of stock performance among the measures tested from 1951 to 1994. This is indirectly confirmed in Fisher (1984), where stock appreciation is described as usually requiring stocks to become more popular. This is easier if stocks start out being less popular. From 1979 to 1991, Barbee et al. (1996) reported that sales-to-price ratios and *debt-to-equity* (D/E) *ratios* explained larger proportions of stock returns than either book-to-price ratios or market capitalization. Further, sales to price ratios captured the roles of D/E ratios and provided the most consistent power to explain stock returns.

In addition, O'Shaughnessy (1996) calculated that holding the fifty stocks with the lowest P/S ratios turned $10,000 into $5.93 million, an annualized return of over 16 percent. This greatly outperformed portfolios holding stocks with the lowest P/E ratios ($1.23 million) and the lowest P/B ratio stocks ($3.59 million). The P/S ratio also outperformed in more short periods and with less risk. This performance was further enhanced when combined with momentum strategies.

O'Shaughnessy (1996) also reported P/C ratios to be good predictors of stock returns. This ratio is less subject to the vagaries of accounting that impact firm earnings per share. Lakonishok et al. (1994) observed that over the twenty-two-year period ending 1990, the 10 percent of stocks with the lowest P/C ratios had average five-year returns of over 20 percent, compared with over 9 percent for the 10 percent of stocks with highest P/C ratios. Low P/C ratio stocks also outperformed high P/C ratio stocks in eighteen of twenty three-year periods.

Positive earnings surprises are one of the technical indicators discussed later, its versions are noted below. Research has observed that stocks with reported earnings greater than expected earnings outperform benchmark indices. Hester (2000) also reported findings for the twenty years ending 1993. Three-month annualized returns of stocks with low P/E ratios and positive earnings surprises outperformed the benchmark index by 20 percent as contrasted with over 6 percent for stocks with high P/E ratios. Low P/E ratio stocks also have less downside risk.

Company stock repurchase plans have been observed as signaling that these stocks will outperform benchmark indices. Ikenberry et al. (1995) analyzed over 1,200 repurchase plans for the period 1980–90. Average returns of repurchased stocks over four-year holding periods were over 12 percent above the benchmark index. Coupled with low P/E ratios, the average returns of repurchased stocks over the same period were over 45 percent above the index. When firms think their shares are a good buy, investors should take heed.

The typical value criteria used by portfolio managers are illustrated by William Nasgovitz, Heartland Value fund manager. As reported in Barbee (1997c), the first four criteria are most important: (1) low P/E ratio relative to the market; (2) high cash flow, especially free cash flow net of uses; (3) low P/B ratio; (4) low long-term debt; (5) earnings momentum; (6) large insider investment; (7) management favors shareholders; (8) undervalued or hidden assets not on the balance sheet; (9) small investor interest; and (10) a catalyst that will cause value to be recognized.

For example, Tweedy Browne mutual fund investment advisors are value investors. They follow textbook value investing as defined by Benjamin Graham, the father of value investing. The Graham rules are summed up in Sivy (1995). Tweedy buys companies for less than net current asset value, diversifies the risk of bad stocks versus unloved stocks by investing broadly, and is very patient with turnover less than ten. It also look for insider purchases of stock. As reported in *Mutual Funds* (1999), Sir John Templeton's investing philosophy is to "buy at the point of maximum pessimism; buy value, not market trends or economic outlook; recognize the difficulty of outperforming the market; and an investor who has all the answers does not even understand the questions." Templeton is the father of international mutual fund investing.

As reviewed in Paluch (1997c), many mutual fund portfolio managers buy stocks others are buying because it is safer to be average than to fail trying to be excellent. And then there are the mavericks – portfolio managers without fear who buy the unloved and patiently wait to harvest returns. They favor small-cap. value stocks with the balance divided between small-cap. growth or blend stocks. These portfolio managers go their own way (no herding) and are patient in waiting for turnaround performance. They are willing to take the heat waiting for this to occur. Shareholders in these funds must also be patient, but, nonetheless, alert in change in portfolio managers. These original mutual funds are good diversifiers, with returns not highly correlated with those on benchmark indices. As a result, when original funds are bad, they are really bad.

Other variants of value investing

Some portfolio managers differentiate several other types of value investing. The first is earnings growth value investing, which seeks stocks with growth prospects undervalued by the market. This is very close to growth investing if companies with above-average earnings growth prospects are considered. Second is free cash flow investing, which seeks companies with excess cash flows that can be used for acquisitions, dividend increases or share repurchases. Third is comparative value investing, which seeks stocks selling below historical valuations or those of their peers. And fourth is net asset value investing, which seeks stocks selling for less than breakup values of net assets or spinoff values of subsidiaries or divisions. This approach is probably closest to what early value investors had in mind, especially as couched in terms of asset values relative to market values.

Fund families and investment style

Differences in investment style are also seen at the level of the mutual fund giants, Fidelity and Vanguard. However, they have become more alike in diverse offerings of managed and indexed funds. Nonetheless, Rekenthaler (1995) characterized Fidelity as "lavish, high flying and stock oriented" and Vanguard as "miserly, conservative, and bond oriented." This overstatement reflects the low-cost philosophy espoused by former Vanguard chairman, John C. Bogle. His legions of fans are known as Bogleheads. Both fund families strive to be best within the confines of their strategies. Fidelity is less high-flying than before and places more constraints on portfolio managers to invest consistently with fund investment objectives. Vanguard, on the other hand, has become king of low-cost index funds and developed more breadth in its managed equity fund offerings.

Value versus Growth checklist

Table 39 provides a checklist with definitions for value and growth measures and ratio definitions. Investors should complete the checklist to determine whether the results are consistent with the domestic equity fund categories and investment styles for other types of funds as reported in Morningstar, in this case for Windsor II (table 40). The required information may be reported in fund prospectuses, statements of additional information, newspaper and magazine interviews with portfolio managers, Morningstar, and other providers, including online, of fund information. In-depth interviews with portfolio managers, such as reported in *Barron's*, are particularly helpful for this purpose. As identified, Windsor II is a large-cap. fund that uses *bottom-up investing*, a value approach.

The checklist assists in delineating variants of investment style among mutual funds. For example, the Merger Fund values firms that are currently or likely to be engaged in merger talk, and then seeks arbitrage profits from the opportunities that develop. This *merger arbitrage* provides generally stable returns by taking long and short positions, respectively, in undervalued shares of firms to be acquired and overvalued shares of firms acquiring them.

The checklist also includes allowances for mutual funds like the Franklin Mutual Series funds, once the active domain of Michael Price. These funds focus on undervalued stocks, "asset plays," and bankruptcies. This combination is unusual, but has been very successful. The portfolio managers are bottom-up investors who seek stocks beaten down owing to earnings disappointments or adverse legal decisions, but which have specific situational catalysts for change. These catalysts include mergers, new CEOs, asset spinoffs, and stock repurchase plans. Bankruptcies and distressed securities often provide special situations because their values are not market-driven. They also look for companies with stock selling at deep discount to potential value if managed for the benefit of shareholders. In these cases, portfolio managers may work behind the scenes as major stockholders to "encourage" change. Or the fund may work publicly by nominating board members and leveraging this representation to encourage change. Because their holdings are not market but specific case driven, they tend to do relatively best in down and sideways markets.

The type of hardball activism used by Franklin Mutual Series funds is becoming more frequent. Funds are finding activism increasingly more profitable than simply giving up on particular undervalued stocks and liquidating large positions. Garrity (1999) identified five factors that contribute to increased fund activism. The first factor is size – mutual funds have assets of almost $7 trillion, which gives them plenty of financial leverage to press companies for changes designed to increase share prices. Second, funds have seen how activism can improve portfolio performance by forcing company management and boards of directors to act to increase stock prices and shareholder wealth.

A third reason is the increased prominence of socially responsible funds. These funds, discussed previously, invest only in companies that survive screens designed to weed out those with defined undesirable products and behaviors, such as cigarettes and Twinkies. However, Buss (1997) stated that their performance is relatively poor because they tend to shun large-cap. stocks (where the bad guys are located) and, therefore, overweight riskier small-cap. stocks. *Mutual Funds* (2000) reported a new socially responsible bond fund that refuses to invest in US Treasury bonds because of defense expenditures.

A fourth reason, related to the second, is that funds are increasingly holding more concentrated portfolios, with perhaps as few as twenty securities, and necessarily taking larger positions in each. As larger shareholders, funds have the need, as well as the leverage and potential, to encourage changes that will increase share prices. And, finally, there is the opportunity presented when company stock prices are less than acquisition values. This provides funds with an incentive to push for the sale of the companies to capture the larger acquisition value.

Black-box growth strategies

Black-box strategies represent the use of quantitative methods in growth investing. These methods are increasingly used by mutual funds to enhance investment style allocation, stock selection ability, and portfolio allocation. These strategies apply the computational capacity and speed of computers to bring new power to fundamental growth and technical methods of security analysis. They provide portfolio managers with near real-time information concerning the particular strategies or variables that best explain current fund performance and securities benefiting from these attributes.

Use of the term "black box" implies that users may not understand the models applied. Black-box strategies include portfolio insurance, genetic algorithms, artificial intelligence (expert systems), chaos theory, market risk neural models, symbolic reasoning, machine learning, complex systems theories, and more. The purpose here is not to discuss these various techniques, but to note that they are applied with varying degrees of effectiveness in practice. For example, Burton (1997) reviewed the failure of portfolio insurance during the October 1987 crash. Leinweber and Arnott (1995) reviewed genetic algorithms, Fried (1999) reviewed artificial intelligence, and Wong et al. (1992), Penn (1994b), and Starer and Balzer (1995) reviewed neural network applications. Brown et al. (1998) successfully applied artificial intelligence to Dow theory, a historically important method of technical analysis. Angel (1994) reviewed chaos theory and its implications for money management. On a larger scale, Coy and Woolley (1998) reviewed the disaster of a supposedly market-neutral hedge fund partnered by two Nobel laureates.

The approaches used by so-called *quant funds* may be described generally as real-time supplements to fund growth analysis. Ronald (1999c) categorized these funds as either pure quant funds or hybrid quant funds. Pure quant funds literally rely almost solely on computer models to select securities. Of course, the human decision process is normally programmed into the models. Hybrid quant funds also use computer models, but portfolio decisions incorporate both computer outputs and qualitative insights and judgment.

Barbee and Deshpande (1997) interviewed John Bogle, Jr., then with NI Growth fund, to get the "plain-English lowdown" on quantitative investing. Quantitative investing is, one, disciplined, not emotional; two, it provides market information more rapidly; and, three, you get more precise answers than with fundamental analysis. Some elements of fundamental analysis can be quantified, but not all. Bogle Jr. described the role of quantitative analysis in investment analysis as follows: "The market is a fire hose, constantly shooting information. The quicker you see, capture, analyze, and respond to that information, the better your investment results." The models run "[m]inute by minute." The quant model is supplemented by fundamental and risk analysis of value stocks.

Quant funds often use momentum strategies. Price and earnings momentum are often used because they have worked well in recent years. But there are several types of momentum strategies. *Earnings-estimate momentum* funds buy when analysts upgrade stock earnings estimates. *Earnings-momentum* funds buy when firms announce improved earnings, expected or not. *Price-momentum funds* buy when stock prices move upwards – classic momentum strategy. And *earnings-surprise momentum* funds buy when firms report earnings above expectations. Interestingly, most portfolio managers do not admit to using price momentum, but they do see others using it.

Ronald (1999c) also provided brief examples of approaches used by several quant funds. Most of these do not appear to be particularly high-tech, but Barr Rosenberg's Market Neutral fund is such a fund. The fund's market-neutral strategy (discussed below) balances holdings of undervalued stocks against short positions (short selling) in overvalued stocks. Fidelity TechnoQuant Growth (great name) applies technical analysis of historical price and trading volume data. The fund does not appear to use new analytical techniques but faster computers. Oppenheimer Main Street fund applies fundamental analysis plus macroeconomic trends to select stocks. Again, the fund does not appear to use new analytical techniques, but faster computers. BGHG Growth searches for stocks with rapidly accelerating earnings growth. Computer speed enables fast execution based on findings. SSGA Small Cap. fund relies on valuation and growth rate factors to select small-cap. stocks. Once more, computers provide more rapid execution.

Vanguard Growth and Income Fund uses technology to enhance returns on the S&P 500 Index by giving larger weights to undervalued stocks with higher growth rates. The fund is a high-test version of the Vanguard 500 Index with slightly more risk. As reported by Saler (1997), lead portfolio manager George Sauter "believes market inefficiencies are present, but the odds are against any person or computer consistently finding them. . . . We are doing everything we can to outperform, but there is a better-than-average chance we will be underperformers."

Market risk neutral strategy

The *market risk neutral strategy* implies the use of dream methodologies to limit portfolio volatility in good and bad markets. Regnier (1998) and Rowland (1998) reviewed the Barr-Rosenberg Market Neutral fund, which the former describes (tongue in cheek) as "Barr Rosenberg's science project." The fund invests in about 600 stocks identified as undervalued and sells short another 600 stocks determined to be overvalued. The proceeds of short selling are invested in ninety-day Treasury bills. The objective of this approach is to make money if the market declines or if it advances. To select stocks for this strategy, 15,000 stocks in 160 industry sectors are evaluated, using 200 different financial ratios. The goal is to earn about six percentage points above the ninety-day Treasury bill rate, which is the long-term average return on large-cap. stocks. The fund has done this while incurring only about 33 percent of the volatility of these stocks. The fund's 2.5 percent expense ratio is very high and provides a significant hurdle for performance.

It is too early to tell whether market neutral strategies will perform well for mutual funds over time. But Ronald (1998a) quoted Nobel laureate William Sharpe as stating that market neutral funds will "revolutionize the investment management industry." As noted, market neutral funds make money if the prices of stocks held increase more than the prices of stocks sold short increase and lose money. The fund also makes money if the prices of stocks sold short increase more than the prices of stocks decrease and lose money. The fund earns the ninety-day Treasury bill rate in either case. The versions of the basic strategy vary among the six market neutral funds, much as differences in fundamental analysis exist among funds.

However, the jury is still out on the proven performance of market neutral funds, especially with their low tax efficiency due to short-term capital gains and very high expense ratios. Moreover, this strategy does have risk. A skeptic of Rosenberg's strategy sums it up in Rowland (1998): "So he's going to beat the market not once but twice." Portfolios cannot be perfectly hedged, and large losses have occurred in hedged portfolios. These funds may also leverage their returns with borrowed money, which adds more portfolio volatility. Until they had been proven over time, Regnier (1998) advised fund investors "to stay neutral on market-neutral funds."

MORNINGSTAR MUTUAL FUND REPORTS

Tables 40–2 are reprinted or generated from Morningstar CD-ROM or binder products. The tables provide two convenient but distinct summary reports for Windsor II, its category, and the fund surrogate for the benchmark index. Tables 40a and 41a are reprinted from *Morningstar Principia Pro*, while table 42a was created using Morningstar (1998b) to generate an analogous peer category for Windsor II. Table 40a identifies Windsor II's category as large-cap. value, which describes its investment style. Note that, as a domestic equity fund, Windsor II's category was identified using the equity style box, rather than its category defined and its investment style identified by style boxes (as discussed above for other fund types). Tables 40b, 41b, and 42b are reprinted from *Morningstar Principia Pro's* "Morningstar Mutual Funds on Demand" file, originally published in *Morningstar Mutual Funds*, the original binder service (Morningstar, 1998a).

Morningstar reports are about as close as one can get to one-stop shopping. These reports and much more, including detailed fund data and fund and industry commentaries, are from *Morningstar Principia Pro for Mutual Funds*, a monthly/quarterly CD-ROM product, *Morningstar Mutual Funds*, a loose-leaf service, and *Morningstar FundInvestor*, a monthly publication. All are available by subscription, and the latter two are often available in public libraries. This type of information and much more are also available from Morningstar online at morningstar.net.

DIVERSIFICATION RISK: VALUE VERSUS GROWTH (TABLE 43)

The purpose of table 43 is to identify differences in the diversification risks of large-cap. value and large-cap. growth funds represented by Vanguard Value Index and Vanguard Growth Index, respectively. These two index funds are the value and growth components of the Vanguard 500 Index, a blended value/growth style fund representing the S&P 500 Index. The value fund is composed of some 150 S&P 500 Index stocks with small P/B ratios.

The value mutual fund most closely mimics the S&P/BARRA Value Index. The value fund has a much smaller median market cap. portfolio and percentage of giant/large-cap. stocks than the growth index. But it is a large-cap. fund, nonetheless. A smaller market cap. is expected because undervalued stocks more likely exist among smaller stocks often trading in less efficient markets. The growth fund includes some 350 S&P 500 Index stocks with high P/B ratios. The fund most closely mimics the S&P/BARRA Growth Index.

The table 43 diversification risk measures include eight investment style risk measures, cash asset allocation risk, market liquidity risk, returns distribution risk, industry sector concentration risk, and securities concentration risk. Relative to table 38, table 43 excludes Morningstar Category, method of security analysis, investment style, geographic concentration, asset allocation, and Value Line portfolio safety and timeliness.

Morningstar Category and investment styles are excluded because the analysis compares large-cap. value and large-cap. growth funds using eight measures of investment style. Geographic concentration and asset allocation are omitted because both funds are domestic stock portfolios. Methods of security analysis are also omitted because both funds are passively managed index funds. Value Line safety and timeliness are omitted because both funds are representative of the domestic large-cap. market. The table does not include Windsor II, its category peer group, and its benchmark index or surrogate, which are included and discussed beginning with table 44.

Value and growth indices

Kelley (1996b) compared the value and growth indices based on the behavior of value and growth funds. Value funds find opportunities to buy undervalued stocks in the cyclical nature of the market for selected industries. On the market down side, value funds buy bad news stocks at less than intrinsic value (fair market value). As the market improves, value investors harvest returns as stocks return to fair market value. Growth funds do not focus on cyclically undervalued stocks. They find opportunities to buy undervalued stocks given their expected earnings growth rates or related expectations. They harvest returns as the market recognizes these expectations and prices them at fair market value.

Granzin (1999b) noted that the Vanguard Growth Index Fund's performance has been very high. The fund is indexed to domestic large-cap. growth stocks, and its P/B ratio is about 50 percent higher than the Vanguard Index 500 Fund. It also carries a higher P/E ratio, higher P/C ratio, larger earnings growth rate, slightly higher beta, and larger standard deviation (total risk). The fund's market cap. size is about twice that of the Vanguard 500 Index. The portfolio is overweighted in three industry sectors: technology, health, and consumer staples.

Nonetheless, its three-year and five-year performance is consistent and near the very top of its category, reflecting rapid portfolio earnings growth, a beta only a touch higher than the S&P 500 Index, and low-risk.

Vanguard 500 Index performance epitomizes large-cap. growth funds in recent years, a time when value fund performance has lagged. Value funds have suffered net redemptions, and numerous portfolios have been liquidated or rolled over into other family funds. Historically, growth stocks or value stocks have higher performance for five or so years, and then the other takes its turn. The result? Over longer periods value and growth stock returns average about the same. For example, Bogle (1994) reported that from 1973 to 1992 growth funds and value funds had average annual returns of 10.1 percent and 11.0 percent, respectively.

John Neff on value investing

Nonetheless, memories appear short and some investors are concerned that value funds will never again have their day. Famed value investor and former mutual fund manager John Neff (1999) disagrees with this grim outlook for value investing:

> Low-P/E investing is not a casualty of the latest new era. Far from it. Stock market excesses invariably lead investors toward what is currently fashionable. Signaling the end of trends gone too far, inflection points mark broad shifts in investor sentiment from bullish to bearish. They hand low-P/E investors the chance to capture extraordinary gains, when worthy, out-of-favor stocks regain the market's attention.

Neff buys unloved stocks, but only if he has confidence in their earnings projections. This includes undervalued technology stocks that satisfy ruthless investment criteria.

Value plus growth investing

In reality, many mutual fund managers use both value and growth styles, thus the Morningstar blend investment style. Kelley (1996b) determined that combining value and growth funds may create substantial portfolio style overlap (discussed above) because growth funds tend towards sector concentration.

To examine this issue, funds were grouped as value or growth based on their P/B ratios, the single most commonly used measure of value (smaller ratios) versus growth (larger ratios) investing. Style overlap was seen in comparisons of the particular industry sectors favored by value and growth funds and by value and growth indices. *Value* funds invest smaller portfolio proportions in utilities, energy, financials, and consumer durables than do value indices. Industrial cyclicals are the only exception. These are typical value sectors. Value funds invest larger proportions in consumer staples, services, retail, health, and technology than do value indices. These are typical growth sectors. Thus value portfolio managers do not avoid more aggressive, undervalued growth sectors.

On the other hand, *growth* funds invest smaller proportions of their portfolios in consumer staples and health than do growth indices. But growth funds invest larger proportions in services, retail, and technology than do growth indices. These are typical growth sectors. Growth funds invest larger proportions in energy, financials, and consumer durables than do value funds. But growth funds invest smaller proportions in utilities and industrial cyclicals than do growth indices. These are typical value sectors. Thus value and growth style managers are not limited to particular traditional industry sectors, but value fund managers more so than growth funds.

In summary, the value indices invest 80 percent of assets in traditional value industry sectors, while value funds invest only 60 percent of assets in these sectors. The other 40 percent are concentrated in traditional growth industry sectors, such as technology, services, and health. Further, value funds invest only about 50 percent as much as the value index in energy and utilities, but almost three times as much in health and technology.

Bogle on style overlap

This style overlap in industry sectors is also seen in the stocks held. John C. Bogle (1994) noted a great deal of overlap in the top ten stocks held by both value and growth funds. Phillip Morris is the largest mutual fund holding in both value and growth funds. FNMA and Merck are the second and third largest fund holdings. They rank from second to fifth among both value and growth funds. The next six largest fund holdings include PepsiCo, Pfizer, American International Group, Royal Dutch, General Electric, and Bristol-Myers Squibb. They rank from second to twentieth among both value and growth funds. Thus some stocks are seen as undervalued by both value and growth funds, but probably for different reasons. Nonetheless, it has been shown that portfolio managers herd their holdings to feel comfort in numbers if performance lags. To the extent that this is so, investors should consider index funds to get average performance with lower expenses, lower trading costs, and higher tax efficiency than with managed portfolios.

Assessing diversification constraints and risk

Analysis of table 44 finds that large-cap. value mutual funds have less diversification risk than large-cap. growth funds. This is to be expected. Large-cap. value funds have less investment style risk as measured by seven of eight risk measures, and less return diversification risk, industry sector concentration risk, and security concentration risk. Large-cap. value funds are more risky along several dimensions: a tad smaller correlation of portfolio returns with their benchmark index (more unsystematic risk) and higher prices paid for stocks per unit of historical three-year earnings growth rates. Large-cap. value fund investing also has more liquidity risk, with respect to the proportion of giant/large-cap. size stocks and median market cap. size.

More specifically, table 44 indicates the Vanguard Value Index fund is less risky than the Vanguard Growth Index fund with respect to all measures except R^2, PEG ratio, median market cap., and percentage of giant/large-cap. size. These and the other measures are defined in the table. Discussion of modern portfolio measures and Morningstar Risk measures is also provided in Meyer (1993) and Paluch (1995). These measures include Morningstar Risk, beta, R^2, and standard deviation. That the combined use of these measures is more useful than single measures in assessing fund risk is not their only advantage.

The value fund's larger R^2 reveals slightly more unique risk, which is measured by $1 - R^2$. In this case, the value fund has only 5 $(1 - 0.95)$ percent unique risk and the growth fund only 4 percent $(1 - 0.96)$, each measured relative to the market's defined R^2 of 100 percent. Unique risk is thus computed by deduction, and represents the proportion of variability in portfolio returns not explained by the market. But note that the value fund's standard deviation of mean returns (total risk) is smaller than the growth fund. This difference in unique risk would probably be larger if the value index included smaller-cap. stocks.

R^2 and beta: a note

Regnier (1997d, f) discussed the application of R^2 and beta in the context of mutual funds. R^2 is a measure of fund risk relative to market risk and is useful in identifying whether combining several funds will reduce overall risk. For example, assume one fund has an R^2 less than 70 percent and another an R^2 of 90 percent, both measured with respect to the S&P 500 Index. Of the two funds, only the former fund will reduce diversification risk if added to a holding of an S&P 500 Index fund. The beta statistic measures the slope of the linear relationship between fund and market returns, so-called systematic risk. That is, there is a relationship between a fund's R^2 and its beta. The simple rule is that if R^2 is less than 70 percent, beta is a less reliable measure of the sensitivity of fund returns.

Consistent with this discussion, Rekenthaler (1994b) discussed the use of R^2s to identify similarly diversified mutual funds. The more alike fund R^2s, the more similarly diversified they are. Barbee (1998b) investigated the actual size and similarity of R^2s among Morningstar fund categories. The analysis was based on the correlation of category returns for three-year and five-year periods. The largest category correlation coefficients are 93 for large-cap. value and large-cap. growth funds, 93 for small-cap. value and small-cap. growth funds, 88 for large-cap. value and small-cap. value funds, and 85 for large-cap. growth and small-cap. growth funds. The smallest category correlations are 79 for large-cap. value and small-cap. growth funds and 83 for large-cap. growth and small-cap. value funds. Thus the largest reduction in two-asset portfolio risk requires equal amounts of average large-cap. value funds and small-cap. growth funds.

A large R^2 is therefore desirable in the overall context of portfolio diversification as a means of minimizing portfolio unsystematic risk, leaving mostly undiversifiable market risk. This is not to say, however, that some mutual fund managers do not purposely take on large amounts of unique risk rather than being clones of market indices. Small R^2s are therefore characteristic of these funds, often value funds with idiosyncratic investment styles. For example, the Franklin Mutual Series funds depend on their ability to select "turnaround stocks," often financially distressed, rather than acting like "closet clones" of market indices. Such funds implicitly assume they can produce returns commensurate with their brand of portfolio risk.

Table 43

As seen in table 43, the value mutual fund's PEG ratio is 1.02 times the market's ratio, and the growth fund's ratio is 0.97 that of the market. The ratio is computed by dividing Morningstar's

P/E ratio by the portfolio's three-year annual earnings growth rate. Past growth rates are used for convenience rather than expected growth rates, but used together they could reflect to what extent expectations differ from recent actual rates. These ratios indicate that the value fund pays a bit more per unit of three-year earnings growth rates than the growth fund. This is not expected unless one considers how value funds work, and perhaps not even then. Peters (1993) sorted stocks by their PEG ratios and discovered that stocks with low ratios greatly outperformed those with high ratios.

PEG and P/E ratios

In general, to the extent that current P/E ratios correctly represent future earnings growth, PEG ratios using then current growth rates can appear quite high and risky. Value funds favor companies that they believe undervalued based on market expectations of earnings growth. If fund earnings expectations disappoint when realized, then too high a price will have been paid. This is the downside loss potential inherent in current high PEG ratios. Value funds also favor stocks that have beaten down prices for reasons that have nothing to do with company financial fundamentals. This strategy works *if* later confirmed correct by higher market prices, especially if accompanied by earnings growth. The general caveat in high current PEG ratios is the potential downside risk if realized future earnings or market valuations are disappointing.

As suggested, P/E ratios must be placed in perspective. Stocks with high earnings growth rates normally have high P/E ratios, but cyclical stocks sometimes provide an exception. During a recession, the P/E ratios of depressed cyclical stocks are often extraordinarily large. The reason is that the traditional P/E ratio is computed using the last twelve months' earnings per share, while the market is looking ahead to improved post-recession earnings. Thus P/E ratios must be used and interpreted with care along with other measures. For example, above-average P/E ratios, earnings growth rates, and P/B ratios suggest growth strategies. But a value strategy may be reflected in recession high P/E ratios accompanied by below-average earnings growth rates and P/B ratios.

Versions of P/E ratios

Another caution with the use of P/E ratios is that there are different versions of this measure. The trailing P/E ratio is computed by dividing a stock's current price by the sum of reported earnings per share for the four most recent quarters. This is the traditional definition. The current P/E ratio divides the price by the sum of the most recent two quarters and forecast (see *Value Line Investment Survey*) of the next two quarters' earnings per share. The third definition is the projected P/E ratio that divides the price by the sum of forecast earnings per share for the next four quarters (see *Value Line Investment Survey*). The fourth definition is the market P/E ratio of the average stocks in a stock index, such as the S&P 500 Index, using either the trailing or the projected P/E ratio versions (see *Barron's*). The fifth definition is the industry P/E ratio of the particular stock being analyzed, and using the same definitions for both. The last definition is the historical P/E ratio that applies the annual trailing P/E ratio version for each of several past years and averages them.

DIVERSIFICATION CONSTRAINTS AND RISK DATA: VANGUARD WINDSOR II, CATEGORY PEERS, AND MARKET INDEX

As discussed, tables 40–2 provide information for analyzing specific and overall mutual fund degrees of diversification and risk for Windsor II's diversification constraints relative to its peer group category and the widely used S&P 500 Index. The Vanguard 500 Index Fund is the surrogate for the benchmark index in those cases where it provides more readily available data.

Table 41 represents the S&P 500 Index through its convenient surrogate, the Vanguard 500 Index Fund. The S&P 500 is a market-cap weighted index of approximately 75 percent of the value of the domestic market, and over 70 percent of all money invested in index funds. This index is most often used for benchmarking market performance, but its large-cap. focus is far from a comprehensive index of the domestic stock market.

As explained by Fisher (2000), the largest thirty stocks in the S&P 500 Index then represented nearly 60 percent of its total value, and the other approximately 470 stocks represented the balance. If the largest (smallest) 100 stocks disappeared from the index, it would decline by 75.3 (1.5) percent, respectively. This is indeed the index of giant/large-cap. stocks, but its performance is driven more by its thirty largest stocks than is widely known. Whether or not actively managed funds outperform the index is primarily determined by whether large-cap. or small-cap. stocks are performing best. During the last fifteen years, large-cap. stocks outperformed small-cap. stocks and the index correspondingly outperformed actively managed funds. It has been observed that when the S&P 500 Index outperforms the small-cap. Russell 2000 index by seventy or more basis points, it also outperforms actively managed funds, and conversely.

DIVERSIFICATION RISK: VALUE/GROWTH INVESTMENT STYLE (TABLE 44)

Stress testing funds

As reported in Middleton (1997), diversification constraints and risk provide a systematic way to stress-test mutual funds. For example, how well will a fund perform if interest rates increase? Is the portfolio overbalanced in interest rate sensitive securities? Look at industry sector concentration and securities concentration. How well prepared is the fund if a problem comes? Look at its cash ratio, net cash inflow, stock/bond allocation, and income/capital gains distribution. Has the portfolio been reviewed? Look at its market liquidity and portfolio safety and timeliness. How volatile is the fund? Look at its price-to-earnings ratio, portfolio earnings growth rate, beta, R^2, and standard deviation. How well has the fund figured out what to do in the past? Look at its Jensen alpha and other risk/return performance measures, including the Treynor Index and Sharpe Index (discussed later). Does the portfolio manager know what's going on? Look at education, experience, and tenure as portfolio manager. These measures provide many useful ways to determine fund health.

Diversification concepts discussed and applied to Windsor II in table 38 are now measured and judged as excellent, acceptable, or unacceptable. The analysis uses empirical data to identify differences in degrees of diversification and risk for Windsor II, its category peer group, and the benchmark index or its surrogate. Table 44 identifies whether Windsor II's *actual* value/growth investment style is appropriate for its Morningstar large-cap. value category in table 40a. The comparison of Windsor II with its category is always most important because it represents Windsor II's peer group. Both the S&P 500 Index and Windsor II are large-cap. portfolios.

The S&P 500 Index is the most widely used and available benchmark, even though it may not be the most accurate benchmark index for investment styles of particular funds. The Vanguard 500 Index Fund is often the surrogate for the S&P 500 Index because of the ready availability of information, such as table 41. As discussed by Barbee (2000), the Vanguard 500 Index fund has provided ten-year average annualized returns in excess of 17 percent, which places the fund in the seventh percentile (first is best) of its category. The fund was launched in 1976, but did not take off until after the October 1987 market panic and sell-off. The fund benefited from the outperformance of large-cap. stocks that became even more dominant during the 1990s.

This performance has attracted assets in excess of $90 billion. The fund has a super-low expense ratio of 0.18 percent – 85 percent lower than the average equity fund. The fund's portfolio turnover has never exceeded 10 percent. This success story has led to numerous competing index funds and funds benchmarked to other market indices. However, the fund's performance is a function of large-cap. domination of small-cap. stocks, and nothing is forever.

The measures in tables 44–51 identify whether Windsor II's individual diversification constraints are more, equally, or less risky than its category, especially, and the market. These overall results are also judged as excellent, acceptable, or unacceptable and are summarized in table 52. Several constraints in table 38 are excluded from subsequent analysis and discussion because the focus is less conceptual and applied only to Windsor II, its peer group category, and benchmark index. Windsor II has a large-cap. value Morningstar Category and investment style, active portfolio management, domestic portfolio, stock asset allocation, domestic geographic concentration, and stock asset allocation. Windsor II's constraints also reflect its comparison with its large-cap. value category. Thus the parameters of this analysis and discussion are more constrained than if the focus was on a fund relative to attainable global diversification (tables 6 and 38).

The investment style risk measures in table 44 include those most often used to differentiate value/growth investing: P/E ratio, P/B ratio, and, more recently, the P/C ratio. As reviewed in Ronald (1998c), the P/C ratio is increasingly preferred over the P/E ratio because it is less subject to the vagaries of accounting and measures that essential ingredient, net cash inflow. Lakonishok et al. (1994) sorted stocks by their P/C ratios and observed large differences in returns. The return differences are somewhat larger than those observed by sorting stocks by B/P (the reverse of P/B). The price-to-book ratio is a major factor differentiating fund returns.

The related risk measures include three-year earnings growth rate, R^2, beta, standard deviation of mean returns, and computed PEG ratio. Less risk and more risk identifies for each measure whether Windsor II has more or less relative risk than its category and the market. For example, smaller P/E, P/B, P/C, and PEG ratios indicate that funds are paying less per unit of earnings, book value, cash flow, and earnings growth rate, respectively. Thus less risk is illustrated in each case.

Risk measures again

As discussed above, a large R^2 indicates that variability in fund returns is explained more by market than by unique factors – less unsystematic risk. Conversely, a large $(1 - R^2)$ indicates that variability of returns is significantly explained by unique, non-market factors. A large beta indicates more sensitivity to given changes in market prices – more systematic risk. A large standard deviation of mean returns indicates more total return volatility – more total risk. The importance given to risk assessment should also reflect that risk measures are better predictors of future returns than past returns. Risk profiles, individual and composite, appear quite stable over time.

The performance implications of PEG ratios are reported in Fitch (1997). Each PEG ratio was computed by dividing the stock's P/E ratio by forecasts of five-year earnings growth rates. The P/E ratio was computed using forecast earnings per share for the next twelve months. PEG ratios of over 5,000 mid-cap. stocks going back to 1982 were analyzed. Stocks with PEG ratios less than 0.75 had annual returns over 19 percent, those with PEG rations between 1.0 and 1.25 had annual returns over 16 percent, and those with PEG ratios over 2.0 had annual returns of nearly 11 percent. The conclusion is that stocks with PEG ratios less than 1.0 are undervalued, those with PEG ratios between 1.0 and 1.25 are fairly priced, and those with PEG ratios over 1.25 are overvalued.

R^2 may also be used to determine how closely mutual fund families correlate their funds with investment objectives. Rekenthaler (1996a) examined the twenty largest fund families. Putnam has the highest R^2 at 88.5 percent and Merrill Lynch has the smallest at 72.8 percent. It was also determined that R^2s are most consistent for equity-income, aggressive growth, and growth and income funds, with R^2s generally over 70 percent. The growth and small company investment objectives are much more diverse. Only a weak correlation exists between fund family R^2s and performance.

Dziubinski and Ronald (1997) examined various risk measures to determine which work best to anticipate the size of losses in market downturns. Beta is the least reliable, followed by the P/E ratio. Price/earnings ratios may be inflated by small earnings, especially in concentrated portfolios. The most reliable measures are Morningstar Risk and standard deviation of mean returns. Based on the data, the following guidelines appear warranted: (1) limit the standard deviation to 10–15 percent (aggressive funds), (2) limit Morningstar Risk to 1.0–1.3 (aggressive funds), and limit concentration in any single sector to 25 percent.

Table 44

Table 44 (and tables 45–51) also identifies those risk differences that reveal significantly more/less mutual fund risk. Significantly more risk is determined if, as the case may be, the fund's measure is 10 percent or more larger/smaller than its category or the market index, as appropriate. Experience has shown the 10 percent rule to be effective in judging whether differences are significant or not. Of course, more sophisticated methods could be used, but this simple rule appears to work quite well. It is applied here and in the relevant tables that follow.

Value/growth investment style

Based on the 10 percent rule, table 44 indicates that Windsor II's investment style and related measures are either less risky or significantly less risky than its *category* except for its standard deviation, beta, and PEG ratio. Windsor II's beta is 1.01 times its category and is slightly more risky. Its standard deviation is 1.02 times its category and is also slightly more risky. However, the PEG ratio is 1.63 times its category and is significantly more risky. Windsor II's PEG ratio indicates that it is paying much more for each unit of earnings growth.

Moreover, Windsor II's investment style and related measures are significantly less risky than the *market* for all measures except R^2 and PEG ratio. Again, the 10 percent rule is applied. Its R^2 is 0.97 that of the market. It is expected to be smaller, and it is, but the difference is not significant. Its PEG ratio is 1.38 times the market ratio, and this difference is significant.

Thus table 44 indicates that Windsor II's value investment style and related risks are excellent (generally less risk) relative both to its category and to the market index or its surrogate. The category comparison is more relevant because it represents the peer group, which is not the case here for the market index. Based on these consistent findings, Windsor II's *overall* investment style risk is also excellent (generally less risk). The large PEG ratio is the only worrisome finding.

DIVERSIFICATION RISK: CASH ASSET ALLOCATION (TABLE 45)

Cash asset allocation represents the ratio of cash assets relative to total assets (cash ratio). Cash assets include bank operating balances and interest-bearing money market securities, such as US Treasury bills, marketable certificates of deposit, bankers' acceptances and repurchase agreements. Cash assets are defined as having sufficiently high credit quality and short maturity that they bear little default and interest rate risk. However, it is usually assumed that the larger a mutual fund's relative allocation to cash assets, the smaller its risk and return.

Mutual funds use cash assets for several purposes. First, there are checkbook balances required for operating purposes, such as paying expenses. Second, there may be additional cash balances reflecting market timing decisions made in anticipation of decreases/increases in stock prices. Interestingly, mean mutual fund cash ratios that lie outside normal bounds are considered *contrarian indicators* if accompanied by either very high or very low market expectations.

Schaeffer (1999) determined that contrarian investing is not the same as value investing. Value investors buy stocks that are fundamentally cheap and sell those that are fully priced. Contrarians buy stocks when market expectations are unreasonably low and sell them when they are unreasonably high. An extreme example of the latter has been seen in stock valuations that imply very high rates of earnings growth *forever*, hence the phrase "Priced for perfection."

Mean mutual fund cash ratios that are atypically outside historical normal ranges are considered bullish/bearish market indicators, respectively. This behavior is based on the observation that fund portfolio managers (and others for that matter) are wrong when their market outlook is excessively exuberant or pessimistic. Under these extreme conditions, the signal is that the market is likely to go the opposite direction from that implied by the atypically sized mean fund cash ratio. The fact that fund cash balances at historical extremes are considered contrarian signals speaks loudly to how well fund portfolio managers are doing as market timers. In a way, this is truly one of the great ironies of one of the major stated advantages of mutual funds – professional portfolio managers.

The third use of cash assets is to anticipate shareholder timing decisions, which include net cash inflows from share purchases, redemptions, and exchanges to other family funds. For example, funds often increase cash to meet shareholder redemptions based on the latter's expectation of market declines. This anticipation of shareholder behavior can make funds into market timers for reasons divorced from their portfolio approach or desires.

Cash balance issues

The issue of mutual fund cash balances for other than operating purposes runs counter to the passive asset allocation strategy described and advocated previously. The cash bucket provides needed cash, and for funds to hold what in effect is redundant cash is to unbalance the desired asset allocation and reduce portfolio returns. Further, Alexanian (1993) calculated that fully invested mutual funds outperform partially invested portfolios by 0.3 percent annually. Penn (1994a) observed that funds with typically large cash positions do not perform well long-term. Worse, large cash balances can even fail to protect fund assets during market declines.

Mutual funds that hold extra cash balances are explicitly or implicitly timing the market. The point is that cash beyond operating needs is inconsistent with passive asset allocation. Investors using chapter 6 asset allocation provide for cash needs in the cash bucket. Additional cash held by funds is redundant and reduces portfolio returns over time. Quinson (1998) summed up one aspect of the cash problem in the statement that cash doesn't rally in a bull market.

However, Kelley (1995b) determined that the mutual funds that performed best over the then last three and five-year periods were not those with the smallest ranges of cash flows. The funds that performed worst had wide ranges of cash balances, and those that performed best had moderate ranges. Funds with cash ratios ranging from 15 percent to 35 percent performed better than those with ratios ranging from 0 percent to 5 percent and over 50 percent. The best cash ranges for performance do not carry over to risk, however. Fully invested funds have less risk. Overall, flexible cash strategies work better than doctrinaire approaches to market timing.

Table 45

Table 45 identifies differences in cash asset allocation for Windsor II and its peer group, as measured by their cash ratios. The more balanced the proportions of cash and other non-cash securities, the larger the degree of diversification and the less the cash asset allocation risk. The S&P 500 Index or its surrogate Vanguard 500 Index is excluded because it is a market benchmark, not an actual portfolio. The Vanguard 500 Index is passively managed to simulate the actual index and, accordingly, holds only very small operating cash balances. Its portfolio is managed only to mimic the effective portfolio composition and performance of the S&P 500 Index.

The latest year and mean cash ratios for the last five years are provided for Windsor II and its peer group. However, in this case the cash ratios are from CDA/Wiesenberger's *Mutual Fund Directory* (1994–8) growth and income investment objective. They are surrogates for Morningstar's less readily available time series data for its large-cap. value category.

As indicated in table 45, Windsor II's 1998 cash asset allocation as measured by its cash ratio is much smaller than its category: 1.7 percent versus 5.9 percent. This difference represents a smaller degree of diversification (less liquidity) with significantly more cash asset allocation risk. Note, however, this risk discussion is exclusive of the issue discussed above concerning the redundancy of cash assets beyond what is needed for operating purposes. However, Windsor II's five-year mean cash ratio is only slightly smaller than its category: 6.5 percent versus 6.9 percent. It represents a slightly smaller degree of diversification with a bit more cash asset allocation risk. This small difference is insignificant.

But, as noted above, Windsor II's policy is to hold about 5 percent in cash assets. Thus its current cash ratio has a larger degree of diversification and less cash asset risk than its stated policy. Taking both the current and five-year mean ratios into consideration, but especially the former, Windsor II's overall cash asset allocation risk is unacceptable. This finding is summarized in table 52. However, only the current cash ratio is more risky, which suggests this may be a temporary situation. But, if Windsor II reverts to its stated policy of 5 percent cash assets, it will continue to have unacceptable cash asset allocation risk.

Net cash inflow

Net cash inflow (NCI) is a basic determinant of cash asset allocation. These data are aggregated in ICI (1998). For an individual fund, they represent the *net* cash inflow from the sale of new shares less outflow from share redemptions and exchanges to other mutual funds. The net cash inflow may, of course, be negative. An ample net cash inflow has several advantages. First, it allows a portfolio manager to take advantage of new investment opportunities without having to sell securities from the current portfolio. This saves management time, expenses, and trading costs. Second, it enables funds to pay shareholder redemptions without having to sell securities. Again, this saves time, expenses, and trading costs. And, third, its allows a portfolio manager to increase cash assets without having to sell securities.

However, the positive effect of cash inflows on mutual fund asset size can also cause problems. As assets grow, mutual funds find it more difficult to invest in small-cap. stocks. There may be too much cash to satisfy diversification requirements and investment criteria, either by purchasing additional stocks or additional shares of stocks currently held. As a result, portfolio managers are forced to buy larger-cap. stocks, which limits further implementation of their small-cap. investment style. The more unique the style, the less likely it can be successfully applied as assets grow beyond their optimal size. Not surprisingly, the level of mutual fund performance is generally unsustainable beyond some level of assets under management.

The larger issue then becomes why do mutual fund managers allow assets to grow beyond optimal levels? The answer reveals a basic conflict of interest between fund managers and shareholders. Zweig (1996) described this conflict answer quite graphically: You make the most money when the fund reaches its optimum size and sticks to it. But the fund manger makes money by collecting fees; the larger a fund gets, the more fees it pays the manager – regardless of how well it does for you. This issue of fund performance and asset size is also discussed later.

Net cash inflow: computation example

In the absence of specific information identifying a mutual fund's net cash inflow (NCI), the following equations, first in general form and then in specific form, may be used:

$$NCI_{n+1} = (TNA_{n+1} - TNA_n) - CG_{n+1}$$

$$CG_{n+1} = (NAV_{n+1} - NAV_n)(NSO_n)$$

or

$$CG_{n+1} = (TNA_{n+1} - TNA_n)(TNA_n/NAV_n)$$

where NCI_{n+1} = net cash inflow, year $n+1$; TNA_{n+1} = total net assets, year $n+1$; TNA_n = total net assets, year n; CG_{n+1} = unrealized capital gains, year $n+1$; NAV_{n+1} = net asset value per share, year $n+1$; NAV_n = net asset value per share, year n; NSO_n = net shares outstanding, year n.

For example, Windsor II's net cash inflow for 1998 (October 31) follows:

$$NCI98 = (TNA98 - TNA97) - CG98$$

$$CG98 = (TNA98 - TNA97)(TNA97/NAV97)$$

$$NCI98 = (\$29,639,000,000 - \$22,568,000,000) - (\$22,568,000,000/\$29.36)$$

$$= \$7,071,000,000 - \$768,664,850$$

$$= \$6,302,335,150$$

The alternative CGn+1 equations used are italicized because the data are directly available in Windsor II's annual report (1998). However, the first equation would be more accurate, because the number of shares outstanding is not rounded. Use of the first capital gains (CG) equation in this particular case requires subtracting the 1998 net *increase* in shares outstanding from 1998 net shares outstanding to arrive at 1997 net shares outstanding.

Next, to gain a relative measure of the size of NCI98, it may be divided by TNA97:

$$\text{Increase in NCI98 (\%)} = NCI98/TNA97$$

$$= \$6,302,333,150/\$22,568,000,000$$

$$= 27.9\%$$

As seen in table 42b, the category's NCI98 is 5.7 percent. Thus Windsor II's has a very ample NCI98 relative to its category. Ideally, the NCI should be calculated for each of the last five years to determine its normal size and variability (standard deviation). As reported in table 45, Windsor II's overall net cash inflow appears excellent. This finding is summarized in table 52. It should be noted that net cash inflows for individual funds may be purchased on a weekly basis from AMG and monthly from FRC and Strategic Insight.

The amount and consistency of net cash inflows are an important determinant of mutual fund returns. The good news is that Lallos (1997b) observed a constant base of mutual fund assets. For domestic equity funds, total monthly cash flow amount to less than 1 percent of assets. However, individual funds and categories of funds may not assume that ample net cash inflows are automatic and may be simply extrapolated into the future. Experience indicates these net cash inflows are quite variable (positive and negative), both absolutely and relatively, and both intra-year and inter-year. For example, Vanguard 500 Index Fund's net cash inflow ranged from a low of $370 million in 1990 to $1.1 million in 1994. It was highest in 1991 when it reached $2.2 billion. Vanguard 500's net cash inflow was also inconsistent relative to two comparable funds.

Net cash inflow: issues

As noted, it may not be assumed that individual and aggregate mutual fund NCIs are automatic. There are several reasons for this, but a few examples are illustrative. On a macro level, NCIs vary with the degree of investor optimism/pessimism concerning short-term, especially, and long-term economic and market outlooks. In the short term, cash generally flows to "hot funds of the month", and conversely for those that are cold. This is especially so for particular fund categories and sector funds that invest in single industries, such as electronics, which are alternately hot or cold. Net cash inflow also follows star portfolio managers for as long as they are so perceived by their followers, and these perceptions appear to allow for a bad year every now and then. But, as discussed above, too much NCI can increase fund asset size to the point where portfolio managers are less able to apply their investment style effectively.

But it is market timers that cause the largest problems for fund managers and investors practising long-term strategies. Carlson (1999) reported that 80 percent of trading costs are caused by less than 20 percent of fund shareholders. In addition to larger trading costs, market timer activity increases fund management expenses, generates additional taxable capital gains distributions for core shareholders, reduces potential returns from forced sales of securities, and, by increasing cash ratios, acts as a cash drag on fund returns, which is especially large in rising markets.

Underlying some of this activity is that investors are redeeming and purchasing mutual fund shares at increasing rates. Investor holding periods are becoming shorter, which is also symptomatic of long-running bull markets. *Mutual Funds* (1999) reported investors reacting to rather than anticipating market moves. They invest more as the market climbs and peaks, and redeem more as the market retreats. This suggests that investors are nervous about the level of market valuations and are moving in and out in efforts to squeeze a bit more from an aging bull, without being the last person to own it. This will likely prove the worst kind of market timing.

Lallos (1997b) determined that, over the last three years, net cash inflows of no-load funds are 40 percent more volatile than those of load funds, which are apparently buffered by sales intermediaries. But both types have large cash outflows during market downturns. Even as cash flowed into mutual funds, the percentage of domestic stock funds with net cash outflows ranged from 30 percent to 50 percent in any given month. The figures are also large for bond funds (55–67 percent) and international funds (40 percent).

Moreover, the returns generated by active investor trading of mutual funds are smaller than if investors had used dollar averaging – invested a consistent sum each month. The differences in performance varied by fund category. From best to worst performance they are mid-cap. value, small-cap. value, large-cap. value, mid-cap. blend, large-cap. blend, large-cap. growth, mid-cap. growth, small-cap. blend, and small-cap. growth. The performance is thus worst in small-cap. and growth funds, especially small-cap. growth.

To counter the frequent trading activity of market timers, Carlson (1999) reported more than 300 funds now impose redemption fees to discourage this activity, which is up almost 50 percent since 1997. These fees generally range from 1 percent to 2 percent on shares held less than ninety or 180 days. Moreover, fund supermarket Charles Schwab & Co. extended its 0.75 percent redemption fee from ninety to 180 days. More funds are also limiting the number of redemptions allowed in a given time period, say, eight a year.

DIVERSIFICATION RISK: MARKET LIQUIDITY (TABLE 46)

As reviewed in ICI (1997), the issue of market liquidity is important because mutual funds provide shareholders with instant liquidity by continuously standing ready to redeem shares upon demand. To be able to do this, funds must have portfolios that are sufficiently liquid and/or bank or other lines of credit. Funds value their portfolios daily, using market value and fair value rules, as appropriate. Fair value is used where there are no "readily available market quotations" to determine what a seller "might reasonably expect to receive" upon current sale. The process of valuing fund portfolios has become more complex as the diversity of types of securities held has increased, some of which are illiquid or have limited liquidity.

An asset is considered *liquid* (marketable) if it can be traded quickly with the relative certainty of no more than a small price change, assuming no new and relevant market information. This "price continuity" of liquid markets requires both market "depth" and "breadth," which refers, respectively, to a large *number* of buy/sell orders representing a large *volume* of shares at prices just above and below the current market price.

Illiquid securities

The SEC defines illiquid securities as those that may not be sold in the "ordinary course of business within seven days" at approximately their portfolio value. Mutual fund holdings of illiquid securities are limited to 15 percent (10 percent for money market funds). This limitation reflects concern that funds (1) maintain sufficient portfolio liquidity to meet redemption requests, (2) maintain sufficient management flexibility in choice of securities to sell in meeting redemptions, and (3) contain the valuation problems inherent with significant holdings of illiquid securities. Fund directors have ultimate responsibility for determining asset liquidity, but day-to-day responsibility rests with the investment advisor following written guidelines.

In general, securities are considered "liquid" unless presumed "illiquid" by SEC regulations or by fund policy following regulatory guidelines. Illiquid securities include restricted securities, repurchase agreements with maturities over seven days, certain municipal lease obligations, and collateralized mortgage obligations (CMOs). The legal classification of restricted securities includes private placements (mostly fixed-income securities) and so-called Rule 144(a) unregistered securities, so identified in shareholder reports. Restricted securities include those with liquidity and pricing concerns, but which are exempt from the disclosure requirements of public offerings. Private placements and 144(a) securities are sold direct to investors, rather than through public offerings.

This rule by exception results in some actually illiquid securities being assumed to be liquid. For example, *exotic (custom) derivatives* are legally liquid, even if illiquid or not liquid in large quantities. Further, the liquidity of international securities, especially emerging market securities, can be affected by several factors, including currency convertibility and repatriation limitations. However, the SEC does state that junk bonds, direct loans and loan participations, certain warrants and options, venture capital, and small business investments may be illiquid, depending on the facts.

Derivatives

Derivatives are securities whose value depends wholly or partly on the performance of some underlying security. In general use, derivatives include warrants, options, and futures contracts. Futures contracts include commodities, interest rates, stock indices, and international currencies. Concern about their liquidity and safety has grown with the large number of mutual funds using them, and the occasional fund loss horror story. Moreover, the numerous types of derivatives funds use adds to the confusion. Derivative securities are defined and discussed in Sharpe et al. (1999), Bodie et al. (1996), and Jones (1998). ICI (1994) also discussed the regulation of derivatives, including options, futures, forward contracts, bond swaps, structured notes, and CMOs.

The history of bond mutual fund use of derivatives has been less than sterling. For example, Damato (1994) surveyed funds, with fourteen having losses year to date. The funds with larger losses made greater use of derivatives, which may have signaled efforts gone bad or efforts to play catch up. Rekenthaler (1994a) summarized this history as costly lessons from Ginnie Mae (GNMA) funds in 1986, option income funds in 1987, junk bond funds in 1989–90, short-term world income bonds in 1992, and mortgage-backed derivatives funds in 1994. These funds all featured: (1) new, safe strategies, (2) free lunches of market returns and lower risk, (3) complex strategies, and (4) inadequate disclosure. Any fund that markets itself using this language should be avoided. There are no free risk/return lunches and risk may be explained quite simply.

Mutual funds thus use derivatives for several purposes. As described by Eileen Sanders (1993), derivatives are used to: (1) invest in markets that are normally restricted; (2) provide convenient and inexpensive ways of investing cash or tilting portfolios without large trading costs; (3) increase flexibility to aggressively or conservatively invest in particular markets; and (4) invest defensively to hedge portfolio risk. In fact, Beese (1994), a former SEC commissioner, called for legislation allowing funds to make greater use of derivatives to manage risk, a common practice in other types of businesses that hedge against unexpected price or interest rate changes.

The use of derivatives varies by type of mutual fund. Equity funds, US Treasury bond funds, and corporate high-yield funds are light users of derivatives. Medium users include all other types of bond funds, with the exception of short-term global bond funds that are heavy users. Some 60 percent of these latter bond funds have significant holdings of structured notes. Overall, exposure to derivatives is not a major problem, but problems there are in particular funds.

Updegrave and Misra (1994) surveyed retail bond and money market mutual funds about their use of derivatives, and only 51 percent responded. But what was learned may be summarized as follows: (1) most funds use derivatives sparingly, (2) money market funds do not hold derivatives, and (3) some funds have reduced their derivatives risk exposure. However, Eileen Sanders (1993) concluded that mutual fund advisors go out of their way to avoid making any real disclosure, such as motivations for the use of derivatives, the risks involved, and the actual performance implications.

One fund takes disclosure in the right direction by defining derivatives, noting their use to manage (reduce) risk, and warning of incorrect use in the form of exotic, highly leveraged securities. The fund states that it may use derivatives in four ways: (1) to hedge the volatility of bond holdings, (2) to enhance returns without disproportionate risk, (3) to establish security positions more efficiently than can be obtained with traditional investments, and (4) to capitalize on specific securities or market outlooks. Of the four, the second and fourth uses involve additional risks. Unfortunately, the fund does not provide actual use and performance. Such words as "enhance" and "to capitalize" may signal increased portfolio risk.

Special securities

As discussed in Sanders (1995), Morningstar uses the term *special securities* to indicate those types of securities that investors may not expect to find in portfolios. The special securities measures indicate whether particular mutual funds use securities that call for additional information and concern. Are they used to enhance returns or reduce risk? Derivative contracts normally incorporate forecasts, such as the direction and extent of changes in interest rates, and such forecasts are often way off the mark.

Morningstar searches fund prospectuses and statements of additional information to identify the types of securities that are permitted, those that are permitted but not held, and those that are prohibited. Next, it examines each security in the portfolio to determine the extent of exposure to derivatives. There are three categories of special securities in table 40b: (1) restricted/illiquid securities, (2) emerging market securities, and (3) options/futures/warrants. The first two categories are each measured as a percentage of assets and the third as yes/no. These securities are discussed in Jones (1998).

Restricted/illiquid securities include those legally defined above as restricted securities which are so identified in shareholder reports. They also include securities with potential liquidity problems, including securities that trade in developing country markets and collateralized mortgage obligations. The latter offer different priority claims on interest and principal payments. Collateralized mortgage obligations are discussed in Sharpe et al. (1999). Mortgage-backed securities are discussed in Ronald (1998b).

Restricted/illiquid securities also include *structured notes*, custom-made derivatives for specific needs. The value of structured notes may depend, for example, on price changes of specified commodities, interest rates, and currency exchange rates. They may be highly leveraged or used to reduce risk. Phillips (1994) reported a Treasury bond fund that suffered a major loss from an inverse floating-rate note (IFRN), misleadingly listed as a floating-rate note in a footnote. This was a serious distortion because floating-rate notes are conservative securities, while so-called *inverse floaters* are highly leveraged and volatile. Not even sophisticated investors would have been forewarned by this misleading disclosure.

However, inverse floaters have not generally been foisted on unsuspecting investors. Municipal bond fund use of inverse floaters, as described by Eileen Sanders (1994), is a case in point. Funds that make "only" moderate use of inverse floaters face only moderate losses when interest rates increase more than expected. Moreover, most (not all) funds disclose enough about the inherent risks that concerned investors are forewarned. There has been enough history to know that funds using inverse floaters are more risky than those that do not.

On a positive note, Kelley (1995a) determined that less than 2 percent of equity funds hold any exotic derivatives or structured notes, and most such holdings are small. Equity funds make greater use of futures and options than bond funds, but less than 50 percent of equity funds use them. Derivatives are primarily used to hedge risk, such as currency risk. The use of derivatives by bond funds ranges from nil to fairly prevalent. Nonetheless, not all derivatives are inherently risky. So-called *plain vanilla derivatives* are routinely used for hedging or quickly deploying cash. They are straightforward and involve no more risk than conventional bonds.

Nonetheless, investors should search portfolio listings and footnotes for signals of risky derivatives. For bond funds, the signals include the terms "interest only" (IO), "principal only" (PO), and "structured notes." For municipal bond and money market funds, the signal is "inverse floating rate notes" (IFRN). These signals are important because the magnitude of losses can be huge. For example, one bank investment advisor had to invest over $67 million to cover derivative losses in several "government" money market funds.

Options, futures, and forward contracts include both those used to enhance returns and those used to reduce risk. Investors should be alert because managers often use them to boost returns at the margin. Ronald (1999a) examined the use of futures by equity and bond funds. For example, bond funds may sell Treasury futures to protect portfolios against increasing interest rates. International funds may buy currency futures to lock in exchange rates. Index funds may buy index futures when they are undervalued relative to index stocks. Equity funds may also leverage portfolios with futures in an effort to increase returns.

Enhanced index funds

Enhanced index funds make adjustments in indexed portfolios in an effort to add value. So far, more has been promised than delivered. In order of risk, Zweig (1999b) identified several types of enhanced index funds. First are leveraged funds that borrow or use derivatives to enhance returns in bull markets and limit losses in down markets. These funds appear to provide less on the up side than they hurt on the down side. Second are tilted funds that attempt to enhance index returns by buying more of undervalued and less of overvalued stocks. These funds appear to have trouble identifying which stocks are which. Third are amalgamated funds that attempt to add to index returns by mixing short-term bonds with stock index futures contracts.

The futures track the market with small down payments, and the bonds are supposed to add a bit to index returns. As discussed below, sometimes it is better to keep it simple and settle for indexed returns, which usually outperform most funds.

Barbee (1998a) examined enhanced index funds and concluded that they are "hardly no-lose propositions." These funds use various strategies, including buying stocks with growth characteristics and price momentum, overweighting index sectors with price momentum, and buying the index and selling calls against it. Performance is, of course, tied to the indices they mimic, which means they are not always having favorable returns. In addition, efforts to enhance returns generate higher expenses than pure index funds. They should only be held in tax-deferred accounts to the extent they realize short-term gains from sales of derivatives.

Barbee also discussed the use of options to reduce risk in enhanced index funds. This strategy works best in times of market volatility with stock returns declining. The basic strategy is to sell calls on indices represented by the portfolios. This provides funds with premiums. If index prices increase, fund gains are called away by option holders. If index prices fall, funds bear the losses. But, in either case, funds keep the option premiums, which provide returns in the former case and cushion losses in the latter cases.

The key to investment in enhanced mutual funds is not automatically to avoid them if they use derivatives, but to determine whether disclosure is appropriate for the inherent risks involved. Improved disclosure is sorely needed to properly forewarn investors. The complexity of some derivative strategies has been a problem because many fund advisors do not, for whatever reason, explain the risk implications under normal and turbulent market conditions. Perhaps they do not understand the risks themselves, such as the implications of large unexpected increases in interest rates. Inadequate disclosure compounds what fund advisors do not know or do not disclose by not giving investors at least the opportunity to learn what they should know about the risks. These risk assumptions and implications may normally be explained by the right source, but this source is not usually the funds. One may remember the disastrous results of the large hedge fund motivated by two Nobel laureates.

Thus concerned investors should invest only in mutual funds that practise forthcoming disclosure. Avoid funds that do not fully disclose and explain the underlying risk assumptions and implications of their derivative strategies. And, even then, investors should not invest unless the risk assumptions and implications are verified by knowledgeable sources. The safest strategy for investors who wish to keep things simple is to avoid funds that use strategies they do not understand. It is not difficult to find funds that do not use derivatives. An even better alternative for funds and investors is for the SEC to standardize the disclosure of derivatives use and its risks.

Table 46

Table 46 identifies differences in the portfolio percentages of giant/large-cap. stocks, median market cap., and special securities for Windsor II, its large (cap.) value category, and the market represented by the Vanguard 500 Index. The larger a mutual fund's market cap. size and its median market cap, the smaller its degree of diversification but the less its market liquidity risk. That is, large market cap. reflects less diversification in a global sense, but also less risk, owing to the relatively more liquid markets they trade in. On other hand, the more balanced a fund's proportion of special securities to other securities, the larger its degree of diversification but the more its special securities risk. These securities generally trade in less liquid markets or, as in the case of restricted securities and some types of derivatives, not at all.

A mutual fund's market liquidity risk is best estimated from the liquidity of the secondary markets in which its portfolio holdings trade, such as the New York Stock Exchange. Absent market-defined measures of liquidity risk in Morningstar, liquidity risk is estimated here from the market cap. of the securities in the portfolio plus any use of special securities. The larger a mutual fund's market cap., for example, the more likely its securities trade in highly liquid (low-risk) markets.

Table 46 indicates that Windsor II's combined percentage of giant/large-cap. stocks is much more than 10 percent larger than its *category*. It has a smaller degree of diversification and significantly less giant/large-cap. size risk. The same condition and conclusion holds for its median market cap. Unfortunately, there is no measure of special securities for the category. Windsor II holds no special securities, which represents a small degree of diversification, but with low market liquidity risk on its own merits. Thus Windsor II has significantly less market liquidity risk than its category peer group with respect to both market cap. and median market cap.

Windsor II's percentage of giant/large-cap. stocks is a bit larger than the *market*, represented by the Vanguard 500 Index Fund. Windsor II has a smaller degree of diversification but a bit less giant/large market cap. risk. This is unexpected, given that value funds normally invest in smaller stocks, but the difference is insignificant based on the 10 percent rule. However, median market cap. funds have the expected result that Windsor II's median market cap. is much more than 10 percent smaller than the market, which indicates a larger degree of diversification with significantly more median market cap. risk. The surrogate market index also holds no special securities, at least not generally, which reflects no diversification but low special securities risk on its own merits. This is as it should be because the Vanguard 500 Index mimics the S&P 500 Index, which holds only its defined portfolio.

Although the market liquidity results are mixed, they tend to favor Windsor II. Thus its overall market liquidity risk is excellent (generally less risk) relative to its category and the market index surrogate. Again, its category comparisons are most relevant. But, also, value funds are not expected to have larger proportions of giant/large market cap. than the market surrogate, but Windsor II does. Thus Windsor II's *overall* market liquidity risk is excellent (generally less risk) compared with both its category and the market surrogate. These findings are summarized in table 52.

DIVERSIFICATION RISK: RETURNS DISTRIBUTION (TABLE 47)

Returns distribution risk reflects the proportions of income (dividend) returns and capital gains returns, as measured by the ratio of income returns to total returns. Alternatively, income and capital gain distributions paid to shareholders could be used, but investors are more accustomed to thinking in terms of investment returns, not the mix of shareholder distributions. Income (dividend) returns are generally more stable than capital gains returns, thereby reflecting less returns distribution risk.

Table 47 identifies differences in returns distribution (proportions of income versus capital gains) risks, for Windsor II and the market index, represented by the Vanguard 500 Index Fund. The category is omitted because a time series of returns distributions is not readily available. The more representative the proportions of income and capital gains to total returns, the larger the degree of diversification and less the returns distribution risk. Windsor II's 1998 ratio of income return to total return is 7.6 percent and the figure is only 4.2 percent for the Vanguard 500 Index. The Windsor II ratio is much more than 10 percent larger than the market index surrogate, which is a larger degree of diversification with significantly less income distribution risk. Windsor II's mean 1994–8 income return to total income ratio is 9.6 percent versus 6.8 percent for the market. Again, the Windsor II income ratio is much more than 10 percent larger than the market, which is a larger degree of diversification with significantly less returns distribution risk. Thus Windsor II's overall returns distribution risk is excellent compared with the market surrogate. This finding is summarized in table 52.

DIVERSIFICATION RISK: INDUSTRY SECTOR CONCENTRATION (TABLE 48)

Table 48 identifies differences in industry concentration risk for Windsor II, its category, and the market surrogate, the Vanguard 500 Index. The smaller Windsor II's industry sector concentration, the larger its degree of diversification and the less its industry sector risk. Diversification by industry sector is a common way to achieve classic portfolio risk reduction. A readily accessible way of measuring this risk is to go to table 41a and sum the percentages of the three largest (top three) industry sector holdings as related to the total portfolio. Morningstar defines ten industry sectors, which are described in Regnier (1997c). If the sum of the top three sectors is *relatively* large, for example, the portfolio has a smaller degree of diversification with more industry sector concentration risk.

Industry sector concentration

The common sense of this issue is that with just a few industry sectors represented in a portfolio, the chances are greater that the sectors are highly correlated. If so, then the major advantage of diversification in reducing risk can easily be lost or diminished. For example, Zweig (1998) reported the correlations among industry sectors. Banks are highly correlated (0.50 or more) with computers, entertainment, home building, and insurance. Computers are highly correlated with banks, entertainment, home building, household products, and insurance. Household products match closely with computers, electric utilities, insurance, and telephone. And insurance is highly correlated with banks, computers, entertainment, home building, and household products. The other relationships are less strong.

Another commonsense reason for broad industry sector diversification is the appearance sometimes of herd behavior among portfolio managers. Given the competition for performance, some portfolio managers are quick to follow the sale of securities in industries that have become unpopular for reasons that may or may not justify their sale. A well diversified portfolio dampens the impact of this behavior on portfolio performance. This same logic supports broad diversification in terms of particular stocks held (discussed next). Further, this herd behavior can provide opportunities for value investors to purchase undervalued, unpopular stocks.

Table 48

As seen in table 48, Windsor II's industry sector concentration (51.3 percent) is slightly smaller than its category (52.2 percent), which indicates a bit larger degree of diversification and slightly less industry sector concentration risk. However, Windsor II's top three industry sector holdings are more than 10 percent larger than the market surrogate (45.6 percent), which indicates a smaller degree of diversification with significantly more industry sector concentration risk.

The possible explanation for this latter finding may be that value funds (and growth funds for that matter) focus on different industry sectors than the market index. This is seen in table 49, where industry sector proportions of value and growth funds are compared with the blended value/growth market index. Value portfolios are much more concentrated in utilities, energy, financials, consumer durables, and services sectors, about the same in industrial cyclicals, and much less so in consumer staples, retail, health, and technology. Thus, depending on the fund's particular top three sector mix, it could be more concentrated than the market index, as is the case here. Nonetheless, Windsor II's overall industry sector concentration risk is acceptable, with slightly less risk than its category, the primary comparison, and much more risk than the market index. This finding is summarized in table 52.

DIVERSIFICATION RISK: SECURITY CONCENTRATION (TABLE 50)

Table 50 identifies differences in security concentration risk for Windsor II, its category, and the Vanguard 500 Index market surrogate. Security concentration refers to the percentage of portfolio assets invested in the ten largest stock holdings. Arnott (1994) analyzed domestic equity funds with the not surprising result that risk generally decreases as diversification increases. And it does not take many securities to be well diversified. But the correlation between risk and the average size of holdings is weak, which is possible because effective diversification also requires low covariance among the holdings. Interestingly, portfolios with more concentrated security holdings, the type that requires stock-picking ability, have slightly smaller returns.

Security concentration issues

Mutual fund portfolios may become more concentrated by the success of their holdings. Diversified mutual funds may invest no more than 5 percent of assets in one security. But, less known, this restriction does not apply to individual holdings that *subsequently* increase in value to more than 5 percent of assets. For example, Paluch (1994a) observed that only 8 percent of funds have multiple stocks each representing more than 5 percent of assets.

Portfolio diversification by number of security holdings is the classic way to achieve portfolio risk reduction. A readily accessible way to measure this risk is to go to table 41a and use the "Assets in top ten holdings percentage" as related to the total portfolio. The assumption here is that the fund is primarily an equity fund, but this process can also be applied to bond funds. It is also assumed that if the top ten percentage is relatively small, for example, the portfolio has a large degree of diversification with a small security concentration risk. Conversely, funds that carry a large percentage of assets in their top ten holdings are more likely to be influenced by how well a few holdings perform.

For example, Paluch (1994a) observed that domestic equity funds with more than 35 percent of assets in the top ten have not only above-average risk, but below-average returns. Funds with less than 10 percent of assets in the top ten have the best performance – below-average risk and slightly above-average returns. Dziubinski (1997) observed that concentrated funds generally underperform less concentrated funds with respect to risk and return. This is interesting because of the recent introduction of mutual funds with several star portfolio managers. The portfolios are divided among the portfolio manager so that each can purchase only the best stocks. Each portfolio manager is supposed to be given conditions favorable to outperformance. However, thus far these funds have not performed as hoped.

However, not all studies agree that concentrated portfolios do not perform well (discussed again in chapter 10). Studies have identified concentrated portfolios as one attribute of portfolio managers who have outperformed over time. In fact, as discussed by Arnott (1995), portfolios of consistent winners are concentrated both by number of holdings and by industry sectors. This is consistent with these portfolio managers being excellent long-term stock pickers and not constrained to single investment styles.

Table 50

As seen in table 50, Windsor II's security concentration (28.4 percent) is more than 10 percent smaller than its category peer group (33.0 percent), which indicates a higher degree of diversification with significantly less security concentration risk. However, Windsor II's top ten security holdings are much more than 10 percent larger than the market index surrogate (19.7 percent), which indicates a smaller degree of diversification and significantly more security concentration risk. The reason for this latter finding is influenced by the nature of the index. It must hold its defined set of 507 securities. On the other hand, the managed Windsor II portfolio includes "only" the 287 securities that meet its investment criteria. Thus Windsor II's overall security concentration risk is acceptable, with much less risk than its category, the primary comparison, and much more risk than the market. This finding is summarized in table 52.

DIVERSIFICATION RISK: VALUE LINE SAFETY AND TIMELINESS (TABLE 51)

Value Line ratings

Value Line safety ratings (financial quality) and *Value Line timeliness ratings* (twelve months' performance outlook) provide another approach to identifying the degree of mutual fund portfolio diversification and risk. The use of these ratings for the assessment of mutual fund portfolio quality and investment timeliness also requires Morningstar data.

The *Value Line Investment Survey* is recognized as a useful source of predictions of stock performance. These predictions are reflected in its timeliness ratings. There is evidence that indicates abnormal returns exist, but only during the three days around publication dates. This is consistent with some degree of market efficiency. Other evidence indicates that abnormal returns go beyond the three-day period, but attributes them to "post-earnings announcement drift" following earnings surprises, rather than to Value Line's information.

Peterson (1995) reviewed various performance findings and focused on Value Line's "stock highlights" report, which includes only stocks with the highest timeliness rating. The stock highlights provide useful investor information, with strong abnormal returns over the three-day publishing period that is unrelated to post-earnings announcement drift. Thus Value Line is considered a useful source of stock timeliness and perhaps quality, as well.

The *Value Line Investment Survey* includes one-page reports on 1,700 stocks that include twenty-three series of financial and operating statistics for the each of the last fifteen years and forecasts for three to five years. The survey includes industry and economic analysis and commentary as well. Value Line's data are highly regarded for accuracy and it is one of the most, if not *the* most, widely used services providing investment information, especially by individual investors.

Value Line safety and timeliness ratings are thus quite appropriate and helpful in assessing the financial health and short-term market outlook of mutual fund portfolios. Value Line's statistical analysis ranks 1,700 stocks from highest suitability to "lowest suitability" for performance over the next twelve months. The 100 "most suitable" stocks are rated 1, the next 300 stocks are rated 2, the next 900 stocks are rated 3, the next 300 are rated 4, and the 100 "least suitable" stocks are rated 5. Statistical analysis also rank-orders each stock for "safety" as measured by downside risk. Each stock is assigned a rating, from "lowest risk" (1) to "highest risk" (5). Any non-rated securities should receive a 5 rating in the interests of conservatism.

Value Line's timeliness and safety ratings each identify a mutual fund's degree of diversification and risk relative to its category and the market surrogate. Timeliness and safety act as diversification constraints. For example, a fund portfolio rated 1 for timeliness provides a below-average degree of diversification, but above-average quality concentration. That is, the portfolio is focused on stocks with high Value Line ratings for expected performance over the next twelve months.

Table 51

Table 51 identifies differences in timeliness and safety risks for Windsor II, its category, and the market surrogate. To do this, the top fifteen security holdings, their percentage of the total portfolio, were provided by Morningstar (1998b), and their safety and timeliness ratings were obtained from *Value Line Investment Survey* (1998). The "Overview: Large Value" category lists its fifteen largest holdings, which acts as a constraint on the number of holdings analyzed for Windsor II and the market surrogate, the Vanguard 500 Index. The top fifteen should include only equity securities, the focus here being primarily equity funds.

The top fifteen obviously represent those securities comprising the largest percentages of the portfolio, but they are used here for their ready availability and convenience. It would be more correct to use all holdings, but in defense of the approach taken it may be noted that Windsor II and the Vanguard 500 Index have 287 and 507 holdings, respectively (tables 40a and 41a). Complete Windsor II and Vanguard 500 Index portfolio listings are in their semi-annual and annual reports (and online for some funds).

As seen in table 51, both portfolio safety and portfolio timeliness scores are computed for Windsor II, its category, and the market surrogate. Both mean and weighted average mean ratings are provided, as well. Weighted average ranks are more accurate than simple mean ranks because each stock is weighted by its relative importance among the top fifteen. For example, Windsor II's weighted and unweighted means for timeliness are 3.5 and 3.4, respectively. In many cases, like this one, the average scores are about the same, but this is certainly not always the case. Larger differences occur, for example, when a few securities dominate the others in size.

Computation of weighted average scores requires the percentage portfolio holding of each of the fifteen stocks to be scaled to a percentage of 100 percent, which implicitly assumes the top fifteen represent the entire portfolio. Each security's weighted rating is then multiplied by its Value Line rating and summed for the portfolio's overall score. If simple averages are used, only the means of the timeliness and safety ratings are calculated.

The findings are also summarized in table 52. Remember, *small* Value Line ratings indicate *high* safety and high timeliness. The weighted mean safety scores are 2.7 and 1.6 for Windsor II and its market surrogate, respectively. The fund's safety score is more than 10 percent larger (worse) than the market (10 percent rule). Thus Windsor II's more representative degree of diversification signals significantly more safety risk than its category. The same finding of a more than 10 percent difference in the fund's weighted mean safety score (2.7) applies to its category (2.2), as well. Windsor II's more representative degree of diversification signals significantly more safety risk than its category. The conclusion, therefore, is that Windsor II's overall safety risk is unacceptable relative to its peer group.

Turning to timeliness risk, Windsor II and the market have weighted-mean scores of 3.5 and 2.9, respectively. The fund's timeliness score is much more than 10 percent larger (worse) than the market. Thus Windsor II's less representative degree of diversification represents significantly more timeliness risk than the market. However, the fund's weighted mean timeliness score (3.5) represents a more representative degree of diversification than its category (3.8), but only insignificantly so. Windsor II's more representative degree of diversification signals slightly less timeliness risk than its category. Windsor II's overall timeliness risk is therefore acceptable, but only marginally so, properly giving most weight to its peer group. The safety and timeliness findings are summarized in table 52.

DIVERSIFICATION RISK: OVERALL ASSESSMENT (TABLE 52)

Table 52 includes summaries of each diversification risk: (1) value/growth investment style, (2) cash asset allocation, (3) market liquidity, (4) returns distribution, (5) industry sector concentration, (6) portfolio concentration, (7) Value Line safety, and (8) Value Line timeliness. There are three excellent, three acceptable, and two unacceptable diversification risks, and an overall assessment of acceptable relative to Windsor II's peer group category and the market index, where applicable. Thus Windsor II's performance as summarized in table 52 is deserving of further evaluation in the chapters that follow. This overall assessment follows that for fund attributes and portfolio manager background in table 27.

CHAPTER EIGHT

MUTUAL FUND PERFORMANCE MEASURES AND BUY/ SELL DECISION CRITERIA

Risk has always been a matter of measurement and gut.
(*Peter L. Bernstein, Peter L. Bernstein Inc., in* Financial Analysts Journal,
January/February 1995)

Unrelenting pressure to outperform has taken away from the manager the incentive to use judgment when it is needed to protect principal or reduce risk or losses when markets are at dangerous levels.
(*Walter M. Cabot, in* Financial Analysts Journal, *July/August 1998*)

We buy scary stuff.... Sometimes we get killed.... Don't come crying to us if we lose all your money, and you wind up a Dumpster Dude or a Basket Lady rooting for aluminum cans....
(*Robert Loest, IPS New Frontier Fund, in* Wall Street Journal, *January 27, 2000*)

This chapter has several goals. The first is to present, discuss, and apply CDA rate of return data and performance measures. The latter include R^2, beta, standard deviation, CDA rating, expense ratio, and CDA Jensen Alpha. The second goal is to present, discuss, illustrate, and apply four computed risk/return measures: Jensen Alpha, Adjusted Jensen Alpha, Treynor Index, and Sharpe Index. The third goal is to summarize Vanguard Windsor II's rates of return, performance measures, computed risk/return measures, and Morningstar measures as excellent, acceptable, or unacceptable (tables 66–7). The fourth goal is to bring together the decision criteria in tables 27, 52, and 66–7 and summarize them in table 68 for purposes of making a buy/sell decision for Windsor II.

The data are from CDA/Wiesenberger (1993–7) and Morningstar (1998). CDA/Wiesenberger provides CDA annualized rates of return, six CDA performance measures, and data for four computed risk/return performance measures generated for ten-year, five-year, three-year, and one-year (where appropriate) periods for each of the years ending 1993–7 (as available).

Morningstar provides risk/return ratings, risk ratings, and return ratings, and computed risk/return ratings are identified for ten-year, five-year, and three-year periods.

The CDA/Wiesenberger data represent Windsor II, its CDA growth and income investment objective, and the S&P 500 Index. This investment objective does not equate with Windsor II's large-cap. value category, but is the nearest to the Morningstar category. To avoid confusion, Windsor II's CDA investment objective is also called "category." The resultant ranking and trend tables indicate the mutual fund's performance for each measure for each time period relative to its category and the benchmark index. The fund's performance is then judged excellent, acceptable, or unacceptable for each of four rate of return time periods, each of six CDA performance measures, and each of three time periods for each of four risk/return performance measures. Next, composite ranks/trends are also judged as excellent, acceptable, or unacceptable for overall rates of return, overall CDA performance measures, and overall risk/return performance for each of four measures. The resultant Morningstar ratings also indicate relative performance for each measure and are similarly judged for each time period and overall.

CDA/Wiesenberger data are useful here because fourteen years of historical data are required to compute for the mutual fund, its category, and the market their performance measures for ten years ending each of the years 1993–7. Vanguard Windsor II was not in business for this entire fourteen-year period, specifically 1984 and part of 1985. As a result, analysis of Windsor II, its category, and the market necessarily excludes the ten-year periods ending 1993 and 1994, leaving only the years ending 1995–7. Windsor II's prospectus (1998) and annual report (1997) are relevant to the analysis.

CDA ANNUALIZED RATES OF RETURN

Table 53 presents the CDA/Wiesenberger (1993–7) measures of ten-year, five-year, three-year, and one-year annualized rates of return for Windsor II, its growth and income category, and S&P 500 Index for each of the years ending 1993–7. As stated, the ten-year performance comparisons of Windsor II, its category, and the S&P 500 Index are limited to the ten years ending 1995–7.

Based on table 53, table 54 identifies Windsor II's return ranks and trends compared with its category and the benchmark index (S&P 500 Index). That is, it identifies how well Windsor II performed relative to the other assets in serving ten-year, five-year, three-year, and one-year investment horizons, and whether Windsor II's performance trends are improving or not. This table indicates whether Windsor II's annualized returns profile best serves long-term or short-term investors, if any. The answers are in the relative performance *ranks* and *trends* of each asset.

Table 54 indicates that the S&P 500 Index ranks first overall for the ten-year investment horizon, as measured by its ranking total of 3 for the ten-year periods ending 1995–7. Windsor II ranks second for the ten-year horizons, and the category ranks third. Windsor II's ranks for the other time horizons make it clear that it performs very well indeed. Windsor II ranks first in five-year, three-year, and one-year horizons, as well as second in ten-year horizons. This is not the usual finding. Generally, results are more mixed, with different assets ranking first in one or more horizons. The category ranks third in all holding periods ending 1995–7.

A simple method is used to determine whether the asset ranks in table 54 reflect positive (improving) trends, constant (no) trends, or negative (worsening) trends. The sums of the latest two ranks (1996 and 1997) are compared with the sums of the earliest two ranks (1993 and 1994). The trend is considered positive (negative) if the sum of the latest two ranks is smaller (larger) than the sum of the earliest two ranks. The trend is constant if the sums are equal. Note, small (large) sums indicate high (low) performance ranks. As noted above, in the case of ten-year annualized returns, Windsor II, category, and benchmark index trends are category and market trends are based only on ranks for the years ending 1995–7. Thus Windsor II's positive ten-year ranking trend is based only on its number one 1997 ranking relative to its number two 1995 ranking.

Overall, Windsor II's annualized return performance rankings for the four investment horizons are excellent. Windsor II ranks second for ten-year horizons and first in all others. And, with the exception of the negative trend for the five-year horizon, Windsor II's ranking trends are all positive. Thus Windsor II's performance is acceptable for investors with ten-year investment horizons and excellent for all investors with five-year or less investment horizons.

A few additional comments are in order. Note that the S&P 500 Index ranks are both higher and more consistent for ten-year horizons than shorter horizons. This is to be expected because the index represents average market performance, which therefore averages out extreme high and low individual stock returns, especially over time. As an aside, this evidence reflects the strength of long-term investing in index funds that mimic market performance – investors get near market returns (not a small feat among managed funds) and more consistent *relative* returns, that is, less relative volatility of returns.

US Treasury bill (one-year) rankings are included to identify the performance of the risk-free rate. Note how much more consistent Treasury bill return rankings are for all investment horizons, but especially note their one-year rankings. Treasury bills consistently have the lowest rankings, except for 1994, when Windsor II and its category had negative returns. Treasury bills thus provide downside protection with positive returns when the market falters. The short-term return rankings of the other three risky assets are quite mixed, perhaps even somewhat random (walk). This suggests that consistent relative performance from short-term investing in particular risky assets is problematic at best.

And, finally, note that Windsor II consistently outranks its category, which makes a statement for Windsor II's portfolio managers in the most relevant of the ranking comparisons. As noted, Windsor II has generally high and positive return ranks for all investment horizons.

CDA PERFORMANCE MEASURES

Table 55 presents a menu of risk, expense, and risk/return measures computed in CDA/ Wiesenberger (1993–7) for each of the years 1993–7. The risk measures are beta, R^2, standard deviation, and CDA rating. The first three measures are conceptually the same as discussed previously. These modern portfolio statistics are computed using linear regression over the last thirty-six-month periods. The dependent variable is the asset's monthly return less the monthly risk-free Treasury bill return, expressed in continuously compounded form. The independent variable is the S&P 500 Index's monthly return, also reduced by the monthly Treasury bill return and also expressed in continuously compounded form. R^2 is the equation's coefficient of determination and measures the percentage of variation in asset returns attributed to variation in market index returns. In effect, the R^2 measures the extent to which a portfolio's diversification mimics the market index. Standard deviation measures the asset's total risk and reflects the dispersion of asset returns converted to monthly compounding. Beta measures the sensitivity (systematic risk) of asset returns relative to changes in the S&P 500 Index. Statistically, it is the slope of the regression line. The larger an asset's R^2, the more reliable its beta is as a measure of systematic risk.

The CDA rating is a composite rating of performance over past market cycles. The percentile asset ratings range from the first (best) to ninety-ninth (worst). Two up markets and two down markets are used, if available, but not less than one of each type market. Extra weight is given to most recent performance and ratings are reduced for inconsistency. Smaller CDA ratings represent less volatile returns, and vice versa. The expense measure is the expense ratio defined previously, and the risk/return performance measure is the Wiesenberger *CDA Jensen Alpha* (discussed below).

Before the CDA/Wiesenberger data were entered in table 55, those measures with defined values were entered. These values represent standards of comparison for identifying mutual fund and category performance relative to the S&P 500 Index. The following variable values are defined for the market: R^2, beta, and CDA Jensen Alpha Index. The market's R^2 was entered as 100 percent because, as the market, it represents the norm against which other asset R^2s are computed and compared. For example, an R^2 of 90 indicates that 90 percent of the variance of an asset's returns are explained by variability in market returns.

Next, the market beta (systematic risk) was entered as 1.00 (100 percent) because it represents the norm against which the sensitivity of asset returns relative to given changes in market returns are compared. The betas of other assets may be larger than, equal to, or smaller than the market beta of 1.00, in which cases their returns are more, equal to, or less sensitive to given changes in market returns.

Several other variables are not applicable to the benchmark index. The index's CDA rating is "n.a." because the rating is computed only for mutual funds. Each fund's percentile is computed relative to the fiftieth percentile assigned to the fund with the median CDA rating. The expense ratio for the S&P 500 Index is entered as n.a. because the index is a performance benchmark, not an actual fund.

The CDA Jensen Alpha risk-adjusted return measure is entered as zero for the S&P 500 Index. The market index's alpha is the benchmark against which portfolio manager performance is compared. That is, the size and sign of the alpha indicate whether particular managers have added/subtracted portfolio returns relative to the unmanaged benchmark index. This measure is discussed below, but here it is enough to say that alpha indicates how well portfolio managers are doing in increasing returns relative to the market for the same level of systematic risk.

Table 56 identifies how closely Windsor II's CDA performance measures compare with its category and the benchmark index for the years 1993–7. The market index ranks first by definition with the largest R^2 (100 percent), Windsor II ranks second with a constant trend, and the category ranks third. Windsor II's portfolio diversification thus matches the benchmark index's diversification more closely than does its category. Thus variability in Windsor II's returns is explained more by variability in market returns than is the case for its category. Windsor II and its category are expected to have smaller R^2s because the market index necessarily reflects only market-related risk. However, Windsor II has less non-market, residual risk than its category. Overall, Windsor II's R^2 (diversification) is acceptable, especially appropriately giving most weight to its performance relative to its category.

Implicit in this finding is that bearing only market risk is preferable to market plus residual, "other" risk. This is consistent with the notion of eliminating all but market risk through optimal portfolio diversification. But, as discussed, some mutual funds have small R^2s, reflecting their measured use of unique strategies. These funds have both market risk and sizable unique risk.

The category ranks first, with the smallest beta, Windsor II ranks second and its rank is constant, and the market index ranks third (beta equals 100 percent). Small betas indicate small systematic risk. Windsor II's beta is smaller than the market's 1.0, but larger than the category's beta. Thus Windsor II's has less systematic risk than the market index, but more than its category. Windsor II's returns are less sensitive than market index returns for given changes in market returns, but more so than its category. This translates to less systematic risk for Windsor II than the market index, but more than its category. This is not surprising because the category necessarily averages individual fund betas. Overall, Windsor II's beta (systematic risk) is acceptable, appropriately giving most weight to its performance relative to its category. Implicit in this finding is that small systematic risk is preferable to large.

The category ranks first, with the smallest standard deviation, Windsor II ranks second with constant trend, and the market index ranks third. Small standard deviations indicate low total risk of returns. Windsor II's annual rankings are not as consistent as for its R^2 and beta rankings. Thus Windsor II has less total risk, measured absolutely by variability of returns, than the market, but more than its category. This finding is not surprising, because Windsor II is a large-value fund and the market is, in effect, a more risky blended value/growth fund. Also, the category necessarily averages individual fund standard deviations. Overall, Windsor II's total risk is acceptable, again appropriately giving most weight to its performance relative to its category.

The category's CDA rating ranks first, with the largest smallest percentile rating, and Windsor II ranks second, with a negative trend. The benchmark index is not rated. Small CDA ratings (percentiles) indicate high ranking with low risk. Windsor II's annual CDA ratings are not as consistent as its R^2 and beta rankings. Windsor II's CDA ratings are lower than its category as determined in more recent years. Thus Windsor II has more risk than its category in good and bad markets. However, table 55 indicates only small differences in annual ratings. Thus Windsor II's overall CDA rating is acceptable, but its negative trend indicates continuing second best ratings.

Moving from risk measures to the expense ratio, Windsor II ranks first, with the lowest expense ratio and a constant trend, and the category is second. The benchmark index has no expenses. Small expense ratios indicate more cost-effective funds. Annual Windsor II and category rankings are consistent, but table 55 reveals large annual differences in expense ratios favoring Windsor II. This finding is not a surprise because Vanguard is known for low expenses, and the category necessarily averages individual fund expense ratios. Thus Windsor II's overall expense ratio is both excellent and consistent.

The CDA Jensen Alpha is the last of these performance measures. As explained below, each asset's alpha is correctly compared only with the S&P 500's alpha of zero. Thus the Windsor II and its category alphas are each compared only with the market index, which ranks second to each. Windsor II's alpha ranks first, but its ranking trend is negative. The category also ranks first, and its ranking trend is also negative. As seen in table 55, annual Windsor II and category alpha scores are not consistent. Windsor II and its category show negative alphas in one year and two years, respectively. Thus Windsor II's overall alpha is excellent, but it negative ranking indicates that change may be on the way.

COMPUTED RISK/RETURN PERFORMANCE MEASURES

One problem in comparing the performance of assets is how to rank them when one has both low risk and return and the other both high risk and return. This is a form of the old apples and oranges problem. This dilemma may be resolved by appropriate use of one of several performance measures that combine risk and return attributes in a single number (index). These composite risk-adjusted performance measures are discussed in Jones (1998) and detailed in Sharpe et al. (1999).

Table 57 presents CDA return data for Windsor II, its category, and the S&P 500 Index that are required to calculate the Jensen Alpha, Adjusted Jensen Alpha, Treynor Index, and the Sharpe Index for the ten years, five years, and three years ending each of the years 1993–7. One-year data are inadequate for these measures. Again, ten-year performance comparisons are made only for each of the years 1995–7. Note that CDA/Wiesenberger provides annual returns, which may normally be less desirable than monthly/quarterly return data, but they do have the advantage of convenience consistently applied.

Jensen Alpha

The *Jensen* (1968) *Alpha* (more commonly, Jensen coefficient or Jensen's differential return measure) may be used to evaluate portfolio manager skill for historical time periods. *Alpha* is the difference between a portfolio's actual return and its expected return given the portfolio's systematic risk and the CAPM. Significantly positive alphas are interpreted as evidence of superior portfolio manager skill. This skill may reflect several factors, such as the ability to select securities, low expenses, and/or market timing. Significantly negative alphas are interpreted as evidence of inferior portfolio manager performance. Alphas that are statistically not different than zero (the market index alpha) suggest performance equal to the market index on a risk-adjusted basis.

This said, the alphas here have not been tested for significant differences from the market's zero alpha. Statistically significant alphas are much less common than insignificant ones. But, as a general guide, positive alphas are good (the larger the better), and negative alphas are not. Positive alphas are observed less often than negative ones and most all alphas are insignificant from zero. For convenience, investors should give particular attention to funds with alphas in the ballpark of 5 or higher. Empirically, when alphas of 5 are included with other popular variables in fund screens, fewer than ten funds are normally identified.

As stated above, a mutual fund's Jensen Alpha is correctly interpreted only relative to the market index's defined zero alpha. The reason is that each asset's beta normally differs in size, which makes performance comparisons among assets with different levels of systematic risk problematic. The market index is the benchmark to which active portfolio managers attempt to generate *abnormal returns*. Thus Windsor II's Jensen Alpha should not be compared with its category's alpha, but only in identifying whether Windsor II's portfolio managers added returns in excess of the unmanaged market index.

The historical Jensen Alpha equation is a rearrangement of the basic Jensen Alpha regression equation that estimates beta and computes alpha. The equation relates portfolio and market mean returns and mean abnormal returns for a given period to the portfolio's systematic risk measured by beta. This more convenient equation is used because CDA/Wiesenberger has independently estimated betas.

Jensen Alpha equation

The Jensen Alpha equation is computed as follows:

$$J_i = r_i - [r_f + (r_m - r_f)B_i]$$

where J_i = Jensen Alpha, asset i, where $i = p$ for portfolio, the mutual fund, in this case Windsor II, or $i = m$ for market, the S&P 500 Index, or $i = c$ for category, in this case the growth and income category; r_i = mean rate of return, asset i, for defined intervals, in this case, ten years, five years, and three years ending each of the years 1993–7; r_f = mean risk-free rate of return, in this case, one-year US Treasury bills (intervals and years as above for r_i); r_m = mean rate of return, market (as above for r_i); B_i = CDA beta, asset i, approximated as that for the year ending the defined period (as above for r_i).

The CDA estimated betas used here were computed for the thirty-six months ending each of the years 1993–7. They are, therefore, precisely correct only for the three years ending each year. But, here, investor convenience wins by using the CDA betas for all holding periods ending each year. Therefore, the betas in table 55 for each of the years 1993–7 are used. Of course, this does not preclude estimating betas statistically with additional data points or utilizing sources of better betas. One problem is finding a readily available source for betas computed for rolling five and ten-year periods. For illustrative purposes here, the simple approach to beta is used.

As an example of applying the Jensen Alpha, Windsor II's alpha for the five years ending 1997 was 3.40. It was computed using the 1997 beta in table 55 and 1997 CDA return data in table 57:

$$J_p = 21.56 - [4.18 + (21.02 - 4.18)0.83]$$

$$= 3.40$$

Jensen Alpha (tables 58–9)

Table 58 presents the ten-year, five-year, and three-year Jensen Alpha for Windsor II, its category, and the market index for each of the years ending 1993–7, but ending 1995–7 for ten-year horizons. Based on this table, table 59 next identifies alpha ranks and trends for Windsor II and its category and compares each with the market index. For example, it identifies how well Windsor II's portfolio managers performed in serving ten-year, five-year, and three-year investment horizons, and whether its performance trends are positive, negative, or constant. That is, this table indicates whether Windsor II's Jensen Alpha profiles best serves long-term or short-term investors, if any.

Table 59 indicates that Windsor II's Jensen Alpha outranks the S&P 500 Index in all ten-year horizons ending 1995–7, all five-year periods except that ending 1994, and all three-year horizons. Windsor II's relative performance trends versus the market are constant for ten-year horizons and positive for both five-year and three-year horizons. The market outranks the category in ten-year periods ending 1995–7 and also three-year periods. The category outranks the market only in five-year horizons. Windsor II's ranks and trends make it clear that its portfolio managers performed extremely well compared with the market index in all investment horizons, and consistently so. Again, as discussed above, this level of performance is certainly not the norm.

Adjusted Jensen Alpha

An *adjusted Jensen Alpha* is needed to compare alphas among different assets, that is, to be able to rank the alphas of alternative mutual fund investments. The regular Jensen Alpha may be correctly used to determine whether a particular mutual fund's portfolio manager has generated abnormal returns as represented by a positive alpha. To make such a comparison among funds, however, each fund's Jensen Alpha must be divided by its beta to adjust its alpha for differences in systematic risk among the funds. If the betas are approximately the same, the rank order of funds using the adjusted Jensen Alpha will approximate those using the Jensen Alpha.

Adjusted Jensen Alpha equation

The Adjusted Jensen Alpha equation is computed as follows:

$$\text{Adj. } J_i = J_i / B_i$$

where Adj. J_i = Adjusted Jensen Alpha, asset i, and B_i = CDA beta, asset i, (as defined above). As an example of applying the Adjusted Jensen Alpha, Windsor II's Adjusted Alpha for the five years ending 1997 was 4.10. It was computed using the 1997 beta in table 55 and the Jensen Alpha for the five years ending 1997 in table 58:

$$\text{Adj. } J_p = 3.40/0.83$$
$$= 4.10$$

Adjusted Jensen Alpha (tables 60–1)

Table 60 presents the ten-year, five-year, and three-year Adjusted Jensen Alpha for Windsor II, its category, and the benchmark index for each of the years ending 1993–7, but ending 1995–7 for ten-year horizons. Based on this table, table 61 next identifies Adjusted Jensen Alpha ranks and trends for Windsor II, its category, and the market index. For example, it identifies how well Windsor II's portfolio managers performed in serving ten-year, five-year, and three-year investment horizons, and whether its performance trends are positive, negative, or constant. That is, this table indicates whether Windsor II's Adjusted Jensen Alpha profiles best serves long-term or short-term investors, if any.

Table 61 indicates that Windsor II's Adjusted Jensen Alpha ranks first in all ten-year horizons ending 1995–7 and all five-year and three-year periods. Windsor II's relative performance trends are constant (as are the category and S&P 500 trends, as well) for ten-year horizons and positive for five-year and three-year horizons. The S&P 500 Index ranks second in ten-year periods ending 1995–7 and in three-year periods. The category ranks second only in five-year periods. Windsor II's ranks and trends again make it clear that its portfolio managers perform extremely well compared with its category and the market in all investment horizons. Again, this level of performance is certainly uncommon.

Treynor Index

The *Treynor* (1965) *Index* (more commonly, Treynor ratio or Treynor reward-to-volatility ratio) seeks to relate portfolio return to its risk. The measure was developed in Treynor (1965). It distinguishes systematic and total risk by implicitly assuming that portfolios are well diversified. In developing this measure, Treynor introduced the concept of the characteristic line whose slope measures the relative volatility of mutual fund returns, the beta coefficient.

To make such a comparison among funds, however, each fund's Jensen Alpha must be divided by its beta to adjust its alpha for differences in systematic risk among the funds. If the betas are approximately the same, the rank order of funds using the Adjusted Jensen Alpha will approximate those using the Jensen Alpha.

Treynor Index equation

The Treynor Index equation is computed as follows:

$$T_i = (r_i - r_f)/B_i$$

where T_i = Treynor Index, asset i, where $i = p$ for portfolio, the mutual fund, in this case Windsor II, or $i = m$ for market, the S&P 500 Index, or $i = c$ for category, in this case, growth and income category; r_i = mean rate of return, asset i, for defined period, in this case, ten years, five years, and three years ending each of the years 1993–7; r_f = mean risk-free rate of return, in this case, one-year US Treasury bills (intervals and years as above for r_i); B_i = CDA beta, asset i, in this case approximated as that for the year ending the defined period (as above for r_i).

As an example of applying the Treynor Index, Windsor II's index for the five years ending 1997 was 20.94. It was computed using the 1997 beta in table 55 and 1997 CDA return data in table 57:

$$T_p = (21.56 - 4.18)/0.83$$
$$= 20.94$$

Treynor Index (tables 62–3)

Table 62 presents the ten-year, five-year, and three-year Treynor Index for Windsor II, its category, and the market index for each of the years ending 1993–7, but ending 1995–7 for ten-year horizons. Based on this table, table 63 next identifies the Treynor Index ranks and trends for Windsor II, its category, and the market. For example, it identifies how well Windsor II performed in serving ten-year, five-year, and three-year investment horizons, and whether its performance trends are positive, negative, or constant. That is, this table indicates whether Windsor II's Treynor Index best serves long-term or short-term investors, if any.

Table 63 indicates that Windsor II's Treynor Index ranks first in all ten-year horizons ending 1995–7 and five-year and three-year periods. Windsor II's relative performance trends are positive for all horizons. The S&P 500 Index ranks second in ten-year and three-year periods. The category ranks second only in ten-year periods. Windsor II's ranks and trends make it very clear that it has performed exceptionally well compared with its category and the market in all investment horizons. Again, this exceptional level of performance is uncommon.

Sharpe Index

The Sharpe (1966, 1994) Index (more commonly, Sharpe ratio or Sharpe reward-to-variability ratio) is based on the author's work in *capital market theory*. The index uses a benchmark based on the capital market line. The Sharpe Index relates the portfolio's mean abnormal returns for a given period to its total risk measured by the standard deviation of returns. The equation identifies portfolio abnormal returns per unit of total risk.

Sharpe Index equation

The Sharpe Index equation is computed as follows:

$$S_i = (r_i - r_f)/SD_i$$

where S_i = Sharpe Index, asset i, where $i = p$ for portfolio, the mutual fund, in this case Windsor II, or $i = m$ for market, the S&P 500 Index, or $i = c$ for category, in this case, growth and income; r_i = mean rate of return, asset i, for a defined period, in this case, ten years, five years and three years ending each of the years 1993–7; r_f = mean risk-free rate, in this case, one-year US Treasury bills (intervals and years as above for r_i); SD_i = standard deviation, asset i, of returns (as above for r_i).

As an example of applying the Sharpe Index, Windsor II's index for five years ending 1997 was 1.10. It was computed using the 1997 beta in table 55 and 1997 CDA return data in table 57:

$$S_p = (21.56 - 4.18)/15.84$$
$$= 1.10$$

Sharpe Index (tables 64–5)

Table 64 presents the ten-year, five-year, and three-year Sharpe Index ranks and trends for Windsor II, its category, and the market index for each of the years ending 1993–7, but ending

1993–5 for ten-year horizons. Based on this table, table 65 next identifies Sharpe Indices for Windsor II its category, and the market. For example, it identifies how well Windsor II has performed in serving ten-year, five-year, and three-year investment horizons, and whether its performance trends are positive, negative, or constant. That is, this table indicates whether Windsor II's Treynor Index best serves long-term or short-term investors, if any.

Table 65 indicates that Windsor II's Sharpe Index ranks third in ten-year horizons ending 1993–5, but rebounds to first in both five-year and three-year periods. Windsor II's relative performance trends are constant for ten-year and three-year periods and positive for five-year periods. The S&P 500 Index ranks first in ten-year periods and second in five-year and three-year periods. The category ranks second in ten-year and five-year periods and third in three-year periods. Windsor II does less well in the ten-year periods than the Jensen and Treynor indices, which rank Windsor II first in all horizons. The implication is that, for this one measure, Windsor II's total risk performance was less effective than its systematic risk performance. But, for all four measures and all investment horizons, Windsor II's overall performance has been outstanding and nearly consistently so!

Composite measure relationships

The relationships among the composite measures are explained in Wilson and Jones (1981) and Sharpe et al. (1999). The Sharpe Index uses the standard deviation and evaluates portfolio performance on the basis of return and diversification. The measure may be used to rank portfolios on the basis of historical performance. The Treynor Index considers only portfolio systematic risk, and also may be used to rank historical portfolio performance. Neither measure provides, as does the Jensen Alpha, the percentage by which a portfolio outperforms or underperforms its market index.

The Jensen Alpha also considers only portfolio systematic risk (beta). As discussed above, the Jensen Alpha should not be used to rank portfolio performance, but the Jensen Alpha is adjusted for this very purpose. The Adjusted Jensen Alpha and Treynor indices rank portfolios identically.

The Adjusted Jensen Alpha, Treynor and Sharpe indices rank well diversified portfolios identically. But, for less diversified portfolios, the Sharpe Index may rank portfolio perform-ance differently than the other two indices. For example, the Sharpe Index may find that a portfolio underperformed the market that the Adjusted Jensen Alpha and Treynor indices find outperformed the market. The reason for any difference in risk-adjusted performance ranking lies with the risk measure used. The Sharpe Index measures total risk (standard deviation) while the others measure only systematic risk (beta).

For example, the implication of the difference in risk measure becomes apparent when ranking two portfolios, one with only market risk and the other also including unique (non-market) risk. The Sharpe Index penalizes the ranking of the latter portfolio, but the other indices would not because they measure only systematic risk. This general finding has import-ant implications for investors. If investors presently hold well diversified portfolios, then the Adjusted Jensen Alpha or the Treynor Index should be used to rank incremental mutual funds being considered for purchase. However, if the mutual funds under consideration represent a significant portion of the total portfolio, then Sharpe is the appropriate measure to use.

The Treynor and Sharpe indices use average returns and risk-free rates (table 57). The Jensen Alpha does also in the equation form presented above, but its basic regression equation form requires individual period returns and risk-free rates.

Potential problems

Composite risk-adjusted performance measures have potential problems, however. These issues, capital market theory, and the CAPM are discussed in Jones (1998), Sharpe et al. (1999), and Elton and Gruber (1995). Because the performance measures are derived from capital market theory and CAPM, they share the same assumptions. These assumptions include: (1) use of the US Treasury bill rate to proxy the risk-free rate; (2) investors borrow/lend at the same risk-free rate; and (3) use of a market index to proxy the true market portfolio, especially as international investing gains importance.

Portfolio rankings are sensitive to the choice of particular benchmark index used to proxy the market portfolio, for example, the S&P 500 Index used here. Because beta is sensitive to the particular market index used, portfolio rankings can be made dependent on the choice of market index. This problem has no obvious solution because of the impossibility of forming a real-world portfolio with the same portfolio composition as a market index that also replicates its returns. Market indices are artificial constructs without operating expenses and trading costs. The result is that market indices set performance standards that are too high relative to what even passively managed index funds can generate.

Problems in identifying true market portfolio also present a challenge to CAPM. Such a portfolio would be a completely diversified global portfolio, but this portfolio is unobservable. Capital market theory and the CAPM assume the market portfolio can be proxied by a market index. However, the beta estimated is not a clear-cut risk measure because it can be sensitive to the market index chosen, even given that commonly used indices are highly correlated. This implies that portfolio rankings can change with the particular market index used. The required use of a market index other than the true market portfolio means it is impossible to test the validity of the CAPM. What is being tested is the efficiency of a particular market index. Further, Jensen Alpha, Treynor, and Sharpe should each be independent of its risk measure. However, this relationship is sometimes positive and other times negative.

As implied in a previous discussion, these risk-adjusted performance measures do not distinguish portfolio manager luck from skill. This explains, for example, why attempts to forecast mutual fund performance based on the size of Jensen Alphas have been generally unsuccessful. The length of time necessary to establish portfolio manager skill is much longer than the time periods included in risk-adjusted performance measures, or any other measures for that matter. Nonetheless, judgments must be formed and decisions made, and risk-adjusted performance measures serve this purpose.

The various risk/return performance measures also use the US Treasury bill rate to proxy the risk-free rate of interest. This is done because the risk-free rate has no real-world counterpart, analogous to the relationship between market indices and real portfolios. Portfolio ranking can be made dependent on choice of risk-free rate. For example, if the Treasury bill rate is, in fact, too low, it becomes easier for portfolios with risk-free and risky assets to show superior relative performance. Conversely, if a higher risk-free rate is used, it becomes more difficult for these portfolios to show superior relative performance. The risk-free rate problem also impacts performance rankings for portfolios leveraged by borrowing at rates higher/lower than real risk-free rates.

The Jensen Alpha and Treynor Index are based on the CAPM in their use of beta to measure risk. If the CAPM prices assets incorrectly, then these measures are also inappropriate. For example, Barbee (1997) discussed mutual fund alphas and noted that they depend on estimated portfolio betas, which in turn depend for reliability on large R^2s, say at least 70 percent. Because of these and other problems, *arbitrage pricing theory* (APT) was developed in an effort to provide a better alternative to CAPM. The APT model explains returns using a linear function of several common factors. However, the Sharpe Index measures risk with the standard deviation (total risk), which is not dependent on CAPM, APT, or the ability to identify the true market portfolio. These provide good reasons to favor the Sharpe Index, if only for portfolios that are not well diversified.

As discussed previously, attribution analysis is used in efforts to explain the why of portfolio performance. Was a particular mutual fund's performance due to market timing skill, or lack thereof, and/or stock selection skill, or lack thereof? The composite risk-adjusted performance measures do not provide the why, but the hope is that they provide generally accurate rankings of composite portfolio performance.

CDA RETURNS, PERFORMANCE MEASURES, AND COMPUTED RISK/RETURN PERFORMANCE MEASURES (TABLE 66)

Table 66 summarizes Windsor II's performance as identified in tables 54, 56, 59, 61, 63, and 65. Three types of performance measures are provided: CDA annualized rates of return and CDA performance measures in sections A and B, respectively, and computed risk/return performance measures in section C. Windsor II's individual performance is provided by performance measure, performance rank, time trend performance, and overall performance assessment. Windsor II's performance time trends are provided to identify future performance for each measure, assuming no change in trend. The discussion is limited to individual and overall assessments to keep explanations as simple as possible. There are twenty-two individual assessments and six summary assessments.

As seen table 66, section A, Windsor II's CDA rate of return performance is very strong. The fund's annualized rates of return are excellent in three of four investment horizons and acceptable for ten-year horizons. This suggests that Windsor II's return performance is best in less than long-term horizons. This is not the best outcome for long-term investors. Nonetheless, Windsor II's overall rates of return are excellent.

Windsor II's CDA performance measures in section B do not provide consistent results because they include three different types of measures: risk, expense, and risk/return. Windsor II's expense ratio is excellent, which is typical for Vanguard funds, and its CDA Jensen Alpha is also excellent. These are strong findings. However, the other four measures are acceptable: R^2, beta, standard deviation, and CDA rating. These are different risk measures. Overall Windsor II's CDA performance measures are acceptable. The expense ratio is assessed as in table 52, and its small size is very important. The CDA Jensen Alpha's assessment is consistent with the computed Jensen Alpha discussed in section C. These two versions of Jensen Alpha were computed using monthly versus annual data, respectively. The story of the CDA performance measures is strong returns, strong risk-adjusted performance, and acceptable risk along several dimensions. The overall assessment is therefor acceptable.

Windsor II's computed risk/return performance measures in section C are identified as excellent in eleven of twelve individual assessments of four performance measures. The Jensen Alpha, Adjusted Jensen Alpha, and Treynor Index are excellent in each individual and each overall assessment. The Sharpe Index is the only exception to this pattern. Its ten-year performance is unacceptable compared with its category and the S&P 500 Index. However, assessments of the shorter-term horizons for the Sharpe Index are excellent. The overall performance of the Sharpe Index is therefore acceptable. Because assessment of the Sharpe Index differs from the excellent assessments of the other three measures, it is important for investors to use the measure most consistent with their portfolio diversification and investment horizon. The overall assessment of the four computed risk/return measures is excellent, given the caveat just noted.

MORNINGSTAR RATING AND RISK AND RETURN PERFORMANCE MEASURES (TABLE 67)

Morningstar also provides readily available measures of risk, return, and risk/return performance. These measures are the risk-adjusted Morningstar Rating (one to five stars), Morningstar Risk, and Morningstar Return. These latter two measures may also be worked together to provide a relative measure of risk/return performance. Table 67 presents these measures for Windsor II, its category, and the benchmark index.

As noted previously, Blume (1998) and Sharpe (1998) critiqued Morningstar measures. Sharpe found them of limited use for selecting individual mutual funds or constructing fund portfolios. Zweig (1996) discussed the computation of star ratings and what they are and are not.

Later, Zweig (2000) reported the characteristics of Morningstar star ratings, both good and bad: (1) one month's or a year's performance can significantly change a fund's rating (unstable ratings), (2) funds operating for ten or more years maintain their rating better than funds with just three years of history (consistency is good), (3) ratings do well in predicting poor fund performance (good), but not excellent performance (bad, but typical), and (4) funds with three to five stars perform about the same (not precise measures).

Morningstar Risk is a measure of a mutual fund's downside volatility relative to other funds in its broad investment class (equity, taxable bond, municipal bond or hybrid). It is computed monthly for each of the last three, five and ten-year periods. Monthly fund returns are plotted relative to Treasury bill returns. The sum of the amounts by which fund returns trail Treasury bill returns is divided by the number of months. This number is compared with the distribution of the scores of the other funds to assign a risk score. The average number is assigned a score of 1 and the other funds are scored relative to 1. A score smaller (larger) than 1 indicates less (more) than average downside risk.

As discussed in Meyer (1993), Morningstar Risk penalizes funds for underperformance, which is consistent with investor fear of losing money. It is a relatively consistent measure of downside volatility because Treasury bill returns are more stable than stock/bond returns. However, its does not allow comparisons between broad asset classes.

Morningstar Return is a measure of a mutual fund's return relative to other funds in its broad investment class, net of any loads and redemption fees. It is computed monthly for each of the last three, five and ten-year periods. Monthly fund returns are plotted relative to Treasury bill returns. The sum of the amounts by which fund returns exceed Treasury bill returns is divided by the number of months. An adjustment is made to prevent negative returns from distorting the data. The adjusted average number is assigned a score of 1 and the other funds are scored relative to 1. A score smaller (larger) than 1 indicates less (more) than average returns.

The Morningstar (star) Rating incorporates risk and return into a star ranking for the last three, five, and ten-year periods. The rating is determined by subtracting a mutual fund's Morningstar Risk from its Morningstar Return score. This remainder is compared with a distribution of such scores for its broad investment category. Fund scores in the top 10 percent receive five stars, those in the next 22.5 percent receive four stars, those in the middle 35 percent receive three stars, those in the next 22.5 percent receive two stars, and those in the bottom 10 percent receive one star. The ratings are computed monthly for the last three, five, and ten years. This measure is not shown in table 67 because each of its return and risk components is included.

However, the three Morningstar risk-adjusted ratings are used to compute overall Morningstar (star) ratings. These are the ratings in table 67. The Morningstar Ratings are computed for each broad investment class. For funds with ten-year histories, the time periods are weighted 50 percent for the ten-year period, 30 percent for the five-year period, and 20 percent for the three-year period. For funds with five-year histories, the time periods are weighted 60 percent for the five-year period and 40 percent for the three-year period. And, of course, funds with three-year histories are weighted 100 percent by this history.

Table 67 indicates that Windsor II's Morningstar Rating is "four star" for each investment horizon. The only comparison is with the "five star" S&P 500 Index because category ratings are not available. Windsor II's lower rating is a concern because it is a large-cap. value fund and the benchmark index is equivalent to a more aggressive large-cap. blend fund. But, without a comparison with its peer group, this finding is not as important as one with the peer group would be. Without a primary comparison with its category, Windsor II's overall Morningatar Rating is acceptable.

Windsor II's Morningstar Risk scores are not significantly different (10 percent rule) than its category and the market index for each horizon. This is partly a concern because the S&P 500 Index is a more aggressive blended category than Windsor II. But, based on the closeness of Windsor II's Morningstar Risk with its category, its overall assessment is acceptable.

Windsor II's Morningstar Return scores are higher (10 percent rule) than its category in all investment horizons. But, not unexpectedly, the return scores are also consistently lower than the market index. The market index proxies a more aggressive portfolio. Therefore, Windsor II's Morningstar Returns are overall excellent, given primary comparison with its category.

BUY/SELL DECISION CRITERIA (TABLE 68)

These criteria and their overall performance assessments are brought forward to table 68. The performance criteria in the first section are the summary assessments of fund attributes and portfolio manager background. The second includes return measures, risk measures, and diversification risk measures. The third section includes measures that combine risk and return elements. Each criterion's performance assessment is weighted on a scale of 3 (excellent), 2 (acceptable), and 1 (unacceptable). This in turn is weighted by its importance to the investor and a weighted overall score computed. The weighted score indicates a buy or sell decision.

Table 68, first section, includes fund attributes and portfolio manager background from table 27. Fund attributes include loads/fees, overall shareholder service, Loeb trading cost, tax efficiency, and shareholder disclosure. The attributes are ranked excellent/acceptable and given a performance score of 2.50. Portfolio manager background is ranked excellent and given a score of 3.00.

Table 68, second section, includes CDA rates of return and CDA performance measures from table 66, diversification risk from table 52, and Morningstar Risk and Return from table 67. CDA performance measures include R^2, beta, standard deviation, CDA rating, expense ratio, and CDA Jensen Alpha. Diversification risk includes value/growth investment style, cash asset allocation (plus net cash inflow), market liquidity, return distribution, industry sector concentration, portfolio concentration, Value Line safety, and Value Line timeliness.

CDA rates of return are ranked excellent and given a score of 3.00, and CDA performance measures are acceptable, with a score of 2.00. Diversification risk is acceptable and given a score of 2.00. Morningstar Risk is acceptable with a score of 2.00, and Morningstar Return is excellent with a score of 3.00. These risk and return measures are one-dimensional, unlike those in the next section.

Table 68, third section, includes Morningstar Rating and computed risk/return measures, the former from table 67 and the latter from table 66. The risk/return measures include Jensen Alpha, Adjusted Jensen Alpha, Treynor Index, and Sharpe Index. The Morningstar Rating is assessed acceptable and given a score of 2.00. The computed risk/return measures are assessed excellent with a score of 3.00. The measures in the third section integrate risk and return. This assessment should be weighted towards the risk/return measures that are consistent with the investor's portfolio diversification, as discussed previously.

The selection criteria in table 68 indicate that Windsor II is overall excellent/acceptable, with a weighted score of 2.43. However, the importance of each criterion varies by investor. In this case, the importance assessments are the author's choices. Therefore, table 68 also includes sample percentage weights of the relative importance of each criterion to the investor. The total of these weights, of course, is 100 percent. Next, performance scores are assigned to each criterion. The fund's overall score thus represents the perceived importance and performance rating of each criterion. The importance weights assign 30 percent of performance to the first set of criteria, 45 percent to the second set, and 25 percent to the third set. This breakdown is useful for determining the reasonableness of the investor's importance weights. As seen in table 68, Windsor II's total weighted performance score is 2.43, which is overall excellent/acceptable. On this basis, Windsor II is a buy if not owned and a hold if owned.

This evaluation could also be done on a more specific basis by restating table 68 to reflect each individual measure (for example, ten-year Jensen Alpha is excellent) in table 27 and tables 66–7. But, in any case, these tables should be reviewed before weighting the criteria and assigning performance ratings.

A second method is also used to score Windsor II's performance. The criteria are unweighted and individual performance scores are simply summed and averaged. Windsor II's overall unweighted performance score is 2.39, which is only 0.04 less than the weighted performance score. This small difference indicates that, in this case, investor weights do not significantly change the overall performance score. The consistency of the two overall scores make a strong case for Windsor II as a large-cap. value fund.

In cases where the differences between weighted and unweighted total performance scores are large, alternative, but reasonable, importance weights should be tested to determine the sensitivity of overall performance scores to different assumptions. However, in cases, such as table 68, where the difference between unweighted and weighted overall performance scores are small, say less than 10 percent, it may not prove important to test the sensitivity of alternative importance weights.

Discussions of which investment style stock and bond allocations should be included in chapter 6's stock/bond asset allocation follow this chapter. In practice, these determinations should be made before assessing the desirability of a particular fund for a particular investment style category. Windsor II is a buy, subject to the need for funds in its category and no other fund with a higher total weighted performance score.

CHAPTER NINE

MUTUAL FUND PERFORMANCE AND PORTFOLIO INVESTMENT STYLE ALLOCATIONS

[F]or enhanced investment performance: Reduce management fees, cut high turnover, cap. the size of large funds and institute incentive fees.

(*John C. Bogle, Vanguard Group, in* **Barron's**, *November 1997*)

[T]he true test of an enduring investment strategy is not whether it works at any given time, but whether it works over time. And, international investing does.

(*Jason Zweig, in* **Money**, *December 1998*)

It takes so long to determine whether outperformance is real or just plain luck, that hiring an active manager is an act of faith.

(*Ted Aronson, Aronson & Partners, in* **Money**, *January 1999*)

Personally, I think indexing wins hands down. After tax, active management just can't win.

(*Ted Aronson, Aronson & Partners, in* **Money**, *February 1999*)

Indexing's key advantage is long-term outperformance.

(*Gus Sauter, Vanguard Group, in* **Morningstar FundInvestor**, *November 1999*)

While it is true that all [mutual funds] will lag the index, no investor will own all of them. As an investor, you add value through manager selection.

(*Bill Miller and Legg Mason, in* **Morningstar FundInvestor**, *November 1999*)

When an asset class does relatively well, an index fund in that class does even better.

(*Dunn's Law, in* **Efficient Frontier**, *April 1999*)

Putting together a good bond fund can be as easy as keeping costs low and not getting too fancy. . . .

(*Eric Jacobson, in* **Morningstar FundInvestor**, *September 2000*)

This chapter has several goals. The first goal is to review the various issues relevant to identifying the appropriate types of stock and bond allocations within the table 35 stock/bond allocations. The stock and bond allocations are based on review and discussion of relevant topics, including market anomalies (exceptions), value versus growth stock performance, small-cap. stock versus large-cap. stock performance, large fund versus small fund performance and domestic versus international stock/bond allocations, including currency risk.

The second goal is to identify the stock and bond investment style allocations for particular stock/bond allocations. The allocations are as follows: 80/20 (or 90/10) domestic/international stock, 60/40 domestic and international large-cap./small-cap. stock, 50/50 domestic and international stock value/growth investment style, and 70/30 domestic/international bonds. The portfolio allocations within various stock/bond allocations are shown and illustrated for a 60/40 stock/bond allocation in table 70.

The third goal of the chapter is to determine whether actively or passively managed (index) funds are appropriate. This discussion includes the pros and cons for both stock funds and bond funds. The fourth goal is to recommend specific index funds for each stock and bond portfolio investment style allocation.

Various of these issues are also covered in Bodie et al. (1996), Reilly and Brown (1997), Jones (1999), Sharpe et al. (1999), and Dreman (1998). Several studies are presented in detail to provide specific results, but also to identify their place in the larger research context.

In sum, the following discussion reviews selected studies of mutual fund performance as well as studies with implications for mutual fund performance.

MARKET ANOMALIES

Anomalies represent exceptions to the theory of efficient markets that have not been explained away by theory or arbitraged away by investors. In the latter case, anomalies have a way of disappearing once investors start applying them in efforts to earn abnormal returns. Trades motivated by anomalies act to drive prices back to fair value and normal returns. In the former case, if it appears a strategy generates abnormally high risk-adjusted returns, the reason may be that markets are less than efficient or the method of adjusting returns for risk is flawed. If markets are efficient, then anomalies should not exist. All stocks along the security market line should have equal risk-adjusted returns because their prices reflect all public information about each security's risk. Further, it is not possible to use past returns to predict the distribution of future returns. As stated by Clements (2000): "Past performance is a rotten guide to future results. But that hasn't deterred investors."

Nonetheless, various applications of fundamental analysis provide anomalies to efficient markets theory. That is, there are certain stock characteristics that make it possible to identify stocks that will have above-average risk-adjusted returns, and vice versa. Tests of market efficiency normally use the CAPM's beta as the risk measure. However, when anomalies are present, the empirical relationships between risk and return differ from those predicted by theory. Tests of anomalies involve joint hypotheses – they consider whether markets are efficient, but at the same time the results are also dependent on the risk measure used in the asset pricing model. These are tests both of efficient markets *and* of the methods used to adjust returns for risk. For example, normal use of CAPM and beta may reveal an anomaly when, in fact, the findings reflect flawed methods of adjusting returns for risk. The assumptions underlying methods of risk adjustment are usually more questionable than those underlying efficient markets theory.

Among anomalies that persist (or may persist), several have implications for mutual fund investors. These "effects" are most often reported in academic research, and include the P/E ratio, P/B ratio, small-cap. size, momentum effect and reversal effect. Several other anomalies are discussed in other chapters. The P/E ratio effect indicates the tendency of stocks with low P/E ratios to outperform those with high P/E ratios. The P/B ratio effect indicates the tendency of stocks with low ratios to outperform those with large ratios. The small-firm effect indicates the tendency for total and risk-adjusted returns to decrease as stock market caps increase.

The momentum effect indicates the tendency for stocks that performed well (poorly) to continue to do so short-term. The *reversal effect* (*mean reversion*) indicates the tendency for stocks that performed well (poorly) to perform poorly (well) medium to long-term. The P/E and P/B anomalies are widely used criteria for distinguishing the likely outperformance of value versus growth stocks. These anomalies thus rationalize the validity of value investing. The small-firm effect anomaly is widely used as a criterion for distinguishing the likely outperformance of small-cap. versus large-cap. stocks.

PERFORMANCE: VALUE VERSUS GROWTH STOCKS

For many years it has been argued that value investment (strategies) styles outperform the market. This premise has been the focus of many research studies, but it is only fair to say that the final word has yet to be written. However, the first lasting word on this issue was by Benjamin Graham, the father of value investing, in Graham and Dodd (1934). Graham advocated buying stocks selling at low prices relative to underlying assets or earning power. In sum, value investors look for undervalued stocks while growth investors look for stocks with superior anticipated earnings growth. Should value or growth investment styles be given preference in equity allocation?

Value investing is a type of fundamental analysis based on the premise that superior returns may be earned by buying undervalued stocks – stocks with low prices relative to earnings, dividends, historical prices, book assets, cash flow, and/or other measures. Growth stocks are described as having high prices relative to these measures.

However, before proceeding, investment icon Warren Buffett's thoughts on value and growth investing are reported by McDonald (1998). Buffett stated that "the two approaches are joined at the hip." Growth is always a component in calculating fund value, a variable that can be positive or negative and of enormous or negligible importance. Use of the term "value investing" is redundant. After all, investing means to seek value that justifies the price paid.

Value investing often connotes the purchase of stocks with low P/E and P/B ratios and high dividend yields. But these variables are not determinative of undervalued stocks. Similarly, stocks with high P/E and P/B ratios and low dividend yields are not necessarily inconsistent with value purchases. Growth investing says little about value. Growth may have positive or negative impacts on value. Growth benefits only when firms can invest incremental returns to create market value.

Berry (1997) examined the "value" of value investing based on its returns for the one and three years following the market highs of 1937, 1967, 1972, 1987, and 1992. In the years following market highs, low P/E stocks appreciated by 3 percent and high P/E stocks fell by almost 2 percent. In the three years after market highs, low P/E stocks outperformed high P/E stocks by over 7 percent. Value stocks clearly provided a cushion following market highs, while growth stocks performed worse because investor expectations rise at market highs and disappoint in market downturns.

Table 43 illustrates differences in value versus growth investing style based on the Vanguard Value Index Fund and Vanguard Growth Index Fund. These two funds represent the value and growth components of the Vanguard 500 Index Fund. The value fund is less risky than the growth fund across many dimensions, including investment style, market liquidity, returns distribution, industry sector concentration, and security concentration. Value versus growth investing was also discussed previously. Value and growth investment styles are introduced and discussed with respect to mutual fund classification, explaining variance of returns, benchmarking performance, and identifying portfolio manager investment style.

Here, the goal is to determine whether stock allocation favors the use of value or growth stocks. That is, in the context of Morningstar style boxes, should value, growth or blend styles be favored in equity allocation? This is an important issue because, as discussed, asset and equity allocations are both important in explaining variance in returns. For mutual fund investors the essential issue is whether value or growth investing is more rewarding long-term.

Undervalued stocks may also reflect the *neglected-stock effect*, which identifies the tendency of small-cap. stocks to be undervalued because they are neglected by large institutional investors. Undervalued stocks could also reflect the *liquidity effect*, which is related to the other small-cap. effects discussed above. This effect indicates the tendency of small-cap. stocks to provide larger returns to compensate for larger trading costs in less liquid small-firm markets.

Basu study

Most research supports the finding that value investing based on such criteria as large B/P ratios, E/P ratios, and C/P ratios (for computational purposes) have produced superior returns over long periods of time. Basu (1977) examined the relationship between stock P/E ratios and their returns. Stocks were divided into five P/E classes (from high to low) and the risk and return of each class computed. Risk-adjusted performance measures indicate that low P/E stocks outperform the market and high P/E stocks underperform the market. The bottom line is that P/E ratios include valuable information, which is inconsistent with market efficiency based on public information. The real conclusion may be that returns were not properly adjusted for risk.

In later studies, the superiority of value investing has been variously attributed to: (1) compensation for risk bearing (for example, Fama and French, below); (2) suboptimal investor behavior in overvaluing glamour stocks (for example, Lakonishok et al. below); and (3) errors in investor expectations of value and growth stock growth rates (for example, LaPorta et al. below). These studies overlap in various ways, especially the latter two studies. The superiority of value investing as a general finding is consistent with Morningstar's use of the nine-cell category style box to distinguish value versus growth investment styles.

Fama and French study

Fama and French (1992) made the case for value investing using monthly stock data from three major exchanges for the period 1963–90. The return behavior of stocks ranked first by B/P ratios and second by E/P ratios was determined. These are the two measures most commonly used to distinguish value and growth stocks. Large ratios represent value stocks and small ratios growth stocks.

A clear positive relationship exists between B/P ratios and average stock returns. But high B/P ratios may operate as a risk measure for troubled firms with book values greater than stock prices. There is a U-shaped relationship between E/P ratios and average stock returns. As E/P increases, average returns first decline and then increase. Value stocks outperform growth stocks over the period.

Fama and French's results indicate the usefulness of value/growth criteria for classifying mutual funds. The results also indicate the usefulness of large-cap./small-cap. style criteria for classifying funds. A clear inverse relationship exists between stock cap. sizes and average returns. Small-cap. stocks have larger average returns than large-cap. stocks. But B/P ratios are stronger than cap. size in explaining stock returns. The bottom line is that value investing produces larger returns because value stocks are fundamentally riskier. Interestingly, beta has no power to explain stock returns following adjustments for market caps and B/P ratios. This finding created a cottage industry debating whether "beta is dead."

William Bernstein (1999e) followed Fama and French and examined the risk and returns of value and growth stocks for the years 1963–99. The (rounded) percentage performance results tabulated here were noted.

	Annualized return	Total risk	Largest annual loss
Small value	17	19	31
Small growth	10	23	51
Large value	15	15	28
Large growth	12	16	45

These return and risk findings are quite clear: small value outperforms small growth, and large value outperforms large growth. When risk/return are combined by dividing risk by return, large value has the least risk per unit of return, and small value ranks second.

The performance of value and growth investment style for the years 1976–99 is seen in table 69. Over this period, small value performed best 33 percent of the years (best record) and has by far the largest terminal wealth. Large value performed best 13 percent of the years and has the sixth largest terminal wealth. Small growth performed best 13 percent of the time and has the third largest terminal wealth. And, large growth performed best 25 percent of the time and has the seventh (worst) largest terminal wealth.

Lakonishok et al. Study

Lakonishok et al. (1994) made the case for value investing based on suboptimal investor behavior in overvaluing glamour stocks. The analysis includes stock data for the years 1963–90.

Since Graham and Dodd (1934), it has been argued that value investing outperforms the market. Value investing calls for buying stocks with low prices relative to earnings, dividends, historical prices, book assets, and other measures. Stocks with high E/P ratios, high B/P ratios, and high C/P ratios earn higher than market returns. Also, stocks that are extreme losers outperform the market over the following several years.

Value strategies work because they are contrary to the popular strategies followed by other investors. Popular strategies have variously been challenged for extrapolating past earnings growth too far into the future, assuming a trend in stock prices, overreacting to good or bad news, or equating a good company with a good stock. Investors tend to overbuy glamour stocks that have done well, with the result they are overpriced. They also tend to oversell stocks that have done poorly, with the result that out-of-favor value stocks are underpriced.

Contrarian investors outperform the market by betting against these popular strategies. They buy underpriced value stocks and sell overpriced glamour stocks. Value investors have also produced superior returns because they invest in stocks that are riskier. Value stocks tend to have higher fundamental risk, and their higher returns compensate for this risk.

In conclusion, Lakonishok et al. established three propositions. First, value style stocks outperformed glamour stocks over the period 1968–90. Second, this outperformance occurred because the actual future growth rates of earnings, etc., of glamour stocks were much lower than they had been or than they were expected to be based on their P/E ratios. Investors have consistently overestimated the future growth rates of glamour stocks relative to value stocks. Third, value strategies appear no more risky than glamour strategies, and the reward for risk does not seem to explain the higher returns on value stocks.

The weight of evidence supports the view that value stocks have been underpriced relative to their actual risk and return attributes. Value stocks provide 10–11 percent more in average annual returns than growth stocks. But, once established, how can the underpricing of value stocks persist for such long periods? The first reason may be that investors know less about value stocks. These are not the large and widely followed glamour stocks. Also the case for value stocks may not have been persuasive, especially prior to quantitative stock analysis and portfolio selection and evaluation tools.

A second reason may be that the value in value investing results from data snooping, which exists only by finding after-the-fact patterns in data. However, this is unlikely, because similar results have been observed in several time periods, in both domestic and international markets.

Zweig (1999b) used the Motley Fool Web site as an extreme example of data snooping. This site has popularized the idea that investors can outperform the market by following strategies that have no basis in rational theory. After the fact, it is easy to identify common attributes of stocks that did well and offer these attributes as a strategy that outperforms the market. Zweig concluded that these coincidental attributes based on perfect hindsight and no theoretical basis are "investment hogwash in its purest form."

A third reason is a systematic pattern of expectational errors by investors. Investor expectations of glamour stock earnings growth and returns are excessively tied to past growth rates and returns, despite actual future returns undergoing reversion to the mean. Investors expect glamour stocks to continue growing faster than value stocks, but they are systematically disappointed. This behavior pattern is also seen when earnings growth expectations are measured by five-year forecasts, rather than by P/E or P/C ratios.

These return differences between value and growth stocks are best explained by individual and institutional investor preferences for glamour stocks. There are several possible reasons for this. First, investors make judgment errors in extrapolating the past growth rates of glamour stocks. Too much emphasis is placed on recent past history and not enough on rational analysis. This is a common behavioral shortcoming. Second, while institutional investors should be rational, they prefer glamour stocks because these stocks appear more prudent and justifiable to fund shareholders and management. But glamour stocks are not really more prudent – they earn smaller returns and do not carry less risk.

Third, and related to the earlier discussion, most investors, portfolio managers, and fund management have shorter investment horizons than required for value investing to pay off. Value investing requires patience to realize abnormal returns, and three to five years is too long for most investors, portfolio managers, and fund managers to wait. Portfolio managers do not want to underperform benchmarks (*tracking error*) for any length of time, fearing loss of assets and/or their jobs. They also do not tilt portfolios towards value and its superior risk/return profile. As a result, portfolio managers do not aggressively arbitrage away the superior returns provided by value stocks. The initial existence of higher returns of value stocks appears due to investor judgment errors and institutional-investor preferences for safe portfolios.

Evidence of higher returns to value stocks over time and across countries suggests that the behavioral and institutional factors underlying them are pervasive and enduring. This difference in returns can explain why portfolio managers underperform the market by over 100 basis points a year before expenses.

LaPorta et al. study

LaPorta et al. (1997) made the case for value investing based on expectational errors by stock investors over the period 1971–93. Simple value strategies based on several ratios have produced superior returns over many years. One explanation is that these results are due to the higher risks of value stocks, as measured by high B/P ratios. But another explanation is that there is little evidence of additional risk. Value stocks are underpriced relative to their risk/return attributes for behavioral and institutional reasons.

Superior returns on value stocks are due to expectational errors made by investors in extrapolating past growth rates too far into the future. Earnings growth rates are predictable only one to two years into the future. But the P/E ratio differences between value and growth stocks reflect expectations that past growth rates will persist longer than is reliably predictable. Value stocks provide larger returns because the market slowly realizes that the earnings growth rates for value stocks are higher than initially expected, and conversely for growth stocks.

In conclusion, expectational errors about future earnings prospects are important to the superior returns of value stocks. Stock earnings surprises in the five years after portfolio formation are systematically positive for value stocks and negative for glamour stocks. Event returns for glamour stocks are significantly lower than glamour returns on the average day. This is inconsistent with a risk premium as the cause of higher returns on value stocks. Overall, in the first two to three years after portfolio formation, return differences from earnings announcements explain about 25–30 percent of annual return differences between value and glamour stocks. This percentage falls to 15–20 percent over years 4 and 5. The results for NYSE stocks are weaker, which suggests these stocks adjust to news more continuously.

The persistence of positive earnings surprises on value stocks long after portfolio formation is consistent with the finding that superior returns on value stocks persist long after portfolio formation. But the size of earnings surprises decreases more rapidly than annual return differences, which suggests that learning about future earnings prospects may not explain all of the return differences.

The superior long-lived returns of value versus glamour stocks have several explanations. First, investors may prefer investing in good companies with overvalued stock prices, but perceived as less risky, rather than undervalued value stocks. Second, institutional portfolio managers may favor well known glamour stocks because they are easier to justify to investors and bosses as prudent investments.

Other studies

O'Shaughnessy's (1996, 1997) widely noted book used 1954–94 data to test the returns of portfolios comprised of various combinations of value and cap. size investing. The key is to identify stocks using a combination of performance-enhancing variables and to follow the strategy consistently over the long term. Six simple value investing strategies were observed to be useful in combination: (1) lowest P/E, (2) lowest P/B, (3) lowest P/C, (4) lowest P/S (sales), (5) highest D/P, and (6) highest price momentum. The strategies were tested using large-cap. and medium-cap. stocks (all market) and largest-cap. stocks (large stocks).

The two best performing portfolios each generated annualized returns of a bit over 18 percent. The best strategy is applied annually and includes fifty all-market stocks with earnings increases for five consecutive years and P/S below 1.50. This simple strategy outperformed the S&P 500 Index in all thirty-two rolling ten-year holding periods. The strategy combined all-market stocks with earnings momentum and conservatively priced shares. The second best strategy is applied annually and includes fifty all-market stocks with the largest prior year earnings increases and lowest P/S ratios.

There are several other key findings. First, small-cap. stocks outperform all strategies, but there is insufficient market liquidity for profitable trading. Second, the strategy of buying stocks with the largest prior year earnings increases works periodically, but not long-term. And, third, all-market stocks outperformed large stocks over time, owing to smaller-cap. stocks.

However, there are findings that disagree with O'Shaughnessy's results. Barbee et al. (1996) determined that only the P/S ratio consistently explained stock returns over the period 1979–91. William Bernstein (1999b) analyzed the performance of each two-way (pairwise) comparison of the six ratios for all-market stocks and large-cap. stocks. The major and combined strategies were not tested. Bernstein stated that the analysis suffers from the peril of accepting back-tested strategies for future use. For large-cap. stocks, there are no pairwise combinations of the six individual strategies that statistically outperform the others. For all-market stocks the findings are better. The low P/S ratio strategy outperforms both low P/E and high D/P strategies. But the low P/S strategy is not significantly distinguishable from the low P/B and low P/C strategies.

Fama and French (1998) also investigated the value versus growth investment style issue in international markets. For the years 1974–94, there is a strong return premium to value investing, both domestically and internationally. Sorting on the B/P ratio, value stocks outperform growth stocks in twelve of thirteen major markets. The difference in average returns for high and low B/P ratios among global markets is over 7 percent per year. There are similar value premiums when sorting on E/P ratios, C/P ratios, and dividend yields, as well. The value premium also applies to the volatile emerging markets.

PERFORMANCE: SMALL-CAP. VERSUS LARGE-CAP. STOCKS

Small-cap. versus large-cap.

The small-firm effect refers to the tendency for small-cap. stocks to outperform large-cap. stocks over time. In earlier years, the performance of small-cap. versus large-cap. stocks shifted quite frequently. For example, small stocks outperformed large stocks from 1932 to 1934, and again from 1938 to 1945. Large-cap. stocks outperformed small-cap. stocks from 1935 to 1937 and, again, from 1946 to 1958. The small-cap. anomaly, when it appears, may be partly due to the much larger trading costs of small-cap. stocks. Another possibility is that beta (systematic risk) may not capture the true risk of small-cap. stocks when estimating risk-adjusted returns. There is also less information available on small-cap. stocks, which may explain why neglected stocks earn abnormal returns. Abnormal returns to small-cap. stocks are seen in both domestic and international markets.

Should small-cap. or large-cap. stocks be given priority in equity allocation? As discussed above, Fama and French (1992) observed an inverse relationship between cap. size and average returns. The performance of value versus growth stocks differs depending whether they are large-cap. or small-cap. stocks. The value/growth and large-cap./small-cap. issues are both discussed as elements of investment style and equity allocation.

The impact of cap. size on returns is also seen in Morningstar (1998) based on the relative returns of the Vanguard Index Small Cap. Stock Fund and the Vanguard 500 Index Fund, the large-cap. index fund. The 500 Index Fund has outperformed the Small Cap. Fund since 1993. Further, the 500 Index Fund outperformed the Small Cap. Fund in eight years: 1987, 1989–90, and 1994–8. And the Small Cap. Fund outperformed the 500 Index Fund in 1988 and 1991–3. The 500 Index Fund had an annualized return over 18 percent, versus nearly 11 percent for the Small Cap. Fund. In cumulative terms, a $10,000 investment in the 500 Index Fund grew to $54,951 over the last ten years versus $27,745 for the Small Cap. Fund.

As noted above, abnormal returns provided by small-cap. stocks may be an anomaly to efficient markets theory. This anomaly came to particular attention in Banz (1981), where, for the forty years ending 1975, total and risk-adjusted returns decreased as stock market caps increased. Average annual returns of stocks in the smallest size quintile were nearly 20 percent larger than average returns in the largest size quintile. But in the fifteen years since the study, large-cap. stocks have outperformed small-cap. stocks by more than two percentage points a year.

In later studies, the small-firm effect came to be called the *January effect* because annual abnormal returns are largely obtained in the first five trading days in January. Small-cap. stocks have more variable returns than large stocks, and are therefore more likely to be sold prior to year end for tax losses and window dressing but repurchased in January. The January effect has become less significant as more investors have attempted to profit from it. As stated above, this is a common outcome for anomalies – they are arbitraged away as they become well known.

Barbee (1999a) may have seen arbitrage in action in the finding that portfolio performance would have been improved if mid-cap. stocks had been substituted for small-cap. stocks over the past twenty years. Moreover, a 40/60 mid-cap. stock/S&P 500 Index portfolio allocation has less risk and about the same return as a 40 percent allocation to small-cap. stocks.

Finally, Damodaran (1998) analyzed three commonly used criteria for classifying value/growth stocks to determine the explanatory variables for each. Based on a sample of 1,400 firms, efforts were made to explain determinants of P/E ratios, P/B ratios, and P/S ratios. The P/E ratio was not significantly explained using a regression of expected five-year earnings growth, dividend payout, and beta. But P/B was significantly explained by a regression of expected five-year earnings growth, dividend payout, beta, and return on equity. And P/S was significantly explained by a regression of expected five-year earnings growth, dividend payout, beta, and net income to sales.

However, the P/S ratio has become widely used to justify market valuations of stocks with no earnings and no short-term prospects of any, but which are, nonetheless, following the "yellow-brick road to Oz" and a bright future based on technology. Does the term Internet stock come to mind?

Other issues

The debate concerning the relative size of large-cap. versus small-cap. returns continues, but Updegrave (1999) reported findings favoring large-cap. stocks. First, small-cap. returns are biased upwards because indices exclude subsequent failed and delisted stocks. On average, small-cap. stocks that leave the Nasdaq lose over 50 percent of value. When index returns are reduced to reflect these losses, the small-cap. return advantage disappears. Thus small-cap. index returns are inflated by survivor bias, which means the returns are partly illusory.

Second, the reported returns of small-cap. indices were not actually available to investors. Small-cap. stocks tend to trade in quite illiquid ("thin") markets, in which only a few hundred shares trade per week, and nearly 60 percent of the smallest shares do not trade at all. Thus any significant trades in such illiquid markets would have driven share prices up 20–40 percent from the prices at which the first shares were acquired. Again, small-cap. index returns are partly illusory.

A third argument is related to the second. Trading costs and portfolio turnover are significant. The bid–ask spreads on small-cap. stocks may be three or more times those of large-cap. stocks. These spreads reflect thin markets and greater risk. Thus, once more, small-cap. index returns are partly illusory.

A fourth and final argument is related to the fact that stock price increases typically occur over just a few days each year. That is, it is difficult for new stock purchasers to obtain annual index returns, which means small-cap. index returns are partly illusory to recent investors.

So, until the style winners, value or style and large-cap. or small-cap., are determined for long-term mutual fund investors, it is reasonable to diversify both by equity allocation (value/growth) and by cap. size. Based on domestic market capitalization, a 75/25 large-cap./small-cap. allocation is generated. The S&P 500 Index and the Russell 1000 index each approximate the vast majority of the total domestic market value, and the Russell 2000 represents the remainder.

However, the S&P 500 Index must be used with caution because it is not quite what it is generally assumed to be – the large-cap. universe. As a cap.-weighted index, the S&P 500 Index is dominated by the thirty largest stocks, of which twenty-five are growth stocks. This means there is no such thing as an equivalent size large-cap. value portfolio. Fisher (1998) noted that the ten largest stocks have the same impact on the index as the smallest 300 stocks. The thirty largest stocks skew the index, with an average cap. size of $60 billion, while the smallest stocks have an average cap. size of $10 billion.

As an example of the S&P 500's split personality, Zweig (1999e) reported that 90 percent of domestic equity mutual funds underperformed the S&P 500 Index in 1998. Worse, 42 percent of index stocks lost money as the overall index reached record heights. Fully one-third of the value of the S&P 500 Index is determined by just 5 percent of its stocks.

Based on the dichotomy in cap. size within the S&P 500 Index, Fisher (1998) suggested several rules for evaluating performance of real large-cap. and small-cap. stocks. First, if large caps are outperforming small-cap. stocks, the ten largest stocks in the S&P 500 Index will outperform the index. Second, equal weights of the 300 smallest stocks in the S&P 500 Index perform more like the Russell 2000 small-cap. index than the S&P 500 Index. Third, since the late 1980s, it has only been necessary to own equal amounts of the ten, fifteen, twenty-five or thirty largest stocks in the S&P 500 Index to outperform the overall index. This explains why most portfolio managers fail to beat the index. They must buy stocks with cap. sizes below $60 billion, unless they limit holdings to the thirty largest stocks in the index, which is not common practice. Fourth, historically, small-cap. stocks outperform large-cap. stocks in the first third of bull markets following bear markets, and large-cap. stocks perform best in the later stages of bull markets and throughout bear markets. Fifth, what works for outperforming the S&P 500 Index with its real large-cap. stocks does not work for the Russell 2000. When small-cap. stocks are performing best, stay focused on the S&P 500 Index, and attempt to beat it with $5 billion to $10 billion small-cap. stocks.

TWEEDY BROWNE ON VALUE AND SMALL-CAP. INVESTING

In Tweedy Browne (1992) the firm's investment philosophy is described as it relates to value/small-cap. investing and the supporting research literature. Summaries of forty-four individual studies are provided and organized into six approaches to value investing: (1) "Assets bought cheap," (2) "Earnings bought cheap," (3) "Investing with the inner circle . . . ," (4) "Stocks that have declined in price," (5) "Stocks with smaller market capitalization," and (6) "Interrelated [multiple variables] investment characteristics."

The study concluded by noting the attributes associated with earning abnormal stock returns. First, companies selling at low prices relative to net current assets, book value, and/or earnings often have many of the attributes associated with abnormal returns. Current earnings are often depressed relative to prior earnings, especially companies selling below book value. Stock prices are frequently low relative to cash flow, and dividend yield is often large. Company market capitalizations are generally small and company stock prices have often declined significantly. Corporate officers, directors, and other insiders have been accumulating shares.

Companies are frequently repurchasing shares in the market. Prices are often selling at discounts to estimates of company sale or liquidation values. When several of these attributes are combined, the results are undervalued stocks.

Second, these attributes are correlated with abnormal returns, but most lack conclusions concerning the pattern, sequence, or consistency of returns over subsets of longer measurement periods. Lakonishok et al. (1994) observed fairly consistent results over one-year holding periods and increasingly consistent results over three-year and five-year holding periods for low P/B and low P/C ratios. This increasing performance edge was seen in 43 percent of market declines over twenty-two years, and in 10 percent of the months with the largest largest percentage gains.

In Tweedy Browne's experience, it is possible to invest in stocks at prices significantly less than the underlying values of companies. Two examples of this are closed-end funds selling at discounts and companies selling for less than the cash value net of liabilities. These exceptions to efficient markets appear recurrently, but it is impossible to say whether such bargains will produce abnormal returns or what the pattern, sequence, or consistency of the returns will be. The underlying Tweedy Browne philosophy is summed up as follows: "[T]here have been recurring and often interrelated patterns of investment success *over very long periods of time*, and we believe that helpful perspective and, occasionally, patience and perseverance, are provided by an awareness of these patterns. . . . Patience and perseverance are required to capture these returns."

PERFORMANCE: LARGE FUNDS VERSUS SMALL FUNDS

The issue of size is also relevant for mutual funds, but here the focus is on fund asset size. As discussed previously, letting fund assets soar normally benefits investment advisors more than shareholders. Smaller funds have advantages that may translate to larger returns than for larger funds. For example, Wermers (2000) determined that small funds have better stock selection skills than large funds. Smaller funds are able to take larger positions (for them) in stocks of just about any cap. size. This facilitates a larger potential number of stocks in which they may invest. Thus they are less constrained by diversification requirements, which means they are normally able to invest only in stocks they really want to own. And smaller block trades lower trading costs relative to larger funds. These are normal performance advantages. Optimal asset size is also affected by the fund investment objectives and market cap. size of the stocks they hold. The optimal size of index funds with all cap. sizes that mimic the entire domestic market would be out of sight larger than the optimal size of sector funds that buy growth stocks. Optimal fund size increases with the market value of the stocks that are eligible to be purchased based on fund investment objectives and styles.

Zweig (1999d) also explored the reasons why small mutual funds may initially perform well and quickly increase in size. The first is just plain luck (perhaps not all luck) in opening funds just when the market has bottomed out – perfect timing. The second reason is temporary waiver of fund expenses to enhance performance and attract more investor dollars. And, again, the third reason is that small share blocks can be traded quickly and relatively inexpensively, unless less liquid securities in thin markets are held.

Mutual funds with small asset bases are small for one or more reasons. Some are just poor performers, and others are new, unknown, and untested. In this latter case, investors should require experienced portfolio managers before investing in new funds. Everything else being equal, investors should focus on small funds that limit asset growth, either by action or by explicit policy. The best place to find such funds is in families that have a history of limiting asset growth and consider investors as owners rather than customers. Unfortunately, the list is very short.

As noted, new mutual funds are small and there is always a degree of uncertainty involved in such investments. Less than 50 percent of new funds outperform their peers in the first year. Because of new fund uncertainties, Zweig (1996c) offers the following investor guidelines. First, invest in fund families known for success in offering new funds. Wolde and Young (2000) assist in this effort by presenting ten dysfunctional fund families to avoid, in general. Second, make sure the fund's investment objective (category) is appropriate. Third, be alert to expense ratios; they are large for new funds. Fourth, do not expect immediate performance miracles, even from star portfolio managers. Fifth, invest for the long term and minimize taxes. And, sixth, make sure investor risk preferences are consistent with the likelihood of volatility as portfolio managers try to get noticed for performance.

In addition to explicit action and policies limiting asset size, mutual funds also use less direct ways of limiting asset size. One way is not to hype funds, but to take advantage of small asset size to generate good returns. Other ways include the imposition of large initial purchase requirements, such as $10,000 or more, redemption fees, and direct/indirect prohibitions on known market timers. Some boutique funds apply strategies best suited for maintaining small asset bases. These specialty shops normally apply methodologies best suited for small portfolios and/or market segments. Boutiques may purposely limit asset size and remain independent of large fund families. They may also decline to distribute shares through brokers or fund supermarkets, and neither do they spend large amounts on advertising.

Mutual funds that purposely limit asset growth deserve special commendation for not following the usual route of growing the asset base far beyond optimal size to generate larger advisory fees. Zweig (1996c) reported that funds need only $200 million in assets before they start to make money for investment advisors. And Regnier (1997a) noted that smaller funds tend to be value funds or large-cap. funds. Hot small growth funds, in particular, tend not to stay unnoticed or small for long.

Mutual funds are subject to strategic changes, such as portfolio liquidations, mergers, changes of portfolio managers, and changes in market cap. Small-cap. funds appear to be very vulnerable to change. For example, Wright and Sanders (1996) examined the fate of twenty-seven small-cap. funds. Only five funds survived without change. Most funds experienced more than one change. For simplicity, each change is counted separately. Seven changes involved merging funds into other funds. Two funds were liquidated. Twelve changes represented changes from small-cap. to mid-cap. funds. Nineteen changes resulted in new portfolio managers. And two changes were made in investment style. Of the five funds surviving without change, only one outperformed its category over ten years. The five funds are all no-load in respected families, and three closed to new purchases at least once.

Asset size also differentially impacts the performance of value and growth mutual funds. Over a five-year period, Barbee (1998b) reported that value funds perform better than growth funds as asset size increases. Nonetheless, both value and growth funds have increased risk as asset size increases. But all cap. sizes of value funds deliver increased risk-adjusted returns as asset size increase. The same does not hold for growth funds. Their risk-adjusted returns quickly become negative and trail off as asset size increases.

The reason for this difference in risk-adjusted returns lies primarily with trading costs. As mutual funds' asset size increases, block size trades are larger, which increases trading costs. The trading costs of growth funds tend to increase more than those of value funds. Part of the reason is that growth funds are competing for the popular merchandise, while value funds look for unloved orphans. But, perhaps more important, growth funds have a higher portfolio turnover. Kinnel (2000) summed up the implication for trading costs in the statement that "[h]igh turnover, smaller caps, and big assets are an ugly mix." A strategy dependent on rapid portfolio turnover is vulnerable when asset growth increases trading costs.

PERFORMANCE: DOMESTIC STOCKS VERSUS INTERNATIONAL STOCKS

As discussed, all four model asset allocation portfolios (table 35) include international stocks. This is rational because for over forty years the benefits of international diversification have been emphasized. The reason: investing in international indices reduces the volatility of domestic portfolios because of the smaller correlation between international and domestic indices. It should therefore be no surprise that Paluch (1996a) reported that nearly 25 percent of domestic equity funds with assets over $1 billion have least 10 percent of assets invested overseas. This is also not surprising for funds in large fund families that have spent huge sums to establish expertise and operations overseas. But this may be surprising to investors who have focused on the much better performance of domestic stocks in recent years.

Solnik and other studies

The good news in international investing is that investors can mimic international indices by holding only domestically traded securities. It is not necessary to invest in securities that only trade overseas. In brief, Errunza et al. (1999) indicated that, based on 1976–93 data, most of the diversification benefits of internationally traded securities could be obtained with homemade (domestic) international diversification. Homemade portfolios include securities with claims on international assets that trade domestically, such as country closed-end funds, multinational corporation stocks, and mutual funds. The analysis indicates that: (1) investors can hold domestically traded securities to mimic those trading overseas; (2) the benefits of international diversification can be largely exhausted by investing only in domestically traded securities; and (3) homemade portfolios correct for the low correlation of domestic indices with internationally traded securities. Thus there is no need to take on the additional risks of direct international investing to gain the benefits of international investing.

In spite of the better performance of domestic stocks in recent years, the arguments for international investing are still quite compelling. In the first place, the domestic market is now only 50 percent of world stock market capitalization. So why should the opportunities for favorable returns and reduced portfolio risks be limited? There are international economies that are growing more rapidly than the United States, and there are also opportunities from gains in currency exchange rates. Although the correlations between markets change over time, there remain sizable opportunities for diversifying risk. And, this includes both stocks and bonds. While international markets move together when worldwide events take place, such as oil embargoes, in other times and over time they provide sufficient opportunities for risk diversification.

As a bonus, Rekenthaler (1995b) observed that the returns of domestic mutual funds with international holdings are more consistent than funds with only domestic holdings. This is seen in funds with global and international portfolios over three four-year rolling periods. Not surprisingly, the winners are characterized as having (1) low expenses, (2) substantially the same portfolio managers, (3) value or blend investment styles with low P/B ratios, and (4) no routine currency hedging. Their investment advisors were early entrants into international investing and have strong research capabilities overseas. These select funds either avoid currency hedging by holding international currencies or hedge international currencies back into dollars only occasionally. They tend to take the long view that currency movements even out over time. The dollar's long decline has made this an easy but also profitable strategy.

For the period 1971–98 Solnik (2000) observed that domestic *stock* markets are most closely correlated with the world portfolio (0.83) and Canada (0.70), and least correlated with Italy (0.26) and Japan (0.27). Domestic *bond* markets (in dollars) offer excellent diversification opportunities. They are most closely correlated with Canada (0.62), Germany (0.31), and the Netherlands (0.31), and least correlated with Italy (0.21) and Switzerland (0.22). These relationships are very conducive for reducing portfolio risk.

Moreover, it should not be assumed that low correlations exist only between domestic and international stocks. Similar disparities exist between large-cap. and small-cap. domestic stocks and between value and growth domestic stocks. These are the causes of the performance differences between these asset classes and justify including each investment style in Morningstar's category style boxes.

Also, over the period 1971–98, Solnik (2000) observed that the risk/return profiles of global *bond* portfolios greatly dominate domestic (only) bond portfolios. The minimum risk bond (only) portfolio was identified as 70 percent domestic and 30 percent international. Further, international bond allocations could be as large as 50 percent and still provide significantly larger returns with no additional risk than domestic (only) bond portfolios. This proportion of domestic/international bond allocations appears reasonable.

Next, Solnik (2000) examined the performance of domestic versus international stock portfolios. The risk/return profiles of global stock portfolios greatly dominate domestic (only) stock portfolios. For example, global stock portfolios with the same risk level as domestic stock portfolios would earn nearly three percentage points more in average annual returns.

As discussed by Barbee (1997b, 1998c), the traditional global minimum risk large-cap. stock portfolio is 70/30 S&P 500/EAFE. More recently, the minimum risk portfolio has been identified as 80/20 S&P 500/EAFE indices. This target allocation of pension plans is also 80/20 domestic/international large-cap. stocks. Moreover, William Bernstein (1995) optimized 80/20 as the minimum risk domestic/international large-cap. stock portfolio. Thus an 80/20 domestic/international stock portfolio allocation is both a conservative and reasonable recommendation for both large-cap. and small-cap. stocks.

Solnik (2000) also examined the volatility of the 80/20 domestic/international stock portfolio mix for the years 1971–97. Consistent with the 80/20 domestic/international stock minimum risk portfolio, the global stock portfolio has always been less risky than a domestic (only) stock portfolio. Despite temporary increases in domestic/international market correlations during world crises, international diversification has added value at all times.

Barbee (1998e) reconciled the poor five-year returns of international mutual funds (8.4 percent) versus domestic mutual funds (17.2 percent) within the 80/20 constraint on domestic/international stock portfolio allocations. First, international stock funds now provide more diversification than during the late 1970s and early 1980s. Over the past twenty years, the proportion of variance of returns that each type of stock explains of the other (R^2) has ranged from 53 to 80. But the 80/20 domestic/international stock allocation has not added risk-adjusted value relative to a domestic (only) portfolio. The bottom line is that the 80/20 domestic/international stock portfolio allocation may require years to pay off, but, long-term or short-term, does it make sense to assume anything less for future global growth?

Moreover, it is not difficult to find appropriate geographically diversified international mutual fund portfolios. Kelley (1995) determined that the average diversified international fund has 40 percent of its assets in Europe, 20 percent in Japan (higher then than later), and 20 percent in emerging markets. There are also good opportunities for investors seeking funds in particular countries. They include regional and single-country mutual funds and single-country closed-end funds, the latter generally selling at a discount to net asset value.

However, this is not to say that domestic/international stock allocations protect portfolios from short-term downturns. Only money market funds can do that. But international markets are not significantly more risky than domestic markets. For example, the average five-year and ten-year standard deviations of returns of European stock funds are about the same as domestic large-cap. growth funds.

Solnik (2000) also examined the 1980–90 diversification benefits of domestic/international stock *and* bond portfolios. The results are very pro international/domestic investing. Global stock/bond portfolios are more efficient than domestic (only) stock/bond portfolios, with twice the return for the same risk. In addition, global stock/bond portfolios are more efficient than global bond (only) portfolios or global stock (only) portfolios. International securities make a strong contribution to portfolio efficiency, both as international stock and as international bond additions. The global stock/bond portfolio is the dominant stock and/or bond portfolio.

Paluch (1996d) observed that it is more difficult to find effective diversification abroad than it is domestically. Japan represents about 40 percent of the EAFE stock index. The index funds tracking this index have been much more volatile than actively managed funds – the opposite of the domestic case. International indexing is more often a decision to concentrate geographically because investment style categories are less useful overseas than domestically.

This finding led Morningstar to use style box categories only for domestic equity funds. Investment style becomes blurred overseas because, for example, international funds might consider what would be a value stock domestically as a growth stock based on the country, rather than the stock. Thus country allocations play a much larger role than investment style in international fund performance. The relationship of high risk/return for domestic small-cap. funds does not generally hold overseas. What evidence there is suggests lower returns overseas. But international small-cap. stock funds are more effective than domestic large-cap. funds as risk reducers in domestic portfolios.

In the context of this discussion, Dziubinski (1999) recommended mutual fund investors take several steps to reduce the volatility of international investing: (1) limit fund investments in volatile emerging markets, (2) limit fund investments in Japan, which are overweighted in the EAFE index, (3) focus on large-cap. funds with *both* value/growth investment styles, (4) favor stock funds that rarely or never hedge exchange risk (currency risk) to minimize volatility, and (5) focus on funds with below-average expense ratios. The focus on low-expense international stock funds is particularly important because average expense ratios are 1.70 percent, versus 1.40 percent for domestic stock funds.

International exchange risk

International exchange risk is one of the major types of risks previously defined. Management of this risk is an important decision for mutual funds investing in international securities. Moreover, while currency movements can significantly impact returns, funds typically provide very little in the way of effective shareholder communication. For example, by how much did currency exchange rates impact fund returns last year? What is the portfolio's current exposure to currency movements, and what is the potential impact on returns? What is the fund's policy concerning the management of currency risks (hedge versus non-hedge) and how is it implemented, and what are the risk/return pros/cons of the policy?

As discussed by Lohmeier (1996), the lack of a stated policy concerning *hedging currency risk* is, in effect, an implicit decision not to hedge. Policies are explicit, even if not so stated, if funds always/sometimes hedge currency risk. The consequences of each policy decision differ. If portfolios are unhedged, dollar increases against other portfolio currencies reduce returns, and vice versa for declines in dollar value. Unhedged funds benefit from stable or declining dollar exchange rates. This policy benefited from the pre-1990s decline in value of the dollar. To be hedged is not always to be safe, however. Fully hedged portfolios can lose more than unhedged ones if asset returns are also considered. Portfolio managers who hedge only at particular times are basically timing exchange rates. And, of all markets, currency exchange rates are perhaps the most difficult to forecast correctly.

Dollar returns from international stock holdings are increased/decreased by changes in the value of the international currency relative to the dollar. Currency risk is inherent in international exchange transactions and is caused by currency fluctuations, such as when converting British pounds sterling to US dollars when the value of the dollar has increased relative to the pound. It is the additional source of variability in returns on international assets for domestic investors caused by currency fluctuations. For example, this risk (good or bad) occurs when US investors sell British stock and exchange the proceeds into US dollars. If the dollar devalued relative to the pound sterling while the British stock was owned, investors would receive an exchange bonus in dollars. The reverse would be true if the dollar increased in value relative to the pound. Domestic investors investing abroad thus benefit from a weak dollar exchange rate, and vice versa.

Arnott (1996) stated that currency hedging is less widespread among mutual funds than is assumed. Many world bond funds hedge currency risk, but only about one-third of all international stock funds do so frequently. The remaining two-thirds do so infrequently or never. Hedging is more frequent among top-down (broad trends) portfolio managers than it is among managers who select attractive stocks wherever they are located. Most international stock funds hold less than 10 percent of their assets in dollars. While currency movements provide additional risks for fund portfolios, active currency hedging also runs the risk of poor timing.

As reviewed in Penn (1994), currency exchange rates, like other market traded assets, respond to supply and demand. Exchange rates are very sensitive to expectations concerning the strength of economies. Countries with a strong trade balance typically have a strong currency because international demand for their products and services requires payment in their currency. For example, the long-term deficits in US trade balances thus weaken the dollar. High interest rates resulting from tight monetary policy also increase demand for the particular currency as international investors purchase the high-yielding bonds. The reverse is also true.

Exchange rate risk can be hedged in several ways. Solnik (2000) discusses these instruments and strategies in detail, along with the construction and management of international portfolios. The primary derivatives used for protecting against currency risk are currency futures (most commonly used), forward contracts, and option contracts. Portfolio managers adapt their hedging strategies given their expectations concerning asset performance in dollars and changes in exchange rates. The basic approach is to hedge the international currency values of international assets. Currency futures are used to hedge the international currency values of international assets. This involves selling short currencies in the amounts of asset values. In multicurrency portfolios, hedging involves the use of futures in the major currencies. Currency options are used to protect against adverse currency movements, while maintaining the profit potential from favorable currency movements.

However, Penn (1994) noted that currency risks do not affect all international portfolios to the same degree. For example, falling interest rates may cause a particular currency to decline in value and for stock prices to increase. Gains in stock prices are typically larger than losses due to declining exchange rates. But the risk is larger for international bond portfolios. Again, assuming decreasing interest rates, bond prices increase, but the increases are typically smaller than losses due to declining exchange rates. Thus many bond portfolios are partly dedicated to currency risk management.

Funds with international bond holdings often buy dollar futures contracts that allow them to sell specified amounts of particular international currencies for dollars at fixed exchange rates. These contracts reduce dollar portfolio losses from the devaluation of international currencies. But hedging can also cause funds to miss currency gains. If, for example, a fund buys a futures contract in dollars, and the international currency gains against the dollar, the fund incurs both costs and misses the dollar gain from the international currency devaluation. The key to profitable hedging is the ability to forecast currency exchange rates – another application of market timing and all its uncertainties. As a result, some funds do not hedge, knowing that unfavorable short-term changes in exchange rates are common, but over time tend to even out.

Nonetheless, the short-term performance implications of hedging can be significant. Rothschild (1998) computed that 23 percent of 1996 international fund returns were due to hedging, but only 13 percent in 1997. As an experiment, another fund ran duplicate portfolios hedged and unhedged. Over six months, the hedged portfolio outperformed the unhedged portfolio by two percentage points. Morningstar provides information on how frequently particular funds hedge their portfolios.

However, contrary to expected results, William Bernstein's (1999d) Markowitz-type optimizer determined that European currencies have great importance in efficient portfolios of global assets and currencies, most especially in high and moderate risk portfolios. The conclusion is "that unhedged international exposure is the way to go. . . . In the long run, currency exposure reduces overall risk, and probably increases return. . . ."

As reviewed by Winston and Bailey (1996), the debate whether or not to hedge international portfolios is long-standing. One side states that hedging provides free lunches of risk reduction to international portfolios, and a second states that hedging costs are prohibitively high for all but the largest international portfolio allocations. There are two basic strategies for managing currency risk. The first is passive currency management that implements permanent controls over portfolio currency exposure. This involves a policy decision that the additional volatility of uncontrolled currency exposure is unacceptable and should be reduced or eliminated. The second is *active currency management*, a form of market timing that manages portfolio exposure to currency exchange risk based on short-term forecasts of mispriced currencies. This active approach is expected to increase portfolio risk, not reduce it. Both approaches are hedging, but only passive currency management is actual hedging. Of the many positions on the desirability of hedging, Froot (1993) observed that hedging can reduce the short-run variance of portfolio returns, but that over the long term it increases the return variance of many portfolios.

Alternatively, Winston and Bailey (1996) provided an indirect approach to hedging currency risk that avoids the costs of actually implementing currency hedging policies. The approach is based on Sharpe's (1992) "effective asset mix." The idea is that *hedged* international stocks behave more like domestic assets in the *total* global portfolio. That is, hedging reduces the diversification benefit of international investing for the *entire* global portfolio. The implication is that exposure to domestic stocks may be increased and exposure to international stocks decreased with little or no adverse effect on the volatility of total global portfolios.

Historically, hedged international stocks have less volatility than unhedged international stocks, but, in the context of the total portfolio, substituting hedged for unhedged international assets reduces diversification and increases risk. Because hedging international assets is similar in some ways to increasing domestic assets, investors could increase domestic assets as superior to hedging international assets in reducing portfolio risk. For example, from 1972 to 1995, portfolios of hedged international stocks, domestic stocks, bonds, and short-term cash assets were no less risky than portfolios with smaller allocations of unhedged international stocks, along with proportionately larger allocations of domestic stocks and cash equivalents. Again, these unhedged portfolios have no adverse effect on portfolio variance.

As applied to the model stock/bond allocations in table 35, Winston and Bailey's (1996) approach could be approximated by reducing international stock allocations by 50 percent and adding the amount reduced to domestic stock allocations. Most important, the resulting international stock allocation should *not* be invested in hedged funds. This method provides computational ease in the context of the reasonably small international stock sub-allocations in most of the model stock/bond allocations. Alternatively, investors could invest either in funds that *never* hedge or in funds that *always* hedge. In either case, the return implications are about the same over the long term, but the hedging case is more volatile. Another alternative is for investors to invest equal amounts in otherwise substitutable hedged and unhedged funds to average out (stabilize) currency returns and risk over time.

All-weather portfolios

All-weather portfolios are broadly diversified long-term portfolios designed to work in all types of markets. These funds can provide an alternative for investors who wish to have their portfolio allocations and sub-allocations made by others. The allocations available to investors are quite wide – the proportions of stocks/bonds vary widely. Hickey (2000) reported that all-weather funds hold an average of 40 percent bonds, but can range to 70 percent or more.

One of the most enduring all-weather portfolios was created by Gerald Perritt in 1968, and periodically revised. One version included equal amounts of seven types of securities, including gold. Perritt's portfolio outperformed the S&P 500 Index with less risk for the years 1968–84. As reported by Burns (1997), the most recent portfolio includes equal amounts of four asset classes: cash, stocks, bonds, and gold. Real estate was omitted from this version because most investors have too much personal real estate. International stocks were also omitted because about 25 percent of operating earnings of S&P 500 stocks are derived overseas. However, this does not preclude international stocks from adding value in the optimizer. Also, the cash asset would be held in the cash bucket.

Burns adapted Perritt's portfolio to his "couch potato" portfolio, which is designed for inactive investors – his version of the chapter 6 model portfolios. This is the type of investor recommended for passive asset allocation portfolios. The Burns portfolio has two assets, one the Vanguard 500 Index fund and the other the Vanguard Total Bond Market Index fund. A 50/50 stock/bond allocation generated annualized returns of nearly 12 percent for ten years and nearly 14 percent for fifteen years. In comparison, the S&P 500 Index had annualized returns over 15 percent for ten years and nearly 17 percent over fifteen years. By changing the stock/bond allocation to 75/25, the portfolio had annualized returns of nearly 14 percent for ten years and over 15 percent for fifteen years. Consistent with earlier findings, portfolios do not have to be complex to do well.

BOND MUTUAL FUNDS

Bond mutual funds have taken a beating in more recent years in their efforts to compete with equity funds for investor dollars. Bond mutual fund assets are now less than equity fund assets, as the long bull market has attracted huge amounts to stock funds that in years past would have gone to bond funds. For example, Dziubinski (2000a) reported that bond funds held 50 percent of fund assets in 1989, but by 1999 they held 21 percent. However, as previously discussed, bonds play an important role in portfolio stock/bond allocations. And bond funds were discussed with respect to their Morningstar categories and investment style.

Bond mutual funds with loads played an important role in converting bank CDs to bond funds during the 1980s. Purcell (1994) reported that high fund yields (income distributions) made it easier to hide high sales loads and expense ratios, including 12b-1 fees. However, this is not the case when interest rates are low and loads/expenses represent even larger proportions of total returns. Portfolio managers find it very difficult to overcome these costs and continue to pay high yields. The nature of bond funds finds few consistent star portfolio managers, which is made even more unlikely by the efficiency of heavily traded bond markets. As a result, many funds attempt to adjust for high loads/expenses by investing in more volatile and less-liquid securities, including derivatives. But the general impact of low interest rates is reduced levels of fund performance.

Bond fund characteristics

As seen in table 7, bond mutual funds offer various investment objectives defined in terms of types of bonds, bond credit quality, and portfolio average maturity. More specifically, bond funds variously include debt securities issued by the US Treasury, government agencies, corporations, and municipalities (general and state-specific).

Credit quality ranges from US Treasury (the highest credit grade) to government agency (the next highest quality grade), to investment grade (AAA to BBB), and to high-yield non-investment grade (BB to D). Bond fund maturities are classified as short-term (one to five years), intermediate-term (five to ten years), and long-term (over ten years). Bond credit quality is based on the issuer's ability to pay the stated coupon interest rate and repay the principal at maturity. These characteristics affect the risk/return profiles of bond funds.

Maturity is a major characteristic because changes in bond mutual fund portfolio values are positively related to portfolio duration. Duration measures bond maturity based on the weighted average time for the remaining cash proceeds to be received. The longer the portfolio duration, the larger the sensitivity of bond portfolios to interest rate changes. Rekenthaler (1994a, b) determined that duration is most meaningful when fund R^2s are high, such as 90 percent. The larger the R^2, the larger the proportion of variance in bond fund returns due to duration. Duration is often inaccurate as a measure of interest-rate sensitivity because of fund holdings of other securities, including convertible bonds, international bonds, international stock, and derivatives. And duration is usually more accurate for small rather than large interest rate changes. As a result, duration and interest-rate sensitivity are most closely correlated in high-quality bond funds with consistent types and quality of holdings.

Bond fund myths and rules

While equity mutual funds normally outperform bond funds, Zweig (1997d) reviewed the up side of bond fund performance and identified several myths and rules concerning investing in bond funds. First, bond returns are not always much lower than stock returns. When interest rates fall, bonds often outperform stocks. Also, stock returns in recent years are not normal in absolute terms or relative to bond returns. In the long run, stock returns reflect dividend yields of ±3–4 percent and earnings growth rates of ±6–7 percent, for total returns in the ±9–12 percent range.

Second, there are times when bond returns are high enough to achieve long-term goals. At 7 percent, ten-year bonds double the principal in ten-plus years. Third, stocks and bonds together provide increased diversification. While stock and bond returns are highly correlated in the short term, over the longer term – say, five years – their returns are less than 50 percent correlated. And, fourth, it is better to buy bonds directly than buying bond funds only if the investor has the time, skill, and cash needed for proper diversification.

Further, bond fund returns are more predictable than stock returns. For example, Zweig (1997d) reported that domestic stocks have lost at least 10 percent eight separate times since 1926. This contrasts sharply with intermediate Treasury bonds. Bond funds also outperform stock funds when interest rates fall sharply and stock fund returns are around or below long-term annualized returns. On the down side, bond funds generate relatively large amounts of taxable interest income, which makes then more desirable holdings in tax-deferred accounts.

Next, the rules for investing in bond mutual funds include the following. First, by knowing their risk preferences and investment horizons, investors can select appropriate bond fund durations (discussed below) to avoid unnecessary interest-rate risk. The sensitivity of bond prices to interest-rate changes is lessened by buying bonds of short duration. Interest-rate risk can be largely eliminated by closely matching bond duration to investment time horizon. Second, the largest enemy of bond fund yields and total returns is fund expenses/loads/fees. They comprise a large proportion of bond interest income. There is a high negative correlation between bond fund expenses and total returns.

Third, the appropriate measure of bond returns is not yield, but total return (yield plus capital gains/losses), the same measure used for stock funds. High bond fund yields and low risk do not go together. Fourth, historically, bond funds that perform well and survive are those that invest consistently with their fund names as correctly reflecting their actual investment objectives. The SEC requires them to invest 80 percent of assets, as suggested by their names. And fifth, bond funds are usually tax-inefficient, so place taxable funds in tax-deferred accounts or buy municipal bond funds.

Gillis (1995) reported another myth implicit in the argument whether bonds or stocks will outperform over the long term. This argument when applied to bond mutual funds fails to recognize that the more bond funds attempt to outperform stock funds, the less they provide traditional bond benefits. Unfortunately, many bond funds pander to investors chasing yields. Numerous funds that "play the yield game" have taken on more risk to maintain yield, which has often resulted in capital losses in their portfolios. The easy remedy for avoiding the myth of yield as the return is simply for investors to focus on total return. The more bond funds take on equity characteristics, the greater the risk to portfolio value.

Bond funds versus bonds

Bond mutual funds provide both advantages and disadvantages compared with investor direct ownership of bonds. Individual bonds can provide stability of principal value *if* held to maturity, as well as fixed coupon interest payments. Bond funds cannot provide this advantage because they hold bond portfolios with various maturities. The portfolio does not mature at a given point in time. Individual bonds also provide specific maturities. Bond funds do not provide this because they continuously hold portfolios of bonds with different maturities. However, bond funds usually have relatively consistent average maturities, which enables investors to select maturity ranges with reasonable confidence that they will be maintained.

In addition, investors can buy new Treasury bonds at low cost direct from the Treasury. This avoids bond mutual fund expenses and loads on Treasury securities, but does not provide access to the wider range of bonds that may be desirable for diversification. Funds have more expertise to deal with lower-quality bond trades in less liquid markets and routinely handle bonds redeemed prior to maturity. Further, directly owned bond portfolios need to be large enough – say, $100,000 – to be able to provide needed diversification by bond type, maturity, and credit quality. These directly owned portfolios also require expertise and time for portfolio management. Investors must take direct action to maintain average maturity in self-directed portfolios.

Bond mutual funds also provide the advantages offered by mutual funds generally. These advantages include portfolio diversification, explicit choice of investment objective, professional management, instant shareholder liquidity by redemption, the potential for no-fee shareholder transaction costs, automatic reinvestment of interest payments, and the array of other fund shareholder services. Automatic reinvestment provides compounding of interest payments at market rates and convenience.

On the other hand, bond funds may have several disadvantages compared with direct bond ownership. These disadvantages include fund expenses, fund trading costs due to portfolio turnover, constraints on shareholder tax planning, and regulatory issues impacting fund investors.

Bogle study

Expenses have an inordinate impact on bond mutual fund returns. To measure this impact, Bogle (1999b) examined four types of bond funds: (1) municipal bonds, (2) short-term US Treasury bonds, (3) intermediate-term Treasury bonds, and (4) intermediate-term bond funds (normally corporate bond funds). In three of four types of funds, bond funds in the low-cost quartile outperform funds in the high-cost quartile by amounts closely equivalent to the differences in expense ratios. In the fourth type of bond fund, returns on the funds in the low-cost quartile are only slightly higher than those in the high-cost quartile, but high-cost funds hold more risky portfolios.

This higher degree of bond mutual fund risk is seen along three dimensions. First, durations are longer, which increases the sensitivity of portfolio market values to changes in levels of interest rates. Second, monthly returns are more volatile than peer groups. And, third, portfolio credit quality is lower, as measured by Standard & Poor's ratings.

For each of the highest to lowest expense quartiles of short-term Treasury bond funds, for example, duration ranges from 2.3 years, 2.4 years, 2.4 years, and 1.9 years, respectively. The higher are fund expenses, the more duration risk there is as funds take on more risk in efforts to earn higher returns and offset higher expenses, such as anticipating changes in interest rates. In turn, the volatility of portfolio returns ranges from 0.69 percent, 0.70 percent, 0.58 percent, and 0.53 percent, respectively. The higher fund expenses, the more the volatility of portfolio returns as funds attempt to increase returns to offset them. And, finally, credit quality, as measured by percentage of Treasury securities in the portfolio, ranges from 92 percent, 95 percent, 99 percent, and 97 percent, respectively. In general, the higher expenses, the lower the credit quality of the portfolio, again in efforts to increase returns and offset higher expenses.

To identify the impact of expenses on five-year annualized returns, the returns of each type of bond fund were reduced by the expense ratios. For example, for each of the highest to lowest expense quartiles of short-term Treasury bond funds, gross returns were reduced by 26 percent, 15 percent, 12 percent and 7 percent, respectively. The other types of bond funds also suffered significant reductions in returns. By comparison, index bond funds experienced just a 3 percent reduction in gross returns. This illustrates the major reason behind the statements of those who favor indexed bond funds.

Measuring returns

Shareholder returns on bond funds have three components, the same as equity funds: current income (interest income, net of expenses), distributions of realized capital gains, and increases/

decreases in net asset value from unrealized capital gains. Interest income is measured as a percentage of net asset value – the yield. The yield is important to shareholders relying on steady sources of income. Bond funds have several methods for advertising and paying current larger income distributions to shareholders. These include low expenses, investing in higher-risk bonds, changing average portfolio maturity in anticipation of changes in interest rates (market timing for bond funds), and maximizing current yields and distributions.

Bogle (1999b) described the method for maximizing current yield. Funds buy Treasury notes at premium (above face value) and then advertise and pay the full coupon (stated) rate to shareholders, net of expenses. These yields are high when premiums are not amortized against current income, but rather are charged against net asset value over time. This maximization of current yield thus guarantees future reductions in net asset value. As premium bonds approach maturity, their prices reduce toward face value. Charging premiums against net asset value also reduces fund assets over time, thereby reducing the asset base for generating future returns. In other games, funds buy bonds selling at discount to face value and add the accretion of discount to advertise high yields.

The yields advertised by bond mutual funds can also differ from yields computed using the required "SEC yield." The SEC yield is computed using a specified formula that assumes bonds are held to maturity. In practice, bond funds often sell bonds before maturity, but some overall assumptions are required to provide comparable yields among funds. The SEC requires this yield in response to the games funds have played with advertised yields and yield computations over the years. This is not to say, however, that all bond funds play accounting games to advertise high yields. Some few funds do not. Differences in accounting for bond premiums make it all the more important for investors to focus on total returns, rather than only the yield component. Rekenthaler (1994c) further discusses and explained these sham practices.

Sanders (1996) tested the impact of these bond mutual fund practices on their future income yields. Funds that paid the largest yields five years ago usually did not pay the largest cumulative dollar yields over the next five years. Only sixteen of the funds that paid the highest yields were among the fifty funds that paid the largest cumulative dollar yields over the next five years. As discussed above, the major reason is that many funds earlier maximized yields and then subsequently charged amortized premiums to net asset value.

Bond fund risks

Bond mutual funds to varying degrees are subject to the risks discussed previously. But the most significant risks for *domestic* (only) funds are interest-rate risk (the number one risk), income risk (somewhat analogous to market risk), call and prepayment risks (also somewhat analogous to market risk), credit risk (analogous to financial risk), and inflation risk.

Interest-rate risk refers to declines in net asset values due to increases in interest rates. Income risk refers to the impact of declining market interest rates on fund income and yield distributions. This risk is most significant for short-term bond funds because their bonds obviously mature frequently. The proceeds are thus reinvested in bonds paying lower market interest rates. Call risk and prepayment risks are also important. They are the risks that bonds will be redeemed prior to maturity. This happens when debtors refinance the debt to take advantage of lower interest rates. Funds must normally reinvest these proceeds at lower market interest rates. Credit risk is variously important depending whether, for example, bond funds invest in US Treasury bonds or junk bonds. Credit quality refers to the ability of the borrower to repay the debt according to the terms of the agreement. The higher the credit rating, the lower is the default risk or chance of ratings downgrade. Inflation risk is especially important to bond investors who depend on current yield distributions, which lose purchasing power over time owing to inflation.

Kelley (1996) studied bond mutual fund risk and reported how to assess it. Fund use of derivatives has often been an unpleasant surprise to investors. The most effective way to analyze fund risk is to determine portfolio concentration. Fund portfolios with more than 25 percent of fund assets invested in one sector have been susceptible to sharp downturns. Other warning signs of risk include standard deviations of returns in excess of 10–15 percent and Morningstar Risk greater than 1.0 and ranging to 1.3 for aggressive funds. Funds with apparent low risk based on one of the following measures can still be risky: Morningstar Risk, beta, and standard deviation. The usefulness of the measures also varies.

Bond fund risk strategies

Bond mutual funds employ several diversification strategies to minimize losses due to increases in interest rates. Purcell (1993) found that these strategies include: (1) investing in less rate-sensitive corporate and high-yield bond funds, and international and global bond funds; (2) investing in bond funds with limited maturities; and (3) investing in intermediate-term bond funds. The latter offer approximately 90 percent of long-term returns with only about 50 percent of the volatility.

Because bond mutual fund returns are so sensitive to interest rate changes, Dziubinski (1998d) provides investor guidelines. But, first, it is useful to compare bond fund management prior to and after 1994. In 1994 the Federal Reserve raised interest rates five times, with the result that the average return on long-term bond funds was −6 percent. The good old days for bond funds were characterized by maximum bond yields, but also by changing portfolio maturities based on interest-rate forecasts and the use of customized exotic derivatives to boost yields.

Since then, there has been much less investor interest in load funds and, most important, funds have learned the hard lesson and now manage portfolios more conservatively. Bond funds typically focus on total return (yield plus capital gains), use duration to limit downside interest rate risk, and use plain vanilla derivatives.

One of the hard lessons for bond mutual funds has been efforts to boost returns by forecasting changes in interest rates. Interest rate forecasting is often a major aspect of fund portfolio management, but this is a dangerous occupation. It is very difficult to forecast rates consistently better than by not forecasting them. In general, sophisticated interest rate forecasting models are less accurate than naive forecasts of no change in rates. Published short-term forecasts by economists generally appear more accurate than forecasts of no change, but this is not the case for longer-term forecasts.

Short-term interest rates have a tendency to follow a mathematical process that extrapolates recent rates. This appears analogous to momentum investing in stocks. Major bond markets appear somewhat efficient, with Treasury bond markets very efficient. The implication is that it is difficult to forecast interest rates more accurately than by simply assuming no rate changes. Sharpe et al. (1999) discussed this issue with references.

While it has been proven risky for bond mutual funds to make portfolio adjustments based on interest rate forecasts, there is no question that bond funds reduce portfolio risk, and low-cost funds provide higher returns than high-cost funds. Both taxable and non-taxable bond funds should be considered, to determine which generate higher after-tax returns, including both federal and state taxes.

The best compromise solution for the bond mutual fund part of the stock/bond allocation (table 35) is to take the middle ground. This means to moderate potential gains and losses from interest rate moves by focusing on intermediate fund duration. This approach is consistent with Paluch's (1997c) rules that require investors to focus on (1) funds with intermediate-term duration, (2) funds with low expense ratios, (3) fund total returns, not just yields, and (4) fund diversification across bond types. For example, during the last six bear markets for Treasury bonds, equal portions of Treasury bonds, junk bonds, and international bonds earned higher returns (three times) or had smaller losses (also three times) than Treasury bond funds. These diversified investments can be satisfied by *multi-sector bond funds* that buy all types of bonds or funds of funds that hold only bond mutual funds.

So what are satisfactory substitutes for bond mutual funds that follow the siren song of interest rate gurus? Such an example is the Vanguard Total Bond Market Index Fund (table 70). This type of fund is appropriate for stock/bond allocations, especially when portfolio and management simplicity is desired. Investors can index the *domestic* bond/stock allocations with two funds – the Vanguard Total Stock Market Fund and the Vanguard Total Bond Index Fund. Further, investors can index international equity markets with the Vanguard Total International Index Fund.

The Total Bond Market Index fund's portfolio is representative of the domestic bond market, with about 67 percent of its portfolio in the highest-quality bonds. This fund is worthy of consideration if for no other reason than its very low 0.2 percent expense ratio, which benefits from passive portfolio management. But, there is more. Returns are in the thirteenth or fourteenth percentile of its category for the last three and five years, which means it has outperformed the vast majority of funds in its category, both indexed and actively managed. The fund's portfolio has an average maturity of about eight years, but, more important, its portfolio duration is only about four years. The fund's downside risk is therefore quite limited – a one percentage point increase in interest rates has a downside portfolio risk of only about 4 percent of assets.

Bond fund performance

Bonds have not been subjected to the same intensive study as stocks. Less is known of the variables that are important in explaining bond returns. Elton et al. (1995) attempted to correct this lack by analyzing the returns of 123 bond funds for the years 1980–92. Bond returns are studied both with respect to given periods of time and over time. The variables tested include (1) stock index returns (expected economic conditions), (2) default risk, (3) term (maturity) risk, (4) unexpected changes in inflation, (5) unexpected changes in economic performance,

(6) bond index market returns, and (7) options (derivatives) risk. Unexpected changes in economic variables are based on changes in expectations, using survey data.

The most inclusive model is important in explaining bond mutual fund returns and expected returns over time. The defined return indices are most important to explaining patterns of bond fund returns over time. The addition of the defined fundamental variables provides the largest improvements in explaining expected returns. Overall, bond fund returns in general are negatively related to unexpected increases in anticipated inflation. These increases are captured in higher interest rates. And bond fund returns in general are negatively related (positive for corporate bonds) to unexpected increases in anticipated economic activity (GNP). Increased economic activity tends to increase interest rates and lower bond prices.

The average percent of explained bond mutual fund mean returns contributed by each variable is dominated by the aggregate bond market index, which represents 73 percent. Unexpected changes in inflation and GNP explain 14 percent and 5 percent, respectively, and the other variables explain only 8 percent.

The negative impact of bond mutual fund expenses on no-load fund returns varies from about 0.75 percent to 1.5 percent a month. The situation is not much improved when expenses are added back. Average returns before expenses are minus 3.5 basis points relative to the index. Thus there is no evidence that, on average, portfolio managers provide superior returns even if their services are free. In conclusion, expenses are the major cause of bond fund underperformance. Thus it is important for investors to buy low-expense funds, such as low-cost index bond funds.

To visualize how these allocations and assumptions work to define the portfolio parameters of a model portfolio for moderate-risk investors with growth portfolio investment objectives (table 34), refer to table 70. The findings, less value/growth allocations, are the same as in table 35. Table 70 includes portfolio sub-allocations for each stock/bond allocation and an example of the process based on a 60/40 stock/bond allocation. The holdings in the 60/40 stock/bond allocation are 18 percent domestic large-cap. value *and* 18 percent domestic large-cap. growth. Next, are 6 percent holdings in domestic small-cap. value *and* 6 percent domestic small-cap. growth. The largest (and only) bond holdings are 28 percent domestic bonds and 12 percent international bonds.

Close and not so close variations of table 70 are widely available from major fund families, investment advisors, brokerage firms, financial planners, and the like. Each has its own emphasis, but they are generally similar for given investment objectives. Interestingly, Vanguard's John C. Bogle is reported by Stevens (2000) to have a 58/42 stock/bond allocation in the Vanguard funds in which he invests. The 58 percent stock allocation is forty-two percentage points indexed and sixteen percentage points actively managed. The 42 percent bond allocation is forty percentage points indexed and two percentage points actively managed.

Table 70 incorporates the long-term performance realities of each style of equity fund investment and domestic/international bond funds. The portfolio mix represents the importance of asset allocation and style allocation relative to specific fund selection. Each particular allocation also reflects the objective of risk minimization and the general inability to make accurate market and investment style forecasts. Investors should make certain the portfolio allocations they choose are those they can live with in good times and bad, and over time. Reasoned changes may of course be made as personal conditions change, but care must be exercised to prevent these adjustments being disguised versions of market timing.

ISSUES IN STOCK AND BOND FUND PERFORMANCE: INDEXING

Thousands of articles have been published on stock and mutual fund performance, including the tax implications. What mutual fund investors need is an assessment of what the current truth is. To this end, Sharpe et al. (1999), Bodie et al. (1996), Jones (1998), and Reilly and Brown (1997) provided coverage and references concerning mutual fund performance. McGinn (1999) discussed the major stock indices benchmarked by index funds and a listing of the larger index funds. The focus here and in the sections that follow is to identify strategies that mutual fund investors can use to (1) assist in implementing and rebalancing passive stock/bond allocation portfolios, or (2) add to or substitute for passive allocation.

Another important issue for mutual fund investors is whether to buy actively managed portfolios or passively managed indexed portfolios. Indexing versus managed portfolios has been one of the great controversies. For one reason, many investors and portfolio managers believe it is un-American to settle for average returns. This belief is strongly held by many despite the fact that Bogle (1999b) reported that 79 percent of all surviving equity funds failed to beat the market index during the first twenty years of index funds. This issue is discussed more thoroughly in the context of stock funds below.

Vanguard 500 Index Fund was the first retail domestic index mutual fund. As reviewed by Lowenstein (1999), when the fund opened in 1976 it was called Bogle's Folly, after then Vanguard chairman, John C. Bogle. The fund attracted all of $11 million the first year, a major disappointment. The fund remained open only because it was the boss's project. The fund did not reach $10 billion in assets until 1995, almost twenty years later. Well, the Vanguard 500 Index is far from the only index fund today, but it retains its premier position as both largest mutual fund and largest index fund, with over $110 billion in assets. The fund's benchmark index is, of course, the S&P 500 Index, the most widely used benchmark index. In fact, the index represents only about 75 percent of the domestic market, the large-cap. portion.

To take this point a bit further, Nocera (1999) reported James Riepe of T. Rowe Price as stating the S&P 500 Index is "a large-cap. growth fund." The implication is that the popularity of S&P 500 index funds is explained by the performance of large-cap. growth stocks, not that they are index funds. Well, maybe. Nonetheless, Nocera's conclusion is seen in the title of his article: "The Age of Indexing. Indexing has won."

Wells Fargo Investment Advisors introduced indexed portfolios in a few pension plans in 1969–71. Over the years, especially in the early years of the Vanguard 500 Index, index funds received a great deal of mostly negative press. But they finally received their just do when Ellis (1975) concluded that the premise that professional portfolio managers can beat the market "appears to be false." This statement aroused much anger, dismay, and, even to this day, disbelief among many of his peers. Indexing is an idea that took a long time to earn its proper role in managing money.

Academic support for indexing is primarily traced to Malkiel (1973), who concluded that chimpanzees throwing darts at the *Wall Street Journal* stock listing could select portfolios as well as the experts. The recommendation is to buy widely diversified stock index funds. By the late 1970s, most academics agreed that the stock market was reasonably efficient. However, since then, research has observed anomalies that challenge the theory. These efforts appear to be increasingly successful, but the battle continues.

Clements (1998) reported several investor beliefs and behaviors that make it difficult for individual investors to invest in index funds. First, investors think they can beat the market, but they are overconfident and overly optimistic. Second, investors believe there is order in the market, if only they knew the key. They cannot believe that the market is random. Third, investors use investment newsletters because they want to be told the key to the market, but newsletters do not provide superior advice, especially after trading costs. Fourth, investors want to be able to take credit for good performance and blame others, such as newsletters, for poor performance.

Efficient markets and index funds

In Malkiel (1995, 1998, 1999a, b), support of index funds based on efficient markets theory of stock prices and the random walk is again reviewed and renewed. The most lucid summary of Malkiel's position is in Burton (1999b). The theory states that when new information arises about stocks or the market, the news spreads quickly and is immediately incorporated into securities prices. This theory is associated with the random walk, which characterizes a price series in which subsequent price changes are random. Based on efficient markets, if information is immediately incorporated into securities prices then tomorrow's price changes are dependent on tomorrow's information and are independent of today's price changes. The arrival of news to the market is unpredictable and therefore price changes based on news are unpredictable and random. To the extent that markets are efficient, the anomalies are not dependable sources of abnormal returns.

By the 1970s, researchers had generally accepted that markets are efficient. A historical series of prices appears to provide no helpful information in predicting future price movements. Further, prices incorporate fundamental information so rapidly and efficiently that both uninformed and informed investors could earn equivalent returns. By the 1980s, however, there were numerous challenges to efficient markets. Stock returns from period to period are not independent, being positively correlated over short periods and negatively so over longer periods. Seasonal and day-of-the-week price patterns were identified.

Moreover, there appears to be a considerable degree of predictability of stock returns based on initial dividend yields, market cap. size, P/E ratios, and P/B ratios. However, predictability of returns does not necessarily imply market inefficiency. Tests of return predictability may reflect rational variation over time in expected returns. Tests of efficiency are joint tests of both the return pattern being tested and the asset-pricing model used.

Nonetheless, the strength of various patterns of return predictability suggests that the 1970s version of efficient markets was unwarranted. Predictable patterns of returns have been interpreted as implying the existence of superior risk-adjusted returns. Measures of mutual fund returns suggest that funds can outperform the market, at least before expenses. But, because funds that terminated operations were often excluded from performance figures, overall fund returns include survivor bias of about 150 basis points. Once returns are adjusted to eliminate this bias, fund returns tend to underperform the market after expenses, but also before expenses except loads. There is no evidence of abnormal returns.

Small-cap. stocks tend to outperform large-cap. stocks over time, and stocks with low P/E and P/B ratios tend to outperform those with high ratios. But these small ratios may actually represent higher risk, requiring higher returns. High dividend yields have tended to outperform low yields historically, but today's low yields reflect low interest rates. Further, the fact that so few portfolio managers outperform the market index gives practical support to market efficiency.

In conclusion, there is no reason to abandon the idea that markets are remarkably efficient. Most investors benefit from buying low-expense index funds, rather than trying to select funds with hot hands. The advantage of passive portfolio management holds – active management generally fails to provide abnormal returns, but it does generate higher investor taxes. A compromise solution is discussed below.

Sauter and Miller on indexing

Would you believe that a mutual fund portfolio manager who manages over $100 billion in assets could be relatively unknown, except by professionals? This lack of publicity agrees with George Sauter, who is Vanguard's head of index funds. He not only manages the first domestic index fund, the hugely successful Vanguard 500 Index, but also twelve other Vanguard index funds. But there is more. Sauter also is the sole portfolio manager of an actively managed mid-cap. growth fund, and he shares portfolio management duties for two other managed portfolios, including Vanguard Windsor II.

Barbee (1997a) described Sauter's quantitative approaches to both passively and actively managed funds. These approaches reflect Sauter's guiding philosophy about market efficiency. That is, indexing assumes markets are efficient – no information is available to separate stocks that will perform well from those that will not. Active portfolio management, on the other hand, is analogous to "indexing with information." It is this information, along with low expenses and defined risk levels, that makes it possible for funds in less efficient small-cap. markets to beat the market. This description speaks quite accurately to the realities of market efficiency and its impact on fund performance.

In DiTeresa (1999a), Vanguard's active and passive portfolio manager, George Sauter, provides a succinct description of the power of indexing:

> Indexing's key advantage is long-term outperformance. Look at the Morningstar style-box categories and you'll find that in every one, the indices beat the majority of funds over the long haul. That wasn't just chance, and there's good reason to expect the pattern to continue. A lot of people think the argument for indexing is that the market is efficient, that each stock's price reflects the current value and the future prospects of the underlying company. I do think the market is *relatively* efficient, but I want to make a more robust argument than that for indexing.
>
> Simply put, investing is a zero-sum game. All investors collectively own the market, so as a whole, they must get the market rate of return. Some investors can outperform, but if they do, it requires others to underperform. Unlike the children of Lake Wobegon, not all investors are above average.

As seen in table 21, index mutual funds, especially no-load funds, have a built-in advantage because of lower expenses and trading costs and higher tax efficiency. Large-cap. market indices typically have only a few changes in the stocks they include in the index. This stability translates to very low portfolio turnover for large-cap. index funds – thus lower realized and taxable capital gains. However, because index funds do not trade their portfolios, they would have large realized capital gains if the market crashed and investors redeemed with urgency. The remaining shareholders would pay the entire (large) tax bill. They also do not hold cash balances other than for operating purposes, which means more assets at risk if the market crashes.

Legg Mason mutual fund portfolio manager Bill Miller takes a different slant on the relative merits of indexing and active management. Miller stated that while everyone talks about the performance of the average mutual fund, no one actually buys the average fund, the implication being that there are both good and poor performing portfolio managers. Thus the way to add value is through portfolio manager selection, "[and] there are a number of funds that have, on average, beaten the S&P over time." However, this does not solve the problem for investors, who have to be able to identify the portfolio managers who will perform well.

Miller considers himself a value investor, an investor who has outperformed the S&P 500 Index for ten straight years through 2000. From this performance, contrasted with that of other value managers, it is obvious he is not a traditional value investor. Many consider Miller a growth investor, based on his holdings of technology stocks that have appreciated far beyond any reasonable concept of "fair value," as defined by traditional value investors. His response is that the fair value of these holdings has increased and continues to exceed market values. In any case, this argument worked well in a market dominated by large growth stocks. And the fund had a smaller negative return than the S&P 500 Index in 2000.

As discussed by DiTeresa (1998b), Miller believes the market is efficient over the long term, but not necessarily at any given point in time. The market eventually corrects mispriced securities. Miller has been successful in buying two types of mispriced stocks. One type is stocks that grow longer or faster than the market expects. The second type is stocks that have been beaten down in price, but come back in price sooner than expected. He does not sell stocks when they reach prices assessed as fair value when purchased, and this is where he differs from typical value investors. Miller is indifferent to being called a value or growth investor because he says he values businesses, not stocks. Miller holds securities until they catch up with his forward-looking constantly updated value assessments. This has allowed him to hold on to technology stocks with greatly elevated prices from time of purchase, such as Dell.

Interestingly, Miller described the S&P 500 Index as "a very successful actively managed portfolio." A committee selects the stocks – they do not simply choose the 500 largest market-cap companies. The portfolio is diversified to be broadly representative of the US economy. The companies are industry leaders with financial strength and have been in business for a number of years. The stocks have adequate trading volume to make them easy (and cheap) to trade. Is should be noted that the index also includes internationally based companies. This selection process is one that individual investors could also do on a more limited scale.

Indexing stock funds

Dziubinski (1998b) and DiTeresa (1999a) provided the Morningstar take on managed versus index mutual funds, following Sauter and Miller. In both studies, the point is made that both active and passive mutual funds have a role in portfolios. DiTeresa concludes that investing in domestic large-cap. stocks favors indexing, with low expenses and low turnover. Investing in small-cap. stocks favors *selected* actively managed funds or indexing in general. Investing in international stocks favors either active or passive, depending on location. Indexing is strong for developed countries, but Japan adds volatility to indices. Active management is best for emerging markets or specific regions. Finally, investing in bonds also favors either indexing or active management, depending on the type of bonds. Active management can add value in some types of bonds.

DiTeresa reported that actively managed equity funds that outperform index funds have very similar characteristics: (1) very low (50 percent less than average) portfolio turnover, (2) large industry sector concentration (50–60 percent invested in two sectors), (3) large portfolio concentration (30 percent or more invested in the top ten holdings), and (4) very small (less than category average) expense ratios. As discussed previously, industry and portfolio concentration implies higher risk. These high-performing portfolio managers are thus able to increase both risk and return. To simplify the fund search process, Peltz (1998) reported the ratings of 735 large equity funds, including the likely future ranges of their performance potential. And, to simplify the choice of portfolio managers and fund advisors, Henderson and Ward (2000) reported an All Century Team of past and present players.

Dziubinski (1998b) compared the performance of mutual fund categories relative to benchmark indices. Performance was computed for five-year periods ending each of the last five years. Preference for indexing among domestic stock funds varies by investment style. The percentage of times each category outperformed its benchmark follows:

1 Large-cap. growth   2 (6)
2 Large-cap. blend   0 (4)
3 Large-cap. value   31 (17)
4 Mid-cap. growth   33 (n.a.)
5 Mid-cap. blend   47 (30)
6 Mid-cap. value   53 (n.a.)
7 Small-cap. growth   47 (91)
8 Small-cap. blend   100 (54)
9 Small-cap. value   53 (81)

The percentages in parentheses represent later findings in DiTeresa (1999a). The results are generally consistent as being either larger/smaller than 50 percent. The major exception being small-cap. growth's much better managed fund performance.

Based on the broader Dziubinski (1998b) findings, indexing appears appropriate for all three large-cap. investment styles, especially large-cap. growth and large-cap. blend, and the mid-cap. growth category. On the other hand, active portfolio management is a must for small-cap. blend funds. For mid-cap. blend, mid-cap. value, small-cap. growth, and small-cap. value funds, the percentages are close to 50/50. In these cases, decisions whether to index or not should be based on analysis of particular funds versus benchmarks.

International stock mutual funds provide an almost unanimous preference for active portfolio management. The percentage of funds in each area that outperformed benchmark indices follows:

1 World (global)   63
2 International   65
3 Europe   37

4	Latin America	51
5	Pacific	59
6	Japan	73
7	Diversified emerging markets	78

Only in heavily large-cap. Europe does indexing outperform active management. The percentages are nearly 50/50 in Latin America, which suggests that the decision whether to index or not should be based on comparison of particular funds versus the benchmark. But all other regions provide a consistent preference for managed portfolios. Thus active portfolio management remains alive and well, internationally.

Indexing bond funds

And, last, taxable bond funds provide a mixed preference for indexing. The percentage of each type of bond fund that outperformed its benchmark index follows:

1	Long-term bonds	41
2	Intermediate-term bonds	57
3	High-yield bonds	47

Indexing outperforms actively managed bond mutual funds in two of three cases, but the percentages are nearly 50/50 for high-yield bond funds. This suggests that the decision to index high-yield bond funds or not depends on the comparison of particular funds with the benchmark. Only intermediate-term bond funds outperform the benchmark index more than 50 percent of the time. But the performance of long-term and high-yield bond funds does not overwhelmingly favor indexing. While the odds favor indexing for all but intermediate-term bonds, it could be argued that indexing is overall a satisfactory solution for bond funds. Expenses heavily influence bond funds, and indices have very low expenses.

Further, as discussed by Rekenthaler (1995a), the performance advantage of indexing bond mutual funds varies with the specific type of bond. As noted above, indexing bond funds does not always outperform actively managed bond funds. However, Treasury bond funds do make a great case for indexing. The percentage of government bond funds that underperform the benchmark index ranges from 82 to 93, going from one-year to ten-year performance. The reasons for this are the high degree of efficiency in this market plus expense ratios over 1 percent. Portfolio managers must get up very early indeed to overcome these long odds.

For tax-deferred or low tax rate investors, corporate bond funds offer better chances of outperforming the index. This market is not as efficient as the Treasury bond market, and corporate bond fund expense ratios are lower in spite of the higher yields they pay. Because of their broader range of credit quality, corporate bond funds benefit more than Treasury bonds can from the risk reduction effects of diversification. Municipal bond funds make sense for investors taxed at marginal rates of 28 percent or higher. State-specific bond funds also allow citizens to exempt their income distributions from state taxes, as well. Municipal bond funds also have the lowest average expense ratios. Of course, in all cases, bond fund portfolio risk increases as average maturity increases.

Indexing and fund categories

The Dziubinski (1998b) and DiTeresa (1999a) findings are generally consistent with the greater efficiency of large-cap. markets, but they are also affected by the particular benchmarks applied. For example, the Russell 2000 small-cap. index is easier to outperform than the S&P 500 Index because there are some 6,000 small-cap. stocks to choose from. Also, the index benchmarks are aggregated and do not reflect the performance of individual funds. There remains hope of outperformance for particular managed funds, especially small-cap. and international funds, but the question remains, which particular funds?

Relevant to the performance of mutual fund categories versus benchmark indices is William Bernstein's (2000a, b) discussion and test of Dunn's Law. This law states that when a particular asset class, such as large-cap. value, does well, its benchmark index does even better. The reason is that benchmark indices have more style purity than actively managed funds in the same asset class. But is this so for all asset classes, given the premise that indexing works best in efficient large-cap. markets and less so in less efficient small-cap. stocks markets?

Analysis of ten asset classes for each of the last five years noted little differences in the efficacy of indexing between best and middling-performance asset classes. Only the worst-performing asset classes having relatively poor performing indices. Over the five-year period, the performance of index benchmarks versus managed funds in all ten asset classes was the thirty-second percentile (first is best).

If proven, Dunn's law would rebut the first part of the claim that some asset classes (small caps) are inefficient enough that actively managed funds are best, but passive management is best in more efficient (large cap.) classes. If so, this could provide closure to the debate concerning the efficacy of index fund performance versus actively managed funds in domestic markets. Dunn's law does not apply abroad because style purity does not exist in particular countries and regions, and international fund portfolio managers are usually constrained by geography.

Indexing and fund managers

Dziubinski (1998a) and Arnott (1998) examined differences in performance by active and passive portfolio managers. This study is interesting because mutual fund performance was compared with what it would have been without making any portfolio changes. One-year fund portfolio performance was compared with what it would have been if no changes were made during the year. In general, fund managers added little to returns, but they increased volatility. The results by cap. size and style were mixed. Large-cap. funds just about performed the same in either case. Only active management of small-cap. value and small-cap. blend funds increased returns *and* reduced total risk. Active management of mid-cap. growth and small-cap. growth funds increased returns, but did not significantly reduce risk. On the other hand, active management of mid-cap. value funds reduced risk, but did not significantly increase returns.

Thus these findings are supportive of passive portfolio management for large-cap. funds, selective active portfolio management of mid-cap. funds, and active management of small-cap.

funds. That is, markets for large-cap. stocks are more efficient than for small-cap. stocks. Analysis of the performance of experienced portfolio managers with above-average returns reported only seventeen managers who significantly increase returns *and* lower risk.

Thus, while index mutual funds have numerous advantages, it should not be assumed they may properly be purchased without analysis. To this point, Lucas (1993) provided several caveats to the purchase of specific index funds. Investors should *not* assume: (1) all index funds have low expenses; (2) only one benchmark index is needed to track the performance of all index funds; (3) all index funds do not use derivatives or other such strategies; (4) international index funds are equally advantageous as domestic ones; (5) all benchmark indices of particular fund categories are comparable; and (6) index funds are equally advantageous for all cap-size stock funds and bond funds.

S&P 500 Index performance

So why does the S&P 500 Index so often outperform the majority of mutual funds, indexed or managed? Again, the reasons may also be inferred from table 21. Here the actual index (not the index fund) has no survivor bias, expenses, trading costs, loads/fees, cash reserves drag, and shareholder taxes from portfolio turnover. And, as Clements (1999d) noted: "Not everyone can pick funds. Really." That is, most fund portfolio managers do not outperform the benchmark index, and the reasons are several.

As implied above, portfolio managers that set fair value sell prices at purchase are also setting limits on positions by selling stocks that have performed well. On the other hand, stocks selected for inclusion in the S&P 500 Index perform as they will once selected. Which approach performs best depends on the relative performance of the particular stocks held/sold and their replacements.

The way the S&P 500 Index is constructed affects its relative performance. As reviewed by Phillips (1994), the S&P 500 Index is a market capitalization weighted measure of stock performance which gives proportionately more weight to the largest market-cap stocks. However, Morningstar and other measures of average fund performance are unweighted by cap. size, which gives more relative weight to small-cap. funds. Over time, equal-weighted fund averages have a performance advantage over the market-cap weighted S&P 500 Index to the extent that small-cap. funds perform better than large-cap. funds. On the other hand, equal-weighted fund averages give more relative weight to the higher expense ratios of small-cap. funds.

Other benchmark indices

DiTeresa (1998a) reported that the use of index mutual funds has increased with the development of more and more index benchmarks for specific market segments. The Institute for Econometric Research (1998a) provided a summary of long-term returns and other attributes of each index fund for thirteen different indices, including forty-three S&P 500 Index funds. Further, there are now benchmark indices for each of Morningstar's nine domestic equity fund categories, as well as for each of its seven global geographic areas of international funds. There are also bond indices for each of the three bond maturity investment styles. Against these benchmark indices twenty notable index funds are listed, each designed to mimic a particular benchmark index. None of the index funds is equally adept at minimizing tracking error and none has the same expense ratios. Vanguard sponsors all but six of these index funds.

New index funds are now being designed for narrower market segments because the broad indices are generally indexed by several funds. For example, there is a Vanguard index fund for each of the growth and value stock categories in the S&P 500 Index. Steps to take in evaluating index funds are also presented. In this regard, it is again noted that funds that index large-cap. markets are generally leaders in low expenses and tax efficiency. And index funds that charge loads deserve no consideration.

Wang (1999) also considers indexing the "right way to invest." The funds are from Morningstar sources. For a 60/40 stock bond allocation, the Vanguard Total Bond Market Index Fund or Schwab Total Bond Market Fund is recommended for the bond allocation. There is no international bond index fund. For the 60 percent stock allocation, the recommended funds are the Vanguard REIT Index Fund (15 percent), the Schwab International Stock Index Fund (10 percent), the Schwab Small-cap. Index Fund or Vanguard Small-cap. Index Fund (10 percent), and the Schwab 1000 or Vanguard 500 Index Fund (25 percent). The domestic stock allocations could also be assigned to the T. Rowe Price Total Stock Market Index Fund or the Vanguard Total Stock Market Index Fund. Wang does not list the Vanguard Total International Stock Index Fund as an alternative to the Schwab International Stock Index Fund. But, again, the simplicity of index fund portfolios is offered.

Other types of index funds

While simple can be good, not all index mutual funds are boring mimics of market indices. Several fund families offer *enhanced index funds*. These funds are designed for market timers who wish to quickly and easily move in and out of the market. In one type of enhanced fund, betas are leveraged up by the use of derivatives that allow them to control more than a dollar's worth of stock for every dollar invested. They provide investors with larger than market returns if purchased just before market increases and, conversely, larger losses if purchased before market declines. DeBlasi (1999a) reported that leveraged index funds are risky. They have trailed the market for long periods of time, and sometimes they lose money in increasing markets. Only in down markets do they perform the way they are supposed to, falling farther and faster than benchmarks. Some funds have large minimum investment requirements to discourage market timers. But who else would be interested in these funds?

Enhanced index funds are another variety of index fund. These safe-sounding funds attempt to provide returns higher than a specified index, but with only market risk. They vary in the index benchmark targeted and on the characteristics of the index they attempt to match, such as P/E ratio, dividend yield, beta, sector concentration, and cap. size. That is, they vary in the market anomaly they attempt to exploit. Many different means are used to enhance returns, but they include derivatives-based techniques and security-level techniques. Each technique has risks. Zweig (1999c) discussed three types of enhanced index funds, but concluded that they provide "a jumble of erratic performance, higher risks, higher taxes, and higher expenses." Riepe and Werner (1998) studied eight funds, but only two provided enhanced returns while exhibiting characteristics reasonably consistent with the S&P 500 Index. The term "enhanced index funds" appears to be a misnomer – these are actively managed funds.

RECOMMENDED PORTFOLIO ALLOCATIONS

At this point, it is useful to identify the recommended international/domestic stock and bond portfolio investment style allocations within the table 35 stock/bond allocations. The case for indexing is strong and is followed here. Model investment style allocations are provided for various stock/bond allocations in table 70, along with detailed allocations for an assumed 60/40 stock/bond allocation. The approach taken is conservative and designed for long-term portfolios. Index funds should be used for at least the 80–90 percent of the portfolio. This optional supplemental use of actively managed funds is discussed in chapter 10.

However, it should be noted that index funds do not generally provide the precise portfolio allocation possible with individual actively managed funds with specific focus. Index funds by their nature replicate the performance of particular market indices, which include the proportions of large-cap./small-cap. and value/growth stocks in the particular index.

1   *Stock/bond asset allocation.* A passive (indexed) stock/bond asset allocation determined by identifying investor risk preference and matching it to a portfolio investment objective (table 34), which in turn is matched to a particular stock/bond allocation (table 35), along with rebalancing and a cash bucket. The investment style allocations for the various stock/bond allocations are included in table 70.

2   *Domestic/international stock allocation.* Eighty/twenty passive domestic/international stock allocation, taken from the optimized minimum risk *large-cap.* allocation and the discussion above. This allocation is more conservative than the 65/35 optimized domestic/international *small-cap.* allocation. The 80/20 overall allocation for both large-cap. and small-cap. domestic/international funds is also more computationally efficient. However, as discussed, the 20 percent international stock allocation may be reduced to 10 percent to avoid the need to consider hedged funds. The table 70 bond allocations assume an 80/20 domestic/international allocation for the purposes of discussion.

3   *Domestic and international large-cap./small-cap. allocation.* Sixty/forty passive large-cap./small-cap. allocation within the domestic/international stock allocation. This allocation is less conservative than the approximately 75/25 domestic large-cap./small-cap. market value allocation. This allocation is also less conservative in less developed international markets, where a small number of large stocks dominate market values. The 60/40 allocation is a conservative compromise between the greater stability of large-cap. stocks and the potential higher returns of small-cap. stocks. A 50/50 allocation would not be unreasonable. The 60/40 large-cap./small-cap. international allocation can only be approximated with the use of broad-based index funds, but this limitation does not apply to domestic index funds (discussed below).

4   *Domestic and international stock value/growth investment style.* Fifty-fifty passive value/growth investment style within both domestic and international stock allocations. This balanced allocation reflects the difficulty in determining which style mutual fund will

outperform and for what period of time. There is a historical tendency for each style to outperform the other for a number of years, but over time the returns of the two styles are quite similar. The 50/50 international value/growth investment style allocation can only be approximated by broad-based index funds, but the 50/50 domestic value/growth large-cap. allocation may be provided by the Vanguard Growth Index and Value Index in lieu of the Vanguard 500 Index Fund (discussed below).

While the studies discussed above indicate the outperformance of value stocks, the same does not apply to value mutual funds. Also, the allocation may not apply equally to international markets because they likely have a larger proportion of growth stocks, but, beyond this, country is more important than investment style in explaining international fund returns.

5   *Domestic/international bond allocation.* Seventy/thirty domestic/international mix within the bond fund allocation, based on Solnik's minimum risk optimized allocation discussed above. The 70/30 domestic/international bond allocation can only be approximated by domestic bond index funds in the same fund family as the stock index funds (discussed below).

BOND AND STOCK FUND RECOMMENDATIONS: SIMPLE IS GOOD

If investors consider bonds as primarily for asset allocation, index bond funds should be used, at least as the core bond portfolio. This is the simplest and perhaps best way to represent the table 70 bond allocation. Bond index funds generally have the twin advantages of low expenses and very competitive returns. Further, active bond portfolio managers do not generally add enough to portfolio returns to compensate for expenses, trading costs, loads/fees, and taxable distributions. Jacobson (2000a) reported that the best bond shops are Vanguard, PIMCO, and Fidelity. Vanguard funds are primarily discussed here because they offer the widest range of low-cost index funds with excellent shareholder services for individual investors. This is not to say, however, that index funds offered by other fund families should be excluded from consideration (see Morningstar).

The PIMCO International Bond Institutional Fund (see Morningstar) is recommended for the international portion of the 70/30 domestic/international bond allocation. The PIMCO fund is actively managed and has a large minimum purchase, but this bond fund family counts icon William Gross among its portfolio managers.

The Vanguard Total Bond Market Index Fund (table 71) is recommended for the domestic portion of the 70/30 domestic/international bond allocation. This fund has moderate duration, very low expenses, and indices the entire domestic bond market. For high-bracket taxable accounts, managed national tax-exempt municipal bond funds should be considered as partial or complete domestic bond allocation replacements, especially the Vanguard Intermediate Term Tax-exempt Municipal Bond Fund (see Morningstar). The municipal bond funds are not index funds.

In fact, for even greater simplicity, or to maintain an index-only bond portfolio, the Vanguard Total Bond Market Index Fund could be used for the entire domestic and international bond allocation. The advantage is simplicity, but with loss of international portfolio diversification and its performance contribution.

For managed funds, the Vanguard GNMA Fund and/or the Vanguard Inflation-protected Fund (see Morningstar) should be considered as partial or complete domestic bond allocation replacements. The GNMA fund's duration is approximately three years and its performance closely follows the Vanguard Total Bond Market Index Fund. The annual return on the Vanguard Inflation-protected Fund is increased by the inflation rate to maintain investor purchasing power.

The Vanguard Total Stock Market Index Fund (table 72) is recommended for the domestic portion of the 80/20 domestic/international stock allocation in table 70. This fund is bench-marked to the Wilshire 5000, which includes 7,000 stocks, good and bad, and thereby tracks the entire domestic stock market and its large-cap./small-cap. and value/growth stocks. This index is approximately 75/25 large-cap./small-cap. Interestingly, Bogle (1999b) computed that a 65/35 allocation of the Vanguard total domestic market stock and bond index funds provides 98 percent of the combined returns of domestic stock and bond markets over the past fifty years.

The Vanguard Total International Stock Index Fund is recommended for the international portion of the 80/20 domestic/international stock allocation, both for its coverage and for its simplicity. The fund is benchmarked to the MSCI Total International Index, which tracks approximately 1,700 international stocks, including value and growth. This low-cost (for international funds) fund of funds invests in Vanguard's European Stock Index Fund, Pacific Stock Index Fund, and Emerging Markets Stock Index Fund, based on each fund's proportion of the MSCI Total International Index: approximately 60 percent European, 30 percent Pacific, and 10 percent emerging markets.

These individual Vanguard international funds are in turn benchmarked to MSCI indices for each geographic area. The European fund is matched to the MSCI Europe Index that includes some 550 stocks in fifteen countries. The Pacific fund is matched to the MSCI Pacific Free Index that includes some 500 stocks in six countries and markets, especially Japan. The emerging markets fund is matched to a liquid version of the MSCI Select Emerging Markets Free Index that includes over 600 stocks in sixteen countries and markets. Moreover, these specific Vanguard international index funds should be purchased to downplay a particular international market, such as long declining Japan.

For high tax bracket accounts, the Vanguard Tax-managed International Fund (see Morningstar) should be considered as a partial or complete replacement for the Vanguard Total International Stock Index Fund. And, to avoid investment in emerging markets, the Vanguard Developed Markets Index Fund (see Morningstar) should be considered as a replacement for the Vanguard Total International Stock Index Fund. This developed markets fund of funds benchmarks only the MSCI European and Pacific indices.

To recap, the simplest Vanguard index fund portfolio includes the Total Stock Market Index Fund, the Total International Stock Index Fund, and the Total Bond Market Index Fund. With these three index mutual funds and the actively managed PIMCO international bond fund it is possible to own the world. Simple can be good! And, in three cases, near market returns are to be had without any risk of losing star portfolio managers. In the index funds, active portfolio management has been replaced by the use of statistical sampling and analysis programs to track benchmark index performance. This also requires skill, but these funds are proven benchmark trackers. And, if additional portfolio diversification is desired, 5–10 percent of the total portfolio could be invested in the Vanguard REIT Index Fund and/or Vanguard

High Yield Corporate Fund (see Morningstar). These funds offer low correlation with the returns of other portfolio securities.

These three Vanguard index mutual funds and the PIMCO international bond fund should be allocated based on table 70. For example, for a 60/40 stock/bond allocation and an 80/20 domestic/international stock allocation, 48 percent would be invested in the Vanguard Total Stock Market Index Fund, 12 percent in the Vanguard Total International Stock Index Funds, 28 percent in the Vanguard Total Bond Market Index Fund and 12 percent in the PIMCO international bond fund. For convenience, as noted, the entire 40 percent bond allocation could be invested in the Vanguard Total Bond Market Index Fund.

Alternatively, with four rather than three index mutual funds, the 60/40 domestic large-cap./small-cap. portfolio allocation in table 70 may be explicitly recognized by two other Vanguard index funds in lieu of the Total Stock Market Index Fund. The Vanguard 500 Index Fund and Vanguard Small-cap. Index Fund (see Morningstar) alternatives provide distinct allocations of domestic large-cap. and small-cap. stocks. The Vanguard 500 Index is benchmarked to the S&P 500 Index, the most widely used benchmark of large-cap. fund and stock market performance. The Vanguard Small Cap. Fund benchmarks the Russell 2000, the most widely used small-cap. index. The Vanguard 500 Index Fund could thus be used for the table 70 29 percent large-cap. stock allocation and the Vanguard Small-cap. Index Fund for the 19 percent small-cap. stock allocation.

For managed mutual funds, the Vanguard Tax-managed Growth and Income Fund and the Vanguard Growth and Income Fund (see Morningstar) should be considered as partial or complete replacements for the Vanguard 500 Index Fund. The former provides tax-managed portfolio management for high tax-bracket accounts and the latter an enhanced S&P 500 Index portfolio. Also, for high tax-bracket accounts, the Vanguard Tax-managed Small-cap. Fund (see Morningstar) should be considered as a partial or complete managed fund replacement for the Vanguard Small-cap. Index Fund.

Specific recognition of the 50/50 domestic value/growth stock allocation in table 70 could be obtained by replacing the Vanguard 500 Index Fund with its composite funds, the Vanguard Growth Index Fund and the Vanguard Value Index Fund (see Morningstar). Specific recognition of the 50/50 international value/growth stock allocation in table 70 (but not for the 60/40 international large-cap./small-cap. allocation) could be obtained by replacing the Vanguard Total International Index Fund with the *managed* Vanguard International Growth Fund and Vanguard International Value Fund (see Morningstar).

As noted, the text analysis process culminates in table 68, and table 73 provides this process in summary form to facilitate fund selection, including cases where more than one index fund has been identified as acceptable. Consistent with using a minimum number of mutual funds, table 73 also notes again that domestic bond index funds may be used for convenience in the table 70 domestic/international bond allocation. In addition, the stock index funds discussed above should be used to meet the table 70 stock investment style allocations. Table 73 thus provides a vital summary checklist of the text approach to selection of index mutual funds.

CHAPTER TEN

ACTIVELY MANAGED VERSUS PASSIVELY MANAGED FUNDS: THE SEARCH FOR MANAGERS

In chapter 9 it was recommended that index mutual funds should comprise the core of the portfolio, such as 80–90 percent. This leaves room, if investors so desire, to add actively managed funds identified as having outstanding portfolio managers. Thus the first goal of this chapter is to explore ways of identifying outstanding actively managed funds. This is not easy, nor is there a single documented approach for identifying such funds.

The second goal is to update and review the active versus index funds controversy, along with other related fund performance issues. And, finally, the third goal is to review selected articles that bear on fund performance issues.

FUND PERFORMANCE AND PORTFOLIO MANAGER ATTRIBUTES

Arnott, Odelbo, and Bryant studies

Arnott (1995) examined the management attributes of high-performing equity mutual funds to see what separates them from the pack. The data are based on seventeen larger-cap funds that outperformed the index in at least thirty-seven of forty-nine rolling five-year periods. These attributes complement the evaluation of portfolio manager background in table 13.

The attributes identified appear quite reasonable and not unexpected. They include (1) veteran portfolio managers; (2) consistent rather than headline performance; (3) independent thinkers; (4) the use of fundamental analysis applied to predominantly value investment styles and measures; (5) contrarian investors *par excellence*; (6) conviction in judgment reflected in riskier concentrated portfolios – sectors and individual stocks; (7) long-term investment horizons and below-average portfolio turnover; and (8) portfolio managers listed by name – no management teams, but no long lists of individuals either. These attributes also mirror successful managers of international funds.

Odelbo (1995) has a slightly different slant on these attributes. Great investors, such as Warren Buffett of Berkshire Hathaway (not a mutual fund), do not follow one investment style exclusively – they look for undervalued winners across the board. Neither do they practise what mere mortals should do in the way of indexing, asset allocation, or style analysis. They do not build portfolios beginning with particular stock/bond allocations based on risk tolerances. But neither is there hard statistical evidence of their performance superiority.

To keep some perspective on the difficulties in assessing portfolio managers, Morningstar, the fund analysis company, selects an annual Portfolio Manager of the Year. Bryant (2000) examined the subsequent performance of past winners with mixed results – no surprise there. A bit more than 50 percent of the managers outperformed most comparable funds (peers). Six managers stood out in subsequent performance, three managers did very well, and three managers did not so good. Those who tried to time the market had the least reliable returns. And those managers with the most reliable returns appeared a bit contrarian with reasonable-size portfolios.

Chevalier and Ellison study

Finally, Chevalier and Ellison (1999) tied together this discussion of mutual fund portfolio managers by examining whether age, the composite SAT scores of their undergraduate colleges, current tenure as a portfolio manager, and the possession of an MBA degree have performance implications. Given the attention to star managers, can the case be made that some managers are statistically better than others? The hot hands strategy suggests some performance persistence, but does any of this reflect stock selection ability or particular personal attributes?

A sample of 492 portfolio managers of growth and growth and income mutual funds was analyzed. The first step examines whether differences in portfolio manager *characteristics* produce different abnormal returns. Younger managers with degrees from high-SAT colleges and MBA degrees earn higher abnormal returns. The latter two variables are very significant. Differences in annual returns between managers who graduated from colleges with the highest and average SAT scores are about one percentage point. Older portfolio managers appear to fare much worse than younger managers. Differences in annual returns between portfolio managers with one-year age differences are about nine basis points. Differences in returns between the oldest and youngest portfolio managers are about 4.6 percentage points. Portfolio managers with MBAs add about sixty-three basis points to annual returns. But portfolio manager tenure adds only slightly to annual performance. These differences appear too large to be due only to superior ability to select stocks.

The second step examines whether differences in portfolio manager *behavior* explain differences in mutual fund abnormal returns. The portfolios of managers who graduated from high-SAT colleges and hold MBA degrees have more systematic risk. Portfolios of managers with long tenure have significantly less systematic risk. Portfolios of older managers have only slightly more systematic risk. The higher returns of portfolio managers with MBAs are due to higher systematic risk. However, the higher returns of younger portfolio managers are not.

The hot hands strategy suggests that differences in expenses are associated with performance differences. Portfolios managed by graduates of higher-SAT colleges are larger and have both lower expenses and lower turnover (the latter two both significant). Portfolios managed by MBAs are also larger, with both lower expenses and lower turnover (only size is significant). The portfolios of older portfolio managers are smaller, with higher expenses.

Expenses are very important in explaining risk-adjusted returns. Interestingly, portfolio turnover has a positive effect on performance when included with expenses. The combination of high turnover and expenses may reflect high research expenses. Nonetheless, expenses are not sufficient to explain the superior performance of younger portfolio managers from select colleges. Their portfolios also have lower turnover.

The third step examines whether differences in portfolio manager *investment styles* explain differences in fund abnormal returns. First, portfolio managers with MBAs have a significant tendency to buy glamour stocks with small book-to-price ratios. Second, older managers have a greater tendency to use momentum strategies. Finally, each additional year of manager age reduces performance by four basis points. The performance difference between thirty-year-old and fifty-five-year-old portfolio managers is about one percentage point per year.

The fourth step examines whether good mutual fund managers beat the market. The average fund's abnormal returns are less than 75 percent of expenses. Portfolio managers of funds with mean characteristics are expected to beat the market if they graduated from the highest-SAT colleges, but not significantly. Overall, 38 percent of the funds are expected to beat the market, but only about 14 percent have significantly large abnormal returns.

Overall, there are differences in mutual fund portfolio performance that cannot be explained by portfolio manager behavior. Fund managers who graduated from high-SAT colleges have higher performance. The results suggest that a subgroup of portfolio managers has stock-picking ability. More surprising, some portfolio managers are expected to beat the market even taking expenses into consideration. Older portfolio managers do not perform as well as younger managers. This could be due to different career concerns – younger portfolio managers are more likely to be fired for underperformance. It could also be because older managers are less educated or less skilled and/or because the good ones leave the industry at younger ages.

MUTUAL FUND SELECTION AND TIEBREAKERS

The selection process for the selection of mutual funds can be simplified greatly by investing only in index funds. This simpler strategy may even provide better performance than the use of actively managed funds. And, even for investors who insist on investing in actively managed funds, it is nonetheless recommended that index funds comprise the core holdings of their portfolios. Singularly indexed or both indexed and actively managed, these fund holdings should match the investment style allocations in table 70, or some other model portfolios.

The text process for assessing *stock index mutual funds* is summarized in table 73. The table notes that fund allocations should follow the allocations in table 70. In addition, the stock index funds and managed bond fund recommended in chapter 9 should provide the core portfolio. As discussed previously, the text analysis process culminates in table 68, but table 73 provides this process in summary form to facilitate fund selection, including cases where more than one index fund has been identified as acceptable.

Tables 74–5

The text process for the selection of *actively managed mutual funds* that culminated in table 68 is summarized in table 74. In cases where more than one fund with the same investment style is found acceptable in table 68, table 74 also provides guidelines for the use of table 75 tiebreakers. The use of actively managed funds also means that investors should review their holdings based on comparison with other funds. This involves the same analysis process that culminates in table 68.

The tiebreakers are surrogates for identifying portfolio managers likely to have superior stock selection skills. As discussed previously, portfolio manager tenure is normally too short to identify superior performance on a probabilistic basis. The selection of talented portfolio managers is also made more difficult because superior performance tends to be limited to short-term momentum in performance.

This problem of identifying superior portfolio managers is evidenced in Bryant (2000), where the subsequent performance of twenty-three Morningstar Managers of the Year was analyzed. All of the managers were found to have one trait in common – they are audacious. Audacity did not pay off for all of the managers, however. Several funds suffered from ill-advised portfolio concentration and poor market timing. However, as discussed below, concentration can prove profitable in value portfolios with low turnover.

The tiebreakers in table 75 indicate that mutual fund portfolio managers associated with high performance are (1) disclosed to shareholders, (2) known for their investment style, (3) younger than average, (4) well educated, (5) and have above-average tenure as portfolio manager. Two other tiebreakers indicate that fund outperformance is associated with eclectic, wide-ranging contrarian-driven value investment styles, in which portfolio managers are patient (low portfolio turnover), opportunistic, and seek undervalued stocks of any market cap. size. In these cases, fund portfolios may include both small-cap. and large-cap. investment styles.

Interestingly, two other table 75 attributes indicate that mutual fund outperformance is associated with concentrated portfolios and not by the use of either asset or style allocation. Portfolios are concentrated both by industry sector and by holdings of individual stocks. These portfolio managers are confident in their judgment and buy lots of shares! The lack of diversified portfolios built without asset allocation and style allocation is not recommended for investor fund portfolios, but these individual funds may be selected for use within particular portfolio allocations.

The justification for this eclectic (or perverse, if you prefer) behavior appears to be its association with superior stock selection ability – a rare skill, indeed. Concentrated portfolios do not create superior returns, but they are characteristic of portfolio managers who earn superior returns. In these cases, portfolios are concentrated because only a limited number of stocks satisfy strict value selection criteria. The use of concentrated portfolios also appears quite consistent over time.

Mutual funds with characteristics described above also have other table 75 portfolio attributes associated with fund outperformance. In addition to the measures noted above, they include: (1) below-average asset size and above-average stability, (3) below-average systematic risk (beta), (4) a high degree of tax efficiency, (5) below-average expense ratios, and (6) relatively steady performance over time. These attributes are consistent with value investing. Table 74 and its references to table 75 and supplementary table 76 thus provide vital summary checklists of the text approach to the selection of managed mutual funds.

Portfolio concentration

As discussed, table 75 supports concentrated portfolios, but in the right hands. Hester (2001) reported that the fewer the number of stocks held, the greater the odds they will outperform the market. This was seen in a study of 12,000 portfolios for ten-year and eighteen-year periods. The odds of 250 stock portfolios beating the market are one in fifty, but for fifteen stock portfolios they are one in four. There are two caveats, however. Portfolio diversification remains essential to volatility reduction in all size portfolios. These allocations may represent investment style categories or other unique styles. Nonetheless, concentrated portfolios are normally more volatile.

Thus stock selection ability is very important in concentrated portfolios. This skill accompanied by risk reduction is essential to outperformance of successful concentrated portfolios. But these abilities are not sufficiently in common among portfolio managers to assume all concentrated portfolios are appropriate for investors. Stout (1997) thus warned that investors should concentrate with care in selecting mutual funds with concentrated portfolios. The average fund with a concentrated portfolio has not increased performance by concentration. In general, fund returns across investment styles decline over various time periods as the number of holdings decreases. Moreover, the range of fund returns increases as diversification decreases. The implication for the average portfolio manager is that portfolios become more risky the more concentrated they are. However, a case may also be made for concentration within diversified portfolios. When diversified portfolios are adjusted for number of holdings, the funds that invest more heavily in their largest holdings are likely to outperform.

There are a few more twists to the portfolio concentration issue. Surz (1998) observed that diversification hampers skilled managers by limiting the size of individual equity positions and nudging them toward the index portfolio. He stated that "in this context, diversification by an active portfolio manager can be viewed as a hedge against lack of skill . . . and some managers have laid off their business risks on to the client." This is seen in increasing portfolio R^2s once boutique portfolios trend away from star portfolio managers. These trends may even increase risk as portfolio managers tread unfamiliar waters. There is a significant opportunity cost in returns by moving even from portfolios of fifteen to thirty stocks. Increasing diversification causes these opportunities to decrease at decreasing rates. Surz stated that "the diversification drag on skill is estimated to *exceed 80 basis points* per year." This cost could be even larger in tax-efficient portfolios with low turnover and "loss harvesting."

The implications of concentrated portfolios as they apply to large-cap. mutual funds are also discussed in Haslem and Scheraga (2001a, b). Two variants of value and one of growth investment style are identified. One value style has significantly more security concentration and industry sector concentration than both the other value style and the growth style, as measured by percentage of assets in the top ten stock holdings and percentage of assets in the top three industry sector holdings, respectively.

This value style also has significantly more cash concentration than the other value style and the growth style, as measured by percentage of cash to total assets. As a result, this value style also has significantly smaller stock holdings than the other two styles, as measured by percentage of stock holdings to total assets. In addition, it has a smaller concentration in international stock holdings than the other value style.

Both value styles have statistically equal rates of return (one and three years), Morningstar Rate of Return Category Rank, Morningstar Worst Three Months Rate of Return, and R^2. They also have statistically equal beta, total risk (standard deviation), Jensen Alpha, and Sharpe Index. Thus the value style with higher security and industry sector concentration hedges these risks with larger concentrations of cash and smaller concentrations of stock and international stock. Value styles may therefore concentrate differently yet still come out the same with respect to return and risk/return performance measures.

The growth style has the highest Morningstar Risk, lowest Morningstar Bear Market Rank, largest beta and standard deviation, and lowest Jensen Alpha and Sharpe Index score. Thus the growth style has more risk and lower composite risk/return performance than the value styles.

But, interestingly, the value and growth styles have statistically equal rates of return (one and three years), Morningstar Category Rank, Morningstar Worst Three Months Rate of Return, Morningstar (star) Ratings, R^2s, management fees, and sales charges. Thus, with equal rates of return, but more risk and lower risk/return performance, the growth style has lower risk-adjusted performance than the value styles.

The tiebreakers between the value and growth styles must therefore be portfolio manager stock selection skill, which is seen in lower risk (beta and total risk, among others) and higher composite risk/return (Jensen and Sharpe) performance. In fact, the growth style's management addition to returns (Jensen Alpha) is negative.

Thus, before selecting particular value style mutual funds with concentrated assets as discussed above, it is important to validate their composite risk/return performance, especially as represented by high Jensen Alphas and Sharpe Index scores, but also by the risk measures noted above. But, without this confirmation of lower risk and risk/return performance, the search for the best managed value funds continues.

If value style risk and risk/return performance support the finding of stock selection ability, then at least in this case there may be truth in the statement reported in Burton (1998): "You concentrate to create wealth; you diversify to preserve it." And, as quoted by Buffett: "Diversification is a protection against ignorance." The great investors are also patient investors, as quoted by Buffett in chapter 7: "Inactivity [buy and hold] strikes us as intelligent behavior." A bit overstated, perhaps, but it makes a point, if you can find the next Buffett. The search is important because history tells us that the few really great investors (portfolio managers) are eclectic in their search for undervalued stocks. They do not necessarily adhere to particular investment styles, but they do look for value where they can find it.

SUPERSTARS REDUX

Tweedy Browne (n.d.) observed that value investing is the single attribute in common of nine very experienced star portfolio managers. Performance records of seven of these managers discussed by Buffett (1984) were computed in Shahan (1986). The seven portfolio managers outperformed the S&P 500 Index by an annual average of between 7.7 percentage points and 16.5 percentage points over periods ranging from thirteen years to twenty-eight years. None of the managers outperformed the index in each and every year. In fact, underperforming the index in 30–40 percent of the years is the norm while still attaining superior long-term performance. Further, periods of underperformance did not predict favorable future results, and periods of outperformance did not predict future favorable performance.

Tweedy Browne's value approach to fund portfolio management is found in table 76's checklist of desirable attributes of actively managed funds. These findings are very compatible with table 75 and, together, they provide a good summary of the text's message. Then table 77 provides a checklist of mutual fund myths that act as a cynical guide to the interpretation of fund representations and claims.

The dedicated value investors at Tweedy Browne also have a Hall of Fame. These portfolio managers are found in Tweedy Browne (n.d.) and include: (1) Bill Ruane, Sequoia Fund; (2) Walter Schloss; (3) Charles Munger; (4) Richard Geurin; (5) Stan Perlmuter; (6) Tweedy Browne partners (the data support them); and (7) John Neff, of the original Windsor Fund.

To conclude this discussion, Adam Smith (1999) identified several past and present super-star managers. These money managers are judged based on their career contributions, given the years it takes to prove superior ability. The Hall of Fame includes: (1) Benjamin Graham, father of value investing; (2) Warren Buffett, Graham's student without peer; (3) Phillip Fisher, growth investing with good management; (4) T. Rowe Price, theory of growth investing; (5) Sir John Templeton, international value investing; (6) John C. Bogle, low-cost index funds; (7) Peter Lynch, "Buy what you know"; and (8) George Soros, global "macro" investing. It will be remembered that Lynch's performance with the Fidelity Magellan Fund has been statistically identified as superior.

Portfolio managers likely to be added to such lists include Michael Price, retired value investor of the then Mutual Series funds; Mason Hawkins, Longleaf funds; Bill Miller, Legg Mason Value funds; and William Gross, PIMCO bond manager. There will also be others who invest with their investors. For the original ideas of these and many other superstars of investment management, see Ellis (1997).

ACTIVELY MANAGED VERSUS INDEX FUNDS

The age-old issue in mutual funds is whether portfolio managers add value relative to passively managed index funds. Wermers (2000) answered this question by reviewing the findings to date and providing further analysis. The study covers the twenty years 1975–94, and includes 1,788 funds that existed some time during that period. The data make it possible to examine actively and passively managed fund returns at both stock holdings and net return levels and to determine the sources of the disparity.

These data make it possible to decompose returns and attribute them to particular portfolio characteristics (investment styles): (1) superior stock selection skills for particular portfolio characteristics (investment style), (2) returns attributable to particular portfolio characteristics, (3) trading costs attributable to particular portfolio characteristics, (4) expenses and fees attributable to particular portfolio characteristics, and (5) differences between gross portfolio returns and net fund returns due to non-stock holdings.

Most studies conclude that actively managed mutual funds underperform passively managed portfolios. Also, fund net returns are negatively related to expenses, which are generally higher for actively managed funds. Moreover, the higher portfolio turnover, the lower fund net returns relative to benchmark indices. The general conclusion: buy low-expense index funds. The impact of fund expense ratios also differs by fund investment style.

Burton (1999a) examined the percentage of high-cost and low-cost stock and bond funds that outperformed their category mean returns. On average, 59 percent and 42 percent of low-cost and high-cost stock funds, respectively, outperform their categories. Low-cost funds outperform 70 percent of both large-cap. value and international stock funds. But low-cost funds outperform only 54 percent of small-cap. funds, while high-cost funds outperform 53 percent. Small cap. appears to be the only category where expenses do not differentiate performance. On average, 66 percent and 29 percent of low-cost and high-cost bond funds outperform their categories. Thus low costs are very important in differentiating bond performance, more so than for stock funds. Low-cost funds outperform 73 percent of short-term bond funds and 72 percent of intermediate-term bond funds.

Other studies examined mutual fund holding of stock rather than total portfolio holdings including non-stock securities. Active portfolio managers have the ability to select stocks that outperform benchmark indices before fund expenses are deducted. This ability is particularly pronounced for growth funds, which outperform benchmark indices. Much of this performance reflects the ability to hold stocks with style characteristics that increase returns. Funds following value strategies outperform those following passive management strategies.

The average mutual fund expense ratio is about 100 basis points a year, compared with eighteen basis points for the Vanguard 500 Index Fund. Based on industry equity assets exceeding $3 trillion, the difference in expense ratios amounts to an additional $20 billion a year for active portfolio management. This is in addition to the higher trading costs of actively managed funds. The key question then becomes whether industry stock selection skills are sufficient to compensate for the additional trading costs incurred and the expenses and fees charged.

Mutual funds also tend to follow investment styles, such as holding small-cap. stocks, value stocks, and stocks with high past returns. These characteristics follow the discussion above of small-cap. versus large-cap. stocks, value (small P/B ratios) versus growth stocks, and momentum (trend-following) investing. Stocks with these characteristics outperform others. These three characteristics are powerful intra-year predictors of patterns in stock gross returns, but the higher portfolio gross returns they generate may not be translated into higher *net* returns owing to larger implementation costs. Overall, active portfolio managers exhibit some stock selection ability and earn higher gross returns, but only by an amount equal to expenses and trading costs. No timing ability is observed.

Wermers (2000) reported several trends in the mutual fund industry over the twenty years of the study. First, growth funds have become most popular, reflecting their high performance. Second, funds have become more fully invested in stocks, versus non-stock bond and cash assets. This increase has increased portfolio returns, as reflected in high returns on growth stocks and the stock market, generally.

Third, while mutual fund portfolio turnover has more than doubled over the period, from 35 percent to 70 percent, total trading costs have declined from 104 to 48 basis points. This cost reduction follows the general decline in such costs, but also improved trade execution made possible by technology. Institutional trading costs (commission and market impact) are dependent on the particular market, trade size, market cap., stock price, and whether the trade is a buy or sell.

Fourth, expense ratios increased from 65 to 99 basis points, due to larger proportions of new, small funds and substitution of 12b-1 fees for loads. The sum of increased expense ratios and decreased trading costs has remained relatively constant. Each represents about 80 basis points of the difference between gross and index returns.

Wermers observed that average broadly diversified equity mutual fund portfolios outperform gross returns on a broad market index by 130 basis points per year. Of these 130 basis points, 71 basis points are from the ability to *select* stocks that outperform their characteristic matched benchmarks. The remaining 55–60 basis points are explained by portfolio manager ability to choose higher returning portfolio characteristics, as measured by style (B/P), cap. size and momentum (prior year returns). In this regard, funds show preferences for small-cap. stocks, growth stocks and momentum stocks, as compared with the market index. Although growth stocks earn lower average returns, returns of small-cap. and momentum stocks more than compensate for this. The result is that funds hold stocks with characteristics that outperformed the market index over the twenty-year period.

Although the average fund outperforms the gross return on the index by 130 basis points, its net return is 100 basis points lower than the index. The 230 basis point spread between fund gross and net returns is due to several factors. About seventy basis points are explained by lower returns on fund non-stock holdings, such as cash assets. And, the remaining 160 basis points are approximately evenly split between expense ratios and trading costs. Thus fund stock holdings outperform the index by almost enough to cover costs – thirty basis points short. In fact, stocks held by funds outperformed the S&P 500 Index in thirteen of twenty years.

To test the value of actively managed mutual funds, it is important to know whether the associated higher trading activity is related to stock selection ability. The highest-turnover funds trade about ten times more than the lowest-turnover funds. Although high-turnover funds have higher trading costs and expenses, they also hold stocks with higher returns. Their stock holdings outperform the lowest turnover funds by 430 basis points a year, with much of this difference (220 basis points) explained by holding stocks with higher-return characteristics. Most of the remaining difference is due to stock selection ability (120 basis points) and slightly better timing ability (90 basis points). On the other hand, high turnover funds have much larger trading costs (240 basis points) and slightly higher expenses (28 basis points) than low turnover funds. But they did have higher net returns than the Vanguard 500 Index Fund over the period. These findings differ from other findings in this text. The debate on such issues continues.

Wermers thus observed that mutual funds hold stocks that significantly outperformed the market index over the twenty-year period. This is consistent with findings that fund portfolio managers have stock selection ability. However, fund *net* returns significantly underperform the same indices. Lower returns on fund holdings of non-stock securities contribute to this difference. Gross and net fund returns are highly correlated, which indicates that expenses and trading costs do not eliminate the returns from stock selection ability. However, fund portfolio managers do not exhibit significant ability to time the characteristics of the stocks they hold. Funds show preferences for small-cap. stocks, growth stocks, and momentum stocks relative to the market portfolio. They earn higher returns with small cap. and momentum stocks, but lower returns with growth stocks (relative to value).

Relevant to the controversy discussed above concerning the attributes of index funds, the returns of managed funds and the passively managed Vanguard 500 Index Fund are compared.

The pro-index argument is that the Vanguard 500 Index outperforms the majority of actively managed funds in any given year because of low expenses and low trading activity. Further, active portfolio managers do not have the ability to select stocks that outperform the market index by enough to cover expenses and trading costs.

The study shows that the Vanguard 500 Index Fund's gross returns track the S&P 500 Index very closely. The fund's expense ratio decreased from 46 basis points in 1977 to 19 basis points in 1994. Other recent competitive aspects of this decline are discussed in chapter 9. The fund's expense ratio contrasts with average index fund expense ratios of 30–40 basis points. Trading costs of the Vanguard 500 Index are estimated at less than ten basis points a year, which is a large cost advantage. Over the period, the Vanguard 500 Index had average net returns of 13.3 percent, the same as the unadjusted average net returns of mutual funds. Each fund also had several negative performance measures.

However, Wermers concluded "that the claims of the Vanguard fund management are *not* overwhelmingly supported by unadjusted net returns." The average fund holds stocks with characteristics providing higher returns that compensate for higher expenses and trading costs. Actively managed funds have higher net returns than the Vanguard 500 Index Fund. But – and it is an important "but" – this return advantage of actively managed funds is lost if adjusted for the risk of their higher return portfolios. If the returns of funds with higher return characteristics are considered compensation for risk, the average actively managed fund underperforms the Vanguard 500 Index Fund by 87 basis points.

CAN ACTIVELY MANAGED MONEY BEAT THE MARKET?

By Russ Wermers

In the following essay, Professor Russ Wermers, University of Maryland, reviews current research findings on mutual fund performance. There are some differences from previous research, which reflect the latest findings. The essay provides a synthesis of these findings, some of which are discussed above (and below).

US equity mutual fund managers currently control over $3 trillion in stocks. So-called active fund managers control the great majority of these stock portfolios (roughly 90 percent of total assets by year 2000). These managers aggressively add stocks to (and liquidate stocks from) their portfolios in an attempt to beat the S&P 500 Index. Their fund companies just as aggressively advertise the track records of well performing funds in an attempt to attract new money from retail investors.

For example, recent television ads for the Fidelity family of funds prominently feature the most famous mutual fund manager in the world (and the former manager of the Fidelity Magellan fund), Peter Lynch. A more recent technology fund superstar is Scott Schoelzel of the Janus 20 fund – Mr. Schoelzel was named the world's best equity fund manager by *Mutual Funds* magazine for 1998, having produced a return of 74 percent compared with the S&P's return of 29 percent.

But there is another side to this story, told most aptly (and most frequently!) by John Bogle, former senior chairman of the Vanguard fund family. Mr. Bogle thinks that most mutual funds waste investor money by trading too frequently and by charging excessive expenses. This message has not been lost on investors. The Vanguard 500 Index fund, the largest index fund in the United States, now manages about $100 billion dollars, roughly the same size as the largest actively managed fund in the United States, the Fidelity Magellan fund. (For an update on the relative fortunes of these two bellwether funds, see www.investorhome.com/magic/.)

Who should individual investors trust with their money? In a *Journal of Finance* study (Wermers, 2000), I conduct what I believe to be a definitive study into this issue over the 1975–94 period. Although many researchers have evaluated the abilities of mutual funds in the past, I have the advantage of a new, state-of-the-art dataset that contains not only the net returns of mutual funds, but also the actual stock holdings of the funds. Having stock holdings data allows me to simultaneously analyze mutual funds at both the stock holdings level and at the net returns level, something not possible in the past. In addition, I use new performance evaluation techniques that were developed with co-authors at Northwestern University, the University of Texas at Austin, and Yale University in another *Journal of Finance* article (Kent et al., 1997). These new evaluation metrics basically separate the total return on stock holdings into that due to fund manager talents in picking stocks (regardless of the manager's chosen style), manager talents in moving into certain stockholding styles (such as holding small stocks) at just the right time, and returns earned by the manager by holding certain styles over the long run (such as managers who preferentially invest in small stocks).

Let's go back to my current study. The decomposition mentioned in its title traces the sources of performance as well as the costs associated with each mutual fund's stock-picking program. The idea is to measure the sources and uses of returns, in detail, to better understand the pluses and minuses of actively managed money. First, the good news. My study finds that the average dollar invested in mutual funds is managed by a stock picker who can beat the S&P 500 Index by 1.5 percent per year. Now, this may not seem like much, but this is the average dollar – some mutual funds beat the S&P by double-digit percentages over several year periods. Now, the bad news – the 1.5 percent per year is at the stockholding level. The net return of this average dollar is 0.8 percent per year below the S&P 500 Index. Actually, this news is not all that bad, as even index funds underperform the S&P by about this amount (although they have done better in recent years owing to cost-cutting practices).

The reasons for this 2.3 percent per year difference between stock returns and net returns? First, expenses charged by the funds for managing and running the operation (and for profits!). Second, trading costs incurred by actively turning over the stock portfolio. These two sources of costs explain about 1.6 percent per year. The remaining 0.7 percent per year is due to the need of stock fund managers to keep some liquid assets in place – roughly 10–15 percent of a stock fund's assets are tied up in short-term cash investments to hedge against the onset of investor redemptions. These non-stock assets have been a significant drag on the performance of funds, but represent an important liquidity-based service to shareholders in funds.

In a related study, Edelen (1999) finds that mutual fund holdings of cash explain the supposed underperformance of mutual funds at the net return level (which has been documented by many papers over the years). Since, as Gruber (1996) argues, smart money chases past mutual fund returns, knowing that returns persist, funds end up holding more cash when they are successful in picking stocks. This cash effect dilutes their performance, and Edelen finds that the average performance of the mutual fund industry (at the net return level) is zero, controlling for the diluting effect of investor inflows. This finding directly agrees with my study.

Do heavy traders perform better?

My study finds that the average dollar invested in an actively managed fund has done just about as well as the average dollar invested in an index fund. That's the first piece of (reasonably) good news provided by my study. An even better finding is that funds trading most aggressively do much better than index funds, even after accounting for their higher expenses and trading costs. For example, the 40 percent of funds trading most aggressively each year beat the Vanguard 500 Index fund, on a net return level, by about 1.5 percent per year. Note that this superior performance is after deducting the much higher trading costs and somewhat higher expense ratios incurred by mutual funds that trade most aggressively. My study shows that a significant portion of the superior performance is due to these funds picking stocks, within their style specialization, that beat other stocks (having the same style characteristics). For example, growth funds pick growth stocks that beat an average growth index by about 2 percent per year.

It is important to note that this positive news on the relation between trading activity and performance is not fully settled. Indeed, Carhart (1997) finds a negative relation between style-adjusted performance and turnover, where my study finds a more complex picture. As mentioned above, my study finds a positive relation between turnover and (unadjusted) net returns, and a U-shaped relation between turnover and style-adjusted net returns. That is, the highest and lowest turnover funds, which are the most active funds and index funds, respectively, exhibit the best style-adjusted net returns.

Do managers with "hot hands" exist?

Where does my research leave the individual investor who is looking for a superior mutual fund? It at least gives that investor hope of finding a superior fund, as my study shows that such funds definitely exist. In fact, in another recent study (Kosowski et al., 2001), we look at the question of whether the top performing funds over the 1962–94 period were simply lucky. That is, if we look at the performance of several hundred mutual funds over a long period of time, we would certainly expect that a few would achieve very high returns due simply to having a run of luck over that period.

Our study addresses this problem through a statistical technique called "bootstrapping," where we adjust for the luck factor. We find that the best performing mutual funds exhibited performance levels that far exceeded the levels one would expect by luck alone. Thus superior funds do exist, meaning that fund managers and analysts at some mutual funds have the ability to identify mispriced stocks. Unfortunately, our study also finds that inferior funds also exist, even controlling for a possible run of bad luck over a long time period. This can be interpreted as the fund management not having skills in finding mispriced stocks, at least to the degree necessary to cover the expenses and trading costs of the fund.

However, the real issue investors care about is how to identify superior (and inferior!) funds. Should we look simply for high-turnover funds? Should we simply rank funds on their past net returns (as Morningstar does)?

Carhart (1997) provides a partial answer for this question by studying the predictability of mutual fund net returns. He finds that there is strong predictability when using the past-year net return of funds as the ranking variable – last year's best funds tend to be this year's best as well. However, he attributes all of this predictability to the momentum effect in stock returns – now a well known anomaly that finds that the highest-return stocks of one year have following-year returns that usually beat the market (as shown by Jegadeesh and Titman, 1993, and Chan et al., 1996). Controlling for momentum, he finds no evidence of persistent stock-selection skills among managers.

In a new study (Wermers, 2001), I take another look at the persistence issue, using my previously mentioned database of mutual fund stock holdings and net returns. In this study, I try several ways of identifying superior funds, including sorting funds on their past one-year and three-year net returns, as well as looking at the long-term performance of funds with the highest levels of turnover.

I find that last year's winning funds beat last year's losers (ranked on the net return of last year) by about 5 percent during this year (at the net return level). These winners also beat the S&P 500 Index by about 2 percent. Of course, these results were already documented by Carhart (1997), but I find the further surprising result that these winning funds continue to beat losers during the second year after the ranking period by about 2.5 percent.

What accounts for the strong persistence in the first-year performance spread between past winners and losers? I address this question by decomposing the winner–loser spread into the portion that is related to differences in style investing, differences in stock-picking talent (independent of the chosen style of investing), differences in expenses, and differences in transaction costs between past winning and losing funds. I find that, of the 5 percent spread during year 1, about 4 percent is due to winners benefiting from the momentum effect (also found by Carhart, 1997). The remaining 1 percent of the spread is due to winning funds picking stocks better than losing funds (not found by Carhart, 1997).

When I repeat this decomposition to determine the sources of the spread in second-year returns, I find that essentially all of the 2.5 percent can be explained by winners (again) benefiting from stocks with momentum. That is, the superior stock-picking talents of winners do not persist for a second year.

The finding of second-year momentum, at first blush, is quite surprising – the momentum effect normally lasts for only one year, yet these winning funds somehow find a way to continue to ride momentum during a second year. The answer to this puzzle appears to be related to the cash flows that consumers invest in winners; for example, the top 20 percent of funds of last year (ranked on net returns) grow by 20 percent this year through cash inflows alone (i.e. not including growth through investment returns). These winning funds use this large amount of incoming cash to change the composition of their equity portfolios – they add new momentum stocks to their portfolios to replace those stocks for which momentum has faded. In contrast, losing funds experience a slight cash outflow during the first year, which constrains them from rebalancing their portfolios. Certainly, these funds could sell stocks, then replace them with other stocks, but they appear to be reluctant to do so – perhaps owing to the transaction costs and/or the taxable capital gains that they would incur.

While this study is still under way, I find the strongest evidence of "hot hands" among growth funds having the highest levels of turnover. Specifically, those growth funds that trade most frequently tend to pick stocks better than other funds for at least four years – these frequent traders also beat other funds at the net return level for this four-year period.

It is also important to look at the net returns generated by past winning funds, after adjusting for style. Although some investors consider style investing (such as investing in small stocks, value stocks, or momentum stocks) to be related to risk, this issue is currently under debate in the finance profession. To be specific, Daniel and Titman (1997) present findings that suggest that the return premium to value stocks is an anomaly, while Davis et al. (2001) argue that this premium is related to the higher risk inherent in value stocks. Also, Jegadeesh and Titman (1993) and Titman and Jegadeesh (2001) find that momentum stocks outperform the market, while Conrad and Kaul (1998) show that this anomaly may be related to the higher risk in momentum stocks.

However, for those who believe that style-based returns are a compensation for bearing risk, I also examine the style-adjusted net returns provided by past winning mutual funds to complete the persistence picture. At first glance, these "alphas" (the return or value added that remains after adjusting for the risk or style of a mutual fund) are disappointing – past winners actually have negative alphas once we control for the size (large cap. versus small cap.), book-to-market (growth versus value), and past return (momentum) styles used by these funds. However, when I control for the negative influence of investor cash flows to winning funds (as described previously), I find that winning funds exhibit an alpha of zero. Thus a mutual fund investor who believes that the higher returns that can be earned by style investing are related to risk, and therefore should not be rewarded, should be indifferent between chasing winning funds and investing in an index fund. In fact, the investor may prefer an index fund, since such funds do not suffer from the hot money effect that chasing winning actively managed funds involves.

The performance of value versus growth funds and small-cap. funds versus large-cap. funds

A final issue of interest is whether funds with a certain style of investing beat funds in other style categories. This question is somewhat complex, as the answer depends on whether the investor believes that style investing is related to risk. For example, an investor may believe that the high returns that normally accrue to value stocks may simply be a compensation for the riskier nature of these stocks.

Since many researchers have discussed the value premium and the small-stock premium, one may easily look at such studies to find a period of time when value funds beat growth funds, or when small stock funds beat large stock funds. (Both happened during 1975–83.) One may also find periods of time when the opposite occurred (e.g. growth funds and large-cap. funds performed well during 1995–9).

Therefore, I will instead focus on the performance of funds, controlling for their style specialization – not because I necessarily believe that style-based returns are a compensation for risk, but because this is the main unanswered question, in my opinion. That is, value funds frequently beat growth funds (with the notable exception of the past several years), but can value funds pick value stocks better than growth funds pick growth stocks?

In Chen et al. (2000), we look at the ability of, for example, value-fund managers to buy value stocks that outperform other growth stocks. In measuring this ability, we first classify funds based on their actual stock holdings at a given point in time, and not on their stated investment policy. This classification method allows us to avoid the problem of funds that say one thing and do something entirely different. In general, we find the following:

1   Growth-fund managers show abilities to pick stocks that outperform other stocks of the same style category. Although growth-fund managers usually buy large-cap. growth stocks, we find that, when they buy value stocks and/or small-cap. stocks, they often find stocks that outperform other stocks in the same style category.
2   Value-fund managers show little ability in picking value stocks that outperform other value stocks. When value-fund managers buy stocks in other style categories, their failure to find well performing stocks continues.
3   Large-cap. growth funds pick stocks at least as well as small-cap. growth funds, and large-cap. and small-cap. value funds show poor ability in picking stocks.

Given this evidence, how can actively managed value funds continue to exist? In the past, it appears that value managers survived simply by buying low P/E stocks, then holding them for several years in the hope of profiting from a reversal of fortune. This strategy, which is central to a value manager, has provided investors with a return premium above the market that has been substantial during long time periods – yet it apparently does little to uncover mispriced stocks, other than using a value strategy. However, with the advent of index value funds, it may become more difficult for actively managed value funds to survive, given their higher expenses.

Conclusions

Can actively managed mutual funds beat the market? Although the issue is not fully settled, my current take on it is that it depends on your view toward style-based returns. If you view the value effect, the small-cap. effect, and the momentum effect as being purely based on risk, then you will be disappointed in the average actively managed fund – simply put your money in a low-expense index fund.

However, if your view is that a manager should be rewarded for producing high net returns that are due to a certain type of style-based investing that paid off, then you might do well investing in an actively managed fund with a reasonable fee. This, of course, depends on whether the returns generated by the style in question can be captured through a low-expense index fund (such as an index fund that invests in large portfolios of low P/E stocks in an attempt to capture the value premium).

In either case, I think there is some evidence that superior funds do exist, even if you are an investor who believes that style investing amounts to taking on more risk. However, I am not yet confident that an amateur investor (like me) can find these funds through easy-to-use analytical tools. I'll let you know when I find something of interest. You can follow my research on this subject through my Web site: http://www.rhsmith.umd.edu/finance/rwermers/index.htm.

MUTUAL FUND PERFORMANCE: SELECTED ISSUES

The following discussion reviews selected studies of mutual fund performance and studies with important implications for mutual fund performance. These studies represent a small sample from the large literature with direct or indirect relevance to the issue of fund performance.

Malkiel studies

Malkiel (1995, 1998, 1999a, b) asks whether there are dependable, predictable patterns in stock market prices that suggest markets are inefficient. These issues are also treated in Evans and Malkiel (1999). As noted, there appears to be considerable predictability in returns when sorted by variables such as dividend yield, market cap. size, P/E ratio, and P/B ratio. The strength of certain predictable patterns in stock prices led to the conclusion that the 1970s version of efficient markets was too simplistic.

The view concerning the returns available from actively managed mutual funds has also changed. Earlier studies find that fund performance after taxes is inferior to portfolios of randomly selected stocks with equivalent risk. Fund managers did not appear to have private information. Later studies revealed fund managers who have enough private information to offset expenses. Others find fund returns net of expenses provide abnormal risk-adjusted returns, depending on the benchmark index used. A "hot hands" phenomenon was isolated where investors may earn abnormal risk-adjusted returns by buying funds with recent good performance.

There is strong evidence supporting hot hands in mutual fund returns. Funds that achieve above-average returns continue to do so. Part of this persistence is due to the persistence of expense ratios. Funds that have the lowest expense ratios are likely to outperform high-expense funds persistently. When winners are defined as outperforming the median last-year performance funds, considerable persistence in returns was noted during the 1970s. An opposite cold hands phenomenon was also noted.

Analysis of mutual fund expenses identified an extremely large negative relationship between fund expense ratios and net performance. This is expected because there is no reason for operating expenses and 12b-1 distribution fees to increase net returns. Failure to find a significant relationship between performance and advisory expenses suggests that fund investors do not benefit from investment advisory expenses. When fund expenses are added back to form gross returns, there is essentially no relationship between gross returns and expenses. There is only an insignificant positive relationship between gross returns and investment advisory expenses. The large impact of expense ratios on net returns may also reflect the positive correlation between expenses and portfolio turnover.

Over the 1971–9 period, winners repeated almost 67 percent of the time. The same results are seen over one quarter or over two years. The relationship changed during the 1980s. The hypothesis of no persistence in returns may not be rejected. It is very hard to conclude there is much predictability in mutual fund returns. This breakdown in persistence occurred across all investment styles, such as growth funds.

The important issue is whether the findings of persistence in mutual fund returns are economically significant. Is there a strategy that will produce abnormal returns? The results over the twenty-year period suggest caution. The strategy of buying the best-performing funds worked very well through 1981 (the bull market began in 1982), but then decreasingly so with inferior returns during the last years of the 1980s through 1991. There is no dependable strategy of generating abnormal returns based on the belief that fund returns persist.

In conclusion, Malkiel confirms that mutual fund managers do not outperform the market, in general. There was evidence of hot hands during the 1970s, but it was not strong, and it broke down considerably during the 1980s. Investment strategies designed to exploit the persistent patterns in prices are tested. The strategy that would have generated large abnormal returns in the 1970s produced inferior returns during the 1980s.

There is some evidence of short-term persistence (momentum) in stock prices over days, weeks, and months. Market prices do not follow a perfect random walk because stock returns may be positively correlated for short periods of time. Evidence of "considerable performance persistence" was identified during the 1970s, but not during the 1980s. The 1970s represent a temporary anomaly from the position in Malkiel (1973). However, this anomaly may not represent true market inefficiency, because momentum investors who pay trading costs are not able to outperform buy-and-hold strategies. However, Clements (1999c) reported that over the last twenty-three years an annual strategy of purchasing the ten top-performing diversified no-load funds would have outperformed average returns by over seven percentage points!

Malkiel also found the expected negative relationship between non-advisory expenses (including 12b-1 fees) and net fund returns. However, if fund portfolio managers add signific- antly to fund returns, there should be a positive relationship between net fund returns and investment advisory expenses. But there is a negative relationship. Further, when expenses are added back to returns, gross returns and expenses have essentially no relationship. Active portfolio management thus generally generates lower returns, but also tends to create higher taxes. Most investors would be better served by low-cost index funds than attempting to select active portfolio managers with hot hands.

Further, momentum strategies are not profitable over the long term because returns revert to the mean. This is reflected in negatively correlated returns over periods of three or four years. However, reversion is stronger in some periods than in others. Reversion also gives support to contrarian strategies that buy (sell) stocks that have been performed well (poorly) for the past several years. Analysis identified strong statistical evidence of mean reversal and non-randomness over three-year and five-year periods. Stocks with very large (small) returns over three-year and five-year periods have small (large) returns in the next three to five years. But the returns in the subsequent period are similar for both groups. The reversals prove to be true mean reversals, not opportunities to exploit contrarian strategies profitably. These reversals may be consistent with efficient markets because interest rates move up and down requiring stock returns to adjust to be competitive with bonds. In sum, it may not be possible to profitably exploit contrarian strategies.

What are the implications for mutual fund performance? Buy index funds, not actively managed funds, and invest long-term. Momentum and contrarian strategies are not profitable over the long run.

Carhart study

Carhart (1997) analyzed the existence of persistence in mutual fund returns. Performance per- sistence does not reflect superior portfolio managers' stock selection skills. Predictability of stock returns is explained mostly by factors in common and differences in fund expenses and trading costs. The only persistence anomaly is the persistent underperformance of the lowest-return funds.

William Bernstein (1999c) agreed. He tested the persistence of the top thirty funds for each of five five-year periods over the next five years ending 1998. In each following period, the S&P

500 outperformed the top thirty funds which performed best for the previous period. Thus the five-year "alpha man" (abnormal returns) became "ape man" (less than average returns) over the following five years.

Persistence of mutual fund performance is often seen but not well explained. Evidence of persistence has been seen over short horizons of one to three years and attributed to hot hands or investment strategies in common. Predictable fund returns have also been observed over long horizons of five to ten years and attributed to information differences or stock selection ability. Much of the long-term persistence in fund performance is due to persistence in expense ratios. For example, Bogle (1999b) determined that 92 percent of the shortfall between index and managed fund returns is due to expenses. While asset allocation dwarfs other sources of total returns, total returns are "severely impacted by costs."

Carhart's (1997) study included nearly 1,900 diversified equity funds using annual returns computed monthly for the years 1962–93. Fund returns were sorted into deciles (portfolios) by annual performance and tracked by performance the next year. Funds were also sorted into deciles by abnormal returns over the past three years and tracked by performance the next year.

Carhart's analysis indicates that momentum in one-year stock prices accounts for the hot hands effect. Funds with higher one-year returns have them because they by chance hold large positions in last year's winning stocks, not because they successfully follow momentum strategies. Hot hands funds only infrequently repeat their abnormal performance. The hot hands effect contrasts with findings that momentum strategies produce higher performance prior to fund expenses and trading costs. Funds that follow one-year momentum strategies earn significantly lower returns after expenses. Trading costs therefore offset the gains from momentum trading.

Mutual fund expenses, portfolio performance, and load fees significantly impact performance. Mutual fund expenses have at least a one-for-one negative impact on performance, and turnover also negatively impacts performance. Trading costs reduce performance by about 0.95 percent of a trade's market value. Variations in costs per transaction also explain part of performance differences. Load funds substantially underperform no-load funds. After adjusting for the relationship between expenses and loads, and omitting the worst-performing funds, load funds underperform no-load funds by about eighty basis points a year.

Mutual fund portfolio managers provide little evidence of stock selection ability. Funds with high past management performance also demonstrate high future performance and returns. However, this future performance is not significantly due to management skill. The best past performance funds appear to earn back their expenses and trading costs, but the majority of funds underperform by their investment expenses and costs.

Carhart finds that much of the persistence in equity mutual fund short-term returns is explained by factors in common, expenses, and trading costs. A strategy of buying last year's top-decile performing funds and selling the lowest-decile funds produced an annual rate of 8 percent. Of this 8 percent, 4.6 percent is due to differences in cap. size and one-year momentum. Differences in expense ratios explain 0.7 percent, and differences in trading costs explain 1 percent. Basing the analysis on longer horizons of past returns finds smaller differences in returns, of which all but 1 percent are explained by factors in common and investment expenses. The unexplained difference in returns is largely seen in the underperformance of bottom-decile funds.

Mutual fund performance is negatively related to fund expense ratios, portfolio turnover, and loads/fees. Expense ratios reduce fund returns by a bit more than one for one, and turnover reduces returns by 0.95 percentage points for each buy-and-sell trade. Trading costs also explain some of the differences in performance among the highest and lowest decile funds. Excluding the lowest-decile funds, load funds underperform non-load funds by 0.80 percent, exclusive of actual loads. This is partially explained by higher portfolio turnover and trading costs.

Carhart finds little evidence of skilled or informed portfolio managers. Mutual funds with above-average past management performance demonstrate above-average management performance and returns in subsequent periods. However, the future returns do not reflect significant management performance. The higher gross returns of high-performing funds earn back their investment expenses and costs.

Overall, the evidence is consistent with market efficiency, in spite of the effects of cap. size, P/B ratios, and momentum. As stated, most funds underperform by the amount of their investment expenses and costs. Buying last year's winners is a feasible strategy for capturing one-year momentum effects in stock returns. This practice shifts trading costs to long-term fund investors. However, more funds are limiting fund access to momentum investors and charging various types and amounts of transaction fees to compensate for the costs.

The study concludes with three lessons. First, investors should avoid mutual funds with persistently poor performance. Second, funds with high returns last year have higher than expected returns next year, but not beyond. And, third, fund expense ratios, loads/fees, and trading costs have a direct negative impact on performance. Strategy and investment costs account for almost all of the predictability of fund returns.

Zweig (1997b) reviewed Carhart (1997) to identify lessons for mutual fund investors. First, low-cost index funds should provide the core of investor portfolios. Second, recent fund performance should not be used as a guide to long-term winners. Performance persistence is short-term and turnover among hot hands funds is high. Third, broadly based funds earn competitive returns with less risk than aggressive funds. Fourth, high average returns also bring along higher risk. And, fifth, check funds for low expense ratios, low portfolio turnover, and high tax efficiency.

A study by Elton et al. (1993) is consistent with the market efficiency in Carhart (1997). From 1965 to 1984 the abnormal returns of load mutual funds were more negative than no-load funds. This suggests little reason to buy the average load fund, if any. Abnormal returns of funds with high expense ratios are also more negative than funds with low expense ratios. And abnormal returns of funds with high turnover rates were more negative than those funds with low turnover rates.

The study concludes that markets are efficient, but, nonetheless, it may be appropriate to make revisions in portfolio risk levels or dividend yields. Frequent portfolio revisions to exploit market inefficiencies are doomed to failure, owing to trading costs. Actively managed funds do not outperform passively managed funds over extended periods. This latter point reflects that the average investor cannot outperform the market because "investors are the market."

The bottom line is that persistence of mutual fund performance may well lie at the extremes. There may be a small number of exceptional managers, but note again the statistical burden of proof of *persistence* and size of abnormal returns discussed previously. But, for portfolio managers in general, such performance is likely a matter of chance. Samuelson's (1989) analysis of superstar portfolio managers did not reveal any easily duplicated strategies that guarantee high performance. However, this does not preclude publications from hyping "Managers of the Year."

Contrarian and momentum strategies: other studies

To the extent that momentum and contrarian strategies offer dependable abnormal returns, markets are not efficient. As discussed, if short-term momentum strategies work, past winner portfolios persist in positive abnormal returns, and loser portfolios persist in negative returns. If longer-term contrarian strategies work, past loser portfolios revert at some point to winner portfolios, and conversely for winner portfolios. However, if markets price assets efficiently, these two strategies should have abnormal profits approximating zero.

Mutual funds that use momentum strategies focus on stocks with either accelerating price momentum or earnings momentum, with every expectation of soon replacing them with even hotter stocks. Paluch (1996b) noted that momentum funds are easy to identify by their traits in common: (1) five-year earnings growth rates twice the market rate, (2) P/E ratios 1.25 times the market P/E; (3) portfolio turnover in excess of 100 percent; (4) Morningstar Risk in excess of 1.0; (5) Morningstar Bear Market ranks between 8 and 10; and (6) Morningstar Worst Three Months Performance in excess of 8 percent.

Mutual fund use of momentum strategies began in the 1980s and provided returns well above those of average domestic equity funds. Of course, this performance was aided by the bull market in those years. Momentum investing has become so widely used that it is now considered a distinct investment style. But, just as momentum funds have grown, they are also very volatile. The high points of fund momentum investing have also been accompanied by occasional flameouts as returns flounder and investors redeem. These funds are akin to growth funds, but "growth funds on steroids." However, the bull market that began in 1982 was not for ever, and this strategy in inconsistent with buy-and-hold strategies. For investors desiring some fun on the wild side, momentum funds should be limited to 10 percent of the portfolio set aside from passive asset allocation and long-term investing.

Sharpe et al. (1999) reconciled the results of six studies that variously identified abnormal contrarian or momentum returns over different periods of portfolio formation and testing. These strategies are opposite sides of the coin. Momentum investors buy stocks that have recently risen in price in the expectation that they will continue to rise. Contrarian investors take the unpopular side of the market. They buy unloved stocks selling below fundamental values owing to excessive investor pessimism and sell stocks trading above fundamental values owing to excessive investor optimism. Neither strategy should generate abnormal returns if markets are efficient, but investor overreaction is a tenet of behavioral finance.

Overall, the six studies included data from 1926 to 1989. The studies determined that contrarian strategies have merit for very short price formation and testing periods of one week to a month and from three to five years. The momentum strategy has merit for periods of six months to one year, a middle ground. The problem with both strategies, but especially the contrarian strategy, is high portfolio turnover with resultant high trading costs.

Dreman (1998) provided data supporting forty-one rules for successful contrarian investing. For the years 1970–96, a low P/E ratio, but also low P/C and P/B ratios, provide above-market returns when applied to the small end of large-cap. stocks. Further, Paluch and Kelley (1996), followed by Dziubinski (1998c), examined mutual fund use of contrarian strategies for the period 1987–96. Funds were selected based on their current popularity measured by percentage changes in net cash inflows. The results indicate that 78 percent of unpopular funds (not widely held) in a given year outperform average equity funds over the next one, two, and three-year periods. Also, in twenty-one of twenty-seven periods, unpopular funds outperform average equity funds over the following one, two, and three-year periods. Unpopular funds outperformed popular funds in twenty-four of twenty-seven periods. The strategy is best applied to tax-efficient no-load funds and deep-discount closed-end funds. Closed-end funds are traded on exchanges, with prices normally at discount or, less often, at premium to net asset value.

In a sequel study, Barbee (1999b) analyzed the outperformance of popular and unpopular categories of equity mutual funds back to 1987. Popularity was again measured by percentage change in net cash inflow. Unpopular funds outperform average funds 78 percent of the time over the next three years. Moreover, 89 percent of unpopular funds outperform the currently *most* popular funds. Barbee stated: "This [contrarian] strategy is the closest investing gets to a sure thing." Well, maybe. It is easiest to implement when investing new money, selling funds, and rebalancing portfolios to desired allocations. More important, this strategy may be applied to the equity style allocations within the passive stock allocations under these conditions. These results were confirmed in DiTeresa (2000).

In a review of momentum investing for the years 1981–98, the Institute for Econometric Research (1998b) examined equity mutual fund returns for momentum over numerous time periods. Subsequent strong and poor fund returns (five classes each) were computed for each of the next thirteen weeks, twenty-six weeks, fifty-two weeks, two years and five years for each of the previous thirteen weeks, twenty-six weeks, fifty-two weeks, two years and five years – nine tests in all. The results show that superior returns are available from using short-term performance criteria after each quarter and at the end of the year to select funds for purchase or sale. But, more interestingly, and counter to most momentum studies, a longer-term perspective is even more rewarding. Prior performance, such as two years or, better, five years, improves the odds for superior performance based on demonstrated portfolio manager ability and efficacy of portfolio investment style.

In table 78, the benefits of momentum investing are provided in the performance of all equity mutual funds for each of the most recent thirteen, twenty-six, and fifty-two weeks and one, two, and five years. The annualized returns of the worst and best performing funds in these prior periods is computed for each of the thirteen, twenty-six, and fifty-two weeks and one and two-year subsequent periods. The three performance returns indicated by a raised *a* appear particularly interesting. These returns are based on the 10 percent of funds with best/ worst prior performance. These choices indicate the periods of highest subsequent performance that also have large differences in best/worst performance. Also, two of the three performance comparisons require only fifty-two weeks' prior performance data. This study indicates that momentum investing has merit over longer periods than the six studies summarized above.

Gruber study

Gruber (1996) attempted to solve a mutual funds paradox. Why do there continue to be increased numbers of actively managed mutual funds when their average performance has been inferior to that of index funds? By most any performance measure, funds underperform market indices. Data from 270 mutual funds and nine closed-end funds for the period 1985–94 were used. A so-called four-index model explained 89 percent of the variability in fund abnormal returns. The four indices represent market returns, differences in small-cap. and large-cap. fund returns, differences in growth and value fund returns, and abnormal bond fund returns.

The Gruber study found persistence in mutual fund performance, and some investors invest as if aware of the persistence. Among the major findings are the following: (1) mutual funds underperform average indices by about 65 basis points a year; (2) fund expense ratios average 113 basis points and exceed the value added by portfolio managers; (3) index funds outperform managed funds, owing to smaller expense ratios; (4) load funds perform worse than no-load funds over any horizon; (5) the model captures the investment objectives that impact performance; (6) closed-end funds usually sell at discount to net asset value because expectations of management performance are "priced," but not so in mutual funds – they sell at net asset value; (7) the model forecasts future risk-adjusted performance better than past returns; (8) funds do *not* price superior management performance into expenses – top-performing funds have lower expense ratios than bottom-performing funds and increase them more slowly; (9) investors do chase fund performance, as measured by the relative amount of new cash inflows; (10) new cash flows follow predictors of performance and earn higher returns than average active and passive funds; and (11) after-tax returns of momentum strategies differ for tax deferred and taxable actively managed and index funds, but favor active management.

The four-factor model as applied to deciles of performance provides the strongest results in forecasting future mutual fund risk-adjusted performance. Buying the top decile of funds ranked using one or three-year selection periods provides significantly larger returns. As noted above, there is persistence in fund returns, and some investors invest as if aware of this persistence. Their new cash flows follow the predictors of future performance, and the risk-adjusted returns they earn are positive and larger than the average returns of both active and passive funds. Thus past fund performance can partly explain future performance.

The next question is, why do investors stay invested in mutual funds predicted to perform poorly? They do so despite the fact that average mutual funds have negative risk-adjusted returns and are outperformed by index funds. And, as opposed to closed-end funds, investors pay for each dollar under management. The answer is there are two distinct "clienteles" for mutual funds: sophisticated and disadvantaged. The "sophisticated clientele" recognizes that future fund performance is partly predictable from past performance. This is because fund prices do not reflect the quality of management – priced at net asset value. These investors act as if they recognize this, based on the fact that their flows of new cash in and out of funds follow the predictors of performance. In fact, the statistical relationship between the predictors and cash flows is very high. These investors benefit from this action because the risk-adjusted returns they earn on new cash flows over ten years are positive and above the returns earned by both the average active and passive funds. This clientele invests the larger percentage of new cash flows that earn positive risk-adjusted returns – returns larger than benchmark index returns.

On the other hand, there is the "disadvantaged clientele" that includes (1) unsophisticated investors attracted by non-rational information, such as advertising; (2) institutionally disadvantaged investors constrained by pension plans to underperforming funds; and (3) tax-disadvantaged investors holding funds with large capital gains that make them inefficient to sell.

The overall performance implications of Gruber's two investor clienteles follow: (1) the total amount invested in mutual funds underperforms index benchmarks; (2) flows of cash invested primarily by sophisticated investors perform better than benchmarks; (3) flows of cash into best performing funds are larger than flows out of poor performing funds, owing to disadvantaged investors; (4) flows of new cash in and out of funds underperform the model that predicts future risk-adjusted returns better than do past returns, again owing to disadvantaged investors; and (5) worst-performing funds are eliminated over time. Thus investment in actively managed and passively managed mutual funds is more rational than usually assumed.

Zweig (1996a) reviewed Gruber's (1996) persistence effect to determine whether it is a profitable mutual funds strategy: buy last year's winners and hold them one year. The surprising strength of return persistence is noted, but caution is called for based on findings by Sharpe and Malkiel that fund performance is becoming less persistent, and "the evidence is far from conclusive." Also, investors would have to own twenty-two funds each year and trade them up to 440 times over ten years. The high fund portfolio turnover would also generate high investor transaction costs and taxes each year. Gruber does not advise investing in this way; the study's purpose was to find out why some investors buy actively managed rather than index funds.

Zheng study

Zheng (1999) took a different tack and investigated the ability of mutual fund investors to select high-performing funds. The study follows Gruber's (1996) finding that newly invested cash flows in funds earn higher than average returns. This issue of investor ability also arises because of the huge supply of data, books, and articles that has followed the huge demand for detailed information and investment advice concerning mutual funds. This demand suggests that many investors use the information to make decisions. The bottom-line question then becomes: Can investors forecast fund performance? The study investigates whether investor purchase and sale decisions are able to predict fund performance, and whether investors are smart in fund selection.

Numerous studies find that mutual funds underperform the market index, but others find some evidence of portfolio manager skill. The focus of Zheng's study is twofold. Do investors have Gruber's *smart money effect*, where new cash flows to funds predict performance? And, do investors have an "information effect," where new cash flows to funds have information that can be used to make abnormal returns? The smart money effect does not require implementation of trading strategies, but strategies must be able to be implemented for the information effect to exist.

The performance measure allows for active strategies based on macroeconomic conditions and style effects. It applies predetermined measures of time-varying expectations and controls for variation due to public information. A portfolio strategy should not be regarded as having superior performance if it can be replicated using readily available public information. The method determines whether the smart money effect is due to rational response to macroeconomic variables or style variables, such as B/P ratios and related measures.

The test results support the smart money effect. Investors are able to select mutual funds by moving cash from poor to good performers. Returns and risk-adjusted returns for funds with new cash inflows are significantly higher than for funds with new cash outflows. But, overall, the trading strategies suggest there are no significant abnormal returns from constructing portfolios with new cash inflows. There is no evidence that active investors can outperform the market, except for evidence of the information effect in small funds.

The smart money effect cannot be completely explained by investors chasing past performance. A significant percentage is explained by performance variations in the "repeat winner" strategy. Superior returns are earned primarily by cash flowing in and out of small funds rather than large funds. The smart money effect is therefore likely due to fund-specific information investors use to make fund choices.

In conclusion, it is important to know whether portfolio managers can outperform the market, but Zheng also wants to know whether investors can generate reasonable returns using mutual funds. Different strategies are tested based on the smart money effect. Cash flows are the dollar changes in fund net assets from this source only. The results confirm the smart money effect – new cash flows money can forecast short-term equity fund performance. Funds that get new cash perform significantly better than those that lose cash. Overall, there is no evidence that the smart money strategy outperforms the market, and there is no evidence that investors in general can outperform the market. However, there is evidence that positive cash flows to small funds outperform the market.

Also, significant evidence supports the information effect for small funds – new cash flows contain information that can be used to outperform the market. The smart money effect is shorter-lived than performance persistence. It reverses after thirty months, for the performance rankings both of positive and of negative cash flow funds. The smart money effect cannot be completely explained by the hot money strategy that chases performance. However, a significant percentage of performance differences reflect variations in repeat winner strategies. The smart money effect is due to fund-specific information. The hot money strategy is based on performance signals, such as positive or negative abnormal returns. Finally, the view that load-fund investors are less informed than no-load fund investors is rejected. The higher cost of buying load funds may make their cash flows appear even smarter.

Zweig (1998c) took the opportunity afforded by the later published Zheng (1999) study to warn about what the study does not say. Investors could have beaten the market by up to 2.4 percentage points a year if they had invested in small no-load funds that were attracting new cash inflows. But this return was not attainable for ordinary fund investors. The strategy calls for trading up to 100 funds every three months. As such, any trading costs or tax liabilities will produce negative returns. And it does no good to hold the funds for a year, because they lose any abnormal returns of the strategy.

Wermers on herding

Wermers (1999) analyzed mutual fund trading activity from 1975 to 1994 to determine whether funds herd when they trade, and, if so, does herding act to stabilize or destabilize stock prices? That is, do institutional investors flock together when they trade, with some investors following others? To investigate the degree to which herding is related to positive-feedback (momentum) trading styles, the tendency of funds to herd into (out of) stocks that are past winners (losers) is examined.

The media report as if institutional investors trade together and move in and out of stocks in a manner inconsistent with stock fundamentals. The alleged results are more market volatility and focus on short-term earnings rather than long-term strategies. The presence of fads in stock prices suggests that investors with similar styles trade together.

There are four possible explanations for institutional investors trading together. First, portfolio managers may disregard private information and trade with the crowd, rather than suffer possible loss of reputation by acting differently. Second, portfolio managers may act together because they receive information that is highly correlated. Third, portfolio managers may infer private information in the prior trades of more informed investors. Fourth, institutional investors may share an aversion to particular stock characteristics, such as high risk and low liquidity.

Most mutual funds use positive-feedback trading strategies to select stocks that outperform prior to expenses. There is also a tendency for investment newsletters to herd. These trading patterns contribute to serial correlation in daily returns. Herding is also seen in stock trade imbalances among mutual funds. Large dollar buy imbalances usually follow prolonged periods of positive abnormal returns, which evidences follow-the-leader behavior. Large dollar imbalances in purchases and sales of stock have also been attributed to chance, not herding.

If mutual funds buy stocks in a destabilizing manner, stock price increases should be followed by decreases. If bought in a stabilizing manner, stock price increases should not be followed by price decreases. To determine whether herding is related to positive-feedback trading styles, the tendency of funds to herd into (out of) stocks that are past winners (losers) must be examined. This behavior reflects herding if stocks tend to have large imbalances between the number of buyers and sellers.

Wermers identified only a small level of mutual fund herding in the average stock. Mutual funds are equally likely to herd when buying/selling stocks. But there is a much higher level of herding by growth versus income oriented funds. Growth funds have less precise information about future stock earnings than income funds. There is also a much higher level of herding in small-cap. stocks, especially when selling. Funds have an aversion to stocks that recently suffered a significant price decline. Further, there is also a higher level of herding in stocks with extreme prior-quarter returns. Herding occurs more often on the buy side of high past return stocks and on the sell side of low past return stocks. This implies that momentum strategies followed by growth funds are important sources of herding. There is little evidence of window dressing.

Mutual funds are rewarded by herding. Stocks bought in herds have significantly higher abnormal returns during subsequent quarters than stocks sold in herds, especially due to underperformance of stocks sold. The next quarterly difference in abnormal returns of stocks most strongly bought and sold is over 2 percent, and is mainly seen in small-cap. stocks. The difference in herding small-cap. stocks is over 4 percent.

Overall, stock price changes from herding are not destabilizing. Price changes appear permanent and they speed the market price adjustment process. Herding is based on private information using fundamental analysis, not on reputational concerns. There is little sign of price reversals for high price and earnings momentum stocks after the twelve-month momentum effect. The momentum effect is not caused by irrational (short-run price impact) positive-feedback strategies, but by the delayed reaction of investors to information in past earnings and returns. Mutual fund herding plays an important role in this process because it is related to rational positive-feedback strategies. Herding also provides power in explaining future stock returns, adjusted for momentum in returns. The linkage of momentum patterns in stock prices with trading patterns among mutual funds supports momentum as an anomaly.

Unexpected inflows of cash to mutual funds are strongly correlated with concurrent returns on market indices. There is little evidence that inflows are correlated with past returns (feedback trading) or future returns. Also, there is little evidence of a correlation between levels of herding and either expected or unexpected cash inflows. Feedback trading and trading impacts on stock returns are due to decisions by portfolio managers and not to investor trading strategies.

Falkenstein study

Falkenstein (1996) investigated equity mutual fund holdings to determine their revealed preferences for various stock characteristics. The behavior of over 2,200 funds was analyzed for the years 1991 and 1992. Fund analysis by sector, age, and size suggests that their preferences for stock characteristics are generally consistent, except for stock cap. size. The strongest finding is that fund preferences are not totally driven by risk proxies. The major surprise is lack of differentiation among funds – estimated variable coefficients are very stable across fund subsectors. Little diversity in the characteristics of portfolio holdings is observed. The only significant diversity is cap. size of holdings, and, except for the small-cap. subsector, funds clearly prefer large-cap. stocks.

The revealed characteristics that drive mutual fund stock portfolios are: (1) general aversion to small-cap. stocks, (2) preference for liquidity (focus on trading costs), (3) constrained preference for stocks with higher idiosyncratic (not beta) volatility (focus on relative rather than absolute performance and minimizing lowest volatility stocks), (4) avoidance of stocks with few recent major news stories (focus on investor recognition), and (5) preference for stocks of successful, older firms (seasoned stocks).

With respect to these points, mutual funds appear to behave more like outsiders than insiders. Preference for glamour stocks – successful growth stocks with low P/B ratios – helps them justify their portfolios to investors. Mutual funds employ trend following using herding, which may also contribute to preference for these types of stocks.

Interestingly, Graham (1999) observed that investment newsletters herd on the well recognized *Value Line Investment Survey*. Herding appears to increase with (1) the size of the newsletter's reputation, (2) the degree of correlation of private information among securities analysts, and (3) the strength of prior information. Not surprisingly, Metrick (1999) observed no evidence of newsletters with superior stock selection skills, either short-term or long-term.

International momentum studies

To conclude the discussion of momentum strategies, it is useful to know whether they can be effectively applied internationally. Rekenthaler (1995b) noted that mutual funds that invest overseas have an advantage over domestic funds. They keep on winning and not just over the short term. The funds that outperform also have attributes in common with domestic outperforming funds. This differs from the domestic finding that fund returns have short-term momentum but revert over longer periods of time.

Rouwenhorst (1998) analyzed a sample of 2,190 stocks from twelve European countries over the years 1978–95, and identified medium-term continuation of fund returns (local currency). A momentum strategy that buys past winners and sells past losers earns about 1 percent a month. This momentum holds in all markets and among all stock cap. sizes, but especially small-cap. stocks. The outperformance is very similar to domestic findings and lasts about one year. European and domestic momentum strategies appear to have a factor in common that drives strategy returns. The strategy returns are inconsistent with efficient markets and its betas are not dependent on market conditions. Instead, losers have higher betas in up markets and lower betas in down markets than winners.

Value versus growth funds: other studies

The value versus growth story (noted above) becomes less clear, however, when examining the returns of value and growth mutual funds. Historically, one investment style generally provides better returns for six to seven years, or so, and then the other style dominates. Style cycles appear to correlate with business cycles, but the historical business cycle paradigm has been absent for the most part since early in the Reagan administration. This is important because this "growth" environment has generally favored growth stocks. For an example of what happened to a leading value fund during this period, see Barbee (1998d); for a discussion of what has happened to value stocks in general, see Cooley (2000).

The result of these and other factors is the failure of value mutual funds to match the performance of growth funds. Value funds *underperformed* growth funds by more than one percentage point a year for the twenty-one years ending 1998. Yet the Wilshire index of small value stocks outperformed its large growth index by nearly one percentage point a year. The value advantage appears to apply only to *small* value stocks, not mutual funds. Even this advantage disappears for all but the smallest companies when the January outperformance is removed. Among the largest 20 percent of companies, there is no performance difference between value and growth stocks.

Barbee (1998f) analyzed the Fama and French (1992) B/P ratio to see why mutual fund performance has not followed Fama and French's findings. Over the past five years, large-cap. funds outperformed small-cap. funds, and value funds narrowly outperformed growth funds. First, only a small number of funds have been in business long enough for comparison with Fama–French stock returns. Second, those small cap. funds that survive typically do not stay small – they evolve into large-cap. funds. Third, Fama–French's low P/B definition of value style is not everyone's definition of value. And the big number four reason for different results is trading costs, which are not included in the Fama–French computations.

The Fama–French counter-argument to Barbee is that most value mutual funds are not true value funds. Why? The long bull market has placed true value managers under growing pressure as the historical pattern of alternating value versus growth dominance has been largely replaced by a growth emphasis. They have responded by including growth stocks as a means of staying competitive with growth funds. Otherwise, their relative performance in this market would be even worse. Even if value stocks do outperform growth stocks over the long term, the long term could be as long as thirty years.

The performance impact of indexing on mutual fund value/growth investment styles is seen in Morningstar (1998), based on the relative returns of the Vanguard Value Index and the Vanguard Growth Index. The Growth Index outperformed the Value Index in each subsequent year beginning with 1994. Since 1992, a $10,000 investment in the Growth Index has grown to

$35,706 versus $30,367 for the growth category, and $30,245 for the Value Index. It is also interesting that the lower-risk Value Index has the same (almost) cumulative value as the growth category and also outperformed its category ($30,245 versus $27,182). These findings suggest that index funds should be given careful consideration relative to actively managed funds.

So should investors favor one or the other investment style? As noted above, the historical pattern of value versus growth dominance has been stretched to new lengths since the early 1980s. How long will this pattern continue, and will the old pattern return? The first answer is when the market realizes that growth and high growth rates are not eternal. Once the market paradigm changes, however, it is still uncertain whether some semblance of an old business cycle will return. What should be done on the way to thirty years is to cover all bases by diversifying across value/growth investment styles, if for no other reason than to reduce portfolio risk. A 50/50 value/growth allocation appears reasonable for both domestic and international stock allocations because the predominance of one style can last years. For example, Hester (1999) reported that value style portfolio managers "can trail the market for up to a third of an extended investment period and still end up with better returns [than growth managers] for the entire term."

This conclusion is also supported by Ibbotson's (1997) findings, discussed previously. When mutual fund performance is compared with value/growth style benchmarks, over 54 percent of one-year winners (above the median) repeated the next year. A majority of winners repeated in thirteen of sixteen years. There are also funds that, based on value/growth style, perform above the median in a majority of years measured from one year period to the next. Extending the performance period from one year to three years, 42 percent of the funds in the top quartile remained in the top quartile and 62 percent remained in the top half. Nonetheless, Ibbotson concluded it is easier to predict which funds will outperform style benchmarks than to predict which investment styles will perform the best. Thus it appears reasonable to diversify across value/growth styles. Updegrave (1999) summarized the value/growth issue as well as the small-cap./large-cap. performance issue discussed below.

Morningstar investment style boxes may cause performance problems for mutual funds when portfolio managers stay in the same cap. size category to maintain "style purity." As noted, style purity is useful to investors seeking portfolio style balance, but can reduce fund returns when stocks are sold as they move the portfolio to larger cap. sizes. As discussed by Zweig (1999f), style categories are supposed to be descriptive of mutual fund portfolios, not prescriptive. Investors in small-cap. funds should worry more about the size of the fund's assets than portfolio cap. size. They should also favor funds that limit asset growth beyond $3 billion to $4 billion.

Fund portfolio turnover: other studies

Previously, a positive relationship was identified between portfolio turnover and trading costs. Here the issue becomes returns, which, of course, are net of trading costs. Paluch (1997a) observed that funds with high portfolio turnover generally underperform buy and hold port-folios. But this is not to say that some investment styles can not use turnover effectively. Analysis of the return added/subtracted by turnover observed that active portfolio turnover adds some value to large-cap. growth funds, but reduces it for large-cap. value and large-cap. blend funds. In the mid-cap. range, active turnover adds some value to mid-cap. blend and mid-cap. growth, but reduces it for mid-cap. value funds. And, finally, active turnover definitely adds value to small-cap. value and small-cap. growth funds.

The positive results of turnover for small-cap. funds are derived in spite of higher trading costs, which is implied to mean that timing is more important than trading costs for small-cap., but not for large-cap., funds. Further, small-cap. markets are less efficient than large-cap. markets, which provide more opportunities to find greatly undervalued stocks. And, finally, small-cap. funds with small asset bases can trade more quickly with less market impact. Nonetheless, small-cap. funds with high portfolio turnover are more risky than small-cap. funds with low turnover.

Lowenstein (1997) also examined this issue and made a good case for less active portfolio turnover, especially for large-cap. value and large-cap. blend funds. The benefits of turnover are also fairly small for other investment styles. Low turnover is called for in markets with large trading costs and illiquid securities, such as in emerging markets. Any advantage of high turnover in small-cap. value and growth funds is less so after turnover-generated taxes.

Koski and Pontiff study

Koski and Pontiff (1999) investigated mutual fund use of derivatives and the performance implications. Derivatives can be useful tools for improving the utilization of information, risk management, and trading cost reduction. These uses contrast with popular press descriptions of derivatives as speculative, high-risk securities. Elimination of the "short-short rule" in 1997 promoted increased use of derivatives. This rule had eliminated the pass-through tax advantage for funds that realized more than 30 percent of capital gains from securities held less than three months.

Mutual fund use of derivatives can affect returns in three ways. First, funds that use derivatives can have more or less risk than other funds, depending whether they are used to hedge or speculate. Second, their use can improve portfolio performance thanks to either lower trading costs or better use of information. Third, derivatives use can affect fund relationships between fund risk/returns over time.

Data for the study included 679 domestic equity funds with four different investment objectives for the period 1992–4. Overall, approximately 21 percent of funds use derivatives, with specific use ranging from about 17 percent of small-cap. funds to 27 percent of aggressive growth funds. The primary attribute driving derivative use is membership in fund families, especially large families, which is significantly positively related to portfolio turnover, absence of loads, and whether they are growth and income funds, and, marginally, to small fund asset size and age.

Importantly, funds using derivatives have neither reduced risk by hedging nor increased risk by speculation. Fund risk is associated with investment objectives and investment style, but not derivative use. There are no significant differences in various risk measures and higher moments of return distributions between funds that use and those that do not use derivatives. Funds that use derivatives combine them with non-derivative securities to maintain portfolio risk/return consistent with non-derivative users. Fund performance does not change with derivative use.

The results indicate that changes in risk are negatively related to prior performance, but the relationship is weaker for funds using derivatives. This is consistent with the use of derivatives to reduce risk. The negative prior return/risk relationship is consistent with gaming to achieve managerial performance payments and with cash flows, but more so with cash flows. And, finally, the use of derivatives is significantly related to systematic risk, but not to unique risk. This suggests the use of stock index derivatives rather than specific stock derivatives.

CHAPTER ELEVEN

MUTUAL FUNDS: THE NEXT GENERATION

> Buy [SPDRs] as a core holding and forget about it.
> (*Ram Kolluri, Global Value Investors, in* **Wall Street Journal,** *June 27, 2000*)
>
> The benefits of the iShares will really accrue to long-term investors who have the time to see the benefits of low cost and tax efficiency compound.
> (*Lee Kranefuss, Barclays Global Investors, in* **Wall Street Journal,** *June 27, 2000*)
>
> Add it all up, and exchange-traded funds have a small, but undeniable, edge [over mutual funds].
> (*Jonathan Clements, in* **Wall Street Journal,** *June 27, 2000*)

Mutual funds have enjoyed many years of success and growth on a scale not previously experienced in the financial services industry. Not a few multimillionaires have been made from managing mutual funds and advising their portfolios (and, hopefully some fund investors, as well). The success of fund investment advisors has not usually been a bad thing for fund investors in an absolute sense, far from it. But, relatively, investors would have been much better off investing in an industry characterized by fund alignment with investors as shareholders and effective price competition.

The first goal of this chapter is to discuss the current state of the mutual fund industry following the decade of the 1990s. This decade was characterized by lack of price competition among funds, focus on fund advertising, changing investor attitudes, the development of online mutual funds, industry shortcomings and alternative investments. The key question is whether the mutual fund industry will proactively adapt to the increasingly significant reality and threat of exchange-traded funds, or will it opt out of the race for dominance in obtaining investor dollars?

The second goal is to describe the nature of exchange-traded funds (ETFs). They are discussed along several dimensions, including the concept, what they are and are not, exchange trading, direct exchange mechanism, tax-free exchanges, arbitrage, benchmarking market indices, tax efficiency and types of risk.

The third goal is to discuss the major ETFs. These include Spiders, Diamonds, Cubes, HOLDRs, iShares, and WEBS, along with their shareholder distributions and fees/expenses.

The fourth goal is to present current and future ETF developments and the implications for mutual funds. The key issue is whether the development and growth of ETFs sound the prologue for proactive fund industry growth and importance, or do ETFs represent the epilogue for mutual fund dominance? The answer lies with the mutual fund industry, including expenses.

MUTUAL FUNDS SINCE THE 1990S

But, before further discussion, it may be useful to review the position of the mutual fund industry following the heady market performance of the 1990s. Or, as Damato (2000a) so concisely put it: "The '90s are over – deal with it." First, the industry is maturing and funds will find it more difficult to obtain and maintain assets. Second, industry maturity is also seen in the fact that mutual funds are now a staple in most households, as individual and/or as pension plan accounts. Thus, third, traditional means of distributing particular fund shares will continue to broaden, as funds seek asset growth. Fourth, the relatively low cost and high performance of index funds will continue to make them increasingly accepted as alternatives to managed funds. Fifth, the increasing market share of index funds will continue the decline in the former mystique of star portfolio managers. The amazing performance of the bull market has spoiled some fund investors, who have come to expect high returns as an entitlement. Thus, sixth, the return to more normal returns will continue to slow investment in mutual funds and encourage investment in other investment vehicles.

Non-price competition

Unfortunately, the mutual fund industry is characterized by non-price competition. A more price-competitive industry would have a history of decreasing investor costs per fund and higher net returns as new funds enter the industry. After all, financing some computers and small management teams is not in the same league as financing robots and assembly lines in the automobile industry. There would be significant declines in sales loads, fees, and expense ratios, analogous to what happened when brokerage commission became competitively priced.

John C. Bogle, former Vanguard chairman, has no doubt that price competition is lacking in the mutual fund industry. This point is made quite clear in Lowenstein (1999), where Bogle stated: "Nobody competes on price." To see this, it is only necessary to examine size and trends in fund expense ratios, but also fund expenses as percentages of investment income. Also, note the expense ratios of tightly run broadly based index funds, and compare them with the ratios of actively managed funds and their "average" below-average returns. Fund investors often pay above-average expenses for below-average returns.

How has all of this happened? Perhaps the fault lies with investors. Not all mutual fund shareholders are experienced or knowledgeable investors. But this is true of customers of many products, and is certainly not unique to the fund industry. How many drivers really know how automobiles work and what competitive prices are? But mutual fund investors have been slow to shift assets to low-cost funds, though this is changing, owing to the performance of index funds. In the past, investors may have been hindered in moving assets by benign neglect, a strong market, or faith in star portfolio managers. But this mindset is changing.

In a more price-competitive industry, mutual funds would have engaged more proactive, shareholder-oriented, and knowledgeable directors. Their talents would have been required to form strategic plans, approve expenses, and provide oversight in a price-competitive market. The reality, however, has been that fund directors are selected more so for being known quantities with interests compatible with in-house fund management. If industry price competition were alive and well, fund managers would select directors who could help them, rather than simply join them on the road to higher directors' and advisory fees.

Advertising

As noted, the overall objective of previous mutual fund advertising was asset growth. Advertising hyped performance and star portfolio managers, both generally based on short-term performance. This siren song of fund advertising was very successful in attracting new assets. Advertising was the medium, performance was the message, and expenses and risk were "just" small and omitted residuals. That is, what are a few expenses compared with double-digit returns? The questions and answers are changing as "returns come back to earth."

More recently, and increasingly, the overall primary objective of mutual fund advertising has moved from performance to achieve asset growth to a defensive stance focusing on asset retention. The major cause for this change has been the below-par performance of actively managed funds and their star portfolio managers versus the higher but boring performance of passively managed index funds. The result of this performance differential has been the increasing trend for the bulk of new monies invested in funds to go to brand name fund families, index funds, and highly rated funds. But this new advertising focus has also angered investors, such as investment newsletter publisher Doug Fabian. He is quoted in Tam (1998) as saying: "I think funds do a better job of marketing now than managing money." His reaction has been to buy only index funds and unit investment trusts. Increased price competition would certainly cause another change in the focus of fund advertising.

Changing investor attitudes

The recent history of relatively higher returns for large-cap. index mutual funds has apparently made fund shareholders more sensitive (finally!) to fund load, fees, expenses, and after-tax returns. And, as investor sensitivity to these factors grows and becomes increasingly more significant, price competition will increasingly drive investment decisions towards index funds. Taking the extremes, investors will more so view funds as commodities than as unique boutiques with star portfolio managers. But even the dominance of index funds will not be able to prevent further change in the nature and relative importance of the mutual fund industry. In fact, eventual industry dominance by index mutual funds and price competition will actually accelerate the threat of and movement towards new investment vehicles.

The changing nature of competition in the mutual fund industry as it pertains to price competition and the threat of new investment vehicles also has a corollary in changing investor attitudes towards mutual funds. As suggested above, growing numbers of investors appear to be ending their love affair with mutual funds, often based on one or more of the fund shortcomings summarized below. Cataloging these flaws may appear to be a bit like "top ten" lists of fund industry and fund manager failures, but the dissatisfactions and implications for the industry are real.

As noted in Santoli (2000b), changing investor attitudes are clearly seen in the slowing of the amounts being invested in mutual funds. Net cash inflows were $171 billion in 1999 compared with an excess of $300 billion in *each* of the years 1997 and 1998. Moreover, Tam (1998) reported growing investment in individual stocks, but also REITS, unit investment trusts and limited liability partnerships. For larger accounts, more investors are enjoying the cachet of personal portfolio managers (noted below), while others enjoy what cachet is left by investing with big name hedge fund managers.

In response to slowing mutual fund net cash inflows, Santoli (2000b) found the expected result. Fewer new funds are being formed (not that any more are needed!). Only 206 new funds were created in 1999, a ten-year low. The potential market for fund shares has lessened, with 50 percent of households currently owing fund shares. The impact is vividly seen in fund redemptions. In 1999, almost 50 percent of funds suffered actual net cash outflows (redemptions). And about two-thirds of what net cash inflows there were went, in order, to industry giants Vanguard, Janus, Fidelity, Alliance and PIMCO.

Large mutual fund families are actively broadening product lines to gain market share at the expense of mid-size and boutique funds. It has been estimated fund families must have at least $100 billion to remain or become viable. To this end, fund distribution strategies have been broadened to include both direct-market funds and indirect-market funds, which differ with respect to packages of loads, fees, and expenses. Traditional no-load and low-load fund families are offering loaded share classes for distribution through fund supermarkets, full-service brokers, discount brokers, and financial advisors. Discount brokers include those owned by fund investment advisors, such as Fidelity, Vanguard and T. Rowe Price.

The changes in investor attitudes towards mutual funds also reflect the very success many investors have had by investing in mutual funds. A growing number of investors appear spoiled by unsustainable past returns, unhappy with average returns, and, as successful investment experts, bored with mutual funds. Take the combination of changing attitudes along with the significant wealth many fund shareholders have accumulated, and you have investors with a real attitude. Now that many fund investors have generated large portfolios, they want personal attention in managing them. These experts want to "play in the big leagues with big league players (advisors) and their big league toys."

This change in investor attitude has also been noted by ICI chairman John Brennan (1999), also chairman of the Vanguard Group (of all things). Brennan cautioned industry fund managers not to be complacent. The industry must capitalize on opportunities if it is to continue to serve its investors. ICI president Matthew Fink (1999) then specified six steps for continued industry success: (1) support legally mandated fiduciary responsibilities; (2) face change head-on and propose needed laws, regulations, and voluntary measures; (3) support strong regulation by the SEC as sole regulator; (4) guard against unfounded assertions of problems, such as shareholders' panic when market prices fall and fund cash flows drive stock prices; (5) work to ensure investors make informed decisions by improving mandated disclosure; and (6) improve investor education concerning risks/returns, asset allocation, diversification, and long-term investing. It is interesting that specific competitive issues were not discussed with specific recommendations.

Online mutual funds

Investor dissatisfaction with mutual funds has led to one of the great mutual fund ironies (not that there is anything wrong with ironies) – online sites that permit bored experts and others to design and manage their "own" mutual fund portfolios. The several Web sites appear to provide viable alternative investment vehicles, but this is not all for the good. They are also designed (explicitly or implicitly) to attract and encourage investors who are active traders, and who as a group are underperformers. The irony is that these *online mutual funds* are directed to investors who *think* they can manage portfolios as well those "underperforming, overpaid" portfolio managers. And the largest irony is that one online fund founder was formerly one of "those" fund advisors/portfolio managers.

What, then, are the underlying business model assumptions of online mutual funds? The first must be that it is more profitable to provide investors with personalized portfolios than it is to be one of those "underperforming" fund investment advisors/portfolio managers. But what is this assumption based on? Is it a good faith belief in the ability of individual investors to manage portfolios effectively? Or, more likely, is it a belief that individual investors *think* they can effectively manage portfolios? In either case, there would be vindication if investors actually proved they could manage portfolios effectively, and so much better for the company.

On a positive note, however, Santoli (2000a) and Taggart (2000) described these online sites as providing real mutual fund advantages, including lower costs, customized individual portfolios, control over tax planning, and adherence to a particular investment style of choice. Based on investor completion of personal profiles, including measurement of risk tolerances, suggested asset allocations are generated along with lists of five to forty stocks derived from one of ninety strategies. The strategies may be back-tested to see how they worked in particular past market environments. The provider performs all of the quantitative analysis.

Once investors have agreed to particular plans, they purchase tailormade portfolios with securities held in safe keeping. Portfolios are set up as buy-and-hold portfolios with annual rebalancing and updates. Investors may sell individual holdings and also decide whether to take taxable gains and losses. The appeal of these online alternatives to mutual funds will be limited to investors who currently manage their own portfolios or desire to do so.

Industry shortcomings

However, as reported by Clements (2000d), John C. Bogle continues to have a less generous view of the industry. This is seen here in his criticism of mutual fund portfolio turnover, the parameters of which have changed from "reasonable patience" to "short-term momentum" investing. Up to the 1980s, mutual fund portfolio turnover was about 15 percent a year, but now it is about 90 percent annually – due to trigger-happy portfolio managers with resulting high trading costs and high capital gains taxes. Investors have followed this volatile course, as well. Since the 1960s, investor turnover has declined from once every fourteen years to once every two and a half years. This decline is partly due to investor performance chasing and advertising emphasizing short-term performance.

Over the 1980s and 1990s, the proportion of closed and merged funds increased from 2 percent to 5 percent per year – owing to poor managers and poor concepts. Fund expense ratios have doubled over the last forty years, increased 65 percent over the last twenty years, and reached 1.59 percent in 1999. The expenses of the least costly funds have increased 27 percent since 1980. Expenses compound over time. Large-cap. stock funds had annualized returns of 12.2 percent over the last fifteen years, compared with 16.7 percent for an S&P 500 Index fund – just 73 percent of indexed returns.

The changing attitude towards mutual funds is also revealed in Nocera's (1998) heated comments. He reportedly gave up on mutual funds and sold them all when a core holding's portfolio manager changed for the fourth time within a few months. As a result, he provided an off-the-record laundry list of problems (or "hates," as he calls them) facing mutual funds: (1) "too many damn funds," (2) "they're too damn big," (3) "performance doesn't matter the way it used to," (4) "refusal to give customers a break on fees," (5) portfolio managers have a "herd mentality," and (6) "bad funds get folded into good ones." Nocera sees the industry's bottom line problem as follows: "[T]he fund industry has gotten greedy. . . . What a shame, no – what a crime."

After the heat from Nocera, Zweig (1998a) brought a cooler head. But he also provided a long list of mutual fund flaws that must be corrected to make them effective competitors: (1) "funds cost too much"; (2) "funds are too big for your own good"; (3) "funds are too taxing"; (4) "managers are trigger-happy"; (5) "managers move around too much"; (6) "too many managers act like sheep"; (7) "fund directors lack backbone"; (8) "funds report in gibberish"; (9) "there are too many funds"; and (10) "funds are getting too complicated."

In turn, Burton (1997) also took aim at the "sins" of mutual fund portfolio managers that require change if funds are to be effective competitors. The shortcomings are not all widely discussed, but they include: (1) "hugging the index" – charging for active management and finding safety in the herd by "closet indexing"; (2) "racing the clock" – end-of-year moves to "jazz up" lagging portfolio performance and save bonuses with risky short-term strategies; (3) "stalling the clock" – near end-of-year moves to "clean up" portfolios to reduce risk and ensure performance and bonuses to date; (4) "chasing performance" – high portfolio turnover and lack of consistent strategy in incessant efforts to "get on the hot performance bandwagon"; (5) "chasing yield" – focus on high bond yields to the detriment of longer-term bond fund total returns; (6) "baiting and switching" – fund names and/or investment objectives that correlate poorly with actual portfolios; and (7) "getting cold feet" – holding excess cash when nervous about market levels, rather than managing entire portfolios.

These three fund observers have thus laid out an extensive checklist of improvements required by mutual funds and investment advisors. Changes in the nature of mutual fund competition, changes in fund investor attitudes, fund disadvantages previously discussed, and the enumerated lists of fund shortcomings suggest problems for the mutual fund industry.

Alternative investments

A most visible signal of investor dissatisfaction with mutual funds is the large shift of assets to *individually managed accounts*. These accounts provide large portfolios with real investment advisors and customized portfolios, not cookie cutter allocations. Price (2000) reported that assets in these accounts have tripled over the last three years to $425 billion. The lowering of management fees has promoted this shift in assets. Past fees could be as high as 3 percent of assets, but now they average 1.9 percent and online management rates are even less, ranging from 1.0 percent to 1.75 percent. These rates are not competitive with domestic ETFs! The accounts are reviewed in Bierck (2000).

But, realistically, the performance of alternatives to mutual funds is often problematic for the same risk and net after-tax returns achievable with low-cost mutual funds and lower-cost ETFs. For example, Rekenthaler (1998) quoted fund manager Ralph Wanger as saying: "You should never run a mutual fund if somebody will pay you to run a hedge fund." Why? Because they have very large fees, typically 2 percent of assets and 20 percent of returns. They also have leveraged (borrowed funds) portfolios of stocks, short positions in stocks, and derivative positions. Ibbotson (2000) reviewed hedge fund performance and concluded that, while some have had very favorable results, the future is less bright owing to growing competition. With their large fees, investors should avoid hedge funds unless they have complete confidence in the ability of the managers to outperform the markets. And who will these managers be over time?

In addition to shifts of investor assets to online mutual funds, individually managed accounts, and hedge funds, there are other types of investing being pitched to investors. These alternatives include (1) no-load dividend reinvestment plans for individual stocks (DRIPs), (2) direct stock purchase plans without commission (DSPs), (3) individual stocks with commission through brokers, (4) initial public offerings (IPOs), and (5) equity and index linked notes (traded derivatives). These securities are discussed in Charles Carlson (1999), Zweig (1998b), Monroe (2000), Willis (2000), and Fishman (1999), respectively. But none of these investments provides the same range of advantages as mutual funds.

But, for all of the mutual fund shareholder dissatisfaction and increasing range of alternative investments, Clements (2000c) concluded that: "Unless you're getting exceptional advice, low-expense no-load stock funds [and ETFs] look awfully attractive." Moreover, Clements (2000b) suggested that small mutual fund investors, bored or not, already have "toys" comparable to "big league investment toys" in the form of index funds. Professor Statman is quoted to make this point: "Disney and McDonald's are for kids. Vanguard index funds are for adults. Kids enjoy Disney parks and get to see Snow White. Adults enjoy owning Vanguard index funds and the feeling of being responsible." (Couldn't resist.) But this is not to say that mutual funds lack for need of serious improvements.

NATURE OF EXCHANGE-TRADED FUNDS (ETFs)

With all of the alternative investments noted above, the fact is that exchange-traded funds (ETFs) or, for short, *index shares*, are the real threat to mutual funds. Wiandt and McClatchy (2002) reported that as of mid 2001 there were 169 ETFs operating globally, 103 in the United States, with $95 billion in assets under management. This contrasts with assets of $65.6 billion at year end 2000. This relatively new class of securities represents a major lower-cost threat to mutual funds and closed-end funds.

The growing tide of investor cash into ETFs will accelerate, owing to their numerous advantages, but there are also disadvantages relative to mutual funds, especially to pure no-load mutual funds. The advantages and disadvantages of ETFs are summarized in table 79. Several of these advantages may be underappreciated. The following discussion focuses on some of the major ETF issues.

Warehouse receipts concept

As reported in Lucchetti and Brown (2000), Nathan Most, formerly head of new products at the American Stock Exchange (AMEX), adapted the warehouse receipts concept in creating ETFs. The development of ETFs occurred at a time the AMEX was desperate for new revenue-producing products. Now, trades in index shares represent over 67 percent of total trading volume. But this success has not been in a vacuum. The New York Stock Exchange and other exchanges in the United States and abroad are sure to follow.

Warehouse receipts represent marketable evidence of ownership of specific types and grades of commodities stored for safe keeping in bonded warehouses. These receipts facilitate buy/ sell transactions of warehoused commodities. The key idea is that warehouse receipts may be bought and sold, but the actual commodities remain unmoved in warehouses. In fact, the formal names of index shares include "depository receipts," "receipts" or "deposit shares," witnessing their debt to traditional warehouse receipts.

The warehouse receipt concept allows separation of the functions of fund management from exchange trading. As with warehouse receipts, when index shares trade, the underlying port-folios remain secure in custodial vaults, which helps keep trading costs low. In fact, for example, iShares index shares (discussed below) are held in book entry form by the Depository Trust Company, as owner of record.

What they are and are not

The early generation of ETFs organized as unit investment trusts with limited, but long, lives under the 1940 Act. This structure was selected because it is inexpensive and easy to operate. There is also little managerial discretion in managing the portfolios. Today, how-ever, most all ETFs are organized as hybrid mutual funds that are not strictly based on the traditional model for mutual funds or closed-end funds. Mutual fund and unit investment trust ETFs both require "exemptive relief" from sections of regulations under both the 1940 Act and the 1934 Act, as well as from NASD. Index shares may be used in the same strat-egies that apply to common stock. For example, index shares may be sold short and purchased on margin. Perhaps most important, index shares trade continuously on the AMEX, and ETFs also issue and redeem index shares in return for in-kind portfolios of stocks (dis-cussed below). It is because of these in-kind portfolios that ETFs are also called "basket securities."

As noted in Zigler (2000a), there are differences in the regulation of ETFs that are unit investment trusts and those that are hybrid mutual funds. First, unit trust ETFs have fixed rather than perpetual lives. Second, unit trust ETFs must replicate index portfolios, rather than benchmark indices using statistical sampling techniques. This limits the kinds of indices unit trust ETFs may benchmark and still qualify as regulated investment companies. Third, unit trust ETFs suffer from *dividend drag* and may not immediately reinvest dividends at the portfolio level, but must accrue them in non-interest-bearing accounts until distributed to shareholders. And, fourth, unit trust ETFs may not profit from lending their securities or use derivatives to manage portfolios.

Exchange-traded funds combine essential aspects of both stocks and mutual funds. Like many stocks, index shares are exchange traded, with prices determined by supply and demand. Like index mutual fund shares, index shares represent proportionate ownership in underlying stock portfolios generally designed to track the performance of identified benchmark indices. These benchmarks include broadly based domestic indices, narrowly based sector indices, and international market indices. For example, Spiders (discussed below) index shares evidence ownership in portfolios matched to the S&P 500 Index.

Both index shares and closed-end fund shares are traded like common stock, but ETFs are not closed-end funds. Further, ETFs have mechanisms (discussed below) that generally prevent the large discounts to net asset values so often found in closed-end funds. Like mutual funds, the number of outstanding index shares continuously changes, but ETFs are not traditional mutual funds.

However, ETFs are similar to index mutual funds in the way they are managed. One aspect is even less complex because shareholder redemptions are normally made on the AMEX, not from actual portfolios. The upshot is that ETFs are generally less costly competitors, especially compared with actively managed funds, but compared with index funds as well. Nonetheless, it is likely that actively managed ETFs and indexed bond ETFs will be developed. Actively managed ETFs will have inherent disadvantages, such as higher expenses and ongoing portfolio changes. These changes will occur while at the same time ETFs must provide continuous portfolio transparency (discussed below).

Movie time

One way to describe the threat of ETFs to mutual funds is to use 1930s MGM color movies, such as *Robin Hood*, as a metaphor. Here goes. The guys outside the castle are trying to rescue the good guys imprisoned by the bad guys inside the castle. Groups of ETFs (lords with knights under their banners) are approaching the King of Fundom's castle. The ETFs have been identified, but not confirmed as a threat. The castle drawbridge has not been raised. One group of ETFs flies the Bogle banner, the king's most annoying lord. What does it all mean? To find out, the king dials 1-800-Vanguard. "There must be a mistake," he says. "Lord Bogle is approaching the castle with knights under his banner." But the usually polite sales representative is quick to the point: "There is no mistake, your majesty. Bogle's ETFs and the others are there to free your prisoners (fund shareholders)." Before the king can hang up, the ETFs have crossed the drawbridge, entered the castle, and "requested" the release of the good guys and their gold (fund assets). Stay tuned. A major battle will follow, but the ETFs are already within the walls.

Exchange trading

The AMEX is an auction market that provides market liquidity with continuous trading and small minimum size trades. Continuous trading is an advantage of index shares because mutual funds trade only when net asset values are computed after the market close. Index shares generally represent ownership in index portfolios but trade like regular common stock on the AMEX. Index shares are traded in round lots of 100, or multiples thereof, or in trades less than 100 shares.

Index shares are also as liquid and flexible as common stock. They can engage in the same conservative, speculative, or hedging strategies of ordinary common stock, such as short selling and purchases on margin, and may also be used to quickly invest or receive cash. Index shares can also be used in combined strategies with closed-end and mutual funds, such as hedging downside risk.

Trades of index shares on the AMEX are executed through broker/dealers. These trades are subject to brokerage commission and fees and trading costs. Trading costs include bid–ask spreads and the price impact of large trades. Over time, these costs may well exceed the costs of trading mutual fund shares, especially for active traders.

However, the cost of trading may be reduced by the use of online and other discount brokers. McReynolds (1998) reported index share trading costs at only about 6c a share. But, in any case, index share trading costs are larger than for pure no-load mutual funds with zero shareholder transaction costs. This suggests that investors in index shares should employ buy-and-hold strategies with large and infrequent trades. The situation is less clear for funds with diverse types and amounts of loads and fees, including no-load funds with annual 12b-1 fees. Case-by-case analysis is needed in these instances. In any case, both investor sales of index shares and redemptions of mutual fund shares have potential capital gains tax implications.

Direct exchange mechanism

While most index share trades take place on the AMEX, this is not the case for the million-dollar direct exchange trades of institutional and large portfolio investors. These "authorized participants" include specialists and broker-dealers. Broker-dealers primarily act on behalf of customers, while specialists make the market in specific index shares and trade for their own account.

On the buy side, participants "create" (purchase) required minimum block-size *creation units* of index shares of specific ETFs. Participants pay for the creation units with defined stock portfolios that match the composition of the particular benchmark indices. These securities are delivered to custodian banks that, in turn, deliver the index shares to the participants at settlement. These exchanges take place after the market close. Creation units represent specified fractions of the values of specific benchmark indices that range from one-fifth to one-hundredth of the market value. Creation units normally comprise 50,000 index shares (ranging from 25,000 to 600,000), or multiples thereof. For example, the prices of iShares creation units range from about $3 million to $8 million. In sum, authorized participants, usually specialists, gather enough of the underlying benchmark shares to form the required multiple (say, 50,000 shares) of index shares.

On the sell side, authorized participants package required minimum block-size *redemption units* of index shares of specific ETFs. These transactions are common to specialists. ETFs pay for redemption units with disclosed in-kind stock portfolios that match the composition of the particular benchmark indices. Custodians also make these exchanges after the market close.

On the down side, both creation and redemption unit exchanges are not free – there are transaction costs. For example, standard iShares creation and redemption fees range from $500 to $12,000 per unit, but they apply to all investor transactions on a given trading day.

As discussed in Wiandt and McClatchy (2002), cash components ordinarily accompany both creation and redemption unit exchanges. On the redemption side, participant cash payments include creation fees as well as any accruals, such as dividends and interest, that have not been reinvested in index shares. On the creation side, participant cash payments may be positive or negative.

Tax-free exchanges

But, on the up side, the exchange of index shares for disclosed in-kind stock portfolios are "tax-fee exchanges" under the tax code. The upshot is that, unlike mutual funds, ETFs do not ever realize capital gains when they redeem redemption units. Neither is there a performance drag from cash assets set aside to meet investor redemptions. These are important advantages for ETFs. Moreover, these tax-free exchanges allow investors to unbundle the in-kind portfolios and take any available tax losses by selling the shares. Mutual funds cannot provide these savings.

Investors incur potential capital gains taxes when they buy and then sell index shares. They also do so when they buy the stocks for a creation unit and then sell these same stocks received in a redemption unit. ETF investors incur tax liabilities in the same way common stock investors do. These transactions also incur trading costs.

Arbitrage

Index share discounts/premiums from net asset values of the underlying stock portfolios are normally very small. The reason for this small difference is arbitrage, which is made effective by exchange trading and tax-free direct exchanges. Wiandt and McClatchy (2002) reported that the redemption/creation process is working well in this regard. Using intraday net asset value estimates of domestic ETFs, 91 percent of the intraday values were between index share bid–ask prices. The average spread was $0.21, with an average of 0.36 percent. Dunn (2000) also reported that premiums/discounts from net asset values are "narrow and fleeting." Zigler (2000a) reported that the difference between net asset value and the $150 market price of SPDR 500 (discussed below) is about 3c per share.

On the other hand, not all studies show small discounts/premiums on index share prices. Wiandt and McClatchy (2002) reported two such studies. One found that index shares can trade at significant discounts/premiums to net asset values for extended periods, especially international index shares. The other study found that twenty-one ETFs traded at discounts/premiums in excess of fifty basis points for a total of 2,921 rolling four-day periods from inception through April 2000. Again, international index shares have the largest discounts/premiums. However, calculations of discounts/premiums may suffer inaccuracies, especially for less traded international ETFs. In general, Wiandt and McClatchy (2002) concluded that "as long as the underlying stocks can trade, it is highly unlikely that significant premiums/discounts to the underlying net asset value will develop, because specialists and other large traders will take advantage of those anomalies."

To make the tax-free exchange mechanism workable for arbitrageurs, ETFs also provide portfolio transparency. This disclosure includes the composition of the actual stocks and the specific shares that will comprise redemption units that day. Also, the values of underlying portfolios are disclosed throughout the trading day, so arbitrageurs can act on any discrepancies between index share market prices and the net asset values of the underlying portfolios. Arbitrageurs thus know the exact stock portfolios they will receive in exchange for their redemption units. And bid–ask spreads of index shares are available on the AMEX throughout the trading day. Mutual funds do not provide this portfolio transparency. They are required to disclose portfolios twice a year. Also, the prices of mutual fund shares purchased or redeemed are not normally known until the close of the trading day, when net asset values are computed.

Opportunities for profitable arbitrage may be seen in cases where index shares sell at discount to the net asset values of underlying portfolios. In these cases, arbitrageurs buy index shares on the AMEX, package them as redemption units, redeem them for the underlying portfolios, and then sell the stocks. Specialists are most active in making unit redemptions for arbitrage purposes. If they are successful, cost of the index shares is less than the amounts received from unbundling the portfolios and selling stocks.

Benchmarking market indices

ETF shares provide returns that normally correspond closely to their benchmark indices. This is more so for domestic than for international ETFs (discussed below). Index share prices thus vary directly but not necessarily perfectly with changes in the net asset values of underlying stock portfolios. Index shares are priced by supply and demand on the AMEX, which may result in small discounts or premiums to the net asset values of the underlying portfolios (exception discussed below). On the other hand, mutual funds trade only at net asset value, but closed-end funds often trade at significant discounts to net asset values.

Organization of early ETFs as unit investment trusts has an important implication for their ability to effectively benchmark small international market indices. As noted, unit trust ETFs are mandated to replicate fully the portfolio composition of specific benchmark indices. This precludes closely tracking small international market benchmark indices and still meeting SEC and IRS diversification requirements. These limitations are especially significant in small international markets with low liquidity and high trading costs. But hybrid mutual fund ETFs and index mutual funds are not subject to these limitations. Mutual fund ETFs use statistical sampling techniques to "optimize" (capture) the performance of benchmark indices. Even so, tracking errors occur.

Tax efficiency

The tax-free exchange mechanism also works to make ETFs tax-efficient. Mutual funds that receive redemption requests must provide cash. This, of course, has potential tax implications for shareholders. Not so for ETFs – they send stock portfolios along with no tax implications. ETFs also use "inventory control" to enhance tax efficiency. The portfolios exchanged for redemption units are managed to minimize the realization of capital gains. The specific shares provided in exchanges are those with the largest unrealized capital gains. And shares sold to meet changes in the composition of benchmark indices are those with the smallest unrealized capital gains.

That ETFs are indexed portfolios works to make them tax-efficient in the same way it works for index mutual funds. ETFs have minimum portfolio turnover with minimum realized capital gains and taxable shareholder distributions. Even if minimized, stock trades due to changes in the composition of the benchmark indices can prove exceptions.

These various factors all work to minimize distributions of realized capital gains to investors. By so doing, investors have greater control over tax planning, such as unbundling stocks to take tax losses. This contrasts with mutual funds that often have large unrealized capital gains overhanging current shareholders. Active portfolio management realizes capital gains that must be distributed to current shareholders. Potential realized capital gains from overhangs are especially relevant when net cash inflows diminish or are negative from shareholder redemptions. In these cases, current remaining shareholders are subject to proportionally larger future capital gains distributions.

In addition to table 79, AMEX (2000a) provided a list of ETF advantages: (1) continuous trading, (2) ability to build portfolios quickly, (3) may be bought on margin and sold short, (4) no sales loads (but commission), (5) low management and sponsor fees, and (6) tax efficiency. Zigler's (2000b) list of ETF advantages includes: (1) index fund-like performance, (2) diversification – broadly based indices available, (3) liquidity – trade any time during the day, (4) flexibility – same advantages as common stock, (5) cost effectiveness – low management fees and transaction costs, and (6) tax efficiency – minimal capital gains, thanks to low portfolio turnover and no redemption transactions.

Types of risk

Domestic ETFs are subject to numerous risks, similar in general to those facing mutual funds. Specifically these risks include: (1) market risk, (2) asset class risk, (3) specific fund (investment style/cap size) risk, (4) passive (not active) management risk, (5) tracking error risk, (6) lack of insurance or guarantees risk, (7) concentration risk (some funds), (8) derivatives risk, and (9) market trading risks (market prices at discount to net asset values; also lack of market liquidity). Mutual funds do not sell for less than net asset values, but closed-end funds often do, and significantly.

International ETFs are subject to these risks and others, including security risk, currency risk, emerging market risk, non-diversification risk (of some funds) and trading risks. These same risks generally apply to other securities traded domestically and internationally, as well. But small international market ETFs are often very volatile and should be held in diversified portfolios for the long term, not for trading.

MAJOR EXCHANGE-TRADED FUNDS

The major ETFs are identified by the acronyms Spiders, Diamonds, Cubes, iShares (including WEBS), and HOLDRs. These ETFs are discussed in turn.

Spiders

State Street Global Advisors first offered Standard & Poor's Depositary Receipts (SPDRs, hence "spiders") in 1993. SPDRS Trust, Series 1, is the original SPDR 500, which represents portfolios matched to the S&P 500 Index and trades at one-tenth its value. This first Spider was organized as a unit investment trust, but later ones were organized as mutual funds. Spiders rank first, with over $24 billion in assets. Burton (2000b) noted that SPDR 500 would be one of the thirty largest mutual funds and fifth largest among index mutual funds.

Not surprisingly, Richardson (1998) reported that institutional investors represent 65 percent of SPDR 500 trading volume. And most of this volume is from short-term market timers. Clements (2000a) reported that Spiders are held an average of nineteen days! In spite of such irrational behavior, this is not to say that long-term investors should not hold ETFs in lieu of, or in addition to, index funds. Domestic ETFs have lower expense ratios than mutual funds with the same investment objectives.

More recently, additional Spiders have been offered. These additions are the S&P Mid Cap. 400 SPDRs, thus "Mid Cap. Spiders" and Select Sector SPDRs, thus "Select Sector Spiders." Mid Cap. Spiders are portfolios matched to the S&P 400 Mid Cap. Index and trade at one-fifth its value. S&P Select Sector Spiders are portfolios matched to each of nine S&P industry benchmark indices and trade at one-tenth their value. Select Sector Spiders are akin to diversified sector mutual funds that trade like stocks.

As discussed in the report "Sector Sensations" in *Mutual Funds* (1998), Sector Spiders compete directly with several of Fidelity's thirty-nine sector mutual funds, which together had annualized returns of 23 percent from 1991 to 1997. But Sector Spiders are less costly than Fidelity sector funds. Sector Spiders have lower average expense ratios (0.65 percent versus 1.52 percent) and lower transaction costs (brokerage commission versus 3.1 percent loads and exchange fees). Sector Spiders provide very serious competition for sector mutual funds.

Diamonds

"Dow Jones Industrial Average Model New Deposit Shares," thus "Diamonds," were first offered as a unit investment trust in early 1998. Diamonds, Trust Series I, are portfolios matched to the Dow Jones Industrial Average (DJIA) and trade at one-hundredth of its value. Over $2 billion is invested in Diamonds, and individual investors represent 80 percent of trading volume. Diamonds are used as single holdings or elements in multiple security strategies.

Cubes

"Nasdaq-100 Tracking Stocks" are identified by the AMEX ticker symbol QQQ, thus "Cubes." Cubes were first offered as unit investment trusts in 1998. Cubes are the most heavily traded ETF and rank second in size, with over $24 billion in assets. Cube portfolios are matched to the Nasdaq 100, the technology subcategory of the Nasdaq Index. Cubes are considered a play on technology by sector investors and market timers. Not surprisingly, Cubes are very volatile and are primarily traded by short-term market timers. Clements (2000a) reported that Cubes are held for an average of four days (!), which appears to reflect online day trader positions.

HOLDRs

In 1998, Merrill Lynch created "Holding Company Depository Receipts," thus "HOLDRs." These "exchange traded baskets" or "grantor trusts" differ from unit trust and mutual fund ETFs. Original offerings of HOLDRs were priced to include 2 percent underwriting fees.

HOLDRs differ from other ETFs in several major ways. First, HOLDR shareholders are proportionate beneficial owners of underlying portfolios formed under depositary trust agreements. Second, the stocks held are not matched to benchmark indices. Each HOLDR represents a portfolio of twenty to fifty stocks for each of twenty narrow industry sectors, such as biotechnology. Unlike mutual funds, HOLDRs' portfolio concentration is not limited by diversification requirements. HOLDRs are thus very concentrated versions of sector mutual funds. Caution is urged except when they are used as elements in overall diversified portfolios.

Merrill Lynch selects the stocks and determines their initial portfolio weights based on market capitalization and liquidity. The portfolios are unmanaged and the number of stocks remains fixed, with the exception of changes due to corporate restructuring. Any cash received is distributed to shareholders. Third, HOLDRs are very tax-efficient. The lack of portfolio rebalancing along with the in-kind process of creation/redemption of HOLDRs shares minimize trading costs and the realization of capital gains that must be distributed. Fourth, trusts expire in forty years, unless terminated earlier for specified reasons. And, fifth, HOLDRs are created and redeemed by the trusts only in minimum round lots of 100 HOLDRs, or multiples thereof, that represent whole share amounts. These round lots are therefore designed for large investors. However, HOLDRs are also accessible to smaller investors, who can buy and sell them on the AMEX through commission brokers.

There are no portfolio management fees, but there are small creation/redemption unit fees and custodial fees. HOLDRs investors pay trust issuance fees of up to $10 per round lot purchased. Quarterly custody fees of $2 per 100 HOLDRs are also imposed, subject to the availability of cash from dividends and distributions. These very low fees are designed to encourage investor arbitrage transactions that maintain HOLDRs prices at or very near the net asset values of underlying portfolios. That is, if HOLDRs trade at discount, arbitragers will buy them, exchange them for portfolios, and sell the higher-priced stocks for arbitrage profits.

But Solodar and Seiler (2001) found that HOLDRs trade at an average discount of 8 percent to net asset value and the discounts are persistent. The discount is explained as possibly due to asymmetric investor information about or different interpretation of individual stocks in the HOLDRs, fluctuations in investor sentiment which impound additional risk, HOLDRs' complexity, which encourages sales in difficult markets, and high portfolio volatility.

iShares and WEBS

Barclays Global Fund Investors first offered "Individual Shares," thus "iShares," organized as mutual funds, in 1996. Barclays Global Fund Investors is a subsidiary of Barclays Global Investors. Barclays is the world's second largest money manager, with assets of nearly $800 billion. Only Fidelity Investments is larger. But, Barclays is also the world's largest manager of index funds, not Vanguard! Interestingly, Barclays' San Francisco-based subsidiary was formerly Wells Fargo Investment Advisors, the 1960s creators of institutional indexed portfolios. Vanguard originated its S&P 500 Index Fund in the mid 1970s. Additional information is to be found in iShares prospectus (1999, 2000) and Zigler (2000a, b).

iShares are advertised as having several advantages: (1) work like stocks, (2) track like index funds, (3) can be traded whenever the market is open, (4) shield investors from the costs of shareholder activity in funds, (5) tax-efficient, (6) cost-effective (low management fees), (7) offer the instant diversification of indexing and more, and (8) investments are transparent (a number of iShares fully replicate underlying indices, the components of which are disclosed monthly).

iShares comprise four series of index shares totaling fifty-four separate portfolios. The first series is iShares MSCI Index Fund Shares, which has baskets of stock matched to each of nineteen Morgan Stanley Country Indices, the benchmark indices. They trade at one-tenth the market value of benchmark indices. This earliest Barclays series was initially, but is no longer, known as "World Equity Benchmark Shares," thus "WEBS" (used following).

WEBS are similar to closed-end country funds except they do not trade at such large discounts to net asset value. The tax-free direct exchange mechanism and AMEX trading are designed so that arbitrageurs will ensure that iShares trade at or very close to net asset value. However, their narrow focus can generate very volatile returns, especially in emerging markets. Used individually, rather than as elements of diversified portfolios, WEBS are single country bets that attract market timers. As concentrated portfolios, WEBS have high security concentration risk and high market liquidity risk, as defined previously.

Diversification requirements pose real problems for WEBS benchmarked to small international market indices. As reviewed in Karmin (1999), the five largest mutual fund holdings cannot exceed 50 percent of portfolio value. But this is literally impossible for ETFs in small international markets. WEBS are similarly constrained by IRS regulations that limit single security holdings to a maximum of 25 percent of total portfolio value. For example, in Malaysia, two or three stocks represent most of the value of the index. Further, it may be literally impossible for WEBS to buy all stocks in the benchmark indices, owing to low market liquidity and high trading costs.

The result? As reported by Richardson (1998), the average WEBS portfolio represents only about 60 percent of the market value of benchmark indices. This means much less than perfect correlation between WEBS and market index returns. Karmin (1999) reported that the correlation of WEBS to country benchmark indices ranges from 96 percent in Sweden to 77 percent in Malaysia, the latter a relatively illiquid market.

As a result, it is not surprising that William Bernstein (2000) found WEBS to have large benchmark index tracking errors. The average WEBS earns 1.81 percentage points less than its index. Tracking errors also increase with higher portfolio turnover. For each 14 percent of average portfolio turnover, there is a 1 percent loss of return. WEBS portfolio turnover averages about 15 percent, which is much higher than for domestic index funds. In addition to this bad news, the average expense ratio is 1.32 percent.

The second iShares series is the Russell Series Index Funds, which has portfolios matched to each of the Russell 3000 Index (total market index), the Russell 2000 Index, the Russell 1000 Index, and six Russell subcategory benchmark indices defined by investment style. The third iShares series is the S&P Series Index Funds. This series includes portfolios matched to the S&P 500 Index, S&P/TSE 60 Index (Toronto index), S&P Europe 350 Index, S&P MidCap

400 Index, S&P SmallCap 600 Index, and each of six S&P/Barra benchmark indices defined by investment style. The fourth series is the Dow Jones Series Index Funds. This series has baskets of stock matched to the Dow Jones US Total Market Index and each of fourteen Dow Jones industry sector benchmark indices. More iShares funds will soon follow.

Shareholder distributions

Exchange-traded funds are required to make shareholder distributions at least annually. The actual frequency varies with the legal form of organization. Burton (1999) reported that Spiders, Diamonds, and Cubes, as unit investment trusts, must hold portfolio dividends in low-earning cash accounts until they are paid to investors quarterly, or monthly, for Diamonds. Worse yet, iShares MSCI Index Fund Shares (formerly WEBS) normally pay distributions annually. This drag is especially harmful to returns when the market is rising, but is also advantageous to returns in falling markets. Luchetti (1999) reported the dividends drag as large enough for Spiders to underperform the Vanguard 500 Index Fund over the past six years. In any case, however, Topkis (2000) reported that both Spiders and Vanguard 500 Index are over 96 percent tax-efficient.

However, the dividends drag does not apply to mutual fund ETFs. Dividends are reinvested automatically when received. Select Spiders and iShares series index shares provide automatic reinvestment of dividends plus any realized capital gains. iShares also plan to lend securities to short sellers (as brokers do) and invest the income in repurchase agreements and futures contracts pending dividend distributions.

Distributions represent investment income net of management and other fees plus net realized long-term or short-term capital gains. Dividends and net short-term realized capital gains are taxable as ordinary income. Distributions of net long-term realized capital gains, net of short-term capital losses, are taxable as long-term capital gains, regardless of how long investors have held the index shares. Exchange-traded funds holding international securities may also be subject to international taxes. As noted, investor trades of index shares on the AMEX have potential capital gains tax implications. Investor sales of index shares held for more than one year are considered long-term capital gains, and those held for one year or less are considered short-term capital gains.

Fees and expenses

Fees and expenses deducted from ETF investment income include management fees, any 12b-1 fees, and "other" expenses. These expenses and fees vary greatly by ETF and invest-ment advisor, and may be net of temporary expense waivers. For example, all nineteen iShares MSCI Series Funds have 0.25 percent 12b-1 fees included in expense ratios ranging from 0.94 percent to 1.43 percent. Several iShares MSCI funds were subsidized initially by fee waivers. However, iShares MSCI funds have higher expense ratios than any of Vanguard's international mutual funds. Additional competition will undoubtedly reduce these charges.

However, expense ratios are much smaller for other iShares index fund shares. The expense ratios of iShares S&P Series Index Fund Shares range from a low of 0.09 percent to 0.60

percent. The expense ratios of Dow Jones Series Index Fund Shares range from 0.20 percent to 0.60 percent, and from 0.15 percent to 0.25 percent for Russell Series Index Fund Shares. The expense ratios of the S&P 500 Index Fund Shares are lowest at 0.09 percent. The expense ratios of the Russell 1000 Index Fund Shares are second, at 0.15 percent. The expense ratios of the S&P 500/BARRA Growth Index Shares and S&P 500/BARRA Value Index Shares are third, at 0.18 percent. And, finally, the expense ratios of Russell 3000 Index Fund Shares and Russell 2000 Index Fund Shares are 0.20 percent.

As noted in Traulsen (2000), most domestic ETFs have no 12b-1 fees and lower expense ratios than even the least costly counterpart mutual funds, including Vanguard funds. For example, Vanguard's Viper 500 will have lower expenses than its Index 500 fund. But, as noted above, international iShares do not have lower expenses than international mutual funds. Overall, lower expense ratios will increasingly be the most important competitive edge ETFs have over index mutual funds, especially managed funds.

CURRENT AND FUTURE DEVELOPMENTS

As suggested above, the fact that Vanguard so quickly applied for SEC approval to offer ETFs says much about the future of the mutual fund industry. The first Vipers were approved in 2001 and more are to follow. Vanguard has several objectives in offering "Vanguard Index Participation Equity Receipts," thus "Vipers." First, the new Viper class will provide new assets to manage, but their low costs will also protect Vanguard against loss of index fund assets to other EFTs.

Second, Vipers will facilitate Vanguard's objective of separating market timers from buy-and-hold investors, but in a way that enables them to serve both types of investors without penalizing either. Vipers will be designed for institutional market timers, thereby shielding long-term mutual fund investors from costly trading behaviors. The expense and fee structures of Vipers and counterpart mutual funds will reflect this objective (and already have for mutual funds).

Vanguard has not been successful at barring market timers from their mutual funds, but the effort must have been limited because their identities are not unknown. Further, stated limits on telephone exchanges and the imposition of redemption fees have not discouraged market timers, but these penalties have been too low to discourage timers. Mutual fund penalties must be made significant if Vanguard really wants to separate market timers and long-term investors. Vanguard will attempt to do this for current shareholders by temporarily them to switch to Vipers at no cost – no brokerage fees. This will allow investors to buy mutual funds and convert to Vipers without fees. This is, of course, a marketing strategy for gathering large amount of dollars into Vipers. Retirement accounts will be excluded from the conversion to prevent brokerage commission from being applied to each future pension contribution.

Third, Vipers will facilitate Vanguard's goal of remaining the lowest-cost provider. Vanguard has the current asset base and economies of scale to accomplish this. Vipers will have lower expense ratios than Vanguard's counterpart mutual funds, but Vanguard will not have to provide direct shareholder services to Viper investors who originate through brokers and other sales agents. Services will be provided by brokers and financial advisors, whom Vanguard can serve more inexpensively. The exceptions are those Vanguard fund shareholders who convert to Vipers.

Kahn (2002) noted that Vipers do have a significant weakness relative to other index shares. The first Viper is a multiple share class of an existing index mutual fund. Because of this single portfolio, Viper investors share the same degree of tax efficiency as their cohort index mutual fund investors.

It was originally planned that the first Vipers would be matched to the benchmark indices of Vanguard's five most prominent index funds: Vanguard 500 Index Fund, with assets over $100 billion at its peak; Total Stock Market Fund; Growth Index Fund; Small Cap. Index Fund; and Value Index Fund. In fact, in 2001, the honors for being first went to Total Stock Market Vipers. Extended Market and Small Cap. Vipers will follow.

IMPLICATIONS FOR MUTUAL FUNDS

The increasing tide of ETF offerings and assets is coming from several directions. First, while retail ETFs originated in the United States, much innovation continues to occur internationally, such as the introduction of actively traded ETFs. Second, Vanguard's lead in ETFs encourages but also forces competitive mutual fund families to follow suit or lose assets under management. As reported by Lucchetti (2000c): "It's really a case of Vanguard's premier brand name putting the *Good Housekeeping* seal of approval on exchange-traded funds." And the threat of ETFs to mutual funds is clearly evidenced by Vipers' lower expense ratios compared even with Vanguard's mutual funds that match the same benchmark indices. Third, as noted, Vanguard will soon have a broader range of ETFs matched to narrower benchmark indices. Thus mutual funds will be faced with Vanguard ETFs across the range of broadly and narrowly defined market indices.

Fourth, the NYSE, Nasdaq, and major international markets are scrambling to compete with AMEX for dominance in ETF markets. And they have the resources to do so effectively. Price competition from various markets and new offerings of ETFs will become significant, which will reduce investor ETF trading costs and fund expense ratios. Fifth, current ETF investment advisors will soon offer new funds that compete more broadly with one another, including subcategory index benchmarks. Sixth, other large money managers will soon offer ETFs that compete broadly with current offerings. And, seventh, larger mutual fund investment advisors will offer their versions of Vipers matched to both broadly based and narrowly defined index benchmarks. Those fund advisors that enter the ETF market early on will broaden their offerings over time.

The upshot of ETF growth will be loss of financial services market share by mutual funds and less growth in assets under management, especially funds without established brand names and major indexed portfolios. There will be increased growth in the number of acquisitions of small fund families by larger ones. Those acquiring will include fund investment advisors attempting to defend themselves against loss of asset base, but also those offering index funds and ETFs and seeking to increase assets under management to compensate for smaller expense ratios.

The performance of ETFs with lower expenses, minimal distributions of capital gains, and continuous trading (see also table 79) will attract huge amounts of assets from individual and institutional investors, market timers, and buy-and-hold investors alike. This growth will increase as mutual fund investors become more price (and cost) sensitive, thereby increasing investment in index mutual funds.

Dominance of price competition will signal that mutual funds have become commodities matched to benchmark indices rather than remaining brands with star portfolio managers and unique investment styles – all due to the success of index funds. The message in mutual fund advertising will thus change to price, as well. This very movement to index mutual funds will accelerate the movement of investors and their investments to ETFs.

As the competitive game becomes ever more focused on price, this will work to the principal advantage of ETFs. Institutional investors, such as pension funds, will flock to ETFs with the increasing importance of management fees and expenses in selecting institutional portfolio managers. The mutual fund industry will either sink or swim, depending on its reaction to the new wave of ETFs – adapt to the new reality forcefully and quickly or go the way of CDs during the 1980s. This should be an interesting time for investors with higher net after-tax performance based on lower costs.

So what will be the future of the mutual fund industry? Will the ETF threat spark a reactive *prologue* for new, price-competitive growth along with ETFs in the mutual fund industry, or will the threat sound an *epilogue* to industry growth and success? The answer lies with the application of today's new entrepreneurial-style manager to the "old world" of mutual fund management.

The threat is real and has been recognized elsewhere, For example, Morningstar's Don Phillips made the following statement in Rowland (2000): "The fund industry's monopoly on the American investor's mind is in jeopardy like never before." And Coy (1998) provided a view of the twenty-first-century financial revolution that goes beyond just mutual funds. And, if this was not enough, in December 2000 net cash inflows for mutual funds and ETFs were $11.6 billion and $10.8 billion, respectively.

In addition to the 169 ETFs in ten countries, Wiandt and McClatchy (2002) stated that fifty more will follow shortly. Some observers even believe there will be 1,000 ETFs by 2004! In fact, some believe ETFs will replace mutual funds as more types of index shares are offered globally, regionally, and by country, such as actively managed, fixed-income, specific investment style, and narrow sector. Wiandt and McClatchy concluded that:

> [f]or the long-term investor, ETFs cost about as much to own as the least expensive index funds and perhaps even a bit less. . . . The one feature that no mutual fund can match is the simplicity, freedom and flexibility of owning an instrument that is bought and sold like a stock.

CHAPTER TWELVE

ECONOMIC AND MARKET INDICATORS: KNOWLEDGE, NOT FAITH

All of the forecasts of disaster that have been made in my lifetime have one thing in common. The disasters have not occurred. And all of the disasters that have occurred have one thing in common. They have not been forecast.

(*Contrarious, in* **Worth,** *October 1993*)

It's like I told my mother: A market is at its worst when it looks like it is at its best.

(*Jim Rogers, in* **Worth,** *May 1997*)

The yield curve never lies.

(*William Wilson, Comerica Bank, in* **Bloomberg Personal Finance,** *December 1997*)

The investor who spends fifteen minutes a year on macroeconomics wastes ten minutes.

(*Peter Lynch, Fidelity Investments, in* **Morningstar FundInvestor,** *December 1999*)

The crowd [investor expectations] is right during the trends but wrong at both ends.

(*Humphrey Neill, in* **Bloomberg Personal Finance,** *July/August 1999*)

The first goal of this chapter is to provide selected menus of both economic and market indicators frequently cited in discussions of market timing. This chapter is optional and provided for the sake of investor knowledge of these frequently used indicators, not as an argument for market timing.

It may seem inconsistent to provide this chapter on economic and market indicators having previously discussed the failures of market timing. It is for this reason that the discussion of indicators is the last chapter in the book – an optional topic. As discussed previously, the practice of market timing by portfolio managers has been widely discredited. So why provide this discussion of indicators? First, there are mutual fund investors who wish to try their own luck at timing the implementation of buy/sell decisions. This is not necessarily a bad thing if investors realize the dangers, but wish some indication of the context of the market based on indicators. The guiding principle in these cases is "knowledge", not "faith."

As an aside, however, there is some good news for the usefulness of market indicators. Pruitt and White (1988) developed a *multi-rule system* that incorporates several individual technical indicators in one technical indicator. The indicators include past price movement strategies (filter rules), cumulative trading volume, price momentum, and moving averages. The composite indicator outperformed the market from 1976 to 1985, net of transaction costs, timing of trades, and risk.

Second, mutual fund investors need to be cognizant of market timing tools and interpretations because their use is widespread among professional investors as, for example, a regular topic on *Wall Street Week*. Most investment houses engage in both fundamental analysis and technical analysis as a means of being all things to all investors, including market timers. If the practice of technical analysis using economic and market indicators thus affects investment decisions, even if wrongly, investors need to know the enemy and how they are impacted by it.

Third, mutual fund investors who follow long-term investment strategies based on stock/bond and investment style allocations (discussed previously) should, by definition, make fewer portfolio changes than short-term "investors." Thus fund investors who follow the text approach should not make portfolio changes based on economic and market indicators, but only when change is called for within the construct of passively managed long-term portfolios. In these cases, it might not be unreasonable to consider the context of the market to assist in deciding whether such changes should be implemented now or in the next month or so. The damage should be minimized by fewer portfolio decisions. Nonetheless, for investors to think they should actively time the market is to put faith in a fantasy of self-deception. The only hope for mutual fund investors who also wish to time the market is to manage their portfolios long-term and thereby be subject to fewer portfolio decisions and timing errors.

The second goal of the chapter is to illustrate the use of each menu of economic and market indicators as applied to implementing the buy/sell decision for Vanguard Windsor II (tables 80–1). To do this a selected number of economic and market indicators are individually assessed and then combined to determine whether the buy/sell decision should be implemented now or later.

The third goal of this chapter is to provide a large menu of both economic and market indicators to provide a broad range of indicators for assessing the economic and market outlooks.

IMPLEMENTING THE BUY/SELL DECISION

Having said this, let us assume mutual fund investors are interested in knowing whether they should implement a particular mutual fund buy/sell decision now or in the next month or so. This buy/sell decision has been based not on market timing, but on needed portfolio changes. That is, are conditions favorable to the implementation of buy/sell decisions, or should they wait a month or so?

The overall economic and market outlook should therefore be scanned, using numerous technical indicators to determine whether to make the buy/sell decision this month or perhaps no sooner than next month. This process is illustrated and applied to timing the buy decision for Windsor II if not held. Should Windsor II be purchased now or later? If later, the economic and market indicators should be reviewed again each month.

The process for making the mutual fund buy/sell decision and timing its implementation is the same in either case. Only the buy/sell decision is different. The diehard approach taken here determines whether buy/sell decisions are likely to produce larger returns if implemented now or later. "Later" is interpreted as no sooner than next month and then again based on analysis of economic and market indicators. To minimize the depth of the analysis, the approach here focuses on current short-term "trends" in the indicators, but with monthly reassessment.

Technical and fundamental approaches

Before beginning, it should be noted that those who forecast the market are roughly divided into two camps: technical and fundamental. This is analogous to the use of technical and fundamental analysis to select securities. Technical analysis of the market is based primarily on identifying and interpreting trends in market measures, such as moving averages. The "trend is your friend" until a reversal pattern appears. Fundamentalists follow economic indicators to make market forecasts. For example, analysis of corporate earnings, inflation rates, and interest rates might be used to judge whether the current market P/E ratio is justified.

Both technical and fundamental market forecasters make use of investor sentiment, but its use is normally attributed more to technical analysis. As discussed previously, behavioral finance has given investor sentiment a new lease of life. Traditional finance believes investors cannot rationally expect to beat the market except by taking on more systematic risk than the market. Behaviorists believe that opportunities for abnormal returns are provided by psychological errors in the way investors think and act. These errors cause securities prices to deviate from fundamental values.

Professional forecasts

The focus here is on the interpretation of selected economic and market indicators to assess the overall likelihood that buy/sell decisions should be implemented now or in the near future. This assessment is based on the totality of economic and market findings, and does not pretend to extend the outlook beyond the current "trends" in the data. But, once indicators have been interpreted and the timing of the decision implementation has been determined, it is useful, nonetheless, to validate the findings with respected sources to see whether the reassessments are in order.

But investors should not automatically assume their assessments are wrong. There is enough error around for everyone. The approach suggested provides more insight than simply relying on overall economic or market forecasts provided by others. Investors are quite capable of interpreting particular indicators, and, besides, the record of professional forecasters appears almost random. Thus dedicated mutual fund timers should do no worse than professional forecasters over time. As discussed in Zweig (2000), for example, one has only to look back to the forecasts made at the end of the 1980s for Japanese stocks, emerging market stocks, small-cap. stocks, international stocks, and the year-by-year forecasts of the DJIA.

Ability to forecast business cycles accurately has yet to be improved by developments in business cycle theory. As discussed in Chatterjee (2000), early economic thought believed each cyclical phase of the economy carries within it the seed that generates the next cyclical phase. That is, the economy is forever in a self-sustaining cycle that precludes sustained stable performance. The cure is to apply aggressive countercyclical policies or institutional reforms, as appropriate. Modern theory is based on a random, "shock-based" view of business cycles. That is, business cycles are caused by random shocks to the economy. Later, these shocks were linked with deviations in labor productivity. However, the issue remains unsettled. The random movements in productivity are themselves due to erratic movements in as yet unspecified factors.

Moreover, Sherden (1998) examined forecaster accuracy in several fields of this $200 billion industry. Almost all forecasters have records no better than flipping a coin. The Federal Reserve predicted only three of six turning points in gross domestic product from 1980 to 1995, and missed both inflation points. The forecasting skill of economists was found to be "about as good as guessing." Stock market gurus occasionally make correct predictions, but "the likelihood of a repeat performance is remote." One such person made the correct forecast in only five of thirteen market calls. Long-term, this is worse than making forecasts by flipping a coin.

If this is discouraging, investors may wish to consider using the Super Bowl winner as the market forecast. In the years when the original NFL was the establishment and the AFL the upstart, an NFL victory was a bullish indicator, and vice versa. This "indicator" has lost its luster with team expansion and conference realignment. Or, as reported by Mathieu (1993), investors could call the private money management firm that uses astrology to manage its portfolio. Or they could invest in the randomly identified stocks in the *Wall Street Journal's* ongoing contest between "dart portfolios" and those selected by investment professionals.

Information sources

There are many online sites that provide economic and market charts, indicators, and data. Examples are listed in the appendix. The *Wall Street Journal's* Web site is excellent one-stop shopping (interactive.wsj.com) for the validation process. The site has very useful and time-saving archives, and also includes access to *Barron's* excellent and comprehensive menu of economic/market data and indicators (www.barrons.com). *Barron's* provides its Market Laboratory: Economic Indicators, Market Laboratory (market indicators), and Pulse of the Economy indicators. The Board of Governors of the Federal Reserve System's (BOG) Beige Book summarizes regional economic conditions prepared by each Federal Reserve bank (www.bog.frb.fed.us). The Federal Reserve Bank of St. Louis provides visuals and data for over eighty indicators, both online (www.stls.frb.org) and in its *National Economic Trends*.

Choice of indicators

Choice of indicators, evidence notwithstanding, usually boils down to those measures investors find most insightful in gaining a feel for the context of economic and/or market conditions. There are no best indicators or economists for judging all economic/market scenarios. However, Mueller (2000) provided a general framework that explains the economy's prosperity over recent years, and which may be used as a general framework for assessing economic trends and the selection of the "best" indicators for this purpose. These "seven engines for prosperity" include (1) population demographics, (2) deregulation, (3) reduced tax rates, (4) trade liberalization, (5) the revolution in technology, (6) welfare reform, and (7) monetary policy.

The technological revolution has been and continues to be the single most important contributor to prosperity. Babyboomers represent the largest population age group at the same time they are at peak income potential. Deregulation has worked to make the affected industries much more cost-effective and price-competitive. Tax cuts have encouraged investment and entrepreneurial activities. Welfare has increased the labor supply in a tight labor market. Last, but certainly not least (and perhaps most), monetary policy has stabilized the economy be anticipating changes in economic and market conditions. Downturns have been softened and inflation has been minimized.

The approach here recommends assessing the economic outlook and market outlook within this framework by using those indicators most likely to be relevant in particular scenarios. How are the economy and market doing and is change likely to be for the better or worse? The precise answer to this question is, of course, never known in advance. A more limited objective is set here, one that helps time the implementation of buy/sell decisions a bit better than by flipping a coin. Once the economic framework has been reviewed, the approach taken is very short-term, *au courant*, and analogous to the momentum strategy used by some growth investors. All that is asked here is whether an indicator's current short-term "trend" (hopefully, not noise) suggests more of the same or more or less in the economic/market outlook.

ECONOMIC INDICATORS: DISCUSSION AND SAMPLE MENU

Before discussing each sample economic indicator, a discussion of some commonly used indicators by market economists is useful. As an example of the outlook information available to individual investors, Garzarelli's (1996) newsletter employed fourteen variously weighted indicators to arrive at scores indicating a bullish or a bearish market outlook. These indicators provide a good sample of the types used by forecasters. The most heavily weighted indicator was the ratio of S&P 500 Index cash flow yield from operating earnings to the average of ninety-day Treasury bill rates and thirty-year Treasury bond yields. This indicator was given by far the most weight. Next in importance were the mutual fund cash ratio (below 5.5 percent is bearish) and the percentage of bullish investment advisors (70 percent or more is bearish). Next in importance were the S&P 500 earnings forecast, the industrial production forecast, the ninety-day Treasury bill rate (cyclical high is bearish), and the ratio of the ninety-day Treasury bill rate to the discount rate (one or more is bearish). The P/E ratio of S&P 500 Index earnings forecast (fair market value forecast) followed.

The least important of the Garzarelli indicators are the ratio of coincident leading economic indicators to lagging economic indicators (ratio peaks are bearish), free reserves in the banking system (positive is bullish), the ratio of the Fed. funds rate to its year-ago level (increase is bearish), the Treasury yield curve (downwards or constant slope is bearish), real and nominal M2, M1, and M3 money supply growth rates (slowing is bearish), and the ratio of real M3 money supply growth to the GDP growth rate (a ratio of one or less is bearish).

With all of the indicators available, which ones are most closely followed? An informal survey of articles using multiple indicators found frequent reference to the advance/decline

line (several versions), market P/E ratios, market dividend yields, and divergence of market indices. The latter indicator often refers to divergence between an increasing DJIA and a decrease in either the DJIA Utilities Index (increase in interest rates), S&P 500 Index or Nasdaq (quality stocks the last to decline). Among individual sell signals commonly found are the ratio of the ninety-day Treasury bill rate to S&P 500 Index yield, index of leading economic indicators, divergence of advance/decline line and S&P 500 Index, and divergence of DJIA and S&P 500 Index.

Several economic and market indicators are often presented in efforts to arrive at "the consensus outlook." Since 1982, sets of indicators warning of market decline normally find concern with historically high and increasing P/E ratios, historically small and decreasing market dividend yields, divergence and decline in advance/decline lines relative to increasing DJIA, and divergence and decline in the S&P 500 or Nasdaq indices relative to increasing DJIA.

The sample economic indicators, data trends, and outlook implications are summarized in table 80. These individual economic indicator assessments (discussed below) are combined judgmentally to determine whether the economic outlook is positive, negative, mixed, or neutral (positive in this case).

Next, the summary economic outlook is entered in table 81. Then the sample market indicators, data trends, and outlook implications are summarized in table 81. These individual market indicator assessments (discussed below) are combined to determine the overall economic and market outlook as positive, negative, mixed, or neutral (mixed in this case). The assessments in tables 80 and 81 were validated using such sources as the *Wall Street Journal* and *Barron's* Web sites. No need to reconsider the indicator assessments was found. Following tables 80–1, table 82 presents a more complete checklist of both economic and market indicators, which serves to provide a wider range of assessment. This more complete treatment of indicators should be used to validate the table 80 economic outlook and the table 81 market outlook.

Next, the individual sample economic indicators that comprise table 80 are presented in figures 12.1 through 12.11. These are followed by the individual indicators that comprise table 81, which are presented in figures 12.12 through 12.14 and tables 83–6. Each indicator discussion includes data trends and outlook implications.

Next, the overall economic and market outlook identified in table 81 may be validated using table 87, which follows the individual economic and market indicator discussions. This table has been found empirically useful for the purpose. It includes both a "time to buy" checklist and a "time to sell checklist." If, for example, the buy side had a predominance of "no" responses, this would be consistent with the table 81 finding of a negative market outlook. That is, both tables agree that Windsor II should be purchased later. However, if, on the other hand, Windsor II is a sell and the sell side had a preponderance of "yes" responses, that would also be consistent with the table 81 finding of a negative market outlook. That is, both tables agree that Windsor II should be sold now.

Gross domestic product growth rate (last four quarters), figure 12.1

This most widely used indicator represents the growth rate of the basic measure of the nation's output of goods and services. Continuing positive growth, particularly with low inflation, is a positive sign for future growth. Gross domestic product and GDP growth rates are illustrated

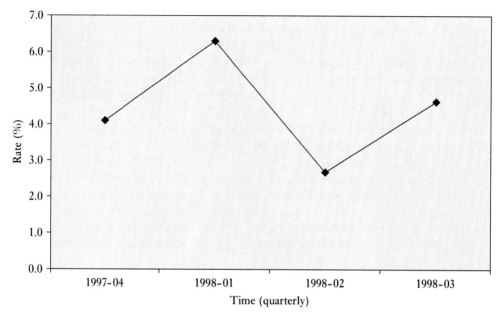

Figure 12.1 GDP and growth rate (last four quarters): SAAR 1997-04, $8,254.5 billion (4.1 percent growth); 1998-01, $8,384.2 billion (6.29 percent); 1998-02, $8,440.6 billion (2.69 percent); 1998-03, $8,538 billion (4.64 percent). Source: http://bos.business.uab.edu. Reproduced with permission.

in figure 12.1, which indicates mixed positive growth rates and an increase in GDP over the last four quarters. This growth pattern signals a mixed, positive economic outlook for more of the same.

Index of industrial output (last six months), figure 12.2

This index provides a relative measure of the nation's industrial output. It is a second basic measure of economic output. The index is illustrated in figure 12.2, which reveals small output decreases for the last two months following four months of mixed increasing and decreasing output. These last two months are slightly negative signals of economic output, but one that is yet to be confirmed.

Unemployment rate (last six months), figure 12.3

This indicator represents a measure of the nation's economic activity in human terms. It is the percentage of unemployed workers based on those actively seeking employment. A strong economy requires a large labor force. The unemployment rate is illustrated in figure 12.3, which shows a fairly persistent increase in unemployment rates over the last six months. This trend appears to be a slightly negative signal for economic growth, but one that has yet to be confirmed.

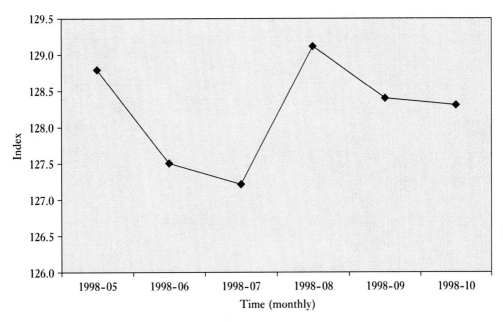

Figure 12.2 Index of industrial output (last six months): 1998-05, 128.8; 1998-06, 127.5; 1998-07, 127.2; 1998-08, 129.1; 1998-09, 128.4, 1998-10, 128.3. Source: http://www.dismal.com. Data provided by Economy.com.

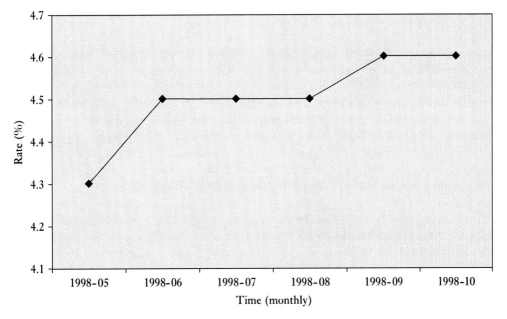

Figure 12.3 Unemployment rate (last six months): 1998-05, 4.3 percent; 1998-06, 4.5 percent; 1998-07, 4.5 percent; 1998-08, 4.5 percent; 1998-09, 4.6 percent; 1998-10, 4.6 percent. Source: http://www.dismal.com. Data provided by Economy.com.

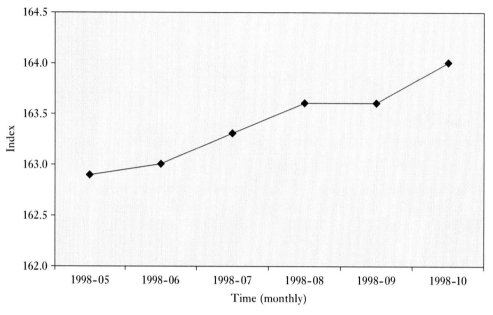

Figure 12.4   Consumer price index (last six months): 1998-05, 162.9; 1998-06, 163.0; 1998-07, 163.3; 1998-08, 163.6; 1998-09, 163.6; 1998-10,164.0. Source: http//bos.business.uab.edu. Reproduced with permission.

Consumer price index (last six months), figure 12.4

Inflation is measured here in its most popular form representing that facing consumers in the products and services they purchase. The index is based on the cost of a fixed "market basket" of goods and services purchased by consumers. A decline in inflation is desirable unless it is accompanied by a severe fall in the level of economic activity. The index is illustrated in figure 12.4, which indicates a slow, consistent price increase for each of the last six months. This moderate increase in consumer prices is a slightly negative signal for economic growth.

M2 money supply growth rate (last six months), figure 12.5

Money supply growth rates reflect the impact of the Federal Reserve in encouraging/discouraging the extension of credit by controlling the growth of the money supply, here measured in its more popular form. As the money supply growth rates increase, short-term interest rates fall, thus contributing to economic expansion. M2 includes M1 money plus savings deposits, small time deposits, money market funds, overnight repurchase agreements, and overnight eurodollars. M1 money is transactions-oriented and includes currency in circulation, demand deposits, and interest-bearing, checkable deposits.

The short-term and long-term results of increasing M2 growth rates differ. Measured over ten-year periods, annual M2 growth rates, annual inflation-adjusted GDP growth rates, and

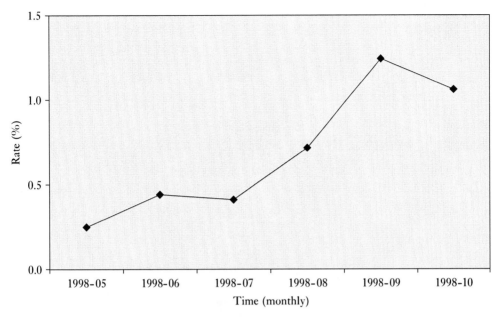

Figure 12.5 M2 money supply and growth rate (last six months): 1998-05, 4177.53 (0.25 percent growth); 1998-06, 4196.1 (0.44 percent); 1998-07, 4213.19 (0.41 percent); 1998-08, 4243.15 (0.71 percent); 1998-09, 4295.56 (1.24 percent); 1998-10, 4341.24 (1.06 percent). Source: http://bos.business.uab.edu. Reproduced with permission.

annual inflation rates move together. That is, long-term average annual increases in M2 growth rates correlate with long-term annual increases in inflation rates. In the short run, however, increases in the M2 money supply growth rate typically contribute to lower interest rates and stimulate demand for consumer and business durable goods, housing, and producer goods and services by lowering costs and prices. Declines in M2 money supply growth rates usually contribute to higher interest rates, with results opposite of those above.

Focusing on the short run, figure 12.5 illustrates a positive, but mixed, increase in M2 growth rates over the last six months. This pattern is a positive signal of continued economic growth with modest inflation.

Excess reserves (last six months), figure 12.6

An increase in excess bank reserves reflects the impact of the Federal Reserve in encouraging/ discouraging extension of credit. Investors should attempt to determine what the Federal Reserve is likely to do. No other institution has such a large impact on the price and availability of money for lending and investing. *Excess reserves* are the difference between the amount of actual member bank reserves (for lending and investing) and the amount required to be held by the Federal Reserve. The amount of excess reserves provides a measure of the relative tightness or ease of monetary policy. Increases in excess reserves typically contribute to increased bank liquidity and lower interest rates, and vice versa.

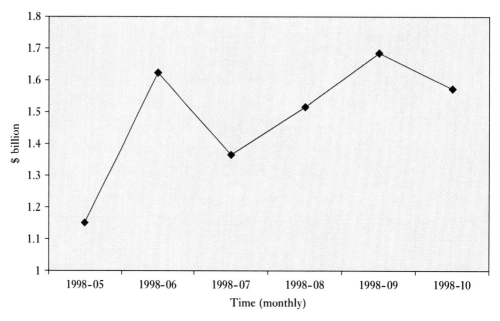

Figure 12.6 Excess reserves (last six months): 1998-05, $1.15 billion (−14.5 percent growth); 1998-06, $1.62 billion (40.87 percent); 1998-07, $1.37 billion (−15.74 percent); 1998-08, $1.51 billion (10.84 percent); 1998-09, $1.68 billion (11.3 percent); 1998-10, $1.57 billion (−6.65 percent). Source: http://www.stls.frb.org. Data provided by Federal Reserve Bank, St. Louis.

Figure 12.6 illustrates a mixed pattern of positive and negative growth rates in excess reserves, but with an overall increase in excess reserves over the last six months. This overall but choppy growth is a positive signal for economic expansion.

Free reserves (not shown) are a more specific measure of the impact of Federal Reserve actions on the price and availability of credit. Free reserves are excess reserves net of borrowed reserves. If excess reserves are larger than borrowed reserves, the difference represents *net free reserves*. If excess reserves are smaller than borrowed reserves, the difference is *net borrowed reserves*. This particular measure is noted because net free reserves are positive signals of economic expansion, and, conversely, net borrowed reserves are negative signals.

Treasury securities yield curve (latest chart), figure 12.7

The shape of the yield curve of ninety-day Treasury bills relative to thirty-year bonds indicates market expectations of future interest rates. The yield curve plots market yields for short- to long-term debt securities of the same credit quality, usually Treasury securities. An upward-sloping yield curve signals higher expected interest rates and a strong economy. For example, a one-year rate thirty years from now will be higher than the current one-year rate. Conversely, a relatively flat or, especially, a downward-sloping yield curve signals lower expected interest

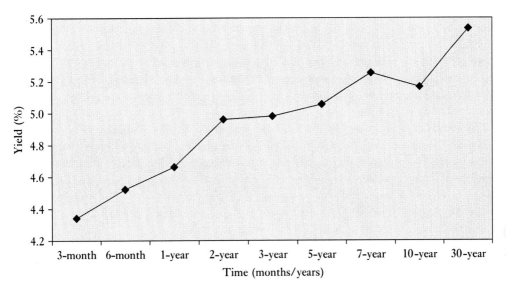

Figure 12.7 Treasury securities yield curve, November 30, 1998. Three-month interest rate 4.34 percent, six-month 4.52 percent, one-year 4.66 percent, two-year 4.957 percent, three-year 4.982 percent, five-year 5.05 percent, seven-year 5.249 percent, ten-year 5.167 percent; thirty-year 5.526 percent. Source: http://quicken.garvininfo.com.

rates and a weak or recessionary economy (Ronald, 1998). Thus the upward-sloping yield curve in figure 12.7 is a strong positive signal for continued economic growth.

The Federal Reserve's monetary actions are primarily felt in the short end of the term structure (yield curve). For example, short-term changes in nominal one-year Treasury bill rates are primarily due to changes in the inflation outlook, changes in real GDP output, and changes in real Federal funds rates. The Federal Reserve's 1990s baseline annual inflation rate was 3 percent, with a target rate of 2–3 percent. These factors become less important as the terms to maturity reflected in the yield curve increase.

The Treasury yield curve generally provides more accurate economic forecasts than professional economists on average, especially changes in direction. It also generally provides more accurate forecasts of recession than other technical indicators, including changes in the S&P 500 Index. But, like everything else in an uncertain world, it is by no means infallible.

The yield curve is important because it indicates the *yield spread* (long-term yields less short-term) between short and longer-term Treasury securities, usually measured using ten-year Treasury bonds and ninety-day Treasury bills. The larger the changes in yield spreads, the larger the expected changes in GDP growth rates. Changes in the yield spread generally explain a sizable proportion of changes in real GDP growth rates, looking out one (especially) to three years. Graza (1997) reported that when yield spreads are zero or negative, real GDP growth rates become increasingly negative as spreads decline. The probability of recession also reaches 90 percent when the yield spread reaches −2.5 percent. And, when spreads are positive, real GDP growth rates become increasingly positive as spreads increase.

The forecast is generally based on the one-year forward interest rates implied in the yield curve. At any point in time, the return on a long-term bond of a given maturity equals that provided by a series of one-year securities up to the bond's maturity. More specifically, the forecast is based on the one-year forward interest rates implied in the yield curve for Treasury zero coupon bonds, which pay no interest. The slope of the plots of the implied rates provides the interest rate forecast. The forward rates generally provide more accurate forecasts than those made by economists.

In a world of perfect foresight, the yield curve would be flat. But, in an uncertain world, it is normally upward-sloping, because long-term bonds bear greater risk if future interest rates prove to be higher than expected. The result is a risk premium in long-term yields. When a recession is expected, long-term rates fall immediately to equalize their expected holding period returns to a succession of one-year bonds over the same period. Yields on securities with different maturities decline by different amounts, depending on how much of the present value of future repayments will occur during the recession period.

As noted above, a recession is normally signaled by an inverted (downward-sloping) or flat yield curve. In fact, "Yield Curve Forecast" (1997) reported that since World War II there has never been a recession without the yield curve first "going flat" (no slope) or inverting. This source also provides the yield curve of one-year forward rates. The yield curve is flat or inverted when the difference (spread) between normally higher long-term rates and short-term rates is narrow or negative, respectively. The Federal Reserve narrows the spread when it raises short-term rates to cool down an overheated economy and prevent inflationary pressures. More specifically, zero or negative yield spreads are generally followed by negative GDP growth over the next twelve months. Over time, a zero to very small negative yield spread indicates about a one-third probability of a recession, and a very large negative yield (±400 basis points) almost promises one. Thus a flat or inverted yield curve is a negative signal of the economic outlook.

The relationship between the yield curve and future *stock prices* is also quite consistent over time. An upward-sloping yield curve is "normal" because investors are overall risk-averse and demand a yield premium to compensate for the greater risks inherent in long-maturity debt securities. An upward-sloping yield curve is generally followed by increases in the S&P 500 Index over the next twelve months.

Thus the upward-sloping yield curve illustrated in figure 12.7 is a positive signal for stock market performance. Conversely, an "abnormal" downward-sloping yield curve is generally followed by declines in the S&P 500 Index over the next twelve months. Thus a forecast of increasing interest rates implies an increasingly strong economy with higher stock prices, and vice versa for a forecast of declining interest rates.

Forecasting short-term interest rates: a note

As a tool to validate the yield curve's forecast, the "original Taylor model" is helpful. As discussed by Hester (1997), the Taylor model computes a desired federal (Fed.) funds rate and compares it with the actual rate. If the desired Fed. funds rate is larger (smaller) than the actual rate, the Federal Reserve is likely to increase (decrease) short-term interest rates. The desired Fed. funds rate is computed as follows:

$$DFF = 2 + AIF + 0.50(AIF - DIF) + 0.50(AGDP - PGDP)$$

where DFF = desired Fed. funds rate (percent), AIF = actual inflation rate (percent), DIF = desired (acceptable) inflation rate (2 percent), AGDP = actual GDP growth rate (percent), and PGDP = potential non-inflationary GDP growth rate (2.25 percent). For example, assuming the actual inflation rate (AIF) is 2.2 percent and the actual GDP growth rate (AGDP) is 2.0 percent, the desired Fed. funds rate (DFF) is 5.3 percent. Assuming the actual Fed. funds rate is 5.5 percent, then the model calls for the Federal Reserve to act to lower short-term interest rates.

However, a difference in actual and desired Fed. funds rates does not mean the Federal Reserve is necessarily going to change short-term interest rates. It has been argued that the Taylor model is designed for explaining what the Federal Reserve has done rather than what it should do. But Taylor disagrees. As reported by Wessell (2000), Taylor believes the Federal Reserve should follow his model to determine what it should do about interest rates, not to explain just what it did about rates.

The focus of the Taylor model on Fed. funds is quite appropriate because this short-term rate is much more highly correlated with economic activity than long-term interest rates. Baum (2000) reported that the correlation between changes in Fed. funds rates and GDP growth rates is negative. This is to be expected, because increased interest rates depress GDP growth. About 29 percent of the variance in GDP growth rates is explained by changes in Fed. funds rates alone. This is no surprise, because monetary policy is transmitted through bank reserves, and Fed. funds rates represent the price of borrowed reserves.

Hester (1997) also reported an expanded Taylor model called the Harris model. This more recent model requires assumptions of a non-accelerating inflation rate of unemployment, average returns on the S&P 500 Index, and average growth rates of the CRB index of industrial production. These variables are less definitely determined than those in the Taylor model. However, the Harris model may at least be used to confirm the results of the Taylor model.

Yardeni (1999) also provided a simplified version of the Federal Reserve's stock valuation model. The model estimated the stock market as 41 percent overvalued! This was at a time when the consensus forecast of earnings growth for the foreseeable future was 15 percent, the highest it has ever been recorded. The subsequent performance of the stock market, especially the Nasdaq, has confirmed that the stock market was "clearly priced for perfection."

Index of consumer confidence (last six months), figure 12.8

The Conference Board publishes the index of consumer confidence. The index is a measure of consumer sentiment based on current conditions and those expected in six months. The expectations component is weighted more heavily. The index is based on a mail survey of 5,000 households that samples consumer evaluations of current and future conditions. A strong economy depends to a large degree on consumer spending. The index attempts to assess the likelihood that consumers will spend based on the degree of optimism reflected in their evaluation of current and future conditions.

The index is illustrated in figure 12.8, which reveals a decline in consumer confidence in five of the last six months. This negative trend is a negative signal for the economic outlook based on a decline in consumer spending.

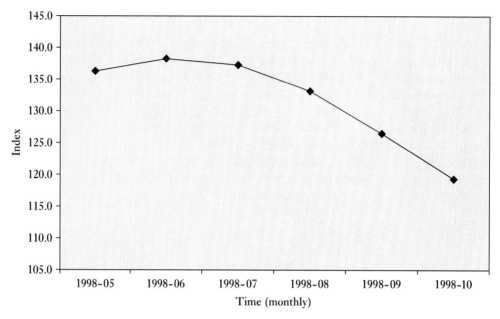

Figure 12.8 Index of consumer confidence (last six months): 1998-05, 136.3; 1998-06, 138.2; 1998-07, 137.2; 1998-08, 133.1; 1998-09, 126.4; 1998-10, 119.3. Source: http://www.dismal.com. Data provided by the Conference Board® Consumer Confidence Index™.

Federal budget deficit (last four quarters), figure 12.9

This indicator measures whether or not the federal government is stimulating/overstimulating the economy by running deficits, the historical pattern. Following deficits in the first two quarters, surpluses appeared in the last two quarters, of which the third-quarter surplus is huge. This appearance of budget surpluses is consistent with the 1990s economic scenario of large real growth in GDP, increased productivity, reduced unemployment, and lowered inflation. The levels of inflation and economic growth were unusually stable. In this scenario, budget surpluses allow a reduction in debt and reduce upward pressure on interest rates, which is good for economic growth with low inflation. These budget surpluses have occurred even though government spending has increased, financed by the larger tax revenue resulting from larger incomes in prosperous times.

The budget surplus/deficit illustrated in figure 12.9, indicates a "trend" towards surplus in the third quarter but less so in the last quarter. This budget trend is a positive signal for a robust economy with low interest rates.

Index of coincident economic indicators (last six months), figure 12.10

This composite index is one of three used to anticipate turning points in the business cycle. The index includes broad measures that tend to summarize the state of actual business activity,

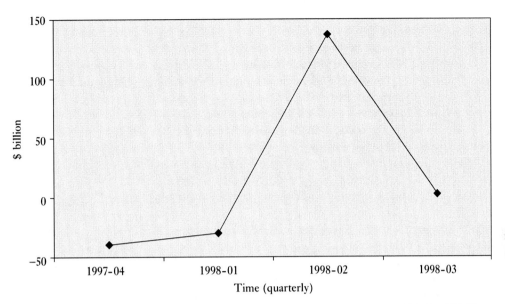

Figure 12.9   Budget deficit (last four quarters). Month 1: 1997-04, −$35.96 billion; 1998-01, −$25.37 billion; 1998-02, −$124.602 billion; 1998-03, −$24.08 billion. Month 2: 1997-04, −$17.34 billion; 1998-01, −$41.76 billion; 1998-02, −$38.778 billion; 1998-03, −$11.16 billion. Month 3: 1997-04, $13.63 billion; 1998-01, −$13.81 billion; 1998-02, $51.1 billion; 1998-03, $38.17 billion. Budget deficit/surplus: 1997-04, −$39.67 billion; 1998-01, −$30.2 billion; 1998-02, $136.925 billion; 1998-03, $2.93 billion. Source: http://www.dismal.com. Data provided by Economy.com.

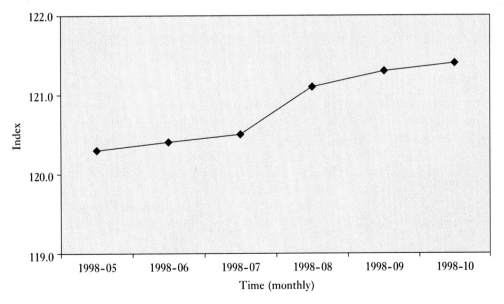

Figure 12.10   Index of coincident economic indicators (last six months): 1998-05, 120.3; 1998-06, 120.4, 1998-07, 120.5; 1998-08, 121.1; 1998-09, 121.3; 1998-10, 121.4. Source: http://bos.business.uab.edu. Reproduced with permission.

both from the input and from the output sides. The index attempts to confirm expectations and to give some precision to broad economic swings. The index includes those indicators most likely to change at the *same time* (coincident) as a peak or trough in economic activity. The coincident index includes industrial production, personal income less transfer payments, non-agricultural employment, and manufacturing and trade sales. This index attempts to determine whether the economy is currently reflecting a change in its direction.

The index of coincident economic indicators is illustrated in figure 12.10, which reveals a steady increase in the index in each of the last six months. This increase in the index is a positive signal for a continuation in economic growth.

Index of leading economic indicators (last six months), figure 12.11

This is the most watched composite index because it attempts to call turns in the economy before they happen. The index represents anticipation of business decisions, investment and production, and flows to economic stocks. This tendency to lead provides signals of change in general economic conditions. The index includes those indicators most likely to change in *anticipation* (lead) of peaks and troughs in economic activity.

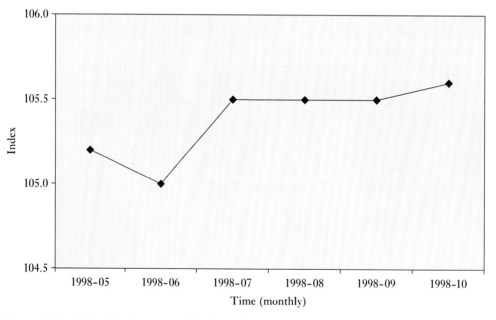

Figure 12.11   Index of leading economic indicators (last six months); 1998-05, 105.2; 1998-06, 105.0; 1998-07, 105.5; 1998-08, 105.5; 1998-09, 105.5; 1998-10, 105.6.
Source: http://bos.business.uab.edu. Reproduced with permission.

The index comprises eleven indicators, including the S&P 500 Index. The logic of including the market index is that it represents an expectation of future economic conditions. The index also includes consumer sentiment, real M2 money supply, and changes in sensitive materials prices. The leading index has forecast more recessions than actually occurred, but when it is correct it provides about a nine months' lead of business cycle peaks.

The index is illustrated in figure 12.11, which indicates a mixed but overall increase in the index over the last six months. The increase in the index is a positive signal for continued economic growth.

Overall economic outlook (table 80)

As discussed above, the results of figures 12.1 through 12.11 are summarized in table 80. The economic indicators provide mixed signals of the economic outlook – seven are positive and four are negative. Nonetheless, the consensus economic outlook is positive, based on GDP growth, money supply growth rates, upward-sloping yield curve and the index of leading economic indicators. The moving averages are strong. These findings were also validated from other sources, but no reason was found requiring reassessment of the overall economic outlook.

Thus, subject to the buy decision summarized in table 68 and the positive economic outlook summarized in table 80, Windsor II should be purchased now. Also, if Windsor II is currently owned, it should continue to be held. However, the final overall implementation decision depends on the market outlook summary and combination of economic and market outlooks in table 81.

As noted by Barbee (1998), investors should also be alert to the different impacts of economic scenarios on stock performance. In recessions, consumer staples and health care stocks do well because people must have what they sell. Cyclical stocks and high-yield junk bonds do poorly when the economy is weak. In the last recession, in 1991, inflation was expected to increase and this meant good performance for commodities, gold, real estate, and inflation-indexed bonds, all of which are inflation-proof. Bonds and stocks not tied to hard assets did poorly. In an out-and-out deflation characterized by a fall in prices and the consumer price index, longer-term bonds and high dividend paying stocks do best. Which securities perform worst? The answer is securities that do best in inflationary times.

MARKET INDICATORS: DISCUSSION AND SAMPLE MENU

There are probably a "million" different market indicators, but most are generally no more accurate (probably less so) than flipping a coin. Fosback (1994) eased the task of finding useful indicators by testing forty-nine technical indicators and a number of stock selection theories. Fosback provides an efficient way to consider technical indicators frequently used in making economic and market forecasts. The report "General Market Indicators" (2000) provides fourteen "psychological" indicators, along with their highs/lows and dates for both the last five years and last twelve months. The essence of these indicators and more is included in table 82. *Market Edge* (1999) provides nine sentiment indicators and an overall indicator, including two discussed in this chapter.

If the *weak-form efficient markets theory* is correct, technical indicators are of no value in forecasting returns because the historical data are already reflected in current market prices. However, more recent evidence suggests that the performance of selected technical indicators may reflect anomalies to efficient market theory. If so, some technical indicators are likely to be valid predictors of market performance.

The approach here is not to engage in a debate over market efficiency, but simply to use economic and market indicators to gain insight into the current context of the securities market. It is not assumed that any one indicator or the other has a good forecasting record: most do not. But, based on the overall preponderance of the indicator evidence, it is hoped it provides some help in timing the implementation of buy/sell decisions. The indicators also are helpful in gaining some understanding of those commonly used in the investment community.

For now, it is enough to note recent support for technical analysis as reviewed by Damodaran (1998). Historically, efficient markets theorists have condemned technical analysis as useless in finding undervalued stocks. More recently, however, this assessment has been somewhat altered by strong evidence of predictable patterns in stock prices. However, investors must be aware of technical indicators based on *data mining* (*data snooping*) which underlies much of the market newsletters. If historical data are punished enough, technical indicators will be found that would have generated superior returns over that particular time period. Frequently, however, these indicators lack a theoretical premise and more often they do not work outside the particular historical time period.

These findings of useful (profitable) technical indicators are of two basic types. The first type is the long-term price reversal. These price reversals are stronger in five-year returns than in one-year returns. Loser portfolios have been found to outperform winner portfolios over the following sixty months, and vice versa. This finding is consistent with market overreaction and correction in long return intervals. The second type of technical indicator is price momentum. This indicator operates opposite from long-term price reversal. A strategy of buying the winners and selling the losers over the last six months and holding the winners for six months provides excess returns. Much of this return is due to delayed investor reaction and occurred largely around positive and negative earnings announcements.

This is not to say, however, that behaviorists find all technical market indicators valid. Some of the technical indicators discussed below may be based on errors in investor thinking. For example, in a review of behavioral finance, Shefrin (2000) found the appealing advisor confidence index (table 84) a better predictor of the past than of the future. Nonetheless, such indicators are widely used and provide insight into how the market may be impacted by investors following these indicators.

The sample market indicators, data trends, and outlook implications are summarized in table 81. These sample market indicators are individually discussed in figures 12.12 through 12.14 and tables 83–6. Each indicator discussion includes data trends and outlook implications. These individual indicator assessments are combined judgmentally in table 81 to determine whether the market outlook is positive, negative, mixed, or neutral (negative in this case). Next, the summary market outlook is entered and combined judgmentally with the summary market outlook in table 81 to determine the overall economic and market, outlook as positive, negative, mixed, or neutral. The assessments were again validated with no need to reconsider them. Again, table 82 presents a more complete checklist of both types of indicators.

It should be remembered that current market value is a forecast precursor of economic activity. Thus any change in market outlook implies a change in expected economic activity as measured in the market. Current market level represents the present value of expectations concerning aggregate firm risk/return performance as impacted at both micro and macro levels. This representation is not always proven correct because of future uncertainties and because investor psychology tends to go to extremes before reversing.

The following discussion of sample market indicators provides the information summarized in table 81. The discussion of each includes data trends and outlook implications. The assessments have again been validated independently. No need to reconsider indicator assessments was found.

NYSE cumulative daily breadth relative to DJIA (latest chart), figure 12.12

The breadth of the market (advance/decline line) indicator is a traditional measure of the extent to which the entire market is participating in changes in the market index. In this case, the number of stocks increasing in price less the number decreasing in price is computed daily. The difference, which may be positive or negative, is plotted daily or on a cumulative weekly

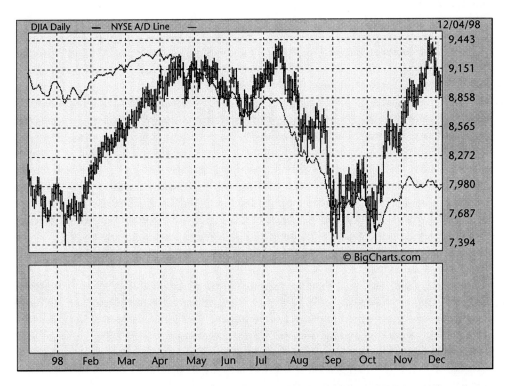

Figure 12.12 NYSE cumulative daily breadth (advance/decline line) relative to DJIA. Source: http://www.bigcharts.com. Copyright © 1998–2001 Marketwatch.com. Historical and current end-of-day data provided by FT Interactive Data. Intra-day data provided by S&P Comstock.

basis. The advance/decline line works best when plotted along with the DJIA. When the two series move together, there is said to be *confirmation* of the continuation of the trend, but when they do not, there is *divergence*, which signals a change in market outlook, normally negative. If both series are increasing (decreasing) the majority of stocks on the NYSE are confirming the change in direction of the index. That is, trends in the DJIA are confirmed by the breadth (or lack thereof) of participation among the stocks on the NYSE. When the advance/decline line confirms the index's upward movement, the market is considered technically strong versus technically weak when it diverges from the index's upward movement.

In figure 12.12, the advance/decline line diverged from the trend of the DJIA in October and the market reversed direction in December. This divergence and apparent weakness in the index are a negative signal of a market downturn under way.

Fosback (1994) found that a modified advance/decline line provides better forecasts than the usual version. An up trend (down trend) is defined when the current weekly reading is higher (lower) than the average reading for the last forty-two weeks. An up trend in the advance/decline line correctly signaled a bull market in progress in the vast majority of cases, but a down trend correctly signaled a bear market in progress in only a minority of cases.

DJIA 200 day and 100 day moving averages relative to DJIA (latest charts), figure 12.13

Moving averages are a well known technical measure for analyzing markets and individual stocks. Moving averages and other technical indicators use historical data to generate decision rules for buying and selling securities. Moving averages are constructed for individual stocks, mutual funds, and market indices. The basic idea is that when a mutual fund's net asset value is above its moving average, a buy is signaled, and a sell is signaled when its net asset value is below its moving average. To compute the moving average each day, the oldest day's net asset value is deleted, today's net asset value added, and the moving average recomputed. The larger the number of days' net asset values in a mutual fund's moving average, such as 200 days versus 100 days, the more gradually the moving average changes for a given latest day change.

Most studies find that moving averages provide mixed performance relative to buy-and-hold strategies. The traditional and most widely published moving average of market performance is the thirty-nine-week moving average (200 day moving average here) of the DJIA. There are many differences in the details and interpretation of moving averages, but the basic idea is captured in figure 12.13, where daily index values fluctuate around an always more gradually changing moving average.

The 200 day and 100 day moving averages are illustrated in figure 12.13. Both indicate one buy signal and one sell signal in the latest year. The sell signal flashed when the index value crossed the moving average from above, and, conversely, the buy signal flashed when the index value crossed the moving average from below. However, because the 200 day moving average changes more gradually than shorter-period moving averages, it generally signals fewer buy/sell decisions. This is most apparent when the market is choppy, not when the market is in a broad up trend as portrayed here.

In choppy markets, the increased number of buy/sell signals may cause investors to lose money resulting from "whipsawing" – repeated buying/selling that may cause investors to sell

Figure 12.13   (a) DJIA 100 day moving average, (b) DJIA 200 day moving average.
Source: http://www.quicken.com.

at lower prices following sell signals than purchase prices following buy signals. In effect, this amounts to sell low and buy higher. Moving averages attempt to signal trades once they have been confirmed, which means trades will not be made at best prices. But trades would not be executed at best prices in any case because, for example, it is not possible to know the lowest price until after it occurs.

To assist investors identify sell signals, Jones (1998) reported three rules using the DJIA moving average. First, sell if the daily index value is below its moving average, advances toward its moving average, fails to cross it, and then retreats. Second, sell if the moving average increases, flattens out or declines, and the index value crosses the moving average from above. Third, sell if the index value rises above its moving average, but the moving average is declining.

As seen in figure 12.13, the recent year index values for both the 200 day and 100 day moving averages moved sharply higher than the moving averages. These two indicators provide a positive signal for the continuation of strong market performance. But note that the 100 day moving average flashed its sell signal at a higher price than the 200 day moving average. Further, it flashed its buy signal at a lower price than the 200 day moving average. The down side to this is that the 100 day moving average typically requires more frequent trading, trading costs, and capital gains taxes than the 200 day moving average.

From a single mutual fund investor's perspective, any additional trading caused by the use of moving average strategies would not have significant costs other than any transaction fees and more frequent taxable events. But what may be true for one investor is not true for the aggregate of fund investors. The more frequently funds trade to meet the purchase/sale requirements imposed by the aggregate implementation of moving average strategies, the smaller fund and shareholder returns will be. These additional costs would normally more than offset any additional aggregate shareholder returns from the use of moving average strategies. And the fewer the days in the moving average, the more frequent the requisite buy/sell signals.

From a performance standpoint, what is the best length of moving average? The Institute for Econometric Research (1994c) compared the performance of ten moving average strategies against a buy-and-hold strategy. Five of ten moving average strategies outperformed a simple buy-and-hold strategy, but all ten strategies have less risk, ranging from 24 percent to 37 percent. In order of profitability (no taxes or trading costs), the five most profitable moving averages are the 75 day, 100 day, 50 day, 125 day, and 150 day moving averages. The 200 day moving average does not rank in the top five. The 75 day moving average is clearly the most profitable, and the 100 day moving average ranks second. Moving averages look most promising when measured using risk-adjusted returns.

From 1982 to 1991, implementation of the 75 day moving average called for twenty-six round-trip transactions versus twenty-one for the 100 day moving average. The 75 day moving average required not quite three round-trip trades a year, and the 100 day moving average required over two round trips a year. However, the unprofitable 200 day moving average required less than one and a half round trips a year.

The finding of improved risk-adjusted returns using moving averages is consistent with the findings in Brock et al. (1992) and reported by Sharpe et al. (1999). Two versions and a related version of a 200 day moving average strategy of the DJIA from 1897 to 1986 were tested. In the first, buy/sell decisions were made *daily* using basic moving average decision rules. If the index value is larger (smaller) than the moving average value, the decision is to buy (sell) the index. Average daily returns were computed for buy days and sell days, which varied in length. If the stock market is efficient, the average daily returns of each type of day should be approximately the same.

The first version of the 200 day moving average strategy had annual returns of 10.7 percent from following buy signals and −6.1 percent from sell signals. The difference in returns, including transaction costs, is a huge 16.8 percentage points! But this strategy has the potential for frequent trading that can whipsaw investor returns. The other two strategies use fixed-length buy/sell holding periods to minimize whipsawing returns by frequent trading. These versions have 18.6 and 17.6 percentage point differences in buy/sell returns.

The results of the study provide apparent anomalies to the theory of efficient markets. The three versions of a 200 day moving average strategy provided only small differences in performance, but the conclusion is the same for all.

Mutual fund cash asset ratio (latest), figure 12.14

Cash asset allocation was noted (table 45) as one of Vanguard Windsor II's diversification risks. Here, this ratio represents all mutual funds, using *Barron's* term, liquid asset ratio. William Bernstein (1999) considers the cash ratio "[t]he best market indicator ever." P/B and P/E ratios are uncharted territory, given the market's long-standing high valuations. The cash ratio explained 31 percent of annualized S&P 500 Index returns for the *next* three years.

The mutual fund cash ratio operates as a contrarian indicator. That is, portfolio managers are overly bearish (bullish) about the direction of the market when cash ratios are historically large (small). The irony is that the aggregate market forecasts made by the professional mutual fund managers of the size of cash ratios held are generally wrong at the historical extremes – either unusually large or unusually small.

A further irony is the argument that actively managed funds are less risky than index funds because they hold cash assets. But, as noted above, the reverse is more likely true because funds tend to hold very large/small cash accounts at the wrong times with respect to market risk or lack thereof. The total risk of index funds based on the S&P 500 is also less than the risk of the average managed fund.

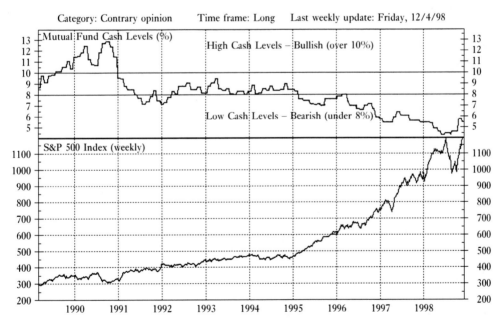

Figure 12.14 Mutual fund cash levels (ratios). Source: http://www.marketgauge.com. Data provided by Winninginvesting.com.

Also, if funds vary their cash ratios, investors must manage their cash positions in light of fund cash ratios. As stated by Quinson (1998b), the question for investors is "Who controls your cash crop?" The fact that fund cash ratios are wrong-sized at the extremes suggests that investors may be less anxious holders of cash assets.

However, before continuing, Quinson (1998a) argued that the cash ratio may be becoming less of a contrarian indicator. High cash ratios were correctly bullish indicators during the mid 1970s and in 1982 and correctly bearish signals in 1972, 1973, and 1976. Following cash ratios of 8.5 percent or less, six-month market returns were small to negative during the 1970s and 1980s. But, during the 1990s, 8.5 percent cash ratios were followed by 8.5 percent returns over the next six months. In the 1990s market environment, it made sense for mutual funds to be fully invested. The importance of mutual fund cash ratios was diminished because of huge net cash inflows that provided liquidity. But the 1990s experience is not for ever.

Figure 12.14 presents a graphical representation of bullish market signals (cash ratios over 10 percent) and of bearish signals (cash ratios less than 8 percent). Cash levels are less than 6 percent, which signals a negative market outlook. Alternatively, or together, the Fosback Index may also be used to determine whether fund cash asset ratios signal positive or negative market outlooks.

The Institute for Econometric Research (1994a) and Fosback (1994) found the *Fosback Index* to be the most accurate forecaster of market performance over the index's fifty-five-year history. Mutual fund portfolio managers have not been accurate in timing key turning points in market performance. They tend to hold too much cash when they should hold little, and vice versa. When interest rates are high, funds have an incentive to hold short-term money market securities, such as Treasury bills, commercial paper, and bank CDs. The index may be applied to particular equity funds or to equity funds in general.

Fosback Index

The Fosback Index's normal cash asset ratio was determined empirically to be 3.2 percent plus 70 percent of the commercial paper interest rate. A positive computed Fosback Index indicates excessive mutual fund pessimism about the market outlook, reflected in excessive cash holdings. These large cash ratios available for investment are, in fact, bullish for the market. A negative index indicates excessive fund optimism about the market outlook, reflected in small cash holdings. These small cash ratios available for investment are bearish for the market. The Fosback Index is thus a contrarian indicator – a positive index equals too much cash due to an overly pessimistic market outlook and vice versa. For example, if the computed index is 10 percent and funds are holding 12 percent in cash, the index is a positive 2 percent and funds are holding too much cash.

The Fosback Index is computed as follows:

$$FI = CCR - \{3.2\% + 0.7(CPR)\}$$

where FI = Fosback Index, CCR = current average mutual fund cash ratio, and CPR = current commercial paper rate. Assuming commercial paper interest rates are zero, the 3.2 percent cash ratio represents operating purposes, including shareholder redemptions. In this case only, the cash ratio has no opportunity cost because no returns are forgone by holding cash assets. The

3.2 percentage is close to the minimum 4.1 percent cash ratio held by funds since 1970. Thus, when funds hold more cash assets than needed for operating purposes, to this extent they are implicitly or explicitly making a market forecast.

In the relatively few times the Fosback Index has been 2.5 percent or larger, substantial market advances followed. The contrarian interpretation is that portfolio managers are wrong (too bearish) when they hold such large cash balances. The correct market forecast is much more likely to be positive, not negative.

If the Fosback Index is between 0 percent and 2.5 percent, mutual fund cash balances are normal. The correct market forecast is for the continuation of current market conditions. No contrarian signal is given in this case. The index should be interpreted for what it says, not for what it does not say. For example, if the index is 0 percent, holdings of fund cash assets are in equilibrium – they do not implicitly or explicitly forecast a market change.

If the Fosback Index is less than 0 percent, fund portfolio managers are signaling a positive (fully invested) market forecast. The contrarian interpretation of this is that portfolio managers are wrong (too bullish) when they hold such small cash balances. The correct market forecast is much more likely to be negative, not positive.

The computed Fosback Index is −1.62 percent. This was computed using the equation above. The average mutual fund cash ratio is 5.5 percent and the rate on one-month directly placed commercial paper is 5.6 percent, both reported in *Barron's*. Thus:

$$FI = 5.5\% - \{3.2\% + 0.70(5.6\%)\}$$

$$= 5.5\% - 7.12\%$$

$$= -1.62\%$$

The negative Fosback Index appears to signal a bullish market outlook based on the market forecast implicit in fund cash ratios. However, the correct (contrarian) interpretation of the Fosback Index is a negative signal for the market outlook. This interpretation also agrees with figure 12.14, which indicates that fund cash ratios over 10 percent are bullish and those less than 8 percent are bearish. These scores are matched against the S&P 500 Index to show how the ratios relate to market performance.

Technical indicators: a detour

The mutual fund cash ratio is one of a class of technical indicators based on the premise of irrational investor behavior, such as overoptimism or overpessimism. Damodaran (1998) identified several types of technical behaviors. In the first type of behavior, investors overreact to information announcements. Investors tend to overweight recent information and underweight prior information. Technical indicators based on this premise include the set of generally discredited odd-lot trading rules, which are based on the "individual investors are bozos" argument. Other technical indicators include mutual fund cash asset ratios (above) and measures of investment advisor sentiment (below).

In the second type of behavior, investor mood swings lead to shifts in the supply of and demand for securities. This untreated behavior is tracked by the breadth of the market and moving average indicators, both discussed above. In the third type of behavior, investors assimilate and understand information more quickly than markets. This is the cornerstone of technical analysis and argues that markets are less efficient than stated in theory. Technical analysis is based on the notion that historical patterns in market and security data can be used to earn excess returns. Evidence of this behavior is found in stock price drifts following significant news announcements, such as announcements of earnings surprises and earnings estimate changes (below). Drifts reflect gradual movement towards new equilibrium prices. Price drifts are used by momentum investors who buy/sell stocks based on their recent relative price strength.

In the fourth type of behavior, markets are driven by external forces beyond investor control. This behavior is consistent with the chorus in Greek literature. One such model, the Elliott wave, posits that markets move in both short-term and long-term waves, of which the latter may last for a century or more. *Market Science* (1997) reviewed a version of this model called the Coppock curve, which forecasts the stock market using a long-term momentum oscillator. "Yield Curve Forecast" (1997) also features current measures of investor confidence, market momentum, market risk, yield curve forecast, and special studies. The most famous technical approach to the market is the Dow theory, which holds that the market follows daily, secondary, and primary (four or more years) trends.

The fifth and final type of behavior is based on two assumptions. First, there are smart investors who earn superior returns and, second, other investors can also benefit by following their lead. This behavior is tracked by specialist short sales (table 82) and insider buying and selling transactions (below).

Investors Intelligence Advisor Confidence Index (last three), table 83

This indicator is provided by *Investors Intelligence*, an investment advisory service, and is based on a weekly sample of some 135 investment advisory services. As with extreme values of mutual fund cash ratios, this indicator has also been identified as a contrarian signal when the greatest proportion of respondents are either largely optimistic or pessimistic. Again, it is ironic that professional advisory services are often wrong at the extremes. Apparently, they are too busy following the herd to know where the cliff is. It is also not always easy to determine whether advisory services are optimistic or pessimistic. They often state one thing short-term and another long-term, and hedge their views to allow rationalization later without admitting mistakes. Perhaps for these reasons, this indicator often signals the wrong market outlook.

Nonetheless, this indicator is interesting because it attempts to measure the market expectations of those writing for investors. It also provides two interpretations, one for bullish investment advisors and another for bearish investment advisors. If 55 percent or more of advisors are bullish, this is a contrarian bearish signal. If 50 percent or more of advisors are bearish, this is a contrarian, bullish signal. Percentages outside these amounts are neutral, non-contrarian signals.

As seen in table 83, nearly 57 percent of investment advisors continue to be bullish, which is a contrarian, negative signal for the market outlook. Also, only 31 percent of advisors are bearish, which is interpreted as neutral and non-contrarian.

DJIA P/E ratio (last three) and *Barron's* consensus DJIA P/E Ratio (latest), table 84

These two P/E ratio indicators reflect how much the market is paying for the trailing earnings per share and next year's expected earnings per share represented by the DJIA. These indicators are interpreted relative to historical relationships. From the end of World War II up to the 1990s, yearly *high* P/E ratios have ranged from about eight times trailing twelve-month earnings per share to briefly over twenty-four times, and the high midpoint is fifteen or sixteen times earnings. Yearly *low* P/E ratios have ranged from about six times earnings to nineteen times earnings, and the low mid point is about twelve times earnings. The long-term golden mean P/E ratio is about fourteen times earnings. Also, buying stocks when P/E ratios are eight times earnings has never failed to be a profitable move. Needless to say, the 1990s were atypical of anything yet experienced, including the size of P/E ratios. Does anyone want a tulip bulb (2000)?

Wu and Wang (2000) examined the traditional relationship between earnings yields (E/P) and future stock returns. Earnings yields predict stock returns over a much longer period than previously found. Earnings yields are correlated with future returns and growth. Earnings yields often predict 40–50 percent of variations in cumulative ten to twenty-year returns, and the ability to do so generally increases with the time horizon. The strongest prediction is for the period ending year 14, and the weakest is for year 1. There is a positive relationship between earnings yields and future stock returns, and a negative relationship between earnings yields and future earnings growth. Low earnings yields predict low future cumulative stock returns and high earnings growth over long horizons.

The two indicators in this section are evaluated using historical relationships, not the 1990s versions. Table 84 indicates the DJIA P/E ratio recently increased then declined, but at 24.3 it is historically out of sight and must be considered a negative signal for the market outlook. Table 84 also indicates a current DJIA P/E ratio of 22.4, based on consensus operating earnings estimates. When applied to the higher consensus earnings estimates for next year, the P/E ratio falls to 19.3. But, even if they are realized, the P/E ratio is at the historical high end of the distribution and must also be considered a negative signal for the market outlook.

As an aside, Nocera (1998) found that *consensus earnings estimates* (the consensus of financial analysts) have completely subsumed the reality of corporate earnings. Firms have found that beating consensus earnings estimates has become more important to share price increases than actual earnings. The result is a type of short-term momentum investing – buying stocks of companies that have exceeded earnings estimates and selling those that have not.

DJIA dividend yield (latest three), table 84

Historically, yearly *high* dividend yields ranged from about 4 percent to 8 percent, with a high mid point of 5 percent. Yearly *low* dividend yields ranged from about 2 percent to 6.5 percent, with a low mid point of 4 percent. The long-term mean dividend yield is about 4.2 percent. Historically, when stocks were overpriced with yields less than 3 percent, stock prices declined over the next year. Small stock yields make bond yields more competitive. Also, when stocks were priced conservatively, with yields over 7 percent, stock prices increased over the next year. Again, this precedes the 1990s.

Wu and Wang (2000) also examined the relationship between current dividend yields and future stock returns. Dividend yields predict stock returns over a much longer period than previously found. Dividend yields are correlated with future returns and growth, which gives them predictive power. Dividend yields have this power because they can forecast the mean-reverting component of future returns and the permanent component of future earnings growth. Mean-reversion of returns is attributed to time-varying expected returns reflecting future economic activity. Behaviorists attribute it to market overreaction or speculative bubbles. The dividend ratio is low when dividends are expected to decrease or grow more slowly, and it is high when expected future returns are high.

Dividend yields often predict 40–60 percent of variations in cumulative ten to twenty-year dividends, and the ability to do so generally increases with the time horizon. The strongest prediction is for the period ending year 19, and the weakest is for year 1. There is a positive relationship between dividend yields and future stock returns, and a negative relationship between dividend yields and future dividend growth. Low dividend yields predict low future cumulative stock returns and high dividend growth over long horizons.

Moreover, current dividend yields and earnings yields show strong, positive correlation. Dividend yields are also positively autocorrelated and current dividend yields lead earnings yields. Overall, there is a positive correlation between dividend (earnings) yields and future stock returns. And there is a negative correlation between dividend (earnings) yields and future dividend (earnings) growth.

Table 84 also indicates that the DJIA dividend yield has increased only very slightly, to 1.69, which is very low historically. Keeping a historical perspective, this very low yield must be considered a negative signal for the market outlook.

Insider transactions (latest ratio of current dollar value of buy versus sell transactions), table 85

This indicator is a revised measure of traditional insider transactions that weighs the buy versus sale sides of these trades by their relative dollar volume. "Insiders" are persons with access to corporate inside information. Insiders are legally defined as corporate officers, directors, or large stockholders. Their insider buy/sell transactions are assumed motivated by informed knowledge of corporate developments and future prospects.

The focus here is on the market outlook rather than that of particular corporations. But large insider trading of particular company stocks has generally provided useful information. Fosback (1994) reported that during bull markets stocks with large insider buying performed better than the market, which performed better than stocks with large insider selling. During bear markets, stocks with large insider buying declined less than the market, which declined less than stocks with large insider selling.

Insider sales are more often motivated by personal needs than insider purchases, such as paying college tuition, diversifying portfolios, and selling shares received from options. As reported by Sturm (1999), insider purchases signal important information, but insider sales do not. Moreover, it has been found that: (1) insider purchase portfolios outperformed the market over a ten-year period by over 7 percent per year (but reporting delays would reduce actual investor returns from this strategy); (2) insider purchases are stronger signals at small to mid cap. size firms; (3) insider transactions by CEOs signal the most information, followed by officers, directors, and large shareholders; and (4) insiders typically act as contrarian investors and buy shares when prices are depressed.

As seen in table 85, the latest insider sales totaled $2.92 billion and insider buys totaled $876.3 million. This is a ratio of sales to purchases of 3.33 to one, which is a negative signal of the market outlook. A better estimate of the outlook may be obtained by reviewing these data for several time periods.

Earnings surprises (latest ratio of number of positive versus negative surprises), table 86a

Earnings surprises occur when a corporation's actual quarterly/annual reported earnings are either larger (a "positive surprise") or smaller (a "negative surprise") than the consensus forecast. Positive surprises usually have a positive impact ("pop") on the prices of particular stocks, and vice versa for negative surprises. Peters (1993) found that companies that have negative surprises are likely to have more of the same in subsequent quarters. Picerno (2000a) reported that earnings surprises are the second most used indicator by institutional investors. The others include *return on equity* (ROE; ranks first), earnings estimate changes (ranks third), and earnings momentum (ranks fourth). The average institutional investor includes seven variables in their forecast models. The models range from very simple to very technical.

Picerno (2000b) also reported several pointers for identifying stocks with potential earnings surprises: (1) stocks that surprised the most on a four-quarter basis tend to produce the largest surprises, but the latest quarter is most important; (2) compute the *standardized unexpected earnings* (SUE) to identify stocks that will have the largest surprise effect on the share price; (3) use estimates of the most accurate analysts in computing SUE; (4) especially consider stocks that also beat their *whisper numbers* as well as analyst estimates; (5) be alert to implications of pre-announcement news; and (6) follow small stocks where the prospect of earnings surprises has not been fully incorporated into market prices. Brown (1997) provided a review and synthesis of research findings.

Table 86a indicates three positive and three negative earnings surprises, which is a one-to-one ratio. This ratio is a neutral signal of the market outlook. Again, a better estimate of the outlook may be obtained by reviewing these data for several time periods.

Earnings estimate changes (latest ratio of number of positive to negative changes), table 86b

Earnings estimates changes differ from earnings surprises. "Estimates" refer to consensus earnings forecasts for the current quarter, and "surprises" refer to actual earnings for the last quarter. Taken together, they give insight on the short-term progression of corporate earnings, by noting whether earnings are or are not coming in better or worse than expected.

Table 86b indicates that the ratio of negative (eight) to positive (four) earnings estimates changes is two to one. This ratio is a negative signal of the market outlook. This negative signal suggests that the next quarter's earnings surprises may be more negative than those in the last quarter.

Market outlook and overall economic and market outlook (table 81)

As discussed above, table 81 includes summary results of figures 12.12 through 12.14 and tables 83–6. The market indicators are generally negative: eight negative, one positive, and one neutral. Of the negative signals, the three P/E ratio and dividend yield indicators could be counted as one because they tend to generate consistent signals. Even so, six indicators are negative, one is positive, and one is neutral. The general consensus is a negative signal for the market outlook.

The consensus negative market outlook is suggested by the level of the market (very large P/E ratios and very low dividend yield), neutral/negative earnings progressions, negative advance/decline line, very small mutual fund cash ratio, and flagging investor confidence. The moving averages are strong.

Thus, based only on the negative *market* outlook summarized in table 81, Windsor II's buy decision should be implemented later. The timing depends on monthly reassessment of market indicators. Overall, the *combined* positive economic outlook and negative market outlook (table 81) provide a mixed signal of the overall outlook (so "helpful," but so typical). Again, the buy decision should be implemented later. The economy is strong and growing, but the stock market is technically weak, with the likelihood of increased volatility and downside risk, at least in the short term. So stay tuned to market indicators next month before buying Windsor II.

Economic and market outlook: validation

As noted, table 82 provides an expanded checklist of indicators to validate the table 80 and table 81 economic and market outlooks. These indicators should be assessed as yes or no, where yes/no is a positive/negative signal for either the economy or the market outlook. Table 82 also includes several contrarian indicators that, when at extreme values, signal the opposite outlook than suggested. That is, when investors are extremely optimistic or pessimistic, they are wrong. Thus, when these indicators are, for example, very optimistic, the correct signal is the opposite one of pessimism.

Also, as discussed above, table 87 provides another checklist for validating economic and market outlooks. Its buy side and sell side assessments may also be used to validate the table 80 and table 81 economic and market outlooks.

FINAL COMMENT

Thank you for accompanying me on this trip to Fundom. I would appreciate receiving your thoughts on fund issues at jhaslem@rhsmith.umd.edu. I hope you now realize there is much to know about mutual funds. I also hope you now have this knowledge and realize that proper mutual fund investing is not particularly difficult. Mutual fund investing can be pleasant and rewarding over time. The secret is not to be ruled by emotion and cognitive errors. This is not easy to do, but dedication to long-term investment horizons and concepts of behavioral finance have important lessons to guide us in this regard.

finis

ONLINE REFERENCES TO MUTUAL FUND AND RELATED INFORMATION (INCLUDING ILLUSTRATIONS)

bos.business.uab.edu [www.economagic.com] (wide range of economic and financial data, including Federal Reserve, Bureau of Labor Statistics, Department of Commerce, and commodity and stock price indices)

cbs.marketwatch.com (market commentary, data, and tools)

finance.yahoo.com (research information)

interactive.wsj.com (*Wall Street Journal*, including *Barron's* Online)

mfcafe.com (information for fund industry insiders)

moneycentral.com (company reports, analysis, and evaluation)

money.cnn.com (business and market news and analysis)

stats.bls.gov (Bureau of Labor Statistics; employment data)

quote.yahoo.com (breaking news)

www.armchairmillionaire.com (long-term investing)

www.barra.com (investment style measures)

www.barrons.com (single best site for market and economic data and indicators, including mutual fund liquid assets ratio)

www.bigcharts.com (customized indicator chart construction)

www.bloomberg.com (Treasury and international yield curves; earnings surprises; earnings momentum; projected five-year earnings growth; relative strength strategy; P/E ratios; and earnings per share variability)

www.bog.frb.fed.us (Federal Reserve Board Beige Book summary of regional economic outlooks with data and indicators)

www.bondpage.com (bond quotes and research tools)

www.bondresources.com (bond information and search tools)

www.bondsonline.com (yield curve; data, news, and articles)

www.briefing.com (market commentary and analysis)

www.brill.com (broad-based mutual fund site)

www.bulldog.com (rankings of analyst performance)

www.businesscycle.com ("future inflation gauge")

www.cboe.com (Chicago Board of Options Exchange; volatility index indicator)

www.clearstation.com (technical analysis and charting tools)

www.companysleuth.com (consolidated types of research information)

www.crc-conquest.org (Conference Board's consumer confidence index and composite indices of economic indicators, including interpretation)

www.directadvice.com (financial planning tools)

www.dismal.com (economic indicator charts and analysis)

www.earningswhispers.com (earnings surprises)

www.economic-charts.com (economic charts, including corporate net cash flow and industry capacity utilization)

www.economy.com (large source of economic and financial data)

www.edgar-online.com (guide to SEC's Edgar Web site of fund filings at www.sec.gov)

www.edgarscan.com (guide to SEC's Edgar Web site of fund filings at www.sec.gov)

www.efficientfrontier.com (research source for portfolio theory and asset allocation)

www.fairmark.com (investor tax planning)

www.financecenter.com (over 100 planning calculators)

www.financialengines.com (retirement planning tools and calculators)

www.finportfolio.com (customized Markowitz-type optimizer)

www.freeedgar.com (guide to SEC's Edgar Web site of fund filings at www.sec.gov)

www.ft.com (*Financial Times* global market news)

www.fundalarm.com (portfolio manager changes)

www.fundsinteractive.com (fund news and trends)

www.gainskeeper.com (portfolio tax calculators)

www.hoovers.com (large number of company reports and data)

www.hulbertdigest.com (fund newsletter performance)

www.ibcdata.com (fund and money market fund data)

www.icefi.com (Internet Closed End Funds Investor; data and services)

www.ici.org (Investment Company Institute; industry studies and developments, including mutual fund cash inflows/outflows; online investor resources)

www.idayoinvestor.com (fund portfolios)

www.indexfunds.com (index funds and ETFs)

www.indexfundsonline.com (index funds)

www.insiderscores.com (timeliness of insider trades)

www.investor.com (portfolio tracking tools and research information)

www.investorama.com (fund screens and directory of finance sites – 12,500 links)

www.investorbroadcast.com (current company announcements and archives)

www.investoreducation.org (clearing house of investor education sites)

www.investorsquare.com (screens for 9,500 funds)

www.ishares.com (Barclay's exchange traded funds)

www.lionshares.com (tracks stock institutional ownership)

www.marketedge.com (nine sentiment indicators and interpretation)

www.marketguage.com (advance/decline line and mutual fund cash ratio)

www.marketguide.com (earnings information from SEC filings)

www.marketocracy.com (measures performance of potential mutual fund portfolio managers)

www.marketscience.com (yield curve; interest rate forecasting; long-term market momentum oscillator: market volatility; market confidence ("animal spirits"); and risk index)

www.maxfunds.com (follows new and small funds)

mfcafe.com (broad fund industry information)

www.mfea.com (Mutual Fund Education Association; direct mail funds)

www.ml.com (Merrill Lynch research and analysis)

www.morningstar.com (single best site for mutual fund data, measures, and analysis; projected five-year earnings growth; also ETFs)

www.multex.com (company research and reports, including earnings estimate revisions, earnings momentum, projected earnings growth rates, P/C ratios, relative strength strategy, P/E ratios, and earnings per share variability)

www.nasd.com (National Association of Securities Dealers; investor education site)

www.oid.com (*Outstanding Investor Digest* site)

www.outercurvefinance.com (proprietary technical analysis tools)

www.personalfund.com (calculates fund loads, fees, and trading costs)

www.personalwealth.com (Standard & Poor's fund news and recommendations)

www.prophetfinance.com (chart making tools and technical analysis)

www.quicken.com (fundamental analysis and evaluation; moving averages and cumulative daily breadth; personal finance software)

www.quickreilly.stkwtch.com (psychological indicators and index moving averages)

www.quote.com (screens for 7,500 funds)

www.russell.com (Frank Russell Company information on asset allocation and performance)

www.schwab.com (fund supermarket)

www.sec.com (SEC Edgar site with regulatory actions, investor information, litigation, fund filings, interactive tools)

www.sheldonjacobs.com (no-load funds and portfolios)

www.smartmoney.com (interactive fund tools)

www.socialfunds.com (socially responsible funds)

www.starmine.com (ranks analyst performance)

www.stls.frb.org (Federal Reserve Bank of St. Louis *National Economic Trends* and indicators)

www.stocktrader.com (especially Treasury yield curve)

www.10kwizard.com (guide to SEC's Edgar Web site of fund filings at www.sec.gov)

www.thestreet.com (market commentary, data, and tools)

www.thewhispernumber.com (earnings surprises)

www.thomsoninvest.net/FirstCall (earnings surprises; earnings estimate revisions; earnings momentum)

www.traders.com (understanding and use of technical analysis for market prediction)

www.treasurydirect.gov (no-fee direct purchase of Treasury securities)

www.validea.com (tracks analyst recommendations)

www.valueengine.com (market valuation indicator)

www.wallstreetcity.com (company screens using eighty criteria)

www.whispernumbers.com (earnings surprises)

www.worldlyinvestor.com (tracks international companies and economies)

www.yardeni.com (economic analysis, strategy, and forecasts)

www.zacks.com (analysts reports and investor information)

Note: *Barron's* rates financial Web sites annually. Gerlach (2000) reviews twelve useful sites. Pettit (2000) and Brill et al. (2000) review investor Web sites. The Investment Company Institute (2000) lists government, association, and reference sites for investors (www.ici.org).

TABLES

Table 1 Investment Company Act of 1940 and Investment Advisors Act of 1940: summary

Investment Company Act of 1940
The Public Utility Holding Company Act of 1935 required Congress to direct the SEC to study the activities of investment companies and investment advisors. The study results were sent to Congress in a series of reports filed in 1938, 1939, and 1940, causing the creation of the Investment Company Act of 1940 and the Investment Advisors Act of 1940. The legislation was supported by both the Commission and the industry.

Activities of companies engaged primarily in investing, reinvesting, and trading in securities, and whose own securities are offered to the investing public, are subject to certain statutory prohibitions and to Commission regulation under this act. Also, public offerings of investment company securities must be registered under the Securities Act of 1933.

Investors must understand, however, that the Commission does not supervise the investment activities of these companies and that regulation by the Commission does not imply safety of investment.

In addition to the registration requirement for such companies, the law requires that they disclose their financial condition and investment policies to provide investors complete information about their activities. This act also:

- prohibits such companies from substantially changing the nature of their business or investment policies without stockholder approval;
- bars persons guilty of securities fraud from serving as officers and directors;
- prevents underwriters, investment bankers, or brokers from constituting more than a minority of the directors of such companies;
- requires that management contracts and any material changes be submitted to securityholders for their approval;
- prohibits transactions between such companies and their directors, officers, or affiliated companies or persons, except when approved by the SEC;
- forbids such companies to issue senior securities except under specified conditions and upon specified terms; and
- prohibits pyramiding of such companies and cross-ownership of their securities.

Other provisions of this act involve advisory fees, advisors' fiduciary duties, sales and repurchases of securities issued by investment companies, exchange offers, and other activities of investment companies, including special provisions for periodic payment plans and face-amount certificate companies.

Table 1 (*continued*)

Investment Advisors Act of 1940

This law regulates the activities of investment advisors, including advisors to investment companies, private money managers, and most financial planners. With certain exceptions, it requires persons or firms that are compensated for providing advice about investing in securities to register with the SEC and conform to statutory requirements designed to protect their clients.

The most significant of the statutory provisions is the Act's broad prohibition against fraudulent conduct, which has been interpreted by the US Supreme Court as prohibiting violation of the fiduciary duties of an investment advisor to its clients. Among other things, this provision requires an advisor to disclose to clients material facts concerning any conflict of interest the advisor may have with the client, to refrain from taking advantage of the position of trust the advisor occupies without the client's informed consent, and to comply with specific prohibitions the SEC has adopted by rule designed to prevent fraudulent conduct.

The Act requires investment advisors registered with the SEC to maintain books and records according to SEC rules. The agency conducts periodic examinations of investment advisors during which these books and records are reviewed to determine whether the advisor is in compliance with the act as well as the other federal securities laws.

The SEC has the authority under the act to deny, suspend, or revoke investment advisor registration based on a violation by the advisor of the Act or of other laws prohibiting fraud, theft, or other kinds of financial misconduct. In addition, the SEC may impose various forms of sanctions on an investment advisor, including substantial fines, and it may issue a cease and desist order or seek an injunction in federal court prohibiting further violation of the law. The SEC may also recommend criminal prosecution by the US Department of Justice for violation of the Act.

Source: Reprinted with permission from *The Work of the SEC* (SEC, Washington, DC), 1998 (www.sec.gov).

Table 2 Information, please: the prospectus versus the statement of additional information

Area	Prospectus	Statement of additional information
Investment strategy	Describes a fund's basic strategy and risks. States which policies can be altered without shareholder approval	Describes any and all investment strategies the fund could ever use, however unlikely, and their risks
Fees	Lists fund costs, including sales charges, management fees, and 12b-1 fees	Shows how management fees are calculated and how 12b-1 fees are spent. Lists brokerage fees
Performance	Presents three-, five-, and ten-year average annual returns and year-by-year returns over the past decade	Describes how performance and yield numbers are calculated
Management	Discloses a fund's investment advisor and the basis for its compensation. Names the fund's portfolio manager	Lists a fund's directors along with their compensation

Source: Reprinted with permission from Richard Ronald, What is . . . the SAI?, *Morningstar FundInvestor*, December 1998, p. 11.

Table 3 Massachusetts Investors' Trust: the first portfolio, March 1924

Shares	Company	Cost
	Bank and insurance	
3	Boston Insurance	682¼
5	Springfield Fire & Marine Insurance	325
	Industrial and miscellaneous	
10	American Radiator	102⅛
5	American Tobacco	145¼
10	Bates Manufacturing	200
10	Eastman Kodak of New Jersey	107⅝
5	Farr Alpaca	172¾
5	General Electric	232¼
50	General Motors	13¼
10	Island Creek Coal	102½
10	Lowell Bleachery	120
10	Nash Motors	109⅝
5	National Lead	145⅝
10	Naumkeag Steam Cotton	176¼
20	Punta Alegre Sugar	50¾
20	Standard Oil of Indiana	57
20	Standard Oil of New York	40¼
20	Texas	38⅞
5	United Fruit	195¼
10	US Steel	97
15	West Point Manufacturing	135
	Railroad and equipment	
5	American Car & Foundry	160¼
15	American Locomotive	73½
10	Atlantic Coast Line Railroad	120⅝
10	Atchison Topeka & Santa Fe Railway	104
10	Baldwin Locomotive	112⅜
20	Baltimore & Ohio Railroad	57¼
5	Canadian Pacific Railway	147⅜
10	Illinois Central Railroad	106⅜
10	New York Central Railroad	104¾
20	Northern Pacific Railway	56
10	Pullman Car	125¼
10	Southern Pacific	93⅝
20	Southern Railway	60¾
10	Union Pacific Railroad	135
	Public utilities	
5	American Gas & Electric	70½
5	American Power & Light	261
10	American Telephone & Telegraph	121¼
10	Brooklyn Edison	111⅜
15	Consolidated Gas of New York	68¼
10	Edison Electric of Boston	175
15	Massachusetts Gas Companies	71½
40	North American	26¾
10	Southern California Edison	101¼
10	Western Union Telegraph	109⅝

Source: Portfolio reprinted with permission from *Massachusetts Investors Trust, Organized March 1924*, MFS, Boston, MA, 1995.

Table 4 Top fifty stock funds of the bull market, 1998

Fund (symbol)	Category	% annualized gain since Aug. 1, 1982	Value of $1,000 investment ($)
1 Fidelity Select Health Care (FSPHX)	SH	23.8	29,975
2 Spectra (SPECX)	LG	22.7	25,957
3 Fidelity Select Financial Services (FIDSX)	SF	22.6	25,514
4 Fidelity Magellan (FMAGX)	LB	22.4	25,045
5 CGM Capital Development (LOMCX)	MB	22.4	24,983
6 Fidelity Destiny I (FDESX)	LV	22.3	24,748
7 Davis NY Venture A (NYVTX)	LV	21.8	23,085
8 Alliance Technology A (ALTFX)	ST	21.6	22,640
9 Amer. Cent.–Twentieth Century Ultra (TWCUX)	LG	21.5	22,181
10 Sequoia (SEQUX)	LV	21.4	21,890
11 Guardian Park Avenue A (GPAFX)	LB	21.2	21,304
12 Federated Capital App. A (FEDEX)	LB	21.1	20,997
13 AIM Constellation A (CSTGX)	MG	20.9	20,655
14 Fidelity Contrafund (FCNTX)	LB	20.7	19,965
15 Putnam Voyager A (PVOYX)	MG	20.6	19,731
16 IDS New Dimensions A (INNDX)	LG	20.5	19,499
17 AIM Weingarten A (WEINX)	LB	20.1	18,394
18 United Income A (UNCMX)	LB	20.1	18,375
19 SIFE Trust A-I (SIFEX)	SF	20.0	18,246
20 Enterprise Growth A (ENGRX)	LG	20.0	18,139
21 FPA Capital (FPPTX)	MV	19.8	17,729
22 Century Shares (CENSX)	SF	19.7	17,429
23 Washington Mutual Investors (AWSHX)	LV	19.6	17,184
24 Selected American (SLASX)	LV	19.5	17,020
25 Vanguard Index 500 (VFINX)	LB	19.5	16,992
26 Dodge & Cox Stock (DODGX)	LV	19.4	16,867
27 MAP-Equity (MUBFX)	MB	19.3	16,666
28 Fundamental Investors (ANCFX)	LV	19.3	16,563
29 Columbia Growth (CLMBX)	LG	19.2	16,441
30 Acorn (ACRNX)	SB	19.1	16,174
31 Security Equity A (SECEX)	LB	19.1	16,145
32 Putnam Vista A (PVISX)	MG	19.1	16,120
33 Vanguard US Growth (VWUSX)	LG	19.0	16,004
34 Salomon Bros. Opportunity (SAOPX)	LV	19.0	15,986
35 Safeco Equity No Load (SAFQX)	LB	19.0	15,893
36 Nicholas (NICSX)	MB	19.0	15,877
37 Vanguard/Windsor (VWNDX)	LV	18.9	15,806
38 Janus (JANSX)	LB	18.9	15,795
39 Nationwide D (MUIFX)	LB	18.9	15,769
40 Stein Roe Special (SRSPX)	MB	18.9	15,724
41 IDS Growth A (INIDX)	LG	18.9	15,713
42 MFS Massachusetts Inv. A (MITTX)	LB	18.9	15,657
43 Lexington Corporate Leaders (LEXCX)	LV	18.8	15,600
44 Mutual Qualified Z (MQIFX)	MV	18.8	15,492
45 Founders Growth (FRGRX)	LG	18.7	15,408
46 Pioneer Growth A (MOMGX)	LG	18.7	15,334
47 Federated Stock (FSTKX)	LV	18.7	15,311
48 Investment Co. of America (AIVSX)	LB	18.7	15,286
49 Fidelity (FFIDX)	LB	18.6	15,192
50 Oppenheimer Quest Value A (QFVFX)	LV	18.6	15,181
Average US diversified stock funds	–	15.9	–

Source: "Midyear Investment Report '98": the Tables, *Money*, August 1998, pp. 91ff., reprinted by special permission, copyright © 1998 Time Inc.

Table 5   Obligations of investment company directors under federal statutes

---

Investment Company Act of 1940

A Portfolio management
  1 Evaluation of portfolio performance
  2 Annual review and approval of investment advisory contract and subadvisory contracts

B Pricing of shares and valuation and liquidity of portfolio securities
  1 Determine schedule for pricing share net asset value
  2 Valuation of securities – market value versus "fair value"
  3 Guidelines for investment in illiquid securities

C Other portfolio management issues
  1 Compliance with investment policies and restrictions – shareholder approval requirements and "watchdog" role
  2 Specific areas of oversight – repurchase agreements, securities loans, securities purchases
  3 Derivative investments – policies, procedures, and risks

D Distribution of fund shares
  1 Selection of principal underwriter
  2 Rule 12b-1 plans – approval of use of assets for distribution
  3 Multiple classes of shares – plan approval

E Auditing issues
  1 Selection of independent auditor
  2 Guidelines for audit committee, if any

F Transactions involving mutual fund affiliates
  1 Purchases of affiliate underwritings
  2 Transactions with affiliated mutual funds or advisory clients
  3 Use of affiliated broker-dealers
  4 Joint transactions with affiliates, including fidelity bonds and liability insurance
  5 Performance review of service providers, including affiliates

G Custody of mutual fund assets
  1 Use of securities depositories
  2 Use of foreign custodians

H Change of control issues
  1 Change in control of investment advisor
  2 Mutual fund mergers
  3 Other terminations of investment advisory contract

I Money market fund issues
  1 Valuation of shares – "amortized cost" and "penny rounding" methods
  2 Minimum credit risk in portfolio securities
  3 Unrated securities in portfolio
  4 Security rating downgrades
  5 Orderly disposition of securities

Table 5 (*continued*)

J Other issues
    1 Execution of portfolio transactions
    2 Compliance with code of ethics
    3 SEC examination results
    4 Compliance with SEC exemptive orders

Securities Act of 1933 and Securities and Exchange Act of 1934
A Responsible for material facts in public documents
    1 Prospectus and SEC registration statements
    2 Proxy statement and reports to shareholders

Source: Adapted from *Introductory Guide for Investment Company Directors*, Investment Company Institute, Washington, DC, September 1995.

Table 6 Diversification constraints: type and degree

Type of constraint	Degree of diversification with examples	
	Smaller	**Larger**
Portfolio investment objective	Growth (one objective)	Growth and income (multiple objectives)
Method of security analysis (fundamental/technical)	Fundamental	Fundamental and technical
Method of portfolio management (active/passive)	Active management	Active and passive management
Morningstar investment style: Value/blend/growth Large/mid/small-cap.	Value Large cap.	Blend (value and growth) Representative market cap.
Cash asset allocation	Small cash ratio	Large cash ratio
Geographic concentration	Domestic	Global
Asset allocation	Stock allocation	Stock and bond allocation
Market liquidity	Large cap. size market	Representative cap. size market
Return distribution	Capital gains	Dividends and capital gains
Industry sector concentration	Few industry sectors	Diverse industry sectors
Security concentration	Few securities holdings	Many securities holdings
Quality concentration (low-quality/high-quality)	High or low-quality bonds High or low-quality stocks	Representative quality bonds Representative quality stocks

Table 7 Mutual fund investment objectives

Stock funds

Aggressive growth funds seek maximum capital growth; current income is not a significant factor. These funds invest in stocks out of the mainstream, such as new companies, companies fallen on hard times, or industries temporarily out of favor. They may use investment techniques involving greater than average risk.

Growth funds seek capital growth; dividend income is not a significant factor. They invest in the common stock of well established companies.

Growth and income funds seek to combine long-term capital growth and current income. These funds invest in the common stock of companies whose share value has increased and that have displayed a solid record of paying dividends.

Precious metals/gold funds seek capital growth. Their portfolios are invested primarily in securities associated with gold and other precious metals.

International funds seek growth in the value of their investments. Their portfolios are invested primarily in stocks of companies located outside the United States

Global equity funds seek growth in the value of their investments. They invest in stocks traded worldwide, including those in the United States

Income-equity funds seek a high level of income by investing primarily in stocks of companies with good dividend-paying records.

Bond and income funds

Flexible portfolio funds allow their money managers to anticipate or respond to changing market conditions by investing in stocks *or* bonds *or* money market instruments, depending on economic changes.

Balanced funds generally seek to conserve investors' principal, pay current income, and achieve long-term growth of principal and income. Their portfolios are a mix of bonds, preferred stocks, and common stocks.

Income-mixed funds seek a high level of income. These funds invest in income-producing securities, including stocks and bonds.

Income-bond funds seek a high level of current income. These funds invest in a mix of corporate and government bonds.

US government income funds seek current income. They invest in a variety of government securities, including US Treasury bonds, federally guaranteed mortgage-backed securities, and other government notes.

GNMA (Ginnie Mae) funds seek a high level of income. The majority of their portfolios is invested in mortgage securities backed by the Government National Mortgage Association (GNMA).

Global bond funds seek a high level of income. These funds invest in debt securities of companies and countries worldwide, including those in the United States

Corporate bond funds seek a high level of income. The majority of their portfolios is invested in corporate bonds, with the balance in US Treasury bonds or bonds issued by a federal agency.

High-yield bond funds seek a very high yield, but carry a greater degree of risk than corporate bond funds. The majority of their portfolios is invested in lower-rated corporate bonds.

National municipal bond funds – long-term seek income that is not taxed by the federal government. They invest in bonds issued by states and municipalities to finance schools, highways, hospitals, bridges, and other municipal works.

State municipal bond funds – long-term seek income that is exempt from both federal tax and state tax for residents of that state. They invest in bonds issued by a single state.

Money market funds

Taxable money market funds seek to maintain a stable net asset value. These funds invest in the short-term, high-grade securities sold in the money market, such as US Treasury bills, certificates of deposit of large banks, and commercial paper. The average maturity of their portfolios is limited to ninety days or less.

Tax-exempt money market funds – national seek income that is not taxed by the federal government with minimum risk. They invest in municipal securities with relatively short maturities.

Tax-exempt money market funds – state seek income that is exempt from federal tax and state tax for residents of that state. They invest in municipal securities with relatively short maturities issued by a single state.

Source: *Mutual Fund Fact Book*, 37th edn, Investment Company Institute, Washington, DC, 1997, pp. 24–5. Reprinted with permission.

Table 8(a)   Mutual fund loads and fees: Vanguard examples

Loads/fees	Index Emerging Markets	500 Index	US Growth	Windsor II
Sales load on purchases (maximum)	None	None	None	None
Sales load on reinvested dividends	None	None	None	None
Redemption fee	1.00%	None	None	None
Contingent deferred sales charge	None	None	None	None
Exchange fee	None	None	None	None
12b-1 fee	None	None	None	None
Account maintenance fee	$10.00	$2.50[a]	None	None
Transaction charge on purchase	1.00%	None	None	None

[a]   Quarterly.

Source: *Prospectus*, Vanguard International Index Portfolio, April 23, 1998; *Prospectus*, Vanguard Index Trust, April 20, 1998; *Prospectus*, Vanguard US Growth Portfolio, December 12, 1997; *Prospectus*, Vanguard Windsor II, February 26, 1999.

Table 8(b)   Mutual fund loads and fees: Fidelity examples

Loads/fees	Select Electronics	Low-priced Stock	Magellan	Growth and Income
Sales load on purchases[a]	3.00%	3.00%	3.00%	None
Sales load on reinvested dividends	None	None	None	None
Redemption fee	$7.50[a]	1.50%[b]	None	None
Contingent deferred sales charge	None	None	None	None
Exchange fee	$7.50	None	None	None
12b-1 fee	None	None	None	None
Account maintenance fee	$12.00	$12.00	$12.00	$12.00
Transaction charge on purchase	None	None	None	None

[a]   Maximum.
[b]   Ninety days.

Source: *Prospectus*, Fidelity Select Portfolio, April 28, 1998; *Prospectus*, Fidelity Low-priced Stock Fund, September 26, 1997; *Prospectus*, Fidelity Magellan Fund, May 22, 1998; *Prospectus*, Fidelity Growth and Income Portfolio, September 25, 1997.

Table 8(c)   Mutual fund loads and fees: miscellaneous examples

Loads/fees	Janus Worldwide	Kaufmann Fund
Sales load on purchases[a]	None	None
Sales load on reinvested dividends	None	None
Redemption fee	$8.00[b]	0.20%
Contingent deferred sales charge	None	None
Exchange fee	None	None
12b-1 fee	None	0.29%
Account maintenance fee	None	None
Transaction charge on purchase	None	None

[a]   Maximum.
[b]   Wire fee.

Source: *Prospectus*, Janus Equity Funds, February 17, 1998; *Prospectus*, Kaufman Fund, May 1, 1998.

Table 9(a)   Mutual fund multiple share class loads and fees: Franklin Mutual Beacon

Loads/fees	Class		
	Z[a]	I	II
Sales load on purchases[b]	None	5.75%	1.99%
Sales load on reinvested dividends	None	None	None
Redemption fee	None	None	0.99%
Contingent deferred sales charge	None	None	None
Exchange fee	None	None	None
12b-1 fee	None	0.35%	1.00%
Account maintenance fee	None	None	None
Transaction charge on purchase	None	None	None

[a]   Closed to new retail investors.

[b]   Maximum.

Source: *Prospectus*, Franklin Mutual Series Fund, Class Z, May 1, 1998; Class I and Class II, May 1, 1998.

Table 9(b)   Mutual fund multiple share class loads and fees: Fidelity Advisor Equity Growth

Loads/fees	Class			
	A	T	B	C
Sales load on purchases (maximum)	5.75%	3.50%	None	None
Sales load on reinvested dividends	None	None	None	None
Redemption fee	None	None	None	1.00%
Contingent deferred sales charge	None	None	5.00%	None
Exchange fee	None	None	None	None
12b-1 fee	0.25%	0.50%	1.00%	1.00%
Account maintenance fee	None	None	None	None
Transaction charge on purchase	None	None	None	None

Source: *Prospectus*, Fidelity Advisor Equity Growth Fund, Class A, Class T, Class B and Class C, February 28, 1998.

Table 10 Load performance calculator

How to use

The default $1 Initial Investment Amount and 10% Assumed Annual Return are good proxies for assessing the impact of sales loads and fees. However, you can change them to whatever values you wish. Next, complete the table of loads for the different share classes you are evaluating by using the "Tab" key to go from box to box. (We have labeled the classes A, B, C and D for general descriptive purposes only.) A fund's load schedule is presented in the "Fee Table" near the front of its prospectus. Note that most so-called Redemption Fees are really Contingent Deferred Sales Charges levied at the time of redemption on the initial purchase or sale amount, whichever is less. They generally decline over time, and we have allowed for multiple-year entries. When you have filled in the relevant boxes, click on the "Calculate" button below the table.

Initial Investment Amount: $ [1]   Assumed Annual Return: [10] %

Load Calculator	Class A	Class B	Class C	Class D
Maximum Front Load	[ ]%	[ ]%	[ ]%	[ ]%
Maximum Redemption Fee	[ ]%	[ ]%	[ ]%	[ ]%
Annual 12b-1 Fee	[ ]%	[ ]%	[ ]%	[ ]%
Contingent Deferred Charge (Year 1)	[ ]%	[ ]%	[ ]%	[ ]%
Contingent Deferred Charge (Year 2)	[ ]%	[ ]%	[ ]%	[ ]%
Contingent Deferred Charge (Year 3)	[ ]%	[ ]%	[ ]%	[ ]%
Contingent Deferred Charge (Year 4)	[ ]%	[ ]%	[ ]%	[ ]%
Contingent Deferred Charge (Year 5)	[ ]%	[ ]%	[ ]%	[ ]%
Contingent Deferred Charge (Year 6)	[ ]%	[ ]%	[ ]%	[ ]%
Contingent Deferred Charge (Year 7)	[ ]%	[ ]%	[ ]%	[ ]%
Contingent Deferred Charge (Year 8)	[ ]%	[ ]%	[ ]%	[ ]%
Contingent Deferred Charge (Year 9)	[ ]%	[ ]%	[ ]%	[ ]%
Contingent Deferred Charge (Year 10)	[ ]%	[ ]%	[ ]%	[ ]%

Source: Reprinted with permission from *Mutual Funds OnLine* (www.mfmag.com), October 1998.

Table 11 Model mutual fund shareholder services: checklist

(1) Check desired services provided and (2) list desired services not provided:

Types of accounts
  Individual
  TOD
  Joint tenancy
  UGMA/UTMA
  UTOD
  Education IRA custodian
  Trust
  Corporate
  Partnership
  Non-profit organizations
  Executor and administrator
  Conservator and guardian
  Attorney-in-fact

Retirement
  IRA custodian
  Rollover IRA custodian
  Roth IRA custodian
  SEP-IRA custodian
  SIMPLE IRA custodian
  Keogh profit-sharing and/or money purchase trustee
  403(b) Tax-deferred annuity plan
  401(k) Savings and investment plan
  457 Deferred compensation plan

Distribution options
  Reinvestment of dividends and/or capital gains
  Exchange of dividends and/or capital gains
  Dividends and capital gains in cash
  Dividends in cash
  Capital gains in cash

Purchase shares
  Mail purchase by personal check or bank checks
  Mail exchange
  Telephone exchange (excluding retirement accounts)
  Wire transfer from bank
  Automatic services:
    Direct deposit
    Exchange
    Purchase from bank account

Table 11   (*continued*)

Redeem and exchange shares
   Mail redemption and exchange
   Telephone redemption and exchange
   Check-writing redemption on fund account
   Wire transfer and electronic transfer redemption to bank
   Automatic services:
      Redemption to bank
      Exchange
      Distributions to bank: dividends and/or capital gains

Shareholder mailings
   Account statements
   Transaction confirmations
   Tax statements for distributions and redemptions
   Tax statements for retirement distributions
   Taxable income statement for redemptions (average cost)
   Prospectus
   Statement of additional information
   Annual and semi-annual financial reports
   Educational publications
   Fund information publications

Other shareholder services
   Investor centers:
      All services and information
   Automated telephone services:
      Access accounts: balances and history
      Transactions: exchanges and redemptions
      Fund performance information
      Request publications

Online services
   Account and investing services:
      Account balances
      Open account
      Purchase, exchange, and redemption of shares
      Change account name and address
      Add and change account options:
         Dividend distribution options
         Automatic services
         Check writing on account
      Account statements
      Proxy voting
   Brokerage services (see below)

Table 11   (*continued*)

Information services:
  Investor services
  Retirement planning and services
  Education planning
  Fund and market news
  Fund performance
  Shareholder reports
  Investor education
  Investor planning tools
  Portfolio tracking and research
Inquiries

Brokerage services: automated, telephone, and online
  Securities transactions
  Fund family transactions
  Other fund transactions

Summary assessment of fund service quantity and quality
Service quantity:
  A Number of desired services provided (checked): all (based on Vanguard Windsor II).
  B Number of desired services not provided: zero (based on Vanguard Windsor II).
  C Number of desired services provided divided by the total number of desired services (A/A+B):
     100% (based on Vanguard Windsor II).

Assessment of service quantity
  Excellent: ✕ (Vanguard Windsor II).
  Acceptable:
  Unacceptable:

Assessment of service quality
  Ranking in major survey: Excellent (Vanguard Windsor II).

Overall service assessment
  Excellent: ✕ (Vanguard Windsor II).
  Acceptable:
  Unacceptable:

Table 12 Who offers what: a checklist of services

Service	AIM	Alliance	American Funds	American Century	American Express/IDS	Colonial	Dean Witter	Dreyfus	Evergreen Keystone	Federated	Fidelity	Franklin Templeton	Janus	John Hancock	Kemper
Checking from money markets	Yes	Yes	Yes	Yes	Yes	Yes	Yes	Yes	Yes	Yes	Yes	Yes	Yes	Yes	Yes
Checking from other funds	No	Yes	No	Yes	No	Yes[b]	No	Yes[b]	No	Yes	Yes[b]	No	No	Yes[b]	No
Minimum dollar amount for single check	250	100	250	100	2,000	500	500	500	250	1	0/1,000[g]	100	250	100	500
Telephone redemption	Yes	Yes	Yes	Yes	Yes	Yes	Yes[b]	Yes	Yes	Yes	Yes	Yes[e]	Yes	Yes	Yes
Telephone switching	Yes	Yes	Yes	Yes	Yes	Yes	Yes	Yes	Yes	Yes	Yes	Yes	Yes	Yes	Yes
Address changes over phone	Yes	Yes	Yes	Yes	Yes	Yes	Yes	Yes	Yes	No	Yes	Yes	Yes	Yes	Yes
Prices by Touch-Tone	Yes	Yes	Yes	Yes	Yes	Yes	Yes	Yes	Yes	Yes	Yes	Yes	Yes	Yes	Yes
Account info by Touch-Tone	Yes	Yes	Yes	Yes	Yes	Yes	Yes	Yes	Yes	Yes	Yes	Yes	Yes	Yes	Yes
Prices by computer	Yes	Yes	Yes	Yes	Yes	No	No	Yes	No	Yes	Yes	Yes	Yes	Yes	Yes
Account info by computer	Yes	No	Yes	Yes	No	No	No	No	No	No	Yes	Yes[e]	Yes	No	No[c]
24-hour access to account information	Yes	Yes		Yes	Yes	Yes	Yes	Yes	Yes	Yes[c]	Yes	Yes[e]	Yes	Yes	Yes
Live rep hours (eastern time):															
Mon.–Fri.	830a–630p	830a–6p	8a–8p	8a–8p	9a–7p	8a–8p	8a–8p	24 hrs	8a–6p	8a–8p	24 hrs	830a–11p	8a–10p	8a–8p	8a–7p
Sat.	None	None	None	None	None	None	None	24 hrs	None	None	24 hrs	930a–530p	10a–7p	None	9a–4p
Sun.	None	None	None	None	None	None	None	24 hrs	None	None	24 hrs	None	None	None	None
Automatic withdrawal	Yes	Yes	Yes	Yes	Yes	Yes	Yes	Yes	No	Yes	Yes	Yes	Yes	Yes	Yes
Free debit card	No	No	No	No	No	No	Yes[c]	Yes	No	No	Yes[a]	No	No	No	No
Wrap accounts	Yes	Yes	No	No	Yes	No	Yes[d]	Yes	No	No	Yes	Yes	No	Yes	Yes[d]
Margin loans	No	No	No	No	No	No	No	Yes	No	No	Yes	No	No	No	No
Funds sold via MF supermarket	No	No	No	Yes	No	Yes	Yes	Yes	Yes	Yes	Yes	Yes	No	No	Yes
Sells other families' funds	No	Yes	No	No	Yes	No	No	Yes	No	No	Yes	No	No	No	No
Can buy stocks or bonds	No	No	No	No	No	No	Yes	Yes	No	No	Yes	Yes[f]	No	No	No
Capital gains info sent before year end	No	Yes	No	No	Yes	No	No	No	Yes	No	No	Yes	No	No	No
Personal financial advisor for fee	No	No	No	No	Yes	No	No	Yes	No	No	Yes	Yes[f]	No	No	No
Walk-in centers (number if yes)	No	No	No	4	2,000	No	361	27	No	No	82	3	3	No	1
Single statement for all holdings	Yes	Yes	Yes	No	Yes	Yes[g]	Yes	Yes	Yes	Yes	Yes	No	Yes[e]	No	Yes
Investor return reported on statement	Yes	No	No	No	No	No	Yes	No	No	Yes	No	No	No	No	Yes
Provide cost basis for sales	Yes	No	Yes	No	Yes	Yes	Yes	No	No	Yes	Yes	Yes	Yes	Yes	Yes
800 number for information	347–4246	227–4618	421–4120	345–2021	437–3133	345–6611	869–3863	645–6561	690–1593	341–7400	544–8888	342–5236	525–8983	225–5291	621–1048
Web address (http://www._.com)	aimfunds	alliance capital	american funds	american century	american express	lib	deanwitter	dreyfus	evergreen funds	federated investors	fidelity .com	franklin-templeton[c]	janusfunds	j. hancock	kemper

Service	Lord Abbett	Merrill Lynch	MFS	Oppenheimer	Pimco	Pioneer	Prudential	Putnam	Scudder	Smith Barney	T. Rowe Price	USAA	Vanguard	Van Kampen	Waddell & Reed
Checking from money markets	Yes	Yes	Yes	Yes	No	Yes	Yes	Yes	Yes	Yes	Yes	Yes	Yes	Yes	Yes
Checking from other funds	No	No	Yes[b]	Yes[b]	No	Yes[b]	No	No	Yes	No	Yes	No	Yes[b]	Yes	No
Minimum dollar amount for single check	500	0	500	100	NA	500	500	500	100	NA	500	250	250	100	250
Telephone redemption	Yes	No	Yes	Yes	Yes	Yes	Yes	Yes[e]	Yes	Yes	Yes	Yes	Yes	Yes	No
Telephone switching	Yes	No	Yes	Yes	Yes[b]	Yes	Yes	Yes	Yes	Yes	Yes	Yes	Yes	Yes	No
Address changes over phone	Yes	No	Yes	Yes	Yes[b]	Yes	Yes	Yes	Yes	No	Yes	Yes	Yes	Yes	No
Prices by Touch-Tone	Yes	No	Yes	Yes	Yes	Yes	Yes	No	Yes	Yes	Yes	Yes	Yes	Yes	No
Account info by Touch-Tone	Yes	Yes	Yes	No	Yes	No	Yes	Yes[e]	Yes	Yes	Yes	Yes	Yes	Yes	No
Prices by computer	Yes	Yes	No	No	No	No	Yes	Yes[e]	Yes	Yes	Yes	Yes	Yes	Yes	Yes
Account info by computer	No	Yes	No	No	No	No	Yes	Yes[e]	Yes	Yes	Yes	Yes	Yes	Yes	No
24-hour access to account information	Yes	Yes	Yes	No	No	Yes	Yes	No	Yes	Yes	Yes	Yes	Yes	Yes	No
Live rep hours (eastern time):															
Mon.–Fri.	830a–800p	9a–5p	8a–8p	830a–9p	830a–8p	8a–9p	24 hrs	830a–8p	730a–1130p	9a–5p	8a–10p	9a–9p	8a–9p	8a–8p	9a–530p
Sat.	None	None	None	10a–2p	None	None	24 hrs	9a–5p	9a–6p	None	830a–5p	930a–6p	9a–4p	None	None
Sun.	None	None	None	None	None	None	24 hrs	None	9a–6p	None	830a–5p	None	None	None	None
Automatic withdrawal	Yes	Yes	Yes	Yes	Yes	Yes	Yes	Yes	Yes	Yes	Yes	Yes	Yes	Yes	Yes
Free debit card	No	Yes	No	No	No	No	Yes	No	Yes	Yes	No	Yes	No	No	No
Wrap accounts	Yes	Yes	No	Yes[c]	Yes[c]	No	Yes	Yes[c]	No	Yes	Yes	Yes	Yes[c]	No	No
Margin loans	No	Yes	No	No	No	No	Yes	No	Yes	Yes	No	Yes	No	No	No
Funds sold via MF supermarket	Yes	No	Yes	No	Yes	No	Yes	No	Yes	Yes	Yes	No	Yes	No	No
Sells other families' funds	No	Yes	No	No	No	No	Yes	No	Yes	Yes	No	Yes	No	No	Yes
Can buy stocks or bonds	No	Yes	No	No	No	No	Yes	Yes[f]	Yes	Yes	Yes	Yes[g]	Yes	No	No
Capital gains info sent before year end	No	No	No	No	No	No	Yes	Yes	Yes	Yes	Yes	No	Yes	No	Yes
Personal financial advisor for fee	No	Yes	No	No	Yes[b]	No	Yes	Yes[f]	Yes	No	Yes	No	Yes	No	No
Walk-in centers (number if yes)	No	670	No	1	No	No	300	No	5	No	5	No	3	No	120
Single statement for all holdings	Yes	Yes	Yes	Yes	Yes	Yes	Yes	Yes	Yes	Yes	Yes	Yes	Yes	Yes	Yes
Investor return reported on statement	No	Yes	No	No	No	No	Yes	Yes	No	Yes	Yes	No	No	Yes	No
Provide cost basis for sales	Yes	Yes	Yes	Yes	Yes	Yes	Yes	Yes	Yes	Yes	Yes	Yes	Yes	Yes	Yes
800 number for information	821-5129	637-3863	225-2606	525-7048	426-0107	225-6292	225-1852	225-1581	225-2470	451-2010	225-5132	531-8181	523-1154	341-2911	366-5465
Web address (http://www. – .com)	lordabbett	ml	mfs	oppenheimer funds	none	none	prusec	putnaminv	funds. scudder	smith barney	troweprice	none	vanguard	vkac	waddell

[a] Through brokerage account.
[b] On some funds.
[c] Only money-market funds.
[d] Through broker or dealer.
[e] Service to be added in 1997.
[f] $1 million in assets required.
[g] Depends on fund.

Source: William P. Barrett, Fund Families: Best to Worst, *Worth*, May 1997, pp. 76ff, reprinted with permission of *Worth* magazine, May 1997.

Table 13 Portfolio manager background: checklist

Background[a]	Encircle responses: Excellent	Acceptable	Unacceptable
Education			
College degree		X[b]	X
MBA		X	
CFA		X	
MBA and CFA	⊗		
Previous investment experience			
0–5 years[c]			X
5–10 years[c]		X	
10+ years	⊗		
Current tenure as portfolio manager			
0–5 years			X
5–10 years		X	
10+ years	⊗		
Overall background	⊗	X	X

Note: Encircled responses represent Vanguard Windsor II.

[a] Composite background if there is more than one portfolio manager, but with most weight to "lead" portfolio manager.

[b] Acceptable for portfolio managers with ten or more years of previous investment experience.

[c] Move to next experience category if member of successful investment management family.

Table 14   Trading attributes and impact on bid–ask spread, and checklist of mutual fund attributes and relationship to bid–ask spread

	Impact on bid–ask spread	
	Increase	Decrease
A Trading attributes		
Auction (vs. dealer) market trade		×
Brokerage commission	×	
Dealer asymmetric information cost	×	
Dealer inventory holding cost	×	
Dealer order flow imbalance	×	
Dealer order processing cost	×	
Exchange (vs. off-exchange) trade		×
Intermarket competition		×
Investor holding period		×
Investor trading frequency		×
Investor trading immediacy (large opportunity cost)	×	
Market efficiency (resilience)		×
Nasdaq reform		×
Number of competing dealers		×
Number of institutional investors		×
NYSE (vs. Nasdaq) trade		×
Option trading in stock		×
Option margin requirements	×	
Pre- (vs. after) earnings announcement trade	×	
Security included in market index		×
Security market capitalization		×
Security number of shareholders		×
Security price	×	
Security price volatility	×	
Security trading frequency		×
Security trading volume	×	
Specialist agency (vs. principal) firm organization		×
Specialist number of stocks traded	×	
Specialist portfolio market risk	×	
Trade order (block) size	×	

B   Trading cost assessment: Loeb method
Mutual fund trading cost: 2.48%.

Comparative funds (Vanguard 500 Index and peer group) trading costs: 0.40% (index fund), 4.13% (peer group).

Mutual fund cost effectiveness: 0.103%.
Index fund cost effectiveness: 0.014%.
Peer group cost effectiveness: 0.20%.

Table 14 (*continued*)

	Impact on bid–ask spread	
	Increase	Decrease

Mutual fund cost effectiveness breakeven return relative to index fund: 177.1%.
Peer group cost effectiveness breakeven return relative to mutual fund: 40.1%.

Loeb trading cost
Excellent: ✗   (Vanguard Windsor II) (relative to peer group)
Acceptable:
Unacceptable: ✗   (Vanguard Windsor II) (relative to index fund)

Notes: Attributes are not mutually exclusive: some are components and others overlap. See references for detail, especially Coughenour and Shatri (1999).

Table 15   Market capitalization, block size and total spread/price (%)

Capitalization sector ($ million)	Block size ($000)								
	5	25	250	500	1,000	2,500	5,000	10,000	20,000
0–10 (4.58)[a]	17.3	27.3	43.8						
10–25 (10.30)	8.9	12.0	23.8	33.4					
25–50 (15.16)	5.0	7.6	18.8	25.9	30.0				
50–75 (18.27)	4.3	5.8	9.6	16.9	25.4	31.5			
75–100 (21.85)	2.8	3.9	5.9	8.1	11.5	15.7	25.7		
100–500 (28.31)	1.8	2.1	3.2	4.4	5.6	7.9	11.0	16.2	
500–1,000 (35.43)	1.9	2.0	3.1	4.0	5.6	7.7	10.4	14.3	20.0
1,000–1,500 (44.34)	1.9	1.9	2.7	3.3	4.6	6.2	8.9	13.6	18.1
Over 1,500 (57.48)	1.1	1.2	1.3	1.7	2.1	2.8	4.1	5.9	8.0

[a]   Average price of issues in capitalization sector.

Source: Reprinted with permission from T. F. Loeb, Trading Cost: the Critical Link between Investment Information and Results, *Financial Analysts Journal*, May/June 1983, p. 42. © 1983 Financial Analysts Federation, Charlottesville, VA. All rights reserved.

Table 16 Tax efficiency of the 100 largest stock funds in the bull run (%)[a]

Fund	Pretax return	Aftertax return	Tax effic.	Fund	Pretax return	Aftertax return	Tax effic.
Kaufmann	+126	+123	98	American – Washington Mut	+158	+142	90
MFS "B" Emerging Growth	+137	+134	98	AARP Growth and Income	+147	+132	90
Putnam "A" New Oppor	+138	+135	98	Davis "A" NY Venture	+157	+141	90
Vanguard US Growth	+165	+158	96	Janus Twenty	+157	+141	90
Vanguard Indx Totl Stk "Inv"	+145	+139	96	Fidelity Equity Income II	+127	+114	90
Oppnh/Quest Oppor Val "A"	+146	+139	95	Alliance "B" Growth	+123	+111	90
Aim "A" Constellation	+101	+95	94	Bernstein Internatl Value	+72	+65	90
Vanguard Index 500 "Inv"	+161	+151	94	Aim "A" Weingarten	+128	+114	89
Vanguard Primecap	+170	+160	94	Fidelity Value	+117	+104	89
Fidelity Spartan US Eqty Idx	+160	+150	94	United Income "A"	+128	+114	89
Harbor International	+99	+93	94	Vanguard Windsor II	+159	+142	89
Oakmark Fund	+135	+127	94	Fidelity Growth & Income	+147	+131	89
Amer Cent/20th Ultra "Inv"	+119	+111	93	Fidelity Low-Priced Stock	+132	+117	89
Dean Witter "B" Dividend Gr	+123	+114	93	Oppenh "A" Main St In & Gr	+112	+100	89
John Hancock Regl Bnk "B"	+212	+197	93	Mutual Series Discovery "Z"	+130	+116	89
Fidelity Blue Chip Growth	+138	+128	93	Aim "A" Charter	+118	+104	88
Janus Worldwide	+128	+119	93	Dodge & Cox Balanced	+95	+84	88
Fidelity Adv "T" Grth Oppors	+128	+118	92	Fidelity Equity Income	+134	+118	88
Fidelity Contrafund	+130	+118	91	Neuberger Guardian	+115	+101	88
Fidelity Growth Company	+113	+103	91	American – Growth Fd Amer	+112	+99	88
Putnam "A" Voyager	+129	+117	91	American – Invest Co Amer	+127	+112	88
AmExp IDS "A" New Dimens	+133	+121	91	Merrill Lynch "A" Basic Val	+133	+117	88
Merrill Lynch "B" Growth	+107	+97	91	Vanguard Internatl Growth	+61	+54	88
American – Captl Wold G&I	+102	+93	91	Dean Witter "B" Amer Value	+122	+107	88
Fidelity Adv "T" Eqty Growth	+125	+114	91	Prudential "B" Equity	+120	+106	88
Nicholas	+145	+131	90	Aim "A" Value	+125	+110	88
American – EuroPacific Grth	+73	+66	90	American – Captl Incm Bldr	+92	+81	88

Table 16 *(continued)*

Fund	Pretax return	Aftertax return	Tax effic.	Fund	Pretax return	Aftertax return	Tax effic.
PBHG Growth "PBHG"	+85	+75	88	Amer Cent/20th Select "Inv"	+105	+88	84
Scudder Growth & Income	+143	+124	87	Fidelity Destiny I	+145	+122	84
Amer Cent/20th Grth "Inv"	+105	+91	87	Vanguard Star	+98	+82	84
Price New Horizons	+125	+109	87	Seligman Comm & Info "A"	+197	+165	84
Janus Fund	+119	+104	87	Fidelity Puritan	+92	+76	83
American – New Perspective	+96	+84	87	American – Income Fd Amer	+90	+75	83
Putnam "A" Global Growth	+76	+66	87	American – Amcap	+116	+96	83
American – New Economy	+95	+83	87	American – American Mutl	+113	+94	83
MFS "A" Research	+141	+123	87	Merrill Lynch "A" Capital	+101	+84	83
Brandywine	+95	+83	87	MFS "A" Total Return	+84	+70	83
Fidelity Asset Manager	+63	+55	87	Mutual Series Shares "Z"	+123	+101	82
American – SmallCap. World	+78	+68	87	American – Balanced	+87	+71	82
Fidelity Fund	+147	+126	86	Mutual Series Qualified "Z"	+122	+100	82
Fidelity Magellan	+119	+102	86	Templeton "I" Growth	+88	+72	82
Vanguard Wellington	+107	+92	86	Lord Abbett "A" Affiliated	+128	+105	82
Price International Stock	+53	+46	86	Merrill Lynch "A" Glbl Alloc	+74	+61	82
Putnam "A" Vista	+127	+109	86	Vanguard Windsor	+129	+104	81
Price Equity Income	+136	+117	86	Vanguard Wellesley Income	+71	+58	81
Invesco Industrial Income	+100	+85	85	Pioneer II "A"	+109	+88	81
Templeton "I" Foreign	+57	+48	85	Putnam "A" George	+100	+81	81
American – Fundamental Inv	+131	+111	85	MFS "A" Mass Investors Tr	+163	+132	81
Putnam "A" Grth & Income	+130	+111	85	Templeton "I" World	+102	+81	79
Mutual Series Beacon "Z"	+118	+100	85	Franklin "I" Income	+51	+39	76

[a] Performance: January 1, 1994 to April 10, 1998.

Source: Reprinted with permission from "Which Funds Are Most Tax-Efficient?" *Mutual Funds*, June 1998, p. 27.

Table 17 Mutual fund portfolio turnover, ten years ended December 31, 1992 (%)

Level of turnover	Annual portfolio turnover rate	% of capital return	
		Unrealized	Realized
Low (under 25)	16	67	33
Below average (25–50)	36	53	47
Average (51–100)	66	22	78
Above average (more than 100)	150	18	82

Source: Reprinted with permission from John C. Bogle, *Bogle on Mutual Funds: New Perspectives for the Intelligent Investor*, 1994 (Irwin, Burr Ridge, IL), p. 219.

Table 18 Impact of federal taxes on stock and bond returns (%)

Variable	Bonds	Stocks[a] Realization of capital gains		
		Annually (high)[b]	Tenth year (low)[b]	At death (zero)[b]
Pre-tax nominal return	+7.0	+10.0	+10.0	+10.0
Taxes on income	+2.3	−1.0	−1.0	−1.0
Taxes on capital gains	+0.0	−2.0	−1.6	+0.0
After-tax nominal return	+4.7	+7.0	+7.4	+9.0
Inflation rate	−3.0	−3.0	−3.0	−3.0
After-tax real return	+1.7	+4.0	+4.4	+9.0
Pre-tax real return	+4.0	+7.0	+7.0	+7.0
Taxes as a % of real return	58	43	36	14

[a] Dividend yield of 3%; capital growth of +7%; also, table assumes a 33% marginal tax rate for income and 28% for capital gains.
[b] Rate of portfolio turnover.

Source: Reprinted with permission from John C. Bogle, *Bogle on Mutual Funds: New Perspectives for the Intelligent Investor*, 1994 (Irwin, Burr Ridge, IL), p. 211.

Table 19 Investor guidelines for selecting tax-efficient funds: checklist

1 Focus on funds with historically consistent portfolio strategies within well defined guidelines, to minimize unexpected and/or large realized capital gains.

2 Focus on funds and fund families with a history of long tenured portfolio managers and consistent investment styles, to limit large and/or unexpected realized capital gains.

3 Focus both on fund tax efficiency *and* portfolio returns, to enhance shareholder after-tax returns.

4 Focus on funds with high risk-adjusted portfolio returns, to offset generally more aggressive and volatile tax-efficient funds.

5 Focus on funds with long-term buy-and-hold rather than short-term capital gains strategies, to defer realization of capital gains.

6 Focus on funds with very low versus high portfolio turnover strategies, to defer realization of capital gains.

7 Focus on funds using "gain/loss management" strategies, whereby highest cost basis shares are sold first and realized capital gains are maximally offset by realized capital losses.

8 In high tax brackets, consider in-state "municipal" rather than taxable bond funds, to avoid state and federal taxes on ordinary income and enhance "after tax" returns.

9 Focus on funds with capital gains rather than income orientation, to generate unrealized capital gains relative to current taxable distributions of ordinary income.

10 Focus on broad market index funds to minimize realized capital gains from portfolio turnover to replace stocks no longer eligible in the actual index; otherwise, focus on large market capitalization index funds with lower expenses, lower trading costs, and lower performance volatility.

11 Consider funds with derivative security and short-sale strategies, to defer current realization of capital gains.

12 Focus on funds with purchase and sales transaction fees and policies restricting unstable cash inflows/outflows, to minimize realization of capital gains to meet "hot money" redemptions.

13 Focus on funds with stable *net* cash inflows, to minimize realization of capital gains to meet redemptions, ease implementation of portfolio strategies, and increase number of shares to reduce proportionate share of future taxable distributions.

14 Focus on funds with small unrealized capital gains built into net asset value, to defer potential future taxable distributions.

15 Focus on funds with portfolio managers who invest heavily in the funds, to provide incentive for tax efficiency.

16 Purchase funds with higher than category peer group tax efficiency, with absolute goal of achieving after-tax returns of at least 90% of before-tax returns.

Overall assessment: fund tax efficiency

Number of subjective attributes of tax-efficient mutual funds identified: ten (estimate).

Number of identified fund attributes divided by total number of tax-efficiency attributes (sixteen): 67%.

Does the fund have higher tax-efficiency than its category peer group (tables 41b and 43)? Yes

Overall relative tax efficiency
Excellent:
Acceptable: X (Vanguard Windsor II)
Unacceptable:

Table 20 Tax guidelines for mutual fund investors: checklist

1 *Minimize the number of taxable redemptions.* Exchange annual cash needs at one time into money market fund to make payments. Money market funds maintain stable net asset values and avoid capital gains/losses on each payment. Only use automatic withdrawal/exchange plans from money market funds to avoid multiple taxable events, especially if bond funds held.

2 *Do not "buy distributions."* Check expected distributions two months before ownership record date. Defer buying shares before fund distributions, especially large capital gains, until after record date. This avoids immediate tax liability on new purchases.

3 *Recognize potential future taxes in unrealized capital gains.* Unrealized/undistributed capital gains (and also net investment income) defer taxes, but will be realized at some point. The implications are deferred versions of No. 2.

4 *Recognize savings from changes in tax rates.*[a] Reduce taxes by selling funds with gains in current or next year, depending on the timing, nature (ordinary income/capital gains), size and direction of change.

5 *Recognize savings from differences in tax rates on long-term capital gains and ordinary income.*[b] If long-term capital gains tax rates are lower, give preference to realized capital gains over both dividend distributions and short-term capital gains distributions taxed as ordinary income.

6 *Recognize impact of fund tax efficiency on after-tax returns (table 21).* Focus on after-tax returns by recognizing fund tax efficiency. Index and tax-managed funds are usually so advantaged.

7 *Consider tax-efficient funds (table 19).* Focus on tax-managed funds, tax-efficient broad-based index funds, and managed funds with efficient histories, especially if portfolio management is long tenured with significant personal investment.

8 *Consider "good" funds with tax-loss carryforwards.* Funds with reduced net asset values due to realized capital losses use tax carryforwards to offset future realized capital gains.

9 *Take current losses in funds to save.* Sell funds with losses sizable enough to significantly reduce current taxable income. Do so before late-year tax selling and realized capital gains are distributed. Distributions generate investor taxable income even if funds have negative returns. Defer repurchase of desirable funds for thirty days to avoid non-deductible "wash sales." Investors may carry forward their realized capital losses against future realized capital gains for seven years. Short-term losses on sale of tax-exempt funds are reduced by any tax-exempt income distributions. Short-term losses on fund sales are reported as long-term losses if long-term capital gains were distributed.

10 *Take international tax credits.* Take fund payments of foreign taxes as tax credits, or at least as tax deductions.

11 *Consider bond funds with tax-exempt state and federal ordinary income distributions and tax-exempt federal ordinary income distributions.*[c] Determine whether after-tax returns on either type of municipal bond fund exceed after-tax returns on taxable bond funds. Municipal bond income distributions may be taxable under the alternative minimum tax (AMT) and if the fund holds municipal bonds ineligible for tax exemption.

12 *"Sidestep" distributions.* Sell funds with forthcoming distributions if investor gains are less than distributions. If not, take no action. Funds sold with taxable gains may be repurchased the next day.

13 *"Double switch" to maintain portfolio allocations and save taxes.* All else equal, in tax-deferred accounts sell bond funds and buy stock funds with large forthcoming distributions; in taxable accounts, buy the bond funds and sell the stock funds to avoid taxable distributions.

14 *Favor tax-deferred accounts.*[d] Favor tax-deferred accounts relative to taxable accounts, especially for less tax-efficient bond funds versus tax-efficient stock funds and actively managed versus passively managed stock funds in general. Also, favor tax-deferred accounts for less tax-efficient stock funds along with taxable accounts for tax-exempt bond funds – optimal in this combination.

15 *Sell all shares in a fund in one transaction.* Simplifies accounting for taxable gains/losses.

16 *Favor deferral of taxes to current taxes.* A dollar of deferred taxes has a smaller present value than a dollar of current taxes.

Table 20 (*continued*)

17 *Favor "return of capital" distributions.* They are not taxed unless they exceed original cost basis. Investor cost basis reduced by amount of capital distributions.

18 *Take long-term capital gains in bond funds.* Rising interest rates will reduce them, so take them when available.

19 *Sell specific shares to reduce capital gains taxes.* This method of determining cost basis for sale of fund shares normally provides smaller capital gains relative to the average cost method used by funds in reporting to shareholders.

Note: For a review of fund tax issues, see Vanguard Group, *Taxes and Mutual Funds* (Vanguard Marketing, Valley Forge, PA), 1999.

[a] For capital gains tax issues, see Block (2000b).
[b] To determine how far fund net asset value can fall and investor still benefits from waiting for long-term capital gains rate to apply: (1) compute dollar after-tax gains using short-term capital gains tax rate; (2) divide this amount by the long-term capital gains tax rate; and (3) the resulting dollar amount is the breakeven net asset value. If the fund net asset value is above (below) this amount, the investor is better (worse) off by waiting for long-term capital gains rate to apply.
[c] For municipal bond tax issues, see Block (2000a).
[d] For guidelines to types of funds that work best in taxable versus tax-deferred accounts over ten-year, fifteen-year, and twenty-year periods, see Stevens (2000), which refers to www.troweprice.com. The higher the retirement tax bracket and the shorter the investment horizon until retirement, the better it is to keep stocks in taxable accounts and bonds in tax-deferred accounts. Also, see Hartman (1998).

Table 21 Analysis of gross returns: Wilshire 5000 Index and mutual fund types (%)

Variable	Wilshire 5000 Index	Mutual fund type		
		No-load index funds	No-load managed funds	Load managed funds
Gross return	16.0	16.0	16.0	16.0
Survivor bias	n.a.	−1.0[a]	−1.0[b]	−1.0[b]
Operating expenses + trading costs	n.a.	−0.2[c]	−1.3[d]	−1.3[d]
Loads/fees	n.a.	0.0	0.0	−0.5[e]
Cash reserves drag	n.a.	0.0	−0.6[f]	−0.6[f]
Shareholder taxes	n.a.	−0.5[g]	−1.0[h]	−1.0[h]
Net return	16.0	14.3	12.1	11.6
Percentage of Wilshire 5000				
Market Index	100	89	76	73
Percentage of no-load index funds	n.a.	100	85	81

[a] Consistent (but high) estimate with b.
[b] Bogle (1999), p. 129.
[c] Ibid., p. 128.
[d] Ibid., p. 127.
[e] Ibid., p. 128.
[f] Ibid., p. 127.
[g] Estimated from h.
[h] Bogle (1999), p. 129.

Source: Adapted from John C. Bogle, *Common Sense on Mutual Funds: New Imperatives for the Intelligent Investor* (John Wiley, New York, 1999), pp. 127–9.

Table 22 Disclosure issues for improved mutual fund communication

1   Portfolio manager disclosure

   (a)   *Portfolio manager background issues*
      Manager name(s) provided?
      Age provided?
      Education (MBA, CFA) provided?
      Prior investment experience provided?
      Current tenure as fund manager provided?
      Family management company?

   (b)   *Portfolio management issues*
      Lead portfolio manager(s) named rather than "team" or "multiple managers"?
      Advisor rather than subadvisor portfolio management?
      Method and amount of portfolio manager compensation/bonus provided/discussed?
      Consistency of method of portfolio manager compensation with fund objective discussed?
      Amount of portfolio manager's investment in fund provided?
      Dollar amount of expenses disclosed on account statements?

   (c)   *Portfolio performance and investment issues*
      Current performance, including relevant benchmark, provided/discussed?
      Major risks in portfolio discussed in context of economic and market outlook?
      Major portfolio changes discussed?
      Portfolio management and performance discussed in context of stated investment objective, policies, and limitations?
      Portfolio management and performance discussed in context of stated investment philosophy, approaches, and style?
      Fund performance history *excludes* any as "similarly managed" non-fund portfolio?
      Portfolio manager performance history *excludes* any managing another portfolio or fund?
      AIMR-PPS statement of ethical principles cited as guidance to measures of investment performance?

2   Board of directors disclosure

   (a)   *Director issues*
      Names provided?
      Mailing and e-mail addresses provided?
      Education provided?
      Current and previous professional experience provided?
      Service on other boards provided?
      Original relationship to investment advisor provided?
      Method of and reason for selection to board provided?
      Length of tenure provided?
      Compensation and benefits provided?
      Amount invested in fund(s) provided?

   (b)   *Board committee issues*
      Standing committees and members provided?
      Issues before the committees discussed?
      Committee actions and recommendations discussed?

Table 22 (*continued*)

    (c)   *Board decision issues*

        Issues before the board discussed?

        Service contract and other actions and approvals discussed?

        Annual shareholder meetings held and minutes distributed to shareholders?

        Loads/fees and expenses provided/discussed?

        Reduction in loads/fees/expenses approved?

        Role of independent directors discussed?

        Independent directors reported as majority of board that nominates new outside directors?

        Asset size at which fund will be closed to new investors stated/discussed?

        Portfolio performance relative to investment objective, policies, and limitations discussed?

        Pending or concluded litigation and ethics issues discussed?

3   Portfolio disclosure issues

    Monthly lagged portfolio provided online?

    Policy, actual use, risks, and performance implications of foreign, less liquid, and illiquid (nonmarketable) securities, provided/discussed?

    Policy, actual use, method, and performance implications of "fair value" pricing provided/discussed?

    Policy and actual use of derivatives for hedging and income enhancement, including foreign currency transactions, along with discussion of their risks and performance implications?

    Policy, actual use, terms, and performance implications of borrowed funds, including family funds, provided/discussed?

    Code of ethics for personal trading provided, including discussion of any in-house and/or regulatory problems?

    Costs of litigation pending or concluded provided/discussed?

    Tax efficiency and after-tax returns provided/discussed?

    "Dollar-weighted" returns also provided/discussed?

    "Standard" modern portfolio theory *measures of risk, return, and risk/return* provided and discussed individually/together; also in fund advertising?

    Selection policy and use of broker-dealers provided/discussed, including commissions paid versus "best available" execution?

    Policy for use and amounts and categories of "soft dollar" payments received provided/discussed, along with impact on fund commissions and operating expenses?

4   Overall assessment: disclosure

   Number of mutual fund disclosure issues provided: see next.

   Number of disclosed issues provided divided by total number of issues (fifty-five): less than 50%.

   Overall mutual fund disclosure

   Excellent:

   Acceptable: ✕   (Vanguard Windsor II) (relative to average)

   Unacceptable: ✕   (Vanguard Windsor II) (relative to goal)

Table 23   Expense ratios: all mutual funds, 1986–99 (%)

September 30	Expense ratio
1986	1.06
1987	1.19
1988	1.24
1989	1.27
1990	1.29
1991	1.28
1992	1.21
1993	1.21
1994	1.23
1995	1.29
1996	1.38
1997	1.41
1998	1.41
1999	1.46
Increase, 1986–99	38

Source: CDA/Wiesenberger, *Mutual Fund Directory*, (CDA/Wiesenberger, Rockville, MD), December 31, 1986–99.

Table 24(a)   Mutual fund expenses: Vanguard examples (%)

Annual fund operating expenses	Emerging Markets	500 Index	US Growth	Windsor II[a]
Management fees	0.28	0.16	0.39	0.38
Rule 12b-1 fees	None	None	None	None
Other expenses	0.07	0.03	0.03	0.03
Total	0.35	0.19	0.42	0.41

[a]   The Windsor II expense ratio is excellent relative to its peer group.

Sources: Vanguard International Index Portfolio, *Prospectus*, April 23, 1998; Vanguard Index Trust, *Prospectus*, April 20, 1998; Vanguard US Growth Portfolio, *Prospectus*, December 2, 1997; Vanguard Windsor II, *Prospectus*, February 26, 1999.

Table 24(b)   Mutual fund expenses: Fidelity examples (%)

Annual fund operating expenses	Select Electronics	Low-priced Stock	Magellan	Growth and Income
Management fees	0.60	0.76	0.43	0.50
Rule 12b-1 fees	None	None	None	None
Other expenses	0.54	0.26	0.19	0.23
Total	1.14	1.02	0.62	0.73

Sources: Fidelity Select Portfolio, *Prospectus*, April 28, 1998; Fidelity Low-priced Stock Fund, *Prospectus*, September 26, 1997; Fidelity Magellan Fund, *Prospectus*, May 22, 1998; Fidelity Growth and Income Portfolio, *Prospectus*, September 25, 1997.

Table 24(c)   Mutual fund expenses: miscellaneous examples (%)

Annual fund operating expenses	Janus Worldwide	Kaufmann Fund
Management fees	0.65	1.50
Rule 12b-1 fees	None	0.37
Other expenses	0.31	0.02
Total	0.96	1.89

Sources: Janus Equity Funds, *Prospectus*, February 17, 1998; Kaufmann Fund, *Prospectus*, May 1, 1998.

Table 24(d)   Mutual fund expenses: Franklin Mutual examples (%)

Annual fund operating expenses	Beacon		
	Class Z	Class I	Class II
Management fees	0.60	0.60	0.60
Rule 12b-1 fees	None	0.35	1.00
Other expenses	0.17	0.17	0.17
Total	0.77	1.12	1.77

Sources: Franklin Mutual Series Fund, Class Z, *Prospectus*, May 1, 1998; also, Class I and Class II, May 1, 1998.

Table 24(e) Mutual fund expenses: Fidelity Advisor examples (%)

Annual fund operating expenses	Fidelity Advisor Equity Growth			
	Class A	Class T	Class B	Class C
Management fees	0.39	0.39	0.39	0.39
Rule 12b-1 fees	0.15	0.25	0.90	1.00
Other expenses	0.36	0.26	0.36	0.36
Total	0.90	0.90	1.65	1.75

Source: Fidelity Advisor Equity Growth Fund, Class A, Class T, Class B and Class C, *Prospectus*, February 28, 1998.

Table 25 Mutual fund management fees, 1920–96 (%)

Fund inception	Minimum contractual management fee
1920–30	0.38
1930–40	0.43
1940–50	0.52
1950–60	0.53
1960–70	0.56
1970–80	0.58
1980–85	0.64
1985–90	0.68
1990–95	0.67
1995–96	0.72
Increase, 1920–30 to 1995–96	89.5

Source: Amy Arnott, The Rising Tide, *Morningstar Mutual Funds*, October 11, 1996.

Table 26 Fees and expenses

Rank	Company	Large company	Small company	Global	Bond	Rank	Company	Large company	Small company	Global	Bond
1	Vanguard	2	1	2	1	51	Gabelli	49	27	n.a.	n.a.
2	GE	3	n.a.	1	n.a.	52	Kaufmann	n.a.	39	n.a.	n.a.
3	Acorn	n.a.	2	n.a.	n.a.	53	Legg Mason	56	31	n.a.	32
4	Dimensional	1	3	5	2	54	Oakmark	40	n.a.	n.a.	n.a.
5	Lindner	n.a.	n.a.	n.a.	n.a.	55	Merrill Lynch	55	37	28	41
6	GMO	7	4	4	n.a.	56	Federated	44	n.a.	42	38
7	MAS	9	n.a.	3	7	57	State Street	33	n.a.	24	72
8	Schwab	4	n.a.	n.a.	10	58	Evergreen Keystone	45	38	50	14
9	SEI	6		11	9	59	Prudential	58	36	34	47
10	Standish	8	8	16	3	60	Key/Victory	62	35	38	61
11	Dodge & Cox	10	n.a.	n.a.	11	61	American	59	41	30	56
12	Morgan Stanley	18	n.a.	8	6	62	American Express/IDS	60	34	35	57
13	Munder	5	7	6	25	63	Dean Witter	53	n.a.	40	48
14	Portico	14	n.a.	n.a.	8	64	Stagecoach	47	n.a.	n.a.	50
15	Nicholas	13	5	n.a.	15	65	Delaware	65	44	19	66
16	USAA	26	6	20	4	66	Eaton Vance	36	n.a.	n.a.	52
17	Compass	12	n.a.	n.a.	17	67	PBHG	50	n.a.	n.a.	n.a.
18	T. Rowe Price	15	15	9	20	68	Alliance	63	32	46	65
19	One	19	14	n.a.	12	69	Kemper	76	42	43	64
20	Dreyfuss	11	17	13	30	70	Waddell & Reed	67	n.a.	36	59
21	Nations	27	n.a.	14	13	71	Lord Abbett	61	47	48	60
22	JPM	23	11	18	23	72	Vista	75	45	n.a.	43
23	Scudder	21	19	17	21	73	First American	64	n.a.	n.a.	46
24	Columbia	24	n.a.	n.a.	16	74	Norwest	69	n.a.	n.a.	42
25	Neuberger & Berman	17	24	n.a.	19	75	Goldman Sachs	83	n.a.	n.a.	28

Rank	Family				
26	Lazard	29	10	7	34
27	American Century	28	13	27	14
28	Harbor	16	n.a.	10	36
29	Janus	25	12	15	33
30	Montgomery	n.a.	22	n.a.	n.a.
31	Pegasus	20	n.a.	n.a.	26
32	Warburg Pincus	38	21	22	22
33	Robertson Stephens	n.a.	26	n.a.	n.a.
34	Stein Roe	31	n.a.	n.a.	24
35	Pimco	48	30	31	5
36	Invesco	34	25	21	35
37	SoGen	n.a.	n.a.	29	n.a.
38	Parkstone	39	18	n.a.	31
39	Franklin Templeton	22	20	32	45
40	Longleaf	37	23	n.a.	n.a.
41	Sequoia	30	n.a.	n.a.	n.a.
42	Fidelity	43	29	23	27
43	Founders	41	28	26	40
44	Galaxy	32	33	33	39
45	Berger	51	n.a.	n.a.	18
46	Strong	42	n.a.	n.a.	28
47	Brandywine	35	n.a.	n.a.	n.a.
48	Smith Barney	52	16	25	49
49	Nuveen	n.a.	n.a.	n.a.	37
50	MainStay	46	n.a.	12	53
76	Seligman	57	43	n.a.	68
77	Putnam	77	46	41	34
78	AIM	78	40	n.a.	55
79	Oppenheimer	81	50	37	63
80	GT Global	n.a.	49	49	76
81	Pioneer	73	48	52	51
82	Paine Webber	71	n.a.	39	67
83	MFS	70	n.a.	44	70
84	AAL	66	n.a.	n.a.	58
85	John Hancock	74	51	51	74
86	Colonial	79	53	47	73
87	Phoenix	72	n.a.	45	75
88	Selected	54	n.a.	n.a.	74
89	First Investors	84	52	53	78
90	New England	82	n.a.	n.a.	52
91	Van Kampen	80	n.a.	54	78
92	Lutheran Brotherhood	68	n.a.	n.a.	19
93	Benchmark	n.a.	n.a.	n.a.	n.a.
94	Sanford C. Bernstein	n.a.	n.a.	n.a.	n.a.
95	BT	n.a.	n.a.	n.a.	n.a.
96	Diversified	n.a.	n.a.	n.a.	n.a.
97	Kent	n.a.	n.a.	n.a.	n.a.
98	MassMutual	n.a.	n.a.	n.a.	n.a.
99	SSgA	n.a.	n.a.	n.a.	n.a.
100	STI Classic	n.a.	n.a.	n.a.	n.a.

Source: Reprinted by permission of *Worth* magazine, May 1997 (William P. Barrett, Fund Families: Best to Worst, *Worth*, May 1997, pp. 76ff).

Table 27   Mutual fund attributes and portfolio manager background: overall assessments –
Vanguard Windsor II, 1998

Mutual fund attributes and portfolio manager background	Overall (individual) assessments
1 Loads/fees (table 8a)	Excellent
2 Overall shareholder service (table 11)	Excellent
3 Portfolio manager background (table 13)	Excellent
4 Loeb trading cost (table 14)	Excellent, relative to category peer group
5 Tax efficiency (table 19)	Acceptable
6 Shareholder disclosure (table 22)	Acceptable, relative to average
7 Expense ratio (table 24a)	Acceptable
Fund attributes	Excellent/acceptable
Portfolio manager background	Excellent

Source: Tables cited in parentheses.

Table 28   Annualized nominal and real returns on stock and fixed-income securities, 1802–1997 (%)

Security/Time period	Annualized nominal return	Annualized real return
Common stock		
1802–1997	8.4	7.0
1802–1870	7.1	7.0
1871–1925	7.2	6.6
1926–1997	10.6	7.2
Long-term Treasury bonds		
1802–1997	4.8	3.5
1802–1870	4.9	4.8
1871–1925	4.3	3.7
1926–1997	5.2	2.0
Short-term Treasury securities		
1802–1997	4.3	2.9
1802–1870	5.2	5.1
1871–1925	3.8	3.2
1926–1997	3.8	0.6

Source: Abridged with permission from Jeremy J. Siegel, *Stocks for the Long Run*, second edition
(McGraw-Hill, New York), 1998, pp. 13, 15.

Table 29 Probability of achieving at least a given geometric rate of return over various investment horizons (%)

Minimum annualized return	Investment horizon (years)				
	1	5	10	20	30
Real					
+10	43	35	30	23	18
+7	49	49	48	47	47
+5	54	58	61	66	69
0	64	79	87	95	97
−5	74	92	98	99	100
−10	83	98	99	100	100
Nominal					
+10	48	44	42	39	37
+7	54	58	62	66	69
+5	58	67	74	81	86
0	68	85	93	98	99
−5	78	96	99	99	100
−10	86	99	99	100	100

Source: Abridged with permission from Charles P. Jones and Jack W. Wilson, Probabilities Associated with Common Stock Returns, *Journal of Portfolio Management*, fall 1995, pp. 25–6, 28–9.

Table 30 A comparison of terminal wealth levels for two hypothetical risky portfolios

Level of terminal wealth ($)	Chance of being below this level of terminal wealth (%)	
	Portfolio A[a]	Portfolio B[b]
70,000	0	2
80,000	0	5
90,000	4	14
100,000	21	27
110,000	57	46
120,000	88	66
130,000	99	82

Note: Initial wealth is assumed to be $100,000, and both portfolios are assumed to have normally distributed returns.

[a] The expected return and standard deviation of A are 8% and 10%, respectively.
[b] The expected return and standard deviation of B are 12% and 20%, respectively.

Source: Reprinted with permission from William F. Sharpe, Gordon J. Alexander and Jeffrey V. Bailey, *Investments*, fifth edition (Prentice-Hall, Englewood Cliffs, NJ), 1995, p. 170.

Table 31 What's your investment risk preference?

Encircle response	Enter score[a]

1 What are your income needs?
    A I need a steady, current income from my investments
    B Current income is not my main consideration
    C I don't need current investment income

2 What's your investment time frame?
    A Short-term results are important to me
    B Day-to-day changes in the financial markets don't bother me
    C I invest primarily for the long term

3 What's your investment time frame?
    A I can't tolerate any loss of capital
    B I can accept temporary drops in my portfolio
    C I can tolerate a potential loss of 25% or more of my capital in return for the opportunity to make realistic gains

4 What kind of investment returns do you look for?
    A I don't have to beat the "market"
    B I want to match or slightly outperform the "market"
    C Outperforming the "market" is very important to me

5 How much do you need to protect against inflation?
    A Protecting my current income and capital are more important than beating inflation
    B I want current income, but I also want to beat inflation
    C My investments must beat inflation

Total score   9 (Kate)

Investor risk category: 5–7 points: low risk, 8–10 points: modest risk, 10–13 points: moderate risk, 14–15 points: high risk.

[a] Score one point for each A answer, two points for each B answer, and three points for each C.

Source: Abridged from "What's Your Investments Risk Preference?" *Independent Investor's Personal Investing Newsletter* (Fidelity Distributors), November 1986, p. 12.

Table 32   Relationship of socioeconomic characteristics to interest in dividend income and capital appreciation: checklist[a]

Check relevant items:	
Interest in dividend income (lower risk)	**Interest in capital appreciation (higher risk)**
____ Older investor	_X_ Larger portfolio
_X_ Female investor	_X_ Higher education
____ Service worker	____ Housewives or retired or non-employed
____ Lower family income	_X_ Younger investor
____ Separated or divorced or widowed	_X_ Independent decision maker
____ Lower education	
____ Dependent decision maker	

[a]   Kate's responses.

Sources: H. Kent Baker and John A. Haslem, Toward the Development of Client-specified Valuation Models, *Journal of Finance*, 29 (September), 1974, pp. 1255–63; H. Kent Baker and John A. Haslem, The Impact of Investor Socioeconomic Characteristics on Risk and Return Preferences, *Journal of Business Research*, October 1974, pp. 469–76; and H. Kent Baker, Michael B. Hargrove and John A. Haslem, A Test of a Revised Theory of the Investment Life Cycle, *Baylor Business Studies*, 10 (May–July) 1979, pp. 17–33.

Table 33   Matching investor risk categories to portfolio investment objectives and passive asset allocation, 1926–93 (%)

Investor risk category	Portfolio investment objective	Passive stock/bond allocation	Average return[a]	Worst annual loss[a]	Percentage of years with loss[a]
Low	Income	20/80	7	−13	19
Modest	Growth and income	40/60	8	−21	21
		50/50[b]	9[b]	−24[b]	21[b]
Moderate	Growth[c]	60/40	9	−28	22
High	Aggressive growth	80/20	10	−36	26
		100/0[b]	11[b]	−43[b]	28[b]

[a]   Figures rounded.
[b]   Additional data provided for perspective only.
[c]   Includes CDA/Wiesenberger Growth and Income investment objective.

Source: Return and risk data abridged from *Vanguard Investment Planner* (Vanguard Marketing, Valley Forge, PA), 1998, p. 9.

Table 34 Risk categories and investment objectives: overall and subcategories

Risk category	Portfolio investment objective		Investment objective subcategory
1 No risk	"Capital conservation" ("cash bucket"): capital conservation with no chance of loss to meet short-term requirements; no-risk investors	(a)	Money market funds (n.a.) (1) Taxable (2) National tax-exempt (3) State tax-exempt plus appropriate short-term/intermediate-term bond funds
2 Low risk	"Income": current income with low risk; very risk-averse investors	(b)	Government bond (3.29) (4) US government income (5) GNMA
		(c)	Municipal bond (3.08) (6) National bond – long-term (7) State bond – long-term
		(d)	Corporate bond (3.23) (8) Flexible portfolio (9) Income – bond (10) Corporate – bond (11) Income – mixed
3 Modest risk	"Growth and income": capital appreciation with income to limit risk; risk-averse investors	(e)	High-yield bond (7.07) (12) High-yield bond
		(f)	International bond (30.13)[a] (13) Global bond
		(g)	Balanced fund (10.37) (14) Balanced fund
		(h)	– (15) Income – equity
4 Moderate risk	"Growth": capital appreciation and secondarily income; slightly risk-averse investors	(i)	Global stock (11.64) (16) Global equity
		(j)	Growth and income (15.28)
		(k)	Growth (17.78) (17) Growth fund
5 High risk	"Aggressive growth": maximum capital appreciation with commensurate risk; risk-neutral or risk-seeking investors	(l)	Foreign (21.33) (18) International fund
		(m)	Aggressive growth (24.05) (19) Aggressive growth fund
		(n)	Metals (39.82) (20) Precious metals/gold

Notes: Lettered objectives from CDA/Wiesenberger; numbered objectives from Investment Company Institute and chapter 2. Standard deviation of return (in parentheses) from CDA/Wiesenberger.

[a] Unusually large standard deviation: 8.01 in 1997.

Sources: Partly abridged from CDA/Wiesenberger, *Mutual Fund Directory* (CDA/Wiesenberger, Rockville, MD), December 31, 1998; and Investment Company Institute, *Mutual Fund Fact Book*, 37th edn (The Institute, Washington, DC), 1997.

Table 35   Portfolio cap. size investment style allocations for passive stock/bond allocations: four models (%)

Model	Portfolio investment objective				
	Income	Growth and income	Growth	Aggressive growth	
	Stock/bond allocation				
	20/80	40/60	60/40	80/20	100/0
Bernstein simplified					
Domestic large-cap.	5	10	15	20	25
Domestic small-cap.	5	10	15	20	25
International large-cap.[a]	5	10	15	20	25
International small-cap.[b]	5	10	15	20	25
Total	20	40	60	80	100
Siegel					
Domestic large-cap.	10	20	30	40	50
Domestic small-cap.	5	10	15	20	25
International stock[c]	5	10	15	20	25
Total	20	40	60	80	100
Gibson diversified[d]					
Domestic large-cap.	6	12	18	24	30
Domestic small-cap.	2	4	6	8	10
Equity REITs	4	8	12	16	20
Precious metals	2	4	6	8	10
International large-cap. and small-cap.	6	12	18	24	30
Total	20	40	60	80	100
Haslem[e]					
Domestic large-cap.	10	19	29	38	48
Domestic small-cap.	6	13	19	26	32
International large-cap.	3	5	7	10	12
International small-cap.	1	3	5	6	8
Total	20	40	60	80	100

Notes: All portfolio stock allocations adjusted from 100% stock allocation. Actual foreign allocations are larger because approximately 25% of domestic large-cap. earnings are foreign.

[a]   Two parts European, two parts emerging markets and one part Pacific.
[b]   Four parts European and one part Japanese.
[c]   Europe, Far East, and emerging markets equally.
[d]   Cash reallocated because of use here of separate cash bucket.
[e]   Assumptions: domestic/foreign stock allocation: 80/20; domestic/foreign large-cap./small-cap. allocations: 60/40.

Sources: William J. Bernstein, *The Intelligent Asset Allocator* (www.efficientfrontier.com), 1995; Jeremy J. Siegel, *Stocks for the Long Run*, second edition (McGraw Hill, New York), 1998, pp. 284–6; and Roger C. Gibson, *Asset Allocations: Balancing Financial Risk* (Irwin, Burr Ridge, IL), 1990, p. 157.

Table 36   Stock index returns, year ending 1998

Index	(Index fund sampled)	Three-year return	Five-year return
Continental small companies	DFA Continental Small Company	15.15	11.13
Emerging markets (equally weighted)	DFA Emerging Markets	−6.47	n.a.
Small Japanese stocks	DFA Japanese Small Company	−26.00	−12.74
EAFE index	DFA Large Cap. International	9.88	9.57
Pacific rim small companies	DFA Pacific Rim Small Company	−18.78	−14.47
US small–medium companies	DFA US 6–10 Small Company	11.37	12.15
US small companies	DFA US 9–10 Small Company	10.21	13.17
UK small companies	DFA United Kingdom Small Company	6.08	6.71
REITs	DFA/AEW Real Estate Securities	10.56	6.78
S&P 500	Vanguard 500 Index	28.16	23.96
Emerging markets (cap. weighted)	Vanguard Emerg Markets Stock Index	−7.60	n.a.
EAFE–Europe	Vanguard European Stock Index	24.74	19.32
Precious metals stocks	Vanguard Gold and Precious Metals	−16.48	−12.05
US growth stocks	Vanguard Growth Index	33.87	27.79
EAFE Pacific	Vanguard Pacific Stock Index	−11.14	−4.01
US value stocks	Vanguard Value Index	21.91	19.79

Source: Reprinted with permission from William J. Bernstein, The Coward's Update, *Efficient Frontier*, January 1999 (www.efficientfrontier.com).

Table 37   Financial Engines: illustration of portfolio allocations (%)

Asset class	Risk level														
	0.34	0.4	0.5	0.6	0.7	0.8	0.9	1.0	1.1	1.2	1.3	1.4	1.5	1.6	1.64
Short bonds	100	76	53	33	25	25	25	23	8						
Intermediate bonds		9	21	31	25	21	12								
Long bonds				3				5	12.5	11	1				
REITs		5	4	4	4	1									
S&P 500		3	12	19	25	25	25	25	25	25	25	25	4		
Wilshire 4500			2	3	5	14	22	25	25	25	25	25	25	21	
Russell 2000												8	25	79	100
CRSP 9–10								1	2	3	4	8	21		
Big growth								2	4	7	11	25	25		
Big value								1	4	7	11				
MSCI Europe				1	3	6	8	10	11	12	13	3			
MSCI Pacific		1	3	4	5	5	6	6	7	8	9	6			
Emerging markets		3	3	3	3	3	2	2	2	2	1				
Continental small		1	1	1	1										
UK small		2	1	1	1										
% success rate	<5	11	33	46	54	59	63	65	67	68	69	69	67	65	65
Worst annual loss	0	0	0	2	3	5	7	8	10	11	13	15	17	19	20

Source: Reprinted with permission from William Bernstein, Bill Sharpe's Brave New World, *Efficient Frontier*, September 1999 (www.efficientfrontier.com).

Table 38 Diversification constraints versus attainable global diversification: type, degree, and risk, Vanguard Windsor II

Type of constraint	Degree of diversification and examples	
	Smaller	Larger
Morningstar category (see style constraint)	*Large-cap. value*[a]	Large-cap. blend (value and growth)
Method of security analysis (fundamental/technical)	*Fundamental analysis*	Fundamental and technical analysis[a]
Method of portfolio management (active/passive)	*Active management*	Active and passive management[a]
Investment style:		
Value/growth	*Value*[a]	Blend (value and growth)
Large/mid/small cap.	*Large cap.*[a]	Representative market cap.
Cash asset allocation	*Small cash ratio*	Large cash ratio[a]
Geographic concentration	*Domestic*	Global[a]
Asset allocation	*Stock allocation*	Stock and bond allocation
Market liquidity	*Large cap. size market*[a]	Representative cap. size market
Returns distribution	Capital gains	*Dividends and capital gains*[a]
Industry sector concentration	Few industry sectors	*Diverse industry sectors*[a]
Security concentration	Few securities holdings	*Diverse securities holdings*[a]
Quality concentration:		
Value Line safety rating	*Low rating*	Representative market rating[a]
Value Line timeliness rating	*Low rating*	Representative market rating[a]

Overall assessment: mutual fund versus attainable global degree of diversification and risk

Number of mutual fund constraints with larger degree of diversification and less risk (equivalent to attainable global diversification): 3 (returns distribution, industry sector concentration, and security concentration).

Number of above constraints divided by total number of constraints: 3/14 = 27% (fundamental/ technical analysis, active/passive management, cash asset allocation, geographic concentration, asset allocation, market liquidity, returns distribution, industry sector concentration, security concentration, Value Line safety rating, and Value Line timeliness rating).

Notes: Vanguard Windsor II in italic. "Morningstar category" replaces "Portfolio investment objective" (table 6). "Value Line safety" and "Timeliness" replace "Quality concentration" (table 6).

[a] Less relative diversification *risk*.

Table 39 Fundamental analysis and variants of value/growth investment style: checklist

---

Encircle responses:

1 Morningstar investment style (category) approach to fundamental analysis:

    (a)   Value   vs.   Blend   vs.   Growth
               ⊗   ✕   ✕

    (b)   Large cap.   vs.   Mid cap.   vs.   Small cap.
               ⊗   ✕   ✕

2 Variants of fundamental analysis:

    (a)   "Top down"   vs.   "Bottom up"
               ✕   ⊗

3 Variants of value style (circle all applicable):

    (a)   "Normal" value style   ⊗

    (b)   Merger arbitrage   ✕

    (c)   Financially distressed securities/indebtedness   ✕

    (d)   "Enhance" shareholder value   ✕

    (e)   "Special situations"   ✕

    (f)   Other: _____   ✕

4 Variants of growth style (encircle all applicable):

    (a)   "Normal" growth style   ✕

    (b)   "Growth at a reasonable price"   ✕

    (c)   Momentum   ✕

    (d)   Other: _____   ✕

Notes: Encircled responses are Vanguard Windsor II.

Definitions:

1 *Morningstar category*: Funds that invest the same way, as measured by cap. size and value/growth investment style.

2 *Fundamental analysis*: Determination of security "intrinsic value" relative to market price, based on underlying factors, such as expected earnings/dividends, cash flow patterns/horizons, and investor required rates of return.

3 *Value style*: Identification of undervalued securities based on fundamental measures, characterized by low price–earnings and price-to-book ratios.

4 *Growth style*: Identification of undervalued securities based on expected earnings growth rates, characterized by high price–earnings and price-to-book ratios.

5 *"Top down" analysis*: Fundamental analysis that focuses on macro outlook of alternative economies, markets and industries; then on micro analysis of individual companies and securities.

6 *"Bottom up" analysis*: Fundamental analysis that focuses on micro analysis of individual companies and securities; then perhaps on industry and/or economic outlook.

Table 39 (*continued*)

7 *"Normal" value style*: The "classic" value style (No. 3 above).

8 *Merger arbitrage*: Identification of underpriced and overpriced securities in proposed/expected mergers; involves arbitrage using simultaneous long and short positions.

9 *Financial distress*: Company operating cash flows inadequate to meet financial obligations and/or negative balance sheet equity.

10 *Distressed securities/indebtedness*: Identification of underpriced securities/indebtedness of financially distressed firms relative to potential "turnaround" values from financial restructurings with private workouts or bankruptcy, the latter including reorganization, acquisition, or liquidation.

11 *"Enhance" shareholder value*: Identification of underpriced stocks relative to potential values; involves taking and leveraging major share positions to influence or control management and "unlock shareholder value."

12 *"Special situations"*: Identification of underpriced stocks relative to unique "events," including tender offers, mergers and acquisitions, liquidations, spinoffs, reorganizations, and recapitalizations; more broadly defined, they includes opportunities from hidden earnings or assets, new technology, new CEOs, new markets, litigation, and tax rulings.

13 *"Normal" growth style*: The "classic" growth style (No. 4 above).

14 *"Growth at a reasonable price"*: Growth style constrained by maximum price to be paid for expected growth.

15 *"Momentum"*: Growth style based on short-term movements in one or more variants of earnings/price changes/estimates.

Table 40(a)   Morningstar, *Principia Pro for Mutual Funds*, Vanguard Windsor II, December 31, 1998

	Rating ★★★★ 2802 Domestic Equity Funds	Net assets $30,908.1 million	Morningstar category Large value

Investment approach

Equity style
Value Blend Growth

Large	■		
Medium			
Small			

Fixed-income style
Short Int Long

High			
Medium			
Low			

Composition as of 10-31-98

Cash	1.7
US stocks	97.7
Non-US stock	0.6
Bonds	0.0
Other	0.0

Regional exposure % of assets as of 09-30-98

US & Canada	82.5
Europe	1.4
Japan	0.0
Latin America	0.0
Pacific Rim	0.0
Other	0.0

Risk and return profile

Morningstar	3 year 2802 funds	5 year 1702 funds	10 year 732 funds
Rating	★	★	★
Risk	0.73	0.81	0.85
Return	1.61	1.62	1.28

Average historical rating over 127 months: 3.9★s

MPT statistics/other measurements

	S&P 500	Best Fit: S&P 500
R-squared	93	93
Beta	0.88	0.88
Alpha	-1.00	-1.00

	3 year	5 year	10 year
Sharpe ratio	1.18	–	
Std deviation	18.08	15.66	
Mean	24.13	21.29	

12-month yield	1.97%
30-day SEC yield	–
Potential cap. gains exp	27% of assets

Equity portfolio statistics

	Portfolio average	Relative index	Relative category
P/E ratio	24.8	0.75	0.97
P/C ratio	16.2	0.70	0.96
P/B ratio	4.4	0.56	0.90
3 year Earnings Gr %	9.4	0.46	0.60
Mdn Mkt Cap. ($ million)	25,916	0.43	1.25

Fixed-income portfolio statistics

Average eff mat/duration	–/–
Average weighted coupon	–
Average weighted price	–
Average credit quality	–

Turnover ratio %	30%
Assets in top 10 holdings %	28.40
Total holdings	287

Sector weightings as of 09-30-98

	% of Stocks	Relative S&P 500
Utilities	12.4	4.43
Energy	9.9	1.52
Financials	22.2	1.40
Industrial cyclicals	12.7	1.10
Consumer durables	5.8	2.64
Consumer staples	8.6	0.91
Services	16.4	1.11
Retail	5.2	0.79
Health	1.5	0.12
Technology	5.4	0.30

Trailing-period performance

	YTD	1 month	3 month	12 month	3 year Annlzd	5 year Annlzd	10 year Annlzd
Total return % as of 12-31-1998	16.36	2.66	14.92	16.36	24.13	21.29	17.33
+/- S&P 500	-12.22	-3.10	-6.36	-12.22	-4.09	-2.76	-1.87
+/- Wil large value	5.11	2.19	1.12	5.11	3.84	2.27	1.09
% rank within Morningstar category:					24(480)	12(327)	9(208)	16(104)

1 = Best 100 = Worst (number of funds)

Load-adjusted return % as of 12-31-98

	15 year Annlzd	
12 months	–	16.36
5 years	–	21.29
10 years	–	17.33
Inceptions		–

Growth of $10,000

— Vanguard Windsor II
$61,673

— Category average:
Large value
$49,798

— Index:
Standard & Poor's 500
$67,534

100,000
80,000
60,000
40,000
20,000
$10,000
5,000

Calendar year performance

	1988	1989	1990	1991	1992	1993	1994	1995	1996	1997	12-98
Total return %	24.73	27.83	-9.99	28.70	11.99	13.60	-1.17	38.83	24.18	32.38	16.36
+/- S&P 500	8.12	-3.85	-6.87	-1.78	4.37	3.54	-2.49	1.30	1.23	-0.97	-12.22
+/- Wil large value	1.94	2.69	-2.40	3.06	-2.40	0.15	3.17	-4.64	5.10	1.00	5.11

Operations

Family:	Vanguard Group	
Inception:	06-1985	
Manager:	James P. Barrow (et al.)	
Tenure:	10 Years	
Telephone:	800-662-7447	
Objective:	Growth and income	

Ticker:	VWNFX
Minimum initial purchase:	$3,000
Minimum IRA purchase:	$1,000
Minimum auto investment plan:	$3,000
Purchase constraints:	—

Front-end fees:	0.00%
Deferred load:	0.00%
12b-1 fee:	0.00%
Expense ratio:	0.37%
Assets:	$30,908.1 million
NAV:	29.85

Source: Reprinted with permission from Morningstar, *Principia Pro for Mutual Funds* (Advanced Analytics, Vanguard Windsor II), December 31, 1998.

Table 40(b)   Morningstar, *Mutual Funds OnDemand*, Vanguard Windsor II, December 6, 1998

Prospectus objective: growth and income | **Ticker** VWNFX | **Load** None | **NAV** $31.07 | **Yield** 2.0% | **SEC yield** — | **Total assets** $29,638.7 million | **Mstar category** Large value

Vanguard Windsor II seeks long-term growth of capital and income: current income is secondary.

The fund invests primarily in undervalued stocks of medium and large companies, characterized by above-average income yields and below-average price/earnings ratios relative to the stock market. Barrow, Hanley, Mewhinney & Strauss supervises approximately 75% of assets, Equinox and Tukman each supervise approximately 10%, and Vanguard supervises the remainder.

Prior to May 17, 1993, the fund was named Windsor II. From that date until Oct. 27, 1998, it was named Vanguard/Windsor II. Equinox and Tukman replaced Invesco as advisors in Oct. 1991.

Portfolio manager(s)

James P. Barrow, et al. Since 6-85. BS'62 U. of South Carolina Barrow has been with Barrow, Hanley, Mewhinney & Strauss since September 1979. Previously, he spent eight years as a portfolio manager with Republic National Bank.

Historical profile: Return High | Risk Average | Rating ★★★★★ Highest

Investment style: Equity, Average Stock %

Legend: ▽ Manager Change · ▽ Partial Manager Change · ▲ Mgr Unknown After · ▲ Mgr Unknown Before

Fund performance vs. category average: □ Quarterly Fund Return · +/- Category Average · — Category Baseline

Performance quartile (within Category)

History

	1987	1988	1989	1990	1991	1992	1993	1994	1995	1996	1997	10-98
Average Stock %		92%	92%	92%	92%	92%	92%	92%	93%	93%	92%	96%
NAV	10.75	12.81	14.96	12.46	14.89	15.91	17.04	15.82	20.66	23.83	28.62	31.07
Total Return %	-2.14	24.73	27.83	-9.99	28.70	11.99	13.60	-1.17	38.83	24.18	32.38	9.23
+/- S&P 500	-7.40	8.12	-3.86	-6.87	-1.79	4.37	3.55	-2.48	1.30	1.24	-0.98	-5.40
+/- Wilshire LV	-5.73	1.93	2.69	-2.40	3.06	-2.40	0.15	3.18	-4.64	5.11	1.00	4.13
Income Return %	4.97	5.36	5.84	4.93	4.94	3.52	3.23	3.25	3.69	3.07	2.78	0.70
Capital Return %	-7.11	19.36	21.99	-14.92	23.75	8.47	10.37	-4.42	35.14	21.12	29.59	8.53
Total Return % Rank Cat	78	12	22	78	46	32	44	67	7	16	13	16
Income $	0.61	0.57	0.74	0.73	0.61	0.52	0.51	0.55	0.58	0.63	0.66	0.20
Capital Gains $	0.80	0.00	0.61	0.28	0.44	0.22	0.50	0.47	0.69	1.16	2.19	0.00
Expense Ratio %	0.49	0.58	0.53	0.52	0.48	0.41	0.39	0.39	0.39	0.39	0.37	—
Income Ratio %	4.11	4.94	5.29	4.93	4.51	3.72	3.11	3.26	3.27	2.92	2.49	—
Turnover Rate %	46	25	22	20	41	23	26	24	30	32	30	—
Net Assets $ million	1,235.0	1,502.6	2,298.8	2,334.5	3,626.6	5,407.4	7,616.3	7,959.0	11,013.0	15,700.0	24,376.5	29,638.7

Performance 10-31-98

	1st Qtr	2nd Qtr	3rd Qtr	4th Qtr	Total
1994	-4.46	2.62	2.85	-1.98	-1.17
1995	9.86	8.11	10.22	6.05	38.83
1996	6.82	2.99	3.37	9.19	24.18
1997	1.59	14.70	9.07	4.15	32.38
1998	12.79	1.80	-11.82	—	—

Trailing

	Total Return %	+/- S&P 500	+/- Wil Large Value	% Rank All	% Rank Cat	Growth of $10,000
3 month	-1.96	-0.39	0.82	50	37	9,804
6 month	-4.37	-3.97	0.45	54	28	9,563
1 year	16.51	-5.48	4.12	10	11	11,651
3 year average	24.83	-1.15	3.99	3	5	19,451
5 year average	19.60	-1.69	2.29	5	7	24,472
10 year average	16.55	-1.33	0.93	10	12	46,247
15 year average	—	—	—	—	—	—

Tax analysis

	Tax-Adj Ret %	% Rank Cat	% Pretax Ret	% Rank Cat
3 year average	22.01	6	88.7	27
5 year average	17.00	8	86.8	25
10 year average	14.08	12	85.1	26

Potential Capital Gain Exposure: 33% of assets

Risk analysis

Time period	Load-Adj Return [1]	Risk % Rank All	Risk % Rank Cat	Morningstar Return	Morningstar Risk	Morningstar Risk-Adj Rating
1 year	16.51					
3 year	24.83	59	24	2.14	0.73	★★★★★
5 year	19.60	65	50	1.88	0.81	★★★★★
10 year	16.55	63	43	1.40	0.84	★★★★

Average historical rating (125 months): 3.9★s
[1] 1 = low, 100 = high

Category rating (3 year): ① ② ③ ④ ⑤   Worst — Best
Return: High
Risk: Below average

Other measures

	Standard index S&P 500	Best fit index S&P 500
Alpha	0.7	0.7
Beta	0.91	0.91
R-Squared	94	94
Standard deviation	18.31	
Mean	24.83	
Sharpe ratio	1.21	

Portfolio analysis 09-30-98

Share change since 06-98
Total Stocks: 287

	Sector	PE	YTD Ret %	% Assets
⊕ Anheuser-Busch	Staples	24.2	37.55	3.17
GTE	Services	28.2	15.25	2.36
⊕⊖⊕ SBC Communications	Services	23.0	29.30	2.35
⊖⊖ Entergy	Utilities	17.2	0.43	2.26
US West	Services	23.7	32.56	2.21
⊕⊕⊕ Chase Manhattan	Financials	14.6	6.25	2.19
BankAmerica	Financials	13.0	-16.50	2.18
Sears Roebuck	Retail	17.0	0.54	2.15
⊕⊖⊖ Waste Management	Services	28.6	14.99	2.04
Philip Morris	Staples	19.7	16.44	1.94
⊕⊕⊖ Williams Companies	Utilities	62.2	-2.53	1.93
Xerox	Technology	NMF	33.56	1.85
⊕⊕⊖ IBM	Technology	24.3	42.73	1.83
Raytheon Cl B	Industrials	—	—	1.78
⊕⊕⊕ Ford Motor	Durables	3.0	75.22	1.77
⊕⊕⊖ Allstate	Financials	10.7	-3.96	1.75
Tenneco	Industrials	—	—	1.74
⊕⊕⊖ Fort James	Industrials	NMF	6.68	1.70
⊕⊖ Honeywell	Industrials	18.8	17.83	1.68
Baker Hughes	Energy	26.6	-48.90	1.59
⊕ K mart	Retail	24.4	22.83	1.47
American Electric Power	Utilities	15.8	-1.46	1.47
PNC Bank	Financials	14.3	-9.46	1.45
Occidental Petroleum	Energy	—	-30.00	1.43
⊖ Chrysler	Durables	8.8	40.16	1.20

	Stock Port Avg	Relative S&P 500 Current	Hist	Rel Cat
Price/Earnings Ratio	23.1	0.75	0.79	0.97
Price/Book Ratio	4.3	0.58	0.64	0.95
Price/Cash Flow	15.1	0.70	0.76	0.96
3 Year Earnings Growth	12.1	0.67	0.74	0.79
1 Year Earnings Est %	8.9	0.87	—	1.43
Debt % Total Cap.	60.7	1.37	1.25	1.24
Med Mkt Cap. $ million	25,802	0.5	0.7	1.47

Current investment style

Style: Value / Blnd / Growth
Size: Large / Med / Small

(Large Value box filled)

Special securities % of assets 09-30-98

Restricted/Illiquid Secs	0
Emerging-Markets Secs	0
Options/Futures/Warrants	No

Composition % of assets 09-30-98

Cash	8.7
Stocks*	91.3
Bonds	0.0
Other	0.0

*Foreign 1.6 (% of stocks)

Market cap.

Giant	52.9
Large	40.4
Medium	6.6
Small	0.1
Micro	0.0

Sector weightings

	% of Stocks	Rel S&P	5-Year High	Low
Utilities	12.4	4.1	16	2
Energy	9.9	1.3	22	10
Financials	22.2	1.4	28	17
Industrials	12.7	1.0	17	9
Durables	5.8	2.1	7	1
Staples	8.6	0.9	15	6
Services	16.4	1.2	16	6
Retail	5.2	0.8	13	2
Health	1.5	0.1	13	1
Technology	5.4	0.4	6	2

Address:	Vanguard Financial Ctr. P.O. Box 2600
	Valley Forge, PA 19482
	800-662-7447/610-669-1000
Inception:	06-24-85
Advisor:	Multiple
Subadvisor:	None
Distributor:	Vanguard Group
NTF Plans:	N/A

Minimum purchase:	$3,000 Add: $100 IRA: $1,000
Min auto inv plan:	$3,000 Systematic Inv: $50
Sales fees:	No-load
Management fee:	None+(-)-888% P, at cost % A
Actual fees:	Mgt: 0.15% A Dist: —
Expense projections:	3 Year: $12 5 Year: $21 10 Year: $47
Average Brok. commission:	$0.0523 Income Distrib: Semi-Ann.

Total cost (relative to category): Low

Analysis by Amy Granzin 11-20-98

Vanguard Windsor II deserves equal billing with its family's stars.

As its name implies, this fund was something of an afterthought. When the first Windsor closed its doors in the 1980s, this fund was rushed out to meet continuing investor demand. For years it stood in Windsor's shadow and was overlooked by those rushing to put their money in Vanguard 500 Index. But times have changed. Windsor has lagged this fund for the past few years and its 1998 performance has been poor. The index fund is as successful as ever, but in many ways, this fund offers an edge.

The index fund, which is led by higher-growth companies that are less likely to pay big dividends, supplies a 1.3% payout. This fund, on the other hand, yields a heartier 2%. Because manager Jim Barrow employs a yield- and valuation-sensitive stock-picking strategy, the portfolio frequently overweights big dividend-paying electric utilities and established, slower-growing blue-chip names.

But the portfolio's poker growth rate hasn't kept it from competing effectively with the S&P 500 over the past few years. It fails to match the index, but the fund's annual return of 19.6% for the five-year period is very competitive considering its lack of hot growth stocks. Its returns have also come with less risk than the index. Barrow's bias for financials and cyclicals provided the fund with nice numbers during the past few years of low interest rates and solid economic growth. And he has done a fine job of preserving the fund's record recently by retreating into utilities.

Naturally, this fund, with its higher turnover rate and emphasis on yield is slightly less tax-efficient than its index sibling. But it is still more tax-friendly than most in its category. Its low expense ratio also helps to keep the fund in the group's top ranks.

Investors disenchanted with Windsor or wary of the high-P/E index will like this fund.

Source: Reprinted with permission from Morningstar, *Mutual Funds OnDemand*, 34 (1), December 6, 1998.

Table 41(a) Morningstar, *Principia Pro for Mutual Funds*, Vanguard 500 Index, December 31, 1998

Rating ★★★★ 2802 Domestic Equity Funds	Net assets $69,544.7 million	Morningstar category Large blend

Investment approach

Equity style
Value Blend Growth — Large / Medium / Small

Fixed-income style
Short Int Long — High / Medium / Low

Composition as of 10-31-98

Cash	0.6
US stocks	97.0
Non-US stock	2.4
Bonds	0.0
Other	0.0

Regional exposure % of assets as of 30-31-98

US & Canada	97.7
Europe	1.7
Japan	0.0
Latin America	0.0
Pacific Rim	0.0
Other	0.0

Risk and return profile

Morningstar	3 year 2802 funds	5 year 1702 funds	10 year 732 funds
Rating	5★	5★	5★
Risk	0.79	0.82	0.85
Return	2.02	1.98	1.59

Average historical rating over 157 months: 4.0★s

MPT statistics/other measurements

	S&P 500	Best Fit: S&P 500
R-squared	100	100
Beta	1.00	1.00
Alpha	-0.08	-0.08

	3 year	5 year	10 year
Sharpe ratio	1.26	–	
Std deviation	20.46	16.95	15.84
Mean	28.16	23.96	19.04

12-month yield	1.16%
30-day SEC yield	–
Potential cap. gains exp	46% of assets

Equity portfolio statistics	Portfolio average	Relative index	Relative category
P/E ratio	32.9	1.00	1.03
P/C ratio	22.5	0.98	1.01
P/B ratio	8.0	1.03	1.08
3 year Earnings Gr %	17.1	0.83	0.92
Mdn Mkt Cap. ($ million)	57,109	0.96	1.47

Sector weightings as of 10-31-98	% of Stocks	Relative S&P 500
Utilities	3.0	1.07
Energy	7.4	1.14
Financials	16.2	1.02
Industrial cyclicals	12.5	1.09
Consumer durables	2.8	1.27
Consumer staples	10.0	1.06
Services	13.8	0.93
Retail	6.4	0.97
Health	12.5	1.02
Technology	15.6	0.86

Fixed-income portfolio statistics	
Average eff mat/duration	–/–
Average weighted coupon	–
Average weighted price	–
Average credit quality	–

Turnover ratio %	5%
Assets in top 10 holdings %	19.71
Total holdings	507

Trailing-period performance

	YTD	1 month	3 month	12 month	3 year Annlzd	5 year Annlzd	10 year Annlzd	15 year Annlzd
Total return % as of 12-31-1998	28.62	5.81	21.39	28.62	28.16	23.96	19.04	17.64
+/- S&P 500	0.04	0.05	0.11	0.04	-0.06	-0.09	-0.16	-0.25
+/- Wil large blend	-0.43	-0.77	-0.85	-0.43	0.29	1.00	0.30	0.26

% rank within Morningstar category:				17(793)	7(509)	5(347)	11(138)	8(82)

1 = Best 100 = Worst (number of funds)

Load-adjusted return % as of 12-31-98

12 months	28.62
5 years	23.96
10 years	19.04
Inception	–

Growth of $10,000

Vanguard 500 index	$66,417	
Category average: Large blend	$52,758	
Index: Standard & Poor's 500	$67,534	

Calendar year performance	1988	1989	1990	1991	1992	1993	1994	1995	1996	1997	12–98
Total return %	16.22	31.37	-3.33	30.22	7.42	9.89	1.18	37.45	22.86	33.21	28.62
+/- S&P 500	-0.39	-0.31	-0.21	-0.26	-0.20	-0.17	-0.14	-0.08	-0.09	-0.14	0.04
+/- Wil large blend	-0.98	-0.05	0.75	-2.25	-0.78	0.15	3.53	-0.21	1.31	-0.09	-0.43

Operations

Family:	Vanguard Index Trust	Ticker:	VFINX	
Inception:	08-1976	Minimum initial purchase:	$3,000	
Manager:	George U. Sauter	Minimum IRA purchase:	$1,000	
Tenure:	12 Year	Minimum auto investment plan:	$3,000	
Telephone:	800-662-7447	Purchase constraints:	—	
Objective:	Growth and income			

Front-end fees:	0.00%
Deferred load:	0.00%
12b-1 fee:	0.00%
Expense ratio:	0.19%
Assets:	$69,544.7 million
NAV:	113.95

Source: Reprinted with permission from Morningstar, *Principia Pro for Mutual Funds* (Advanced Analytics, Vanguard 500 Index), December 31, 1998.

Table 41(b) Morningstar, *Mutual Funds OnDemand*, Vanguard 500 Index, January 6, 1999

Prospectus objective: growth and income

Vanguard 500 Index Fund seeks investment results that correspond with the price and yield performance of the S&P 500 index.

The fund allocates the percentage of net assets each company receives on the basis of the stock's relative total-market value: its market price per share multiplied by the number of shares outstanding.

Shareholders are charged an annual account-maintenance fee of $10 for accounts with less than $10,000. Prior to Dec. 21, 1987, the fund was named Vanguard Index Trust. Prior to 1980, it was named First Index Investment Trust. From that date until Oct. 27, 1998, the fund was named Vanguard Index Trust 500 Portfolio.

Portfolio manager(s)

George U. Sauter. Since 10-87. BA'76 Dartmouth C.; MBA'80 U. of Chicago. Sauter is a vice president of Vanguard Group, his employer since 1987. Other funds currently managed: Vanguard Morgan Grth, Vanguard Windsor II, Vanguard Explorer, Vanguard Sm Cap. Idx, Vanguard Ext Mkt Idx, Vanguard Pacific Stk Idx, Vanguard Euro Stk Idx, Vanguard Inst Idx, Vanguard Tot Stk Idx, Vanguard Grth Idx, Vanguard Val Idx, Vanguard Emerg Mkt Idx, Vanguard Tax-Mgd Bal, Vanguard Tax-Mgd Gr&Inc, Vanguard Tax-Mgd Cap. App, Vanguard Aggr Grth, Vanguard Total Intl Stk, Vanguard REIT Idx.

Performance 10-31-98

	1st Qtr	2nd Qtr	3rd Qtr	4th Qtr	Total
1994	-3.84	0.40	4.86	-0.05	1.18
1995	9.71	9.49	7.94	6.01	37.45
1996	5.36	4.44	3.05	8.35	22.86
1997	2.64	17.41	7.48	2.84	33.21
1998	13.91	3.29	-9.95	—	

Trailing	Total Return %	+/- S&P 500	+/- Wil Top 750	% Rank All	% Rank Cat	Growth of $10,000
3 month	22.09	0.06	-0.27	12	19	12,209
6 month	7.52	0.04	0.36	7	15	10,752
1 year	23.66	0.00	0.20	5	12	12,366
3 year average	26.58	-0.08	0.82	2	6	20,279
5 year average	22.87	-0.09	1.09	2	5	28,005
10 year average	18.58	-0.16	0.35	6	11	54,951
15 year average	17.15	-0.26	0.34	4	8	107,466

Tax analysis	Tax-Adj Ret %	% Rank Cat	% Pretax Ret	% Rank Cat
3 year average	25.54	4	96.1	7
5 year average	21.75	3	95.1	6
10 year average	17.25	5	92.8	7

Potential Capital Gain Exposure: 44% of assets

Fund data

Ticker	VFINX	
Load	None	
NAV	$108.49	
Yield	1.2%	
SEC yield	—	
Total assets	$69,544.7 million	
Mstar category	Large blend	

Historical profile

Return	High
Risk	Average
Rating	★★★★★ Highest

Investment style: Equity — Average Stock %

Key: ▽ Manager Change · ▽ Partial Manager Change · ▲ Mgr Unknown After · ▼ Mgr Unknown Before

Fund performance vs. category average: □ Quarterly Fund Return · +/- Category Average · — Category Baseline

Performance quartile (within Category)

History

	1987	1988	1989	1990	1991	1992	1993	1994	1995	1996	1997	11-98
Equity %	100%	100%	100%	99%	99%	99%	100%	99%	99%	100%	99%	99%
NAV	24.65	27.18	33.64	31.24	39.32	40.97	43.83	42.97	57.60	69.16	90.07	108.49
Total Return %	4.71	16.22	31.37	-3.33	30.22	7.42	9.89	1.18	37.45	22.86	33.21	21.56
+/- S&P 500	-0.55	-0.39	-0.32	-0.21	-0.26	-0.20	-0.17	-0.14	-0.09	-0.09	-0.14	-0.01
+/- Wilshire Top 750	0.60	-0.98	-0.06	0.76	-2.25	-0.78	0.16	3.53	-0.21	1.31	-0.09	0.48
Income Return %	2.87	4.54	4.49	3.52	3.73	2.88	2.79	2.70	2.86	2.24	1.92	0.90
Capital Return %	1.84	11.68	26.87	-6.85	26.50	4.55	7.11	-1.52	34.58	20.62	31.29	20.66
Total Rtn % Rank Cat	39	35	23	56	51	44	47	19	9	22	13	12
Income $	0.69	1.10	1.20	1.17	1.15	1.12	1.13	1.17	1.22	1.28	1.32	0.81
Capital Gains $	0.17	0.32	0.75	0.10	0.12	0.10	0.03	0.20	0.13	0.25	0.59	0.12
Expense Ratio %	0.26	0.22	0.21	0.22	0.20	0.19	0.19	0.19	0.20	0.20	0.19	—
Income Ratio %	3.15	4.08	3.62	3.60	3.07	2.81	2.65	2.72	2.38	2.04	1.66	—
Turnover Rate %	15	10	8	23	5	4	6	6	4	5	5	—
Net Assets $ million	826.3	1,055.1	1,803.8	2,173.0	4,345.3	6,517.7	8,272.7	9,356.1	17,371.8	30,331.9	49,357.6	69,544.7

Risk analysis

Time period	Load-Adj Return %	Morningstar Return	Morningstar Risk	Risk % Rank All	Risk % Rank Cat	Morningstar Risk-Adj Rating
1 year	23.66					
3 year	26.58	2.23	0.79	63	33	★★★★
5 year	22.87	2.00	0.81	65	32	★★★★★
10 year	18.58	1.60	0.85	63	38	★★★★★

Average historical rating (156 months): 4.0★s
[1] 1 = low, 100 = high

Category rating (3 Year): ①②③④⑤ Worst — Best   Return High · Risk Average

Other measures	Standard index S&P 500	Best fit index S&P 500
Alpha	-0.1	-0.1
Beta	1.00	1.00
R-squared	100	100
Standard deviation	20.05	
Mean	26.58	
Sharpe ratio	1.20	

Portfolio analysis 10-31-98

Share change since 08-98 Total Stocks: 507	Sector	PE	YTD Ret %	% Assets
⊕ General Electric	Industrials	33.5	24.50	3.20
⊕ Microsoft	Technology	59.8	88.78	2.93
⊕ Exxon	Energy	25.1	25.54	1.95
⊕ Coca-Cola	Staples	46.7	5.95	1.87
⊕ Merck	Health	37.3	48.12	1.81
⊖ Wal-Mart Stores	Retail	40.7	91.75	1.73
⊖ Intel	Technology	33.1	53.44	1.68
⊕ Pfizer	Health	45.0	51.28	1.58
⊖ IBM	Technology	26.6	58.95	1.56
⊖ Philip Morris	Staples	21.4	27.40	1.40
⊕ Procter & Gamble	Staples	33.3	11.20	1.34
⊕ AT & T	Services	18.0	3.11	1.26
⊕ Bristol-Myers Squibb	Health	35.3	30.33	1.24
⊕ Johnson & Johnson	Health	31.0	24.95	1.23
⊕ Citicorp	Financials	12.0	-25.50	1.21
⊕ Royal Dutch Petro NY ADR	Energy	20.2	-10.80	1.19
⊕ Lucent Technologies	Technology	NMF	116.00	1.18
⊕ BankAmerica (New)	Financials	18.1	9.03	1.12
⊕ MCI WorldCom	Services	–	95.04	1.10
⊕ Cisco Systems	Technology	80.2	102.80	1.10
⊕ SBC Communications	Services	24.2	33.84	1.02
⊕ American Intl Group	Financials	27.1	29.90	1.01
⊖ Eli Lilly	Health	50.4	30.26	1.00
⊕ Dell Computer	Technology	73.3	189.50	0.93
⊕ Bell Atlantic	Services	30.8	26.23	0.93

	Stock Port Avg	Relative S&P 500 Current	Relative S&P 500 Hist	Rel Cat
Price/Earnings Ratio	31.9	1.03	1.00	1.04
Price/Book Ratio	7.6	1.02	1.00	1.10
Price/Cash Flow	21.9	1.01	1.00	1.01
3 Year Earnings Growth	17.2	0.92	1.00	0.92
1 Year Earnings Est %	9.5	0.93	–	0.81
Debt % Total Cap.	31.4	0.71	1.00	0.98
Med Mkt Cap. $ million	54,088	1.0	1.0	1.55

Current investment style

Style: Value Blnd Growth
Size: Large Med Small

(style box: Large / Blend shaded)

Special securities % of assets 10-31-98

○ Restricted/Illiquid Secs	0
○ Emerging-Markets Secs	0
○ Options/Futures/Warrants	No

Composition % of assets 10-31-98

Cash	0.6
Stocks*	99.5
Bonds	0.0
Other	0.0
*Foreign (% of stocks)	2.5

Market cap.

Giant	54.2
Large	34.5
Medium	10.9
Small	0.4
Micro	0.0

Sector weightings	% of Stocks	Rel S&P	5-Year High	5-Year Low
Utilities	3.0	1.0	9	3
Energy	7.4	1.0	11	7
Financials	16.2	1.0	18	8
Industrials	12.5	1.0	19	12
Durables	2.8	1.0	6	3
Staples	10.0	1.0	15	10
Services	13.8	1.0	18	10
Retail	6.4	1.0	9	5
Health	12.5	1.0	13	8
Technology	15.6	1.0	16	5

Analysis by Scott Cooley 12-18-98

Low costs are only one of Vanguard 500 Index Fund's advantages.

A lot of attention justifiably gets paid to this fund's expense ratio. At 60 basis points below the average for no-load large-blend funds, its costs are low. Its annual levy is also only about half the average for S&P 500 index funds that are available to individuals. (Because of a $10 annual maintenance fee for small accounts, the fund's effective annual expense ratio can be higher, however.)

But even among index funds, low costs aren't this fund's only edge. Manager Gus Sauter has run index money for a decade, and his skills have improved over the years. Indeed, the fund's tracking error – the gap between the return of the index and that of the portfolio – has generally fallen over the past decade. In part that's because Sauter has exploited differences between the cash and futures markets, buying whatever is cheaper at the end of the day. As a result, for the year through November, the fund trails the index by only one basis point, and it's more than 20 basis points ahead of Fidelity's S&P index fund, which currently has lower expenses.

One oft-cited drawback is the fund's huge potential capital-gains exposure. Sauter says that big sales from the fund are unlikely, though, unless the market crumbles – which would reduce the unrealized gains. Vanguard also plans to first sell higher-cost shares, limiting realized gains. With a median market cap. that's higher than its peers, the fund could bleed assets if small caps consistently beat mega-caps, as they did in the late 1970s. Sauter says, however, that simulations (using Vanguard's current tax-minimization strategies) indicate the fund would have paid out capital gains only twice since its inception, and each distribution would have been small.

Thus broad diversification, Sauter's skill and experience, and low expenses continue to be strong selling points for this fund.

Address:	P.O. Box 2600 Valley Forge, PA 19482 800-662-7447/610-669-1000	Minimum purchase:	$3,000 Add: $100 IRA: $1,000
		Min auto inv plan:	$3,000 Systematic Inv: $50
Inception:	08-31-76	Sales fees:	No-load
Advisor:	Vanguard Core Management Group	Management fee:	Provided at cost, at cost % A
Subadvisor:	None	Actual fees:	Mgt: 0.16% Dist: –
Distributor:	Vanguard Group	Expense projections:	3 Year: $6 5 Year: $11 10 Year: $24
		Average Brok. commission:	$0.0181 Income Distrib: Quarterly
NTF Plans:	N/A	Total cost (relative to category):	Low

Source: Reprinted with permission from Morningstar, *Mutual Funds OnDemand* 34 (3), Vanguard 500 Index, January 6, 1999.

Table 42(a) Morningstar, *Principia Pro for Mutual Funds*, average of 514 funds (large value), December 31, 1998

	Rating 3.41	Net assets $967.91 million	Morningstar category

Investment approach

Equity style

Value Blend Growth

410	46	2	Large
33	1		Medium
	2		Small

Fixed-income style

Short Int Long

			High
			Medium
			Low

Composition

Cash	6.2
US stocks	86.8
Non-US stock	4.4
Bonds	0.9
Other	1.4

Regional exposure % of assets

		Relative S&P 500
US & Canada	88.0	–
Europe	3.2	–
Japan	0.1	–
Latin America	0.2	–
Pacific Rim	0.3	–
Other	1.2	–

Sector weightings	% of Stocks	Relative S&P 500
Utilities	5.5	–
Energy	9.0	–
Financials	23.2	–
Industrial cyclicals	15.5	–
Consumer durables	4.8	–
Consumer staples	6.6	–
Services	13.5	–
Retail	5.2	–
Health	8.1	–
Technology	8.7	–

Equity portfolio statistics	Portfolio average	Relative index	Relative category
P/E ratio	25.5	–	–
P/C ratio	16.9	–	–
P/B ratio	4.9	–	–
3 year Earnings Gr %	15.7	–	–
Mdn Mkt Cap. ($ million)	20,212	–	–

Fixed-income portfolio statistics	
Average eff mat/duration	–/–
Average weighted coupon	–
Average weighted price	–
Average credit quality	–

Turnover ratio %	70%
Assets in top 10 holdings %	33.0
Total holdings	96

Risk and return profile

Morningstar	3 year	5 year	10 year
Rating	3.30	3.48	3.27
Risk	0.81	0.84	0.87
Return	1.14	1.17	0.99

MPT statistics/other measurements

	S&P 500	Best Fit:
R-squared	87	–
Beta	0.87	–
Alpha	–4.20	–

	3 year	5 year	10 year
Sharpe ratio	0.94	–	–
Std deviation	17.76	15.24	14.65
Mean	19.74	17.88	15.53

12-month yield	0.95%
30-day SEC yield	0.92%
Potential cap. gains exp	19% of assets

Trailing-period performance

	YTD	1 month	3 month	12 month	3 year Annlzd	5 year Annlzd	10 year Annlzd	15 year Annlzd
Total return % as of 12-31-1998	12.34	3.42	16.50	12.34	19.74	17.88	15.53	14.55
+/- S&P 500	-16.24	-2.34	-4.78	-16.24	-8.48	-6.17	-3.67	-3.34
+/- LB agg	3.67	3.12	16.16	3.67	12.45	10.61	6.27	4.24

Load-adjusted return % as of 12-31-98

12 months	10.15
5 years	17.45
10 years	15.26
Inception	17.83

% rank within Morningstar category: —
1 = Best 100 = Worst (number of funds)

Graph not available

Calendar year performance

	1988	1989	1990	1991	1992	1993	1994	1995	1996	1997	12-98
Total return %	17.63	23.62	-6.36	29.13	10.63	13.78	-0.38	32.48	20.61	26.70	12.34
+/- S&P 500	1.02	-8.06	-3.24	-1.35	3.01	3.72	-1.70	-5.05	-2.34	-6.65	-16.24
+/- LB agg	9.74	9.09	-15.32	13.13	3.23	4.03	2.54	14.01	16.99	17.02	3.67

Operations

Family:	—	Ticker:	—
Inception:	—	Minimum initial purchase:	$319,927
Manager:	—	Minimum IRA purchase:	$4,545
Tenure:	4.2 years	Minimum auto investment plan:	$7,130
Telephone:	—	Purchase constraints:	—
Objective:	—		

Front-end fees:	1.30%
Deferred load:	0.96%
12b-1 fee	0.38%
Expense ratio:	1.31%
Assets:	$967.91 million
NAV:	—

Source: Reprinted with permission as computed from Morningstar, *Principia Pro for Mutual Funds,* Advanced Analytics, Large Value Category, December 31, 1998.

Table 42(b) Morningstar, *Mutual Funds OnDemand*, overview, large-cap. value, December 6, 1998

Large-cap. value funds focus on big companies that are less expensive than the market as a whole. These firms may be out-of-favor with investors due to recent business problems or – more often – they're simply growing slower than other companies. These slow-growers, which usually fall in the utilities, energy, financials, and cyclical sectors, also have their virtues. Such companies tend to pay relatively high dividends and have more-stable stock prices.

Highlights 11-20-98

Biggest Inflows: Familiar names like Legg Mason Value and Vanguard Growth & Income remain popular with investors. It's bank-run funds, however, that are really recording a flood of new assets. First Chicago's Pegasus Equity Income and National City's Armada Equity Income nearly doubled in size during 1998's third quarter.

Biggest Outflows: Once-loved offerings Vanguard Windsor and Neuberger & Berman Guardian have developed two of the bigger asset leaks due to disastrous recent returns. Loss of interest in the still-solid Oakmark fund is a little harder to explain.

Performance 10-31-98

	1st Qtr	2nd Qtr	3rd Qtr	4th Qtr	Total
1995	8.57	8.00	7.26	5.10	32.29
1996	5.32	2.41	2.97	8.19	20.07
1997	1.59	13.53	8.98	0.78	26.57
1998	11.12	–0.76	–12.30		–

Trailing	Total Return %	+/– S&P 500	% Rank All	+/– Wil Large Value	% Pretax Ret	% Rank All	Tax-Adj Ret %	% Rank All	Total
3 month	–2.83	–1.27	15	–0.06					53
6 month	–6.80	–6.40	25	–1.97					61
1 year	8.77	–13.20	29	–3.63					37
3 year average	19.12	–6.87		–1.73					15
5 year average	16.09	–5.20		–1.22					15
10 year average	14.50	–3.38		–1.12					22
15 year average	13.83	–3.28		–3.72					29

Tax analysis		% Pretax Ret	% Rank All
3 year average	15.97	87.1	54
5 year average	13.13	84.8	50
10 year average	11.84	82.2	52

	Total return %	Morningstar risk	Funds in Category
vs. (5 years)	40	30	20	10

Wilshire Large Value

5 year Morningstar risk

Top funds

Best 5 year return %		Lowest 5 year Morningstar risk		Highest 5 year Morningstar rating	
○ Legg Mason Value Prim	27.85	□ Smith Barney Prem Tot Ret B	0.58	Sequoia	
Sequoia	25.85	T. Rowe Price Equity-Income	0.60	Torray	
Torray	22.25	American Mutual	0.61	American Cent Inc & Grow Inv	
Kemper-Dreman High Ret Eq A	21.78	Franklin Equity Income I	0.62	American Cent Equity Gr Inv	
Clipper	21.55	Vontobel US Value	0.63	T. Rowe Price Equity-Income	

History	1987	1988	1989	1990	1991	1992	1993	1994	1995	1996	1997	10-98
Top Decile Average	12.43	30.91	36.61	1.72	45.83	21.66	24.20	5.30	40.82	29.07	35.22	13.46
Total Return %	1.14	17.27	23.45	–6.48	29.41	10.41	13.57	–0.52	32.29	20.12	26.61	3.97
Bottom Decile Average	–12.72	1.11	13.14	–15.37	18.33	0.61	4.71	–8.52	22.12	11.51	16.55	–4.68
+/– S&P 500	–4.12	0.66	–8.23	–3.37	–1.07	2.80	3.51	–1.83	–5.25	–2.83	–6.74	–10.66
+/– Wilshire LV	–2.45	–5.53	–1.69	1.11	3.78	–3.98	0.11	3.83	–11.18	1.04	–4.76	–1.12
Expense Ratio %	1.15	1.30	1.25	1.25	1.24	1.20	1.18	1.21	1.26	1.30	1.31	1.32
Income Ratio %	2.82	3.33	3.60	3.60	3.09	2.49	2.10	2.11	2.12	1.70	1.41	1.18
Turnover Rate %	78	65	65	63	64	58	57	60	62	66	65	75
Net Assets ($ billion)	38.94	44.10	57.72	53.45	70.16	87.72	123.83	142.96	214.87	291.91	422.25	461.60
#Funds, excluding multiple share classes	88	101	107	118	129	153	170	188	208	229	254	263

Risk analysis

	Morningstar Return	Score Risk	Morningstar Risk-Adj Rating
3 year	1.38	0.81	★★★★
5 year	1.29	0.83	★★★★
10 year	1.04	0.89	★★★★
Wtd average	1.18	0.85	★★★★★

Other measures

		Standard Index S&P 500
Standard deviation	17.52	Alpha	–3.40
Mean	18.71	Beta	0.88
Sharpe ratio	0.91	R-squared	88

Morningstar category correlation

Style	Value	Blend	Growth		Size
					Large	Med	Small
	1.00	0.98	0.91		Large		
	0.95	0.90	0.78		Med		
	0.77	0.72	0.65		Small		

Average expense ratios

Front-end load	1.21	Level Load	1.95
Deferred load	1.91	No-Load	.99
Category average	1.32		

Update Amy Granzin, 11-20-98

The game may have changed, but the same players are winning on the large-value field.

This year's third-quarter market correction left a number of casualties among this typically defensive group when financials stocks plunged precipitously. (The category's average fund devotes 23% of assets to these stocks.) While many of these Teflon firms survived 1997's global economic crisis, US banks and brokerages finally tripped up when Russian banks defaulted on their loans this fall, and recession fears reemerged. Funds with heavy exposure to this once "can't lose" sector such as top-ranked Chase Vista Equity Income and Preferred Value understandably suffered.

But for the most part, this group's hierarchy has remained intact in 1998. Bigger median market caps continued to be better, and many financials-heavy funds have managed to land on top. Through October, familiar, if not idiosyncratic, offerings had held their seats in the winner's circle.

Clipper Fund (which hasn't made a false move in years), was vindicated for its once-maligned 35% cash position when the market got rocky. Its one-name wonder compatriot, Sequoia, has also retained its place at the top, despite an astonishing 90% stake in financials, which includes a 34% position in Berkshire Hathaway. Legg Mason Value, another fund that thinks diversification is for wimps and often boasts the group's biggest technology weighting, ranks number one in 1998 and is the best-performing fund in Morningstar's database over the past five years.

While these funds all go their unique ways, there's an important factor that links a lot of the short- and longer-term victors. Most have relatively small asset bases. Clipper's still under $1 billion, and Torray Fund is just over that mark. None of the category's top 10 of 1998 are much larger than $5 billion. On the other hand, some of the swollen funds from bigger shops, such as Vanguard Windsor, which has produced rotten returns over the past 12 months, seem to have seen better days.

This year's affirmation of the status quo should probably reassure nervous investors searching for consistency. Despite considerable market volatility in 1998, those funds that, at base, emphasize fundamental stock-picking just keep coming out ahead.

Source: Reprinted with permission from Morningstar, *Mutual Funds OnDemand* 34 (1), Overview: Large Value, December 6, 1998.

Portfolio analysis 10-31-98

Average number of equity holdings: 89

	% Portfolios in Category	% Net Assets
Philip Morris	65	1.75
IBM	57	1.20
Mobil	53	0.72
Chase Manhattan	48	0.87
Bell Atlantic	48	0.63
Ford Motor	48	0.83
Exxon	46	0.74
AT & T	46	1.36
American Home Products	46	0.92
GTE	45	0.69
Bristol-Myers Squibb	43	0.78
Fannie Mae	41	1.31
El duPont de Nemours	41	0.10
First Union	41	0.87
Texaco	40	0.73

Most common purchases	Value $ million
General Re	1,278.8
Chrysler	1,243.2
IBM	966.1
American Stores	769.5
MCI WorldCom	731.8

Most common sales	Value $ million
Allstate	−481.8
State Street	−474.9
American Home Products	−315.1
Ford Motor	−311.1
General Motors	−305.1

Investment style

	Stock Port Avg	Rel S&P 500
Price/Earnings Ratio	23.8	0.78
Price/Book Ratio	4.5	0.62
3 Year Earnings Gr %	15.3	0.77
Price/Cash Flow	15.8	0.74
Debt % Total Cap.	48.9	1.10
Med Mkt Cap. $ million	17,362.4	0.33
Yield	1.0%	

Sector weightings

	% of Stocks	Rel S&P 500
Utilities	5.3	1.76
Energy	9.3	1.27
Financials	22.6	1.39
Industrials	16.6	1.33
Durables	4.9	1.78
Staples	6.6	0.66
Services	13.3	0.97
Retail	5.3	0.83
Health	7.7	0.62
Technology	8.4	0.54

Market cap.

● Giant	37.7
◐ Large	37.5
○ Medium	21.5
○ Small	2.9
⊘ Micro	0.2

Composition % of assets 09-30-98

Cash	7.1
Stocks*	90.7
Bonds	1.3
Other	0.9
*Foreign (% of stocks)	5.0

Cash inflows

	Cash Flow %	% Total assets Equity	% Total assets All
1994	12.9	19.82	10.26
1995	14.3	20.13	11.65
1996	13.1	20.46	12.66
1997	14.1	21.58	14.29
1998	5.7	21.70	14.22

Table 43 Selected measures of diversification risk: value versus growth. Vanguard Value Index and Vanguard Growth Index Relative to Vanguard 500 Index and each other, 1998

Diversification risk measure[a]	Relative to 500 Index		Value risk relative to growth risk
	Value Index	Growth Index	
Investment style risk			
P/E ratio	0.73	1.22	Less
P/B ratio	0.44	1.55	Less
P/C ratio	0.68	1.22	Less
Three-year earnings growth rate	0.60	1.05	Less
R^2	0.95	0.96	More
Beta	0.97	1.03	Less
Standard deviation	0.95	1.09	Less
PEG ratio[a]	1.02	0.97	More
Cash asset allocation risk			
Cash ratio	n.a.	n.a.	–
Market liquidity risk			
Giant and large market cap. (%)	1.01	1.09	More
Median market cap. ($ million)	0.42	1.71	More
Special securities (%)	n.a.	n.a.	–
Returns distribution risk			
Income return/Total returns (%)	4.75	0.5	Less
Industry sector concentration risk			
"Top three" industry sectors/Total assets (%)	1.30	1.35	Less
Security concentration risk			
"Top ten" securities/Total assets (%)	1.02	1.95	Less

n.a. Not applicable to benchmark market index.

[a] Computed from Morningstar data.

Definitions:

1 *P/E ratio (price/earnings ratio):* Weighted average of the P/E ratios of the stocks in a mutual fund's portfolio. Current stock price divided by its most recent twelve months' earnings per share.

2 *P/B ratio (price/book value ratio):* Weighted average of the P/B ratios of the stocks in a mutual fund's portfolio. Current stock price divided by its book value per share.

3 *P/C ratio (price/cash flow ratio):* Weighted average of the P/C ratios of the stocks in a mutual fund's portfolio. Current stock price divided by its cash flow per share.

Table 43 (*continued*)

4 R^2 (*also R-squared, coefficient of determination*): Proportion of the movements in a mutual fund's portfolio returns that are explained by movements in the market index returns. Measure of sameness of a fund's portfolio relative to the market index.

5 *Beta* (*also β, systematic risk, non-diversifiable risk*): Sensitivity measure of the proportional change in a mutual fund's excess returns for a given change in the excess returns of the market index, where excess returns equal total return less ninety-day Treasury bill returns.

6 *Standard deviation* (*also SD, total risk, coefficient of determination*): Absolute measure of dispersion (total risk) of a mutual fund's returns for the most recent twelve months annualized.

7 *PEG ratio*: P/E ratio divided by weighted average of the most recent three-year earnings growth rates of the stocks in a mutual fund's portfolio. Relative measure of the price paid for each unit of earnings growth rate.

8 *Cash ratio*: Cash assets in a mutual fund's portfolio divided by the portfolio's total value. Relative measure of liquidity in a portfolio.

9 *Giant and large market cap.* (%): Sum of the percentages of a mutual fund's portfolio invested in the two largest categories of stock holdings measured by market capitalization. Relative measure of the liquidity of the markets represented in a portfolio.

10 *Median market cap.* (*$ million*): Median market capitalization of the stocks in a mutual fund's portfolio. Absolute measure of the liquidity of the representative stock in a portfolio.

11 *Special securities* (%): Percentage of a mutual fund's portfolio held in each of two types of above-average risk securities: (a) restricted/illiquid; (b) emerging market; and (c) whether (yes/no) the portfolio includes options, futures or warrants. "Signals" of potential additional portfolio risk.

12 *Income return/total return* (%): Percentage of a mutual fund's returns from interest and dividends. Measure of stability of returns.

13 *"Top three" industry sector/total assets* (%): Percentage of a mutual fund's total assets invested in its three largest industry sectors. Measure of sector concentration.

14 *"Top ten" securities/total assets* (%): Percentage of mutual fund's total assets invested in its ten largest securities holdings. Measure of security concentration.

Sources: *Morningstar Principia Pro for Mutual Funds*, Vanguard Value Index, Vanguard 500 Index, and Vanguard Growth Index, December 31, 1998; *Morningstar Mutual Funds OnDemand*, Vanguard Value Index, December 6, 1998; Vanguard 500 Index, January 6, 1999; and Vanguard Growth Index, January 6, 1999.

Table 44 Measures of diversification risk: value/growth investment style. Vanguard Windsor II, large-cap. value category, and S&P 500 Index/Vanguard 500 Index, 1998

Measure	Fund	Fund relative to:		Fund vs. category	Fund vs. market
		Category	S&P 500		
P/E ratio	24.80	0.97	0.75	Less risk	Less risk[a]
P/C ratio	16.20	0.96	0.70	Less risk	Less risk[a]
P/B ratio	4.40	0.90	0.56	Less risk[a]	Less risk[a]
Three-year earnings growth rate	9.40	0.60	0.46	Less risk[a]	Less risk[a]
		Vanguard 500 Index			
R^2 (1.0 is ideal)	0.93	1.07	0.93	Less risk	More risk
Beta (low is better)	0.88	1.01	0.88	More risk	Less risk[a]
Standard deviation	18.08	1.02	0.88	More risk	Less risk[a]
PEG ratio[b]	2.64	1.62	1.63	More risk[a]	More risk[a]
Risk comparison:					
Overall fund vs. category				Excellent	
Overall fund vs. market					Excellent
Overall fund investment style risk				Excellent	

[a] Significantly more/less risk (10% rule).
[b] Computed from Morningstar data.

Sources: Tables 40(a), 41(a), and 42(a).

Table 45 Diversification risk: cash asset allocation and net cash inflow, Vanguard Windsor II and large-cap. value category,[a] 1994–98

Cash ratio	1994	1995	1996	1997	1998	Mean
(A) Cash asset allocation						
Windsor II	8.0	7.3	8.3	7.1	1.7	6.5
Category	8.3	8.2	6.7	5.4	5.9	6.9
Fund vs. category					More risk[b]	More risk
Overall cash asset liquidity risk					Unacceptable	

(B) Net cash inflow (1998)
Windsor II increase in NCI: 27.9%.
Category increase in NCI (table 42b): 5.7%.

Overall net cash inflow: Excellent.

Note: This measure not applicable to the passively managed Vanguard 500 Index.

[a] Represented by CDA/Wiesenberger Growth and Income investment objective.
[b] Significantly more risk (10% rule).

Source: Cash asset data from CDA/Wiesenberger, *Mutual Fund Directory* (CDA/Wiesenberger, Rockville, MD), December 31, 1994–98. NCI cited above.

Table 46   Measures of diversification risk: market liquidity (market capitalization, median market capitalization, and special securities), Windsor II, overview: large-cap. value, and Vanguard 500 Index, 1998

	Windsor II	Large-cap. value	500 Index
Market cap. (%)			
Giant and large	93.3	75.2	88.7
Medium	6.6	21.5	10.9
Small and micro	0.1	3.1	0.4
Total	100	100	100
Fund vs. category		Less risk[a]	
Fund vs. market			Less risk
Overall fund market cap. risk		Excellent	Excellent
Median market cap. ($ million)			
	25,916	20,212	57,109
Fund vs. category		Less risk[a]	
Fund vs. market			More risk[a]
Overall median market risk		Acceptable	Acceptable
Special securities/total assets (%)			
Restricted/illiquid	0.0	n.a.	0.0
Emerging market	0.0	n.a.	0.0
Options/futures/warrants	0.0	n.a.	0.0
Fund vs. market			Equal risk
Overall fund special securities risk		Excellent	Excellent
Overall fund market liquidity risk		Excellent	Excellent

Notes: *Giant and large*: 250 largest cap. *Medium*: 750 second largest cap. *Small and micro*: 4,000 third largest cap. Total = 5,000 largest cap. sizes.

n.a. = Not available in this source.
[a]   Significantly less/more risk (10% rule).

Source: Tables 40(a–b), 41(a–b), and 42(b).

Table 47 Measures of diversification risk: returns distribution, Windsor II and Vanguard 500 Index, 1994–98 (%)

Assets/returns/risk comparisons	1994	1995	1996	1997	1998	Mean
Windsor II						
Income return	3.25	3.69	3.07	2.78	0.70	n.a.
Capital gains return	−4.42	35.14	21.12	29.59	8.53	n.a.
Total returns	−1.17	38.83	24.18	32.38	9.23	n.a.
Income return/total returns	n.a.	9.5	12.7	8.6	7.6	9.6
500 Index						
Income return	2.70	2.86	2.24	1.92	0.90	n.a.
Capital gains return	−1.52	34.58	20.62	31.20	20.66	n.a.
Total returns	1.18	37.45	22.86	33.21	21.56	n.a.
Income return/total returns	n.a.	7.6	9.8	5.8	4.2	6.8
Fund relative to market					Less risk[a]	Less risk[a]
Overall fund returns distribution risk					Excellent	

Notes: Data not available for category. *n.a.* Not applicable.

[a] Significantly less risk (10% rule).

Source: Tables 40(b) and 41(b).

Table 48 Measures of diversification risk: industry sector concentration, Windsor II, Vanguard 500 Index and average of 514 funds (large value), 1998

Asset/risk comparison	"Top three" industry sectors to total assets (%)
Windsor II	51.3
500 Index (market surrogate)	45.6
Large-cap. value category	52.2
Fund relative to category	Less risk
Fund relative to market	More risk[a]
Overall fund industry sector concentration risk	Acceptable

[a] Significantly more risk (10% rule).

Source: Tables 40(a), 41(a), and 42(a).

Table 49 Measures of diversification risk: value versus growth, industry sector concentration, Vanguard Value Index and Vanguard Growth Index relative to S&P 500 Index and each other, 1998

Industry sector	Relative to S&P 500 Index	
	Value Index	Growth Index
Utilities	2.50	0.00
Energy	2.48	0.14
Financials	1.62	0.45
Consumer durables	2.55	0.14
Services	1.20	0.72
Industrial cyclicals	1.03[a]	1.11
Consumer staples	0.11	1.73
Retail	0.83	0.98[a]
Health	0.17	1.84
Technology	0.41	1.26

[a] Insignificantly different; all others significant (10% rule).

Source: *Morningstar Principia Pro for Mutual Funds*, Vanguard Value Index, and Vanguard Growth Index, December 31, 1998.

Table 50 Diversification risk: portfolio concentration, Windsor II, Vanguard 500 Index and average of 514 funds (large value), 1998

Asset/risk comparison	"Top ten" securities as % of total assets
Windsor II	28.4
500 Index	19.7
Large-cap. value category	33.0
Fund relative to category	Less risk[a]
Fund relative to market	More risk[a]
Overall portfolio concentration risk	Acceptable

[a] Significantly more risk (10% rule).

Source: Tables 40(a), 41(a), and 42(a).

Table 51 Diversification risk: Value Line safety and timeliness, Windsor II, Vanguard 500 Index, and overview: large value, 1998

Stock	% of total	Weighted %	Timeliness	Safety
Fund assets				
Chase Manhattan	3.15	8.91	5	3
Ford Motor	3.09	8.74	5	3
GTE	2.69	7.61	5	2
Sears Roebuck	2.60	7.35	3	3
Anheuser-Busch	2.49	7.04	4	1
IBM	2.42	6.84	3	3
Waste Management	2.40	6.79	2	3
US West Communications	2.14	6.05	3	1
BankAmerica	2.13	6.02	2	3
SBC Communications	2.12	6.00	3	2
Chrysler	2.05	5.80	5	3
K-mart	2.05	5.80	1	4
PNC Bank	2.03	5.74	4	2
Entergy	2.02	5.71	3	4
First Chicago NBD	1.98	5.60	3	3
Total	35.36	100.00		
Mean score			3.4000	2.6667
Weighted average			3.5048	2.6598
Market assets				
General Electric	3.14	12.94	3	1
Coca-Cola	2.15	8.86	3	1
Microsoft	2.04	8.41	1	2
Exxon	1.97	8.12	4	1
Merck	1.66	6.84	3	1
Royal Dutch (NY)	1.52	6.27	5	1
Intel	1.50	6.18	3	3
Philip Morris	1.44	5.94	3	3
Procter & Gamble	1.40	5.77	3	1
IBM	1.33	5.48	3	3
AT&T	1.30	5.36	5	2
Pfizer	1.26	5.19	1	2
Bristol-Myers Squibb	1.23	5.07	3	1
Wal-Mart Stores	1.16	4.78	1	2
Johnson & Johnson	1.16	4.78	3	1
Total	24.26	100.00		
Mean score			2.9333	1.6667
Weighted average			2.9460	1.5894

Table 51 (*continued*)

Category assets				
Philip Morris	1.65	14.04	3	3
AT&T	1.25	10.64	5	2
Chase Manhattan	1.10	9.36	5	3
IBM	1.06	9.02	3	3
Ford Motor	0.98	8.34	5	3
Bristol-Myers Squibb	0.81	6.89	3	1
BankAmerica	0.71	6.04	3	2
General Motors	0.70	5.96	3	3
Exxon	0.66	5.62	4	1
Bell Atlantic	0.64	5.45	3	1
NationsBank	0.63	5.36	3	2
Mobil	0.62	5.28	4	1
GTE	0.57	4.85	5	2
American Home Products	0.35	2.98	3	1
Atlantic Richfield	0.02	0.17	4	1
Total	11.75	100.00		
Mean score			3.7333	1.9333
Weighted average			3.7745	2.2034

Summary findings (weighted average rating)

Safety risk[a]	Rating		Risk
Fund vs. market	2.7 vs. 1.6		More risk[b]
Fund vs. category	2.7 vs. 2.2		More risk[b]
Overall fund safety risk		Unacceptable	

Timeliness risk[a]			
Fund vs. market	3.5 vs. 2.9		More risk[b]
Fund vs. category	3.5 vs. 3.8		Less risk
Overall fund timeliness risk		Acceptable	

[a]   Lower scores: higher quality and timeliness.

[b]   Significantly more/less risk (10% rule).

Source: Earlier dates of tables 40(b), 41(b), and 42(b), supplemented from *Value Line Investment Survey*, 1998.

Table 52 Mutual fund diversification risks and investment styles: overall assessments, Vanguard Windsor II, 1998

Measure	Overall (individual) assessments
A Diversification risks	
1 Value/growth investment style (table 44)	(Excellent)
2 Cash asset allocation (table 45)	(Unacceptable)
3 Net cash inflow (table 45)	(Excellent)
4 Market liquidity (three measures) (table 46)	(Excellent)
5 Returns distribution (table 47)	(Excellent)
6 Industry sector concentration (table 48)	(Acceptable)
7 Security concentration (table 50)	(Acceptable)
8 Value Line safety (table 51)	(Unacceptable)
9 Value Line timeliness (table 51)	(Acceptable)
Overall assessment	Acceptable
B Value/growth investment styles	
1 Table 39	Normal value
2 Table 40a	Value

Source: Tables cited.

Table 53 CDA annualized rates of return, Windsor II, S&P 500 Index, and growth and income category, 1993–7

Holding period	Windsor II	S&P 500 Index	Category
Ten years ending:			
1997	18.1	18.1	14.9
1996	14.6	15.2	12.5
1995	14.4	14.8	12.1
1994	n.a.	14.3	11.8
1993	n.a.	14.9	12.5
Five years ending:			
1997	20.7	20.3	16.5
1996	16.7	15.2	13.2
1995	17.6	16.5	14.6
1994	7.8	8.7	7.8
1993	13.5	14.5	12.4
Three years ending:			
1997	31.7	31.1	24.2
1996	19.4	19.6	14.3
1995	15.9	15.3	12.5
1994	7.9	6.2	6.4
1993	17.9	15.6	15.9
One year:			
1997	32.4	33.4	24.8
1996	24.2	22.8	18.1
1995	38.8	37.5	28.9
1994	−1.2	1.3	−2.4
1993	13.6	10.1	12.4

n.a. Not applicable.

Source: CDA/Wiesenberger, *Mutual Fund Directory* (CDA/Wiesenberger, Rockville, MD), 1993–7.

Table 54   CDA annualized rates of return: ranks and trends, Windsor II, S&P 500 Index, and growth and income category, 1993–7

Holding period	Year holding period ends						Overall rank	Relative time trend
	1993	1994	1995	1996	1997	Total		
Ten years (1995–7)								
Windsor II	n.a.	n.a.	2	2	1	5	2	Positive
S&P 500 Index	1	1	1	1	1	3	1	Constant
Category	2	2	3	3	3	9	3	Constant
Treasury bills	3	3	4	4	4	12	4	Constant
Five years								
Windsor II	2	2	1	1	1	7	1	Positive
S&P 500 Index	1	1	2	2	2	8	2	Negative
Category	3	2	3	2	3	13	3	Constant
Treasury bills	4	4	4	4	4	20	4	Constant
Three years								
Windsor II	1	1	1	2	1	6	1	Negative
S&P 500 Index	3	3	2	1	2	11	2	Positive
Category	2	2	3	3	3	13	3	Negative
Treasury bills	4	4	4	4	4	20	4	Constant
One year								
Windsor II	1	3	1	1	2	8	1	Positive
S&P 500 Index	3	2	2	2	1	10	2	Positive
Category	2	4	3	3	3	15	3	Constant
Treasury bills	4	1	4	4	4	17	4	Negative

n.a.   Not applicable.

Source: Table 53.

Table 55 CDA performance measures: Windsor II, S&P 500 Index, and growth and income category, 1993–7

Performance measure	Windsor II	S&P 500 Index	Category
R squared (%)			
1997	92	100	77
1996	91	100	79
1995	87	100	75
1994	86	100	67
1993	90	100	70
Beta			
1997	0.83	1.00	0.78
1996	0.96	1.00	0.81
1995	0.98	1.00	0.83
1994	0.91	1.00	0.78
1993	0.89	1.00	0.72
Standard deviation			
1997	9.66	11.19	9.68
1996	9.71	9.65	8.89
1995	8.67	8.28	7.97
1994	2.27	2.32	2.25
1993	2.81	2.98	2.61
CDA rating (percentile)			
1997	28	n.a.	24
1996	25	n.a.	23
1995	31	n.a.	28
1994	37	n.a.	38
1993	42	n.a.	42
Expense ratio (%)			
1997	0.39	n.a.	1.43
1996	0.40	n.a.	1.42
1995	0.39	n.a.	1.35
1994	0.39	n.a.	1.28
1993	0.41	n.a.	1.23
CDA Jensen Alpha (%)			
1997	4.3	0.0	0.8
1996	−0.9	0.0	−1.1
1995	0.8	0.0	−0.3
1994	1.9	0.0	0.7
1993	3.2	0.0	3.3

n.a. Not applicable.

Source: CDA/Wiesenberger, *Mutual Fund Directory* (CDA/Wiesenberger, Rockville, MD), 1993–7.

Table 56 CDA performance measures: ranks and trends. Windsor II, S&P 500 Index, and growth and income category, 1993–7

Performance measure	1993	1994	1995	1996	1997	Total	Overall rank	Relative time trend
R squared (%)								
Windsor II	2	2	2	2	2	10	2	Constant
S&P 500	1	1	1	1	1	5	1	Constant
Category	3	3	3	3	3	15	3	Constant
Beta								
Windsor II	2	2	2	2	2	10	2	Constant
S&P 500	3	3	3	3	3	15	3	Constant
Category	1	1	1	1	1	5	1	Constant
Standard deviation								
Windsor II	2	2	3	3	1	11	2	Constant
S&P 500	3	3	2	2	3	13	3	Positive
Category	1	1	1	1	2	6	1	Negative
CDA rating (%)								
Windsor II	1	1	2	2	2	8	2	Negative
S&P 500	n.a.	n.a.	n.a.	n.a.	n.a.	n.a.	n.a.	n.a.
Category	1	2	1	1	1	6	1	Positive
Expense ratio								
Windsor II	1	1	1	1	1	5	1	Constant
S&P 500	n.a.	n.a.	n.a.	n.a.	n.a.	n.a.	n.a.	n.a.
Category	2	2	2	2	2	10	2	Constant
CDA Jensen Alpha								
Windsor II	1	1	1	3	1	7	1[a]	Negative
S&P 500	2	2	2	2	2	10	2	Constant
Category	1	1	3	3	1	9	1[a]	Negative

Ranking key: R squared (%), largest = 1. Beta, smallest = 1. Standard deviation, smallest = 1. CDA rating (%), smallest = 1. Expense ratio, smallest = 1. CDA Jensen Alpha (%), largest = 1.
n.a. Not applicable.

[a] Asset ranks interpreted only relative to S&P 500's defined rating of 2.

Source: Table 55.

Table 57(a) CDA risk/return performance data: Windsor II, S&P 500 Index, growth and income category, and Treasury bills, 1993–7

Year	Windsor II	S&P 500 Index	Category	Treasury bills
1997	32.4	33.4	24.8	5.0
1996	24.2	22.8	18.1	4.7
1995	38.8	37.5	28.7	4.9
1994	−1.2	1.3	−2.1	3.6
1993	13.6	10.1	13.3	2.7
1992	12.0	7.6	9.9	3.2
1991	28.7	30.4	27.2	5.2
1990	−10.0	−3.1	−4.4	7.3
1989	27.8	31.6	22.8	7.8
1988	24.7	16.5	16.9	6.1
1987	−2.1	5.2	0.1	5.2
1986	21.4	18.6	16.9	5.8
1985	n.a.	31.7	26.7	7.3
1984	n.a.	6.2	6.4	9.8

Source: CDA returns from CDA/Wiesenberger, *Mutual Fund Directory* (CDA/Wiesenberger, Rockville, MD), 1993–7.

Table 57(b)   Computed risk/return performance data: Windsor II, S&P 500 Index, growth and income category, and Treasury bills, 1993–7

Holding period (years)	1993	1994	1995	1996	1997
Windsor II mean rates of return					
Ten	n.a.	n.a.	15.37	15.65	19.10
Five	14.42	8.62	18.38	17.48	21.56
Three	18.10	8.13	17.07	20.60	31.80
Windsor II standard deviations					
Ten	n.a.	n.a.	15.78	15.93	15.38
Five	15.70	14.85	15.58	14.95	15.84
Three	9.21	8.12	20.22	20.24	7.32
Category mean rates of return					
Ten	13.58	12.73	12.93	13.05	15.52
Five	13.76	8.78	15.40	13.58	16.56
Three	16.80	7.03	13.30	14.90	23.87
Category standard deviations					
Ten	10.72	11.65	11.93	11.98	11.55
Five	12.32	12.78	12.82	11.28	12.00
Three	9.17	8.09	15.40	15.65	5.36
S&P 500 mean rates of return					
Ten	15.48	14.99	15.57	15.99	18.81
Five	15.32	9.26	17.38	15.86	21.02
Three	16.03	6.33	16.30	20.53	31.23
S&P 500 standard deviations					
Ten	12.40	12.90	13.83	13.99	14.41
Five	15.15	12.91	15.66	14.40	15.30
Three	12.50	4.53	18.88	18.21	7.59
Treasury bill mean rates of return					
Ten	6.07	5.42	5.18	5.07	5.05
Five	5.24	4.40	3.92	3.82	4.18
Three	3.70	3.17	3.73	4.40	4.87

n.a.   Not applicable.

Source: Table 57(a).

Table 58 Jensen Alpha computations, Windsor II, S&P 500 Index, and growth and income category, 1993–7

Holding period	Windsor II	S&P 500 Index	Category
Ten years ending			
1997	2.63	0.0	−0.26
1996	0.10	0.0	−0.87
1995	0.01	0.0	−0.87
1994	n.a.	0.0	−0.15
1993	n.a.	0.0	0.74
Five years ending			
1997	3.40	0.0	−0.76
1996	2.10	0.0	0.01
1995	1.27	0.0	0.31
1994	−0.20	0.0	0.59
1993	0.21	0.0	1.26
Three years ending			
1997	5.05	0.0	−1.57
1996	0.71	0.0	−2.57
1995	1.02	0.0	−0.86
1994	2.09	0.0	1.40
1993	3.42	0.0	4.22

n.a. Not applicable.

Source: Tables 55 and 57.

Table 59 Jensen Alpha: ranks and trends, Windsor II, S&P 500 Index, and growth and income category, 1993–7

Holding period	Year holding period ends					Total	Overall rank[a]	Relative time trend
	1993	1994	1995	1996	1997			
Ten years (1995–7)								
Windsor II	n.a.	n.a.	1	1	1	3	1	Constant
S&P 500 Index	2	2	2	2	2	6	2	Constant
Category	1	3	3	3	3	9	3	Constant
Five years								
Windsor II	1	3	1	1	1	7	1	Positive
S&P 500 Index	2	2	2	2	2	10	2	Constant
Category	1	1	1	1	3	7	1	Negative
Three years								
Windsor II	1	1	1	1	1	5	1	Constant
S&P 500 Index	2	2	2	2	2	10	2	Constant
Category	1	1	3	3	3	11	3	Negative

n.a. Not applicable.
[a] Asset ranks interpreted only relative to S&P 500's defined ranking of 2.

Source: Table 58.

Table 60 Adjusted Jensen Alpha computations, Windsor II, S&P 500 Index, and growth and income category, 1993–7

Holding period	Windsor II	S&P 500 Index	Category
Ten years ending			
1997	3.17	0.0	−0.34
1996	0.10	0.0	−1.07
1995	0.01	0.0	−1.05
1994	n.a.	0.0	−0.20
1993	n.a.	0.0	1.03
Five years ending			
1997	4.10	0.0	−0.97
1996	2.19	0.0	0.01
1995	1.30	0.0	0.37
1994	−0.22	0.0	0.76
1993	0.23	0.0	1.75
Three years ending			
1997	6.08	0.0	−2.01
1996	0.74	0.0	−3.17
1995	1.04	0.0	−1.04
1994	2.29	0.0	1.79
1993	3.85	0.0	5.86

n.a. Not applicable.

Source: Tables 55 and 58.

Table 61 Adjusted Jensen Alpha: ranks and trends, Windsor II, S&P 500 Index, and growth and income category, 1993–7

Holding period	Year holding period ends					Total	Overall rank	Relative time trend
	1993	1994	1995	1996	1997			
Ten years (1995–7)								
Windsor II	n.a.	n.a.	1	1	1	3	1	Constant
S&P 500	3	1	2	2	2	6	2	Constant
Category	1	2	3	3	3	9	3	Constant
Five years								
Windsor II	2	3	1	1	1	8	1	Positive
S&P 500	3	2	3	3	2	13	3	Constant
Category	1	1	2	2	3	9	2	Negative
Three years								
Windsor II	2	1	1	1	1	6	1	Positive
S&P 500	3	3	2	2	2	12	2	Positive
Category	1	2	3	3	3	12	2	Negative

n.a. Not applicable.

Source: Table 60.

Table 62 Treynor Index computations, Windsor II, S&P 500 Index, and growth and income category, 1993–7

Holding period	Windsor II	S&P 500 Index	Category
Ten years ending			
1997	16.93	13.76	13.42
1996	11.02	10.92	9.85
1995	10.40	10.39	9.34
1994	n.a.	9.57	9.37
1993	n.a.	9.44	10.47
Five years ending			
1997	20.94	16.84	15.87
1996	14.23	12.04	12.05
1995	14.76	13.46	13.83
1994	4.64	4.86	5.62
1993	10.31	10.08	11.83
Three years ending			
1997	32.45	26.37	24.36
1996	16.88	16.13	12.96
1995	13.61	12.57	11.53
1994	5.46	3.17	4.98
1993	16.18	12.33	18.19

n.a. Not applicable.

Source: Tables 55 and 57.

Table 63 Treynor Index: ranks and trends, Windsor II, S&P 500 Index, and growth and income category, 1993–7

Holding period	Year holding period ends					Total	Overall rank	Relative time trend
	1993	1994	1995	1996	1997			
Ten years (1995–7)								
Windsor II	n.a.	n.a.	1	1	1	3	1	Positive
S&P 500	3	1	2	2	2	6	2	Constant
Category	1	2	3	3	3	9	3	Negative
Five years								
Windsor II	2	3	1	1	1	8	1	Positive
S&P 500	3	2	3	3	2	13	3	Constant
Category	1	1	2	2	3	9	2	Negative
Three years								
Windsor II	2	1	1	1	1	6	1	Positive
S&P 500	3	3	2	2	2	12	2	Positive
Category	1	2	3	3	3	12	2	Negative

n.a.   Not applicable.

Source: Table 62.

Table 64 Sharpe Index computations, Windsor II, S&P 500 Index, and growth and income category, 1993–7

Holding period	Windsor II	S&P 500 Index	Category
Ten years ending			
1997	0.91	0.95	0.91
1996	0.66	0.78	0.67
1995	0.65	0.75	0.65
1994	n.a.	0.74	0.63
1993	n.a.	0.76	0.70
Five years ending			
1997	1.10	1.10	1.03
1996	0.91	0.84	0.87
1995	0.93	0.86	0.90
1994	0.28	0.38	0.34
1993	0.58	0.67	0.69
Three years ending			
1997	3.68	3.48	3.54
1996	0.80	0.89	0.67
1995	0.66	0.67	0.62
1994	0.61	0.70	0.48
1993	1.56	0.99	1.43

n.a.   Not applicable.

Source: Table 57.

Table 65 Sharpe Index: ranks and trends, Windsor II, S&P 500 Index, and growth and income category, 1993–7

Holding period	Year holding period ends					Total	Overall rank	Relative time trend
	1993	1994	1995	1996	1997			
Ten years (1995–7)								
Windsor II	n.a.	n.a.	2	3	2	7	3	Constant
S&P 500	1	1	1	1	1	3	1	Constant
Category	2	2	2	2	2	6	2	Constant
Five years								
Windsor II	3	3	1	1	1	9	1	Positive
S&P 500	2	1	3	3	1	10	2	Negative
Category	1	2	2	2	3	10	2	Negative
Three years								
Windsor II	1	2	2	2	1	8	1	Constant
S&P 500	3	1	1	1	3	9	2	Constant
Category	2	3	3	3	2	13	3	Constant

n.a. Not applicable.

Source: Table 64.

Table 66 CDA annualized rates of return, CDA performance measures, and computed risk/return performance measures: overall assessments, Windsor II, 1993–7

Performance measure	Windsor II		Overall (individual) assessments
	Rank	Trend	
A CDA annualized rate of return			
Ten years	2	Positive	(Acceptable)
Five years	1	Positive	(Excellent)
Three years	1	Negative	(Excellent)
One year	1	Positive	(Excellent)
Overall (table 54)			Excellent
B CDA performance measure			
R squared	2	Constant	(Acceptable)
Beta	2	Constant	(Acceptable)
Standard deviation	2	Constant	(Acceptable)
CDA rating	2	Negative	(Acceptable)
Expense ratio	1	Constant	(Excellent)
CDA Jensen Alpha	1	Negative	(Excellent)
Overall (table 56)			Acceptable
C Computed risk/return performance measure			
Jensen Alpha:			
Ten years	1	Constant	(Excellent)
Five years	1	Positive	(Excellent)
Three years	1	Constant	(Excellent)
Overall (table 59)			Excellent
Adjusted Jensen Alpha:			
Ten years	1	Constant	(Excellent)
Five years	1	Positive	(Excellent)
Three years	1	Positive	(Excellent)
Overall (table 61)			Excellent
Treynor Index:			
Ten years	1	Positive	(Excellent)
Five years	1	Positive	(Excellent)
Three years	1	Positive	(Excellent)
Overall (table 63)			Excellent
Sharpe Index:			
Ten years	3	Constant	(Unacceptable)
Five years	1	Positive	(Excellent)
Three years	1	Positive	(Excellent)
Overall (table 65)			Acceptable
Overall assessment			**Excellent**

Source: Tables cited.

Table 67   Morningstar rating, risk, returns, and risk/return measures: overall assessments, Windsor II, S&P 500 Index, and large-cap. value category, 1998

Morningstar measure	Windsor II	S&P 500 Index	Category	Overall (individual) ratings
Rating:				
Ten years	4☆	5☆	n.a.	(Acceptable)
Five years	4☆	5☆	n.a.	(Acceptable)
Three years	4☆	5☆	n.a.	(Acceptable)
Overall				Acceptable
Risk:				
Ten years	0.85	0.85	0.87	(Acceptable)
Five years	0.81	0.82	0.84	(Acceptable)
Three years	0.73	0.79	0.81	(Acceptable)
Overall				Acceptable
Return:				
Ten years	1.28	1.59	0.99	(Excellent)
Five years	1.62	1.98	1.17	(Excellent)
Three years	1.61	2.02	1.14	(Excellent)
Overall				Excellent
Overall assessment				**Excellent/ Acceptable**

n.a.   Not applicable.

Source: Tables 40(a), 41(a), and 42(a).

Table 68 Buy/sell decision criteria: scores and weights, Windsor II, 1993–8

Decision criterion	Performance assessment	Performance score	Importance assessment (%)	Weighted score
Fund attributes (table 27)				
1 Fund attributes	Excellent/ Acceptable	2.50	15	0.30
2 Portfolio manager background	Excellent	3.00	15	0.45
Risk and return performance (tables 66, 52 and 67)				
1 CDA rates of return	Excellent	3.00	10	0.30
2 CDA performance measures	Acceptable	2.00	15	0.30
3 Diversification risk	Acceptable	2.00	15	0.30
4 Morningstar risk	Acceptable	2.00	5	0.10
5 Morningstar return	Excellent	3.00	5	0.15
Risk/return performance (tables 66 and 67)				
1 Morningstar rating	Acceptable	2.00	5	0.10
2 Computed risk/return measures	Excellent	3.00	15	0.45
Average performance score		2.50		
Overall weighted score				**2.45**
Overall performance	**Excellent/ Acceptable**			

Note: Performance ranked 3, 2, 1.

Source: Tables cited.

Table 69(a)   Performance of investment styles, 1976–99, by year

Year	Best	Worst
1976	Small value	Large growth
1977	Small growth	Large growth
1978	Small growth	Large value
1979	Small growth	Large value
1980	Large growth	Mid value
1981	Small value	Large growth
1982	Small value	Large growth
1983	Small value	Large growth
1984	Mid value	Small growth
1985	Mid value	Large growth
1986	Large value	Small growth
1987	Large growth	Small growth
1988	Small value	Large growth
1989	Large growth	Small value
1990	Large growth	Large value
1992	Small value	Large growth
1993	Small value	Large growth
1994	Large growth	Small growth
1995	Large value	Small value
1996	Small value	Mid growth
1997	Large value	Mid growth
1998	Large growth	Small value
1999	Mid growth	Mid value

Source: Abridged from Maggie Topkis, There is a Season: Turn, Turn, Turn, *Money*, June, 2000, pp. 50–1.

Table 69(b)   Performance of investment styles, 1976–99, by style

Investment style	Terminal value (and rank)	% best/worst
Small value	**$602,000 (1)**	33/17
Mid value	419,000 (4)	8/4
Large value	345,000 (6)	13/17
Small growth	438,000 (3)	13/17
Mid growth	458,000 (2)	8/8
Large growth	313,000 (7)	25/38
S&P 500 Index	387,000 (5)	100/100

Source: As table 69a.

Table 70(a)   Model portfolio allocations (%)

	Stock/bond allocations				
	20/80	40/60	60/40	80/20	100/0
Stock					
Domestic large–cap. value	5	10	15	19	24
Domestic large–cap. growth	5	9	14	19	24
Domestic small–cap. value	3	7	10	13	16
Domestic small–cap. growth	3	6	9	13	16
International large–cap. value	1[a]	3	4	5	6
International large–cap. growth	1[a]	2	3	5	6
International small–cap. value	1[a]	2	3	3	4
International small–cap. growth	1[a]	1[a]	2	3	4
Bond					
Domestic	56	42	28	14	0
International	24	18	12	6	0
	100	100	100	100	100

Note: The stock allocations are consistent with the Haslem model in table 35 but with the addition of value/growth allocations.

[a]   For stock portfolios under $500,000, add to domestic stocks but maintain their relative proportions.

Table 70(b) Sample portfolio allocations (%)

1 Stock/bond allocation: 60/40
   Stock   60
   Bond   40
                     ___
                     100

2 Domestic/foreign stock allocation: 80/20
   Stock
     Domestic   48
     International   12
   Bond   40
                     ___
                     100

3 Large-cap./small-cap. allocation: 60/40
   Stock
     Domestic
       Large-cap.   29
       Small-cap.   19
     International
       Large-cap.   7
       Small-cap.   5
   Bond   40
                     ___
                     100

4 Value/growth allocation: 50/50 (rounded) and domestic/international bond allocation: 70/30
   Stock
     Domestic
       Large-cap.
         Value   15
         Growth   14
       Small-cap.
         Value   10
         Growth   9
     International
       Large-cap.
         Value   4
         Growth   3
       Small-cap.
         Value   3
         Growth   2
   Bond
     Domestic   28
     International   12
                     ___
                     100

Note: These stock allocations are consistent with the Haslem model in table 35 but with addition of value/growth allocations.

Table 71(a) Vanguard Total Bond Market Index Fund, *Morningstar Principia Pro for Mutual Funds*, December 31, 1998

Rating	Net assets	Morningstar category
★★★★ 1488 Fixed Income Funds	$7,509.7 million	Intermediate-term bond

Investment approach

Equity style
Value Blend Growth — Large / Medium / Small

Fixed-income style
Short Int Long — High / Medium / Low

Equity portfolio statistics	Portfolio average	Relative index	Relative category
P/E ratio	—	—	—
P/C ratio	—	—	—
P/B ratio	—	—	—
3 year Earnings Gr %	—	—	—
Mdn Mkt Cap. ($ million)	—	—	—

Fixed-income portfolio statistics

Average eff mat/duration	8.4 years/4.4 years
Average weighted coupon	7.50
Average weighted price	111.80
Average credit quality	AA

Turnover ratio %	39%
Assets in top 10 holdings %	22.43
Total holdings	3101

Composition as of 09-30-98

Cash	2.6
US stocks	0.0
Non-US stock	0.0
Bonds	97.4
Other	0.0

Credit analysis as of 11-30-98

	% of Bonds
US government	0.00
AAA	67.30
AA	7.70
A	14.40
BBB	10.00
BB	0.60
B	0.00
Below B	0.00
Not rated/not available	0.00

Regional exposure % of non-cash assets

US & Canada	—
Europe	—
Japan	—
Latin America	—
Pacific Rim	—
Other	—

Risk and return profile

Morningstar	3 year 1488 funds	5 year 987 funds	10 year 368 funds
Rating	4★	4★	5★
Risk	0.82	0.89	0.82
Return	0.41	0.45	0.94

Average historical rating over 109 months: 4.0★s

MPT statistics/other measurements

	LB Agg	Best Fit: LB Agg
R-squared	99	99
Beta	0.99	0.99
Alpha	-0.09	-0.09

	3 year	5 year	10 year
Sharpe ratio	0.61	—	—
Std deviation	3.73	4.29	4.33
Mean	7.17	7.21	9.00

12-month yield	—
30-day SEC yield	6.06%
Potential cap. gains exp	3% of assets

Load-adjusted return % as of 12-31-98

12 months	8.59
5 years	7.21
10 years	9.00
Inception	—

Trailing-period performance

	YTD	1 month	3 month	12 month	3 year Annlzd	5 year Annlzd	10 year Annlzd	15 year Annlzd
Total return % as of 12-31-1998	8.59	0.38	0.31	8.59	7.17	7.21	9.00	—
+/- LB agg	-0.08	0.08	-0.03	-0.08	-0.12	-0.06	-0.26	—
+/- LB int govt/corp	0.17	-0.02	0.02	0.17	0.41	0.62	0.49	—
% rank within Morningstar category				18(490)	14(360)	13(236)	29(82)	

1 = Best 100 = Worst (number of funds)

Growth of $10,000

Vanguard tot bond mkt idx
$25,423

Category average:
Interm-term bond
$24,045

Index:
LB aggregate bond
$26,150

Chart axis labels: 100,000 / 80,000 / 60,000 / 40,000 / 20,000 / $10,000 / 5,000

Calendar year performance

	1988	1989	1990	1991	1992	1993	1994	1995	1996	1997	12-98
Total return %	7.35	13.64	8.65	15.25	7.14	9.68	−2.66	18.18	3.58	9.44	8.59
+/− LB agg	−0.54	−0.89	−0.31	−0.75	−0.26	−0.07	0.26	−0.29	−0.04	−0.24	−0.08
+/− LB int govt/corp	0.67	0.87	−0.52	0.62	−0.03	0.90	−0.73	2.87	−0.48	1.57	0.17

Operations

Family:	Vanguard group	Ticker:	VBMFX
Inception:	12-1986	Minimum initial purchase:	$3000
Manager:	Kenneth Volpert	Minimum IRA purchase:	$1000
Tenure:	7 years	Minimum auto investment plan:	$3000
Telephone:	800-662-7447	Purchase constraints:	–
Objective:	Corp bond-high quality		

Front-end fees:	0.00%
Deferred load:	0.00%
12b-1 fee	0.00%
Expense ratio:	0.20%
Assets:	$7509.7 million
NAV:	10.27

Source: Reprinted with permission from Morningstar, *Principia Pro for Mutual Funds,* Advanced Analytics, Vanguard Total Bond Market Index Fund, December 31, 1998.

Table 71(b) Vanguard Total Bond Market Index Fund (revised name), *Morningstar Mutual Funds OnDemand*, August 21, 1998

Prospectus objective: Corp bond – high quality

Vanguard Bond Index Fund Total Bond Market Portfolio seeks to replicate the total return of the Lehman Brothers Aggregate Bond index.

The fund normally invests at least 80% of assets in securities listed on the index. It attempts to keep its portfolio weightings in line with the weightings of the index.

Shareholders are charged a $10 annual account-maintenance fee for accounts with less than $10,000. The fund also offers Institutional shares. Prior to April 23, 1993, the fund was named Vanguard Bond Market Fund. From that date until Jan. 19, 1994, it was called Vanguard Bond Index Fund.

Portfolio manager(s)

Ian A. MacKinnon. Since 12-86. BA'70 Lafayette C.; MBA'74 Pennsylvania State U. MacKinnon is a senior vice president at the Vanguard Group, his employer since 1981. He currently manages several Vanguard fixed-income funds.

Kenneth Volpert, CFA. Since 11-92. BS'81 U. of Illinois; MBA'85 U. of Chicago. Volpert joined Vanguard as an assistant vice president and senior portfolio manager in November 1992. He previously held similar positions with Mellon Bond Associates and Investment & Capital Management Corporation. Volpert currently manages several Vanguard index funds.

Performance 07-31-98

	1st Qtr	2nd Qtr	3rd Qtr	4th Qtr	Total
1994	-2.71	-1.01	0.52	0.55	-2.66
1995	4.81	6.01	1.88	4.41	18.18
1996	-1.91	0.60	1.79	3.12	3.58
1997	-0.62	3.56	3.40	2.83	9.44
1998	1.55	2.36	–	–	–

Trailing

	Total Return %	+/- LB Agg	+/- LB ITGvt/Corp	% Rank All	% Rank Cat	Growth of $10,000
3 month	2.07	0.04	0.34	20	22	10,207
6 month	2.82	0.01	0.34	48	20	10,282
1 year	7.76	-0.11	1.01	55	13	10,776
3 year average	7.99	-0.04	0.96	55	21	12,594
5 year average	6.72	-0.08	0.59	55	24	13,845
10 year average	8.92	-0.23	0.61	56	35	23,501
15 year average	–	–	–			–

Tax analysis

	Tax-Adj Ret %	% Rank Cat	% Pretax Ret	% Rank Cat
3 year average	5.27	22	66.0	39
5 year average	3.96	18	58.9	25
10 year average	6.06	28	67.9	20

Potential Capital Gain Exposure: 3% of assets

Ticker VBMFX	Load None	NAV $10.14
Yield 6.3%	SEC yield –	Total assets $8,003.1 million

Historical profile

Return	Above average
Risk	Average
Rating	★★★★ Above average

History

	1987	1988	1989	1990	1991	1992	1993	1994	1995	1996	1997	07-98
	43%	47%	37%	28%	26%	22%	19%	18%				
NAV	9.20	9.05	9.44	9.41	9.99	9.88	10.06	9.17	10.14	9.84	10.09	10.14
Total Return %	1.54	7.35	13.64	8.65	15.25	7.14	9.68	-2.66	18.18	3.58	9.44	4.18
+/- LB Aggregate	-1.23	-0.53	-0.89	-0.31	-0.76	-0.26	-0.07	0.26	-0.29	-0.03	-0.24	0.05
+/- LB Int Govt/Corp	-2.12	0.67	0.88	-0.52	0.62	-0.03	0.90	-0.73	2.88	-0.48	1.57	0.36
Income Return %	9.17	9.14	9.17	8.78	8.45	7.25	6.66	6.37	7.31	6.50	6.75	3.68
Capital Return %	-7.63	-1.78	4.47	-0.13	6.80	-0.11	3.02	-9.03	10.87	-2.92	2.69	0.50
Total Rtn % Rank Cat	54	71	20	21	71	45	65	19	36	31	26	20
Income $	0.87	0.81	0.80	0.80	0.77	0.70	0.64	0.62	0.65	0.64	0.64	0.37
Capital Gains $	0.00	0.00	0.00	0.00	0.02	0.09	0.12	0.00	0.00	0.00	0.00	0.00
Expense Ratio %	0.14	0.30	0.24	0.21	0.16	0.20	0.18	0.18	0.20	0.20	0.20	–
Income Ratio %	9.01	8.84	8.49	8.60	7.95	7.06	6.24	6.57	6.66	6.54	6.54	–
Turnover Rate %	77	21	33	29	31	49	50	33	36	39	39	–
Net Assets $ million	43.3	58.1	138.6	276.7	848.8	1,059.9	1,540.2	1,730.7	2,405.0	2,952.8	5,010.0	6,174.4

Mstar category Interm-term bond

Investment style Fixed-Income — Income Rtn % Rank Cat

Growth of principal vs. interest rate shifts
- Principal Value $000 (NAV with capital gains reinvested)
- Interest Rate % on 10 Year Treasury
- ▽ Manager Change
- ▽ Partial Manager Change
- ▲ Mgr Unknown After
- ▲ Mgr Unknown Before

$12 / 11 / 10 / 9 / 8 / $7

Performance quartile (within Category)

Risk analysis

Time period	Load-Adj Return %	Risk %Rank All [1]	Risk %Rank Cat [1]	Morningstar Return	Morningstar Risk	Morningstar Risk-Adj Rating
1 year	7.76	37	34			
3 year	7.99	24	29	0.54[2]	0.99	★★★
5 year	6.72	24	24	0.38[2]	0.99	★★★
10 year	8.92	21	21	0.86[2]	0.85	★★★★

Average historical rating (104 months): 4.0★s

[1] 1 = low, 100 = high [2] T-Bill return substituted for category average

Category rating (3 Year)

(1) (2) (3) (4) (5)
Worst — Best

Return	Above average
Risk	Average

Other measures

	Standard index LB Agg	Best fit index LB Agg
Alpha	0.0	0.0
Beta	1.00	1.00
R-squared	100	100
Standard deviation	3.63	
Mean	7.99	
Sharpe ratio	0.86	

Portfolio analysis 03-31-98

Total Fixed-Income: 2745

	Date of Maturity	Amount $000	Value $000	% Net Assets
US Treasury Bond 8.125%	08-15-19	153,074	191,236	3.40
US Treasury Bond 8%	11-15-21	141,364	176,001	3.13
US Treasury Note 6.875%	05-15-06	120,849	129,377	2.30
US Treasury Note 6.625%	04-30-02	96,409	99,676	1.77
US Treasury Bond 8.125%	08-15-21	71,988	90,659	1.61
FHLMC 7.5%	12-01-27	86,855	89,092	1.59
US Treasury Bond 10.375%	11-15-12	55,278	73,227	1.30
US Treasury Note 8.75%	08-15-00	65,325	69,803	1.24
US Treasury Bond 8.875%	08-15-17	47,644	63,079	1.12
US Treasury Note 7.875%	11-15-99	58,823	60,897	1.08
US Treasury Note 5.75%	10-31-02	57,682	57,835	1.03
US Treasury Bond 10.375%	11-15-09	45,624	56,836	1.01
US Treasury Note 7.5%	02-15-05	47,870	52,608	0.94
US Treasury Note 6.75%	06-30-99	51,154	51,891	0.92
FNMA 7%	11-01-27	51,270	51,836	0.92
US Treasury Note 5.875%	07-31-99	51,192	51,393	0.91
US Treasury Note 6.375%	05-15-99	47,724	48,140	0.86
GNMA 7.5%	12-01-27	45,540	46,760	0.83
FHLMC 7%	12-01-27	46,040	46,606	0.83
US Treasury Note 8%	08-15-99	43,799	45,197	0.80

Current investment style

Duration: Short Int Long

Avg Eff Duration[1]	4.4 Years
Avg Eff Maturity	—
Avg Credit Quality	AA
Avg Wtd Coupon	7.46%
Avg Wtd Price	107.16% of par

[1] figure provided by fund: as of 07-24-98

Quality: High Med Low

Duration management as of 07-24-98

Duration Benchmark	LB Aggregate
Benchmark's Duration	4.4 Years
Duration Range	Duration Neutral

Fund's Duration 4.4 ▼

2 ||||||||||||||||||| 8

Years   Category Avg 5.0 ▲   Years

Special securities % of assets 03-31-98

● Restricted/Illiquid Secs	Trace
○ Exotic Mortgage-Backed	0
● Emerging-Markets Secs	Trace
○ Options/Futures/Warrants	No

Credit analysis % of bonds 07-24-98

US Govt	63	BB	0
AAA	7	B	0
AA	6	Below B	0
A	16	NR/NA	0
BBB	9		

Coupon range

	% of Bonds	Rel Cat
0%	0.0	0.01
0% to 7%	36.5	0.91
7% to 8.5%	46.3	1.17
8.5% to 10%	13.1	1.02
More than 10%	4.2	0.73

1.00 = Category Average

Composition % of assets 07-24-98

Cash	0.0	Bonds	100.0
Stocks	0.0	Other	0.0

Analysis by Hap Bryant 08-07-98

Vanguard Bond Index Fund Total Bond Market Portfolio keeps its big guns fixed on target.

This fund seeks to track the Lehman Brothers Aggregate index. Because it's impractical for the portfolio to hold all of the index's names (now more than 6,000 bonds), comanager Ken Volpert has to simulate the benchmark with fewer holdings. To a large degree, his efforts have succeeded: The fund is one of only three intermediate-term bond funds with an R-squared of 100, meaning that the fund's performance is almost completely attributable to the index's movements. Indeed, the fund's trailing returns are almost all within 10 basis points of the index's.

Consistent with this focus, Volpert and Vanguard bond strategist Ian MacKinnon don't alter the fund's duration stance based on interest-rate predictions. Instead, they keep the fund's duration and its sector weightings close to the benchmark's, while making only small sector and issue moves on the margins. For example, Volpert underweights short-term Treasuries relative to the index, using short-term corporates instead, because the latter tend to deliver slightly better returns. The fund's short-term corporate stake is typically 15% of assets, but Volpert will reduce this position when spreads are tight. Still, the fund's above-average stake in Treasuries and agency bonds gives it less credit risk than its typical peer.

This strategy has served as a fine complement to the fund's low-expense mandate. As is the case with many other Vanguard funds, this offering's annual expense ratio (around 20 basis points) is one of the lowest in its category. Vanguard will extract a $10 annual fee from accounts of less than $10,000, however, so small investors don't enjoy its expense advantage to the fullest.

Still, this fund's record of superior returns and minimal credit risk makes it worthy of consideration.

Address:	Vanguard Financial Ctr. PO Box 2600
	Valley Forge, PA 19482
	800-662-7447/610-669-1000
Inception:	12-11-86
Advisor:	Vanguard fixed-income group
Subadvisor:	None
Distributor:	Vanguard Group
NTF Plans:	N/A

Minimum purchase:	$3,000	Add: $100 IRA: $1,000
Min auto inv plan:	$3,000	Systematic Inv: $50
Sales fees:	No-load	
Management fee:	Provided at cost, at cost % A	
Actual fees:	Mgt: 0.01%	Dist: —
Expense projections:	3 Year: $6 5 Year: $11 10 Year: $26	
Income distrib:	Monthly	

Total cost (relative to category): Low

Source: Reprinted with permission from Morningstar, *Mutual Funds OnDemand* 33 (4), Vanguard Total Bond Market Index, August 21, 1998.

Table 72(a) Vanguard Total Stock Market Index Fund, Morningstar, *Principia Pro for Mutual Funds*, December 31, 1998

Rating ★★★★ 2802 Domestic Equity Funds	**Net assets** $8,548.7 million	**Morningstar category** Large blend

Investment approach

Equity style

Value	Blend	Growth	
■			Large
			Medium
			Small

Fixed-income style

Short	Int	Long	
			High
			Medium
			Low

Composition as of 09-30-98

Cash	4.9
US stocks	95.0
Non-US stock	0.1
Bonds	0.0
Other	0.0

Regional exposure % of assets as of 09-30-98

US & Canada	94.4
Europe	0.0
Japan	0.0
Latin America	0.0
Pacific Rim	0.0
Other	1.0

Risk and return profile

Morningstar	3 year 2802 funds	5 year 1702 funds	10 year 732 funds
Rating	4★	4★	—
Risk	0.87	0.87	—
Return	1.69	1.65	—

Average historical rating over 45 months: 4.0★s

MPT statistics/other measurements

	S&P 500	Best Fit: S&P 500
R-squared	97	97
Beta	1.01	1.01
Alpha	−2.68	−2.68

	3 year	5 year	10 year
Sharpe ratio	1.09	—	—
Std deviation	20.45	16.86	—
Mean	25.00	21.50	—

12-month yield	1.19%
30-day SEC yield	—
Potential cap. gains exp	32% of assets

Equity portfolio statistics

	Portfolio average	Relative index	Relative category
P/E ratio	32.2	0.98	1.01
P/C ratio	22.0	0.96	0.99
P/B ratio	7.5	0.96	1.01
3 year Earnings Gr %	18.3	0.89	0.98
Mdn Mkt Cap. ($ million)	29,345	0.49	0.75

Fixed-income portfolio statistics

Average eff mat/duration	—/—
Average weighted coupon	—
Average weighted price	—
Average credit quality	—

Sector weightings as of 09-30-98

		% of Stocks	Relative S&P 500
➡	Utilities	3.8	1.36
◆	Energy	6.2	0.95
$	Financials	17.5	1.10
⚙	Industrial cyclicals	11.9	1.03
⬡	Consumer durables	3.0	1.36
▣	Consumer staples	7.8	0.83
◣	Services	15.9	1.07
▮	Retail	6.2	0.94
✚	Health	12.2	0.99
◨	Technology	15.5	0.86

Turnover ratio %	2%
Assets in top 10 holdings %	18.62
Total holdings	3118

Trailing-period performance

	YTD	1 month	3 month	12 month	3 year Annlzd	5 year Annlzd	10 year Annlzd	15 year Annlzd
Total return % as of 12-31-1998	23.26	6.45	21.51	23.26	25.00	21.50	—	—
+/− S&P 500	−5.32	0.69	0.23	−5.32	−3.22	−2.55	—	—
+/− Wil large blend	−5.79	−0.13	−0.73	−5.79	−2.87	−1.46	—	—
% rank within Morningstar category:				47(793)	39(509)	32(347)		

1 = Best 100 = Worst (number of funds)

Load-adjusted return % as of 12-31-98

12 months	23.26
5 years	21.50
10 years	—
Inception	19.22

Growth of $10,000

Vanguard tot stk mkt index $31,861

Category average: Large blend $29,085

Index: Standard & Poor's 500 $34,671

100,000
80,000
60,000
40,000
20,000
$10,000
5,000

Calendar year performance	1988	1989	1990	1991	1992	1993	1994	1995	1996	1997	12-98
Total return %	—	—	—	—	—	10.62	-0.17	35.79	20.96	31.00	23.26
+/- S&P 500	—	—	—	—	—	0.56	-1.49	-1.74	-1.99	-2.35	-5.32
+/- Wil large blend	—	—	—	—	—	0.88	2.18	-1.87	-0.59	-2.30	-5.79

Operations

Family: Vanguard index trust
Inception: 04-1992
Manager: George U. Sauter
Tenure: 7 years
Telephone: 800-662-7447
Objective: Growth and income

Ticker: VTSMX
Minimum initial purchase: $3,000
Minimum IRA purchase: $1,000
Minimum auto investment plan: $3,000
Purchase constraints: —

Front-end fees: 0.00%
Deferred load: 0.00%
12b-1 fee: 0.00%
Expense ratio: 0.20%
Assets: $8,548.7 million
NAV: 27.42

Source: Reprinted with permission from Morningstar, *Principia Pro for Mutual Funds*, Advanced Analytics, Vanguard Total Stock Market Index Fund, December 31, 1998.

Table 72(b) Vanguard Total Stock Market Index Fund, Morningstar, *Mutual Funds OnDemand*, January 6, 1999

Prospectus objective: growth and income

Vanguard Total Stock Market Index Fund seeks to replicate the aggregate price and yield of the Wilshire 5000 index.

The fund purchases approximately 1,900 of the largest securities in the Wilshire 5000 index (all US stocks that trade regularly on the NYSE, AMEX, or OTC markets), and a representative sample of the rest. The fund may also invest in futures contracts.

Institutional shares, designed for institutional investors, are also offered by the fund. Prior to Oct. 27. 1998, the fund was named Vanguard Index Trust Total Stock Market Portfolio.

Portfolio manager(s)

George U. Sauter. Since +92. BA'76 Dartmouth C.; MBA'80 U. of Chicago. Sauter is vice president of Vanguard Group, his employer since 1987. Other funds currently managed: Vanguard Morgan Grth, Vanguard 500 Index, Vanguard Windsor II, Vanguard Explorer, Vanguard Sm Cap. Idx, Vanguard Ext Mkt Idx, Vanguard Pacific Stk Idx, Vanguard Euro Stk Idx, Vanguard Inst Idx, Vanguard Grth Idx, Vanguard Val Idx, Vanguard Emerg Mkt Idx, Vanguard Tax-Mgd Bal, Vanguard Tax-Mgd Gr&Inc, Vanguard Tax-Mgd Cap. App, Vanguard Aggr Grth, Vanguard Total Intl Stk, Vanguard REIT Idx.

Performance 11-30-98

	1st Qtr	2nd Qtr	3rd Qtr	4th Qtr	Total
1994	-3.71	-0.90	5.62	-0.95	-0.17
1995	9.15	9.23	8.94	4.54	35.79
1996	5.52	4.25	2.81	6.96	20.96
1997	0.65	16.81	9.75	1.52	31.00
1998	13.28	1.84	-12.07		

Trailing	Total Return %	+/- S&P 500	+/- Wil Top 750	% Rank All	% Rank Cat	Growth of $10,000
3 month	21.77	-0.25	-0.59	14	30	12,177
6 month	3.93	-3.55	-3.23	24	49	10,393
1 year	17.76	-5.90	-5.69	13	49	11,776
3 year average	23.05	-3.60	-2.71	6	38	18,631
5 year average	20.44	-2.52	-1.34	6	33	25,344
10 year average	—	—	—	—	—	—
15 year average	—	—	—	—	—	—

Tax analysis	Tax-Adj Ret %	% Rank Cat	% Pretax Ret	% Rank Cat
3 year average	21.99	26	95.4	10
5 year average	19.37	22	94.8	8
10 year average	—	—	—	—

Potential Capital Gain Exposure: 29% of assets

Ticker	Load	NAV	Yield	SEC Yield	Total assets
VTSMX	None	$25.98	1.2%	—	$10,796.4 million

Historical profile

Return	Above Avg
Risk	Average
Rating	★★★★

Investment style

Equity — Above Avg
Average Stock %

▽ Manager Change
▼ Partial Manager Change
▲ Mgr Unknown After
▲ Mgr Unknown Before

Mstar category: Large Blend

Fund performance vs. category average

■ Quarterly Fund Return
+/- Category Average
— Category Baseline

Performance quartile (within Category)

History	1987	1988	1989	1990	1991	1992	1993	1994	1995	1996	1997	11-98
Average Stock %	—	—	—	—	—	97%	98%	98%	98%	97%	95%	98%
NAV	—	—	—	—	—	10.84	11.69	11.37	15.04	17.77	22.64	25.98
Total Return %	—	—	—	—	—	10.41*	10.62	-0.17	35.79	20.96	31.00	15.79
+/- S&P 500	—	—	—	—	—	1.29*	0.57	-1.48	-1.75	-1.98	-2.36	-5.78
+/- Wilshire Top 750	—	—	—	—	—	—	0.89	2.18	-1.87	-0.59	-2.31	-5.29
Income Return %	—	—	—	—	—	2.33	2.42	2.33	2.48	1.94	1.83	0.80
Capital Return %	—	—	—	—	—	8.08	8.20	-2.50	33.30	19.02	29.17	14.99
Total Rtn % Rank Cat	—	—	—	—	—	—	40	41	26	50	35	49
Income $	—	—	—	—	—	0.23	0.26	0.27	0.28	0.29	0.32	0.18
Capital Gains $	—	—	—	—	—	0.00	0.03	0.03	0.09	0.11	0.27	0.05
Expense Ratio %	—	—	—	—	—	0.21	0.20	0.20	0.25	0.22	0.20	—
Income Ratio %	—	—	—	—	—	2.42	2.31	2.35	2.14	1.86	1.65	—
Turnover Rate %	—	—	—	—	—	—	1	2	3	3	2	—
Net Assets $ million	—	—	—	—	—	275.4	512.3	785.7	1,570.9	3,530.9	5,092.7	8,548.7

Risk analysis

Time period	Load-Adj Return %	Risk % Rank¹ All	Cat	Morningstar Return	Morningstar Risk	Morningstar Risk-Adj Rating
1 year	17.76	—	—	—	—	—
3 year	23.05	70	69	1.80	0.86	★★★★
5 year	20.44	70	61	1.65	0.86	★★★★
Incept	18.34	—	—	—	—	—

Average historical rating (44 months): 4.0★s

¹ 1 = low, 100 = high

Category rating (3 year)

①②③④⑤
Worst Average Best

Return — ④
Risk — ②

Other measures	Standard index S&P 500	Best fit index S&P 500
Alpha	-2.9	-2.9
Beta	1.00	1.00
R-Squared	97	97
Standard deviation	19.89	
Mean	23.05	
Sharpe ratio	1.02	

Portfolio analysis 09-30-98

Share change since 03-98 Total Stocks: 3118	Sector	YTD Ret %	PE	% Assets
⊕ Microsoft	Technology	88.78	59.8	2.48
⊕ General Electric	Industrials	24.50	33.5	2.38
⊕ Exxon	Energy	25.54	25.1	1.58
⊕ Merck	Health	48.12	37.3	1.42
⊕ Intel	Technology	53.44	33.1	1.33
⊕ Coca-Cola	Staples	5.95	46.7	1.31
⊕ Pfizer	Health	51.28	45.0	1.27
⊕ Wal-Mart Stores	Retail	91.75	40.7	1.13
⊕ IBM	Technology	58.95	26.6	1.11
⊕ Philip Morris	Staples	27.40	21.4	1.03
⊕ AT & T	Services	3.11	18.0	0.97
⊕ Johnson & Johnson	Health	24.95	31.0	0.97
⊕ Bristol-Myers Squibb	Health	30.33	35.3	0.95
⊕ Procter & Gamble	Staples	11.20	33.3	0.87
⊕ Cisco Systems	Technology	102.80	80.2	0.87
⊕ Lucent Technologies	Technology	116.00	NMF	0.83
⊕ Eli Lilly	Health	30.26	50.4	0.80
⊕ MCI WorldCom	Services	95.04	–	0.80
⊕ Dell Computer	Technology	189.50	73.3	0.78
⊕ SBC Communications	Services	33.84	24.2	0.75
⊕ American Intl Group	Financials	29.90	27.1	0.74
⊕ Schering-Plough	Health	73.52	47.2	0.70
⊕ Bell Atlantic	Services	26.23	30.8	0.69
⊕ BellSouth	Services	58.37	26.7	0.68
⊕ Berkshire Hathaway Cl A	Financials	52.40	37.0	0.65

Current investment style

Style: Value Blnd Growth
Size: Large Med Small

	Stock Port Avg	Relative S&P 500 Current	Hist	Rel Cat
Price/Earnings Ratio	31.1	1.00	1.05	1.02
Price/Book Ratio	7.0	0.95	1.03	1.02
Price/Cash Flow	21.4	0.98	1.02	0.99
3 Year Earnings Growth	18.4	0.99	1.20	0.98
1 Year Earnings Est %	11.8	1.15	–	1.00
Debt % Total Cap.	31.8	0.72	1.02	1.00
Med Mkt Cap. $ million	27,509	0.5	0.6	0.79

Sector weightings

Sector weightings	% of Stocks	Rel S&P	5-Year High	Low
Utilities	3.8	1.3	7	3
Energy	6.2	0.9	9	3
Financials	17.5	1.1	20	6
Industrials	11.9	1.0	17	12
Durables	3.0	1.1	5	3
Staples	7.8	0.8	12	8
Services	15.9	1.2	17	14
Retail	6.2	1.0	8	5
Health	12.2	1.0	12	9
Technology	15.5	1.0	15	7

Special securities % of assets 09-30-98

○ Restricted/Illiquid Secs	0
●● Emerging-Markets Secs	Trace
●● Options/Futures/Warrants	Yes

Composition % of assets 10-31-98

		Market cap.	
Cash	0.0	Giant	41.5
Stocks*	100.0	Large	28.7
Bonds	0.0	Medium	19.7
Other	0.0	Small	7.7
*Foreign	0.1	Micro	2.4
(% of stocks)			

Address:	PO Box 2600
	Valley Forge, PA 19482
	800-662-7447/610-669-1000
*Inception:	04-27-92
Advisor:	Vanguard Core Management Group
Subadvisor:	None
Distributor:	Vanguard Group
NTF Plans:	N/A

Minimum purchase:	$3000	Add: $100 IRA: $1000
Min auto Inv plan:	$3000	Systematic Inv: $50
Sales fees:	No-load	
Management fee:	0.17%	Provided at cost, at cost A
Actual fees:	Mgt: 0.17%	Dist: –
Expense projections:	3 Year: $6	5 Year: $11 10 Year: $26
Average Brok. commission:	$0.0177	Income Distrib: Quarterly
Total cost (relative to category):		Low

Analysis by Steve Chung 12-18-98

Vanguard Total Stock Market Index Fund is an understandable choice.

This fund, like other index offerings, should raise at least two central questions for investors. The first is the subject of much debate and centers on overall market efficiency. Is it possible for active managers to consistently add more value with their investment decisions than the costs they are charging to do so? The second question is related and receives a little less attention, but is perhaps of greater importance. If some active managers can add value above costs, can investors confidently identify those who are skilled enough to do so?

Because this fund's passive strategy eliminates the uncertainty involved in choosing active managers, it might be a good choice for many investors. It's particularly appropriate for those seeking a core holding, or a simple, one-stop shop for equity exposure. That's because it covers more ground then nearly all other equity offerings. The fund is designed to track the Wilshire 5000 index, which includes every large and small stock traded on the major US exchanges. (The fund only actually holds about 3,100 names, because it would be too costly to own every stock.) In addition, at a mere 200 basis points (not including a $10 annual fee for accounts of less than $10,000), its costs can't be beat.

The fund's actual performance hasn't been too shabby, either. Its three- and five-year returns land comfortably in the large-cap. blend group's upper half (though its risk scores are also a bit higher than average). It has also finished every calendar year of its existence in the group's top half. What's more, the fund's low-turnover indexing strategy has helped its aftertax relative returns look even better.

To be sure, investors who think they can pick portfolio managers should probably look elsewhere. However, over time, this fund will be difficult to beat.

Source: Reprinted with permission from Morningstar, *Mutual Funds OnDemand* 34 (3), Vanguard Total Stock Market Index Fund, January 6, 1999.

Table 73 Selection of index mutual funds: summary checklist

1 Invest completely or primarily in pure no-load index funds, but also consider exchange traded funds (chapter 9).

2 Invest long-term and determine investor risk category (table 31), portfolio investment objective (table 34), and passive stock/bond allocation and cap. size investment styles (table 35). The cash bucket is managed outside the investment portfolio.

3 Diversify the portfolio based on the stock cap. size and value/growth investment style allocations determined in table 70. Stock allocations include combinations of value/growth, small-cap./large-cap., and domestic/international style funds. But note that index funds do not generally provide the investment style specificity called for in table 70. They reflect particular markets more than particular investment styles.

4 Also, diversify the portfolio based on the foreign/domestic bond allocations determined in table 70. The domestic bond allocation may also be used for the foreign bond allocation, owing to the lack of an international bond index fund in the same fund family (see text alternative).

5 Build simple portfolios using few broadly based index funds and avoid redundancy of investment style.

6 Invest in fund families that offer funds consistent with core competences. Index fund portfolios are managed to track benchmark market indices.

7 Select among index funds (table 27) with the highest overall assessments of both fund attributes and portfolio manager background (all compared with benchmark market index or index fund surrogate). The factors include load/fees, overall shareholder service, Loeb trading cost, tax efficiency, shareholder disclosure, expense ratio, and portfolio manager background.

8 Select among index funds (table 52) with the highest overall assessment of diversification risks, including value/growth investment style and portfolio safety and timeliness, among others (all versus benchmark market index or index fund surrogate). These findings should be very similar among competing index funds.

9 Select among index funds (tables 66–7) with the highest assessments of annualized rates of return, performance measures, computed risk/return performance measures, and Morningstar measures (all versus benchmark market index or index fund surrogate). These findings should be very similar among comparable index funds, except as impacted by expenses.

10 Select among index funds (table 68) with the highest overall summary performance assessment and weighted score.

11 Select index funds that penalize market timers with fees, but especially those that limit access.

12 Select index funds that treat shareholders as owners, not customers, and that communicate effectively.

Note: The numbered tables refer to those that would be completed for particular funds, not Vanguard Windsor II.

Table 74   Selection of actively managed equity mutual funds: summary checklist and tiebreakers

1   Invest long-term in actively managed stock funds to complement the core holdings of stock index funds selected by the process summarized in table 73.

2   Complement core holdings of stock index funds with actively managed stock funds that maintain the asset and investment style allocation consistent with table 70.

3   No changes are required in the bond index fund allocations, but if managed bond funds are desired review the PIMCO bond funds in Morningstar.

4   Build simple portfolios using few actively managed stock funds and avoid redundancy of investment style.

5   Invest in fund families that offer stock funds consistent with core competencies.

6   Select stock funds with excellent portfolio background and favor those managed by qualified members of successful family investment management companies (table 13).

7   Select stock funds (table 68) with at least excellent/acceptable overall fund attributes and portfolio manager background (all versus the same investment style category).

8   Select stock funds (table 52) with at least excellent/acceptable diversification risks, including investment style and portfolio safety and timeliness (all versus the same investment style category).

9   Select stock funds (tables 66–7) with at least excellent/acceptable overall annualized rates of return, performance measures, Morningstar measures, and especially excellent overall computed risk/return performance measures (all versus the same investment style category).

10   Select stock funds with the same investment style that ranks highest in table 68.

11   Select stock funds that penalize market timers with fees, but especially those that limit access.

12   Select stock funds that are yet small enough to facilitate the continuation of successful strategies, especially in fund families with a history or policy of limiting fund asset size.

13   If more than one stock fund has been identified in table 68 as meeting requirements for a particular investment style, first validate the portfolio manager's background as excellent (table 13). If so, use a series of tiebreakers to determine whether portfolio manager and fund attributes are consistent with those in table 75, which are associated with fund outperformance.

14   To implement the table 75 tiebreakers, first determine whether the portfolio manager is disclosed and investment philosophy and strategy disclosed. Then determine whether the portfolio manager's professional attributes are consistent with the following attributes. First, determine whether the portfolio manager has a contrarian value investment style (tables 39, 40a, 44 and prospectus) consistent with attribute No. 6. If so, second, determine whether the fund has a low portfolio turnover (table 40a) consistent with attribute No. 7. If so, third, determine whether the portfolio manager follows attribute No. 8 and does not use asset and style allocation. If so, review tables 66–7 to determine whether this policy has provided superior risk/return performance, especially Jensen Alpha Index and Sharpe Index scores. If so, fourth, determine whether the portfolio managers's portfolio concentration is consistent with attribute No. 9, as measured by industry sector (table 48) and individual securities holdings (table 50). If so, review table 55 to determine whether the fund's R^2 is small, reflecting a large amount of unique portfolio risk. If the responses thus far are predominantly consistent with "yes" responses in table 75, the "picture" emerges of a competent and confident portfolio manager with stock selection ability based on a unique contrarian-driven value investment style.

15   Next, determine whether the stock fund portfolio is consistent with attributes 10–14 in table 75. First, determine whether the fund has a low beta risk (table 55). Second, determine that fund assets have not "ballooned," but remain conducive to superior performance (net assets per year, table 40b). Third, determine whether the fund is tax-efficient (tax analysis, table 20). And, fourth, determine whether the fund's performance is relatively steady over time (table 53).

16   Thus if a particular stock fund's portfolio manager and fund attributes are predominantly consistent with table 75, and superior to competing funds, then the fund is a "buy", subject to validation by predominantly "yes" responses in table 76, and any efforts to time the decision (tables 80–1).

Note: The table numbers refer to those that would be completed for particular funds, not Vanguard Windsor II.

Table 75 Portfolio manager and fund attributes of high-performing actively managed funds: checklist

---

Encircle the number of questions where the response is "yes"

1 Is the (real) lead portfolio manager disclosed and his or her investment philosophy and strategy discussed?
2 Is the lead portfolio manager's age below average for a portfolio manager?
3 Is the lead portfolio manager's tenure as manager above average?
4 Did the lead portfolio manager graduate from a high-SAT college?
5 Does the portfolio manager have an MBA and/or CFA?
6 Does the lead portfolio manager have an eclectic, wide-ranging and opportunistic investment style couched predominantly in a contrarian-driven value strategy?
7 Does the portfolio manager have a patient investment horizon evidenced by low portfolio turnover?
8 Does the portfolio manager avoid the use of asset allocation or style allocation (not for "regular" investors)?
9 Is the portfolio concentrated by industry sector and/or individual stocks with more unique risk (not for "regular" investors)?
10 Does the portfolio have below-average systematic risk for its investment style category?
11 Are the fund's assets relatively stable and below average in size for its investment style category?
12 Is the fund tax-efficient for its investment style category?
13 Does the fund have a below-average expense ratio for its investment style category?
14 Does the fund maintain a relatively steady course in relative performance over time?

Note: A predominance of "yes" answers provides positive signals for particular actively managed funds.

Sources: Adapted from Judith Chevalier and Glenn Ellison, 1999, Are Some Mutual Fund Managers Better than Others? Cross-sectional Patterns in Behavior and Performance, *Journal of Finance*, 54 (June), pp. 875–94; and other sources.

Table 76 Selection attributes of actively managed mutual funds: another checklist

---

1 Uses fundamental analysis to understand company businesses and applies contrarian value investment style – "value investor *par excellence*."[a]

2 Eclectic value investment style defies consistent style classification – searches for "bargains" where they exist without limits on cap. size.

3 Independent thinker (not a committee) with conviction in judgment – not a "closet" index fund and does not use asset or style allocation and may hold concentrated portfolios (not for "regular" investors).

4 Remains fully invested in stocks only – no efforts to market time.

5 Keeps trading cost low – low portfolio turnover in usually liquid markets.

6 Investment advisor and portfolio manager act as owners with significant personal investment.

7 Acts continuously to improve research capability, but not necessarily backed with large research staff.

8 Veteran portfolio manager (one or two) who built the performance record is disclosed and still on board.

9 Performance record that of a mutual fund only.

10 Expense ratio below average with a history of decline.

11 Asset size has not "ballooned" and the fund is willing to close to new investors to maintain performance.

12 Long-term contrarian investor with below-average variability of returns – history of consistent investment style and performance – not "flashy" or trendy.

13 Fund family has excellent reputation for stock selection and limited patience with underperforming funds.

---

[a] For a treatment of value investing style and its results, see Tweedy Browne (1992). For a financial planning perspective of fund selection, see Stevens (1999).

Sources: Adapted from Tweedy Browne, *Ten Ways to Beat an Index* (Tweedy Browne Company, New York), n.d.; Carla Fried et al., The Money *One Hundred*, 1998: The World's Best Mutual Funds, *Money*, June, 1998, pp. 66ff.; Amy C. Arnott, What Makes for a Consistent Winner? *Morningstar Investor*, October 1995, pp. 1–2, 4; Catherine G. Odelbo, No Easy Answers, *Morningstar Investor*, October 1995, 41; Amy Granzin, Finding a Focused Fund, *Morningstar FundInvestor*, February 2000, 6–7; Kunal Kapoor, The Truth about Focused Funds, *Morningstar FundInvestor*, October 2000, 1–3; and other sources.

Table 77 Fifty-plus mutual fund "myths"

---

1 Current law and regulation provide adequate shareholder disclosure.
2 Mutual funds and investment advisors are one and the same entity.
3 The quantity and quality of shareholder services are comparable.
4 Expense ratios have declined for the average fund over time.
5 Trading costs are small and of little consequence.
6 Fund tax efficiency is of little consequence to after-tax performance.
7 The average portfolio manager has long tenure.
8 Portfolio manager backgrounds are routinely disclosed.
9 The average portfolio manager is significantly invested in the fund.
10 The average outside director is significantly invested in the fund.
11 Large funds perform better than small funds.
12 Shareholders voice concerns at annual shareholder meetings.
13 Fund performance histories represent only the fund.
14 Funds execute trades at the lowest possible cost.
15 Outside directors have a record of reducing expenses.
16 A fund's investment advisor manages the portfolio.
17 Fund names and investment objectives mirror investment styles.
18 Outside directors effectively select directors.
19 Bond funds perform better than stock funds over time.
20 Risks to portfolio returns and value decrease as the investment period increases.
21 Shareholder risk preferences closely match portfolio investment objectives.
22 Risks related to portfolio diversification are comparable, especially among peers.
23 Measures of fund performance are comparable, especially among peers.
24 Portfolio managers are skilled at timing the market.
25 Economic and market forecasts are usually close to the mark.
26 Large-cap. funds outperform small-cap. funds.
27 Growth funds outperform value funds.
28 Momentum investing is a risky scheme.
29 Adding international stocks to portfolios increase risk.
30 Actively managed portfolios outperform passively managed portfolios.
31 Adding additional funds increases portfolio diversification.
32 The average fund outperforms its benchmark market index.
33 No-load funds have no loads.
34 Funds indexed to the S&P 500 Index have total market diversification.
35 Money market funds have never "lost a dime."
36 Load funds outperform no-load funds.
37 Funds have lower expenses than exchange-traded funds.
38 Funds with high portfolio turnover perform best.
39 Expenses are more important to the performance of stock funds rather than bond funds.
40 "Hot" performing funds normally "stay hot" over time.
41 High-performing bond funds have high gross yields.
42 Load charges are comparable for large and small purchases.
43 Funds sold direct to investors do not have sales loads.
44 Stock selection skill is the major cause of differences in fund performance.
45 Most shareholders invest too heavily in stock funds.
46 Fund shareholders are well diversified globally.
47 Index funds guarantee only average performance.

Table 77 (*continued*)

48 Recommendations of investment newsletters, radio and television programs, and investment magazines provide above-average returns.[a]

49 Increase returns by purchasing funds just before shareholder distributions are made.

50 Junk-bond funds are too risky for typical portfolios.

51 Brokers are key to obtaining "best deals" in funds.

52 Sell funds immediately upon hearing of a market decline.

53 New "fund concepts" have a history of high returns.

54 Tax-exempt municipal bond funds have larger after-tax returns than taxable bond funds.

55 Adding risky securities to portfolios reduces diversification.

56 Sell only the amounts needed to simplify tax record keeping.

57 Current portfolio managers are responsible for prior fund performance.

58 Stock funds are too risky for retirement portfolios.

59 Outside directors ensure the primacy of shareholder interests.

60 Index funds do not perform well in international markets.

Notes: Each myth is false as an absolute or total truth. Myths of rational investor behavior are discussed in chapter 6.

[a] In general, forget Dogs of the Dow, Motley Fools, *Forbes's* Honor Roll, Wall Street Week, *Barron's* Roundtable, *Wall Street Journal* Dartboard Portfolios, funds of funds, Morningstar Managers of the Year, and investment newsletters. But remember *Value Line Investment Survey* and Morningstar for data and analysis of funds.

Sources: Adapted from Jason Zweig, Twelve Deadly Fund Myths . . . and How to Profit from Them, *Money*, February, 86ff., 1996; Jonathan Clements, The Twenty-five Facts every Fund Investor should Know, *Wall Street Journal*, March 5, 1993, C1ff.; Jonathan Clements, Debunking some Mutual Fund Myths, *Wall Street Journal*, March 16, 1999, C1; John C. Bogle, *Bogle on the Secret to Investment Success*, Vanguard Group, April 6, 1999 (www.vanguard.com); and numerous other sources.

Table 78   Performance of momentum strategies

Performance period		Prior % of best and worst (%)	Subsequent best/worst performance (%)
Prior	Next		
13 weeks	13 weeks	50	12.1/10.8
13	13	10	12.0/8.6
26	13	50	12.1/11.4
26	13	10	12.2/9.6
26	26	50	12.0/11.6
26	26	10	11.5/11.0
52	13	50	14.4/11.4
52	13	10	14.5[a]/8.5
52	26	50	13/11.8
52	26	10	14.4/8.0
52	52	50	13.5/11.6
52	52	10	14.6[a]/8.8
2 years	52	50	12.5/11.1
2	52	10	13.0/8.0
2	2 years	50	12.6/11.0
2	2	10	12.6/7.0
5	1	50	11.3/10.2
5	1	10	13.3/5.9
5	2	50	13.3/11.7
5	2	10	15.2[a]/7.1

[a]   Largest returns with large performance differences.

Source: Abridged from Institute for Econometric Research, *Mutual Fund Hot Hands: Go with the Winners*, Special Bonus (The Institute, Fort Lauderdale, FL), April 1998.

Table 79   Exchange-traded funds versus mutual funds: checklist of advantages and disadvantages

Exchange-traded funds: advantages

1   The AMEX provides market liquidity and continuous trading at or near current market prices for index shares. Continuous trading provides more flexibility in rebalancing portfolios. Prices are determined by supply and demand. Index shares may be traded in small lots and the trading strategies available to common stock are also available for index shares.

2   Most index share transactions are executed on the AMEX, especially less than block-size trades. Bid–ask spreads are not unreasonable, and brokerage commission and fees can be reduced by online and/or discount brokers. But index share trading costs favor buy-and-hold strategies.

3   Large investors may also directly purchase and redeem index shares packaged as minimum block-size creation/redemption units. Creation/redemption units are purchased/redeemed in exchange for stock portfolios that match specific benchmark indices. But there are purchase and redemption fees.

4   Investor exchanges of redemption units for in-kind baskets of stock are tax-free exchanges. Exchange-traded funds do not sell stocks with potential capital gains to meet redemptions and there are no performance "drags" from holdings of cash assets. Investors may also unbundle portfolio shares received and sell them for any tax losses.

5   AMEX trading and tax-free direct exchanges with continuous portfolio transparency facilitate arbitrage that maintains index share prices at or very near net asset values of underlying portfolios. Arbitrageurs buy index shares selling at discount to net asset values on the AMEX, directly exchange redemption units for underlying stock portfolios, and sell unbundled stocks on the AMEX for more than paid for index share redemption units.

6   Exchange-traded funds are very tax-efficient, owing to direct tax-free exchanges, portfolio transparency, index portfolios, and control over the specific composition of underlying stock portfolios. Index portfolios are not actively managed, which minimizes turnover and realized capital gains. Shares of stock with the largest unrealized capital gains are exchanged for redemption units to minimize realized capital gains. Shares with the smallest unrealized capital gains are sold to meet changes in the composition of benchmark indices and to minimize realized capital gains.

7   Domestic exchange-traded funds are inherently less costly to manage than traditional domestic mutual funds. They have lower expense ratios than actively managed domestic mutual funds and also most index funds with the same benchmark indices.

8   Exchange-traded funds and mutual funds provide "instant" diversification, with broadly based portfolios or "homemade" portfolios with allocations of narrowly focused exchange-traded funds, such as foreign/domestic, specific country, investment style and/or industry sectors.

9   Exchange-traded funds provide access to benchmark indices and global sectors not (yet) available from mutual funds.

10 Investors may practise cash management by temporarily "sweeping" cash inflows into index shares.

Exchange-traded funds: disadvantages

1   Index share trading costs are higher than pure no-load mutual funds with zero shareholder transaction costs. This difference is increased by market timing and dollar cost averaging strategies that trade frequently, even given online and/or discount brokerage commission and small bid–ask spreads.

2   Investor purchase and redemption of creation and redemption units are subject to fees, which are higher than for pure no-load mutual funds.

3   Exchange-traded fund brokers generally provide less in the way of diversity and quality of shareholder services than mutual funds.

Table 79 (*continued*)

4 Exchange-traded fund index shares risk selling at discounts (also premiums) to net asset values of underlying stock portfolios, though arbitrage normally keeps them small. But index shares can trade at significant discounts/premiums for extended periods, especially in small, less liquid international markets. HOLDRs have proven to have large discounts to net asset value.

5 No sponsor of both exchange-traded funds and index mutual funds has yet matched the annual returns of the Vanguard 500 Index Fund.

6 Exchange-traded funds often have large tracking errors in matching the performance of small international market benchmark indices. These indices do not provide the required portfolio diversification, and markets have low liquidity and high trading costs. Tracking error derives from the use of statistical methods to approximate benchmark performance. These exchange-traded funds also have higher expense ratios and higher portfolio turnover and trading costs than comparable mutual funds.

7 The performance and liquidity of exchange-traded fund shares have yet to be severely tested in major market declines.

8 The settlement period for index share trades is three days, but it is overnight for mutual fund redemptions.

Table 80 Sample economic indicators: outlook summary

Economic indicators	Data trend	Implications for economic outlook
1 GDP growth rate (figure 12.1)	Increasing	Positive
2 Industrial output index (figure 12.2)	Decreasing	Negative
3 Unemployment rate (figure 12.3)	Increasing	Negative
4 Consumer price index (figure 12.4)	Increasing	Negative
5 M2 money supply growth rate (figure 12.5)	Increasing	Positive
6 Excess reserves growth rate (figure 12.6)	Increasing	Positive
7 Treasury securities yield curve (figure 12.7)	Upward sloping	Positive
8 Consumer confidence index (figure 12.8)	Decreasing	Negative
9 Federal budget deficit (figure 12.9)	Decreasing to Surplus	Positive
10 Coincident economic indicators index (figure 12.10)	Increasing	Positive
11 Leading economic indicators index (figure 12.11)	Increasing	Positive
Economic outlook	**Positive (seven of eleven indicators)**	

Source: Figures cited.

Table 81 Sample market indicators: outlook summary, overall economic and market outlook

Market indicators	Data trend	Outlook implication
1 NYSE cumulative daily breadth (with DJIA Index) (figure 12.12)	Negative	Negative
2 DJIA moving averages, 100 day and 200 day (figure 12.13)	Positive	Positive
3 Mutual funds cash ratio (figure 12.14)	Negative	Negative
4 *Investors Intelligence* Advisor Sentiment Index (bullish advisors) (table 83)	Neutral	Negative
5 DJIA P/E ratio (table 84)	Positive	Negative
6 Consensus DJIA P/E ratio (table 84)	Negative	Negative
7 DJIA dividend yield (table 84)	Neutral	Negative
8 Insider transactions (table 85)	Negative	Negative
9 Earnings surprises (table 86a)	Neutral	Neutral
10 Earnings estimates changes (table 86b)	Negative	Negative

Market outlook **Negative (eight of ten indicators)**

Overall economic and market outlook Mixed[a]
(including table 80)

[a] Economy "positive", but market technically weak ("negative").

Source: Figures and tables cited.

Table 82 Economic and market indicators: selected checklist

Encircle the number of indicators with "yes" responses:

A   Economic indicators (see *Barron's* first)
1   Is the GDP growth rate increasing?
2   Is the index of industrial output increasing?
3   Is the unemployment rate decreasing?
4   Is the consumer price index stable or falling?
5   Is the M2 money supply growth rate increasing?
6   Are excess reserves increasing?
7   Is the Treasury yield curve upward-sloping?
8   Is the consumer confidence index increasing?
9   Is the federal budget deficit decreasing?
10 Is the index of coincident economic indicators increasing?
11 Is the index of leading economic indicators increasing?
12 Is the ratio of the index of coincident economic indicators to the index of lagging economic indicators stable (not peaking)?
13 Have reserve requirements been reduced?
14 Are Fed. funds and Treasury bill rates lower than discount rate?
15 Have margin requirements either been increased or decreased?
16 Have there been two successive decreases in discount rate, margin requirements or reserve requirements?
17 Is the capacity utilization rate less than 81%?
18 Is the Fed. funds rate decreasing and the Treasury yield curve upward-sloping?
19 Is the Bridge-CRB Index of commodity futures prices stable or declining?
20 Are net free reserves increasing?
21 Is the ninety-day Treasury bill yield decreasing?
22 Is the ratio of ninety-day Treasury bill yield to discount rate decreasing?
23 Are M1, M2, and M3 money supply measures increasing in both nominal and real terms?
24 Is the ratio of real M3 money supply growth rate to real GDP growth rate greater than 1?
25 Is the CIBCR Leading Inflation Index stable or declining?
26 Is the ratio of thirty-year Treasury bond yield to fifty-two-week moving average of thirty-year Treasury bond yield less than 90%?
27 Is the ratio of federal budget deficit to GDP declining or budget in surplus?
28 Is the CRB spot futures (inflation) index steady or decreasing?
29 Is the ECRI future inflation guide steady or decreasing?
30 Is the National Association of Purchasing Managers' (NAPM) Index above 44?

B   Market indicators (see *Barron's* first)
1   Is NYSE cumulative daily breadth increasing with and not diverging from DJIA?
2   Is DJIA above its *Investor's Business Daily* 100 day and 200 day moving averages and increasing?
3   Is the mutual fund cash ratio 10% or above?
4   (a) Is the *Investors Intelligence* Investor Sentiment Index of Bullish Advisors 35% or less?[a]
    (b) Is the *Investors Intelligence* Investor Sentiment Index of Bearish Advisors 50% or more?[a]
5   Is the DJIA P/E ratio less than 18–20?
6   Is the P/E ratio of consensus DJIA operating earnings (next twelve months) lower than current DJIA P/E ratio and less than 18–20?
7   Is the DJIA dividend yield above 3–4%?

Table 82   (*continued*)

8   Is the ratio of the dollar volume of insider transactions buying to dollar volume of insider transactions selling greater than 1?

9   Is the ratio of the number of positive earnings surprises to the number of negative earnings surprises greater than 1?

10 Is the DJIA Utility Index increasing along with DJIA (not diverging)?

11 Is the NYSE Specialist Short Sales Ratio of specialist shares sold short to total shares sold short less than 45%?

12 Is the ten-day moving average of the CBOE put/call ratio greater than 50–60/100?[a]

13 Is the absolute sum of the CPI inflation rate and the DJIA P/E ratio 20 or less?

14 Is the ratio of S&P 500 Index earnings yield (next four quarters) to ten-year Treasury bond yield greater than 1?

15 Is the number of weekly IPOs small or decreasing?[a]

16 Is the percentage of bullish futures traders to total futures traders small and/or decreasing?[a]

18 Is the percentage of bullish economists to total economists small and/or decreasing?[a]

19 Is the ratio of bullish advertisements in *Barron's* to bearish advertisements in *Barron's* small and/or decreasing?[a]

20 Are foreign dollar purchases of US stocks small and/or decreasing?[a]

21 Is the University of Michigan Investor Sentiment Index less than 60%?[a]

22 Is the CBOE Market Volatility Index (VIX Index) below its twenty-day moving average?[a]

23 Is the ratio of ten-year Treasury bond yield to S&P 500 Index dividend yield less than 2.5?

24 Is the dividend yield spread between yield on thirty-year Treasury bonds and DJIA dividend yield between 3.0% and 5.75%?

25 Is the ratio of the average of S&P 500 cash flow and operating earnings to the average of thirty-year Treasury bond yield and ninety-day Treasury bill yield above 1.95?

26 Is the average equity allocation recommended by major investment firms less than 60%?[a]

27 Is the spread between high-yield bond (BBB) yields and ten-year Treasury bonds narrowing?

28 Is the yield on Fed. funds futures (subtract contract price from 100) declining?

29 Is the spread between nominal and real yields on ten-year Treasury bonds increasing?

30 Is the thirty-year Treasury bond yield more than 10% less than its fifty-two-week moving average?

31 Is the ratio of S&P 500 earnings yield to ten-year Treasury bond yield greater than 1?

32 Is the average investment manager's recommended portfolio stock allocation less than 50%?[a]

33 Are discounts on closed-end funds stable or increasing?[a]

Interpretation: A preponderance of "yes" answers in one or both sections signals an overall positive economic and/or market outlook.

[a]   Contrarian indicator.

Notes: For these and other indicators, see Fosback (1994), Shim et al. (1994), Rogers (1994), Hildebrand (1992), Garzarelli (1996), Stack (1994a, b), Niemira and Zukowski (1994), Graza (1997, 1998a, b, c), Schaeffer (1998, 1999a), Investors Business Daily (2000), Barron's (2000), Market Edge (1999), and National Economic Trends (2000). Graza and Ungar (2001) review five essential indicators. See Shefrin (2000) for a behavioral finance view of technical market indicators.

Table 83   *Investors Intelligence* Advisor Sentiment Index (last three weeks)

Sentiment	Last week (December 4, 1998)	Two weeks ago (November 27, 1998)	Three weeks ago (November 20, 1998)
Bullish	56.9	57.9	57.0
Bearish	31.0	29.8	31.6
Correction	21.1	12.3	11.4
Outlook Negative			

Source: http://interactive.wsj.com. Data provided by *Investors Intelligence*.

Table 84   DJIA market measures

A: DJIA P/E ratio (last three observations)

	Last week (December 4, 1998)	Two weeks ago (November 27, 1998)	Three weeks ago (November 20, 1998)
DJIA P/E ratio	24.3	25.1	21.0

Outlook Negative

B: Consensus DJIA P/E ratio (current estimate for this and next year)

	1998 P/E	1999 P/E
Consensus DJIA P/E ratio	22.4	19.3

Outlook Negative

C: DJIA dividend yield (last three observations)

	Last week (December 4, 1998)	Two weeks ago (November 27, 1998)	Three weeks ago (November 20, 1998)
DJIA dividend yield (%)	1.69	1.63	1.68

Outlook Negative

Source: http://interactive.wsj.com.

Table 85   Insider transactions, non-bank companies, November 30, 1998 (ratio of current dollar value of buy/sell transactions)

Company name	% change in holdings	No. of insiders	No. of shares	$ value (million)
Buy				
Genzyme Transgenics	1,416	1	5,000	26,900
Texas Industries	767	2	3,100	77,111
Southern African Fund	575	1	230	2,428
Helix Technology	250	1	500	5,565
Thermo Fibertek	236	1	48,900	245,225
Winter Sports	171	1	116	1,334
Homeland Holding	155	1	600	2,328
Penzoil	100	1	500	17,375
Speigel	69	1	12,000	39,000
Heartport	20	1	75,000	459,000
Total				**876,266**
Sell				
Petsmart	−100	1	94,902	651,027
Ameripath	−56	1	50,000	650,000
Optical Cable Corp	−31	2	4,901	57,379
FNB Corp	−13	1	7,038	198,119
Glenayre Technologies	−11	1	8,000	50,950
Precision Auto Care	−10	1	1,500	6,750
Fort James Corp	−8	1	5,000	196,250
Resmed	−7	3	9,000	525,880
Willis Lease Finance	−1	1	35,000	579,400
Total				**2,915,755**

Dollar value of purchases smaller than dollar value of sales
Overall assessment: negative

Source: http://interactive.wsj.com.

Table 86(a)   Earnings surprises, November 30, 1998 (ratio of current number of positive/negative surprises)

Company name	Quarter ended	Actual EPS	Estimated EPS	% change	No. of analysts
Appid Extrusion	9/30	0.05	0.08	−37.50	2
Avcorp	9/30	0.03	0.06	−50.00	1
Duckwall-Alco	10/31	0.22	0.19	15.79	2
Mediware Info	9/30	0.15	0.12	25.00	1
Todd A-O A	8/31	0.07	0.10	−30.00	1
Vlasic Foods	10/31	0.15	0.13	15.38	6

Ratio (positive:neutral): 3:3
Overall assessment: neutral

Company name	Financial year end	Previous Friday's	Last Friday's

Table 86(b)   Earnings estimates changes, November 30, 1998 (ratio of current number of positive/negative changes)

Company name	Financial year end	Previous Friday's	Last Friday's consensus
Positive			
Laser Vision	April 1999	0.21	0.29
Information A	January 1999	0.20	0.21
Navigante Inte	April 1999	0.67	0.70
Samnmina	September 1999	1.89	1.95
Negative			
Nuevo Energy	December 1999	−0.68	−1.01
Pioneer Natur	December 1999	−0.33	−0.41
Amerada Hess	December 1999	1.33	1.03
Union Pacific	December 1999	−0.32	−0.37
Cross Timbers	December 1999	0.44	0.38
Asarco	December 1999	−1.10	−1.25
Boeing	December 1999	2.09	1.82
Kerr-McGee	December 1999	2.34	2.05

Ratio (positive:negative): 4:8
Overall assessment: negative

Source: http://interactive.wsj.com.

Table 87(a)   The time to buy checklist

"Yes" answers are favorable	Yes	No

The business cycle
1   Is business activity in a down trend, and if so, do you foresee the end of that down trend?
2   Is inflation decelerating?
3   If corporate profits have declined from their previous peak, do you expect them to start turning upward soon?

Monetary policy and interest rates
4   Are short-term interest rates starting to decline?
5   Has the Federal Reserve Board given indications that it will ease restraints on growth of the money supply?

Stock valuations
6   Has the price/earnings ratio of the Value Line composite index fallen to near or even below its level at the market's last cyclical low point?

Sentiment indicators
7   Are mutual funds heavily in cash?
8   Is the odd-lot short-sales ratio very high?
9   Is the specialists' short-sales ratio exceptionally low?
10   Are your friends and business associates pessimistic or apathetic about the market?

State of the market
11   Has the market been declining for many months since its previous cyclical high?
12   Has the market registered a large percentage drop from its previous cyclical high?
13   Has the market recently accelerated its rate of decline, as it typically does in the final stages of bear markets?
14   Has the market rebounded from its last major low point, dropped back to that low point once or twice, and then advanced?

The presidential election cycle
15   Is the next presidential election not much more than two years from now?

Total

Source: As adapted in John A. Haslem, *The Investor's Guide to Mutual Funds* (Prentice-Hall, Englewood Cliffs, NJ), 1988, p. 112.

Table 87(b)   The time to sell checklist

"Yes" answers are worrisome or bearish	Yes	No

The business cycle
1   Is there growing evidence that the business cycle has reached a peak?
2   Is inflation accelerating?
3   If corporate profits are rising, does the current rate of increase appear too strong to last?

Monetary policy and interest rates
4   Are short-term interest rates rising and are they as high as they were at the corresponding stage of the previous upturn?
5   Has the Federal Reserve Board started to tighten monetary policy?

Stock valuations
6   Has the P/E ratio risen near or above its level at the market's last cyclical peak?

Sentiment indicators
7   Are the cash reserves of mutual funds low?
8   Is the odd-lot short sales ratio very low?
9   Is the specialists' short-sales ratio exceptionally high?
10   Are your friends and business associates talking about their winners and feeling euphoric about the market?

State of the market
11   Has the market been advancing for many months since its previous cyclical low?
12   Has the market registered a large percentage gain from its previous cyclical low?
13   Is the advance/decline line underperforming the popular averages – an indication of deteriorating market strength?
14   Has the market dropped below its recent high and climbed back to it a couple of times or more, only to retreat again?

The presidential election cycle
15   Is this the year following a presidential election?

Total

Source: As table 87a.

GLOSSARY

Selected market and technical indicators are discussed in chapter 12.

Abnormal return return on risky asset in excess of that expected for its risk class.

Active/passive currency management use of market timing/passive allocation to manage portfolio exposure to currency exchange.

Active portfolio management and trading behavioral anomaly that investor trading and trading volume are based on overconfidence in interpretation of information.

Actively managed fund (portfolio) traditional fund portfolio management based on active securities selection and trading designed to outperform benchmark index.

Administrator (fund) provider of fund management services and oversight.

Adjusted Jensen Alpha adjustment of Jensen Alpha to allow performance comparisons among portfolios.

Adverse selection costs (costs of asymmetric information with informed traders) securities market maker losses caused by trading with investors who have "insider" information.

All-weather portfolio portfolio allocations designed for performance in any market conditions over time.

Alpha (Jensen) difference between actual excess return and that expected given portfolio systematic risk and the CAPM; significantly positive alphas evidence superior portfolio manager skills, and conversely for negative alphas.

Annual fees (loads) includes any 12b-1 fees (distribution fees) and account maintenance fees.

Annual (and semi-annual) reports mandated periodic fund financial reports to shareholders.

Annualized rates of return (returns) compound average annual returns for particular time periods.

Anomaly behavioral exception to the theory of efficiency of financial markets.

Arbitrage pricing theory (APT) theory that explains returns using linear functions of several common factors.

Arbitrage profits profits from simultaneous purchase/sale of securities with different prices in two markets.

Asset allocation funds funds that use tactical asset management (form of market timing) to allocate among asset classes.

Asset pricing and investor sentiment behavioral anomaly that discrepancies in asset prices from "intrinsic values" are based on the nature and degree of investor optimism or pessimism.

Attainable global diversification degree of fund portfolio diversification attainable globally.

Back-end (deferred) loads paid at redemption includes any redemption fees, contingent-deferred sales charges, exchange fees, and (for convenience) sales (redemption) transaction fees paid into portfolios.

Balanced funds original asset allocation funds that use strategic stock/bond asset allocation.

Behavioral finance (as opposed to "modern finance") application of cognitive psychology to investor decision making versus the rational decisions of "economic man."

Benchmark index (performance benchmark) market index used as standard of performance for actively/passively managed portfolios.

Benchmark style index particular performance standard used to evaluate and maintain desired portfolio investment style.

Benchmark tracking error difference between a fund's return and that of its benchmark market index.

Beta measure of market (systematic) risk.

Biased self-attribution behavioral concept that investors tend to attribute good outcomes to their abilities and bad outcomes to externalities.

Bid–ask spread difference between security bid and ask prices set by market makers.

Black-box strategy use of advanced quantitative models to make or enhance investment decisions (may imply less than complete user understanding).

Blend style (blend) investment style that includes both value and growth styles.

Block trades large orders to buy/sell shares that normally impact market prices.

Bottom-up investing method of fundamental analysis that analyzes particular stocks first before, if at all, analyzing industry and economic outlooks.

Boutique funds "specialty shops" that apply investment approaches best suited for small portfolios and market niches.

Breakeven return return required for fund to be equally as trading cost-effective as the market index/peer group.

Breakpoint discounts (break points) increasingly large front-end load discounts given for increasingly large minimum share purchases.

Business risk increased volatility of a particular security's returns derived from changes in the risk of the particular industry or business.

Buy-and-hold strategy of constructing long-term portfolios with low portfolio turnover.

Capital asset pricing model (CAPM) theory that expected returns on securities are linear functions of sensitivity to changes in market portfolio returns.

Capital gains distribution fund distribution of taxable realized capital gains, net of realized capital losses, to shareholders.

Capital market securities marketable securities with maturities defined as exceeding one year.

Capital market theory theory of the process by which assets are priced in financial markets.

Cash assets (reserves) marketable short-term securities with minimum price volatility quickly convertible to "cash."

Cash bucket account managed outside investment portfolio to meet anticipated and unanticipated cash needs for a defined number of years.

CDA Jensen Alpha (see _Jensen Alpha_) CDA/Wiesenbeger's Jensen Alpha, computed using monthly data.

CDA Rating CDA/Wiesenberger's composite percentile rating of fund performance over past market cycles.

Certainty-equivalent return certain return that provides investors with utility equivalent to expected value of uncertain return.

CFA charter (designation) certification of successful completion of educational program designed for current and prospective investment professionals.

Closed-end fund (closed-end management investment company) fund with generally fixed portfolio and non-redeemable outstanding shares priced by market supply/demand.

Closet indexing managing actively managed fund portfolio to approximate benchmark index performance (to avoid being an outlier).

Cognitive dissonance   behavioral concept that investor memories of past performance are consistently better than actual performance.

Cognitive psychology   as applied to behavioral finance, it reflects the various non-rational behaviors of investors.

Collateralized mortgage obligations (CMOs)   securities designed to improve traditional mortgage pass-through securities with sequential risk classes of cash flows, including interest only, principal only, and Z tranche.

Collectibles (fine arts collectibles)   "other" fine arts that include historical, whimsical, or sentimental art forms, including autographs and memorabilia.

Combined purchase privilege   provision that breakpoint discounts are based on total shareholder investment in family funds; may be extended to pooled family purchases.

Common factors   factors that are in common to security returns generally.

Confirmation   convergence of two or more historically meaningful market indicators that together signal continuation in market outlook.

Consensus earnings estimates   "average" expectation of stock earnings per share by securities analysts.

Constrained attainable diversification   potential constraint on degree of fund portfolio diversification attainable globally.

Constrained optimized allocations   identification of portfolio allocations that ensure minimum/maximum allocations of particular asset classes.

Contingent deferred sales charges (CDSC)   sizable fees designed to discourage investor redemptions before commission to sales agents are paid – typically decline to zero over five or six years.

Contrarian indicator   market indicator for which the interpretation is opposite of finding at extreme values.

Contrarian strategy   behavioral anomaly to efficient markets that seeks out-of-favor, undervalued stocks caused by biased profit forecasts and risk misperceptions.

Country fund   investment company that invests in a single country.

Country (political) risk   increased volatility of security returns derived from changes in risk of firms operating in particular countries due to changes in the ability to convert foreign earnings into dollars.

Creation units   investors "create" (purchase) creation units of index shares of specific ETFs in exchange for minimum block size stock portfolios that generally match specific benchmark indices.

Cross-sectional diversification   portfolios that are diversified in the short term and increase certainty of long-term returns (versus time-series diversification).

Cubes   ETFs benchmarked to the Nasdaq 100 Trust Series I technology index.

Custodian   service provider that holds fund assets in safe keeping and manages cash payments and receipts.

Custom benchmark index (custom style benchmark)   combination of market indices that best reflects portfolio manager's past returns and investment style.

Customer servicing fees (trailing commission)   element of fund distribution expenses paid for sales agent "continuing customer service."

Data mining (snooping)   "punishing" historical data to find technical indicators that would have generated superior returns over the particular period and applying them to the future.

Day traders   "investors" who trade on the basis of intra-day market and technical news (not recommended).

Debt-to-equity ratio (D/E)   company's long-term debt divided by book value of its shareholder equity (%).

Derivatives   class of securities whose value depends wholly or partly on their relationships to underlying securities.

Diamonds   ETFs benchmarked to the DJIA.

Diminishing marginal utility of wealth   increase in utility (satisfaction) diminishes with each increment of wealth.

Direct-market fund   fund that distributes shares direct to investors.

Discount (premium)   amount by which closed-end funds or ETF shares are trading below (above) net asset value.

Disinterested (independent) directors   fund directors not otherwise affiliated with fund investment advisory firms or the funds themselves.

Distributor (principal underwriter)   registered broker-dealer that distributes and redeems fund shares.

Divergence   divergence in trend of two or more historically meaningful market indicators that together signal change in market outlook.

Diversification effect   reduction in portfolio risk provided by appropriate diversification.

Diversification risk   increase/decrease in degree of portfolio risk due to constraint on attainable global diversification.

Diversified (non-diversified) fund   open-end or closed-end fund that meets (does not meet) qualifying legal diversification requirements.

Dividend (income) distribution   fund shareholder distribution of dividend and interest income, plus net realized short-term capital gains; taxed as ordinary income.

Dividend (cash) drag   delayed reinvestment of ETF dividend distributions that constrain returns.

Dividend yield (D/P)   current annual dividend per share divided by share price (%).

Dollar cost averaging   strategy of reducing average cost of portfolio by investing fixed amounts at fixed intervals in good markets and bad.

Dollar-weighted returns   portfolio returns weighted by returns earned on actual amounts invested over a particular period.

Domestic hybrid mutual funds   general class of funds that provide "full diversification" in one portfolio; includes asset allocation funds.

Dow theory   most famous technical approach to the market, which states the market follows daily, secondary, and primary (four or more years) trends.

Downside risk   risk measure that focuses on portion of returns variance that causes asset returns not to meet target returns.

Drift   continuation of momentum in stock returns over the short term that is predictable from prior returns and prior news about earnings.

Duration   measure of bond maturity based on weighted average time for remaining cash proceeds to be received.

Duration dependence   concept that, as duration of speculative bubbles increases, the probability of a crash decreases.

Earnings-estimate momentum strategy   strategy based on buying stocks for which earnings-per-share estimates have been increased.

Earnings-momentum strategy   strategy that buys stocks with increasing earnings per share.

Earnings-surprise momentum strategy   strategy that buys stocks reporting earnings per share above expectations.

Earnings surprises   positive technical market indicator when number of positive earnings surprises exceed negative surprises, and vice versa.

Economic man   the rational investor assumed in modern finance.

Economies of scale   reduction in unit costs associated with increased asset size.

Efficient frontier   set of all efficient portfolios – portfolio with the highest expected return for the least amount of risk.

Efficient markets   securities market in which securities are priced at "intrinsic values"; three versions – weak form, semi-strong form, and strong form.

Efficient minimum-risk global portfolio   portfolio mix of US and international stocks on the efficient frontier that has minimum risk.

Efficient portfolio   portfolio with the highest expected return for a given amount of risk.

Elliott wave   technical model (such as the Coppock curve) which states that market prices move in both short-term and long-term waves, and the latter may last for a century or so.

Emerging market funds   funds that invest in securities in developing countries.

Endowment effect   behavioral concept that investors believe the securities held are preferable to those not held.

Enhanced index fund (leveraged, tilted, and amalgamated)   fund that makes adjustments to indexed portfolios in an effort to increase returns relative to the benchmark market index.

Equity premium puzzle   behavioral anomaly that finds presence of larger equity premiums than dictated by rational markets due to investor loss aversion.

(Equity) risk premium   additional return required for investors to buy stocks rather than risk-free debt.

Equity style allocation   allocation of equity securities by value/growth and cap. size investment styles within the equity allocation determined by stock/bond asset allocation.

Equity style box   Morningstar concept that identifies domestic equity fund's investment style category over past three years.

Excess reserves   excess of actual bank reserves over reserves required held by Federal Reserve – measure of tightness or ease of monetary policy.

Exchange (shares)   redemption of shares in one fund and purchase of shares in another fund within the same fund family.

Exchange risk (currency risk)   increased volatility of security returns derived from changes in risk of operating in particular countries due to changes in conversion rates of foreign earnings into dollars.

Exchange-traded funds (ETFs)   "fund-like" entities with generally indexed portfolios and shares that are exchange traded; also offer direct creation of shares and in-kind share redemption with mechanisms to minimize differences between market share prices and net asset values.

Exotic (custom) derivatives   customized derivative contracts with non-standard terms that are often illiquid.

Expense ratio (fund)   annual fund expenses divided by average total assets – includes management fees, any 12b-1 fees, and "other" operating expenses.

Factor model   model that explains security performance based on both in-common and unique (unexplained) factors.

Fair-value pricing   estimates of closing market prices where actual prices are not available owing to low market liquidity or time-zone differences.

Fee waivers   temporary reductions in fund expenses to attract new investors.

Financial assets   securitized assets, such as mutual fund shares, versus real (tangible) assets, such as gold.

Financial engineers   persons on Wall Street with advanced degrees in mathematical sciences who develop new and advanced investment "products."

Financial institutions   financial service providers, classified as either depository or non-depository institutions.

Financial intermediaries   financial institutions that indirectly channel savings to productive uses, such as banks.

Financial risk   increased volatility of security returns derived from changes in firm risk due to its proportionate use of debt financing.

Financial services industry   industry classification for providers of financial services, including mutual funds.

Fine arts   broad class of fine arts sold and auctioned by major auction houses and dealers, such as fine jewelry, art works, and antiques.

Fixed-income style box   Morningstar concept that identifies bond fund's maturity and credit quality investment style for the current year.

Fixed-income trusts   shorthand for unit investment trusts that invest in fixed-income securities.

Fixed trusts   shorthand for unit investment trusts.

Floating-rate notes   securities with interest rates periodically reset based on defined interest rates.

Fosback Index   contrarian indicator based on size of fund cash assets ratio.

Framing effect   behavioral concept that investor choices among logically identical alternatives are influenced by the way they are presented ("framed").

Free (net free or net borrowed) reserves   excess reserves net of bank borrowed reserves – technical indicator of monetary policy ease or tightness.

Front-end loads (paid at purchase)   sales loads, loads on reinvested dividends, and purchase transaction fees (for convenience) paid into the portfolio.

Fund   shorthand for mutual fund.

Fund selection and allocation   identification of mutual funds for purchase and determination of allocations within identified investment style portfolio allocations.

Fundamental analysis   estimate of security intrinsic value based on analysis of current and future financial attributes.

Fund-specific attributes   variables other than investment style that affect fund performance.

Funds of funds   mutual funds that invest in shares of other mutual funds.

Futures contract   agreement to buy/sell specified number of shares of a particular asset at a specified price and time period.

Gains–loss management   strategy of increasing fund portfolio tax efficiency by taking realized capital losses to offset realized capital gains.

Glamour stocks   well known growth stocks widely considered appropriate investments.

Growth style (growth)   investment style of funds that invest in stocks with superior earnings growth and prospects.

Hedge fund   private investment partnership in which general partners have significant investments; may take portfolio positions and use leveraged and speculative strategies not permitted for mutual funds.

Hedging currency risk   strategy of using currency derivatives to reduce portfolio exposure to exchange rate risk.

Herding   behavioral concept that portfolio managers tend to buy what other institutional investors are buying.

HIFO   selling high cost shares first to minimize realized capital gains.

High-yield bond fund   fund that primarily invests in bonds of lower than investment grade.

HOLDRS   ETFs benchmarked to twenty narrow domestic industry sector indices.

Hot hands (versus cold hands)   attribution of funds with sustained superior (inferior) short-term performance.

Hot money   investor purchases that "chase" hot fund performance.

Hub-and-spoke fund   fund offering multiple share classes appended to new or existing single portfolios.

Illusion of control   behavioral concept in which investors, often short-term, think they know and control more than they actually do about their decisions.

Immediacy (market impact) costs   price concessions "paid" in making immediate trades, especially significant in large block trades.

Index (passively managed) fund   fund with passively managed portfolio benchmarked to a market index.

Index shares tradable ETF shares generally benchmarked to particular market indices.

Indirect-market (sales force) fund fund that distributes (sells) shares to investors through sales agents.

Individually managed accounts investor accounts managed by particular portfolio managers.

Inflation (purchasing power) risk increased volatility of security returns derived from changes in the rate of inflation.

Information-motivated trades trades that increase market maker bid–ask spreads when "motivated" by private information.

Interested (inside) directors fund directors who are affiliated with fund investment advisory firms.

Interest-rate risk increased volatility of security returns due to changes in interest rates.

Intermediation process of acquiring financial assets in the form of shares in mutual funds, rather than acquiring assets directly in financial markets.

Intrinsic (fair market) value estimate of security value based on analysis of current and future financial attributes; theoretically, present value of future cash flows to investors.

Inverse floating-rate notes (inverse floaters) (IFRN) notes with variable interest rates that move opposite to the direction of changes in benchmarked interest rate – a "bet on interest rates."

Investment Advisors Act of 1940 statute that applies to investment advisors, in general; requires fund registration and imposes fiduciary, anti-fraud, and shareholder and SEC disclosure provisions.

Investment advisory fees fees paid to investment advisors for portfolio management services.

Investment company classification of unit investment trusts and management investment companies (open-end and closed-end management companies) under the 1940 Act.

Investment Company Act of 1940 (1940 Act) primary legislation governing mutual funds that provides for SEC regulatory oversight.

Investment management process of implementing investment policy, and includes active portfolio allocation, if any, investment style allocation, security selection and allocation, and portfolio performance evaluation.

Investment management company (management company, investment advisor, investment manager, fund manager, fund advisory firm, fund advisor) fund sponsor that provides portfolio advisory and normally other services.

Investment objective traditionally, type of portfolio securities held to meet particular investor needs, such as "growth" and "growth and income."

Investment policy identification of investor risk preferences, portfolio investment objectives, and stock/bond asset allocation.

Investment style style of portfolio management classified as value versus growth and large-cap. versus small-cap.

(Investment) style allocation allocation of equity securities by value/growth and cap. size investment style, and allocation of fixed-income securities by maturity and credit quality style; within stock/bond asset allocation.

Investment style box Morningstar concept that identifies equity fund value/growth and cap. size investment style for current year.

iShares ETFs benchmarked to fifty-four domestic and foreign market indices.

January effect behavioral anomaly of abnormal early year returns that provide much of annual returns.

Jensen Alpha measure of degree to which portfolio manager skill or lack thereof is added or subtracted from passive portfolio returns.

Large-cap. style (large-cap.) investment style of funds that invest in stocks with large market capitalization.

Lead portfolio manager final arbiter among fund portfolio managers and for oversight of any subadvisor managers.

Letters of intent (statements of intention)   investor commitments to invest specified amounts to qualify for specified breakpoint commission.

Level-load fund   fund share class that imposes 1 percent redemption fees in first year plus annual 12b-1 fees.

Life-stage (life-cycle, lifestyle) fund   asset allocation fund designed to match specific investor investment horizons and risk preferences, which are identified for specific investors through use of planning tools.

Liquid (marketable) asset   asset that can be sold quickly.

Liquidity effect   larger returns on small-cap. stocks that compensate for larger trading costs in less liquid markets.

Liquidity-motivated trades   trades made for liquidity or portfolio rebalancing purposes.

Liquidity risk   increased volatility of security returns derived from changes in market liquidity that change bid–ask spreads.

Load fund   fund that imposes front-end or back-end sales charge.

Loads   traditionally front-end sales charges, but now also level loads (12b-1 expenses effectively acting as loads) and back-end loads.

Loss aversion   behavioral concept that investors weigh losses more heavily than gains.

Low loads   direct-market funds that impose below-average front-end sales loads.

Management (advisory) fees   fund portfolio advisory fees that are the major component in fund total operating expenses.

Management ("managed") investment company   class of investment companies that includes open-end and closed-end funds.

Management team (team management)   term used rather than listing each portfolio manager to convey that no single person "calls the shots."

Market resilience   degree of market efficiency that indicates whether market prices quickly readjust to equilibrium prices owing to investor arbitrage actions.

Market risk (non-diversifiable risk)   increased volatility of security returns derived from changes in the overall level of financial market prices.

Market risk neutral strategy   strategy designed to earn returns in good and bad markets by buying undervalued stocks, selling overvalued stocks short, and investing proceeds in Treasury bills.

Market timing (market timers)   strategy of moving portfolio assets from cash to securities, and vice versa, based on short-term market forecasts; also involves changing portfolio asset allocations (not recommended).

Market value pricing   securities priced daily, normally based on last trade prices and mid points of most recent bid–ask spreads of unlisted securities.

(Markowitz-type) mean variance optimizer   model for optimizing portfolio asset allocation based on original Markowitz model, but modified to enhance applications.

Mean reversion (reversion to mean or mean revert)   tendency for momentum strategies not to be profitable over longer time periods due to reversion of returns to mean levels; provides opportunity for application of contrarian strategies.

Median market capitalization   method of identifying fund cap. size investment style by measuring portfolio capitalization.

Mental accounting   behavioral concept that investors use separate "mental accounts" to simplify complex problems.

Merger arbitrage   strategy of seeking arbitrage profits by buying undervalued shares of firms to be acquired and shorting shares of acquiring firm.

Micro-cap stocks   stocks with the smallest market capitalizations.

Mid-cap. style (mid-cap.)   investment style of funds that invest in stocks with mid-sized market capitalization.

Minimum risk portfolio   portfolio on the efficient frontier with lowest absolute risk.

Miscellaneous fees   "annoying" residual shareholder transaction fees, including account close-out fees, systematic withdrawal plan fees, automatic investment plan fees, and retirement account fees.

Modern finance   "the" dominant investment paradigm that markets are highly efficient and prices determined by rational (not behavioral) investors.

Momentum effect and strategy (persistence, positive-feedback strategy)   stocks with superior past returns continue to outperform "losers" over the short term; evidenced by earnings growth, earnings estimates, earnings surprises, or price behavior.

Money market fund   fund that invests in short-term money market securities and normally maintains $1 net asset value.

Money market securities   short-term debt securities with maturities defined as less than one year.

Morningstar Bear Market Rank   measure of fund performance in past bear markets.

Morningstar Category (category)   domestic equity fund investment style category over last three years.

Morningstar Category Rating   fund risk/return rating relative to its category peer group over the past three years.

Morningstar (star) Rating   fund risk/return rating relative to its broad asset class based on weighted average of its Morningstar Risk-adjusted Rating for each of the three, five, and ten-year periods.

Morningstar Return   measure of excess returns net of loads/fees relative to its broad investment class.

Morningstar Risk   measure of a fund's downside risk volatility relative to its broad investment class.

Morningstar Risk-adjusted Rating   combined measure of Morningstar Rating and Morningstar Return for each of the last three, five, and ten-year periods.

MSCI (EAFE) Index   Morgan Stanley benchmark index for developed countries in Europe, Australasia and Far East.

Multi-advisors   use of "outside" portfolio managers for fund portfolio management; may include a mix of "inside" and outside managers.

Multi-managers   use of two or more subadvisors to diversify portfolio management by investment style.

Multiple managers   use of two or more portfolio managers rather than one lead manager; may be used to diffuse star portfolio manager.

Multiple share classes   share classes (such as A, B, and C) with different sales charge and fee options attached to the same or equivalent portfolios.

Multi-rule system   composite technical market indicator that incorporates several individual indicators.

Multi-sector bond funds   funds that diversify by types of bonds.

Mutual fund (fund)   open-end fund with continuous offering and redemption of shares priced at net asset value.

(Mutual) fund family (fund complex)   inclusive term for all funds operated by a particular investment advisor.

Mutual fund supermarket (fund supermarket)   discount broker that distributes mutual fund shares from numerous fund families.

Myopic loss aversion   behavioral concept that combination of short investment horizon and risk aversion causes more investor regret owing to more frequent negative returns relative to long investment horizons.

Nasdaq   centralized market for bid–ask prices of over-the-counter securities.

National Association of Securities Dealers (NASD)   securities industry self-regulatory authority for pricing, advertising, sales, and ethics; includes mutual fund advisors.

National Securities Market Act of 1996 (1996 Act)   provides for more efficient management of investment companies with more effective and less burdensome regulation.

Neglected-stock effect tendency of small-cap. stocks to be undervalued as they are "neglected" by large institutional investors.

Net asset value (net asset value) total fund assets less liabilities, divided by number of shares outstanding at close of trading.

Net cash inflow (outflow) dollar amount of fund sales exceeds dollar redemptions.

Net free (borrowed) reserves amount of bank reserves less borrowed reserves is positive (negative).

Neutral equity style strategy that focuses only on stock selection, not asset allocation (not recommended).

No-load funds legally, funds with zero or no more than 0.25 percent annual 12b-1 fees (not literally "no load" in the latter case).

No transaction fees (NTF) investor purchases/redemptions of fund shares on fund supermarkets carry no explicit fees.

Non-diversified (diversified) funds open-end and closed-end fund portfolios legally defined as non-diversified (diversified).

Normalized portfolio passive portfolio asset allocations designed to perform well over the long term.

Online mutual funds "personalized" mutual funds managed online by individual investors.

Open-end fund (open-end management investment company) mutual fund with continuous offering and redemption of shares priced at net asset value.

Operating leverage changes in firm risk derived from use of fixed assets as seen in proportion of fixed costs to total costs.

Opportunity (waiting) costs costs from being out of the market and missing return opportunities; perhaps due to market timing.

Option option to buy/sell specified number of shares of a particular stock at a specified price and time period.

Option on futures contract option contract written on futures contract.

Ordinary income mutual fund distributions of dividend and interest income plus net realized short-term capital gains.

"Other" operating expenses component of fund total operating expenses, along with management fees and any 12b-1 fees; represent non-portfolio costs of managing fund.

Outperformance abnormal or relatively superior returns.

Overconfidence behavioral concept that investors overestimate their knowledge and its reliability, more so when they have self-declared expertise.

Overreaction (underreaction) behavioral concept that investors overreact to private information signals and underreact to public signals.

Pass-through tax treatment (tax conduit) IRS qualified regulated mutual funds do not pay taxes on distributions to shareholders, but investors do.

PEG ratio measure of how much is paid for each unit of earnings growth rate; P/E ratio divided by earnings growth rate.

PEGY ratio PEG ratio with dividend yield added to earnings growth rate.

Performance evaluation methods used to compare portfolio performance with its benchmark market index or peer group.

Performance and portfolio transparency degree to which portfolio performance and holdings are currently disclosed to shareholders.

Plain vanilla derivatives derivatives that are not inherently risky; used to hedge risk or invest funds quickly.

Portfolio manager person or persons with responsibility for implementing portfolio strategy.

Portfolio manager style investment style used by portfolio manager; usually includes value/growth and cap. size investment style variables.

Portfolio posting periodic listing of each security holding in the portfolio.

Portfolio pumping end-of-year stock purchases designed to increase prices of the same stocks already held.

Portfolio rebalancing periodic change of current portfolio asset allocation back to its long-term allocation.

(Portfolio) style tilt (static and variable) portfolio asset allocation that favors a particular investment style.

Portfolio turnover percentage of average portfolio holdings that have been replaced over the year.

Price discovery process of determining security prices through buyer/seller interactions that incorporate new information.

Price drift evidence of market inefficiency, where stock prices drift rather than go immediately to new equilibrium prices following earnings announcements.

Price-momentum strategy strategy of buying stocks with increasing prices.

Price-to-book ratio (P/B) price per share divided by book value per share; small relative ratio generally suggests value investing.

Price-to-cash ratio (P/C) price per share divided by cash flow per share; small relative ratio generally suggests value investing.

Price-to-earnings ratio (P/E) price per share divided by earnings per share; small relative ratio generally suggests value investing.

Price-to-sales ratio (P/S) price per share divided by sales per share; small relative ratio generally suggests value investing.

Price transparency degree to which market makers know the size and direction of current buy/sell orders when setting bid–ask prices; enhances market liquidity by lowering bid–ask spreads.

Private securities class of restricted securities that are only traded privately.

Professional portfolio management portfolio managed by person with appropriate education, background, and experience.

Profile (prospectus) fund legal disclosure document that summarizes key information in the prospectus.

Prospect theory behavioral theory of decision making under uncertainty in which investors are risk averse.

Prospectus traditional fund legal disclosure document.

Pure no-load fund fund with no loads or 12b-1 fees.

Quant funds (pure and hybrid) funds that use quantitative techniques and models to perform fundamental and/or technical analysis to select securities.

Random walk weak form version of efficient markets theory that holds changes in stock prices are independently distributed over time (not serially related).

Rate of return (returns) annualized rates of asset returns.

Rational speculative bubbles behavioral concept that it is rational to stay invested during market bubbles because the probability of high returns offset the probability of crashes.

Real estate investment trusts (REITs) trusts that make creditor and/or equity investments in real estate; include equity trusts and bond trusts.

Real (tangible) assets tangible assets, such as gold and real estate.

Real rate of return rate of return, net of inflation rate.

Rebalancing threshhold describes how far actual asset allocations must deviate from desired allocations before portfolios are rebalanced.

Redemption investor sale of shares back to the fund.

Redemption units investors redeem (sell) creation units of index shares of specific ETFs in exchange for minimum block size stock portfolios that match specific benchmark indices.

Registered broker-dealers sales agents regulated by the SEC in their role as fund share distributors (principal underwriters).

Regret behavioral concept that investors feel worse about bad outcomes than they feel good about positive outcomes.

Regulated investment company fund that meets IRS tax conduit regulations and qualifies for pass-through tax treatment.

Representativeness heuristic behavioral concept that investors give too much weight to current evidence as "representative" evidence.

Restricted securities legal classification of private and illiquid securities restricted for fund use; includes private placements and 144 (a) securities.

Return on equity (ROE) measure of performance; net income per share after taxes divided by equity book value per share.

Reversal effect (reversion to mean) behavioral anomaly that funds outperforming in the short run revert to mean returns over the medium to long term.

Rights of accumulation (cumulative quantity discount) investor rights to discounted loads based on promise of breakeven quantity purchases over specified period of time.

Risk aversion investor preference for certain return to uncertain returns with the same expected value; other investors are risk-seeking or risk-neutral.

Risk-free rate return on riskless asset, usually ninety-day Treasury bills.

Risk premium additional return on a risky asset that compensates for additional risk relative to risk-free asset.

Risk/return performance measure performance measure that incorporates both risk and return into a composite index, such as Sharpe.

R^2 **(R squared)** proportion of variance of asset returns explained by variance of market returns; R^2s over 0.70 are considered high.

Rule 12b-1 (12b-1 fees) SEC rule that permits funds to use maximum of 1 percent of fund assets annually to pay for distribution-related expenses; component of fund total operating expenses.

Russell 2000 Index stock index of small-cap. stocks.

S&P/BARRA Growth (Value) Index benchmark market indices for domestic growth (value) stocks.

S&P 500 Index benchmark index for domestic large-cap. stocks; the most used index.

Sector funds funds that invest in a single industry or industry segment, such as technology.

Securities Act of 1933 (1933 Act) original "truth in securities" disclosure legislation for sales of new securities, including mutual fund shares.

Securities Act of 1934 (1934 Act) extends 1933 Act disclosure legislation to outstanding shares, including fund distributors.

Securities and Exchange Commission (SEC) federal agency that regulates investment companies, primarily under the 1940 Act.

Securitized tangible and financial assets that are packaged as securities and publicly traded.

Security market line linear relationship between stock systematic risk (beta) and expected returns; derived from CAPM.

Service providers external firms that provide funds with essential services, such as portfolio management.

Shareholder liquidity measure of the length of time it takes for fund shareholders to access fund shares as spendable bank account balances.

Shareholder transaction costs any shareholder "costs of transacting" with funds, at purchase, redemption, and/or while shares are held.

Sharpe Index measure of portfolio's excess returns relative to its total risk.

Small-cap. style (small cap.) investment style of funds that invest in stocks with small market capitalization.

Smart money effect (also, a strategy) new cash inflows forecast short-term fund performance – funds that get new cash perform significantly better than those that lose cash.

Socially responsible funds   funds that invest only in stocks that meet self-defined criteria as "socially responsible."

Soft dollar payments (arrangements)   specified dollar amounts of research products/services that investment advisors receive in exchange for specified dollar trading commission.

Special securities   Morningstar concept that includes restricted/illiquid securities, emerging market securities, and options/futures/warrants.

Spiders   ETFs benchmarked to the S&P 500 Index.

Spread expenses   trading costs expressed as a percentage of total assets under management.

Standard deviation (of mean returns)   measure of portfolio total risk.

Standardized unexpected earnings (SUE)   measure of difference between actual and expected earnings per share; used to identify stocks that will have the largest surprise effects on share prices.

Star (portfolio) managers (stars)   portfolio managers so designated by presumed ability to out-perform benchmark market indices.

Strategic income bond fund   life-stage fund with bond allocations designed to meet the needs of particular investors.

Statement of additional information (SAI)   fund legal disclosure document that includes what would be "information overload" in the prospectus.

Static tilts   passive investment style allocations based on value/growth and cap. size.

Step-out transactions   investment advisors direct particular broker-dealers to execute trades and "step out" of portions of commission to those making soft dollar payments.

Stock repurchase plans (share "buy-backs")   plans whereby firms purchase and retire some of their shares.

Strategic (passive) asset allocation   relatively constant asset allocations based on long-term market forecasts.

Strategic income bond funds   life-stage funds with varying bond allocations.

Structured notes   bonds with imbedded derivatives designed to meet requirements of particular investors.

Style analysis (performance attribution analysis and equity style management)   process of identifying portfolio manager investment style for purpose of performance evaluation.

Style drift   process whereby portfolio investment style "drifts" from stated investment style.

Style enforcement   monitoring of portfolio manager for style consistency.

Style exposure   extent to which variations in equity fund returns reflect investment style allocations.

Style overlap   fund portfolios' allocations with overlap of investment style.

Style performance persistence   extent to which "winning" investment styles are persistent over short time periods.

Style purity   descriptive of funds that maintain their stated investment style (no style "drift").

Subadvisors   firms employed by investment advisors to manage fund portfolios.

Subchapter M of the IRS Code   provision for qualifying funds as tax-free conduits.

Survivor bias   overestimation of overall fund returns over time by including only the funds that "survived."

Systematic (non-diversifiable) risk   market risk (beta) that cannot be eliminated through portfolio diversification.

Tactical (active) asset allocation   relatively active asset allocations based on short-term market forecasts (form of market timing).

Target maturity funds   newer type of life-stage funds that use investor investment horizons to select funds with appropriate maturity dates.

Tax efficiency   percentage of fund return that translates to investor after-tax return.

Tax-loss carryforwards   net realized capital losses that are carried forward and netted against future year capital gains.

Tax-loss selling   realization of portfolio losses, often designed to offset realized capital gains.

Tax-managed funds funds that explicitly manage portfolios in a tax-efficient manner by minimizing realized capital gains and improving shareholder after-tax returns.

Taylor model model that computes the desired Federal funds rate (versus the actual).

Technical analysis general method of security analysis based on identifying recurring patterns in historical price and volume data of individual securities and/or the overall market.

Theoretical trading cost unmeasurable difference between trade price and market price in the absence of a trade; includes immediacy cost (market impact cost) and opportunity cost.

Time diversification concept that advocates long-term equity investing based on declining risk and stable returns as investment holding periods increase (not valid for reducing risk to terminal portfolio value).

Time-weighted returns usual method of reporting returns based on a share of stock purchased at beginning of particular periods.

Total operating expenses fund payments for management (advisory) fees, any 12b-1 fees, and "other" operating expenses.

Total risk sum of systematic and unsystematic risks measured by standard deviation of mean returns.

Tracking error measure of degree to which a portfolio underperforms its benchmark index.

Trading costs (actual) sum of measurable trading costs for security transactions.

Transfer agent fund service provider that maintains portfolio and general accounting records, and maintains fund records of shareholder accounts and transactions (purchases/redemptions), among others.

Treynor Index measure of portfolio excess return relative to its systematic risk.

Trust certificates (units) "shares" offered by unit investment trusts at net asset value plus fees.

12b–1 fees annual marketing and distribution costs included in fund operating expenses with the effect of annual loads.

Unconstrained optimized allocations Markowitz-type portfolio optimizer that does not specify minimum amounts of particular asset classes.

Unit investment trust (UIT) investment company with a fixed life and fixed portfolio of stocks or bonds.

Unsystematic (diversifiable) risk unique risk that can be eliminated through portfolio diversification.

Utility measure of investor satisfaction provided by an asset.

Value of active management value added to returns by ability of portfolio manager to earn consistent abnormal returns relative to benchmark index.

Value Line **safety ratings** 1–5 rankings of stock financial quality (1 is best).

Value Line **timeliness rating** 1–5 ranking of expected stock performance over the next year (1 is best).

Value style (value) investment style of funds that invest in out-of-favor, undervalued stocks priced at less than "intrinsic value."

Variable annuity fund-like portfolio "wrapped" in insurance contract.

Warrant option that provides the right to buy specific number of shares of a particular stock at a specified price before a specified date.

Weak-form efficient markets theory security prices reflect information in past price and volume data.

WEBS World Equity Barclay Shares; the original international iShares ETFs.

Whisper numbers unwritten earnings estimate updates provided by security analysts.

Wilshire 5000 index for the entire domestic stock market.

Window dressing (dress up) changes made in portfolios prior to end-of-period statements that improve quality and reduce risk.

Wire redemption fees fund fees for wiring investor share redemptions to bank accounts.

Wrap (account) fees broker fees charged for "wrapping" investor securities holdings into one account for private management (expensive).

Yield income component (percent) of total return.

Yield spread difference between short-term and long-term security interest rates (such as reflected on Treasury yield curve).

REFERENCES

GENERAL

Each publication/issue of these references is relevant to the study of mutual funds. From chapter 2 onward they are listed only if cited or if they include tutorials.

CDA/Wiesenberger, 1986– , *Mutual Funds Directory* (CDA/Wiesenberger, Rockville, MD) (annual fund performance history).

Clements, Jonathan, 1995– , *Getting Started, Wall Street Journal* (archives www.wsj.com).

Investment Company Institute, 1998– , *Investment Company Institute* (www.ici.org) (ICI publications and online links to reference, association and US government sources of investor information).

Morningstar, 1998– , *Morningstar Principia Pro for Mutual Funds*, December 31 (CD-ROM).

Morningstar, 1991– , *Morningstar Mutual Funds* (reprinted in *Principia Pro for Mutual Funds*, Advanced Analytics for Principia, CD-ROM).

Morningstar, 1992–95, *Morningstar Five Star Investor*.

Morningstar, 1995–98, *Morningstar Investor*.

Morningstar, 1998– , *Morningstar FundInvestor*.

Morningstar, 1998– , *Morningstar.com* (www.morningstar.com).

Zweig, Jason, 1995– , *The Fundamentalist, Money* (archives www.money.com).

1 UNDERSTANDING MUTUAL FUNDS

Alexanian, Harach, 1993, Sooner or Later: In Investing, Time is Money. *Morningstar Five Star Investor*, June, 1, 8–9.

Barbee, Olivia, 1999, A Close Look at Trusts, *Morningstar FundInvestor*, February, 12–13.

Belsky, Gary, 1992, What Net Asset Value Really Means, *Money*, April, 56.

Block, Julian, 1999, How Trusts Can Enrich Your Heirs, *Mutual Funds*, September, 48–50.

Bogle, John C., 1999, *Common Sense on Mutual Funds: New Imperatives for the Intelligent Investor* (John Wiley & Sons, New York).

DiTeresa, Peter, 1999, Nineteen ninety-nine in Review, *Morningstar FundInvestor*, December, 6–7.

Dziubinski, Susan, 1998, Advice for Seeking Advice, *Morningstar FundInvestor*, November, 12–13.

Dzuibinski, Susan, 1999, Taking Issue, *Morningstar FundInvestor*, March, 21.

Fifty Years of the Dow, 1999, *Time*, February, 52–4.

Fortune, Peter, 1997, Mutual Funds, Part I: Reshaping the American Financial System, *New England Economic Review* (Federal Reserve Bank of Boston), July/August, 45–72.

Fosback, Norman G., 1998, Bailout a Blessing for Mutual Fund Investors, *Mutual Funds*, December, 140.

Fraser, Jill A., 1999, Singular Sensations, *Bloomberg Personal Finance*, June, 72–80.

Fredman, Albert J. and Russ Wiles, 1997, *How Mutual Funds Work*, 2nd ed. (New York Institute of Finance, New York).

Galarza, Pedro et al., 1999, Read This and Reap, *Money*, 95–7.

Gasparino, Charles, 1998, Mutual Funds Get Set for Selling, *Wall Street Journal*, October 15, C1, C25.

Gillis, Catherine, 1992, Tracking Premiums and Discounts, *Morningstar Five Star Investor*, November, 9–11.

Haslem, John A., 1988, *The Investor's Guide to Mutual Funds* (Prentice Hall, Englewood Cliffs, NJ).

Investment Company Institute, 1995, *Introductory Guide for Investment Company Directors*, September (The Institute, Washington, DC).

Investment Company Institute, 1996a, *Mutual Fund Shareholders: The People Behind the Growth*, spring (The Institute, Washington, DC).

Investment Company Institute, 1996b, *The Organization and Operation of a Mutual Fund*, June (The Institute, Washington, DC).

Investment Company Institute, 1997a, *A Guide to Closed-end Funds*, May (The Institute, Washington, DC).

Investment Company Institute, 1997b, *A Guide to Unit Investment Trusts*, May (The Institute, Washington, DC).

Investment Company Institute, 1997c, *Mutual Fund Fact Book*, 37th ed. (The Institute, Washington, DC).

Investment Company Institute, 1998a, *A Guide to Bond Mutual Funds*, January (The Institute, Washington, DC).

Investment Company Institute, 1998b, Closed-end Funds and Mutual Funds (www.icef.com).

Investment Company Institute, 1999a, *Equity Ownership in America, October* (The Institute, Washington, DC).

Investment Company Institute, 1999b, *Profile of Mutual Fund Shareholders*, September (The Institute, Washington, DC).

Investment Company Institute, 1999c, US Household Ownership of Closed-end Funds in 1998, *Fundamentals*, April, 1–3.

Investment Company Institute, 2000a, *A Guide to Mutual Funds*, May (The Institute, Washington, DC).

Investment Company Institute, 2000b, *401(k) Plan Participants: Characteristics, Contributions, and Account Activity*, spring (The Institute, Washington, DC).

Investment Company Institute, 2000c, *Mutual Fund Fact Book*, 40th ed. (The Institute, Washington, DC).

Investment Company Institute, 2000d, Mutual Fund Shareholders' Use of the Internet, *Fundamentals*, July, 1–7.

Investment Company Institute, 2000e, Mutual Funds and the Retirement Market, *Fundamentals*, May, 1–7.

Investment Company Institute, 2000f, US Household Ownership of Mutual Funds in 2000, *Fundamentals*, August, 1–4.

Investment Company Institute and Securities Industry Association, 1999, *Equity Ownership in America*, October (ICI and SIA, Washington, DC).

Jones, Charles P., 1998, *Investments: Analysis and Management*, 6th ed. (John Wiley & Sons, New York).

Karp, Richard, 2000, Doomed Dinosaurs? *Barron's*, February 28, 27–8.

Kunert, Kurt, 1993, Operations Companies Make the Fund Go "Round," *Morningstar Five Star Investor*, November, 2.

Lowenstein, Alice, 1994, Easy Recordkeeping, *Morningstar Five Star Investor*, September, 13.

Malhotra, D.K. and Robert W. McLeod, 2000, Closed-end Fund Expenses and Investment Selection, *Financial Review*, 41, 85–104.

Malkiel, Burton G., 1995, The Structure of Closed-end Fund Discounts Revisited, *Journal of Portfolio Management*, summer, 32–8.

Massachusetts Distributors, n.d., *History and General Information, Massachusetts Investors Trust* (Massachusetts Distributors, now MFS Fund Distributors, Boston, MA).

McLean, Bethany, 1999, Eight Act Now Investment Tips from America's Top Advisors, *Mutual Funds*, September, 34–6.

McReynolds, Rebecca, 1999, The New Way to Avoid Probate, *Mutual Funds*, September, 44–6.

MFS Fund Distributors, 1997, reprint of first portfolio of *Massachusetts Investors Trust, Organized March 1924* (MFS, Boston, MA).

Mid-year Investment Report '98: The Tables, *Money*, August 1998, 91ff.

Montgomery, Leland, 1998, Some of Wall Street's Biggest Players are Mad as Hell, and if They Have Their Way the Cozy World of Closed-end Funds Will Never be the Same, *Worth*, February, 74–80.

Paluch, Susan, 1994, Open-and-shut Case for Closed-end Single-country Funds, *Morningstar Five Star Investor*, December, 10–12.

Paluch, Susan, 1996, Roster Review: A History Lesson, *Morningstar Investor*, August, 8.

Penn, Michael, 1993a, Defining the "Total" in Total Return, *Morningstar Five Star Investor*, December, 2.

Penn, Michael, 1993b, Mutual Fund Investing is a Game Everyone Can Play, *Morningstar Five Star Investor*, September, 2.

Phillips, Don, 1991, Investment Illiteracy, *Morningstar Mutual Funds*, November 1.

Phillips, Don, 1992, A Lesson for Life, *Morningstar Five Star Investor*, December, 32.

Phillips, Don, 1993, Shareholder Education Takes Center Stage, *Morningstar Five Star Investor*, October, 40.

Phillips, Don, 1997, Owner or Consumer? *Morningstar Mutual Funds*, April 25.

Phillips, Don, 1999, Answering What's Answerable, *Morningstar FundInvestor*, December, 44.

Pozen, Robert C., 1998, *The Mutual Fund Business* (MIT Press, Cambridge, MA).

Purcell, Kylelane, 1993a, Keeping the "Trust" in Investment Trusts, *Morningstar Five Star Investor*, December, 40.

Purcell, Kylelane, 1993b, Parent to Child: Passing the Investment Baton, *Morningstar Five Star Investor*, October, 1, 12.

Purcell, Kylelane, 1993c, Prudent Investing Can Be Money in the Bank, *Morningstar Five Star Investor*, November, 40.

Purcell, Kylelane, 1994, The Best Fund Reporting Can Be Problematic Now, *Morningstar Five Star Investor*, October, 42.

Purcell, Kylelane, 1995, A Well-chosen Shift, *Morningstar Five Star Investor*, February, 41.

Ratner, David L., 1998, *Securities Regulation in a Nutshell*, 6th ed. (West Group, St. Paul, MN).

Regnier, Pat, 1995, If It Ain't Broke . . . , *Morningstar Mutual Funds*, August 18.

Regnier, Pat, 1997, What are . . . Closed-end Funds? *Morningstar Investor*, March, 13.

Reid, Brian, 1997, Growth and Development of Bond Mutual Funds, *Perspective* (Investment Company Institute), June, 1–11.

Reid, Brian, 2000, The 1990s: A Decade of Expansion and Change in the Mutual Fund Industry, *Perspective* (Investment Company Institute), July, 1–20.

Reid, Brian and Kimberlee Millar, 2000, Mutual Fund Assets and Flows in 1999, *Perspective* (Investment Company Institute), February, 1–11.

Rekenthaler, John, 1992, Where's the Beef? *Morningstar Mutual Funds*, June 26.

Rekenthaler, John, 1994a, Looking Afield, *Morningstar Mutual Funds*, June 10.

Rekenthaler, John, 1994b, Too Many Funds? *Morningstar Mutual Funds*, August 18.

Rekenthaler, John, 1996. Taking Issue, *Morningstar Investor*, April, 41.

Renberg, Werner, 1998, Bye, Bye, Bonds, *Barron's*, August 3, 22–3.

Ronald, Richard, 1998a, What is . . . the Statement of Additional Information? *Morningstar FundInvestor*, December, 11.

Ronald, Richard, 1998b, What are . . . Unit Investment Trusts? *Morningstar Investor*, February, 13.

Ronald Richard, 1999, What is . . . net asset value? *Morningstar FundInvestor*, March, 11.

Rottersman, Max and Jason Zweig, 1994, An Early History of Mutual Funds, *Friends of Financial History*, 51 (spring), 12–14, 16–20.

Rowland, Mary, 1998, *The New Commonsense Guide to Mutual Funds* (Bloomberg Press, New York).

Sanders, Catherine V., 1997, Send for Help, *Morningstar Investor*, March, 14–16 (includes checklist for selecting investment advisors and their credentials, estate planning needs, and care-giver needs in times of illness).

Sharpe, William F., Gordon J. Alexander, and Jeffery V. Bailey, 1999, *Investments*, 6th ed. (Prentice Hall, Upper Saddle River, NJ).

Sias, Richard W., 1997, Optimum Trading Strategies for Closed-end Funds, *Journal of Investing*, spring, 54–61.

Silberman, H. Lee, 1974, *Fifty Years of Trust, Massachusetts Investors Trust, 1924–74*, November (Massachusetts Financial Services, Boston, MA).

Sobel, Robert, 1998, Two-edged Sword, *Barron's*, July 6, F10.

Stevens, Sue, 2000. Rekenthaler Reaches for Retirement, *Morningstar FundInvestor*, May, 8–9.

"The Prudent Man," 1959, *Time*, June 1, 74–8, 80.

Topkis, Maggie, 1999, How to Choose a Financial Planner, *Mutual Funds*, 38–40.

Tweedy Browne Global Value and American Value Fund, 1998, *Prospectus*, August 1.

US General Accounting Office, 1997, *Mutual Funds: SEC Adjusted its Oversight in Response to Rapid Industry Growth*, May (GAO, Report to Congressional Committees, Washington, DC).

US Securities and Exchange Commission, 1995, *What Every Investor Should Know*, February (SEC, Washington, DC).

US Securities and Exchange Commission, 1997, *The Work of the SEC*, June (SEC, Office of Public Affairs, Policy Evaluation and Research, Washington, DC).

Vanguard Group, 1993, Investment Lessons of a Century from a Fund Pioneer, *In the Vanguard* (Vanguard Marketing), summer, 1, 3.

Whelehan, Barbara M., 1998, Your Road Map to a Winning Portfolio, *Mutual Funds*, September, 38–42.

Whelehan, Barbara M., 1999, Bargain Basement Funds, *Mutual Funds*, September, 67–71.

Whelehan, Barbara M., 2000, Fund ABCs, *Mutual Funds*, August, 47, 48–52.

Willis, Clint, 1999, Present at the Creation, *Mutual Funds*, February, 58–60, 62–3.

Wolper, Gregg, 1994a, Despite Volatility, Single-country Funds Have Their Place, *Morningstar Five Star Investor*, May, 40.

Wolper, Gregg, 1994b, Savor the Flavors of Single-country Funds, *Morningstar Five Star Investor*, June, 1, 10–11.

Wolper, Gregg, 1995, Hitting the High Notes with Closed-end Funds, *Morningstar Investor*, December, 8–9.

Wolper, Gregg, 1997, Opening the Closed-end Door, *Morningstar Mutual Funds*, February 14.

Wolper, Gregg, 1998, Closed-end Activists Set an Example, *Morningstar Mutual Funds*, April 21.

Zweig, Jason, 1996, Why Now May be the Time to Open Your Wallet to Closed-end Funds, *Money*, February, 77ff.

Zweig, Jason, 1998, Stock or Funds, *Money*, April, 93ff.

Zweig, Jason, 1999a, The History of Mutual Funds, Seventy-five Years: Look Back and Learn, *Money*, April, 94ff.

Zweig, Jason, 1999b, The History of Mutual Funds, Seventy-five Years: Risks and Riches, *Money*, April, 96ff.

2   MUTUAL FUND SERVICE ADVANTAGES
3   MUTUAL FUND SERVICE ADVANTAGES: PROFESSIONAL MANAGEMENT

A Day on the Road, 1997, *Janus Report* (Janus Distributors), March, 4, 6–9.

Ackermann, Carl, Richard McEnally, and David Ravenscraft, The Performance of Hedge Funds: Risk, Return, and Incentives, *Journal of Finance*, 54 (June), 833–74.

America's Most Unusual Funds, 1998a, *Mutual Funds*, November, 56, 60–1.

Ang, James S. and Jess H. Chau, 1982, Mutual Funds: Different Strokes for Different Folks, *Journal of Portfolio Management*, winter, 43–7.

Arnott, Amy C., 1995, Tweedy Browne Brings the World Closer to Home, *Morningstar Five Star Investor*, March, 8.

Arnott, Amy C., 1999, Taking Issue, *Morningstar FundInvesor*, January, 21.

Asnes, Marion, et al., 1999, The World's Best Mutual Funds: The Money 100, *Money*, June, 83ff.

Association of Investment Management and Research, 1999, *Chartered Financial Analyst Examination Program* (AIMR, Charlottesville, VA).

Bailey, Jeffery V., 1996, Evaluating Investment Skill With a VAM Graph, *Journal of Investing*, summer, 64–71.

Bamford, Janet, 1998, Learning Through Immersion, *Bloomberg Personal Finance*, June (www.bloomberg.com).

Barbee, Olivia, 1997a, Help! They're Taking Over My Fund Company! *Morningstar Investor*, August, 8–9.

Barbee, Olivia, 1997b, In the Blood, *Morningstar Investor*, May, 10–12.

Barbee, Olivia, 1997c, Taking Issue, *Morningstar Investor*, October, 22.

Barrett, William P., 1997, Fund Families: Best to Worst, *Worth*, May, 76ff.

Beck, Kristine L., Steven B. Perfect, and Pamela P. Peterson, 1996, The Role of Alternative Methodology on the Relation between Portfolio Size and Diversification, *Financial Review*, 31 (May), 381–406.

Bernstein, Peter L., 1997, Rules for Risk Takers, *Bloomberg Personal Finance*, March/April (www.bloomberg.com).

Bernstein, Peter L., 1998, Where, Oh Where are the .400 Hitters of Yesteryear? *Financial Analysts Journal*, November/December, 6–14.

Bernstein, William J., 1999, The Needle and the Haystack, *Efficient Frontier*, July (www.efficientfrontier.com).

Bloomberg, Michael R., 2000, The Trouble with Stars, *Bloomberg Personal Finance*, March (www.bloomberg.com).

Blume, Marshall, 1971, On the Assessment of Risk, *Journal of Finance*, 26 (March), 1–10.

Bogle, John C., 1998, Mutual Funds . . . The Greatest Investment Ever Invented, *Mutual Funds*, April, 66–7.

Boitano, Margaret, 1999, Fund Firms are Clamping Down on Investors Playing Short-term, *Wall Street Journal*, April 5, R3.

Brandstrader, J.R., 1999, No Place Like Home, *Barron's*, April 5, F11.

Brealey, Richard A., 1990, Portfolio Theory versus Portfolio Practice, *Journal of Portfolio Management*, summer, 6–10.

Brill, Marla, 1998, Do You Need a Financial Advisor? *Mutual Funds*, December, 88–91.

Brockman, Christopher M. and Robert Brooks, 1998, The CFA Charter: Adding Value to the Market, *Financial Analysts Journal*, November/December, 81–5.

Brown, Ken, 1999, Fundamental Changes, *SmartMoney*, December, 42, 44.

Brush, John S., 1996, Mutual Funds, Share Repurchases, and Merger and Acquisition Activity, *Journal of Investing*, winter, 23–5.

Burton, Jonathan, 1998a, Partners in Profit, *Bloomberg Personal Finance*, July/August (www.bloomberg.com).

Burton, Jonathan, 1998b, Show Me the Load! *Mutual Funds*, October, 44–9.

Burton, Jonathan, 1999, A Cut Above, *Bloomberg Personal Finance*, May (www.bloomberg.com).

Carlson, Greg, 1998, Elite Personal Services for High Ticket Investors, *Mutual Funds*, October, 36, 38.

Charlson, Josh, 1993, NASD Caps 12b-1 Fees, *Morningstar Five Star Investor*, August, 3.

Chick Funds Beat the Veterans, 1998b, *Mutual Funds*, August, 16–17.

Chordia, Tarun, 1996, The Structure of Mutual Fund Charges, *Journal of Financial Economics*, 41 (May), 3–39.

Cooley, Scott, 2000, Manager Changes: Should You Stay or Should You Go? *Morningstar FundInvestor*, September, 1–3.

Cullen, Lisa R., 1998a, Five Things Funds Can Do to You During a Market Downturn, *Money*, January, 45–6.

Cullen, Lisa R., 1998b, Why the Acquired Mutual Series Funds May be Losing Their Old Appeal, *Money*, January, 48.

Cullen, Lisa R., 1999, In For a Rough Ride, *Money*, April, 40, 43–4.

Curtis, Carol E., 1998, Play with the Pros, *Bloomberg Personal Finance*, January/February (www.bloomberg.com).

Damato, Karen, 2000b, Social Studies: How "Responsible" Funds Differ on Stock Choices, *Wall Street Journal*, March 18, C1, C27.

Davis Schedules the Ultimate Fund Killing, 1999a, *Mutual Funds*, February, 30–1.

DeBlasi, Michelle, 1999, Mutual Funds: To Have and to Hold . . . and Hold, *Bloomberg Personal Finance*, December (www.bloomberg.com).

DeBlasi, Michelle, 2000, Overlap Can Undermine Diversity, *Bloomberg Personal Finance*, July/August (www.bloomberg.com).

Desai, Ravi, 1999, He Went Thataway! *Worth*, June, 79–80, 82.

DiTeresa, Peter, 1999a, Six Ways to Get to Out-of-reach Managers, *Morningstar FundInvestor*, February, 1, 4–5.

DiTeresa, Peter, 1999b, The Morningstar Guide to Major Fund Families, Part 1, *Morningstar FundInvestor*, April, 1, 4–5.

DiTeresa, Peter and Amy Granzin, 1999, Morningstar's Fund Family Portraits, Part 2, *Morningstar FundInvestor*, August, 1–3.

Dziubinski, Susan, 1997, Taking Issue, *Morningstar Investor*, December, 22.

Dziubinski, Susan, 1998, Taking Issue, *Morningstar Investor*, February, 22.

Dziubinski, Susan, 1999a, Taking Issue, *Morningstar FundInvestor*, February, 21.

Dziubinski, Susan, 1999b, Taking Issue, *Morningstar FundInvestor*, July, 44.

Dziubinski, Susan, 2000, Mutual Fund Notables of the 1990s, *Morningstar.com* (news.morningstar.com).

Edgerton, Jerry, 1998a, Does Your Manager Moonlight? *Money*, August, 47–8.

Edgerton, Jerry, 1998b, The Succession Question: Who Would Take Over if Your Manager Resigned? *Money*, April, 39–40, 42.

Egodigwe, Laura S., 2000, Fund Manager Abandons Ship? No Need to Run for the Lifeboat, *Wall Street Journal*, August 4, C1, C19.

Ellis, Charles D. and James Vertin, eds., 1997, *The Investor's Anthology: Original Ideas from the Industry's Greatest Minds* (John Wiley & Sons, New York).

Elton, Edwin J. and Martin J. Gruber, 1977, Risk Reduction and Portfolio Size: An Analytical Analysis, *Journal of Business*, 50 (October), 415–37.

Evans, John L. and Stephen H. Archer, 1968, Diversification and the Reduction of Dispersion: An Empirical Analysis, *Journal of Finance*, 23 (December), 761–7.

Fidelity Growth and Income Portfolio, 1997, *Prospectus*, September 25.

Fidelity Low-priced Stock Fund, 1997, *Prospectus*, September 26.

Fidelity Advisor Equity Growth Fund, Class A, Class T, Class B, and Class C, 1998, *Prospectus*, February 28.

Fidelity Magellan Fund, 1998, *Prospectus*, May 22.

Fidelity Select Portfolio, 1998, *Prospectus*, April 28.

Fishman, Ted C., 1999, Wall Street's Twenty-five Smartest Players, *Worth*, October, 128–46, 149.

Five Views on How Many Funds You Should Own, 1998c, *Mutual Funds*, September, 60–1.

Fosback, Norman G., 1997, A Heretical Idea: Scrap Prospectus Requirement, *Mutual Funds*, February, 12.

Fosback, Norman G., 1998a, At Last: Profiles and Readable Prospectuses, *Mutual Funds*, May, 10, 12.

Fosback, Norman G., 1998b, Let's Put an End to Disclosure Dichotomy, *Mutual Funds*, July, 10.

Franklin Mutual Series Fund, Class I and Class II, 1998a, *Prospectus*, May 1.

Franklin Mutual Series Fund, Class Z, 1998b, *Prospectus*, May 1.

Fund Family Shareholder Association, How Vanguard's Directors Invest, 1998, *Independent Advisor for Vanguard Investors*, June, 1, 4–5.

Gallo, John G. and Larry J. Lockwood, 1999, Fund Management Changes and Equity Style Shifts, *Financial Analysts Journal*, September/October, 44–52.

Garligniano, Jeff, et al., 1999, The *SmartMoney* Thirty Power Brokers, *SmartMoney*, September, 116–28, 130.

Gillis, Catherine, 1994, A Risky Risk Measure? *Morningstar Five Star Investor*, December, 42.

Goetzmann, William N. and Nadav Peles, 1997, Cognitive Dissonance and Mutual Fund Investors, *Journal of Financial Research*, 20 (summer), 145–58.

Graza, Christopher, 1998, Too Much Togetherness, *Bloomberg Personal Finance*, January/February (www.bloomberg.com).

Green, William, 1998, The Rookies, *Money*, November, 140ff.

Griffeth, Bill, 1995, *The Mutual Fund Masters* (Probus Publishing, Chicago).

Guerard, John B., Jr., 1997, Is There a Cost to Being Socially Responsible in Investing? *Journal of Investing*, summer, 11–18.

Hagy, James R., 1998, The Twenty Best Mutual Funds, *SmartMoney*, September, 102–25.

Harrell, David, 1998, See Dick Invest: The Plain Language Prospectus, *Morningstar.Net* (text.morningstar.net).

Harris, Marlys, 1998, All the Money World's a Stage, *Bloomberg Personal Finance*, May (www.bloomberg.com).

Harris, Wayne, 1998, Vanguard Sets New Standard for Funds on the Net, *Mutual Funds*, November, 42.

Harris, Wayne, 1999a, Fidelity in a TKO, *Mutual Funds*, November, 45–6.

Harris, Wayne, 1999b, T. Rowe Price: A Site for Sore Eyes, *Mutual Funds*, November, 52–3.

Harris, Wayne, 1999c, Vanguard Delivers, *Mutual Funds*, November, 49–50.

Hartman, Curtis, 1993, A *Worth* Notes Guide to the Investment Classics, *Worth*, October, 60ff.

Haslem, John A., 1988, *The Investor's Guide to Mutual Funds* (Prentice Hall, Englewood Cliffs, NJ).

Henderson, Barry and Sandra Ward, 2000, All Stars, *Barron's*, January 10, F5ff.

How Fund Families Wipe Away Their Mistakes, 1999b, *Mutual Funds*, May, 22.

Investment Company Institute, 1994a, *Distribution Channels for Mutual Funds: Understanding Investor Choices*, summer (The Institute, Washington, DC).

Investment Company Institute, 1994b, *The Service Quality Challenge: Understanding Shareholder Expectations*, autumn (The Institute, Washington, DC).

Investment Company Institute, 1996, *The Profile Prospectus: As Assessment by Mutual Fund Shareholders*, Volume 1, May (The Institute, Washington, DC).

Investment Company Institute, 1997a, *Mutual Fund Fact Book*, 37th ed. (The Institute, Washington, DC).

Investment Company Institute, 1997b, *Understanding Shareholders' Use of Information and Advisors*, spring (The Institute, Washington, DC).

Jacob, Nancy L., 1998, Evaluating Investment Performance, in Peter L. Bernstein and Aswath Damodaran, eds., *Investment Management* (John Wiley & Sons, New York) (see references).

Janus Equity Funds, 1998, *Prospectus*, February 17.

Jensen, Michael C., 1968, The Performance of Mutual Funds in the Period 1945–64, *Journal of Finance*, 23 (May), 389–416.

Johnson, Abigail, 1998, A Delicate Balance, *Fidelity Focus*, summer, 28.

Johnson, Scott, 1998, Counterpoint: The Case against Mutual Funds, *Mutual Funds*, April, 67–8.

Jones, Charles P., 1998, *Investments: Analysis and Management*, 6th ed. (John Wiley & Sons, New York).

Kaufmann Fund, 1998, *Prospectus*, May 1.

Kelley, Jeff, 1994, A Fine Mess, *Morningstar Mutual Funds*, November 25.

Kelley, Jeff, 1995, Little Excitement for Level Loads, *Morningstar Mutual Funds*, December 22.

Kihn, John, 1996, To Load or Not to Load? A Study of Marketing and Distribution Charges of Mutual Funds, *Financial Analysts Journal*, May/June, 28–36.

King, Benjamin F., 1966, Market and Industry Factors in Stock Price Behavior, *Journal of Business*, 39, Part II (January), 139–80.

Lallos, Laura, 1998, Taking Issue, *Morningstar FundInvestor*, December, 21.

Lemak, David J. and Peruvemba K. Satish, 1996, Mutual Fund Performance and Managers' Terms of Service: Are There Performance Differences? *Journal of Investing*, winter, 59–63.

Levin, Barbara, 1998, Point: Fund Loads Pay for Professional Advice, *Mutual Funds*, May, 74.

Lipschultz, David B., 1999, A Place at the Table, *SmartMoney*, December, 142–7.

Livingston, Miles and Edward S. O'Neal, 1998, The Cost of Mutual Fund Distribution Fees, *Journal of Financial Research*, 21 (summer), 205–18.

Load Performance Calculator, 1998, *Mutual Funds Online* (www.mfmag.com).

Lucas, Lori, 1992a, Another Bad Deal, *Morningstar Mutual Funds*, October 2.

Lucas, Lori, 1992b, Five-year Performance: Then – and Now, *Morningstar Five Star Investor*, November, 2.

Lucas, Lori, 1992c, Subadvisors or Subsidizers? *Morningstar Mutual Funds*, September 18.

Lucas, Lori, 1993, When Good Funds Disappoint, *Morningstar Five Star Investor*, January 1, 9–10.

Lucchetti, Aaron, 2000, Merger Kick for Fund Firms Can Give Investors Surprise Run for Their Money, *Wall Street Journal*, September 5, R1, R5.

Lucchetti, Aaron and Pui-Wing Tam, 2000, What's the Date? It's Key in Funds' Ads, *Wall Street Journal*, April 26, C1, C27.

Lynch, Peter, 1993, Peter Lynch on Portfolio Management, *Morningstar Five Star Investor*, April, 1, 9.

Mains, Norman E., 1977, Risk, the Pricing of Capital Assets, and the Evolution of Investment Portfolios: Comment, *Journal of Business*, 50 (July), 371–84.

Marcus, Alan J., 1990, The Magellan Fund and Market Efficiency, *Journal of Portfolio Management*, fall, 85–8.

Markowitz, Harry, 1952, Portfolio Selection, *Journal of Finance*, 7 (March), 77–91.

Markowitz, Harry, 1961, *Portfolio Selection: Efficient Diversification of Investments*, 2nd ed. (Blackwell, Oxford and Cambridge, MA).

Mayer, Martin, 1998, A Faith Misplaced, *Bloomberg Personal Finance*, November (www.bloomberg.com).

McDermott, Darren, 1999, Young Managers Follow the Herd, *Wall Street Journal*, August 2, C1, C25.

McDonald, Duff, 1998, Annual Retorts: The Sayings of Chairman Warren, *Money*, April, 77–8, 83.

McDonald, John G., 1974, Objectives and Performance of Mutual Funds, 1960–69, *Journal of Financial and Quantitative Analysis*, 9 (June), 311–33.

McFarland, Rich, 1998, Counterpoint: No-load Funds Are the Bargains of Wall Street, *Mutual Funds*, May, 75.

McGough, Robert and Pui-Wing Tam, 1999, Vanguard May Ask Bogle to Quit Board, *Wall Street Journal*, August 12, C1, C21.

McReynolds, Rebecca, 1999, Fathers and Sons, *Mutual Funds*, April, 62–6.

Meyers, Stephen L., 1973, A Re-examination of Market and Industry Factors in Stock Price Behavior, *Journal of Finance*, 28 (June), 695–705.

Misra, Prashanta, 1991, Watch Out For New Ads That Rank Their Funds as No. 1, *Money*, Year End, 28.

Newbould, Gerald D. and Percy S. Poon, 1996, Portfolio Risk, Portfolio Performance, and the Individual Investor, *Journal of Investing*, summer, 72–8.

Nick, Mary, 1996, Focus on: Socially Conscious Investing, *Morningstar Investor*, June, 5.

Niederman, Derrick, 1993, Illusions of Grandeur, *Worth*, November, 136.

Norton, Leslie P., 1998, The Best Fund Managers, *Barron's*, July 20, 33ff.

Norton, Leslie P., 2000, The Best Fund Managers, *Barron's*, February 7, 3ff.

Oakmark Family of Funds, 1998, *Semi-annual Report*, March 31.

O'Neal, Edward S., 1997, How Many Mutual Funds Constitute a Diversified Mutual Fund Portfolio? *Financial Analysts Journal*, March/April, 37–46.

O'Neal, Edward S., 1999, Mutual Fund Share Classes and Broker Incentives, *Financial Analysts Journal*, September/October, 76–87.

Oster, Christopher et al., 1998, Power Brokers, *SmartMoney*, September, 113–25.

Oster, Christopher, 1999, Capital Appreciation, *SmartMoney*, March, 131–5.

Paluch, Susan, 1995, As Lines Blur, Diversification Gets Tougher, *Morningstar Five Star Investor*, February, 12–13.

Paluch, Susan, 1997, Focus on: Family Consistency, *Morningstar Investor*, February, 17.

Penn, Michael, 1994, Despite Ruling, Uncovering Managers Still a Whodunit, *Morningstar Five Star Investor*, March, 38–9.

Phillips, Don, 1991, A Matter of Maturity, *Morningstar Mutual Funds*, September 20.

Phillips, Don, 1992, Sometimes a Great Notion, *Morningstar Mutual Funds*, April 3.

Phillips, Don, 1993a, A Loaded Debate, *Morningstar Mutual Funds*, December 24.

Phillips, Don, 1993b, Lies, Damn Lies, and Fund Advertisements, *Morningstar Mutual Funds*, February 19.

Phillips, Don, 1995, A Lesson from the Masters, *Morningstar Five Star Investor*, March, 3.

Phillips, Don, 1996, The Myth of the Dumb Investor, *Morningstar Mutual Funds*, March 29.

Pozen, Robert C., 1998, *The Mutual Fund Business* (MIT Press, Cambridge, MA).

Prola, Rosemary F., 2000, The Rocket Scientists of Finance, *Smithbusiness Online* (University of Maryland, College Park, MD), spring (www.rhsmith.umd.edu).

Purcell, Kylelane, 1993, Using Shareholder Reports to Find Good Funds, *Morningstar Five Star Investor*, December, 1, 12.

Purcell, Kylelane, 1994a, It's Time to Conquer the Nameless Dread, *Morningstar Five Star Investor*, January, 40.

Purcell, Kylelane, 1994b, Mutual Funds Beat the System (of Unsystematic Risk), *Morningstar Five Star Investor*, June, 2.

Purcell, Kylelane, 1994c, Surprise! Mergers Coming to a Fund Near You, *Morningstar Five Star Investor*, July, 40.

Purcell, Kylelane, 1995, Rookies with Experience, *Morningstar Five Star Investor*, February, 14–15.

Quinson, Tom, 1998, It's All to the Goods, *Bloomberg Personal Finance*, March (www.bloomberg.com).

Rea, John and Richard Marcis, 1996, Mutual Fund Shareholder Activity During US Stock Market Cycles, 1944–95, *Perspective* (Investment Company Institute), March, 1–16.

Regnier, Pat, 1997, '87 Eighty-sixed, *Morningstar Investor*, October, 8–9.

Reilly, Frank K. and Keith C. Brown, 1997, *Investment Analysis and Portfolio Management*, 5th ed. (Dryden Press, Fort Worth, TX).

Rekenthaler, John, 1992a, Up the Down Staircase, *Morningstar Mutual Funds*, February 7.

Rekenthaler, John, 1992b, Shuffling the Cards, *Morningstar Mutual Funds*, March 20.

Rekenthaler, John, 1992c, Who's in Charge? *Morningstar Mutual Funds*, December 25.

Rekenthaler, John, 1993a, A Mutual Fund Mania? *Morningstar Mutual Funds*, October 1.

Rekenthaler, John, 1993b, Blind Faith, *Morningstar Mutual Funds*, October 15.

Rekenthaler, John, 1994a, Narrowing the Search, *Morningstar Mutual Funds*, September 16.

Rekenthaler, John, 1994b, Who's in Charge – Part 2, *Morningstar Mutual Funds*, March 4.

Rekenthaler, John, 1996a, Judging the Book by its Cover, *Morningstar Investor*, January, 41.

Rekenthaler, John, 1996b, Taking Issue, *Morningstar Investor*, August, 41.

Rocco, Bill, 1998a, Fighting Redemptions, *Morningstar Mutual Funds*, August 6.

Rocco, Bill, 1998b, Not So Redeeming After All, *Morningstar FundInvestor*, November, 19.

Rothschild, Oeheme, 1994, Do Too Many Captains Sink the Mutual Fund Ship? *Morningstar Five Star Investor*, November, 10–12.

Rothschild, John, 1998, Peter's Principles, *Fidelity Focus* (Fidelity Distributors), fall, 10–15.

Rudnitsky, Howard, 1998, Are REITs Right? *Bloomberg Personal Finance*, September (www.bloomberg.com).

Saler, Thomas D., 1998a, Buffettology, *Mutual Funds*, November, 62–4.

Saler, Thomas D., 1998b, Order from Chaos, *Mutual Funds*, October, 72–5.

Sanders, Catherine V., 1996a, Chatting with the Masters, *Morningstar Investor*, August, 38–40.

Sanders, Catherine V., 1996b, Dear Shareholder, *Morningstar Mutual Funds*, April 26.

Sanders, Catherine V., 1997a, Gut Reaction, *Morningstar Investor*, November, 8–9.

Sanders, Catherine V., 1997b, How Many Funds Do You Need? *Morningstar Investor*, June, 1, 4–5.

Sanders, Catherine V., 1997c, The Plight of the Fickle Investor, *Morningstar Investor*, December, 1, 4–5.

Sanders, Catherine V., 1998, Taking Issue, *Morningstar Investor*, March, 22.

Sanders, Eileen, 1994, Elder Funds Find Age Doesn't Equal Investment Wisdom, *Morningstar Five Star Investor*, August, 14–15.

Sanders, Jay, 1994, Are Managers with Ivy Roots Better at Making Green? *Morningstar Five Star Investor*, June, 13.

SEC Cracks Down on Fund Mergers, 1999c, *Mutual Funds*, September, 22.

Sharpe, William F., 1966, Mutual Fund Performance, *Journal of Business*, 39, Part 2 (January), 119–38.

Sharpe, William F., Gordon J. Alexander, and Jeffery V. Bailey, 1999, *Investments*, 6th ed. (Prentice Hall, Upper Saddle River, NJ).

Shawky, Hany A., 1982, An Update on Mutual Funds: Better Grades, *Journal of Portfolio Management*, winter, 29–34.

Simon, Ruth, 1997, Invest Smarter by Ferreting Out the Secrets in Fund Prospectuses, *Money*, October, 41.

Sinha, Joe, 1993, Penny-ante Fees Can Drain Investment Dollars, *Morningstar Five Star Investor*, December, 1, 10.

Smith, Adam, 1999, Twelve Minds That Made the Market, *Bloomberg Personal Finance*, December (www.bloomberg.com) (very worthwhile).

Solnik, Bruno, 1974, Why Not Diversify Internationally Rather than Domestically? *Financial Analysts Journal*, July/August, 58–64.

Solnik, Bruno, 2000, *International Investments*, 4th ed. (Addison-Wesley, Reading, MA).

Solnik, Bruno, Cyril Boucrelle, and Yann LeFur, International Market Correlation and Volatility, 1996, *Financial Analysts Journal*, September/October, 17–34.

Statman, Meir, 1987, How Many Stocks Make a Diversified Portfolio? *Journal of Financial and Quantitative Analysis*, 22 (September), 353–63.

Statman, Meir, 2000, Socially Responsible Mutual Funds, *Financial Analysts Journal*, May/June, 3–39.

Tam, Pui-Wing, 1999, An Agent for Change in Fund World, *Wall Street Journal*, September 7, R1, R6.

Tam, Pui-Wing and Bridget O'Brien, 1999, The Luster of the Superstar Manager Fades, *Wall Street Journal*, March 1, R1, R6.

Taylor, Walton R.L. and James A. Yoder, 1996, How Diversified Are Stock Mutual Funds? *Journal of Investing*, spring, 66–8.

Texas Spawns the First City Fund, 1999d, *Mutual Funds*, May, 24.

Tole, Thomas M., 1982, You Can't Diversify Without Diversifying, *Journal of Portfolio Management*, winter, 5–11.

Tweedy Browne Global Value and American Value Fund, 1998a, *Annual Report*, March 31.

Tweedy Browne Global Value and American Value Fund, 1998b, *Prospectus*, August 1.

Uhlfelder, Eric, 1997, Vanguard versus Fidelity, *Mutual Funds*, August, 40–5.

Vanguard Index Trust, 1998, *Prospectus*, April 20.

Vanguard International Index Portfolio, 1998, *Prospectus*, April 23.

Vanguard US Growth Portfolio, 1997, Prospectus, December 12.

Vanguard Windsor II Fund, 1999, Prospectus, February 26.

Waddock, Sandra and Samuel B. Graves, 2000, Performance Characteristics of Social and Traditional Investments, *Journal of Investing*, summer, 27–38.

Wang, Penelope et al., 1999, The Money 100: The World's Best Mutual Funds, *Time*, June, 83ff.

Weitz, Roy, 1999, *Fund Alarm* (www.fundalarm.com).

Whelehan, Barbara M., 1998, Day in the Life of a Winner, *Mutual Funds*, November, 66–72.

Whelehan, Barbara M., 1999a, And the Winner is . . . , *Mutual Funds*, 51–5.

Whelehan, Barbara M., 1999b, For Extra TLC, Pool Your Assets in One Firm, *Mutual Funds*, November, 29–31.

Whelehan, Barbara M., 2000a, Is There Life After Mike? *Mutual Funds*, July, 26.

Whelehan, Barbara M., 2000b, They're *Ba-a-ack:* Loads Proliferate Once More, *Mutual Funds*, February, 29–30.

Willis, Clint, 1999a, Big is Beautiful, *Mutual Funds*, October, 40–1.

Willis, Clint, 1999b, How to Diversify Your Fund Portfolio, *Mutual Funds*, August, 52–7.

Willis, Clint, et al., 1999, The Best Fund Families, *Mutual Funds*, October, 39–48.

You'll Have to Pay to Get Out, 1999e, *Mutual Funds*, December, 29.

Young, Claire, 1998, Growing from Within: The Janus Way, *Janus Report* (Janus Distributors), summer, 4–5, 12.

Young, Lauren, 1998a, Are You Being Served? *SmartMoney*, September, 126–34.

Young, Lauren, 1998b, How the Other Half Lives, *SmartMoney*, November, 68.

Young, Lauren, 1999, Mutual Funds: Leaders of the Pack, *SmartMoney*, September, 105–12.

Young, Lauren, 2000, On Top of the World, *SmartMoney*, January, 104–10.

Zweig, Jason, 1995, Meet America's Most Reliable Fund Manager, *Money*, December, 76ff.

Zweig, Jason, 1996a, Here's a Fund Fee Shareholders Should be Glad to See, *Money*, April, 69.

Zweig, Jason, 1996b, It's Fund Oscar Time. The Envelope, Please, *Money*, December, 65ff.

Zweig, Jason, 19996c, Why You Should Watch Out for Those Sizzling Funds That Shout: "We're No. 1", *Money*, March, 55.

Zweig, Jason, 1998a, A Plague of Mergers, *Money*, November, 83ff.

Zweig, Jason, 1998b, The Best Mutual Fund Family in America, *Money*, August, 63–4, 66.

Zweig, Jason, 2000, Chart Burn, *Money*, April (www.money.com).

Notes: Also, see general references to Morningstar, Clements (archives www.wsj.com), and Zweig (archives www.money.com). The *Journal of Investing*, winter 1997, is a special issue on socially responsible investing; the fall 2000 issue is partly so dedicated.

4 MUTUAL FUND SERVICE DISADVANTAGES
5 MUTUAL FUND SERVICE DISADVANTAGES: EXPENSES

A Last-minute Tax Tip, 1999a, *Mutual Funds*, April, 65–6.

Arnott, Amy, 1993, Unearthing Brokerage Costs, *Morningstar Mutual Funds*, September 3.

Arnott, Amy C., 1995, Lawsuits Run Amok, *Morningstar Mutual Funds*, February 17.

Arnott, Amy C., 1996a, Portfolios Please, *Morningstar Mutual Funds*, July 5.

Arnott, Amy C., 1996b, The Rising Tide, *Morningstar Mutual Funds*, October 11.

Arnott, Amy, 1997, On the Record, *Morningstar Mutual Funds*, July 4.

Arnott, Amy C., 1998, Taxable Events, *Morningstar Mutual Funds*, February 21.

Arnott, Robert, 1998, Trading Costs, in Peter L. Bernstein and Aswath Damodaran, eds., *Investment Management* (John Wiley & Sons, New York).

*art*line, 2001, *The Online Guide to Fine Art* (www.artline.com).

artumbrella, 2001, *The Global Site for Art Sites* (www.artumbrella.com).

Atkins, Allen B. and Eward A. Dyl, 1997, Transactions Costs and Holding Periods for Common Stocks, *Journal of Finance*, 52 (March), 309–25.

Barbee, Olivia, 1997a, A Weak Prognosticator, *Morningstar Investor*, February, 18.

Barbee, Olivia, 1997b, Coming Full Circle, *Morningstar Investor*, September, 14–16.

Barbee, Olivia, 1997c, Focus on: Institutional Funds, *Morningstar Investor*, June, 17.

Barbee, Olivia, 1998a, Does Asset Size Matter? *Morningstar Investor*, March, 1, 4–5.

Barbee, Olivia, 1998b, Land Lovers, *Morningstar FundInvestor*, June, 10–12.

Barbee, Olivia, 1998c, Villain or Fall Guy? *Morningstar Investor*, January, 10–12.

Barbee, Olivia, 1999a, Numbers Do Lie, *Morningstar FundInvestor*, October, 1–3.

Barbee, Olivia, 1999b, Seven Habits of Highly Tax-efficient Investors, *Morningstar FundInvestor*, September, 1–3.

Barbee, Olivia, 1999c, Vanguard Tax-managed Capital Appreciation Foils the IRS, *Morningstar FundInvestor*, May, 12.

Barbee, Olivia and Scott Cooley, 1999, Taking Issue, *Morningstar FundInvestor*, April, 21.

Barrett, William P., 1997, Fund Families: Best to Worst, *Worth*, May, 76ff.

Block, Julian, 2000a, The Deceptive Charm of Tax-free Funds, *Mutual Funds*, February, 91–2.

Block, Julian, 2000b, Sell . . . and Pay Less Tax, *Mutual Funds*, October, 105.

Bogle, John C., 1994, *Bogle on Mutual Funds: New Perspectives for the Intelligent Investor* (Irwin, Burr Ridge, IL).

Bogle, John C., 1997a, A Plea to the Press, *Bloomberg Personal Finance*, May/June (www.bloomberg.com).

Bogle, John C., 1997b, Whose Board? *Bloomberg Personal Finance*, December, 35–6, 38.

Bogle, John C., 1998, Do Mutual Funds Charge You Too Much? Pro: Fund Fees are Beyond Excessive, *Mutual Funds*, October, 80.

Bogle, John C., 1999a, *Common Sense on Mutual Funds: New Imperatives for the Intelligent Investor* (John Wiley & Sons, New York).

Bogle, John, 1999b, Marketing Madness, *Bloomberg Personal Finance*, May, 33–6.

Bogle, John C., Jr., 1997, Big Can be Bad, *Mutual Funds*, February, 82–3.

Boitano, Margaret, 1999, Many Tax-managed Funds Deliver, But Strategy Still Draws Criticism, *Wall Street Journal*, January 7, R16.

Brockman, Paul and Dennis Y. Chung, 1999, Bid–Ask Spread Components in an Order-driven Environment, *Journal of Financial Research*, 22 (summer), 227–46.

Brown, Keith C., W.V. Harlow and Laura T. Starks, 1996, Of Tournaments and Temptations: An Analysis of Managerial Incentives in the Mutual Fund Industry, *Journal of Finance*, 51 (March), 85–110.

Bullard, Mercer, 2000a, Be Aware of Fund Finagling, *Mutual Funds*, November, 112.

Bullard, Mercer, 2000b, Heads in the Sand, *Barron's*, April 10, F32.

Burton, Jonathan, 1997, Cheaper is Better, *Bloomberg Personal Finance*, July/August (www.bloomberg.com).

Burton, Jonathan, 1999, Lean Mean Money Machines: Funds with Low Expenses, *Bloomberg Personal Finance*, July/August (www.bloomberg.com).

Burton, Jonathan, 1998a, Less is More: Our Survey of Fund Fees, *Bloomberg Personal Finance*, May (www.bloomberg.com).

Burton, Jonathan, 1998b, Tax Managed Funds, *Mutual Funds*, July, 27–8.

Burton, Jonathan, 1999, Lean, Mean Money Machines, *Bloomberg Personal Finance*, July/August (www.bloomberg.com).

Burton, Jonathan, 2000, Change on the Exchange, *Bloomberg Personal Finance*, January/February (www.bloomberg.com).

Calian, Sara, 2001, US Fund Firms Hit Foreigners with Higher Fees, *Wall Street Journal*, January 22, C1, and C12.

Carhart, Mark, 1997, On Persistence in Mutual Fund Performance, *Journal of Finance*, 52 (March), 57–82.

CDA/Wiesenberger, 1986–98, *Mutual Fund Directory*, December 31 (CDA/Wiesenberger, Rockville, MD).

Chalmers, John M.R., Roger M. Edelen, and Gregory B. Kadlec, 1999, Evaluating Mutual Fund Managers by the Operational Efficiency of their Trades. Unpublished working paper, Finance Seminar Series, University of Maryland, College Park, MD.

Chan, Louis K.C. and Josef Lakonishok, 1995, The Behavior of Stock Prices around Institutional Trades, *Journal of Finance*, 50 (September), 1147–74.

Clark, Robinson G., 1999, Ten Things the SEC Won't Tell You, *SmartMoney*, May, 147ff.

Clements, Jonathan, 1992, Debate Rages over Whether Funds Charge Too Much, *Wall Street Journal*, May 18, C1, C9.

Collins, Sean and Phillip Mack, 1997, The Optimal Amount of Assets under Management in the Mutual Fund Industry, *Financial Analysts Journal*, September/October, 67–73.

Comparison Shopping, 2000a, *Mutual Funds*, August, 55–7.

Corman, Linda, 1997, Fund Supermarkets: Pay to Play, *Worth Mutual Fund Guide*, 19–20, 23–4.

Corwin, Shane A., 1999, Differences in Trading Behavior across NYSE Specialist Firms, *Journal of Finance*, 52 (April), 721–45.

Costas, Suzanne, 1998, Double Take, *Bloomberg Personal Finance*, July/August (www.bloomberg.com).

Coughenour, Jay and Kuldeep Shastri, 1999, Symposium on Market Microstructure: A Review of Empirical Research, *Financial Review*, 34 (November), 1–27 (trading cost bibliography).

Cullen, Lisa, 1998, Why Funds That Are Closed Still Charge Marketing Fees, *Money*, May, 30–1.

Damato, Karen, 1997, Some Funds Don't Deftly Manage Taxes, *Wall Street Journal*, August 8, C1, C23.

Damato, Karen, 1999a, Funds' Tally of IRS Bite Can be Tricky, *Wall Street Journal*, November 3, C1, C25.

Damato, Karen, 1999b, How Investors Failed to Note a Fund Benefit: A Cut in Fees, *Wall Street Journal*, April 29, C1, C23.

Damato, Karen, 1999c, Mutual Fund Manager, Under Fire, Loses His Dream, *Wall Street Journal*, June 9, C1, C27.

Damato, Karen and Bridget O'Brien, 1999, Insult and Injury: Losses Won't Erase Tax Due on Funds' Distributed Gains, *Wall Street Journal*, October 12, C1, C13.

Damodaran, Aswath, 1998, The Hidden Costs of Trading, in Peter L. Bernstein and Aswath Damodaran, eds., *Investment Management* (John Wiley & Sons, New York).

Dellva, Wilfred L. and Gerard T. Olson, 1998, The Relationship between Mutual Fund Fees and Expenses and their Effects on Performance, *Financial Review*, 33, 85–104.

Double-Tax-Free Funds: Backyard Tax Saving, 1999b, *Mutual Funds*, May, 31–3.

Dziubinski, Susan, 1997, Keeping More of What You Earn, *Morningstar Investor*, November, 1, 4–5.

Dziubinski, Susan, 1998a, Taking Issue, *Morningstar FundInvestor*, May, 22.

Dziubinski, Susan, 1998b, That's Fundertainment, *Morningstar FundInvestor*, August, 8–10.

Easley, David, Nicholas M. Kiefer, and Maureen O'Hara, 1996, Cream Skimming or Profit Sharing? The Curious Role of Purchased Order Flow, *Journal of Finance*, 51 (July), 811–33.

Eleswarapu, Venkat R., 1997, Cost of Transacting and Expected Returns in the Nasdaq Market, *Journal of Finance*, 52 (December), 2113–27.

Espinoza, Galina, 1999, Your Fund's New Best Friend, *Money*, February, 148–51.

Evensky, Harold, 2000, The Truth about Fund Taxes, *Mutual Funds*, December, 118.

Fidelity Advisor Equity Growth Fund, Class A, Class T, Class B and Class C, 1998, *Prospectus*, February 28.

Fidelity Growth and Income Portfolio, 1997, *Prospectus*, September 25.

Fidelity Low-priced Stock Fund, 1997, *Prospectus*, September 26.

Fidelity Magellan Fund, 1998, *Prospectus*, May 22.

Fidelity Select Portfolio, 1998, *Prospectus*, April 28.

Fido to Investors: It's Our Money, 2000b, *Mutual Funds*, September, 23.

Fortin, Rich and Stuart Michelson, 1998, Mutual Funds Trading Costs, *Journal of Investing*, spring, 66–70.

Fosback, Norman G, 1997, Pandora's Box, *Mutual Funds*, August, 10.

Fosback, Norman G., 1999a, Loads, Fees, Taxes . . . Should You *Really* Care? *Mutual Funds*, September, 92.

Fosback, Norman G., 1999b, The Fund Expense Scandal, *Mutual Funds*, May, 100.

Fosback, Norman G., 1999c, 12b-1: The "B" Now Stands for Billion, *Mutual Funds*, July, 100.

Fosback, Norman G., 1999d, Where's a Director When You Need One? *Mutual Funds*, June, 100.

Franklin Mutual Series Fund, Class I and Class II, 1998a, *Prospectus*, May 1.

Franklin Mutual Series Fund, Class Z, 1998b, *Prospectus*, May 1.

Frederick, Jim, 1998, A Trading Strategy for Beating the Spread, *Money*, June, 49–50.

Fried, Carla, 1998, Beat Back Fund Taxes, *Money*, January, 88ff.

Fund Family Shareholder Association, 2000, When Non-profits Profit, *Independent Advisor for Vanguard Investors*, July, 1, 11–12.

Garland, James P., 1997, The Attraction of Tax-managed Index Funds, *Journal of Investing*, spring, 13–20.

Garrity, Mike, 1998a, SEC Finds Frequent Abuse of Soft Dollars, *Mutual Fund Market News*, September 28, 1, 10.

Garrity, Mike, 1998b, SEC to Funds: Improve Soft Dollar Oversight, *Variable Annuity Market News*, October, 1, 20.

Garrity, Mike, 1998c, Yachtman Seeks Directors' Removal: Directors Say, "You're Fired," *Mutual Fund Market News*, September 28, 1, 11.

Gasparino, Charles, 1998a, Mutual Fund Investors Risk Bite from "Soft-Dollar" Deals, *Wall Street Journal*, September 16, C1, C29.

Gasparino, Charles, 1998b, Pain of Mutual Fund Fees is More Acute When the Market is Going Down Than Up, *Wall Street Journal*, August 25, C1, C21.

Gasparino, Charles, 1998c, Trading Rules for Managers Get Stiffer, *Wall Street Journal*, June 25, C1, C31.

Gasparino, Charles and Pui-Wing Tam, 1999, Mutual Fund Boards: No Comfort? *Wall Street Journal*, February 5, C1, C23.

Goldstein, Michael A. and Edward F. Nelling, 1999, Market Timing and Trading in Nasdaq Stocks, *Financial Review*, 34, 27–44.

Good Grief! Is Fund Manager Pay Shrinking?, 1999c, *Mutual Funds*, January, 18.

Green, William, 1998, Do These Guys Deserve $60 Million a Year? *Money*, September, 101ff.

Harris, Diane, 1997, Smart Ways to Shop the New Financial Supermarkets, *Money*, June, 101ff.

Hartman, Kathleen, 1998, The Devil is in the Details, *Morningstar Mutual Funds*, April 6.

Hasbrouck, Joel, 1995, One Security, Many Markets: Determining the Contributions to Price Discovery, *Journal of Finance*, 50 (September), 1175–99.

Haslem, John A., 1988, *The Investor's Guide to Mutual Funds* (Prentice Hall, Englewood Cliffs, NJ).

Hechinger, John, 1999, Fidelity's Value, Long Elusive, Looks to be around $30 Billion, *Wall Street Journal*, June 17, C1, C13.

Howard, Mark, 1993, Judging Real Estate Investment Options, *Morningstar Five Star Investor*, July, 1, 8.

If You're Going with High-cost Funds, You're Stacking the Deck against Yourself, 1999, *Bloomberg Personal Finance*, May (www.bloomberg.com).

Institute for Econometric Research, 1998, *Tax Saving Guide*, January (The Institute, Deerfield Beach, FL).

Institute for Econometric Research, 1999, *Tax Efficiency Ratings* (The Institute, Deerfield Beach, FL).

Investment Company Institute, 1999, *The Report of the Advisory Group on Best Practices for Fund Directors*, June (The Institute, Washington, DC).

Investment Company Institute, 2000, Use of 12b-1 Fees by Mutual Funds in 1999, *Fundamentals*, April, 1–2.

Janus Equity Funds, 1998, *Prospectus*, February 17.

Jeffrey, Robert H., 1998a, Tax Considerations, in Peter L. Bernstein and Aswath Damodaran, eds., *Investment Management* (John Wiley & Sons, New York).

Jeffrey, Robert H., 1998b, Taxes and Performance Evaluation, in Peter L. Bernstein and Aswath Damodaran, eds. *Investment Management* (John Wiley & Sons, New York).

Jeffrey, Robert H. and Robert D. Arnott, 1993, Is your Alpha Big Enough to Cover its Taxes? *Journal of Portfolio Management*, spring, 15–25.

Jones, Jonathan, Kenneth Lehn, and J. Harold Mulherin, 1990, Institutional Investors and Stock Market Liquidity: An Empirical Analysis of the 1980s. Unpublished working paper, Finance Seminar Series, University of Maryland, College Park, MD.

Kaufmann Fund, 1998, *Prospectus*, May 1.

Keim, Donald B. and Ananth Madhavan, 1997, Transaction Costs and Investment Style: An Interexchange Analysis of Institutional Equity Trades, *Journal of Financial Economics*, 46 (December), 265–92.

Kelley, Jeff, 1995a, Double Whammy: Needless Funds and Marketing Zeal, *Morningstar Investor*, November, 41.

Kelley, Jeff, 1995b, Putting Performance First, *Morningstar Investor*, June, 41.

Kelley, Jeff, 1996a, Institutional Funds Put Out the Welcome Mat, *Morningstar Investor*, 1–2, 4.

Kelley, Jeff, 1996b, The Good, the Bad, and the Stingy, *Morningstar Investor*, May, 8–9.

Kostin, David J. and A. Richard Moore, 1997, A New Approach to Valuing Real Estate Investment Trusts, *Dow Jones Asset Management*, November/December, 31ff.

Lallos, Laura, 1994, Value Funds Make Best Use of Tax Shelters, *Morningstar Five Star Investor*, April, 1, 12.

Lammert, Warren B., 1997, Bigger is Better, *Mutual Funds*, February, 82–3.

Latzko, David A., 1999, Economies of Scale in Mutual Fund Administration, *Journal of Financial Research*, 22 (fall), 331–9.

Lauricella, Tom, 1999, Caught in the Crossfire, *SmartMoney*, January, 116–21.

Loeb, T.F., 1983, Trading Cost: The Critical Link between Investment Information and Results, *Financial Analysts Journal*, May/June, 39–44.

Lucchetti, Aaron, 1999a, Capital Gains Distributions Can Turn the End of the Year into a Taxing Time, *Wall Street Journal*, November 1, R1, R7.

Lucchetti, Aaron, 1999b, Click Here to Find Out What Your Fund Costs, *Wall Street Journal*, November 1, R1, R7.

Lucchetti, Aaron, 1999c, Many Fund Firms Resist Fees Based on Results, *Wall Street Journal*, June 18, C1, C23.

Lucchetti, Aaron, 1999d, Personal Trading Troubles Fund Officials, *Wall Street Journal*, June 15, C27.

Lucchetti, Aaron, 1999e, SEC Probes Funds' Commission, *Wall Street Journal*, September 16, C1, C25.

Lucchetti, Aaron, 2000, Are Investors in Mutual Funds Better Served by Less Data? *Wall Street Journal*, June 28, C1, C27.

Madhavan, Ananth and Seymour Smidt, 1993, An Analysis of Changes in Specialist Inventories and Quotations, *Journal of Finance*, 48 (December), 1595–628.

Malhotra, D.K. and Robert W. McLeod, 1997, An Empirical Analysis of Mutual Fund Expenses, *Journal of Financial Research*, 20 (summer), 175–90.

McGough, Robert, 1997, Low "Turnovers" May Taste Very Good to Fund Owners in Wake of Tax Deal, *Wall Street Journal*, July 31, C1, C23.

McGough, Robert, 1998, Robust Fund Industry isn't Lowering Fees, *Wall Street Journal*, May 14, C1, C27.

McLeod, Robert W. and D.K. Malhotra, 1994, A Re-examination of the Effect of 12b-1 Plans on Mutual Fund Expense Ratios, *Journal of Financial Research*, 17 (summer), 231–40.

McMurray, Scott, 1994, Burned Alive, *Worth*, April, 68ff.

Middleton, Timothy, 1997, Funds and Taxes: Keeping It, *Worth Mutual Fund Guide*, 26–7.

Misra, Prashanta and Jason Zweig, 1996, The SEC Looks at whether Vinik Broke the Rules, *Money*, January, 43ff.

Mulvihill, Michael, 1996, A Question of Trust, *Morningstar Mutual Funds*, August 30.

Murphy, Brian P., 1999, Funds with Hidden Tax Breaks, *Money*, August, 40, 42.

Musto, David K., 1999, Investment Decisions Depend on Portfolio Disclosures, *Journal of Finance*, 54 (June), 935–52.

O'Brien, Bridget, 1999, A Little Light Reading? Try a Fund Prospectus, *Wall Street Journal*, May 3, R1, R5.

O'Hara, Maureen, and George S. Oldfield, 1996, The Microeconomics of Market Making, *Journal of Financial and Quantitative Analysis*, 21 (December), 361–74.

Oster, Christopher, 2000, Fees? You Mean Mutual Funds Have Fees? *Wall Street Journal*, July 14, C1, C19.

Pagano, Marco, and Ailsa Roell, 1996, Transparency and Liquidity: A Comparison of Auction and Dealer Markets with Informed Trading, *Journal of Finance*, 51 (June), 579–611.

Paltrow, Scot J., Greg Ip, and Michael Schroeder, 1999, As Huge Changes Roil the Market, Some Ask: Where is the SEC? *Wall Street Journal*, October 11, A1, A10.

Penn, Michael, 1994, Investors Should Cage their Tax Anxieties, *Morningstar Five Star Investor*, January, 1, 10–11.

Perold, Andre, 1988, The Implementation Shortfall: Paper versus Reality, *Journal of Portfolio Management*, spring. Quoted in Bernstein, Richard L. and Frank J. Fabozzi, eds., 1997, *Streetwise: The Best of the Journal of Portfolio Management* (Princeton University Press, Princeton, NJ).

Perold, Andre and Robert S. Salomon, Jr., 1991, The Right Amount of Assets under Management, *Financial Analysts Journal*, May/June, 31–9.

PersonalFund.com (1999), *Mutual Fund Cost Calculator* (www.personalfund.com).

Peters, Donald J. and Mary J. Miller, 1998, Taxable Investors Need Different Strategies, *Journal of Investing*, fall, 37–44.

Phillips, Don, 1993, While the Have-nots Play, the Haves Pay Off, *Morningstar Five Star Investor*, December, 40.

Phillips, Don, 1994, A Trust Retained, *Morningstar Mutual Funds*, September 2.

Phillips, Don, 1995, A Deal with the Devil, *Morningstar Mutual Funds*, May 26.

Phillips, Don, 1997, Slamming the SEC? *Morningstar Mutual Funds*, June 20.

Picerno, Joseph, 1999, Investing's Final Frontier, *Dow Jones Asset Manager*, November/December, 43–6.

Pozen, Robert C., 1994, Fidelity's Code of Ethics, *Fidelity Focus*, spring, 24.

Pozen, Bob, 1998a, Fair-value Pricing, *Fidelity Focus*, spring, 26.

Pozen, Robert C., 1998b, *The Mutual Fund Business* (MIT Press, Cambridge, MA).

Purcell, Kylelane, 1993, Understanding the Intricacies of Tax Liability, Morningstar *Five Star Investor*, September, 1, 12.

Purcell, Kylelane, 1995, Ring 'em Up, *Morningstar Five Star Investor*, January, 3.

Rea, John D. and Brian K. Reid, 1998, Trends in the Ownership Costs of Equity Mutual Funds, *Perspective* (Investment Company Institute), November, 1–15.

Rea, John D. and Brian K. Reid, 1999, Total Shareholder Cost of Bond and Money Market Mutual Funds, *Perspective* (Investment Company Institute), March, 1–8.

Rea, John D., Brian K. Reid, and Travis Lee, 1999, Mutual Funds Costs, 1980–98, *Perspective* (Investment Company Institute) September, 1–11.

Rea, John D., Brian K. Reid, and Kimberlee W. Millar, 1999, Operating Expense Ratios, Assets, and Economies of Scale in Equity Mutual Funds, *Perspective* (Investment Company Institute), December, 1–11.

Regnier, Pat, 1997, Are Mutual Fund Fees Schwabbed Up? *Morningstar Mutual Funds*, May 9.

Regnier, Pat, 1999a, Lonely Crusade, *Money*, April, 120ff.

Regnier, Pat, 1999b, Yachtman Wins One, *Money*, January, 60.

Reilly, Frank K. and Keith C. Brown, 1997, *Investment Analysis and Portfolio Management*, 5th ed. (Dryden Press, Fort Worth, TX).

Rekenthaler, John, 1992a, Costly Maneuvers, *Morningstar Mutual Funds*, March 6.

Rekenthaler, John, 1992b, Puncturing a Few Myths, *Morningstar Mutual Funds*, July 24.

Rekenthaler, John, 1993a, Getting Something for Nothing, *Morningstar Five Star Investor*, July, 32.

Rekenthaler, John, 1993b, Taxing Issues, *Morningstar Mutual Funds*, August 6.

Rekenthaler, John, 1993c, The Big Boom, *Morningstar Mutual Funds*, May 28.

Rekenthaler, John, 1994a, Magellan and Taxes, *Morningstar Mutual Funds*, December 23.

Rekenthaler, John, 1994b, Time Bombs, *Morningstar Mutual Funds*, December 9.

Rekenthaler, John, 1996a, Judging the Book by its Cover, *Morningstar Investor*, January, 41.

Rekenthaler, John, 1996b, Taking Issue, *Morningstar Investor*, July, 41.

Rekenthaler, John, 1996c, Taking Issue, *Morningstar Investor*, November, 41.

Rekenthaler, John, 1996d, Taking Issue, *Morningstar Investor*, September, 41.

Rekenthaler, John, 1997, Read this Column, Save $1,000, *Morningstar Investor*, January, 22.

Ronald, Richard, 1998a, What are . . . Annual Costs? *Morningstar FundInvestor*, May, 13.

Ronald, Richard, 1998b, What is . . . Cost Basis? *Morningstar Investor*, January, 13.

Ronald, Richard, 1999a, What is . . . Tax Efficiency? *Morningstar FundInvestor*, May, 19.

Ronald, Richard, 1999b, What is . . . Turnover Ratio? *Morningstar FundInvestor*, April, 19.

Rowland, Mary, 1998, Get the Air Out, *Bloomberg Personal Finance*, August (www.bloomberg.com).

Sanders, Catherine V., 1995a, More Loaded Questions, *Morningstar Mutual Funds*, June 23.

Sanders, Catherine V., 1995b, The Taxman Cometh, *Morningstar Mutual Funds*, October 13.

Sanders, Catherine V., 1997, Making April Less Taxing, *Morningstar Investor*, February, 1, 4–5.

Sanders, Catherine V., 1998a, Taking Issue, *Morningstar Investor*, January, 22.

Sanders, Catherine V., 1998b, Taking Issue, *Morningstar Investor*, July, 21.

Sanders, Catherine V., 1998c, What You'd Know if We Were King, *Morningstar FundInvestor*, April, 1, 4–5.

Santini, Donald L. and Jack W. Aber, 1996, Investor Response to Mutual Fund Policy Variables, *Financial Review*, 31 (November), 765–81.

Schroeder, Michael, 2001, SEC Chief's Valediction: Beware of the Investment World's Pitfalls, *Wall Street Journal*, January 17, C1, C10.

SEC Town Meetings, 1997, *Mutual Funds*, February, 69–71.

Sharpe, William F., Gordon J. Alexander, and Jeffery V. Bailey, 1999, *Investments*, 6th ed. (Prentice Hall, Upper Saddle River, NJ).

Shivdasani, Anil and David Yermack, 1999, CEO Involvement in the Selection of New Board Members: An Empirical Analysis, *Journal of Finance*, 54 (October), 1829–53.

Simon, Ruth, 1993, How Fund Directors Are Letting You Down, *Money*, September, 105ff.

Sivy, Michael, 1998, T. Rowe's Stock Tops its Funds, *Money*, year end, 31–2.

Sprouse, Mary L., 1997, The Best Ways to Keep the IRS's Mitts away From Your Mutual Fund Profits, *Money*, August, 167–8.

Stevens, Sue, 2000, Should You Shelter Your Bonds or Your Stocks? *Morningstar FundInvestor*, October, 8–9.

Tam, Pui-Wing, 1998a, From Mutual Fund Loser to Tax Time Winner, *Wall Street Journal*, October 12, C1, C13.

Tam, Pui-Wing, 1998b, Some Closed Funds Charge for Marketing, *Wall Street Journal*, December 9, C1, C25.

Tam, Pui-Wing, 1998c, Tax-Efficient Mutual Funds Are Hard Sell in Choppy Market, *Wall Street Journal*, October 8, C1, C23.

Tam, Pui-Wing, 1999a, Fund Firms Push for "Double Duty" Boards, *Wall Street Journal*, August 11, C1, C11.

Tam, Pui-Wing, 1999b, Riding Herd on Mutual Fund Fees, *Wall Street Journal*, February 19, C1, C23.

Tam, Pui-Wing, 1999c, Study Ranks Fund Board Effectiveness, *Wall Street Journal*, October 8, C1, C19.

Tam, Pui-Wing and Aaron Lucchetti, 1999, Vanguard to Publish After-tax Returns, *Wall Street Journal*, October 11, C1, C23.

Tax Loads: A Little Known Burden on Mutual Fund Investors, 1995, *Mutual Funds*, December, 35–6.

Tobias, Andrew, 1999, Heavy Load, *Worth*, October, 83–4, 170.

Treynor, Jack, 1994, The Invisible Costs of Trading, *Journal of Portfolio Management*, fall. Quoted in Bernstein, Richard L. and Frank J. Fabozzi, eds., 1997, *Streetwise: The Best of the Journal of Portfolio Management* (Princeton University Press, Princeton, NJ).

Treynor, Jack, 1999, Zero Sum, *Financial Analysts Journal*, January/February, 8–12.

Tufano, Peter and Matthew Sevick, 1997, Board Structure and Fee-setting in the US Mutual Fund Industry, *Journal of Financial Economics*, 46 (December), 321–55.

Tweedy Browne Fund, 1998, *Annual Report*, March 31.

Umphrey, Willard L., 1998, Do Mutual Funds Charge You Too Much? Con: Dispelling the High Expense Ratio Myth, *Mutual Funds*, October, 81.

Updegrave, Walter L., Prashanta Misra, and Mark Bautz, 1994, How to Be a Smart Mutual Fund Investor, *Money*, September, 70–5, 77.

US Securities and Exchange Commission, 1996, *New Disclosure Options for Open End Management Companies* (SEC, Washington, DC).

US Securities and Exchange Commission, 1998, *Inspection Report on the Soft Dollar Practices of Broker-Dealers, Investment Advisors and Mutual Funds*, September 28 (SEC, Office of Compliance, Inspection and Examinations, Washington, DC).

Vanguard Group, 1998, *Vanguard Tax-managed Funds* (Vanguard Marketing, Valley Forge, PA).

Vanguard Group, 1999a, *Understanding the Tax Acts of 1997 and 1998* (Vanguard Marketing, Valley Forge, PA); also (www.vanguard.com).

Vanguard Group, 1999b, *Taxes and Mutual Funds* (Vanguard Marketing, Valley Forge, PA); also (www.vanguard.com).

Vanguard Index Trust, 1998, *Prospectus*, April 20.

Vanguard International Index Portfolio, 1998, *Prospectus*, April 23.

Vanguard US Growth Portfolio, 1997, *Prospectus*, December 12.

Vanguard Windsor II Fund, 1999, *Prospectus*, February 26.

Ward, Sandra, 1998, Fundom's Dirty Little Secret, *Barron's*, August 3, 35–6.

Welling, Kathryn M., 1998, By the Numbers, *Barron's*, June 15, 40, 42–4.

Whelehan, Barbara M., 1998, Stuck with the Tab, *Mutual Funds*, May, 60–2.

When Tax-free Funds Aren't, 1999d, *Mutual Funds*, July, 75–6.

Which Funds Are Most Tax-Efficient? 1998, *Mutual Funds*, June, 27–8.

Willis, Clint, 1998, Strategies for Tax-conscious Fund Investors, *Mutual Funds*, April, 27, 29.

Windawi, A. Jason, 1994, Wrangling with REITs, *Morningstar Five Star Investor*, October, 3.

Windawi, A. Jason, 1995, Real Estate Funds Have Arrived, *Morningstar Mutual Funds*, March 31.

Wolde, Richard T., 1999, Ten Things Your Fund Supermarket Won't Tell You, *SmartMoney*, September, 161ff.

Wolde, Richard T., 2000, Chicago Hopeless? *SmartMoney*, January, 40.

Yachtman Sues Directors, 1998, *Mutual Funds*, December, 24.

Yachtman Wins One, 1999, *Money*, January, 60.

Yes, Fund Managers Play End-of-quarter Games, 2000c, *Mutual Funds*, April, 24.

Zweig, Jason, 1995, Why You Shouldn't Take Fund Managers' Personal Trading Too Personally, *Money*, November, 66.

Zweig, Jason, 1996a, Today's Hottest Funds are Too Big for their Britches, *Money*, April, 146ff.

Zweig, Jason, 1996b, Why Investors Have No Reason to Fret over the Most Recent Fidelity Flap, *Money*, June, 63.

Zweig, Jason, 1997a, Is That New Fund a Hard-boiled Survivor – or Humpty Dumpty? *Money*, December, 98ff.

Zweig, Jason, 1997b, Your Funds May be Making You Rich . . . But You're Also Getting Robbed, *Money*, February, 62ff.

Zweig, Jason, 1997c, Watch Out for the Year-end Fund Flim Flam, *Money*, November, 130ff.

Zweig, Jason, 1998a, How Funds Can Do Better, *Money*, February, 42ff.

Zweig, Jason, 1998b, Performance Peek-a-boo, *Money Year-End Financial Guide*, December, 55ff.

Zweig, Jason, 1998c, Why Your Portfolio Manager May Work Better in the Dark, *Money*, March, 50ff.

Zweig, Jason, 1999a, Confessions of a Fund Pro, *Money*, February, 73ff.

Zweig, Jason, 1999b, Mutual Fund Tax Bombs, *Money*, July, 55–7.

Note: Also, see general references to Morningstar, Clements (archives, www.wsj.com), and Zweig (archives, www.money.com).

6 LONG-TERM INVESTING IN MUTUAL FUNDS AND STOCK/BOND PORTFOLIO ALLOCATIONS

A Quick Test for Risk Tolerance, 1989, *Fortune/ Investor's Guide*, 97.

Alexander, Gordon J. and Jack C. Francis, 1986, *Portfolio Analysis* (Prentice Hall, Englewood Cliffs, NJ).

Alexanian, Alex, 1993, Sooner or Later: In Investing, Time is Money, *Morningstar Five Star Investor*, June, 1, 8.

Arnott, Amy, 1997, Asset Allocation: Revisiting the Debate, *Morningstar Mutual Funds*, September 22.

Arnott, Robert D. and Frank J. Fabozzi, eds., 1992, *Active Asset Allocation*, rev. ed. (Probus Publishing, Chicago).

Arnott, Robert D. and Robert M. Lovell, 1993, Rebalancing: Why? When? How Often? *Journal of Investing*, spring, 5–10.

Asinof, Lynn, 2000, Web Detectives Help Expose Overlap in Fund Portfolios, *Wall Street Journal*, January 26, C1, C29.

Asness, Clifford S., 1996, Why not 100 percent Equities? *Journal of Portfolio Management*, winter, 29–34.

Asness, Clifford S., 2000, Stocks versus Bonds: Explaining the Equity Risk Premium, *Financial Analysts Journal*, March/April, 96–113.

Baker, H. Kent and John A. Haslem, 1973, Information Needs of Individual Investors, *Journal of Accountancy*, November, 64–9.

Baker, H. Kent and John A. Haslem, 1974a, The Impact of Investor Socioeconomic Characteristics on Risk and Return Preferences, *Journal of Business Research*, 2 (October), 469–76.

Baker, H. Kent and John A. Haslem, 1974b, Toward the Development of Client-specified Valuation Models, *Journal of Finance*, 29 (September), 1255–63.

Baker, H. Kent, Michael B. Hargrove, and John A. Haslem, 1977, An Empirical Analysis of the Risk–Return Preferences of Individual Investors, *Journal of Financial and Quantitative Analysis*, 12 (September), 377–89.

Baker, H. Kent, Michael B. Hargrove, and John A. Haslem, 1979, A Test of a Revised Theory of the Investment Life Cycle, *Baylor Business Studies*, 10 (May, June, July), 17–33.

Barbee, Olivia, 1997, Making the Grade with International Funds, *Morningstar Investor*, July, 1, 4–5.

Barbee, Olivia, 1998a, Focus on: Lifecycle Funds, *Morningstar Investor*, February, 17.

Barbee, Olivia, 1998b, Those Darn International Funds, *Morningstar FundInvestor*, July, 1, 4–5.

Bernstein, Peter L., 1996a, *Against the Gods: The Remarkable Story of Risk* (John Wiley & Sons, New York).

Bernstein, Peter L., 1996b, Are Stocks the Best Place to be in the Long Run? A Contrary Opinion, *Journal of Investing*, summer, 6–9.

Bernstein, Peter L., 1996c, What Prompts Paradigm Shifts? *Financial Analysts Journal*, November/December, 7–13.

Bernstein, Peter L., 1997a, Rules for Risk Takers, *Bloomberg Personal Finance*, March/April (www.bloomberg.com).

Bernstein, Peter L., 1997b, What Rate of Return Can You Reasonably Expect . . . or What Can the Long Run Tell Us about the Short Run? *Financial Analysts Journal*, March/April, 20–8.

Bernstein, William J., 1995, *The Intelligent Asset Allocator* (www.efficientfrontier.com).

Bernstein, William J., 1996a, The Coward's Portfolio – A Modest Portfolio, *Efficient Frontier*, September (www.efficientfrontier.com).

Bernstein, William J., 1996b, The Rebalancing Bonus: Theory and Practice, *Efficient Frontier*, September (www.efficientfrontier.com).

Bernstein, William J., 1997a, The July 1997 Coward's Portfolio, *The Intelligent Asset Allocator*, July (www.efficientfrontier.com).

Bernstein, William J., 1997b, What the Investment Industry Doesn't Want you to Know, *The Online Asset Allocator* (www.efficientfrontier.com).

Bernstein, William J., 1997c, What's the Proper Bond Mix in your Portfolio? *Efficient Frontier*, September (www.efficientfrontier.com).

Bernstein, William J., 1998a, The Appropriate Use of the Mean Variance Optimizer, *Efficient Frontier*, January (www.efficientfrontier.com).

Bernstein, William J., 1998b, The Death of Diversification, *Efficient Frontier*, April (www.efficientfrontier.com).

Bernstein, William J., 1999a, Bill Sharpe's Brave New World, *Efficient Frontier*, September (www.efficientfrontier.com).

Bernstein, William J., 1999b, The Coward's Update, *Efficient Frontier*, January (www.efficientfrontier.com).

Bernstein, William J., 1999c, The Duration of Stocks, *Efficient Frontier*, September (www.efficientfrontier.com).

Bernstein, William J., 2000a, Case Studies in Rebalancing, *Efficient Frontier*, winter (www.efficientfrontier.com).

Bernstein, William, J., 2000b, Factor Rotation, Efficient Frontier, summer (www.efficientfrontier.com).

Bernstein, William J., 2000c, The Best of the Behaviorists, *Efficient Frontier*, winter (www.efficientfrontier.com).

Bhansali, Jayesh D., 1998, Inflation-indexed US Treasury Bonds: An Analysis, *Journal of Investing*, fall, 45–51.

Bhatia, Sanjir, ed., 1995, *Managing Assets for Individual Investors* (Association of Investment Management Research, Charlottesville, VA).

Bierman, Harold, Jr., 1995, Bubbles, Theory, and Market Timing, *Journal of Portfolio Management*, fall, 54–60.

Bodie, Zvi, 1995, On the Risk of Stocks in the Long Run, *Financial Analysts Journal*, May/June, 18–22.

Bodie, Zvi and Dwight B. Crane, 1997, Personal Investing: Advice, Theory, and Evidence, *Financial Analysts Journal*, November/December, 13–23.

Bodie, Zvi, Alex Kane, and Alan J. Marcus, 1999, *Investments*, 4th ed. (Irwin, Chicago).

Bogle, John C., 1991, Investing in the 1990s, *Journal of Portfolio Management*, spring, 5–15.

Bogle, John C., 1999, *Common Sense on Mutual Funds: New Imperatives for the Intelligent Investor* (John Wiley & Sons, New York).

Brennan, M.J., 1995, The Individual Investor, *Journal of Financial Research*, 18 (spring), 59–74.

Brenner, Lynn, 1998, What Goes Where? *Bloomberg Personal Finance*, September (www.bloomberg.com).

Brenner, Lynn, 1999, A Fund for All Ages, *Bloomberg Personal Finance*, December (www.bloomberg.com).

Brinson, Gary P., 1998, Global Management and Asset Allocation, in Richard L. Bernstein and Aswath Damodaran, eds., *Investment Management* (John Wiley & Sons, New York).

Brinson, Gary P., L. Randolph Hood, and Gilbert L. Beebower, 1986, Determinants of Portfolio Performance, *Financial Analysts Journal*, July/August, 39–44.

Brinson, Gary P., Brian D. Singer, and Gilbert L. Beebower, 1991, Determinants of Portfolio Performance II: An Update, *Financial Analysts Journal*, May/June, 40–8.

Brocato, Joe and Steve Steed, 1998, Optimal Asset Allocation over the Business Cycle, *Financial Review*, 33, 129–48.

Brown, Ken, 2000, Fund Diversification Dies a Not Very Slow Death, *Wall Street Journal*, February 7, R1, R5.

Buckman, Rebecca and Ruth Simon, 1999, Day Trading Can Breed Perilous Illusions, *Wall Street Journal*, August 2, C1, C16.

Burns, Scott, 2000a, Aging's New Math, *Worth*, February, 67–8.

Burns, Scott, 2000b, It Pays to Plod, *Worth*, March, 67–8.

Burton, Jonathan, 1998, 'Tis Folly to be Wise, *Dow Jones Asset Management*, March/April, 20ff.

Burton, Jonathan, 1999a, Sharpe Reckoning, *Bloomberg Personal Finance*, January/February (www.bloomberg.com).

Burton, Jonathan, 1999b, Turning over Rocks, *Dow Jones Asset Management*, November/December, 29–32, 34.

Canner, Niko, N. Gregory Mankiw, and David N. Weil, 1997, An Asset Allocation Puzzle, *American Economic Review*, 87 (March), 181–91.

CDA/Wiesenberger, 1998, *Mutual Fund Directory*, December 31 (CDA/Wiesenberger, Rockville, MD).

Chan, Anthony and Carl R. Chen, 1992, How Well Do Asset Allocation Fund Managers Allocate Assets? *Journal of Portfolio Management*, spring, 81–91.

Chandy, P.R. and William Reichenstein, 1993, Market Surges and Market Timing, *Journal of Investing*, summer, 41–5.

Chang, Eric C. and Wilbur G. Lewellen, 1984, Market Timing and Mutual Fund Performance, *Journal of Business*, 57, Part 1 (January), 57–72.

Chieffe, Natalie, 1999, Asset Allocation, Rebalancing, and Returns, *Journal of Investing*, winter, 43–8.

Chopra, Vijay K., 1993, Improving Optimization, *Journal of Investing*, fall, 51–9.

Chow, George, 1995, Portfolio Selection Based on Return, Risk and Relative Performance, *Financial Analysts Journal*, March/April, 54–60.

Chow, George et al., 1999, Optimal Portfolios in Good Times and Bad, *Financial Analysts Journal*, May/ June, 65–73.

Clements, Jonathan, 1998, In the Field of Investing, Self-confidence Can Sometimes Come Back to Haunt You, *Wall Street Journal*, September 22, C1.

Clements, Jonathan, 1999a, Knowing When to Hold, When to Fold, *Wall Street Journal*, August 3, C1.

Clements, Jonathan, 1999b, Why You're Never Too Old for Stocks, *Wall Street Journal*, July 13, C1.

Clements, Jonathan, 2000a, Fixating on Risk Can Sink Investors, *Wall Street Journal*, June 6, C1.

Clements, Jonathan, 2000b, How Market Slumps Can Alter Psychology, *Wall Street Journal*, February 22, C19.

Clements, Jonathan, 2000c, This Crazy Market is Hard to Beat, *Wall Street Journal*, February 1, C1.

Comrey, Andrew L., 1992, Check your Risk Tolerance, *Fidelity Focus* (Fidelity Distributors), spring, 9.

Coval, Joshua D. and Tobias J. Moskowitz, 1999, Home Bias at Home: Local Equity Preference in Domestic Portfolios, *Journal of Finance*, 54 (December), 2045–73.

Cringely, Robert X., 1999, Day Dreaming, *Worth*, October, 41–2.

Curtis, Carol E., 1998, Master Builders, *Bloomberg Personal Finance*, May (www.bloomberg.com).

Daniel, Kent, David Hirshleifer and Avanidhar Subrahmanyam, 1998, Investor Psychology and Security Market Under- and Overreactions, *Journal of Finance*, 53 (December), 1839–85 (references to market anomalies).

DeBondt, Werner F.M. and Richard H. Thaler, 1995, Financial Decision-making in Markets and Firms: A Behavioral Perspective, in R.A. Jarrow, V. Maksimovic, and W.T. Ziemba, eds. *Handbooks in Operations Research and Management Science*: Volume 9, *Finance* (Elsevier, Amsterdam), 385–410.

Delaney, Kevin J., 1998, Fund Tale: The Young and the Aggressive, *Wall Street Journal*, January 23, C1, C25.

DeTocqueville, Alexus, 1840, The Strange Unrest of Happy Men, *Democracy in America* (Oxford University Press, London), 398–419 (excerpt reprinted in *Journal of Portfolio Management*, winter 1976, 71–4).

DiTeresa, Peter, 1998, Invest Well for the Short Haul, *Morningstar FundInvestor*, April, 8–9.

DiTeresa, Peter, 1999a, Balance with Ease, *Morningstar FundInvestor*, June, 10–11.

DiTeresa, Peter, 1999b, Getting to the Finish Line, *Morningstar FundInvestor*, March, 12–13.

Dreman, David, 1998, *Contrarian Investment Strategies: The Next Generation – Beating the Market by Going against the Crowd* (Simon & Schuster, New York).

Efficient Solutions, 1998, *Mean–Variance Optimization: Modern Portfolio Theory* (www.effisols.com).

Ellis, Charles D., 1997, Small Slam! *Financial Analysts Journal*, January/February, 6–8.

Ellis, Charles D., 1998, The Investment Setting, in Peter L. Bernstein and Aswath Damodaran, eds. *Investment Management*, (John Wiley & Sons, New York).

Eng, Li Li, 1999, Comparing Changes in Stockholdings of Different Institutional Investors, *Journal of Investing*, spring, 46–50.

Erb, Claude B., Campbell R. Harvey, and Tadas E. Viskanta, 1996, Political Risk, Economic Risk, and Financial Risk, *Financial Analysts Journal*, November/December, 29–46.

Errunza, Vihang, Ked Hogan, and Mao-Wei Hung, 1999, Can the Gains from International Diversification be Achieved without Trading Abroad? *Journal of Finance*, 54 (December), 2075–107.

Fabozzi, Frank J. and Jack C. Francis, 1979, Mutual Fund Systematic Risk for Bull and Bear Markets: An Empirical Examination, *Journal of Finance*, 34 (December), 1243–50.

Farrelly, Jennifer, 1999, Index Four-Front, *Fidelity Focus* (Fidelity Distributors), winter, 22–3.

Feinberg, Andrew, 1997, Setting a Steady Course, *Worth*, May, 117–18.

Ferson, Wayne E. and Campbell R. Harvey, 1991, Sources of Predictability in Portfolio Returns, *Financial Analysts Journal*, May/June, 49–56.

Fidelity Investments, 1986, What's your Investments Risk Preference? *Independent Investor's Personal Investing Newsletter*, November, 12.

Fidelity Investments, 1988, How Conservative are You? *Investment Vision*, July/August, 5–7.

Fidelity Investments, 1995, *Managing Risk in your Portfolio* (Fidelity Distributors, Boston, MA).

Financial Engines, 2000, *How We Recommend Funds* (app.financialengines.com).

Fisher, Kenneth L., 1998, The Ultimate Contrarian, *Bloomberg Personal Finance*, January/February (www.bloomberg.com).

Fisher, Kenneth L. and Meir Statman, 1999, A Behavioral Framework for Time Diversification, *Financial Analysts Journal*, May/June, 74–87.

Fogler, H. Russell and Darwin M. Bayston, eds., 1984, *Improving the Investment Decision Process: Quantitative Assistance for the Practitioner – and for the Firm*, (Institute of Chartered Financial Analysts, Charlottesville, VA).

Frankfurter, George M., 1993, The End of Modern Finance? *Journal of Investing*, winter, 6–9.

Frankfurter, George M., 1994, A Brief History of MPT: From A Normative Model to Event Studies, *Journal of Investing*, winter, 18–23.

Fraser, Jill A., 1999, Who's Finding Asset Allocation Solutions? *Bloomberg Personal Finance*, December (www.bloomberg.com).

Fuller, Russell J., 1996, Amos Tversky, Behavioral Finance, and Nobel Prizes, *Financial Analysts Journal*, July/August, 7–8.

Galarza, Pedro, et al., 1998, Market Madness, *Money*, November, 101ff.

Garrity, Mike, 1999, Funds Strive to Restrain Market Timers, *Mutual Fund Market News*, October 25, 1, 14.

Gibson, Roger C., 1990, *Asset Allocation: Balancing Financial Risk* (Irwin, Chicago).

Gibson, Roger C., 1996, *Asset Allocation: Balancing Financial Risk*, 2nd ed. (Irwin, Chicago).

Gluck, Andrew, 1995, Running the Right Fund Risks, *Worth*, May, 84, 86–7.

Goetzmann, William N. and Nadav Peles, 1997, Cognitive Dissonance and Mutual Fund Investors, *Journal of Financial Research*, 20 (summer), 145–58.

Grant, James, 1999, The Matter of Logic, *Money*, April, 66–7.

Gray, Jack, 1997, Overquantification, *Financial Analysts Journal*, November/December, 5–12.

Graza, Christopher, 1998, Read the Vital Signs, *Bloomberg Personal Finance*, September (www.bloomberg.com).

Grinold, Richard C. and Ronald N. Kahn, 1995, *Active Portfolio Management* (Probus Publishing, Chicago).

Hanson, Bjorn and Mattias Persson, 2000, Time Diversification and Estimation Risk, *Financial Analysts Journal*, September/October, 55–62.

Haslem John A., 1988, *The Investor's Guide to Mutual Funds* (Prentice Hall, Englewood Cliffs, NJ).

Heckman, Fred, 1988, What is your Aptitude for Taking Risk? *Futures*, November, 51–2.

Henriksson, Roy D., 1984, Market Timing and Mutual Fund Performance: An Empirical Investigation, *Journal of Business*, 57, Part 1 (January), 73–96.

Hertog, Roger and David A. Levine, 1996, Income versus Wealth: Making the Trade-off, *Journal of Investing*, spring, 5–16.

Hirschey, Mark, 1998, How Much is a Tulip Worth? *Financial Analysts Journal*, July/August, 21–33.

Huang, Nellie S. and Jersey Gilbert, 1998, The One Investment Guide You Really Need Now, *SmartMoney*, November, 117–29.

Hube, Karen, 1998, Time for Investing's Four-letter Word, *Wall Street Journal*, January 23, C1, C17.

Hube, Karen, 1999, Investors Will Greet the New Decade Wealthier, But Many Won't Necessarily Be All That Wiser, *Wall Street Journal*, December 15, C1, C22.

Hulbert, Mark, 1996, New Tool for Contrarians, *Forbes*, November 18, 298.

Ibbotson, Roger C. and Gary P. Brinson, 1992, *Global Investing: The Professional's Guide to the World Capital Markets* (McGraw-Hill, New York).

Ibbotson, Roger C. and Paul D. Kaplan, 2000, Does Asset Allocation Explain 40, 90, or 100 percent of Performance? *Financial Analysts Journal*, January/February, 26–33.

Investment Company Institute, 1996, *Shareholder Assessment of Risk Disclosure Methods*, spring (The Institute, Washington, DC).

Investment Company Institute, 1997, *Mutual Fund Fact Book*, 37th ed. (The Institute, Washington, DC).

Investment Company Institute, 1999, IRA Ownership in 1999, *Fundamentals*, December, 1–4.

Investment Company Institute, 2000, Financial Decisions at Retirement, *Fundamentals*, November, 1–5.

Jeffrey, Robert H., 1984, The Folly of Market Timing, *Harvard Business Review*, July/August, 102–10.

Jones, Charles P. and Jack W. Wilson, 1995, Probabilities Associated with Common Stock Returns, *Journal of Portfolio Management*, fall, 21–2, 24–32.

Jones, Charles P. and Jack W. Wilson, 1999, Asset Allocation Decisions – Making Choice between Stocks and Bonds, *Journal of Investing*, spring, 51–6.

Kahneman, Daniel, Paul Slovic, and Amos Tversky, 1982, *Judgment under Uncertainty: Heuristics and Biases* (Cambridge University Press, New York) (classic).

Kadlec, Daniel, 2000, Psyched Out, *Time*, June 5, 96.

Kao, G. Wenchi, Louis T.W. Cheng, and Kam C. Chen, 1998, International Mutual Fund Selectivity and Market Timing during Up and Down Market Conditions, *Financial Review*, 33, 127–44.

Kaplan, Paul D. and Laurence B. Siegel, 1994, Portfolio Theory is Alive and Well, *Journal of Investing*, fall, 18–23.

Keon, Jr., Edward F., 1998, Is the US Market Irrationally Exuberant? *Journal of Investing*, fall, 71–83.

Kiss, Robert M. and Todd B. Johnson, 1996, Equitizing the Cash in your Portfolio, *Journal of Investing*, fall, 24–9.

Klemkosky, Robert and Rakesh Bharati, 1995, Time-varying Expected Returns and Asset Allocation, *Journal of Portfolio Management*, summer, 80–7.

Kon, Stanley J., 1983, The Market Timing Performance of Mutual Fund Managers, *Journal of Business*, 56 (July), 323–47.

Kon, Stanley J. and Frank C. Jen, 1979, The Investment Performance of Mutual Funds: An Empirical Investigation of Timing, Selectivity, and Market Efficiency, *Journal of Business*, 52 (April), 263–89.

Kritzman, Mark, 1994, What Practitioners Need to Know . . . about Time Diversification, *Financial Analysts Journal*, January/February, 14–18 (included in Kritzman, 1995).

Kritzman, Mark, 1995, *The Portable Financial Analyst* (from *Financial Analysts Journal*) (Probus Publishing, Chicago).

Kritzman, Mark, 1998, Risk and Utility: Basics, in Richard L. Bernstein and Answath Damodaran, eds., *Investment Management* (John Wiley & Sons, New York).

Laster, David S., 1998, Measuring Gains from International Equity Diversification: The Bootstrap Approach, *Journal of Investing*, fall, 52–60.

LeBaron, Dean, Gail Farrelly, and Susan Gula, 1989, Facilitating a Dialogue on Risk: A Questionnaire Approach, *Financial Analysts Journal*, May/June, 19–24.

Lee, Cheng F. and Shafiqur Rahman, 1991, New Evidence on Timing and Security Selection Skill of Mutual Fund Managers, *Journal of Portfolio Management*, winter, 80–3.

Levitt, Robert, 1999, How Risky are Equities, Really? *Dow Jones Asset Management*, November/December, 65–6, 68.

Levy, Haim and Yishay Spector, 1996, Cross-asset versus Time Diversification, *Journal of Portfolio Management*, spring, 24–34.

Lowenstein, Alice, 1994a, Good or Bad, Fund Performance Not an Issue of Sex, *Morningstar Five Star Investor*, June, 38–9.

Lowenstein, Alice, 1994b, Life-stage Programs Popular, but of Limited Use, *Morningstar Five Star Investor*, November, 14–15.

Lowenstein, Alice, 1998a, Wielding the Axe, *Morningstar Investor*, February, 14–16.

Lowenstein, Alice, 1998b, Worth the Risk? *Morningstar Investor*, March, 14–15.

Lowenstein, Roger, 1999, Day Trading is for Losers, *SmartMoney*, August, 63–4, 66.

Lowenstein, Roger, 2000, Half Rational or Half Nuts? *SmartMoney*, June, 63–4.

Lucas, Lori, 1992, Promises, Promises, *Morningstar Mutual Funds*, November 2.

MacBeth, James D. and David C. Emanuel, 1993, Tactical Asset Allocation: Pros and Cons, *Financial Analysts Journal*, November/December, 30–43.

Maginn, John L. and Donald L. Tuttle, eds., 1990, *Managing Investment Portfolios: A Dynamic Process* (Warren Gorham and Lamont, Boston, MA).

Mahar, Maggie, 1999a, Should You Sweat Out the Cycles? *Bloomberg Personal Finance*, March (www.bloomberg.com).

Mahar, Maggie, 1999b, Three Wall Street Truths You Can't Trust, *Bloomberg Personal Finance*, March (www.bloomberg.com).

Makoff, Eileen, 1995, Portfolio Optimization: A Peek behind the Magician's Curtain, *Morningstar Investor*, August, 8–9.

Malkiel, Burton G., 1996, *A Random Walk down Wall Street* (W.W. Norton, New York).

Markman, Robert, 2000, A Whole Lot of Bull $*#%!, *Worth*, February, 116–25.

Markowitz, Harry, 1952, Portfolio Selection, *Journal of Finance*, 7 (March), 77–91.

Markowitz, Harry, 1961, *Portfolio Selection: Efficient Diversification of Investments*, 2nd ed. (Blackwell, Oxford).

Markowitz, Harry, 1999, The Early History of Portfolio Theory: 1600–1960, *Financial Analysts Journal*, July/August, 5–16.

Mayer, Martin, 1999, Trading is not Investing, *Bloomberg Personal Finance*, April (www.bloomberg.com).

McCulley, Paul, 2000, Perfect Safety Costs Too Much, *Mutual Funds*, July, 98.

McEnally, Richard W., 1985, Time Diversification: Surest Route to Lower Risk? *Journal of Portfolio Management*, summer, 24–6.

McGinn, Daniel, 1998, Boost your Investment Smarts, *Bloomberg Personal Finance*, September (www.bloomberg.com).

McInish, Thomas H., Sridher N. Ramaswami, and Rajendre K. Srivastara, 1993, Do More Risk-averse Investors have Lower Net Worth and Income? *Financial Review*, 28 (February), 91–106.

McQueen, Grant and Steven Thorley, 1994, Bubbles, Stock Returns, and Duration Dependence, *Journal of Financial and Quantitative Analysis*, 29 (September), 379–401.

Meric, Ilhan and Gulser Meric, 1998, Correlation between the World's Stock Markets before and after the 1987 Crash, *Journal of Investing*, fall, 67–70.

Merrill, Craig and Steven Thorley, 1996, Time Diversification: Perspectives from Option Theory, *Financial Analysts Journal*, May/June, 13–19.

Meyer, Marsha and Don Phillips, 1993, Tip for Building a Solid Fund Mix, *Morningstar Five Star Investor*, April, 1, 8.

Michaud, Richard D., 1998, *Efficient Asset Management: A Practical Guide to Stock Portfolio Optimization and Asset Allocation* (Harvard Business School Press, Boston, MA).

Michaud, Richard D., 2000, A New Design for Portfolios, *Bloomberg Personal Finance*, July/August (www.bloomberg.com).

Morningstar, 2000, *Morningstar Mutual Funds* (binder) or *Morningstar Mutual Funds OnDemand* in *Principia Pro for Mutual Funds*, December 31 (CD-ROM, January 1, 2001).

Nagy, Robert A. and Robert W. Obenberger, 1994, Factors Influencing Individual Investor Behavior, *Financial Analysts Journal*, July/August, 63–8.

Newbould, Gerald D. and Percy Poon, 1996, Portfolio Risk, Portfolio Performance, and the Individual Investor, *Journal of Investing*, summer, 72–8.

O'Brian, Bridget, 2000a, Calculating Retirement? It's No Simple Equation, *Wall Street Journal*, February 7, R1, R5.

O'Brian, Bridget, 2000b, Money Market Funds Suit Many Investors, but Proud Creator Frets about Extra Risk, *Wall Street Journal*, November 6, R1, R4.

O'Brien, Robert, 1999, The Twenty percent Club: Stock Market is on Track for an Unprecedented Five-year Tear, *Wall Street Journal*, November 26, C1–C2.

Odean, Terrance, 1998, Are Investors Reluctant to Realize their Losses? *Journal of Finance*, 53 (October), 1775–98 (see references therein).

Odean, Terrance and Brad Barber, 2000, You are What you Trade, *Bloomberg Personal Finance*, May (www.bloomberg.com).

Olsen, Robert A., 1998, Behavioral Finance and its Implications for Stock Price Volatility, *Financial Analysts Journal*, March/April, 10–18 (includes 40 risk behaviors).

Olsen, Robert A. and Muhammad Khaki, 1998, Risk, Rationality, and Time Diversification, *Financial Analysts Journal*, September/October, 58–63.

Opdyke, Jeff D., 2000, Bumpy Market Reminds Investors to Assess their Risk Tolerance, *Wall Street Journal*, July 14, C1, C11.

O'Shaughnessy, Lynne, 1999, How to Pick a Money Fund, *Mutual Funds*, June, 52–4, 56.

Paluch, Susan, 1997, When Good Research Turns Bad, *Morningstar Investor*, September, 1, 4–5.

Peers, Alexandra, 1987, Psych 101: Investor Behavior, *Wall Street Journal*, November, 1D, 16D–17D.

Peltz, Michael, 1999a, Investors, Start your Engines, *Worth*, April, 104–9.

Peltz, Michael, 1999b, Winner's Curse, *Worth*, February, 1.

Penn, Michael, 1993, Asset Allocation Tries to Mature its Image, *Morningstar Five Star Investor*, August, 1, 10–11.

Perold, Andre F. and William F. Sharpe, 1988, Dynamic Strategies for Asset Allocation, *Financial Analysts Journal*, January/February, 16–27.

Perritt, Gerald, 1994, Overcoming the Bear Market Blues, *Worth*, July/August, 107–8.

Phillips, Don, 1991, Another One Bites the Dust, *Morningstar Mutual Funds*, July 12.

Phillips, Thomas K., Greg T. Rogers, and Robert E. Capaldi, 1996, Tactical Asset Allocation: 1977–94, *Journal of Portfolio Management*, fall, 57–64.

Picerno, James, 1997, Questioning Financial Dogma, *Dow Jones Asset Management*, November/December, 16.

Poindexter, J.C. and Charles P. Jones, 1995, Back to the Future: Making the Asset Allocation Decision in the 1990s, *Journal of Investing*, spring, 29–32.

Power, William, 1990, Merrill Lynch Asks: How Much Risk Can You Take? *Wall Street Journal*, July 2, C1, C14.

Reichenstein, William and Dovalee Dorsett, 1995, *Time Diversification Revisited* (Research Foundation of the Institute of Chartered Financial Analysts, Charlottesville, VA).

Reilly, Frank K. and Keith C. Brown, 1997, *Investment Analysis and Portfolio Management*, 5th ed. (Dryden Press, Fort Worth, TX).

Reiner, Eric L., 1999, In Fine Form, *Bloomberg Personal Finance*, April (www.bloomberg.com).

Regnier, Pat, 1998, Picking Funds for Retirement, *Money*, December, 96ff.

Rom, Brian M. and Kathleen W. Ferguson, 1994, Postmodern Portfolio Theory Comes of Age, *Journal of Investing*, fall, 11–17.

Rosenblatt, Joel, 2000, How Economists Help Predict Behavior Online, *Wall Street Journal*, October 2, B1, B4.

Ross, Stephen A., 1999, Adding Risks: Samuelson's fallacy of Large Numbers Revisited, *Journal of Financial and Quantitative Analysis*, 34 (September), 323–39.

Roszkowski, Michael J. and Glenn E. Snelbecker, 1989, How Much Risk Can a Client Stand? *Best's Review*, August, 44–6, 118–19.

Rowland, Mary, 1990, How Much Risk Can You Take? *Wall Street Journal*, April 8, C1.

Rowland, Mary, 1997, Are You a Performance Pig? *Bloomberg Personal Finance*, May/June (www.bloomberg.com).

Rowland, Mary, 1998, Is Diversification Dead? *Bloomberg Personal Finance*, October (www.bloomberg.com).

Rowland, Mary, 1999, Two-loss Trading, *Bloomberg Personal Finance*, May (www.bloomberg.com).

Saler, Thomas D., 1999a, Getting Rich the Automatic Way, *Mutual Funds*, November, 66–7.

Saler, Thomas D., 1999b, Market Timing Renaissance, *Mutual Funds*, January, 50–2.

Samuelson, Paul A., 1974, Challenge to Judgment, *Journal of Portfolio Management*, fall, 17–19.

Samuelson, Paul A., 1989, The Judgment of Economic Science on Rational Portfolio Management: Indexing, Timing, and Long-horizon Effects, *Journal of Portfolio Management*, fall, 4–12.

Samuelson, Paul A., 1990, Asset Allocation could be Dangerous to your Health, *Journal of Portfolio Management*, spring, 5–8.

Samuelson, Paul A., 1994, The Long-term Case for Equities, *Journal of Portfolio Management*, fall, 15–24.

Samuelson, Paul A., 1997, Dogma of the Day: Invest for the Long Term, the Theory Goes, and the Risk Lessens, *Bloomberg Personal Finance*, January/February, 33–4.

Sanders, Catherine V., 1996a, Chatting with the Masters, *Morningstar Investor*, August, 38–40.

Sanders, Catherine V., 1996b, Focus on: Market Timing, *Morningstar Investor*, September, 5.

Sanders, Catherine V., 1997a, How Many Funds Do You Need? *Morningstar Investor*, June, 1, 4–5.

Sanders, Catherine V., 1997b, Rebalancing Act, *Morningstar Investor*, October, 1, 4–5.

Sanders, Catherine V., 1997c, Staring down the Bear, *Morningstar Investor*, March, 8–9.

Schooley, Diane K. and Debra D. Worden, 1999, Investors' Asset Allocations versus Life-cycle Funds, *Financial Analysts Journal*, September/October, 37–43.

Sharpe, William F., 1975, Likely Gains from Market Timing, *Financial Analysts Journal*, March/April, 60–9.

Sharpe, William F., 1984a, Factor Models, CAPMs, and the APT, *Journal of Portfolio Management*, fall, 21–5.

Sharpe, William F., 1984b, Practical Aspects of Portfolio Optimization, in H. Russell Fuller and Darwin M. Bayston, eds. *Improving the Investment Decision Process: Quantitative Assistance for the Practitioner – and for the Firm* (Institute of Chartered Financial Analysts, Charlottesville, VA), 52–65.

Sharpe, William F., 1987a, *Asset Allocation Tools* (Scientific Press, Redwood City, CA).

Sharpe, William F., 1987b, Integrated Asset Allocation, *Financial Analysts Journal*, September/October, 25–32.

Sharpe, William F., 1990, Asset Allocation, in John L. Maginn and Donald L. Tuttle, eds., *Managing Investment Portfolios: A Dynamic Process* (Warren Gorham & Lamont, Boston, MA).

Sharpe, William F., 1991, The Arithmetic of Active Management, *Financial Analysts Journal*, January/February, 7–9.

Sharpe, William F., Gordon J. Alexander, and Jeffery V. Bailey, 1995, *Investments*, 5th ed. (Prentice-Hall, Englewood Cliffs, NJ).

Sharpe, William F., Gordon J. Alexander, and Jeffrey V. Bailey, 1999, *Investments*, 6th ed. (Prentice-Hall, Upper Saddle River, NJ) (see pp. 822–3 and 873–4 for extensive references to market timing).

Shefrin, Hersh, 2000, *Beyond Fear and Greed: Understanding Behavioral Finance and the Psychology of Investing* (Harvard Business School Press, Boston, MA) (synthesis and bibliography).

Shefrin, Hersh, and Meir Statman, 1995, Making Sense of Beta, Size, and Book-to-Market, *Journal of Portfolio Management*, June, 26–34.

Siegel, Jeremy J., 1998, *Stocks for the Long Run*, 2nd ed. (McGraw-Hill, New York).

Siegel, Jeremy J., 1999, Returns for the Long Run, *Bloomberg Personal Finance*, April, 35–6, 38.

Sinquefield, Rex, 1996, Where are the Gains from International Diversification? *Financial Analysts Journal*, January/February, 8–14.

Sivy, Michael, 1998, How Bad Can it Get? *Money*, October, 130–2.

Slovic, Paul, 1972, Psychological Study of Human Judgment: Implications for Decision Making, *Journal of Finance*, 27 (September), 779–801.

Smalhout, James S., 1997, Too Close to your Money? *Bloomberg Personal Finance*, November (www.bloomberg.com).

Sorensen, Eric H., Keith L. Miller, and Vele Samak, 1998, Allocating between Active and Passive Management, *Financial Analysts Journal*, September/October, 19–31.

Statman, Meir, 1995a, A Behavioral Framework for Dollar Cost Averaging, *Journal of Portfolio Management*, fall, 70–8.

Statman, Meir, 1995b, Behavioral Finance versus Standard Finance, in Arnold S. Woods, ed., *Behavioral Finance and Decision Theory* (Association for Investment Management and Research, Charlottesville, VA).

Statman, Meir, 1999, Foreign Stocks in Behavioral Portfolios, *Financial Analysts Journal*, March/April, 12–17.

Stevens, Dale H., Ronald J. Surz, and Mark E. Wimer, 1999, The Importance of Investment Policy, *Journal of Investing*, winter, 80–5.

Sturm, Paul, 1999, Confidence Game, *SmartMoney*, January, 79–80.

Surz, Ronald J., Dale Stevens, and Mark Wimer, 1999, The Importance of Investment Policy, *Journal of Investing*, winter, 43–8.

Tew, Bernard and Richard Bernstein, 1994, Improving Quantitative Models through Optimization, *Journal of Investing*, winter, 24–30.

Thaler, Richard, 1992, *The Winner's Curse: Paradoxes and Anomalies of Economic Life* (Free Press, New York).

Thaler, Richard H., 1993, *Advances in Behavioral Finance* (Russell Sage Foundation, New York).

Thorley, Steven R., 1995, The Time Diversification Controversy, *Financial Analysts Journal*, May/June, 68–75.

Treynor, Jack L., 1998, Bulls, Bears, and Market Bubbles, *Financial Analysts Journal*, March/April, 69–74.

Treynor, Jack L. and Kay K. Mazuy, 1966, Can Mutual Funds Outguess the Market? *Harvard Business Review*, July/August, 131–6.

Updegrave, Walter, 1998, Breaking the Rules for Retirement, *Money*, December, 86–90, 92–4.

Updegrave, Walter, 1999a, Everything You Think You Know about Investing is Wrong, *Money*, May, 127ff.

Updegrave, Walter, 1999b, Grand Delusions, *Money*, April, 132ff.

VanDerhei, Jack, et al., 1999, 401(k) Plan Asset Allocation, Account Balances, and Loan Activity, *Perspective* (Investment Company Institute), January, 1–19.

Vanguard Group, 1997, *Bear Markets* (Vanguard Marketing, Valley Forge, PA).

Vanguard Group, 1998, *Vanguard Investment Planner* (Vanguard Marketing, Valley Forge, PA).

Vanguard Group, 1999, *Realistic Expectations for Stock Market Returns* (Vanguard Marketing, Valley Forge, PA).

Veit, E. Theodore and John M. Cheney, 1982, Are Mutual Funds Market Timers? *Journal of Portfolio Management*, winter, 35–42.

Volkman, David A., 1999, Market Volatility and Perverse Timing Performance of Mutual Fund Managers, *Journal of Financial Research*, 22 (winter), 449–70.

Wagner, Jerry C., 1997, Why Market Timing Works, *Journal of Investing*, summer, 78–81.

Welling, Kathryn M., 1998, By the Numbers, *Barron's*, June 15, 40, 42–4.

Welsh, James, 1999, Warren Buffet's Fabulous Fund, *Mutual Funds*, June, 42–5.

Wigmore, Barrie A., 1998, Revisiting the Crash of 1987, *Financial Analysts Journal*, January/February, 36–48.

Where to Stash that Cash, 2000, *SmartMoney*, August, 27–8.

Willis, Clint, 1990a, The Ten Mistakes to Avoid with your Money, *Money*, June, 84ff.

Willis, Clint, 1990b, Trying to Time the Market is a Fools' Game – Here's Why, *Money*, 47–8.

Willis, Clint, 1998, How to Build a Bigger Nest Egg, *Mutual Funds*, December, 78–80, 82.

Wilson, Jack W. and Charles P. Jones, 1987, A Comparison of Annual Common Stock Returns: 1871–1925 with 1926–1985, *Journal of Business*, 60 (April), 239–58.

Witty, John, 1999, Get the Fat Out, *Bloomberg Personal Finance*, September (www.bloomberg.com).

Woods, Arnold S., 1997, Behavioral Risk: Anecdotes and Disturbing Evidence, *Journal of Investing*, spring, 8–12.

Woods, Arnold S., ed., 1995, *Behavioral Finance and Decision Theory in Investment Management* (Association of Investment Management and Research, Charlottesville, VA).

Yoo, Peter, 1998, The Long and Short (Runs) of Investing in Equities, *National Economic Trends* (Federal Reserve Bank of St. Louis), October, 1.

You Just Can't Do Better Than Stock Funds, 1998, *Mutual Funds*, July, 25–6.

Zeikel, Arthur, 1995, Memorandum to my Daughter, *Financial Analysts Journal*, March/April, 7–8.

Zhang, Linda H., 1998, Global Asset Allocation with Multirisk Considerations, *Journal of Investing*, fall, 7–14.

Zweig, Jason, 1996, Why You'd be Foolish to Count on a 10 percent Annual Return from your Stock Funds, *Money*, January, 45ff.

Zweig, Jason, 1997a, How to Build a Portfolio that will Keep You Smiling, *Money*, Forecast, 82ff.

Zweig, Jason, 1997b, Learn from the Big Bad Bear: Four Moves that can Help You Survive the Next Stock Crash, *Money*, May, 55.

Zweig, Jason, 1997c, When the Stock Market Plunges . . . Will You be Brave or Will You Cave? *Money*, January, 104ff.

Zweig, Jason, 1998a, Here's How to Use the News and Tune Out the Noise, *Money*, July, 63ff.

Zweig, Jason, 1998b, Risk, Revisited, *Money*, November, 106.

Zweig, Jason, 1999, Confessions of a Fund Pro, *Money*, February, 73ff.

Notes: Also, see general references to Morningstar, Clements (archives www.wsj.com), and Zweig (archives www.money.com). The *Financial Analysts Journal*, November/December, 1999 issue, includes nine articles reviewing and updating behavioral finance. See article bibliographies for additional references; and pp. 58–9 list anomalies, psychological antecedents, and references. The *Journal of Investing*, spring 2000 issue, includes nine articles reviewing and updating global asset allocation, including style allocation. The *Financial Analysts Journal*, January/December 1995 issue, includes the best articles of the past fifty years.

7 PORTFOLIO DIVERSIFICATION RISK AND EQUITY STYLE ALLOCATION

Adler, Michael and Andrew Chun Yi, 1998, Has There Been a Fundamental Change in the Stock Market? *Journal of Investing*, spring, 71–76.

Alexanian, Hrach, 1993, Cash May Have Been an Afterthought, but Not in the '90s, *Morningstar Five Star Investor*, October, 14.

Angel, James J., 1994, Implications of Chaos for Portfolio Management, *Journal of Investing*, summer, 30–5.

Ankrim, Ernest M., 1991, Risk-adjusted Performance Attribution, *Financial Analysts Journal*, March/April, 74–82.

Arnott, Amy, 1994, How Many Eggs? *Morningstar Mutual Funds*, April 15.

Arnott, Amy, 1995, What Makes for a Consistent Winner? *Morningstar Investor*, October, 1–2, 4.

Arnott, Amy, 1996, Bringing in the New, *Morningstar Mutual Funds*, November 11.

Arnott, Amy, 1998a, Digging into Morningstar Risk, *Morningstar Mutual Funds*, September 6.

Arnott, Amy, 1998b, Morningstar's New Style Box, continued, *Morningstar Mutual Funds*, December 21.

Arnott, Robert D., John L. Dorian, and Rosemary Macedo, 1992, Style Management: The Missing Element in Equity Portfolios, *Journal of Investing*, summer, 13–21.

Arrington, George R., 2000, Chasing Performance through Style Drift, *Journal of Investing*, summer, 13–17.

Asness, Marion, et al., 1999, The Money 100, *Money Special Issue*, June, 86ff.

Bailey, Jeffrey V., 1996, Evaluating Investment Skill with a VAM Graph, *Journal of Investing*, summer, 64–71.

Bailey, Jeffrey V. and Robert D. Arnott, 1986, Cluster Analysis and Manager Selection, *Financial Analysts Journal*, November/December, 20–8.

Barbee, Olivia, 1997a, Better than a Crystal Ball, *Morningstar Investor*, August, 18–19.

Barbee, Olivia, 1997b, Focus On: Bear Market Rank, *Morningstar Investor*, November, 17.

Barbee, Olivia, 1997c, Just Your Everyday Fund Company, *Morningstar Investor*, September, 10–12.

Barbee, Olivia, 1998a, Enhanced Index Funds Don't Always Enhance Returns, *Morningstar FundInvestor*, November, 14.

Barbee, Olivia, 1998b, The Superdiversifiers, *Morningstar FundInvestor*, November, 1, 4–5.

Barbee, Olivia, 1999a, Eliminating Overlap, *Morningstar FundInvestor*, January, 12–13.

Barbee, Olivia, 1999b, How to Buy a Small-growth Fund, *Morningstar FundInvestor*, April, 8.

Barbee, Olivia, 1999c, Squeezing Diversification from a Single Fund Family, *Morningstar FundInvestor*, March, 1, 4–5.

Barbee, Olivia, 2000, Vanguard 500 Index, *Morningstar FundInvestor*, January, 12–13.

Barbee, Olivia and Abhay Deshpande, 1997, Illuminating the Black Box, *Morningstar Investor*, March, 10–12.

Barbee, William C., Jr., Sandip Mukherji, and Gary A. Raines, 1996, Do Sales Price and Debt–Equity Explain Stock Returns Better than Book–Market and Firm Size? *Financial Analysts Journal*, March/April, 56–60.

Beese, J. Carter, 1994, Free the Fund Managers! *Barron's*, August 29, 44.

Berkshire Hathaway, 1996, *Annual Report*.

Bernstein, Peter L., 1995, Risk as a History of Ideas, *Financial Analysts Journal*, February, 7–11.

Bernstein, Richard, 1995, *Style Investing* (John Wiley & Sons, New York).

Bierck, Richard, 2000, Heard it on the Radio, *Bloomberg Personal Finance*, July/August (www.bloomberg.com).

Block, Stanley B., 1999, A Study of Financial Analysts: Practice and Theory, *Financial Analysts Journal*, July/August, 86–95.

Blume, Marshall, 1998, An Anatomy of Morningstar Ratings, *Financial Analysts Journal*, March/April, 19–27.

Bodie, Zvi, Alex Kane, and Alan J. Marcus, 1996, *Investments*, 3rd ed. (Irwin, Chicago).

Bogle, John C., 1994, *Bogle on Mutual Funds: New Perspectives for the Intelligent Investor* (Irwin, Burr Ridge, IL).

Bogle, John C., 1999, *Common Sense on Mutual Funds: New Imperatives for the Intelligent Investor* (John Wiley & Sons, New York).

Bonds Behaving Badly? 2000, *Mutual Funds*, October, 23.

Braden, William B., 1995, Modeling Mutual Funds using Linear Regression, *Journal of Investing*, winter, 36–44.

Brandt, Jay T., 1994, Professional Portfolio Managers: An Investigation of Practices and Preferences, *Journal of Investing*, summer, 10–16.

Brill, Marla, 1997, Ratings Shootout: Morningstar versus Value Line, *Mutual Funds*, May, 54–61.

Brill, Marla, 1999, Holy Growth Fund! *Mutual Funds*, June, 66–8.

Brown, Stephen J. and William N. Goetzmann, 1998, Mutual Fund Styles, *Journal of Financial Economics*, 43 (March), 373–99.

Brown, Stephen J., William N. Goetzmann, and Alok Kumar, 1998, The Dow Theory: William Peter Hamilton's Track Record Reconsidered, *Journal of Finance*, 53 (August), 1311–33.

Brush, John S. and Michael E. Anselmi, 1994, Practical Use and Misuse of Beta, *Journal of Investing*, summer, 42–7.

Burton, Johnathan, 1997, The Man who Made the Stock Market Gasp, *Dow Jones Asset Management*, November/December, 20ff.

Buss, Dale D., 1997, Pure Profit, *Bloomberg Personal Finance*, March/April (www.bloomberg.com).

Carbonara, Peter, 1999, What is Intrinsic Value? *Money*, June, 133.

Carlson, Greg, 1999, You'll Have to Pay to Get Out, *Mutual Funds*, December, 29–30.

Carter, Richard B. and Howard E. Van Auken, 1990, Security Analysis and Portfolio Management: A Survey and Analysis, *Journal of Portfolio Management*, spring, 81–5.

CDA/Wiesenberger, 1994–8, *Mutual Fund Directory* (CDA/Wiesenberger, Rockville, MD).

Christopherson, Jon A., 1995, Equity Style Classifications, *Journal of Portfolio Management*, spring, 32–43.

Chung, Steve, 1999, Five Essential Qualities of a Muni-bond Fund, *Morningstar FundInvestor*, June, 8–9.

Coggin, T. Daniel, Frank J. Fabozzi, and Robert Arnott, eds., 1997, *The Handbook of Equity Style Investing* (Frank J. Fabozzi Associates, New Hope, PA).

Coy, Peter and Suzanne Woolley, 1998, Failed Wizards of Wall Street, *Business Week*, September, 114–18, 120.

Cullen, Lisa R., 1997, What You Can Learn from the Missteps at Janus, *Money*, June, 46–8.

Damato, Karen S., 1994, Examining Your Mutual Funds for Derivatives Risk, *Wall Street Journal*, August 11, C1, C26.

Damato, Karen S. and Robert McGough, 1998, New Gauge Measures Mutual Fund Risk, *Wall Street Journal*, January 9, C1, C23.

Delaney, Joan, 1994–5 Five Ways to Reduce Risk, *Mutual Funds*, December/January, 61–4.

DiBartolomeo, Dan and Erik Witkowski, 1997, Mutual Fund Misclassification: Evidence Based on Style Analysis, *Financial Analysts Journal*, September/October, 32–43.

DiTeresa, Peter, 1998a, Finding a Large-cap. Value Fund, *Morningstar FundInvestor*, September, 8.

DiTeresa, Peter, 1998b, Finding a Large-growth Fund, *Morningstar FundInvestor*, May, 8.

DiTeresa, Peter, 1998c, Refining Morningstar's Style Box, *Morningstar FundInvestor*, December, 8–10.

DiTeresa, Peter, 1998d, Taking Issue, *Morningstar FundInvestor*, June, 22.

DiTeresa, Peter, 1998e, The Sector Fund Rules, *Morningstar FundInvestor*, June, 8.

DiTeresa, Peter, 1999, Investing, Pure and Simple, *Morningstar FundInvestor*, May, 1, 4–5.

Dorfman, John, 1998, Ten Ways Earnings Lie, *Bloomberg Personal Finance*, August (www.bloomberg.com).

Dorfman, John, 2000, Price-to-Sales Ratios Can Help You Spot Overvalued and Undervalued Stocks in an Industry, *Bloomberg Personal Finance*, May (www.bloomberg.com).

Dorfman, John, 2001, The World According to GARP, *Bloomberg Personal Finance*, March (www.bloomberg.com).

Dziubinski, Susan, 1997, Focus On: Compact Funds, *Morningstar Investor*, October, 17.

Dziubinski, Susan and Richard Ronald, 1997, Focus On: Risk Indicators, *Morningstar Investor*, December, 17.

Edgerton, Jerry, 1998, Who's That Peering over Your Fund Manager's Shoulder? It's the Fund Style Cop, *Money*, April, 49.

Elton, Edwin J., Martin J. Gruber, and Christopher R. Blake, 1995, Fundamental Economic Variables, Expected Returns, and Bond Fund Performance, *Journal of Finance*, 50 (September), 1229–56.

Fama, Eugene F., 1972, Components of Investment Performance, *Journal of Finance*, 27 (June), 551–67.

Fama, Eugene F. and Kenneth R. French, 1992, The Cross-section of Expected Stock Returns, *Journal of Finance*, 47 (June), 427–65.

Fama, Eugene F. and Kenneth R. French, 1995, Size and Book-to-Market Factors in Earnings and Returns, *Journal of Finance*, 50 (March), 131–55.

Ferguson, Robert and John Moffatt, 1995, Myth and Reality in the World of Factors, *Journal of Investing*, summer, 52–5.

Financial Engines, 2000, *How We Recommend Funds* (app.financialengines.com).

Fisher, Kenneth L., 1984, *Super Stocks* (Dow Jones-Irwin, Homewood, IL).

Fisher, Kenneth L., 1999, High P/Es = Low Risk, *Bloomberg Personal Finance*, June (www.bloomberg.com).

Fisher, Kenneth L., 2000, Passive is Active, Bloomberg Personal Finance, April (www.bloomberg.com).

Fitch, Malcolm, 1997, Six Stocks Pegged to Earn 47 percent, *Money*, June, 114–15, 117.

Fogler, H. Russell, 1990, Common Stock Management in the 1990s, *Journal of Portfolio Management*, winter, 26–35.

Fogler, H. Russell, 1993, A Modern Theory of Security Analysis, *Journal of Portfolio Management*, spring, 6–14.

Fortune, Peter, 1998, Mutual Funds, Part II: Fund Flows and Security Returns, *New England Economic Review* (Federal Reserve Bank of Boston), January/February, 3–22.

Fraser, Bruce W., 1998, Quant Works, *Mutual Funds*, July, 50–2.

Fried, Jeff, 1999, Future Imperfect, *Worth*, March, 63–4.

Gallo, John and Larry J. Lockwood, 1997, Benefits of Proper Style Classification of Equity Managers, *Journal of Portfolio Management*, spring, 47–55.

Garland, Eric, 1999, Lessons from the Master, *Money*, August, 90–3.

Garrity, Mike, 1999, Fund Activism said to be Growing, *Mutual Fund Market News*, October 11, 1, 9.

Gordon, Derek, 1997, Will the Real Value Fund Please Stand Up? *Money*, April, 140–2.

Gottsman, Laura and Jon Kessler, 1998, Smart Screened Investments: Environmentally Screened Equity Funds that Perform Like Conventional Funds, *Journal of Investing*, fall, 15–24.

Grant, James, 1999a, Bargain Hunting, *Money*, February, 70–1.

Grant, James, 1999b, The Matter of Logic, *Money*, April, 66–7.

Granzin, Amy, 1999a, Small-cap. Cornucopia, *Morningstar FundInvestor*, November, 6–7.

Granzin, Amy, 1999b, Vanguard Growth Index, *Morningstar FundInvestor*, September, 14–15.

Graves, Cebra, 1996, Gateway to Diversification, *Morningstar Investor*, May, 10.

Harrell, David, 1997, *The Morningstar Style Universe*, quarterly (text.morningstar.net).

Haslem John A. and Carl A. Scheraga, 2001a, Morningstar's Classification of Large-cap. Mutual Funds, *Journal of Investing*, spring, 79–84.

Haslem, John A. and Carl A. Scheraga, 2001b, "Morningstar's Classification of Large-cap. Mutual Funds": Reply, *Journal of Investing*, spring, 87–9.

Hester, William, 1998, PEGY o' my Heart, *Bloomberg Personal Finance*, August (www.bloomberg.com).

Hester, William, 2000, Fundless Fun, *Bloomberg Personal Finance*, September (www.bloomberg.com).

Higgs, Peter J. and Stephen Goode, 1993, Target Active Returns and Attribution Analysis, *Financial Analysts Journal*, May/June, 77–80.

Holowesko, Mark, 1998, Point: True Value Investing Knows No National Boundaries, *Mutual Funds*, July, 70.

Hughes, Bridget B., 2000, The Pick of the World Stock Category, *Morningstar FundInvestor*, March, 12–13.

Ibbotson, Roger, 1997, Style Conscious, *Bloomberg Personal Finance*, March/April (www.bloomberg.com).

Ikenberry, David L., Josef Lakonishok, and Theo Vermaelen, 1995, Market Underreaction to Open Market Share Repurchases, *Journal of Financial Economics*, 39 (October), 181–208.

Investment Company Institute, 1993, *Piecing Together Shareholder Perceptions of Investment Risk*, spring (The Institute, Washington, DC).

Investment Company Institute, 1994, *Investments in Derivatives by Registered Investment Companies*, August (The Institute, Washington DC).

Investment Company Institute, 1997, *Valuation and Liquidity Issues for Mutual Funds*, February (The Institute, Washington, DC).

Investment Company Institute, 1998, *Trends in Mutual Fund Activity* (Research Department), December.

Jacobs, Bruce I. and Kenneth N. Levy, 1996, High Definition Style Rotation, *Journal of Investing*, fall, 14–23.

Jones, Charles P., 1998, *Investments: Analysis and Management*, 6th ed. (John Wiley & Sons, New York).

Kao, Duen-Li and Robert D. Shumaker, 1999, Equity Style Timing, *Financial Analysts Journal*, January/February, 37–48.

Kelley, Jeff, 1995a, A Hunt for Derivatives Finds Few Culprits, *Morningstar Five Star Investor*, March, 38–39.

Kelley, Jeff, 1995b, Shades of Gray, *Morningstar Mutual Funds*, April 14.

Kelley, Jeff, 1996a, Focus on: Bear Market Indicator, *Morningstar Investor*, February, 5.

Kelley, Jeff, 1996b, Style Matters – But So Does Substance, *Morningstar Investor*, April, 8–9.

Klein, Robert A. and Jess Lederman, eds., 1995, *Equity Style Management* (Irwin, Chicago).

Kurtz, Lloyd and Dan DiBartolomeo, 1996, Socially Screened Portfolios: An Attribution Analysis of Relative Performance, *Journal of Investing*, fall, 35–41.

Lakonishok, Josef, Andrei Shleifer, and Robert W. Vishny, 1994, Contrarian Investment, Extrapolation, and Risk, *Journal of Finance*, 49 (December), 1541–78.

Lallos, Laura, 1997a, The Star Rating, Ten Years Later, *Morningstar Mutual Funds*, April 11.

Lallos, Laura, 1997b, The Virtues of Commitment, *Morningstar Mutual Funds*, November 7.

Lauricella, Tom, 1999, Unhappy Trails, *SmartMoney*, September, 132–8, 140.

Leinweber, David J. and Robert D. Arnott, 1995, Quantitative and Computational Innovation in Investment Management, *Journal of Portfolio Management*, winter, 8–15.

Lockwood, Larry J., 1996, Macroeconomic Forces and Mutual Fund Betas, *Financial Review*, 31 (November), 747–63.

Lowenstein, Alice, 1997, Bond Fund Category Ratings Unplugged, *Morningstar Mutual Funds*, January 31.

Lucchetti, Aaron, 2000, Cash-light Mutual Funds Proliferate, *Wall Street Journal*, April 28, C1, C23.

Makoff, Eileen M., 1995, Risk: The Big Picture, *Morningstar Mutual Funds*, April 28.

Malkiel, Burton G., 1995, Returns from Investing in Equity Mutual Funds, *Journal of Finance*, 50 (June), 549–72.

McDonald, Duff, 1999, How to Find True Value in an Overpriced Market, *Money*, June, 126–30.

McGough, Robert, 1999, No Earnings? No Problem! Price–Sales Ratio Use Rises, *Wall Street Journal*, November 26, C1–C2.

McWilliams, James D., 1995, Beyond Investment Rates of Return – How Were the Numbers Earned? *Journal of Investing*, winter, 80–90.

Merriken, Harry E., 1994, Analytical Approaches to Limit Downside Risk: Semivariance and the Need for Liquidity, *Journal of Investing*, fall, 65–72.

Meyer, Marsha, 1993, Deciphering the Lingo of Risk, *Morningstar Five Star Investor*, February, 1, 8, 32.

Michaud, Richard O., 1998, Is Value Multidimensional? Implications for Style Management and Global Stock Selection, *Journal of Investing*, spring, 61–5.

Middleton, Timothy, 1997, Stress-test your Investments, *Bloomberg Personal Finance*, October (www.bloomberg.com).

Monroe, Ann, 1998, Playing by the Numbers, *Bloomberg Personal Finance*, September (www.bloomberg.com).

Monroe, Ann, 2000, Don't be Boxed in by Style, *Bloomberg Personal Finance*, November (www.bloomberg.com).

Morningstar, 1998a, *Morningstar Mutual Funds* (binder) or Morningstar Mutual Funds OnDemand in *Morningstar Principia Pro for Mutual Funds*, December 31 (CD-ROM, January 1, 1999).

Morningstar, 1998b, *Morningstar Principia Pro for Mutual Funds*, December 31 (CD-ROM, January 1, 1999).

Morningstar, 1998c, Vanguard Windsor II, *Morningstar Net* (www.morningstar.net).

Morningstar, 2000a, *Morningstar Deeper Portfolio Analysis* (www.morningstar.com) (access to portfolio analysis tools).

Morningstar, 2000b, *Morningstar Portfolio X-rays* (www.morningstar.com).

Myers, Randy, 1997, Adjust your Pressure Gauges, *Bloomberg Personal Finance*, March/April (www.bloomberg.com).

Nawrocki, David N., 1999, A Brief History of Downside Risk Measures, *Journal of Investing*, fall, 9–25.

Neff, John, 1999, Traditional Values, *Bloomberg Personal Finance*, November (www.bloomberg.com).

Olsen, Robert A., 1997, Investment Risks: The Experts' Perspective, *Financial Analysts Journal*, March/April, 6–66.

O'Shaughnessy, James P., 1996, *What Works on Wall Street* (McGraw-Hill, New York).

Paluch, Susan, 1994a, Diversification Favorably Tips the Risk/Reward Scales, *Morningstar Five Star Investor*, September, 14–15.

Paluch, Susan, 1994b, P/E in Perspective, *Morningstar Five Star Investor*, October, 13.

Paluch, Susan, 1995, Minding Mutual Fund Risk, *Morningstar Five Star Investor*, January, 38–9.

Paluch, Susan, 1996, Focus on: Microcap Funds, *Morningstar Investor*, October, 5.

Paluch, Susan, 1997a, Focus on: True Mid-cap. Funds, *Morningstar Investor*, March, 17.

Paluch, Susan, 1997b, Sizing up New Funds, Morningstar Investor, June, 18.

Paluch, Susan, 1997c, Where Others Fear to Tread, *Morningstar Investor*, June, 8–9.

Penn, Michael, 1994a, Cash Conundrums, *Morningstar Five Star Investor*, June, 3.

Penn, Michael, 1994b, Neural Net's Next Generation Explores Global Horizons, *Morningstar Five Star Investor*, July, 38–9.

Peters, Donald J., 1993, *A Contrarian Study for Growth Stock Investing* (Quorom Books, Westport, CT).

Peterson, David R., 1995, The Information Role of the Value Line Investment Survey: Evidence from Stock Highlights, *Journal of Financial and Quantitative Analysis*, 30 (December), 607–18.

Phillips, Don, 1994, Tackling the Ills of Illiquid Securities, *Morningstar Five Star Investor*, October, 40–1.

Phillips, Don, 1996, A One-year Star Rating, *Morningstar Mutual Funds*, May 10.

Purcell, Kylelane, 1994a, A New Tool for Bond Funds, *Morningstar Five Star Investor*, April, 14.

Purcell, Kylelane, 1994b, Giving Credit Qualities where Credit is Due, *Morningstar Five Star Investor*, March, 2.

Purcell, Kylelane, 1995, Rookies with Experience, *Morningstar Five Star Investor*, February, 14.

Quinson, Tim, 1998, Who Controls your Cash Crop? *Bloomberg Personal Finance*, May (www.bloomberg.com).

Regnier, Pat, 1997a, Focus on: The Revised Star Rating, *Morningstar Investor*, November, 5.

Regnier, Pat, 1997b, International Style, *Morningstar Investor*, July, 18.

Regnier, Pat, 1997c, What are . . . Sectors? *Morningstar Investor*, October, 13.

Regnier, Pat, 1997d, What is . . . Beta? *Morningstar Investor*, May, 13.

Regnier, Pat, 1997e, What is . . . Market Cap? *Morningstar Investor*, November, 13.

Regnier, Pat, 1997f, What is . . . *R*-squared? *Morningstar Investor*, June, 13.

Regnier, Pat, 1998, Barr Rosenberg's Science Project, *Money*, August, 52.

Rekenthaler, John, 1994a, Mortgage Derivatives: The Lessons, *Morningstar Mutual Funds*, June 24.

Rekenthaler, John, 1994b, Most Similar Funds, *Morningstar Mutual Funds*, May 13.

Rekenthaler, John, 1994c, Putting Risk in its Place, *Morningstar Mutual Funds*, May 27.

Rekenthaler, John, 1995, Average isn't Enough, *Morningstar Mutual Funds*, July 7.

Rekenthaler, John, 1996a, Conformist or Rebel? *Morningstar Mutual Funds*, May 24.

Rekenthaler, John, 1996b, Style Analysis: Part 1, *Morningstar Mutual Funds*, February 16.

Rekenthaler, John, 1996c, Style Analysis: Part 2, *Morningstar Mutual Funds*, March 1.

Remolona, Eli M., Paul Kleiman and Debbie Gruenstein, 1997, Market Returns and Mutual Fund Flows, *FRBNY Economic Policy Review*, July, 33–52.

Renberg, Werner, 1999, Category Killers, *Barron's*, April 5, F10.

Ronald, Richard, 1998a, What are . . . Market-neutral Funds? *Morningstar FundInvestor*, August, 11.

Ronald, Richard, 1998b, What are . . . Mortgage-backed Securities? *Morningstar FundInvestor*, June, 13.

Ronald, Richard, 1998c, What is . . . Price/Cash Flow? *Morningstar FundInvestor*, September, 11.

Ronald, Richard, 1998d, What is . . . Short Selling? *Morningstar Investor*, March, 13.

Ronald, Richard, 1999a, What are . . . Futures? *Morningstar FundInvestor*, June, 19.

Ronald, Richard, 1999b, What are . . . Morningstar Star and Category Ratings? *Morningstar FundInvestor*, February, 11.

Ronald, Richard, 1999c, What are Quantitative Funds? *Morningstar FundInvestor*, July, 17.

Ronald, Richard, 1999d, What are . . . The Morningstar Categories and Style Boxes? *Morningstar FundInvestor*, January, 11.

Rose, Sarah, 1999, Looking beyond the P/E, *Money*, February, 40B–40C.

Rowland, Mary, 1998, A Season to Hedge, *Bloomberg Personal Finance*, June (www.bloomberg.com).

Saler, Thomas D., 1997, Buy the Numbers, *Mutual Funds*, December, 68–72, 74.

Sanders, Catherine V., 1995, Digging into Derivatives, *Morningstar Mutual Funds*, January 6.

Sanders, Catherine V., 1996, A New Language, *Morningstar Investor*, November, 1–2, 4.

Sanders, Catherine V., 1998, Finding a Small-value Fund, *Morningstar Investor*, February, 8.

Sanders, Eileen, 1993, Derivative Use in Mutual Funds Explodes, *Morningstar Five Star Investor*, October, 1, 10–11.

Sanders, Eileen, 1994, Muni-inverse Floaters: No Mixed Messages, *Morningstar Mutual Funds*, July 22.

Schaeffer, Bernie, 1999, True Contrarian – Accept no Substitute, *Bloomberg Personal Finance*, July/August, 30–1.

Shareholders Keep Buying, but Fund Reserves Low, 1999, *Mutual Funds*, October, 34.

Sharpe, William F., 1978, Major Investment Styles, *Journal of Portfolio Management*, winter, 68–74.

Sharpe, William F., 1982, Factors in New York Stock Exchange Returns, 1931–79, *Journal of Portfolio Management*, summer, 5–18.

Sharpe, William F., 1988, Determining a Fund's Effective Asset Mix, *Investment Management Review*, November/December, 59–69.

Sharpe, William F., 1992, Asset Allocation: Management Style and Performance Measurement, *Journal of Portfolio Management*, winter, 7–19.

Sharpe, William F., 1998, Morningstar's Risk-adjusted Ratings, *Financial Analysts Journal*, July/August, 21–33.

Sharpe, William F., Gordon J. Alexander, and Jeffery V. Bailey, 1999, *Investments*, 6th ed. (Prentice-Hall, Upper Saddle River, NJ).

Shefrin, Hersh and Meir Statman, 1995, Making Sense of Beta, Size, and Book-to-Market, *Journal of Portfolio Management*, winter, 26–34.

Siegel, Laurence B. and John G. Alexander, 2000, The Future of Value Investing, *Journal of Investing*, winter, 33–45.

Singer, Brian D. and Denis S. Karnosky, 1995, The General Framework for Global Investment and Performance Attribution, *Journal of Portfolio Management*, winter, 84–92.

Sivy, Michael, 1995, The Six Rules of Investing from Legendary Ben Graham, *Money Forecast*, 23.

Sivy, Michael, 1999, Tools of the Trade, *Money*, April, 71ff.

Soltani, Rameen, 1999, Go after la Creme de la Creme, *Bloomberg Personal Finance*, June (www.bloomberg.com).

Sorensen, Eric H. and Chee Y. Thum, 1992, The Use and Misuse of Value Investing, *Financial Analysts Journal*, March/April, 51–7.

Sortino, Frank A. and Hal J. Forsey, 1996, On the Use and Misuse of Downside Risk, *Journal of Portfolio Management*, winter, 35–42.

Sortino, Frank A. and Lee N. Price, Performance Measurement in a Downside Risk Framework, *Journal of Investing*, fall, 59–64.

Starer, David and Leslie A. Balzer, 1995, Artificial Neural Nets: Cerebrally Smart, but Lamentably Dumb, 1995, *Journal of Investing*, winter, 16–20.

Statman, Meir, 1984, Growth Opportunities vs. Growth Stocks, *Journal of Portfolio Management*, spring, 70–4.

Stevens, Paul S. and Amy Lancellota, 1995, Improving Mutual Fund Risk Disclosure, *Perspective* (Investment Company Institute), November, 1–17.

Surz, Ronald J., 1998a, Cyberclone Peer Groups, *Journal of Investing*, winter, 63–7.

Surz, Ronald J. and Mitchell Price, 2000, The Truth about Diversification by the Numbers, *Journal of Investing*, winter, 93–5.

The Wisdom of Sir John Templeton, 1999, *Mutual Funds*, January, 107.

Traulsen, Chris, 2000, Surveying the Internet Landscape, *Morningstar FundInvestor*, May, 6–7.

Updegrave, Walter L. and Prashanta Misra, 1994, Funds with Hidden Risks, *Money*, December, 132ff.

Value Line Investment Survey, 1998 (Value Line Publishing, New York).

Vanguard Windsor II Fund, 1998, *Annual Report*, October 31.

Vanguard Windsor II Fund, 1999a, *Prospectus*, February 26.

Vanguard Windsor II Fund, 1999b, *Statement of Additional Information*, February 26.

Wang, Penelope, 1997, Best Ways to Pick Winning Stocks, *Money*, May, B1, B4–B6.

Welsh, James, 1998, Take a Wild Ride, *Mutual Funds*, July, 43–4.

Whelehan, Barbara M., 1998, Playing with Options, *Mutual Funds*, October, 50–2.

Whelehan, Barbara M., 1999, P/E Ratios: How High Can We Go? *Mutual Funds*, March, 35–6.

Whelehan, Barbara M., 2000, Small Value, Big Potential, *Mutual Funds*, December, 89–90.

Willis, Clint, 1999, True Value, *Worth*, June, 126ff.

Wolper, Gregg, 2000, Taking Issue, *Morningstar FundInvestor*, March, 44.

Wong, F.S. et al., 1992, Fuzzy Neural Systems for Stock Selections, *Financial Analysts Journal*, January/February, 47–52.

Zweig, Jason, 1996, Today's Hottest Funds are Too Big for their Britches, *Money*, April, 146ff.

Zweig, Jason, 1998, Diversification Pitfalls, *Money*, October, 85ff.

Zweig, Jason, 1999a, Confessions of a Fund Pro, *Money*, February, 73ff.

Zweig, Jason, 1999b, Flavor of the Month, *Money*, March, 65ff.

Note: Also, see general references to Morningstar, Clements (archives www.wsj.com), and Zweig (archives www.money.com).

8 MUTUAL FUND PERFORMANCE MEASURES AND BUY/ SELL DECISION CRITERIA

Balzer, Leslie A., 1994, Measuring Investment Risk: A Review, *Journal of Investing*, fall, 47–58.

Barbee, Olivia, 1997, What is . . . Alpha, *Morningstar Investor*, December, 13.

Bernstein, Peter L., 1995, Risk as a History of Ideas, *Financial Analysts Journal*, January/February, 7–11.

Bernstein, Richard L. and Frank J. Fabozzi, 1997, *Streetwise: The Best of the Journal of Portfolio Management* (Princeton University Press, Princeton, NJ).

Blume, Marshall, 1998, An Anatomy of Morningstar Ratings, *Financial Analysts Journal*, March/April, 19–27.

Cabot, Walter M., 1998, Restrictive Guidelines and Pressure to Outperform, *Financial Analysts Journal*, July/August, 6–10.

CDA/Wiesenberger, 1993–7, *Mutual Fund Directory* (CDA/Wiesenberger, Rockville, MD).

Damato, Karen, 2000a, Read This (and Invest) at Your Peril! Manager Tells Hard Truth in Disclosures, *Wall Street Journal*, January 27, C1, C29.

Elton, Edwin J. and Martin J. Gruber, 1995, *Modern Portfolio Theory and Investment Analysis*, 5th ed. (John Wiley & Sons, New York).

Ferguson, Robert, 1986, The Trouble with Portfolio Management, *Journal of Portfolio Management*, spring. Quoted in Bernstein, Richard L. and Frank J. Fabozzi, 1997, *Streetwise: The Best of the Journal of Portfolio Management* (Princeton University Press, Princeton, NJ).

Fogler, H. Russell, 1995, Investment Analysis and New Quantitative Tools, *Journal of Portfolio Management*, summer, 39–48.

French, Dan W. and Glenn V. Henderson, Jr, 1985, How Well Does Performance Evaluation Perform? *Journal of Portfolio Management*, winter, 15–18.

Grinblatt, Mark and Sheridan Titman, 1994, A Study of Monthly Mutual Fund Returns and Performance Evaluation Techniques, *Journal of Financial and Quantitative Analysis*, 29 (September), 419–44.

Jeffrey, Robert H., 1984, A New Paradigm for Portfolio Risk, *Journal of Portfolio Management*, fall. Quoted in Bernstein, Richard L. and Frank J. Fabozzi, 1997, *Streetwise: The Best of the Journal of Portfolio Management* (Princeton University Press, Princeton, NJ).

Jensen, Michael C., 1968, The Performance of Mutual Funds in the Period 1945–1964, *Journal of Finance*, 23 (May), 389–416.

Jones, Charles P., 1998, *Investments: Analysis and Management*, 6th ed. (John Wiley & Sons, New York).

Khorana, Ajay and Edward Nelling, 1998, The Determinants and Predictive Ability of Mutual Fund Ratings, *Journal of Investing*, fall, 61–6.

Meyer, Marsha, 1993, Deciphering the Lingo of Risk, *Morningstar Five Star Investor*, February, 1, 8, 32.

Modigliani, Franco and Leah Modigliani, 1997, Risk-adjusted Performance, *Journal of Portfolio Management*, winter, 45–54.

Monroe, Ann, 1998, Playing by the Numbers, *Bloomberg Personal Finance*, September (www.bloomberg.com).

Morningstar, n.d., *Advanced Analytics for Morningstar Principia Plus* (Morningstar, Chicago). (Morningstar variable definitions.)

Morningstar, 1998, *Morningstar Principia Pro for Mutual Funds*, December 31 (CD-ROM, January 1, 1999).

Regnier, Pat, 1997, What is . . . Sharpe Ratio? *Morningstar Investor*, August, 13.

Sharpe, William F., 1964, Capital Asset Prices: A Theory of Market Equilibrium under Conditions of Risk, *Journal of Finance*, 20 (September), 425–42.

Sharpe, William F., 1966, Mutual Fund Performance, *Journal of Business*, 39 (January), 119–38.

Sharpe, William F., 1994, The Sharpe Ratio, *Journal of Portfolio Management*, fall, 49–58.

Sharpe, William F., 1998, Morningstar's Risk-adjusted Ratings, *Financial Analysts Journal*, July/August, 21–33.

Sharpe, William F., Gordon J. Alexander, and Jeffrey V. Bailey, 1999, *Investments*, 6th ed. (Prentice-Hall, Upper Saddle River, NJ) (see pp. 872–5 for references to performance evaluation studies).

Simons, Katerina, 1998, Risk-adjusted Performance of Mutual Funds, *New England Economic Review* (Federal Reserve Bank of Boston), September/October, 33–48.

Sortino, Frank A. and Lee N. Price, 1994, Performance Measurement in a Downside Risk Framework, *Journal of Investing*, fall, 59–64.

Surz, Ronald J., 1995, A Methodology for Evaluating Risk-adjusted Returns, *Journal of Investing*, fall, 70–4.

Treynor, Jack L., 1965, How to Rate Management of Investment Funds, *Harvard Business Review*, January/February, 63–75.

Treynor, Jack L. and Kay K. Mazuy, 1996, Can Mutual Funds Outguess the Market? *Harvard Business Review*, July/August, 131–6.

Vanguard Windsor II Fund, 1997, *Annual Report*, October 31.

Vanguard Windsor II Fund, 1998, *Prospectus*, February 20.

Wilson, Jack and Charles P. Jones, 1981, The Relationship between Performance and Risk, *Journal of Financial Research*, 4 (summer), 109–17.

Zweig, Jason, 1996, Don't Wish upon the Stars to Pick Funds, *Money*, July 47.

Zweig, Jason, 2000, The Star System, *Money*, March (www.money.com).

Notes: Also, see general references to Morningstar, Clements (archives www.wsj.com), and Zweig (archives www.money.com). The *Financial Analysts Journal*, January/February, 1995 issue, reprints leading articles over the past fifty years – a history of investment management.

9 MUTUAL FUND PERFORMANCE AND PORTFOLIO INVESTMENT STYLE ALLOCATIONS
10 ACTIVELY MANAGED VERSUS PASSIVELY MANAGED FUNDS: THE SEARCH FOR MANAGERS

Adler, Stephen, 1998, Counterpoint: Move Over, S&P, the Dow is Superior, *Mutual Funds*, June, 71.

Ang, James S., An-Sing Chen, and James Wuh Lin, 1999, Information Sharing, Return Characteristics, and Portfolio Beta: The Case of Mutual Funds, *Journal of Investing*, fall, 54–64.

Ang, James S., Carl R. Chen, and James Wuh Lin, 1998, Mutual Fund Managers' Efforts and Performance, *Journal of Investing*, winter, 68–75.

Annual Five Star Fund Guide, 2000, *Mutual Funds*, June, 61–6, 68–73.

Arnott, Amy C., 1995, What Makes for a Consistent Winner? *Morningstar Investor*, October, 1–2, 4.

Arnott, Amy C., 1996, Putting together the Currency Puzzle, *Morningstar Mutual Funds*, September 27.

Arnott, Amy C., 1998, The Management Payoff, *Morningstar Mutual Funds*, July 6.

Arshanapalli, Bala, T. Daniel Coggin, John Doukas, and H. David Shean, The Dimensions of International Equity Style, *Journal of Investing*, spring, 15–30.

Asness, Clifford S., 1997, The Interaction of Value and Momentum Strategies, *Financial Analysts Journal*, March/April, 29–36.

Banz, Rolf, 1981, The Relationship between Return and Market Value of Common Stocks, *Journal of Financial Economics*, 9 (March), 3–18 (see references therein).

Barbee, Olivia, 1997a, Isn't it Ironic? *Morningstar Investor*, November, 10–12.

Barbee, Olivia, 1997b, Making the Grade with International Funds, *Morningstar Investor*, July, 1, 4–5.

Barbee, Olivia, 1998a, Convertible Funds, *Morningstar FundInvestor*, June, 17.

Barbee, Olivia, 1998b, Does Asset Size Matter? *Morningstar Investor*, March, 1, 4–5.

Barbee, Olivia, 1998c, Enhanced Index Funds Don't Always Enhance Returns, *Morningstar FundInvestor*, November, 14.

Barbee, Olivia, 1998d, The Straight Story on Oakmark, *Morningstar FundInvestor*, August, 14.

Barbee, Olivia, 1998e, Those Darn International Funds, *Morningstar FundInvestor*, July, 1, 4–5.

Barbee, Olivia, 1998f, Turning Stock Research into Mutual Fund Returns, *Morningstar FundInvestor*, December, 1, 4–5.

Barbee, Olivia, 1999a, Mid-cap. Funds: The Small-cap. Substitute, *Morningstar FundInvestor*, June, 1, 4–5.

Barbee, Olivia, 1999b, Our Hot Tip: Buy the Unloved, *Morningstar FundInvestor*, January, 1, 4–5.

Barbee, Jr., William C., Sandip Mukherji, and Gary Raines, 1996, Do Sales–Price and Debt–Equity Explain Stock Returns Better than Book–Market and Firm Size? *Financial Analysts Journal*, March/April, 56–60.

Bary, Andrew, 1997, Bigger isn't Better, *Barron's*, November 17, 25–7.

Basu, S., 1977, Investment Performance of Common Stocks in Relation to their Price–Earnings Ratios: A Test of the Efficient Markets Hypothesis, *Journal of Finance*, 32 (June), 663–82.

Bauman, W. Scott and Robert E, Miller, 1995, Portfolio Performance Rankings in Stock Market Cycles, *Financial Analysts Journal*, March/April, 79–87.

Bauman, W. Scott, C. Mitchell Conover, and Robert E. Miller, 1998, Growth versus Value and Large-cap. versus Small-cap. Stocks in International Markets, *Financial Analysts Journal*, March/April, 75–89.

Bekaert, Geert and Campbell R. Harvey, 1995, Time-varying World Market Integration, *Journal of Finance*, 50 (June), 403–44.

Bergstrom, Gary L., 1975, A New Route for Higher Returns and Lower Risks, *Journal of Portfolio Management*, fall. Quoted in Bernstein, Peter L. and Frank J. Fabozzi, eds., 1997, *StreetWise: The Best of the Journal of Portfolio Management* (Princeton University Press, Princeton, NJ).

Bernstein, Peter L., 1997, Rules for Risk Takers, *Bloomberg Personal Finance*, March/April (www.bloomberg.com).

Bernstein, Peter L., 1998, Where, Oh Where are the .400 Hitters of Yesteryear? *Financial Analysts Journal*, November/December, 6–14.

Bernstein, Peter L. and Frank J. Fabozzi, eds., 1997, *StreetWise: The Best of the Journal of Portfolio Management* (Princeton University Press, Princeton, NJ).

Bernstein, Richard, 1999, What's Nifty about the 50? *Bloomberg Personal Finance*, November (www.bloomberg.com).

Bernstein, William J., 1995, *The Intelligent Asset Allocator* (www.efficientfrontier.com).

Bernstein, William J., 1999a, Historical Returns – Signal or Noise? *Efficient Frontier*, September (www.efficientfrontier.com).

Bernstein, William J., 1999b, Small Cap. Growth Indexing and the Multi-factor Threestep. *Efficient Frontier*, April (www.efficientfrontier.com).

Bernstein, William J., 1999c, The Grand Infatuation, *Efficient Frontier*, July (www.efficientfrontier.com).

Bernstein, William J., 1999d, To Hedge or Not to Hedge, *Efficient Frontier*, July (www.efficientfrontier.com).

Bernstein, William J., 1999e, Value Stocks – Hidden Risk or Free Lunch? *Efficient Frontier*, September (www.efficientfrontier.com).

Bernstein, William J., 1999f, When Indexing Fails, *Efficient Frontier*, April (www.bloomberg.com).

Bernstein, William J., 2000a, Dunn's Law Review – Foreign Funds, *Efficient Frontier*, July (www.efficientfrontier.com).

Bernstein, William J., 2000b, The Dunn's Law Review, *Efficient Frontier*, April (www.efficientfrontier.com).

Berry, Michael, 1997, Too Toppy? Not! *Bloomberg Personal Finance*, January/February (www.bloomberg.com).

Best Funds of the Decade, 2000, *Mutual Funds*, January, 66–8.

Birinyi, Laszlo, 1998, The Educated Investor, *Bloomberg Personal Finance*, August (www.bloomberg.com).

Birinyi, Laszlo, 2000, Ride the Money Flow, *Bloomberg Personal Finance*, October (www.bloomberg.com).

Bodie, Zvi, Alex Kane, and Alan J. Marcus, 1996, *Investments*, 3rd ed. (Irwin, Chicago).

Bogle, John C., 1999a, *Bogle on the Secret to Investment Success*, Vanguard Group, April 6 (www.vanguard.com).

Bogle, John C., 1999b, *Common Sense on Mutual Funds: New Imperatives for the Intelligent Investor* (John Wiley, New York).

Bogle, John C., 1999c, *The Clash of Cultures in Investing: Complexity versus Simplicity*, Vanguard Group, April 6 (see other reports at www.vanguard.com).

Bolster, Paul J., Vahan Janjugian, and Emery J. Trahan, 1995, Determining Investor Suitability using the Analytic Hierarchy Process, 1995, *Financial Analysts Journal*, July/August, 63–75.

Bouquet of Bond Funds, 1996, *Morningstar Investor*, April, 38–40.

Bracker, Kevin and Chris Morran, 1999, Tactical Currency Allocation Revisited: Four Simple Currency Trading Rules, *Journal of Investing*, fall, 65–73.

Brown, Stephen J., 1995, Performance Persistence, *Journal of Finance*, 50 (June), 679–98.

Brown, Stephen J., William N. Goetzmann, and Alok Kumar, 1998, The Dow Theory: William Peter Hamilton's Track Record Reconsidered, *Journal of Finance*, 53 (August), 1311–33 (see references therein).

Bryant, Hap, 2000, Stars and Also-rans, *Morningstar FundInvestor*, March, 6–7.

Brynjolfsson, John, 1999, TIPS are Tops in Total Return, *Bloomberg Personal Finance*, July/August (www.bloomberg.com).

Buffett, Warren, 1984, The Superinvestors of Graham-and-Doddsville, *HERMES* (Columbia University, School of Business), fall, 4–15.

Burns, Scott, 1997, The Joy of Doing Nothing, *Worth*, March, 121–2.

Burton, Jonathan, 1998, Do More with Less, *Bloomberg Personal Finance*, March (www.bloomberg.com).

Burton, Jonathan, 1999a, Lean, Mean Money Machines, *Bloomberg Personal Finance*, July/August (www.bloomberg.com).

Burton, Jonathan, 1999b, Reflections of a Random Walker, *Dow Jones Asset Management*, July/August, 20ff (clearest explanation of indexing and efficient markets).

Burton, Jonathan, 2000, PIMCO: Are They Bond Smart? *Mutual Funds*, November, 77–80.

Calian, Sara, 2000, Vanguard Boosts its European Presence, *Wall Street Journal*, February 17, C27.

Callahan, Craig T., 1998, Point: Investors Should Look Beyond Index Funds, *Mutual Funds*, February, 64.

Carhart, Mark M., 1997, On Persistence in Mutual Fund Performance, *Journal of Finance*, 51 (March), 57–82 (see references therein).

Chan, Louis K.C., Narasimhan Jegadeesh, and Josef Lakonishok, 1996, Momentum Strategies, *Journal of Finance*, 51 (December), 1681–713 (see references therein).

Chaudhry, 2000, January Anomalies: Implications for the Market's Incorporation of News, *Financial Review*, 35, 79–96.

Chaumeton, Lucie, Gregory Connor, and Ross Curds, 1996, A Global Stock and Bond Model, *Financial Analysts Journal*, November/December, 65–74.

Chen, Hsiu-Lang, Narashimhan Jegadeesh, and Russ Wermers, 2000, The Value of Active Mutual Fund Management: An Examination of the Stockholdings and Trades of Fund Managers, *Journal of Finance*, 35 (September), 343–68.

Chevalier, Judith and Glenn Ellison, 1999, Are Some Mutual Fund Managers Better than Others? Cross-sectional Patterns in Behavior and Performance, *Journal of Finance*, 54 (June), 875–94.

Cholerton, Kenneth, Peirre Pieraerts, and Bruno Solnik, 1986, Why Invest in Foreign Currency Bonds? *Journal of Portfolio Managememnt*, summer. Quoted in Bernstein, Peter L. and Frank J. Fabozzi, eds., 1997, *StreetWise: The Best of the Journal of Portfolio Management* (Princeton University Press, Princeton, NJ).

Christie, William G. and Roger D. Huang, 1995, Following the Pied Piper: Do Individual Returns Herd around the Market? *Financial Analysts Journal*, July/August, 31–7.

Christie-David, Rohan and Mukesh Chaudhry, 2000, January Anomalies: Implications for the Market's Incorporation of News, *Financial Review*, 35, 79–96.

Christofi, Andreas C., Panayiotis Theodossiou, and Andreas Pericli, 1999, Time-varying Risk and Return in Global Portfolio Management, *Journal of Investing*, winter, 62–9.

Chung, Steve, 1999, Five Essential Qualities of a Muni-bond Fund, *Morningstar FundInvestor*, June, 8–9.

Clements, Jonathan, 1993, The Twenty-five Facts every Fund Investor Should Know, *Wall Street Journal*, March 5, C1ff.

Clements, Jonathan, 1998, The Truth Investors Don't Want to Hear on Index Funds and Market Soothsayers, *Wall Street Journal*, May 12, C1.

Clements, Jonathan, 1999a, Debunking some Mutual Fund Myths, *Wall Street Journal*, March 16, C1.

Clements, Jonathan, 1999b, Hint: Managers are only as Smart as the Expenses they Charge, *Wall Street Journal*, July 6, R1, R10.

Clements, Jonathan, 1999c, Hot Stocks are Sizzling on Momentum, *Wall Street Journal*, September 7, C1.

Clements, Jonathan, 1999d, Not Everyone Can Pick Funds. Really, *Wall Street Journal*, November 9, C1.

Clements, Jonathan, 2000, History 101: Past is Imperfect Guide, *Wall Street Journal*, May 23, C1.

Cochrane, John H., 1999, New Facts in Finance, *Economic Perspectives* (Federal Reserve Bank of Chicago), third quarter, 36–58.

Coggin, T. Daniel and Charles A. Trzcinka, 2000, A Panel Study of US Equity Pension Fund Manager Style Performance, *Journal of Investing*, summer, 6–12.

Coletti, Richard J., 1995, The Hidden Value of Junk, *Mutual Funds*, December/January, 66–70.

Collins, Patrick J., 1999, Monitoring Passively Managed Mutual Funds, *Journal of Investing*, winter, 49–61.

Conrad, Jennifer and Gautam Kaul, 1998, An Anatomy of Trading Strategies, *Review of Financial Studies*, 11 (fall), 489–519.

Cooley, Scott, 2000, Is Deep Value Investing Dead? *Morningstar FundInvestor*, May, 1–3.

Cuenca, Julie A., 1998, Double-digit Yields, *Mutual Funds*, December, 54–5.

Curtis, Carol E., 1998, Master Builders, *Bloomberg Personal Finance*, May (www.bloomberg.com).

Cutler, David M., James M. Poterba, and Lawrence H. Summers, 1989, What Moves Stock Prices? *Journal of Portfolio Management*, spring. Quoted in Bernstein, Peter L. and Frank J. Fabozzi, eds., 1997, *StreetWise: The Best of the Journal of Portfolio Management* (Princeton University Press, Princeton, NJ).

Dada, Joe, 1993, Is There a Shortcut to International Investing? *Journal of Investing*, winter, 45–7.

Damodaran, Aswath, 1998, Asset Selection: Strategies and Evidence, in Peter L. Bernstein and Aswath Damodaran, eds. *Investment Management* (John Wiley, New York).

Daniel, Kent and Sheridan, Titman, 1997, Evidence on the Characteristics of Cross-Sectional Variation in Common Stock Returns, *Journal of Finance*, 52 (March), 1–33.

Daniel, Kent, Mark Grinblatt, Sheridan Titman, and Russ Wermers, 1997, Measuring Mutual Fund Performance with Characteristic Benchmarks, *Journal of Finance*, 52 (July), 1035–58.

Davis, James L., Eugene F. Fama, and Kenneth R. French, 2001, Characteristics, Covariances, and Average Returns, 1929 to 1997, *Journal of Finance*, 55 (February), 389–406.

DeBlasi, Michelle, 1999a, Pumped Up, *Bloomberg Personal Finance*, June (www.bloomberg.com).

DeBlasi, Michelle, 1999b, Get inside the Market's Head, *Bloomberg Personal Finance*, October (www.bloomberg.com).

DeBlasi, Michelle, 2000, How Tasty is the Newest Net Entree? *Bloomberg Personal Finance*, May (www.bloomberg.com).

DeGennaro, Ramon P. and Dale L. Domian, 1996, Market Efficiency and Money Market Fund Portfolio Managers: Beliefs versus Reality, *Financial Review*, 31 (May), 453–74.

Dennis, Patrick, Steven B. Perfect, Karl N. Snow, and Kenneth W. Wiles, 1995, The Effects of Rebalancing on Size and Book-to-Market Ratio Portfolio Returns, *Financial Analysts Journal*, May/June, 47–57.

Desai, Hemang and Prem C. Jain, 1995, An Analysis of the Recommendations of the "Superstar" Money Managers at *Barron's* Annual Roundtable, *Journal of Finance*, 50 (September), 1257–73.

Desai, Hemang, Bing Liang, and Ajai K. Singh, 2000, Do All Stars Shine? Evaluation of Analyst Recommendations, *Financial Analysts Journal*, May/June, 20–9.

DiTeresa, Peter, 1998a, Finding, an Index Fund, *Morningstar FundInvestor*, November, 8–10.

DiTeresa, Peter, 1998b, Sticking with his Values, *Morningstar FundInvestor*, August, 16–18.

DiTeresa, Peter, 1999a, Indexing and Active Management Duke it Out, *Morningstar FundInvestor*, November, 1–3.

DiTeresa, Peter, 1999b, Sell Signals, *Morningstar FundInvestor*, August, 8–9.

DiTeresa, Peter, 2000, For Popular Returns, Try Unpopular Categories, *Morningstar FundInvestor*, January, 1–2.

Dorfman, John, 2000, Run this Ten-point Test on your Portfolio, *Bloomberg Personal Finance*, October (www.bloomberg.com).

Dow Dogs, 1997, *Mutual Funds*, May, 46–8, 50.

Dreman, David, 1998, *Contrarian Investment Strategies: The Next Generation* (Simon & Schuster, New York).

Dreman, David and Michael A. Berry, 1995a, Analyst Forecasting Errors and their Implications for Security Analysis, *Financial Analysts Journal*, May/June, 30–41.

Dreman, David and Michael A. Berry, 1995b, Overreaction, Underreaction, and the Low P/E Effect, *Financial Analysts Journal*, July/August, 21–30.

Dreman, David N. and Eric A. Lufkin, 1997, Do Contrarian Strategies Work within Industries? *Journal of Investing*, fall, 7–29.

Dziubinski, Susan, 1997, Focus On: Compact Funds, *Morningstar Investor*, October, 17.

Dziubinski, Susan, 1998a, Earning their Keep, *Morningstar FundInvestor*, June, 1, 4.

Dziubinski, Susan, 1998b, Is Indexing Overrated? *Morningstar FundInvestor*, September, 1, 4–5.

Dziubinski, Susan, 1998c, On the Contrary, *Morningstar Investor*, January, 1, 4–5.

Dziubinski, Susan, 1998d, Platform Shoes, Fleetwood Mac – and Bonds, *Morningstar Investor*, February, 1, 4–5.

Dziubinski, Susan, 1999, Foreign Investing for Wimps, *Morningstar FundInvestor*, August, 6–7.

Dziubinski, Susan, 2000a, How to Choose Winning Mutual Funds, *Morningstar.com*, June 23 (news.morningstar.com).

Dziubinski, Susan, 2000b, Mutual Fund Notables of the 1990s, *Morningstar.com*, January 1 (news.morningstar.com).

Edelen, Roger M., 1999, Investor Flows and the Assessed Performannce of Open-end Mutual Funds, *Journal of Financial Economics*, 53 (September), 439–66.

Elliott, Scott M., 1993, Tracking Down the Value of Active Management: The Good News and the Bad, *Journal of Investing*, winter, 62–71.

Ellis, Charles D., 1975, The Loser's Game, *Financial Analysts Journal*, July/August, 19–26.

Ellis, Charles D., 1997, *The Investor's Anthology: Original Ideas from the Industry's Greatest Minds* (John Wiley, New York).

Elton, Edwin J., Martin J. Gruber, Sanjiv Das, and Matthew Hlavka, 1993, Efficiency with Costly Information: a Re-interpretation of Evidence from Managed Portfolios, *Review of Financial Studies*, 6, 1–22.

Elton, Edwin J., Martin J. Gruber and Christopher R. Blake, 1995, Fundamental Variables, Expected Returns, and Bond Fund Performance, *Journal of Finance*, 50 (September), 1229–56 (see references therein).

Erb, Claude B., Campbell B. Harvey, and Tadas E. Viskanta, 1995a, Country Risk and Global Equity Selection, *Journal of Portfolio Management*, winter, 74–83.

Erb, Claude B., Campbell B. Harvey, and Tadas E. Viskanta, 1995b, Do World Markets Still Serve as a Hedge? *Journal of Investing*, fall, 26–43.

Errunza, Vihang, Ked Hogan, and Mao-Wei Hung, 1999, Can the Gains from International Diversification be Achieved without Trading Abroad? *Journal of Finance*, 54 (December), 2075–107 (see references therein).

Evans, Michael K., 1997, Three Ways to Play, *Worth*, March, 64–6.

Evans, Richard E. and Burton G. Malkiel, 1999, *Earn More (Sleep Better): The Index Fund Solution* (Simon & Schuster, New York).

Falkenstein, Eric G., 1996, Preferences for Stock Characteristics as Revealed by Mutual Fund Portfolio Holdings, *Journal of Finance*, 51 (March), 111–35.

Fama, Eugene F. and Kenneth R. French, 1992, The Cross-section of Expected Stock Returns, *Journal of Finance*, 47 (June), 427–65 (see references therein).

Fama, Eugene F. and Kenneth R. French, 1998, Value versus Growth: The International Evidence, *Journal of Finance*, 53 (December), 1975–99 (see references therein).

Ferri, Michael G. and Chung-ki Min, 1996, Evidence that the Stock Market Overreacts and Adjusts, *Journal of Portfolio Management*, spring, 71–6.

Ferson, Wayne E. and Rudi W. Schadt, 1996, Measuring Market Strategy and Performance in Changing Economic Conditions, *Journal of Finance*, 51 (June), 425–61 (see references therein).

Ferson, Wayne E. and Vincent A. Warther, 1996, Evaluating Fund Performance in a Dynamic Market, *Financial Analysts Journal*, November/December, 20–8.

Fisher, Kenneth L., 1998, Yes, Size does Matter, *Bloomberg Personal Finance*, June (www.bloomberg.com).

Fisher, Kenneth L., 2000, Passive is Active, *Bloomberg Personal Finance*, April (www.bloomberg.com).

Fortin, Rich and Stuart Michelson, 1995, Are Load Funds Worth the Price? *Journal of Investing*, fall, 89–94.

Frankfurter, George M. and Elton G. McGoun, 1995, The Event Study: Is It Either? *Journal of Investing*, summer, 8–16.

Frankfurter, George M. and Herbert E. Phillips, 1994, A Brief History of MPT: From a Normative Model to Event Studies, *Journal of Investing*, winter, 18–23.

Fridson, Martin S., 1999, One Man's Junk, *Bloomberg Personal Finance*, September (www.bloomberg.com).

Fried, Carla, 1995, The New Way to Make More Money in Funds, *Money*, August, 68ff.

Fried, Carla et al., 1998, The Money 100, 1998, The World's Best Mutual Funds, *Money*, June, 66ff.

Froot, Kenneth, 1993, Currency Hedging over Long Horizons, *National Bureau of Economic Research*, Working Paper No. 4355, May.

Fund Family Shareholder Association, 1997a, Inflation-indexed Bonds: All You Need to Know, *Independent Advisor for Vanguard Investors, Special Report*, June, 7–10.

Fund Family Shareholder Association, 1997b, Lump Sum Investing, *Independent Advisor for Vanguard Investors, Special Report*, August, 7–10.

Fund Family Shareholder Association, 1998, Vanguard's Investing Baloney, *Investment Adviser for Vanguard Investors, Special Report*, August, 7–10.

Garigliano, Jeff, 1999, Ten Things your Investment Newsletter Won't Tell You, *SmartMoney*, October, 143ff.

Garrone, Francois and Bruno Solnik, 1976, A Global Approach to Money Management, *Journal of Portfolio Management*, summer, 5–14.

Gastineau, Gary L., 1995, The Currency Hedging Decision: A Search for Synthesis in Asset Allocation, *Financial Analysts Journal*, May/June, 8–17.

Gerlach, Douglas, 2000, Cutting Edge Web Sites, *Mutual Funds*, November, 6–64.

Gillis, Catherine, 1995, What a Bond Fund Isn't, *Morningstar Five Star Investor*, March, 41.

Goetzmann, William N. and Roger C. Ibbotson, 1994, Do Winners Repeat? *Journal of Portfolio Management*, winter, 9–18.

Graham, Benjamin and David L. Dodd, 1934, *Security Analysis* (McGraw-Hill, New York).

Graham, John R., 1999, Herding among Investment Newsletters: Theory and Evidence, *Journal of Finance*, 54 (February), 237–68 (see references therein).

Graham, John R. and Campbell R. Harvey, 1996, Market Timing Ability and Volatility Implied in Investment Newsletters' Asset Allocation Recommendations, *Journal of Financial Economics*, 42 (November), 397–421.

Graham, John R. and Campbell R. Harvey, 1997, Grading the Performance of Market-timing Newsletters, *Financial Analysts Journal*, November/December, 54–66.

Grant, James L., 1995, A Yield Effect in Common Stock Returns, *Journal of Portfolio Management*, winter, 35–40.

Granzin, Amy, 2000, Finding a Focused Fund, *Morningstar FundInvestor*, February, 6–7.

Graza, Christopher, 1997a, Ladders, Barbells, and Bullets, *Bloomberg Personal Finance*, November (www.bloomberg.com).

Graza, Christopher, 1997b, Better Measure? *Bloomberg Personal Finance*, December (www.bloomberg.com).

Graza, Christopher, 1997c, Is the Deck Stacked? *Bloomberg Personal Finance*, September (www.bloomberg.com).

Graza, Christopher, 2000, When to Get Out, *Bloomberg Personal Finance*, October (www.bloomberg.com).

Green, William, 1999, The Secrets of Sir John Templeton, *Money*, January, 102ff.

Grinold, Richard C., 1989, The Fundamental Law of Active Management, *Journal of Portfolio Management*, spring. Quoted in Bernstein, Peter L. and Frank J. Fabozzi, eds., 1997, *StreetWise: The Best of the Journal of Portfolio Management* (Princeton University Press, Princeton, NJ).

Gross, William H., 1998, This Time it's Different, *Bloomberg Personal Finance*, April (www.bloomberg.com).

Gross, William H., 2000, Marching to a New Beat, *Bloomberg Personal Finance*, March (www.bloomberg.com).

Gruber, Martin J., 1996, Another Puzzle: The Growth in Actively Managed Mutual Funds, *Journal of Finance*, 51 (July), 783–810 (see references therein).

Gustafson, Keith E. and James D. Miller, 1999, Where has the Small Stock Premium Gone? *Journal of Investing*, fall, 45–53.

Halpern, Philip, Nancy Calkings, and Tom Ruggels, 1996, Does the Emperor Wear Clothes or Not? The Final Word (or Almost) on the Parable of Investment Management, *Financial Analysts Journal*, July/August, 9–15.

Hammond, Dennis R., 1996, Equity Diversification Internationally, *Journal of Investing*, summer, 36–42.

Hanachi, Shervin, 2000, Can the Average US Equity Fund Outperform the Benchmarks? *Journal of Investing*, summer, 45–52.

Haslem, John A. and Carl A. Scheraga, 2001a, Morningstar's Classification of Large-cap. Mutual Funds, *Journal of Investing*, spring, 79–84.

Haslem, John A. and Carl A. Scheraga, 2001b, "Morningstar's Classification of Large-cap. Mutual Funds": Reply, *Journal of Investing*, spring, 87–89.

Haugen, Robert A., 1997, The Race between Value and Growth, *Journal of Investing*, spring, 23–31.

Henderson, Barry and Sandra Ward, 2000, All Stars: The All-century Team, *Barron's*, January, 10, F5ff.

Hensel, Chris R. and William T. Ziemba, 1995, The January Barometer, *Journal of Investing*, summer, 67–70.

Hester, William, 1998a, Danger Lurks in Length, *Bloomberg Personal Finance*, September (www.bloomberg.com).

Hester, William, 1998b, Length Does Matter, *Bloomberg Personal Finance*, August, 21.

Hester, William, 1999, Patience Bears Fruit, *Bloomberg Personal Finance*, March (www.bloomberg.com).

Hester, William, 2001, Put Your Portfolio on a Diet, *Bloomberg Personal Finance*, January/February (www.bloomberg.com).

Hickey, Catherine, 2000, Unearthing the All-weather Domestic Hybrid Fund, *Morningstar FundInvestor*, March, 1–3.

Hirschey, Mark, 2000, The "Dogs of the Dow" Myth, *Financial Review*, 35, 1–16.

Hirschey, Mark, Vernon J. Richardson, and Susan Scholz, 2000, Stock-price Effects of Internet Buy–Sell Recommendations: The Motley Fool Case, *Financial Review*, 35, 147–74.

Holowesko, Mark, 1998. Point: True Value Investing Knows No National Boundaries, *Mutual Funds*, July, 70.

Huberman, Gur and Shmuel Kandel, 1990, Market Efficiency and Value Line's Record, *Journal of Business*, 63 (April), 187–216.

Hulbert, Mark, 2000, *Hulbert Financial Digest*, monthly (rates investment newsletter performance).

Ibbotson, Roger G., 1992, Growth Investing: How Good Do You Have to Be? *Journal of Investing*, summer, 56–64.

Ibbotson, Roger G., 1997, Style Conscious, *Bloomberg Personal Finance*, March/April (www.bloomberg.com).

Indro, Daniel C., Christine X. Jiang, Michael Y. Hu, and Wayne Y. Lee, 1998, Mutual Fund Performance: A Question of Style, *Journal of Investing*, summer, 46–53.

Indro, Daniel C., Christine X. Jiang, Michael Y. Hu, and Wayne Y. Lee, 1999, Mutual Fund Performance: Does Fund Size Matter? *Financial Analysts Journal*, May/June, 74–87.

Institute for Econometric Research, 1994, *How to Make Money from "Wall Street Week,"* Special Bonus Reports (The Institute, Fort Lauderdale, FL), 5–8.

Institute for Econometric Research, 1998a, *Index Funds*, Special Bonus (The Institute, Deerfield Beach, FL), July.

Institute for Econometric Research, 1998b, *Mutual Fund Hot Hands: Go with the Winners*, Special Bonus (The Institute, Fort Lauderdale, FL), April.

Is it Time to Buy Value Funds?, 1999, *Mutual Funds*, July, 24.

Jacobs, Bruce I. and Kenneth N. Levy, 1989, The Complexity of the Stock Market, *Journal of Portfolio Management*, fall. Quoted in Bernstein, Peter L. and Frank J. Fabozzi, eds., 1997, *StreetWise: The Best of the Journal of Portfolio Management* (Princeton University Press, Princeton, NJ).

Jacobs, Bruce I. and Kenneth N. Levy, 1995, Engineering Portfolios: A Unified Approach, *Journal of Investing*, winter, 8–15.

Jacobs, Bruce I., Kenneth N. Levy, and Mitchell C. Krask, 1997, Earnings Estimates, Predictor Specification, and Measurement Error, *Journal of Investing*, summer, 29–46.

Jacobson, Eric, 2000a, Some of the Best Bond Shops, *Morningstar FundInvestor*, September, 6–7.

Jacobson, Eric, 2000b, Taking Issue, *Morningstar FundInvestor*, September, 44.

Jaffe, Sam, 1997, For Safety's Sake, *Bloomberg Personal Finance*, July/August (www.bloomberg.com).

Jankus, Ronald J., 1998, The Recent History of International Diversification, *Journal of Investing*, summer, 67–76.

Jegadeesh, Narasimhan and Sheridan Titman, 1993, Returns to Buying Winners and Selling Losers: Implications for Stock Market Efficiency, *Journal of Finance*, 48 (March), 93–130.

Johnson, Todd B. and Ken A. Schluchter, 1998, Point: Indexing with the S&P is as Good as it Gets, *Mutual Funds*, June, 70–1.

Jones, Charles P., 1998, *Investments: Analysis and Management*, 6th ed. (John Wiley, New York).

Jones, Charles P. and Jack W. Wilson, 2000, Can Recent Extraordinary Stock Returns be Repeated? *Journal of Investing*, summer, 71–2.

Jones, Charles P., J.C. Poindexter, and Jack W. Wilson, 1996, Probable Bond Returns: The Lessons of History, *Journal of Investing*, fall, 69–73.

Jones, Irwin E., 1992, Can a Simplified Approach to Bond Portfolio Management Increase Return and Reduce Risk? *Journal of Portfolio Management*, winter, 70–6.

Jubak, Jim, 1999, Don't You Love Special Effects? *Worth*, November, 33–4.

Kahn, Ronald D., 1997, Three Classic Errors in Statistics, from Baseball to Investment Research, *Financial Analysts Journal*, September/October, 6–8.

Kahn, Ronald N. and Andrew Rudd, 1995, Does Historical Performance Predict Future Performance? *Financial Analysts Journal*, November/December, 43–52.

Kahn, Ronald N., Jacques Roulet, and Shahram Tajbakhsh, 1996, Three Steps to Global Asset Allocation, *Journal of Portfolio Management*, fall, 23–31.

Kapoor, Dunal, 2000, The Truth about Focused Funds, *Morningstar FundInvestor*, October, 1–3.

Keim, Donald B., 1999, An Analysis of Mutual Fund Design: The Case of Investing in Small Stocks, *Journal of Financial Economics*, 51 (February), 173–94.

Kelley, Jeff, 1995, International Funds – Down, But Not Out, *Morningstar Investor*, December, 1–2, 4.

Kelley, Jeff, 1996, Lessons from a Lumping, *Morningstar Investor*, September, 8–9.

Kinnel, Russel, 2000, Close 'em Down, *Morningstar FundInvestor*, February, 44.

Koski, Jennifer L. and Jeffrey Pontiff, 1999, How are Derivatives Used? Evidence from the Mutual Fund Industry, *Journal of Finance*, 54 (April), 791–816 (see references therein).

Kosowski, Robert, Allan Timmerman, Hal White, and Russ Wermers, 2001, Can Mutual Fund "Stars" Really Pick Stocks? New Evidence from a Bootstrap Analysis. Working paper, Department of Economics, University of California, San Diego.

Kritzman, Mark, 1986, How to Detect Skill in Management Performance, *Journal of Portfolio Management*, winter. Quoted in Bernstein, Peter L. and Frank J. Fabozzi, eds., 1997, *StreetWise: The Best of the Journal of Portfolio Management* (Princeton University Press, Princeton, NJ).

Lakonishok, Josef, Andrei Shleifer, and Robert Vishny, 1994, Contrarian Investment, Extrapolation, and Risk, *Journal of Finance*, 49 (December), 1541–78 (see references therein).

LaPorta, Rafael, Josef Lakonishok, Andrei Shleifer, and Robert Vishny, 1997, Good News for Value Stocks: Further Evidence on Market Efficiency, *Journal of Finance*, 52 (June), 859–74 (see references therein).

Lee, Susan, 1996, Sweet and Sour, *Worth*, February, 41–4.

Lohmeier, Andrew, 1996, Focus On: Currency Strategies, *Morningstar Investor*, July, 5.

Lowenstein, Alice, 1997, The Low-Turnover Advantage, *Morningstar Mutual Funds*, August 15.

Lowenstein, Roger, 1999, It Bogles the Mind, *SmartMoney*, October, 71–2.

Lucas, Lorie, 1993, Index Funds are Not All Created Equal, *Morningstar Five Star Investor*, March, 1, 9–19.

Lucchetti, Aaron, 2001, Fund Managers Disagree on the Value of Currency Hedging, *Wall Street Journal*, February 2, C1 and C19.

Mahar, Maggie, 1998, Buy Bonds: That's a Direct Order, *Bloomberg Personal Finance*, June (www.bloomberg.com).

Malkiel, Burton G., 1973, *A Random Walk down Wall Street* 1st ed. (Norton, New York).

Malkiel, Burton G., 1995, Returns from Investing in Equity Mutual Funds, 1971 to 1991, *Journal of Finance*, 50 (June), 549–72 (see references therein).

Malkiel, Burton G., 1997, Hot TIPS? *Bloomberg Personal Finance*, September (www.bloomberg.com).

Malkiel, Burton G., 1998, Still on a Random Walk, *Bloomberg Personal Finance*, July/August (www.bloomberg.com).

Malkiel, Burton G., 1999a, *A Random Walk down Wall Street*, 7th ed. (Norton, New York).

Malkiel, Burton G., 1999b, The Case for Index Funds, *Mutual Funds*, February, 72–5.

Marathe, Achla and Edward Renshaw, 1995, Stock Market Bubbles – Some Historical Perspective, *Journal of Investing*, winter, 63–73.

Maturi, Richard J., 1999, Benchmark for Success, *Mutual Funds*, July, 64–7.

McDonald, Duff, 1998, Annual Retorts: The Sayings of Chairman Warren, *Money*, April, 77–8, 83.

McEnally, Richard W., 1986, Latane's Bequest: The Best of Portfolio Strategies, *Journal of Portfolio Management*, winter. Quoted in Bernstein, Peter L. and Frank J. Fabozzi, eds., 1997, *StreetWise: The Best of the Journal of Portfolio Management* (Princeton University Press, Princeton, NJ).

McGinn, Daniel, 1999, The Ultimate Guide to Indexing, *Bloomberg Personal Finance*, September (www.bloomberg.com).

McGough, Robert and Deborah Lohse, 1997, The "Small-cap. Effect," by Some Accounts, is a Myth, *Wall Street Journal*, February 10, C1, C7.

McQueen, Grant and Steven Thorley, 1999, Mining Fools' Gold, *Financial Analysts Journal*, March/April, 61–72.

McReynolds, Rebecca, 1999, When to Sell, *Mutual Funds*, November, 62–5.

Metrick, Andrew, 1999, Performance Evaluation with Transactions Data: The Stock Selection of Investment Newsletters, *Journal of Finance*, 54 (October), 1743–75 (see references therein).

Meyer, Kenneth R., 1975, The Dividends from Active Portfolio Management, *Journal of Portfolio Management*, spring. Quoted in Bernstein, Peter L. and Frank J. Fabozzi, eds., 1997, *StreetWise: The Best of the Journal of Portfolio Management* (Princeton University Press, Princeton, NJ).

Michaud, Richard O., Gary L. Bergstrom, Ronald D. Frashure, and Brian K. Wolahan, 1996, Twenty Years of International Equity Investing, *Journal of Portfolio Management*, fall, 9–22.

Middleton, Timothy, 1999, A Nice Fit in a Portfolio: Midcap Stocks, *Bloomberg Personal Finance*, September (www.bloomberg.com).

Miller, Edward M., Jr., 1978, How to Win at the Losers' Game, *Journal of Portfolio Management*, fall. Quoted in Bernstein, Peter L. and Frank J. Fabozzi, eds., 1997, *StreetWise: The Best of the Journal of Portfolio Management* (Princeton University Press, Princeton, NJ).

Morningstar, 1997, *The Seven Pillars of Mutual Fund Success* (Morningstar, Chicago).

Morningstar, 1998a, *Morningstar Principia Pro for Mutual Funds*, December 31 (CD-ROM, January 1, 1999).

Morningstar, 1999b, Morningstar Mutual Funds (binder) or Morningstar Mutual Funds OnDemand in *Morningstar Principia Pro for Mutual Funds*, December 31 (CD-ROM, January 1, 1999).

Mosebach, Michael and Mohammad Najand, 1999, Are the Structural Changes in Stock Market Investing Driving the US Stock Market to its Current Levels? *Journal of Financial Research*, 22 (fall), 317–29.

Mulvihill, Michael T., 1996, Focus On: Gold Funds, *Morningstar Investor*, March, 5.

Nocera, Joseph, 1999, The Age of Indexing, *Money*, April, 102ff.

Nofsinger, John R. and Richard W. Sias, 1999, Herding and Feedback Trading by Institutional and Individual Investors, *Journal of Finance*, 54 (December), 2263–95.

Odelbo, Catherine Gillis, 1995, No Easy Answers, *Morningstar Investor*, October, 41.

Oertmann, Peter and Heinz Zimmerman, 1996, US Mutual Fund Characteristics across the Investment Spectrum, *Journal of Investing*, fall, 56–68.

Olsen, Robert A., 1996, Implications of Herding Behavior for Earnings Estimation, Risk Assessment, and Stock Returns, *Financial Analysts Journal*, July/August, 37–41.

Olson, Dennis, John Nelson, Craig Witt, and Charles Mossman, 1998, A Test of the Investors' Daily Stock Rating System, *Financial Review*, 33, 161–76.

O'Neal, Edward S., 2000, Industry Momentum and Sector Mutual Funds, *Financial Analysts Journal*, July/August, 37–49.

O'Shaughnessy, James P., 1996, *What Works on Wall Street* (McGraw-Hill, New York).

O'Shaughnessy, James P., 1997, Analysts' Picks, with a Plus, *Bloomberg Personal Finance*, January/February (www.bloomberg.com).

O'Shaughnessy, Lynne, 1998, Five Best Funds for the Bull Market, *Mutual Funds*, May, 44–6, 48.

O'Shaughnessy, Lynne, 1999, Reach for Higher Returns, *Mutual Funds*, July, 44–9.

Pachetti, Nick, 2000, Masterful Mediocrity, *Worth*, December/January, 73–5.

Paluch, Susan, 1995, Focus On: Convertible Bond Funds, *Morningstar Investor*, May, 5.

Paluch, Susan, 1996a, Focus On: Big Funds, *Morningstar Investor*, April, 5.

Paluch, Susan, 1996b, Raising the Yellow Flag on Momentum Funds, *Morningstar Investor*, March, 1–2, 4.

Paluch, Susan, 1996c, The Kennel Club, *Morningstar Investor*, November, 8–9.

Paluch, Susan, 1996d, When in Rome . . . , *Morningstar Investor*, July, 1–2, 4.

Paluch, Susan, 1997a, Focus On: Portfolio Turnover, *Morningstar Investor*, September, 17.

Paluch, Susan, 1997b, Improving the Odds, *Morningstar Investor*, January, 1, 4–5.

Paluch, Susan, 1997c, The Bond Fund Rules, *Morningstar Investor*, April, 1, 4–5.

Paluch, Susan and Jeff Kelley, 1996, Going against the Crowd, *Morningstar Investor*, January, 1–2, 4.

Papp, L. Roy, 1998, Counterpoint: The World's Best are Right Here in the USA, *Mutual Funds*, July, 71.

Pari, Robert A., 1987, Wall Street Week Recommendations: Yes or No? *Journal of Portfolio Management*, fall, 74–6.

Peltz, Michael, 1998, Mutual Fund Ratings, *Worth*, January, 157ff.

Penn, Michael, 1994, Dealing with the Currency Risk Gremlin, *Morningstar Five Star Investor*, April, 2.

Phillips, Don, 1994, When – and Why – Funds Beat the Market, *Morningstar Five Star Investor*, March, 1, 10–11.

Philpot, James, Douglas Hearth, James N. Rimby, and Craig T. Schulman, 1998, Active Management, Fund Size, and Bond Mutual Fund Returns, *Financial Review*, 33, 115–26.

Picerno, James, 1998, When Worlds Collide, *Dow Jones Asset Management*, March/April, 32ff.

Pruitt, Stephen W., Bonnie F. VanNess, and Robert A. VanNess, 2000, Clientele Trading in Response to Published Information: Evidence from the Dartboard Column, *Journal of Financial Research*, 23 (spring), 1–13.

Purcell, Kylelane, 1993, Portfolio Strategies for Rising Interest Rates, *Morningstar Five Star Investor*, June, 1, 10.

Purcell, Kylelane, 1994, Load Bond Vehicles are Funds Out of Time, *Morningstar Five Star Investor*, September, 42.

Regnier, Pat, 1997a, Great and Small, *Morningstar Investor*, March, 1, 4–5.

Regnier, Pat, 1997b, International Style, *Morningstar Investor*, July, 18–19.

Regnier, Pat, 1997c, What are . . . Inflation Indexed Bonds?, *Morningstar Investor*, April, 13.

Regnier, Pat, 1997d, What's That? *Morningstar Investor*, January, 13.

Reichenstein, William, 1999, Bond Fund Returns and Expenses: A Study of Bond Market Efficiency, *Journal of Investing*, winter, 8–16.

Reilly, Frank K. and Keith C. Brown, 1997, *Investment Analysis and Portfolio Management*, 5th ed. (Dryden Press, Fort Worth, TX).

Riepe, Mark W. and Matthew D. Werner, 1998, Are Enhanced Index Mutual Funds Worthy of their Name? *Journal of Investing*, summer, 6–15.

Rekenthaler, John, 1994a, Duration Arrives, *Morningstar Mutual Funds*, January, 1.

Rekenthaler, John, 1994b, Duration: What Worked – And What Didn't, *Morningstar Mutual Funds*, July, 8.

Rekenthaler, John, 1994c, The Taxable Bond Sham, *Morningstar Mutual Funds*, October, 28.

Rekenthaler, John, 1995a, Bond Funds: The Groundwork, *Morningstar Investor*, November, 1–2, 4.

Rekenthaler, John, 1995b, With International Stock Funds, Let the Winners Ride, *Morningstar Investor*, June, 1–2, 4.

Riepe, Mark W. and Matthew D. Werner, 1998, Are Enhanced Index Funds Worthy of their Name? *Journal of Investing*, summer, 6–15.

Roth, Michael J.C., 1998, Counterpoint: Indexing Makes Good Sense, *Mutual Funds*, February, 65.

Rothschild, Tricia O., 1996, Momentum Investors Pick Up Speed Overseas, *Morningstar Investor*, July, 10–11.

Rothschild, Tricia O., 1997, Focus On: Emerging Markets Funds, *Morningstar Investor*, August, 17.

Rothschild, Tricia O., 1998, Why Yen, Rubles, and Dollars Matter, *Morningstar FundInvestor*, July, 14.

Rouwenhorst, K. Geert, 1998, International Momentum Strategies, *Journal of Finance*, 53 (February), 267–84 (see references therein).

Rowland, Mary, 2000, Twenty-one Funds for the Twenty-first Century, *Bloomberg Personal Finance*, December (www.bloomberg.com).

Samuelson, Paul, 1974, Challenge to Judgment, *Journal of Portfolio Management*, fall. Quoted in Bernstein, Peter L. and Frank J. Fabozzi, eds., 1997, *StreetWise: The Best of the Journal of Portfolio Management* (Princeton University Press, Princeton, NJ).

Samuelson, Paul, 1989, The Judgment of Economic Science on Rational Portfolio Management, *Journal of Portfolio Management*, fall, 4–12.

Sanders, Catherine V., 1996, Yield Doesn't Beget Yield, *Morningstar Investor*, April, 1–2, 4.

Sauter, Gus and Chuck Carlson, 2000, Index Imperative, Bloomberg Personal Finance, June (www.bloomberg.com).

Scherreik, Susan, 1998, Discover the Beauty of Bonds, *Money*, December, 51, 54.

Seix, Christina and Ravi Akhoury, 1986, Bond Indexation: The Optimal Quantitative Approach, *Journal of Portfolio Management*, spring. Quoted in Bernstein, Peter L. and Frank J. Fabozzi, eds., 1997, *StreetWise: The Best of the Journal of Portfolio Management* (Princeton University Press, Princeton, NJ).

Shahan, V. Eugene, 1986, Are Short-term Performance and Value Investing Mutually Exclusive? The Hare and the Tortoise Revisited, *HERMES* (Columbia University, School of Business), spring, 26–30.

Sharpe, William F., 1982, Factors in New York Stock Exchange Returns, 1931–79, *Journal of Portfolio Management*, summer. Quoted in Bernstein, Peter L. and Frank J. Fabozzi, eds., 1997, *StreetWise: The Best of the Journal of Portfolio Management* (Princeton University Press, Princeton, NJ).

Sharpe, William F., 1992, Asset Allocation: Management Style and Performance Measurement, *Journal of Portfolio Management*, winter, 7–19.

Sharpe, William F., Gordon J. Alexander, and Jeffery V. Bailey, 1999, *Investments*, 6th ed. (Prentice-Hall, Upper Saddle River, NJ) (see references therein).

Siegel, Jeremy J., 1995, The Nifty Fifty Revisited: Do Growth Stocks Ultimately Justify their Price? *Journal of Portfolio Management*, summer, 8–20.

Sirri, Erik R. and Peter Tufano, Costly Search and Mutual Fund Flows, *Journal of Finance*, 53 (October), 1589–1622 (see references).

Smith, Adam, 1999, Twelve Minds that Made the Market, *Bloomberg Personal Finance*, December (www.bloomberg.com).

Solnik, Bruno, 2000, *International Investments*, 4th ed. (Addison Wesley Longman, Reading, MA).

Solnik, Bruno, Cyril Boucrelle, and Yann Le Fur, 1996, International Market Correlation and Volatility, *Financial Analysts Journal*, September/October, 17–34.

Sorenson, Eric H., Keith L. Miller, and Vele Samak, 1998, Allocating between Active and Passive Management, *Financial Analysts Journal*, September/October, 18–31.

Sortino, Frank A., Gary A. Miller, and Joseph M. Messina, 1997, Short-term Risk-adjusted Performance: A Style-based Analysis, *Journal of Investing*, summer, 19–28.

Spiedell, Lawrence S. and John D. Graves, 1998, The Case for International Small-cap. Stocks, *Journal of Investing*, winter, 6–10.

Stankowich, D. Kaine, 1998, Taming Inflation, *Mutual Funds*, March, 66–8, 70.

Statman, Meir, 1995, A Behavioral Framework for Dollar-cost Averaging, *Journal of Portfolio Management*, fall, 70–8.

Stevens, Sue, 1999, Top Ten Portfolio Pitfalls, *Morningstar FundInvestor*, September, 8–9.

Stevens, Sue, 2000, Jack Bogle: The Man and his Portfolio, *Morningstar FundInvestor*, September, 8–9.

Stickel, Scott, 1995, The Anatomy of the Performance of Buy and Sell Recommendations, *Financial Analysts Journal*, September/October, 25–39.

Stout, Mike, 1997, Concentrate with Care, *Morningstar Mutual Funds*, October 10.

Sturm, Paul, 1999, The Professor and the Index, *SmartMoney*, May, 79–80.

Sturm, Paul, 2000, Dogs of the Dow, Take 2, *SmartMoney*, July, 71–4.

Surz, Ronald J., 1998, *R*-squareds and Alphas are from Different Alphabets, *Journal of Investing*, summer, 62–6.

Tam, Pui-Wing, 1998, Do Leveraged Funds Deliver Long-term? *Wall Street Journal*, December 2, C1, C21.

Tam, Pui-Wing, et al., 2000a, In the '90s, It Took All Kinds (of Fund Managers) to Succeed, *Wall Street Journal*, January 10, R3, R20.

Tam, Pui-Wing et al., 2000b, Really Bad Mistakes aren't Just for Amateurs, *Wall Street Journal*, January 10, R1, R19.

Thomas, Langdon, Jr., 2000, Miller's Crossing, *SmartMoney*, July, 126–9.

Titman, Sheridan and Narasimhan Jegadeesh, 2001, Profitability of Momentum Strategies: An Evaluation of Alternative Explanations. Working paper, Red McCombs School of Business, University of Texas, Austin, TX.

Topkis, Maggie, 1999, Onward Vanguard Soldiers, *Mutual Funds*, 42–5, 48–9.

Topkis, Maggie, 2000, There is a Season: Turn, Turn, Turn, *Money*, June, 50–1.

Tweedy Browne, n.d., *Ten Ways to Beat an Index* (Tweedy Browne Company, New York).

Tweedy Browne, 1992, *What has Worked in Investing* (Tweedy Browne Company, New York).

Updegrave, Walter, 1999, Everything You think You Know about Investing is Wrong, *Money*, May, 127ff.

Updegrave, Walter, 2001, Looking Backward, *Money*, July, 57, 60–1.

Vanguard Group, 1997a, *Bond Fund Investing* (Vanguard Marketing, Valley Forge, PA).

Vanguard Group, 1997b, Vanguard Plain Talk about Realistic Expectations for Stock Market Returns, *Investor Education*, July 14 (www.vanguard.com) (topics for fund investors).

Vanguard Group, 1998a, *International Investing* (Vanguard Marketing, Valley Forge, PA).

Vanguard Group, 1998b, *Vanguard International Index Portfolios* (Vanguard Marketing, Valley Forge, PA).

Vanguard Group, 1999a, *Index Investing* (Vanguard Marketing, Valley Forge, PA).

Vanguard Group, 1999b, Inside Indexing with Gus Sauter, *In the Vanguard*, spring, 1, 3.

Vanguard Group, 1999c, Bogle on the Secret to Investment Success, *Online Library*, April 6 (www.vanguard.com) (Bogle papers and speeches).

Wang, Penelope, 1997, Make Money Mirroring the Market, *Money*, January, 92–7.

Wang, Penelope, 1999, The Right Way to Index, *Money*, April, 115–16, 119.

Weiss, Andrew M., 1999, Why Institutions Systematically Underperform Broadly Based Market Indices, *Journal of Investing*, spring, 65–74.

Wermers, Russ, 1999, Mutual Fund Herding and the Impact on Stock Prices, *Journal of Finance*, 54 (April), 581–622 (see references therein).

Wermers, Russ, 2000, Mutual Fund Performance: An Empirical Decomposition into Stock-picking Talent, Style, Transactions Costs, and Expenses, *Journal of Finance*, 55 (August), 1655–95 (see references and discussion therein).

Wermers, Russ, 2001, Predicting Mutual Fund Returns. Working paper, Robert H. Smith School of Business, University of Maryland, College Park, MD.

Whelehan, Barbara M., 1997, How to Own the World, *Mutual Funds*, February, 73–4, 76.

Whelehan, Barbara M., 2000a, Fund ABCs, *Mutual Funds*, August, 47, 49–52.

Whelehan, Barbara M., 2000b, Value: A New View, *Mutual Funds*, October, 71–5 (three-dimensional analyzer).

Why Bonds are Weird, 2000, *Mutual Funds*, June, 20–1.

Wignall, Christian, 1994, Does International Investing Still Make Sense? Yes, and Here's Why, *Journal of Investing*, winter, 12–17.

Willis, Clint, 1998, The Best-kept Secret, *Fidelity Focus* (Fidelity Distributors), summer, 8–13.

Willis, Clint, 1999, Are You Forgetting Something? Bonds, *Fidelity Focus* (Fidelity Distributors), spring, 18–22.

Willis, Clint et al., 1999, The Best Fund Families, *Mutual Funds*, October, 39–46.

Winston, Kenneth J. and Jeffery V. Bailey, 1996, Investment Policy Implications of Currency Hedging, *Journal of Portfolio Management*, summer, 50–61.

Witty, John, 1999, Get the Fat Out, *Bloomberg Personal Finance*, September (www.bloomberg.com).

Wolde, Richard T. and Lauren Young, 2000, Dysfunctional Families, *SmartMoney*, July, 139–43.

Wright, Adam and Catherine V. Sanders, 1996, The Only Constant is Change, *Morningstar Investor*, October, 8–9.

Zheng, Lu, 1999, Is Money Smart? A Study of Mutual Fund Investors' Fund Selection Ability, *Journal of Finance*, 54 (June), 901–33 (see references therein).

Zuckerman, Gregory and Joe Niedzielski, 2000, Some Bond Pickers Outperformed in a Decade Filled with Obstacles, *Wall Street Journal*, January 10, R10.

Zwecher, Michael J., 1997, The Relative Performance of Mid-cap. Stock Indices, *Journal of Investing*, summer, 47–52.

Zweig, Jason, 1996a, Peering into a Fund's Past Can't Tell You All You Need to Know about its Future, *Money*, October, 56.

Zweig, Jason, 1996b, Twelve Deadly Fund Myths . . . And How to Profit from Them, *Money*, February, 86ff.

Zweig, Jason, 1996c, When to Take a Wild Ride . . . On a New Fund Rocket, *Money*, July, 96ff.

Zweig, Jason, 1997a, Funds that Really Make Money for their Investors, *Money*, April, 124ff.

Zweig, Jason, 1997b, How to Beat 77 percent of Fund Investors Year after Year, *Money*, August, 136ff.

Zweig, Jason, 1997c, How to Build a Portfolio that Will Keep You Smiling, *Money Forecast Issue*, 82ff.

Zweig, Jason, 1997d, This Summer's Blockbusters . . . Bond Funds, *Money*, June, 134ff.

Zweig, Jason, 1998a, Don't Believe the Bull, Bond Funds Do Have a Place, *Money*, June, 63–4.

Zweig, Jason, 1998b, Invest Globally – Still, *Money*, February, 75ff.

Zweig, Jason, 1998c, Proof that Chasing Hot Funds Will Make You Dizzy, Not Rich, *Money*, May, 46.

Zweig, Jason, 1999a, Confessions of a Fund Pro, *Money*, February, 73–75.

Zweig, Jason, 1999b, False Profits, *Money*, August, 55–7.

Zweig, Jason, 1999c, Flavor of the Month, *Money*, March, 65ff.

Zweig, Jason, 1999d, Looking Out for No. 1, *Money*, November (www.money.com).

Zweig, Jason, 1999e, No Dumping, *Money*, January, 63ff.

Zweig, Jason, 1999f, The Tyranny of Style, *Money*, December (www.money.com).

Note: Also, see general references to Morningstar, Clements (archives www.wsj.com), and Zweig (archives www.money.com).

11 MUTUAL FUNDS: THE NEXT GENERATION

American Stock Exchange, 2000a, *Frequently Asked Questions on Index Share Products*, September 8 (www.AMEX.com).

American Stock Exchange, 2000b, *Index Shares on Broad-based Indices*, September 8 (www.ishares.com).

American Stock Exchange, 2000c, *Index Shares on International Indices*, September 8 (www.AMEX.com).

American Stock Exchange, 2000d, *Index Shares on Sector Indices*, September 8 (www.ishares.com and www.AMEX.com).

Bernstein, William J., 2000. Tangled Webs, *Efficient Frontier*, spring (www.efficientfrontier.com).

Bierck, Richard, 2000, Leave the Fund Fold? *Bloomberg Personal Finance*, March (www.bloomberg.com).

Brennan, John J., 1999, *Chairman's Report*, Investment Company Institute, General Membership Meeting, Washington, DC, May 20.

Brown, Ken, 2000, Hedge Funds' Heat Generates Allure for Mutual Fund Firms, *Wall Street Journal*, August 7, R1, R5.

Burton, Jonathan, 1997, The Seven Deadly Sins of Fund Managers, *Bloomberg Personal Finance*, October (www.bloomberg.com).

Burton, Jonathan, 1999, A Dominant Proposition, *Dow Jones Asset Management*, November/December, 20–2, 24.

Burton, Jonathan, 2000a, Cheap Thrills, *Bloomberg Personal Finance*, July/August (www.bloomberg.com).

Burton, Jonathan, 2000b, Hit Three Nails on the Head, *Bloomberg Personal Finance*, March (www.bloomberg.com).

Carlson, Charles, 1999, Dive Directly into DRIPS, *Bloomberg Personal Finance*, October (www.bloomberg.com).

Carlson, Greg, 1999, Spiders Invade Sector World, *Mutual Funds*, March, 24.

Church, Emily, 2000, Market Wagers, *Worth*, December/January, 77–8, 80.

Clements, Jonathan, 2000a, Flip Side on Exchange-traded Funds, *Wall Street Journal*, June 27, C1.

Clements, Jonathan, 2000b, How Stock Investors Take it Personally, *Wall Street Journal*, August 29, C1.

Clements, Jonathan, 2000c, Racier Bets may not be the Best Route, *Wall Street Journal*, August 15, C1.

Clements, Jonathan, 2000d, Vanguard Founder Blasts Funds' Focus, *Wall Street Journal*, May 16, C1.

Coy, Peter, 1998, The Twenty-first Century Economy: Doing Business, *Business Week*, August, 98, 100–1.

Cox, W. Michael and Richard Alm, 1999, The New Paradigm, *Annual Report, Federal Reserve Bank of Dallas*, 3–25.

Damato, Karen, 2000a, Facing the Future of Funds, *Wall Street Journal*, January 10, R1, R3, R8.

Damato, Karen, 2000b, "Personal Funds" May Challenge Industry, *Wall Street Journal*, October 6, C1, C21.

Dugan, Ianthe, 2000, Once-prosperous Hedge Fund is Torn in Power Struggle over Profits, Control, *Wall Street Journal*, August 4, C1–C2.

Dunn, Patricia C., 2000, Future Vision, *iShares* (Barclays Global Investors), winter, 2–7.

Dwyer, Paula et al., 1998, The Twenty-first Century Stock Market, *Business Week*, August 10, 66–8, 70, 72.

Ennis, Richard M., 1997, The Structure of the Investment Management Industry: Revisiting the New Paradigm, *Financial Analysts Journal*, July/August, 6–13.

Fink, Matthew, 1999, *President's Report*, Investment Company Institute, General Membership Meeting, Washington, DC, May 20.

Fisher, Kenneth L., 2000, Passive is Active, *Bloomberg Personal Finance*, April (www.bloomberg.com).

Fishman, Ted C., 1999, Beyond Mutual Funds, *Worth*, March, 111–15.

Fraser, Jill A., 1999, Singular Sensations, *Bloomberg Personal Finance*, June (www.bloomberg.com).

Fund Family Shareholder Association, 1999, Diamonds and Spiders and Webs, *Independent Advisor for Vanguard Investors*, October, 1, 3–5.

Fund Family Shareholder Association, 2000a, Vanguard Goes ETF, *Independent Advisor for Vanguard Investors*, June, 1, 4.

Fund Family Shareholder Association, 2000b, Viper Venom, *Independent Advisor for Vanguard Investors*, October, 1, 11.

Graza, Christopher, 1999, How to Drive – Defensively, *Bloomberg Personal Finance*, December (www.bloomberg.com).

HOLDRS, 2000, Merrill Lynch, September 10 (www.holdrs.com).

Ibbotson, Roger, 2000, The Hedge Fund Dilemma, *Bloomberg Personal Finance*, March (www.bloomberg.com).

iShares MSCI Series, 1999, *Prospectus*, Barclays Global Investors, December 31.

iShares Russell Series, S&P Series and Dow Jones Series, 2000, *Prospectus*, Barclays Global Investors, May 12.

Kahn, Virginia M., 2002, Not a Better Mousestrap, *Bloomberg Personal Finance*, January/February, 20–2.

Karmin, Craig, 1999, More Efficient WEBS Provide Alternative to Closed End Funds, *Wall Street Journal*, July 6, R16.

Karmin, Craig, 2000, Closed End Country Funds Feel Effects of Alternative Products, *Wall Street Journal*, January 10, R14.

Laderman, Jeffrey M., 1999, Mutual Funds: So Long, Glory Days? *Business Week*, June 28, 30–1.

Laderman, Jeffrey M., 2000, Funds that Trade like Stocks, *Business Week*, April 24, 192, 194.

Liang, Bing, 1999, On the Performance of Hedge Funds, *Financial Analysts Journal*, July/August, 72–85.

Lowenstein, Roger, 1998, Not Reckless Enough, *SmartMoney*, December, 77–8, 80.

Lowenstein, Roger, 1999, It Bogles the Mind, *SmartMoney*, October, 71–2.

Lowenstein, Roger, 2000, Death of the Expert, *SmartMoney*, August, 61–2.

Lucchetti, Aaron, 1999, Trading Pace in Mutual Funds Quicken, *Wall Street Journal*, September 24, C1, C23.

Luchetti, Aaron, 2000a, For Most of the Big Fund Companies, the Name of their Game is to Retain, *Wall Street Journal*, August 7, R1, R5.

Lucchetti, Aaron, 2000b, Tradable Shares Bring Some Buzz to Mutuals, *Wall Street Journal*, June 5, R1, R5.

Lucchetti, Aaron, 2000c, Vanguard Plans Funds to Trade Like Stock, *Wall Street Journal*, May 15, C27.

Lucchetti, Aaron and Ken Brown, 2000, AMEX is Back, Thanks to a Tradable Variety of Index Mutual Funds, *Wall Street Journal*, February 22, A1, A15.

Marmer, Harry S., 1996, Visions of the Future: The Distant Past, Yesterday, Today, and Tomorrow, *Financial Analysts Journal*, May/June, 9–12.

McGough, Robert, 1998, Although the Mutual Fund Party is Hot, a Few Investors Start to Look Elsewhere, *Wall Street Journal*, April 29, C1, C29.

McReynolds, Rebecca, 1998, Spiders and Diamonds, *Mutual Funds*, September, 46–8.

Monroe, Ann, 2000, Shifting from Funds to Stocks, *Bloomberg Personal Finance*, March (www.bloomberg.com).

Nocera, Joe, 1998, Giving up on Funds, *Money*, October, 97–9.

Picerno, James, 1998, Of Hedge Funds and Masters of the Universe, *Dow Jones Asset Management*, March/April, 16.

Picerno, James, 1999a, Closing the Gap, *Dow Jones Asset Management*, September/October, 59–60, 62.

Picerno, 1999b, Hedge Funds in the Twenty-first Century, *Dow Jones Asset Management*, September/October, 28–41.

Price, Susan, 2000, Custom Fit, *Worth*, October, 59–60.

Purcell, Dave and Paul Crowley, 1999, The Reality of Hedge Funds, *Journal of Investing*, fall, 26–44.

Reid, Brian, 2000, The 1990s: A Decade of Expansion and Change in the US Mutual Fund Industry, *Perspective* (Investment Company Institute), July, 1–20.

Rekenthaler, John, 1998, Taking Issue, *Morningstar FundInvestor*, November, 21.

Richardson, Vanessa, 1998, Spiders, Webs, and Diamonds: Basket Securities that Look like Index Funds, *Money*, May, 64A–64B.

Rowland, Mary, 2000, Twenty-one Funds for the Twenty-first Century, *Bloomberg Personal Finance*, December (www.bloomberg.com).

Santoli, Michael, 2000a, Buggy Whip Funds? *Barron's*, June 26, F3–F4.

Santoli, Michael, 2000b, Midlife Crisis, *Barron's*, April 10, F5–F6, F8.

Sector Sensations, 1998, *Mutual Funds*, November, 74–81.

Solodar, Oleg and Michael J. Seiler, 2001, Are HOLDRs a Piece of the Closed End Puzzle? *Journal of Investing*, summer, 65–71.

Stanton, Frank, 1999, What is . . . the S&P 500 SPDR? *Morningstar FundInvestor*, August, 17.

Taggart, Gregory, 2000, Build Your Own Mutual Fund, *Bloomberg Personal Finance*, October (www.bloomberg.com).

Tam, Pui-Wing, 1998, Managed Funds are Facing Defections, *Wall Street Journal*, December 11, C1, C21.

Tobias, Andrew, 2000, A New Fund for a New Millennium, *Mutual Funds*, February, 110.

Topkis, Maggie, 2000, A Guide to Spiders, Webs, and Diamonds, *Mutual Funds*, January, 52–5.

Traulsen, Christopher, 2000, Exchange-traded Funds: What You Should Know, *Morningstar FundInvestor*, August, 1–3.

Uhlfelder, Eric, 1997, How to Own the Dow, *Mutual Funds*, October, 51–2, 54.

Vanguard Gets Snakey, 2000, *Mutual Funds*, August, 22.

Ward, Sandra, 2000, Elephant Man, *Barron's*, April 10, F10–F11.

Wiandt, Jim and Will McClatchy, 2002, *Exchange Traded Funds* (John Wiley & Sons, New York).

Willis, Clint, 2000, Are You In? *Worth*, February, 98–105.

Wolper, Gregg, 1997, What are . . . Webs? *Morningstar Investor*, July, 13.

Zeikel, Arthur, 1996, The Future before Us, *Financial Analysts Journal*, September/October, 8–16.

Zigler, Brad, 2000a, Ask Dr. Index, *iShares* (Barclays Global Investors), winter, 22–3.

Zigler, Brad, 2000b, ETFs 101: FUNDamentals, iShares (Barclays Global Investors), winter, 9–15.

Zweig, Jason, 1998a, How Funds can do Better, *Money*, February, 42, 44–6.

Zweig, Jason, 1998b, Stocks or Funds? *Money*, April, 93ff.

Notes: Also, see general references to Morningstar, Clements (archives www.wsj.com), and Zweig (archives www.money.com). Also, see ETF Web sites: American Stock Exchange (www.amex.com), Barclays Global Investors (www.ishares.com), and Merrill Lynch (www.holdrs.com).

12 ECONOMIC AND MARKET INDICATORS: KNOWLEDGE, NOT FAITH

Anderson, James A., 1998, The Trend is Your Friend, *Money*, April, A1–A4.

Arvedlund, Erin E., 2001, Dueling Indices, *Barron's*, January 29, MW11.

Barbee, Olivia, 1998, Preparing for Worse, *Morningstar FundInvestor*, May, 1, 4–5.

Bary, Andrew, 2000, Model Behavior, *Barron's*, January 24, 22.

Baum, Caroline, 2000, Short Shrift, *Bloomberg Personal Finance*, November (www.bloomberg.com).

Bernstein, William J., 1999, The Best Market Indicator Ever, *Efficient Frontier*, January (www.efficientfrontier.com).

Bierman, Jr., Harold, 1999, The Reasons Stocks Crashed in 1929, *Journal of Investing*, spring, 11–18.

Bierck, Richard, 2000, Inflation Oases, *Bloomberg Personal Finance*, November (www.bloomberg.com).

Birinyi, Laszlo, 2000, Ride the Money Flow, *Bloomberg Personal Finance*, June (www.bloomberg.com).

Bjorgen, Eric, 2001, A Troubling Trend, *Mutual Funds*, January, 30.

Brill, Martha, et al., 2000, Mutual Funds Pullout Web Guide, *Mutual Funds*, November, n.p.

Brock, William, Josef Lakonishok, and Blake LeBaron, 1992, Simple Trading Rules and the Stochastic Properties of Stock Returns, *Journal of Finance*, 47 (December), 1731–64.

Brown, Lawrence D., 1997, Earnings Surprise Research: Synthesis and Perspectives, *Financial Analysts Journal*, March/April, 13–19.

Brown, Melissa R. and Kevin C. Condon, 1995, Estimate Revisions: A Quantitative Study, *Journal of Investing*, winter, 56–62.

Burns, Scott, 1999, The Bond Bard, *Worth*, June, 91–3.

Burton, Jonathan, 1998, Insider Trading, *Mutual Funds*, August, 42–4.

CBO's Growth Outlook, 2000, *National Economic Trends* (Federal Reserve Bank of St. Louis), November, 1–27 (use latest issue).

Chakravarty, Sugato and John J. McConnell, 1999, Does Insider Trading Really Move Stock Prices? *Journal of Financial and Quantitative Analysis*, 34 (June), 191–209.

Chancellor, Edward, 1999, New Era, Old Baloney, *Bloomberg Personal Finance*, December (www.bloomberg.com).

Chang, Saeyoung and David Y. Suk, 1998, Stock Prices and the Secondary Dissemination of Information: The Wall Street Journal's "Insider Trading Spotlight" Column, *Financial Review*, 33, 115–28.

Chatterjee, Satyajit, 2000, From Cycles to Shocks: Progress in Business Cycle Theory, *Business Review* (Federal Reserve Bank of Philadelphia), March/April, 27–37.

Clarke, Roger G. and Meir Statman, 1998, Bullish or Bearish? *Financial Analysts Journal*, May/June, 6–8.

Clements, Jonathan, 2000, Seven Big Myths: Words Not to Live By, *Wall Street Journal*, September 19, C1.

Cole, Kevin, Jean Helwege and David Laster, 1996, Stock Market Valuation Indicators: Is This Time Different? *Financial Analysts Journal*, May/June, 56–64.

Contrarious, 1993, Mutual Funds: The New Stock Market, *Worth*, October, 39–40, 42.

Copeland, Maggie M. and Thomas E. Copeland, 1999, Market Timing: Style and Size Rotation Using the VIX, *Financial Analysts Journal*, March/April, 73–81.

Coughlin, Cletus C. and Daniel L. Thorton, 2000, The Exceptional 1990s, *National Economic Trends* (Federal Reserve Bank of St. Louis), March, 1.

Damodaran, Aswath, 1998, Asset Selection: Strategies and Evidence, in Peter L. Bernstein and Aswath Damodaran, eds. *Investment Management* (John Wiley & Sons, New York).

DeBlasi, Michelle, 1999a, Get Inside the Market's Head, *Bloomberg Personal Finance*, October (www.bloomberg.com).

DeBlasi, Michelle, 1999b, How Slow Will We Grow? *Bloomberg Personal Finance*, April (www.bloomberg.com).

DelPret, Dom, 1999, The Fed. Factor, *Fidelity Focus* (Fidelity Distributors), spring, 23–4.

Dialynas, Chris P. and David H. Edington, 1992, Bond Yield Spreads: A Postmodern View, *Journal of Portfolio Management*, fall. Quoted in Bernstein, Richard L. and Frank J. Fabozzi, eds., 1997, *Streetwise: The Best of the Journal of Portfolio Management* (Princeton University Press, Princeton, NJ).

Dorsey, Thomas, 1997, Analysts' Picks, With a Plus, *Bloomberg Personal Finance*, January/February (www.bloomberg.com).

Dowen, Richard J., 1996, Analyst Reaction to Negative Earnings for Large Well-known Firms, *Journal of Portfolio Management*, fall, 49–55.

Dreman, David N. and Michael Berry, 1995, Analyst Forecasting Errors and their Implications for Security Analysis, *Financial Analysts Journal*, May/June, 30–41.

Eng, William F., 1993, *The Day Trader's Manual: Theory, Art, and Science of Profitable Short-term Investing* (John Wiley Sons, New York).

Epstein, Gene, 1997, Twenty percent Undervalued? *Barron's*, December 11, 24.

Equity Funds Run Out of Cash, 1998, *Mutual Funds*, October, 41.

Evans, Michael K., 1990, Taking the Measure of the Market, *Investment Vision* (Fidelity Distributors), March/April, 18–21, 62.

Fisher, Kenneth L. and Meir Statman, 2000, Investor Sentiment and Stock Returns, *Financial Analysts Journal*, March/April, 16–23.

Fitch, Malcolm, 1998, Why You Should Manage Funds Online, *Money*, 54, 56.

Fosback, Norman, 1994, *Stock Market Logic* (Dearborn Financial Publishing/Institute for Econometric Research, Fort Lauderdale, FL).

Fosback, Norman G., 1998, What's Driving the Market? *Mutual Funds*, November, 116.

Fridson, Martin S., 1998, Spotting the Very Good Years, *Bloomberg Personal Finance*, May (www.bloomberg.com).

Garzarelli, Elaine, 1996, *The Garzarelli Outlook* (Phillips Publishing), July–December issues.

General Market Indicators, 2000, *Investor's Business Daily*, various issues.

Gerlach, Douglas, 2000, Cutting Edge Web Sites, *Mutual Funds*, November, 61–4.

Graza, Christopher, 1997, Yield to the Curve, *Bloomberg Personal Finance*, December (www.bloomberg.com).

Graza, Christopher, 1998a, A Moving Target, *Bloomberg Personal Finance*, February (www.bloomberg.com).

Graza, Christopher, 1998b, Reading the T-leaves, *Bloomberg Personal Finance*, May (www.bloomberg.com).

Graza, Christopher, 1998c, Read the Vital Signs, *Bloomberg Personal Finance*, September (www.bloomberg.com).

Graza, Christopher, 1999, Here's What the Pros do to Overdrive Defensively, *Bloomberg Personal Finance*, December (www.bloomberg.com).

Graza, Christopher, 2000, Is Gridlock Good? *Bloomberg Personal Finance*, June (www.bloomberg.com).

Graza, Christopher and Elizabeth Ungar, 2001, The Only Indicators You'll Ever Need, *Bloomberg Personal Finance*, January/February (www.bloomberg.com).

Harris, Wayne, 1999, Edgar: Comprehensive . . . but Challenging, *Mutual Funds*, July, 42.

Haslem, John A., 1988, *The Investor's Guide to Mutual Funds* (Prentice Hall, Englewood Cliffs, NJ).

Hester, William, 1997, Outguess the Fed, *Bloomberg Personal Finance*, September (www.bloomberg.com).

Hester, William, 1999, Focus on Fed. Funds, *Bloomberg Personal Finance*, October (www.bloomberg.com).

Hildebrand, George, 1992, *Business Cycle Indicators and Measures* (Probus Publishing, Chicago).

Hut One. Hut Two. Our Dow Prediction is . . . , 1999, *Mutual Funds*, April, 32.

Institute for Econometric Research, 1994a, *Fund Timing Index*, Special Bonus Reports, Part 1, (The Institute, Fort Lauderdale, FL), 5.

Institute for Econometric Research, 1994b, *How to Make Money from "Wall Street Week,"* Special Bonus Reports (The Institute, Fort Lauderdale, FL), 5–8.

Institute for Econometric Research, 1994c, *Moving Average Trading Systems*, Special Bonus Reports, Part 5, (The Institute, Fort Lauderdale, FL), 36–40.

Is There Trouble Ahead for the Dow? 1999, *Mutual Funds*, May, 36.

Janjigian, Vahan, 1997, *Forbes* Special Situation Survey: A Study in Market Efficiency, *Journal of Investing*, summer, 65–70.

Jones, Charles P., 1998, *Investments: Analysis and Management*, 6th ed. (John Wiley, New York).

Jones, Irwin E., 1995, What Does the Yield Curve Predict about Interest Rates? *Journal of Investing*, summer, 62–6.

Kleisen, Jay, 2000, The Economic Outlook for 2000: Bulls on Parade? *National Economic Trends* (Federal Reserve Bank of St. Louis), January, 1.

Kopicki, Allison, 1998, Armchair Economist, *Bloomberg Personal Finance*, May (www.bloomberg.com).

Laing, Jonathan, 2000, Don't be Put Off by Bad Breadth, *Barron's*, September 4, 35.

Leefeldt, Ed, 2000, How Can Whispers Help You? *Bloomberg Personal Finance*, January/February (www.bloomberg.com).

Levenson, Alan, 2000, Inside the Fed: How Greenspan Thinks about the Economy, *T. Rowe Price Report*, spring, 13–14.

Mahar, Maggie, 1999, Should You Sweat Out the Cycles? *Bloomberg Personal Finance*, March (www.bloomberg.com).

Marathe, Achla and Edward Renshaw, 1995, Stock Market Bubbles – Some Historical Perspective, *Journal of Investing*, winter, 63–73.

Market Laboratory, 2000, *Barron's*, various issues.

Market Letter – Sentiment Index, 1999, *Market Edge* (Quick & Reilly), April 25 (quickreilly.stkwtch.com).

Market Science, 1997, Note on Forecasting the Stock Market Using the Long-term Momentum Oscillator, *Market Science*, December 16 (marketscience.com).

Mathieu, Paula, 1993, Looking for Investment Advice? Some Say it's in the Stars, *Morningstar Five Star Investor*, November, 13.

McGee, Suzanne, 1997, Technical Analysis Successfully Tests Old Resistance Level of Fundamentalists, *Wall Street Journal*, October 13, C1–C2.

McWilliams, James D., 1984, "Watchman, Tell us of the Night!" *Journal of Portfolio Management*, spring, 75–80.

Mead, Walter R., 2000, Growth: Get Used to It, *Worth*, March, 130–4.

Mueller, Jay N., 2000, Seven Engines of the Economy, *Mutual Funds*, August, 38–9.

Mutual Fund Cash Levels, 1998, *Market Gauge by Data View* (Data View Inc.), December (www.bloomberg.com).

Neal, Robert and Simon M. Wheatley, 1998, Do Measures of Investor Sentiment Predict Returns? *Journal of Financial and Quantitative Analysis*, 33 (December), 523–47.

New York thirty-day Advance/Declines Ratio, 1997, *Market Gauge by Data View* (Data View Inc.), December 10 (www.marketgauge.com).

Niemara, Michael P. and Gerald F. Zukowski, 1994, *Trading the Fundamentals* (Probus Publishing, Chicago).

Nocera, Joseph, 1998, The Trouble With the Consensus Estimate, *Money*, June, 59–60.

Note on Forecasting the Stock Market using the Long-term Momentum Oscillator, 1997a, *Market Science*, December 16 (marketscience.com).

O'Higgins, Michael, 1999, The Bond Bard, *Worth*, June, 91–3.

Online Investor, 2000, Investment Company Institute, September 26 (www.ici.org).

Osler, Carol, 2000, Support for Resistance: Technical Analysis and Intraday Exchange Rates, *Economic Policy Review* (Federal Reserve Bank of New York), July, 53–68.

Peters, Donald J., 1993, Are Earnings Surprises Predictable? *Journal of Investing*, summer, 47–51.

Pettit, Dave, et al., 2000, How to Plumb the Investing Secrets of the Internet, *Wall Street Journal*, May 25, C1, C17.

Phillips, Don, 1999, Answering What's Answerable, *Morningstar FundInvestor*, December, 44.

Picerno, James, 2000a, This Year's Model, *Bloomberg Personal Finance*, June (www.bloomberg.com).

Picerno, James, 2000b, Wheel and Deal, *Bloomberg Personal Finance*, October (www.bloomberg.com).

Picerno, James, 2001, In Search of Perfection, *Bloomberg Personal Finance*, January/February (www.bloomberg.com).

Pruitt, Stephen W. and Richard E. White, 1988, Who Says Technical Analysis Can't Beat the Market? *Journal of Portfolio Management*, spring, 55–8.

Psychological Market Indicators, 2000, *Investor's Business Daily*, various dates.

Quinson, Tim, 1998a, Safe or Sorry? *Bloomberg Personal Finance*, September (www.bloomberg.com).

Quinson, Tim, 1998b, Who Controls your Cash Crop? *Bloomberg Personal Finance*, May (www.bloomberg.com).

Raghavan, Anita, 1992, CRB Futures Index Gets Surprisingly High Marks as Barometer for Forecasting Inflation and Rates, *Wall Street Journal*, October 10, C1.

Reilly, Frank K. and David T. Whitford, 1982, A Test of the Specialists' Short Sale Ratio, *Journal of Portfolio Management*, winter, 12–18.

Reitano, Robert R., 1992, Non-parallel Yield Curve Shifts and Immunization, *Journal of Portfolio Management*, spring. Quoted in Bernstein, Richard L. and Frank J. Fabozzi, eds., 1997, *Streetwise: The Best of the Journal of Portfolio Management* (Princeton University Press, Princeton, NJ).

Research, 1997b, *Market Science*, December 16 (marketscience.com).

Roach, Stephen S., 1999, Fall into the Gap, *Bloomberg Personal Finance*, June (www.bloomberg.com).

Robbins, Marcus, 1997, Expect No Mercy, *Bloomberg Personal Finance*, September (www.bloomberg.com).

Robbins, Marcus, 1999, The Buyback Beacon, *Bloomberg Personal Finance*, March (www.bloomberg.com).

Rogers, Jim, 1997, Top to Bottom, *Worth*, May, 41–4.

Rogers, R. Mark, 1994, *Handbook of Key Economic Indicators* (Irwin Professsional, Burr Ridge, IL).

Ronald, Richard, 1998, What is . . . Yield Curve? *Morningstar FundInvestor*, April, 13.

Rosen, Scott, 2000, It's a Long Way Down, *Mutual Funds*, April, 38.

Schaeffer, Bernie, 1998, Fly Away! *Bloomberg Personal Finance*, September (www.bloomberg.com).

Schaeffer, Bernie, 1999a, A Sentimental Favorite, *Bloomberg Personal Finance*, March (www.bloomberg.com).

Schaeffer, Bernie, 1999b, Tools of the Trader, *Bloomberg Personal Finance*, June (www.bloomberg.com).

Schaeffer, Bernie, 1999c, True Contrarian – Accept No Substitute, *Bloomberg Personal Finance*, July/ August (www.bloomberg.com).

Schaeffer, Bernie, 2000a, Gauging Investor Sentiment on Tech, *Bloomberg Personal Finance*, May (www.bloomberg.com).

Schaeffer, Bernie, 2000b, It's a Judgment Call, *Bloomberg Personal Finance*, January/February (www.bloomberg.com).

Schaeffer, Bernie and Christopher Johnson, 2000, A Nasdaq Pointer for Contrarians, *Bloomberg Personal Finance*, June (www.bloomberg.com).

Sharpe, William F., Gordon J. Alexander and Jeffery V. Bailey, 1999, *Investments*, 6th ed. (Prentice-Hall, Upper Saddle River, NJ).

Shefrin, Hersh, 2000, *Beyond Fear and Greed: Understanding Behavioral Finance and the Psychology of Investing* (Harvard Business School Press, Boston, MA).

Sherden, William A., 1998, *The Fortune Tellers: The Big Business of Buying and Selling Predictions* (John Wiley, New York).

Shim, Jae K., Joel G. Siegel and Jonathan Lansner, 1994, *One Hundred and One Investment Decision Tools* (International Publishing, Chicago).

Slater, Karen, 1989, Do "Moving Averages" Reveal When to Buy and Sell Stocks? *Wall Street Journal*, May 18, C1, C8.

Stack, James B., 1994a, *Personal Profit Guide* (InvesTech Research, Whitefish, MT).

Stack, James B., 1994b, *"Investment Strategies": Tactics and Tradeoffs, InvesTech Special Report* (InvesTech Research, Whitefish, MT).

Stack, James B., 1995, *Uncharted Waters* (InvesTech Research, Whitefish, MT), 1–8.

Stephenson, Kevin, 1997, Just How Bad are Economists at Predicting Interest Rates? (And What are the Implications for Investors?), *Journal of Investing*, summer, 8–10.

Sturm, Paul, 1999, Inside Sources, *Smart Money*, August, 69–71.

Taggart, Gregory, 2000, Star Search, *Bloomberg Personal Finance*, November (www.bloomberg.com).

Taggart, Gregory, 2001, The Inside Track, *Bloomberg Personal Finance*, March (www.bloomberg.com).

The T-bond Outlet, 2000, *Mutual Funds*, November, 44.

The Wonderland of New Economy Investing, 2000, *T. Rowe Price Report*, spring, 1–6.

Thompson, Roger, 1997, Chart Toppers, *Bloomberg Personal Finance*, December (www.bloomberg.com).

Treasury Yield Curve, 1998, *Stocktrader* (Maloney Securities Co.), December 4 (www.stocktrader.com).

Updegrave, Walter L., 1989, Seven Signals that Help You Answer the Toughest Question of All: When to Sell, *Money*, February, 123.

Vergin, Roger C., 1996. Market Timing Strategies: Can You Get Rich? *Journal of Investing*, winter, 79–86.

Wessell, David, 2000, Could One Little Rule Explain All of Economics? *Wall Street Journal*, February 7, B1, B4.

What the Pros See, 2000, *Mutual Funds*, August, 42–5.

White, C. Barry, 2000, What P/E will the US Stock Market Support? *Financial Analysts Journal*, November/December, 30–8.

Witty, John, 2000, Is Inflation Tamed? *Bloomberg Personal Finance*, October (www.bloomberg.com).

Wu, Cunchi and Xu-Ming Wang, 2000, The Predictive Ability of Dividend and Earnings Yields for Long-term Stock Returns, *Financial Review*, 35, 97–124.

Yakal, Kathy, 2000, Cries and Whispers, *Barron's*, January 24, 52.

Yardeni, Edward, 1999, Next: Dow 8000? *Barron's*, September 6, 17.

Yield Curve Forecast, 1997, *Market Science*, December 16 (marketscience.com).

Zaretsky, Adam M., 2000, Overblown Productivity? *National Economic Trends* (Federal Reserve Bank of St. Louis), 1.

Zeikel, Arthur, 1991, Forecasting and the Market, *Financial Analysts Journal*, November/December, 15–18.

Zweig, Jason, 2000, Do the Experts get the Future Right? Does Anybody? *Money*, February (www.money.com).

Note: Also, see general references to Morningstar, Clements (archives www.wsj.com), and Zweig (archives www.money.com).

INDEX

CPSIA information can be obtained at www.ICGtesting.com
Printed in the USA
BVOW062005031212

306993BV00010B/143/P